Design Strategies and Innovations in Multimedia Presentations

Shalin Hai-Jew
Kansas State University, USA

A volume in the Advances in Multimedia and
Interactive Technologies (AMIT) Book Series

Information Science
REFERENCE
An Imprint of IGI Global

Managing Director:	Lindsay Johnston
Managing Editor:	Austin DeMarco
Director of Intellectual Property & Contracts:	Jan Travers
Acquisitions Editor:	Kayla Wolfe
Production Editor:	Christina Henning
Development Editor:	Austin DeMarco
Typesetter:	Cody Page and Tucker Knerr
Cover Design:	Jason Mull

Published in the United States of America by
Information Science Reference (an imprint of IGI Global)
701 E. Chocolate Avenue
Hershey PA, USA 17033
Tel: 717-533-8845
Fax: 717-533-8661
E-mail: cust@igi-global.com
Web site: http://www.igi-global.com

Library of Congress Cataloging-in-Publication Data

CIP Data
Design strategies and innovations in multimedia presentations / Shalin Hai-Jew, editor.
    pages cm
 Includes bibliographical references and index.
 ISBN 978-1-4666-8696-0 (hardcover) -- ISBN 978-1-4666-8697-7 (ebook) 1. Media programs (Education)--Design. 2. Multimedia systems--Design. I. Hai-Jew, Shalin, editor of compilation.
 LB1028.4.D47 2015
 371.33--dc23
                        2015015550

This book is published in the IGI Global book series Advances in Multimedia and Interactive Technologies (AMIT) (ISSN: 2327-929X; eISSN: 2327-9303)

British Cataloguing in Publication Data
A Cataloguing in Publication record for this book is available from the British Library.

For electronic access to this publication, please contact: eresources@igi-global.com.

Advances in Multimedia and Interactive Technologies (AMIT) Book Series

Joel J.P.C. Rodrigues
Instituto de Telecomunicações, University of Beira Interior, Portugal

ISSN: 2327-929X
EISSN: 2327-9303

MISSION

Traditional forms of media communications are continuously being challenged. The emergence of user-friendly web-based applications such as social media and Web 2.0 has expanded into everyday society, providing an interactive structure to media content such as images, audio, video, and text.

The **Advances in Multimedia and Interactive Technologies (AMIT) Book Series** investigates the relationship between multimedia technology and the usability of web applications. This series aims to highlight evolving research on interactive communication systems, tools, applications, and techniques to provide researchers, practitioners, and students of information technology, communication science, media studies, and many more with a comprehensive examination of these multimedia technology trends.

COVERAGE

- Gaming Media
- Internet technologies
- Digital Images
- Multimedia technology
- Mobile Learning
- Audio Signals
- Social Networking
- Web Technologies
- Multimedia Services
- Digital Watermarking

IGI Global is currently accepting manuscripts for publication within this series. To submit a proposal for a volume in this series, please contact our Acquisition Editors at Acquisitions@igi-global.com or visit: http://www.igi-global.com/publish/.

Titles in this Series

For a list of additional titles in this series, please visit: www.igi-global.com

Design Strategies and Innovations in Multimedia Presentations
Shalin Hai-Jew (Kansas State University, USA)
Information Science Reference • copyright 2015 • 505pp • H/C (ISBN: 9781466686960) • US $225.00 (our price)

Cases on the Societal Effects of Persuasive Games
Dana Ruggiero (Bath Spa University, UK)
Information Science Reference • copyright 2014 • 345pp • H/C (ISBN: 9781466662063) • US $205.00 (our price)

Video Surveillance Techniques and Technologies
Vesna Zeljkovic (New York Institute of Technology, Nanjing Campus, China)
Information Science Reference • copyright 2014 • 369pp • H/C (ISBN: 9781466648968) • US $215.00 (our price)

Techniques and Principles in Three-Dimensional Imaging An Introductory Approach
Martin Richardson (De Montfort University, UK)
Information Science Reference • copyright 2014 • 324pp • H/C (ISBN: 9781466649323) • US $200.00 (our price)

Computational Solutions for Knowledge, Art, and Entertainment Information Exchange Beyond Text
Anna Ursyn (University of Northern Colorado, USA)
Information Science Reference • copyright 2014 • 511pp • H/C (ISBN: 9781466646278) • US $180.00 (our price)

Perceptions of Knowledge Visualization Explaining Concepts through Meaningful Images
Anna Ursyn (University of Northern Colorado, USA)
Information Science Reference • copyright 2014 • 418pp • H/C (ISBN: 9781466647039) • US $180.00 (our price)

Exploring Multimodal Composition and Digital Writing
Richard E. Ferdig (Research Center for Educational Technology - Kent State University, USA) and Kristine E.
Pytash (Kent State University, USA)
Information Science Reference • copyright 2014 • 352pp • H/C (ISBN: 9781466643451) • US $175.00 (our price)

Multimedia Information Hiding Technologies and Methodologies for Controlling Data
Kazuhiro Kondo (Yamagata University, Japan)
Information Science Reference • copyright 2013 • 497pp • H/C (ISBN: 9781466622173) • US $190.00 (our price)

www.igi-global.com

701 E. Chocolate Ave., Hershey, PA 17033
Order online at www.igi-global.com or call 717-533-8845 x100
To place a standing order for titles released in this series, contact: cust@igi-global.com
Mon-Fri 8:00 am - 5:00 pm (est) or fax 24 hours a day 717-533-8661

This is for R. Max.

Editorial Advisory Board

Table of Contents

Foreword xv

Preface xvii

Acknowledgment xxii

Section 1
Exploring Online Multimedia

Chapter 1
The Evolution of the (Hidden) Web and its Hidden Data 1
    Manuel Álvarez Díaz, University of A Coruña, Spain
    Víctor Manuel Prieto Álvarez, University of A Coruña, Spain
    Fidel Cacheda Seijo, University of A Coruña, Spain

Chapter 2
Creating Extended-Form Eventgraphs from Social Media Using Publicly Available Software Tools 31
    Shalin Hai-Jew, Kansas State University, USA

Chapter 3
Eavesdropping on Narrowcast Self-talk and Microchats on Twitter 106
    Shalin Hai-Jew, Kansas State University, USA

Section 2
Theories, Models, and Practices for Multimedia Design and Deployment

Chapter 4
Leveraging the Design and Development of Multimedia Presentations for Learners 149
    Lijia Lin, East China Normal University, China
    Amy Leh, California State University San Bernardino, USA
    Jackie Hee Young Kim, Armstrong State University, USA
    Danilo M. Baylen, University of West Georgia, USA

Chapter 5
Audio for Multi-Media Presentations in E-Learning...164
    Hattie Wiley, National Weather Service, USA

Chapter 6
Use of Video to Enhance Education 189
    Brent A. Anders, Kansas University, USA

Section 3
Enhanced Technological Tools for Multimedia Designs

Chapter 7
Static Text-Based Data Visualizations: An Overview and a Sampler 203
    Shalin Hai-Jew, Kansas State University, USA

Chapter 8
Using Microsites as Live Presentation Platforms (with Three Embedded Real-World Cases) 303
    Shalin Hai-Jew, Kansas State University, USA

Section 4
Considering Human Needs in Multimedia Presentations

Chapter 9
Promoting Engagement with Online Presentations 322
    Amy Gaimaro, St. John's University, USA

Chapter 10
Evaluation of Situations Causing Split of Attention in Multimedia Learning Environments via
Eye-Tracking Method...337
    Duygu Mutlu-Bayraktar, Istanbul University, Turkey
    Servet Bayram, Marmara University, Turkey

Section 5
Digital Visualizations for Learning and Knowing

Chapter 11
Conducting Semantic-Based Network Analyses from Social Media Data: Extracted Insights about
the Data Leakage Movement 369
    Shalin Hai-Jew, Kansas State University, USA

Chapter 12
Grounding Cyber: Querying Social Media Platforms, the Web, and Internet for Geolocational
Information 428
    Shalin Hai-Jew, Kansas State University, USA

Section 6
Real-World Cases in Innovative Multimedia Applications

Chapter 13
Rolling NVivo 10 out to a University's Research Community: Live Trainings and a Semantic
Web-Friendly E-Book 526
Shalin Hai-Jew, Kansas State University, USA

Compilation of References 559

About the Contributors 582

Index 586

Detailed Table of Contents

Foreword xv

Preface xvii

Acknowledgment xxii

Section 1
Exploring Online Multimedia

Chapter 1
The Evolution of the (Hidden) Web and its Hidden Data 1
    Manuel Álvarez Díaz, University of A Coruña, Spain
    Víctor Manuel Prieto Álvarez, University of A Coruña, Spain
    Fidel Cacheda Seijo, University of A Coruña, Spain

This paper presents an analysis of the most important features of the Web and its evolution and implications on the tools that traverse it to index its content to be searched later. It is important to remark that some of these features of the Web make a quite large subset to remain "hidden". The analysis of the Web focuses on a snapshot of the Global Web for six different years: 2009 to 2014. The results for each year are analyzed independently and together to facilitate the analysis of both the features at any given time and the changes between the different analyzed years. The objective of the analysis are twofold: to characterize the Web and more importantly, its evolution along the time.

Chapter 2
Creating Extended-Form Eventgraphs from Social Media Using Publicly Available Software Tools 31
    Shalin Hai-Jew, Kansas State University, USA

This chapter explores the feasibility of exploring surprise and unfolding events through the extraction of strategic data from social media platforms and the Web and Internet to form extended-form eventgraphs. "Extended-form eventgraphs" are conceptualized as those involving multivariate descriptors of events: participants, their respective roles, their interrelationships, their messaging, the timeline, related locations, and other event features and dynamics. What are the current extant methods and tools, then, and how are they applied in sequence, and what is ultimately knowable to sketch out an eventgraph based on social media channels? What sorts of real-world human events, which may not be directly "social" or pre-planned, are observable in online spaces? This chapter offers an initial proof-of-concept of a non-scalable manual-based eventgraphing process with two real-world examples: one of a mainstream tracked event and one of a more silent event. Finally, it offers a simple sense of a possible way forward which may be used in whole or in part. The challenge here involves using publicly available software tools for this information capture (versus self-created programs).

Chapter 3

Eavesdropping on Narrowcast Self-talk and Microchats on Twitter 106
    Shalin Hai-Jew, Kansas State University, USA

On Twitter, a range of discourse networks may be extracted showing different types of conversational interactions. While the attention is often on what is trending and large-size high-interactive social graphs, many extracted networks are self-loops and small-group discourse networks based on ad hoc narrowcast conversations. In this exploratory study of microblogging messaging on Twitter, the focus is on microblogging conversations that result in self-loops (self-to-self conversations, individuals microblogging to themselves) and small-group graphs and motifs (one-to-few or few-to-few conversations). This work proposes and tests hypotheses about the various types of seeding #hashtags and keywords that result in different types of ad hoc microblogging microchat network graphs on Twitter.

Section 2
Theories, Models, and Practices for Multimedia Design and Deployment

Chapter 4

Leveraging the Design and Development of Multimedia Presentations for Learners 149
    Lijia Lin, East China Normal University, China
    Amy Leh, California State University San Bernardino, USA
    Jackie Hee Young Kim, Armstrong State University, USA
    Danilo M. Baylen, University of West Georgia, USA

The chapter addresses how multimedia presentations can be designed effectively for learners. Based on the literature, it defines the related terms and discusses the role of human factors during the design and development process of multimedia. Then, it discusses strategies, such as providing learner control and using visual cueing, to design effective multimedia presentations. In addition, various technologies in creating multimedia-based instruction are described. Finally, the chapter discusses evaluation frameworks, as well as the implications for integrating multimedia into educational practices.

Chapter 5

Audio for Multi-Media Presentations in E-Learning 164
    Hattie Wiley, National Weather Service, USA

Although many advances have changed the way we are able record, distribute, and consume audio enhanced or audio based learning materials, audio can still be either a critical driver or an impeding detriment to learner comprehension and retention. Consequently, this chapter reviews the instructional design implications of audio prior to exploring the impacts advances in audio technology, software, and equipment have on the creation of audio enhanced or audio based multimedia presentations for learning, training, or education.

Chapter 6

Use of Video to Enhance Education 189
Brent A. Anders, Kansas University, USA

Even with so many different educational tools and evolutions in techniques of instruction (both pedagogical and andrological approaches), the use of video is one of the most effective means of instructing students. This chapter presents multiple evidence detailing why video can greatly enhance instruction in a multiple of ways to include its use in motivation, explanation (via multi-modalities), and feedback. This chapter will also demonstrate the benefits of using a student-centered/learning-centered instructional video capturing system within the classroom to improve learning for both face-to-face and online learning. Resources and specific examples are provided to demonstrate that video is a fundamental tool that should be used to enhance both the educational process and instructional experience. New uses and video technologies are also addressed for future investigation and incorporation.

Section 3
Enhanced Technological Tools for Multimedia Designs

Chapter 7

Static Text-Based Data Visualizations: An Overview and a Sampler 203
Shalin Hai-Jew, Kansas State University, USA

Data visualizations have enhanced human understandings of various types of quantitative data for many years. Of late, text-based data visualizations have been used informally and formally on the WWW and Internet as well as for research. This chapter describes this phenomenon of text-based data visualizations by describing how many of the most common ones are created, where the underlying textual datasets are extracted from, how text-based data visualizations are analyzed, and the limits of such graphical depictions. While this work does not provide a comprehensive view of static (non-dynamic) text-based data visualizations, many of the most common ones are introduced. These visualizations are created using a variety of common commercial and open-source tools including Microsoft Excel, Google Books Ngram Viewer, Microsoft Visio, NVivo 10, Maltego Tungsten, CASOS AutoMap and ORA NetScenes, FreeMind, Wordle, UCINET and NetDraw, and Tableau Public. It is assumed that readers have a basic knowledge of machine-based text analysis.

Chapter 8

Using Microsites as Live Presentation Platforms (with Three Embedded Real-World Cases) 303
Shalin Hai-Jew, Kansas State University, USA

Live presentations in academic conferences often link to online resources for preview or post-view. Microsites may enhance live and real-time presentations. To examine the human factors and software challenges involved, this chapter offers three real-world partial solutions for interactive microsites that serve multiple purposes. This article focuses on the use of SoftChalk as a core authoring tool to create microsites for live presentations. Three real-world and unique cases (all from 2012) are showcased here: "Using Tableau Public for (Spatial and Trendline) Data Visualization (An Early Exploration and 'TMI' Musing on Data)" at https://softchalkcloud.com/lesson/rtNYCf1K80el9w; "Building and Analyzing Node-Link Diagrams to Understand Social Networks" at https://softchalkcloud.com/lesson/c4d8tSWMCwm39n; and "Building Effective Study Guides for Online Learning and Assessment" at https://softchalkcloud.com/lesson/rFnD0AQX3xRVTa.

Section 4
Considering Human Needs in Multimedia Presentations

Chapter 9

Promoting Engagement with Online Presentations 322
Amy Gaimaro, St. John's University, USA

Educators delivering online presentations face many challenges when teaching in this modality. Lack of student engagement is one such challenge. Students can study online with lackluster learning experiences when participating in a predominately text-based course. Applying multiple instructional strategies to address students' diverse learning styles can provide students with a more engaged online learning experience. Another challenge many educators face, is the need for support and guidance to facilitate effective online learning. More specifically, educators of the twenty-first century are seeking the know-how to move traditional text-based materials into online, media-rich course content. This chapter will examine some of the challenges of delivering quality online presentations. In conclusion, the author will provide examples of strategies for delivering effective online presentations within the virtual college classroom.

Chapter 10

Evaluation of Situations Causing Split of Attention in Multimedia Learning Environments via
Eye-Tracking Method 337
Duygu Mutlu-Bayraktar, Istanbul University, Turkey
Servet Bayram, Marmara University, Turkey

In this chapter, situations that can cause split of attention in multimedia environments were determined via eye tracking method. Fixation numbers, heat maps and area of interest of learners were analyzed. As a result of these analyses, design suggestions were determined for multimedia environments to provide focusing attention to content without split attention effect. Visual and auditory resources should be provided simultaneously. Visual information should be supported with auditory expression instead of texts. Images such as videos, pictures and texts should not be presented on the same screen. Texts provided with pictures should be presented via integration to each other instead of separate presentation of text and picture. Texts provided with videos should be presented via integration to each other instead of separate presentation of text and video. Images should be given via marking important points on images to increase attention.

Section 5
Digital Visualizations for Learning and Knowing

Chapter 11

Conducting Semantic-Based Network Analyses from Social Media Data: Extracted Insights about
the Data Leakage Movement 369
Shalin Hai-Jew, Kansas State University, USA

Network analysis is widely used to mine social media. This involves both the study of structural metadata (information about information) and the related contents (the textual messaging, the related imagery, videos, URLs, and others). A semantic-based network analysis relies on the analysis of relationships between words and phrases (as meaningful concepts), and this approach may be applied effectively to social media data to extract insights. To gain a sense of how this might work, a trending topic of the day was chosen (namely, the free-information and data leakage movement) to see what might be illuminated using this semantic-based network analysis, an open-source technology, NodeXL, and access to multiple social media platforms. Three types of networks are extracted: (1) conversations (#hashtag microblogging networks on Twitter; #eventgraphs on Twitter; and keyword searches on Twitter; (2) contents (video networks on YouTube, related tags networks on Flickr, and article networks on Wikipedia; and (3) user accounts on Twitter, YouTube, Flickr, and Wikipedia.

Chapter 12
Grounding Cyber: Querying Social Media Platforms, the Web, and Internet for Geolocational Information 428
Shalin Hai-Jew, Kansas State University, USA

Tying "cyber" entities, spaces, and events to real-world physical spaces is a critical step in de-mythifying cyberspace. This chapter introduces Maltego Tungsten™, a penetration testing tool, as one method to extract geolocational information from social media platforms, the Web, and the Internet—in order to relate online accounts, emails, aliases, and online-discussed events to specific physical spaces. This tool may be used for general research or applied "oppo" (opposition) or "doxing" (documenting) research of targets. This also discusses how the geolocational information may be further used to extract deeper understandings. Also, Network Overview, Discovery, and Exploration for Excel (NodeXL) is applied for some geolocational information extractions.

Section 6
Real-World Cases in Innovative Multimedia Applications

Chapter 13
Rolling NVivo 10 out to a University's Research Community: Live Trainings and a Semantic Web-Friendly E-Book 526
Shalin Hai-Jew, Kansas State University, USA

At Kansas State University, there has been a concentrated effort to evolve the institution into one of the nation's top 50 research public universities. One small part of that involves the rollout of NVivo to the university's faculty, staff, and graduate students. By the second year of the site license, the campus was on its own to provide training. This effort involved multiple live face-to-face (F2F) trainings and the use of a multimedia e-book. "Using NVivo: An Unofficial and Unauthorized Primer" (http://scalar.usc.edu/works/using-nvivo-an-unofficial-and-unauthorized-primer/index) was written over a several week period (hyper-fast agile development) and released on the Scalar platform in Fall Semester 2014. This chapter addresses how a designed e-book, built on a Semantic Web-friendly platform, harnesses the power of multimedia, digital repositories, the Surface Web, and crowd-sourced feedback.

Compilation of References 559

About the Contributors 582

Index 586

Foreword

Ancient Practices Reborn in Digital Multimedia

Ignore all the current hype about multimedia, and the possibilities for its contributions to education remain.

The *Merriam-Webster Dictionary* defines multimedia as "using, involving, or encompassing several media <a *multimedia* approach to learning>," with the first known use of the term in 1962. In 1994, the IEEE Computer Society launched a bimonthly, peer-reviewed magazine on multimedia with Dr. William Grosky as editor in chief and me as the magazine's IEEE staff editor. At the time—just 20 years ago—everything about multimedia seemed new. Today, "*IEEE MultiMedia* is a quarterly peer-reviewed scientific journal published by the IEEE Computer Society and covering multimedia technologies. Topics of interest include image processing, video processing, audio analysis, text retrieval and understanding, data mining and analysis, and data fusion." These research-advancing topics represent quite a difference from the earliest implementations of multimedia covered by the first issues of the publication—methods and approaches also used by our recent and earliest ancestors.

We don't know when language arose, although some scientists theorize it might have evolved with tool use. Teaching others how to do something is faster and easier when the instructor can tell as well as show students what to do and in what order. We do know that early peoples used plant and mineral dyes and stone tools to create images on cave walls and elsewhere to save their knowledge for their own future use as well as that of their descendants. Centuries later, Homer and other bards used lyres to create a musical framework for sung stories, helping themselves, apprentice bards, and listeners memorize the lengthy tales of their people's history or mythology. This method continued through history, and we still use it today in teaching even our youngest children: think of the ABC or alphabet song.

With organized record keeping and "formal" education came the use of surfaces crafted specifically for text (letters and numbers), including clay, vellum, papyrus, knotted cords, sheets of slate, and paper. These materials were so precious in earlier times that they were frequently reused and sometimes kept in special collections. The first uses involved finance, from individual contracts to tallies of goods and government tax receipts. Later, a few rare libraries collected texts, from histories to myth, with the risk of destruction always present, whether by invaders, weather or geological disasters, or accidental fires. Only the most dedicated scholars could access these records, and then only if they had the time and money to travel to them. The wealthy, including church and government officials, collected their own libraries in a somewhat haphazard fashion, using the professional scribes available to them to make copies or even originals of oral traditions (as happened with Homer's work and the early Danish/English saga of Beowulf).

"Modern" mass education with teachers and classrooms is fairly recent, largely but not entirely supplanting the types of church or tutorial education reserved for the elites and apprenticeship learning for those who became craftsmen. Mechanization disrupted that model, but most people still did not receive any kind of formal education until their governments decided it was valuable for their economies. And the right thing to do for individual human development, of course. The advent of computers and their rapidly growing importance in all facets of our lives, including education of even the youngest students with toy-like electronic devices, arises from an existing tradition of using multiple types of media to pass knowledge to the next generation, something we tend to forget in embracing "new" methods of teaching and learning.

Our effectiveness in using multimedia to support (not supplant) verbal and textual methods remains an open question. Some research shows improved engagement of students when multimedia enlivens the instruction, but not always improved retention. Students who enjoy the class but don't learn the material not only fail to achieve the curricular goals but also fail to advance in their studies. Like any other instructional tools, multimedia tools require thoughtful application to achieve the desired results. Allowing students to use different media to learn in the ways that serve them best works only when they have committed to that learning, the tools are appropriate for the purpose, and the instructors and students have the support they need to use, modify, and create media. That includes demonstrating not just subject knowledge but also multimedia literacy, which might take the form of projects that can develop into an electronic portfolio for lifelong use.

This book, *Design Strategies and Innovations in Multimedia Presentations*, continues research into the *effective* use of multimedia. The authors share their experience, examples, and advice about pedagogy, methods, and tools to weave multimedia into instruction without losing sight of the ultimate goal: student learning. People have used different media from the earliest stages of human development to teach their children and others, and finding ways to apply various types of media in our increasingly digital world builds on an ancient pattern that has served humanity well.

Nancy Hays
EDUCAUSE, USA

Nancy Hays is editor and manager, Publishing, for EDUCAUSE, a nonprofit association and the foremost community of IT leaders and professionals committed to advancing higher education. She joined EDUCAUSE in 2000 to manage the editorial and peer-review process for EDUCAUSE Quarterly, which moved entirely online in 2009 and merged with EDUCAUSE Review and the EDUCAUSE Multimedia programs in 2012 as the association's flagship publication. As editor for EDUCAUSE, Hays works with the editorial, content, and executive teams to determine important trends in the field of higher education information technology, solicit appropriate authors to write on different topics, and develop ideas for publication online. She also runs the peer-review committee and process and oversees the editorial and production teams for EDUCAUSE publications, from conference programs to books. Prior to joining EDUCAUSE, Hays was group managing editor for the IEEE Computer Society, where she started as an assistant editor in 1985. As group managing editor she supervised editorial and production teams and worked with the editors-in-chief and editorial boards for IEEE Computer Graphics and Applications, IEEE Multimedia, IEEE Micro, IEEE Design and Test, and the Annals of the History of Computing. From 1980 to 1985, she held editorial jobs in technology and medical publishing. Hays earned a master's degree in English literature from UCLA in 1980 and three bachelor's degrees from Oregon State University in 1977 (English, economics, and liberal studies).

Preface

Every book involves a boggling amount of focus and hard work. Because a finalized book is never a sure thing, I always wait until the manuscript as fully materialized—the work peer reviewed and revised, the images properly rendered, and the contracts signed—before writing any preface. After all, anything done earlier is premature if there is nothing to actually introduce. This introduction will include a description of the topic, where it fits in the world today, describe the target audience, and suggest how this book may impact the field. Finally, this preface will introduce the backstory of this work along with an overview of its contents.

Today, it's all multimedia. *Design Strategies and Innovations in Multimedia Presentations* takes readers behind the thoughts, designs, and innovations behind the multimedia that people consume today on social media platforms, in online courses, in various presentations (mediated and F2F), in e-books, and elsewhere. Broadly speaking, "multimedia" refers to the uses of multiple mediums of expression or communications. The rarity today is not multimedia but single media: think about the last time you engaged with anything that was just pure and plain text or just imagery. Today, slideshows feature embedded videos, interactive questions, and light games. HTML videos include interactive questions and simulations. E-books contain data visualizations, hyperlinks, interactive simulations, embedded videotaped interviews, and rich media. Online maps are zoomable and pannable; they are viewable in different overlays; there are street views; there are rich layers of data that may be accessed.

Everywhere I turn, there is multimedia richness. Last year, I went to several local conferences and presentations related to the "digital humanities," a catch-all term referring to the uses of computation and WWW-based affordances to enhance work in humanities fields. Rich data corpuses are being transcoded, curated, richly annotated, and shared broadly online. Crowd-sourced research is being used to complement traditional channels of knowing. Social media platforms are being scraped for structural data to analyze human interrelationships and content networks. Many of these tools are free or of nominal expense. In the age of the Social Web, there is a lot of hosting capability for users. There are a variety of web browser and software add-ins that contribute to data extraction capabilities from the WWW and Internet as well as from social media platforms. This data may be extracted and used to draw relational networks for structure mining. Multimedia-based richness is being used to enhance research, teaching, learning, and any number of other endeavors.

In online training systems I've evaluated, there are avatars (voiced-over by professional trainers) engaging from within virtual environments. There are rich agent-based models that use a wide range of dynamic visuals to evoke simplified worlds. In the multiple massive open online courses (MOOCs) that I've taken this past year and into this one, I've benefitted from interactive videos, videos annotated with overlays of information, annotated lecturing with online whiteboards (and document cameras), and media-rich assessments. For various on-campus projects, there are agent-based models that are highly interactive (with wide ranges of possible parameters) and visual. There have been advancements in virtual and game worlds to simulate natural environments, which are being pursued through grant funding. Games for learning are easy to create with authoring tools that have become as easy as inputting contents (and maybe a little basic art). On multiple projects, digital slideshows are easily output for clever interactivity, with visitors able to page through digital slideshows and photo albums.

While there are elements of "wow" in multimedia used for higher education and mainstream learning, more often, the struggles are just to create mere coherence and polish while wielding multimedia authoring tools. Those who work in data visualization have been striving to communicate complex "big data" to researchers and others using multimedia methods because lower-dimensional means are insufficient to convey the ingrained complexity of the data. Proper designs are necessary to help humans intuit meanings from the masses of data in the world, a challenge that Robert Sapolsky has so famously addressed in "People Who Can Intuit in Six Dimensions" (2010).

There is very little an instructional designer does that does not involve some form of multimedia, whether it is in training, instructional design itself, data extractions from social media platforms, data analysis from online survey systems, presenting at conferences F2F or from a distance, or publishing.

The multimedia design aspects. While contents may be born digital on-the-fly, quite a bit of multimedia contents are designed and structured for particular purposes. Even as related authoring technologies have advanced and become much easier to wield (often without much needed in the way of direct coding), designing meaningful and effective multimedia requires plenty of skills: in design, drafting, pre-testing, and effort.

New technologies are created to enable easier capture and sharing of information with others. Some recent examples are screen capture tools (both static and full motion) that harness the computer and built-in webcams and microphones (or mobile devices); and image- and video- editing tools. There are new technologies that enable digital authoring—whether agent-based modeling tools, 3D modeling, gameplay design, diagramming / drawing tools, animations, and others. On a daily basis, I am dazzled by the various multimedia elements while aware of the technologies and design efforts to create these multi-media-rich experiences. The sophistication of authoring tools for the creation of multimedia-based digital learning objects has enabled subject matter experts (SMEs) themselves to create what they want to their exact specifications. For an instructional designer, he or she is in a constant race to maintain relevance.

The goal of this book is to capture some of the methods of designing multimedia to present information, learning, sensations, and experiences. While most people consume multimedia often on a daily basis through the Web and Internet, many may have no idea of the amount of resources, effort, savvy, and design that goes into this creating multimedia. There are usually also gaps in understanding the rules that guide the work—law-based rules of privacy (for the people featured in multimedia), copyright and intellectual property protections, accessibility, and others; further, there are informative guidelines of designing for human perception, cognition, memory, and learning.

De facto media is "multi" by nature, and the term "multimedia" is redundant and likely dated. This topic may be better represented as something about "digital" contents. Multimedia design and delivery methods evolve quickly. The technologies themselves are constantly evolving. Vint Cerf has recently warned of the risks of the loss of digital contributions and proposed a sort of "digital vellum" to ensure that multimedia created today is accessible to people in the future. The dependencies required to access digital contents—the digital file types, basic computer languages, the computer operating systems, the computer hardware—are in constant motion, and at any one time, there are contents lost to large groups of people through the digital "slow fires."

The romance of an Idea. The initial impetus for this work involves the romance of an idea, simply, explaining multimedia design. The romance is almost always a necessity because a rational cost-benefit consideration would likely result in not pursuing the project. A book project takes on about a year in development time, and sometimes, longer; in this case, *Design Strategies and Innovations in Multimedia Presentations* is coming in about a half-year later than initially planned. Actual royalties for the lifespan of a book will not even cover the first weekend of invested work in creating a book. Suffice it to say that the thrill of a book's publication and its going out into the world overbalances the other way and makes up for the huge investments in effort.

The Chapters

Nancy Hays provides a historical sense of multimedia in learning leading up to the present in her excellent foreword, "Ancient Practices Reborn in Digital Multimedia."

The book itself consists of six parts, as follows:

Part 1: Exploring Online Multimedia
Part 2: Theories, Models, and Practices for Multimedia Design and Deployment
Part 3: Enhanced Technological Tools for Multimedia Designs
Part 4: Considering Human Needs in Multimedia Presentations
Part 5: Digital Visualizations for Learning and Knowing
Part 6: Real-World Cases in Innovative Multimedia Applications

The first section describes the informative uses of some online multimedia. There are three chapters in Part 1, "Exploring Online Multimedia." The opening chapter is part of a multi-year study of the Hidden (Deep) Web and its contents. Manuel Alvarez Diaz, Victor Manuel Prieto Alvarez, and Fidel Cacheda Seijo's "The Evolution of the (Hidden) Web and its Hidden Data" describes rich techniques used to understand the contents of the hidden Web, including the identification of multimedia based on identified file types. Chapter 2, "Creating Extended-Form EventGraphs from Social Media using Publicly Available Software Tools," describes strategies to map an in-world event based on the signals available from social media using various extractive software tools and methods. In this work, Shalin Hai-Jew builds on prior works that used tools to map participants chatting about events and their messaging from microblogging sites; the "extended form" perspective strives for a fuller view. Hai-Jew's "Eavesdropping on Narrowcast Self-talk and Microchats on Twitter," Chapter 3, describes the phenomena of individual self-looped self-talk on Twitter as well as small-group conversations. This chapter shows some of the more common uses of microchatting sites not just for popular and trending communications phenomena but quieter forms of communications to meet human needs.

In the next section, the focus is on practical design approaches to multimedia. Part 2, "Theories, Models, and Practices for Multimedia Design and Deployment," consists of three chapters. Lijia Lin, Amy Leh, Jackie Hee Young Kim, and Danilo M. Baylen's "Leveraging the Design and Development of Multimedia Presentations for All Learners" (Chapter 4) engages some solid strategies for the effective design of multimedia for learning. Hattie Wiley's "Audio for Multimedia Presentations in E-Learning"

(Chapter 5) provides a highly readable approach to considering audio in instructional design based on years of design experience. This work refreshingly and expertly addresses a perceptual channel that is not often addressed in the research literature. Brent A. Anders' "Use of Video to Enhance Education" (Chapter 6) provides a practical look at practical considerations in designing video for learning.

The third section focuses on technological tools. Part 3, "Enhanced Technological Tools for Multimedia Designs," is comprised of two chapters. Hai-Jew's "Static Text-Based Data Visualizations: An Overview and a Sampler" (Chapter 7) summarizes a range of text-based data visualizations created from a suite of complementary tools used to represent research. Chapter 8, "Using Microsites as Live Presentation Platforms (with Three Embedded Real-World Cases)," describes the application of online microsites to deliver multimedia contents for use in live presentations. Microsites are those that go beyond an online presentation but include interactivity and often residual resources that may be left online as learning resources.

Part 4, "Considering Human Needs in Multimedia Presentations," contains two chapters that focus on the human element in the consumption of multimedia. Amy Gaimaro's "Promoting Engagement with Online Presentations" (Chapter 9) addresses the very real need to capture learner attention and engagement. This work uses a generational model to understand learner needs and suggests some core preparatory and design approaches. In Chapter 10, Duygu Mutlu-Bayraktar and Servet Bayram use an eye-tracking-based research methodology to understand how particular multimedia layouts engage human attention. In "Evaluation of Situations Causing Split of Attention in Multimedia Learning Environments via Eye-tracking Method," this authoring team empirically builds on the research of multimedia and human attention.

In Part 5, "Digital Visualizations for Learning and Knowing," there are two chapters that focus on the uses of multiple perceptual channels for learning and knowing. Chapter 11, "Conducting Semantic-Based Network Analyses from Social Media Data: Extracted Insights about the Data Leakage Movement," focuses on the application of network analysis to online multimedia data to extract public expressed sentiment. In this work, Hai-Jew uses the data leakage movement and the public discussions around this issue as a "seed" for the research. She focuses on the tight integration of text and visual information as a way of creating awareness and knowing. Chapter 12, "Grounding Cyber: Querying Media Platforms, the Web, and Internet for Geolocational Information," describes how online information may be converted into geolocational data and related back to the physical world. Here, Hai-Jew shows cyberspace as not quite cyber but fully grounded.

The final section, Part 6, "Real-World Cases in Innovative Multimedia Applications," contains one work. Hai-Jew's "Rollling NVivo 10 out to a University's Research Community: Live Trainings and a Semantic-Web Friendly E-Book" describes the use of the Scalar platform to support the rollout of a qualitative and mixed methods data analysis tool to a university. This chapter highlights the importance of harnessing technologies in an innovative way to achieve instrumental aims in a university context.

The text development cycle. Ironically, the editing of a print book is in some ways one of the lesser multimedia-rich endeavors, and there is something pleasantly old-fashioned about a print text (even if most copies of it go out electronically). In a sense, text alone may feel like a kind of sensory deprivation in the current age. Initially, it was thought that this text could address a range of approaches to multimedia presentation: interactive slideshows, multimedia-enriched surveys, games and simulations, narrations, data visualizations, web conferencing presentations, and augmented reality experiences. There were hopes for mobile design elements. It was hoped that there would be some multimedia FX or special effects. I wanted writing on various types of strategies to convey truth—through skilled multimedia-supported artifice. There are so many ways to package information in digital formats. Ultimately, I wanted to capture a sense of where multimedia design is today and how multimedia may be deployed creatively and effectively in different contexts.

When the initial call for chapter proposals went out, I had high hopes that there would be rich angles and insights, given how pervasive multimedia is in the educational and training context and beyond. The tactic was to "cast a wide net" and to be open to the various angles that various writers originated. Some initial chapters that were submitted did not meet book standards for originality, relevance, focus, or overall fit, and the works did not have sufficient cores to build on for revision. The skill set needed to create a coherent chapter based on direct author insights and experiences is a rare one, which requires years to build and maintain. Indeed, much of what is researched and written does not actually make it into peer-reviewed and edited publications. (Ideally, the process should be a supportive and constructive one, and there should be lessons learned from the process—to ultimately enable the author to publish in a quality reviewed work one day.) Another challenge with this text involved a number of authors who proposed topics with workable ideas but whose lives became too busy, and nothing was ever submitted. Follow-through for promised work is also not a given, and there are always some number—even quite renowned and well published individuals—who have too many other commitments to finish the work. In the planning of any book, such "drops" are planned into the final. It can be very difficult to change up the incentives for authors, and I will be the first to admit that the inputs to a chapter are extraordinary.

All the prior challenges were to be expected. What was a surprise to me was how I had miscalculated the pool of potential writers. In fields where there is broad knowledge, such as this one, I assumed that there might be interest in pursuing creative designs and technological applications. There is lot of talented individuals and teams working in various fields that engage multimedia, but it may be that there is less interest in writing for publication. There is certainly tough competition for author talent, and authors are free agents who have every right to shop their work. Sometimes when there is a lot of something going on people do not seem to have the time yet to process what they are doing and therefore do not have something to share with others. Anyway, I really am not sure why this work did not attract as many authors as I would have liked. Ideally, there would have been a wider diversity of works.

I am very delighted that this work did ultimately "make." There are costs to all enthusiasms, and as with all book topics pursued, the works are of interest to me. *Design Strategies and Innovations in Multimedia Presentations* is a culmination of knowledge gained from years in the instructional design trenches and enthusiasms that have been enduring.

Shalin Hai-Jew
Kansas State University, USA

Acknowledgment

First, I would like to thank the authors who contributed. Every chapter requires a lot of expertise and effort. The authors had to come up with original ideas, conduct the research work, write their chapters, and go through a process of peer critique and revision. They have to have the professional trust to share their work broadly in the present and for those who may use this book into the future. From the outside, these aspects may seem fairly simple, but in fact, they are not. Even the work of coming up with original insights and ways to frame the work involves the need to stay up-to-date on the research literature, on in-field techniques, and on a wide range of software tools. The authors have to be in good standing with their respective workplace organizations. The authors have to practice professional self-discipline if they are working alone, and they have to collaborate well with colleagues if they are collaborating on a team. To the authors goes my deepest gratitude.

Next, I would like to extend my thanks to the editorial advisory board members. They were a source of encouragement throughout the work. Nancy Hays, editor of EDUCAUSE Review Online, wrote a spectacular foreword as well further, she is a constant source of friendly professional support, for which I am deeply grateful. I am grateful, too, that they lent their good names and prestige to this project.

Finally, the personnel at IGI-Global were supportive as always. Every book project requires a team to actualize, and I am grateful for their support. Their new book system has made the process easier. Austin DeMarco was especially supportive and has my gratitude.

Section 1
Exploring Online Multimedia

Chapter 1
The Evolution of the (Hidden) Web and its Hidden Data

Manuel Álvarez Díaz
University of A Coruña, Spain

Víctor Manuel Prieto Álvarez
University of A Coruña, Spain

Fidel Cacheda Seijo
University of A Coruña, Spain

ABSTRACT

This paper presents an analysis of the most important features of the Web and its evolution and implications on the tools that traverse it to index its content to be searched later. It is important to remark that some of these features of the Web make a quite large subset to remain "hidden". The analysis of the Web focuses on a snapshot of the Global Web for six different years: 2009 to 2014. The results for each year are analyzed independently and together to facilitate the analysis of both the features at any given time and the changes between the different analyzed years. The objective of the analysis are twofold: to characterize the Web and more importantly, its evolution along the time.

INTRODUCTION

Since its origins, the WWW has been the subject of numerous studies. However, one constant has been and continues to be the analysis of its size. Although it is nearly impossible to compute the exact size of the Web, because it is in constant change, everyone agrees that his size is in the order of billions of documents or pages (Gulli & Signorini, 2005). In this way, the WWW could be considered the largest repository of documents ever built.

Due to the large size of the Web, search engines are essential tools for users who want to access relevant information for a specific topic. Search engines are complex systems that allow, among other things: gathering, storing, managing and granting access to the information. Crawling systems are those which perform the task of gathering information. These programs are capable of traversing and analysing the Web in a certain order, by following the links between different pages.

DOI: 10.4018/978-1-4666-8696-0.ch001

The task of a crawling system presents numerous challenges due to the quantity, variability and quality of the information that it needs to collect. Among these challenges, specific aspects can be highlighted, such as the technologies used in web pages to access to data, both in the server-side (Raghavan & Garcia-Molina, 2001) or in the client-side (Bergman, 2001); or problems associated with web content such as Web Spam (Gyongyi & Garcia-Molina, 2005) or repeated contents (Kumar & Govindarajulu, 2009), etc. To get a detailed enumeration it is necessary to analyse the Web in more detail.

This article presents an analysis of the most important features of the Web and its components and also its evolution over a period of time. Particular emphasis is placed on the use of client/server side technologies. It is very important to remark that the Hidden Web is "hidden" just for the existence of some technologies used in web documents that difficult the task of crawler systems for accessing to it.

The analysis focuses on a snapshot of the Global Web for six different years: from 2009 to 2014. The results for each year are analysed independently and together to simplify the evaluation of the features at any given time and the changes between the different analysed years. The objectives of the analysis are twofold: to characterize the Web and more importantly, its evolution along the time, and also to analyze how its changes affect tools such as crawlers and search engines. So, changing trends are presented and explained.

The structure of this paper is as follows. Background section introduces works related with the study and characterization of the Web. Methodology section shows the methodology followed to characterize the Web. Dataset section explains the dataset used. The analysis section discusses the results obtained for each year, and their evolution through the time. Finally, the future research directions section includes possible future works and the conclusions section summarises the results of the paper.

BACKGROUND

The characterization of the Web is a topic widely studied in the supported literature. Baeza-Yates et al. (Baeza-Yates, Castillo & Efthimiadis, 2007) performed a study which analyses various features of the Web at several levels: web page, web site and national domains. On the other hand, there are several studies that are focused on the Web of a particular country. In 2000, Sanguanpong et al. (Sanguanpong, Piamsa-nga, Keretho, Poovarawan & Warangrit, 2000) presented an analysis of various issues related to web servers and web documents in Thailand. Baeza-Yates et al. presented two articles (Baeza-Yates, Castillo, & Lopez, 2005; Baeza-Yates & Castillo, 2000), which were focused more specifically on the characteristics of the Spanish and Chilean Web, respectively. The Spanish Web was also studied by Prieto et al. (Prieto, Álvarez, & Cacheda, 2013), by comparing the analysis of the Spanish Web with the Global Web in a tree-years period. In 2002, Boldi et al. (Boldi, Codenotti, Santini, & Vigna, 2002) presented an interesting article, where the authors have studied different features (content and structure analysis, web graph, etc.) of the African Web. Gomes et al. (Gomes & Silva, 2005), carried out a study to characterise the community Web of the people of Portugal. The authors studied different features such as: the number and domain distribution of sites, the number and size distribution of text documents, the structure of this Web, etc. Years later, Miranda and Gomes (Miranda & Gomes, 2009) performed a study which presented trends on the evolution of the Portuguese Web, derived from the comparison of two characterizations of a web portion performed within a 5 year interval. This study analyses several metrics regarding content and site characteristics. Modesto et al. (Modesto, Pereira, Ziviani, Castillo, & Baeza-Yates, 2005) presented an article, which analyses the features of approximately 2% of the .br domains. The results have been compared with the results obtained in other studies on the Chilean and Greek Web. Finally, another similar study was performed by Efthimiadis and Castillo (Efthimiadis & Castillo, 2004), where the authors did a characterization of the Greek Web.

On the other hand, there are studies that focus on studying a specific feature of the Web. It is the case of the study presented by Grefenstette and Nioche (Grefenstette & Nioche, 2000), where the authors have analysed the English and non-English language used on the Web. A relevant study was the performed by Bharat et al. (Bharat, Chang, Henzinger, & Ruhl, 2001), which discussed the links between Web sites and its meaning. Other study focused on a particular feature of the Web, was the performed by Downey (Downey, 2001), where the author has analysed models for web page sizes.

There are other studies that focus exclusively on the structure of the Web, such as that conducted by Broder et al. (Broder, Kumar, Maghoul, Raghavan, Rajagopalan, Stata, Tomkins, & Wiener, 2000). In this article they show an analysis of links between pages in the same domain, across domains within the same country and between global domains. In 1999, Huberman and Adamic (Huberman, & Adamic, 1999) carried out a study where the authors characterise the distribution of web pages per web site. According to this study the web pages are distributed among sites following to a universal power law: many sites have only a few pages, whereas very few sites have hundreds of thousands of pages. In 2007, Serrano et al. (Serrano, Maguitman, Boguñá, Fortunato, & Vespignani, 2007) reported a statistical analysis of the topological properties of four different WWW graphs obtained with different crawlers. Another relevant study was presented by Baeza-Yates et al. (Baeza-Yates, Saint-Jean, & Castillo, 2002), where they analyse the structure of the Web, its dynamics and its relationship to the quality of content. Finally, in (Baeza-Yates & Poblete, 2006), Baeza-Yates and Poblete characterise the structure of the Chilean Web.

A relevant part of the Web that has been studied by many authors is the Deep or Hidden Web. This portion of the Web contains those pages that are accessed through web forms or by means of client-side technologies such as JavaScript or Flash. Among the studies, we can highlight the one carried out by Bergman (Bergman, 2001). More recent studies are those performed by Shestakov, in 2011, (Shestakov, 2011a; Shestakov, 2011b). In these papers, the author analyses the problem of Deep Web characterization and treats to estimate the total number of online databases on the Web.

Other aspects that deserve special attention are those related to the similarity of the Web and its decline. A study of the similarity of the Web, is the one performed by Cho et al. (Cho, Shivakumar, & Garcia-Molina, 2000), which proposes a technique to detect replicated documents and collections to improve web crawlers, archivers, and ranking functions used in search engines.

There are several studies with respect to the dynamic and age of Web pages. The most notably of these is that presented by Lewandowski (Lewandowski, 2008), which discusses the evolution of the age of the pages over several years. Fetterly et al. (Fetterly, Manasse, Najork, Wiener, 2003) included a study about the degree of change of each page, and which factors are correlated with change intensity. On the other hand, there are several studies of the Web dynamic. Adar et al. (Adar, Teevan, Dumais, & Elsas, 2009) describe algorithms, analyses, and models for characterizing changes in Web content, focusing on both time (by using hourly and sub-hourly crawls) and structure (by looking at page-DOM, and term-level changes). Other interesting work about the Web dynamic is the performed by Ntoulas et al. (Ntoulas, Cho, & Olston, 2004). They seek to gain improved insight into how Web search engines should cope with the evolving Web. This study is focus on aspects of potential interest to search engine designers: the evolution of link structure over time, the rate of creation of new pages and new distinct content on the Web, and the rate of change of the content of existing pages under search-centric measures of degree of change.

At last, there are studies focused on proposing crawling strategies to improve the performance of crawlers. They are based on the age and dynamics (changes) of web pages. For instance, the work by Brewington and Cybenko (Brewington & Cybenko, 2000) or a study by Cho and Garcia-Molina (Cho & Garcia-Molina, 2003a), where the authors not only discuss the dynamics of web content, but also show methods to try to keep data collections of search engines more up to date. We can also highlight the presented by Cho and Garcia-Molina (Cho & Garcia-Molina, 2003b). This article formalizes the notion of "freshness" of copied data and propose a Poisson process as the change model of data sources. They show that a Poisson process is a good model to describe the changes of Web pages. Other similar study is the performed by Olston and Pandey (Olston & Pandey, 2008), where the authors characterize the longevity of information found on the Web, via both empirical measurements and a generative model that coincides with these measurements. They propose new recrawl scheduling policies that consider longevity.

Numerous studies have examined the Web from different points of view. However, to the best of our knowledge, only our previously presented paper (Prieto, Álvarez, & Cacheda, 2013) has studied the evolution of the main features the Web through time. This article expands the analysis previously presented in (Prieto, Álvarez, & Cacheda, 2013), by extending it to a 6-years period, but focusing on the Global Web. In addition, it puts special interest in features relevant to determine the evolution of the Hidden Web in time, such as the use of client/server side technologies.

METHODOLOGY USED FOR THE ANALYSIS

The analysis of the Web can be performed at various levels of granularity (Björneborn & Ingwersen, 2004). Below we describe the levels we have included in this article, together with the characteristics analysed in each of them, for the six-years period considered. They are also shown in Figure 1.

- Word Level: The study of this level provides information about the vocabulary used on the Web, and the most commonly used HTML tags.
- Content Level: The analysis of this level allows obtaining information about the evolution of the web documents size and its relationship to the useful content. It allows increasing the knowledge about the evolution of the most widely used languages on the Web, and how multimedia file formats, format styles, other types of documents or compression methods usage evolve on the Web. In addition, some meta-tags commonly used in web pages are analysed.
- Web Page Level: At this level, the characteristics of an entire web page are analysed: the length of the URLs/title of web pages and the age of web pages. In addition, we will pay special attention on the level of compression and the similarity of web pages.
- Web Site Level: The study of this level provides the main features of web sites, defined as collections of related web pages common to a domain or subdomain. We analyse the number of links (inlink, outlink, static, dynamic, relative and absolute) on the Web. This allows to know how the Web is growing and modifying its structure, and how this affects search algorithms. We also analyse the technologies used by web servers to build sites. In addition, the Hidden Web, defined as the set of web pages that are not directly accessible through links (Raghavan & Garcia-Molina, 2001) is analysed. When we talk about Hidden Web, we could differentiate two very different parts: the client-side and the server-side Hidden Web. For the client-side Hidden Web and its evolution, we study client-side technologies usage. In order to access server-side Hidden Web, it is

Figure 1. Granularity levels used to analyse the Web

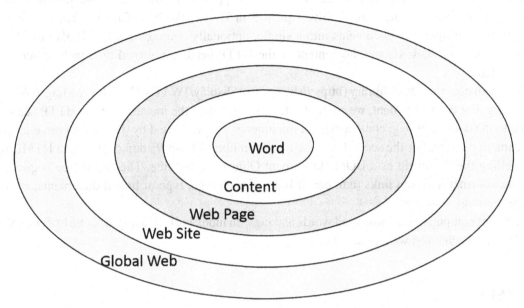

necessary to submit a query on a web form. This part of the Web contains a large amount of data, but its treatment is more complex. The size and the quality of the Hidden Web is important for the crawlers and search engines, to decide whether they should put more resources to process it. In this study, we analyse the evolution in the number of Hidden Web entry points, which are the elements that a crawler has to be able to discover for accessing hidden web content.

- Global Web Level: This level allows obtaining information about the use and evolution of the software used by web servers. In addition, the mainly used configurations for the Exclusion Robots protocol are analysed.

DATASET USED FOR THE ANALYSIS

This section describes the dataset used for studying the Web. We used the data provided by "The Stanford WebBase Project[1]", which is part of the Stanford Digital Libraries Project[2]. In this project, the Stanford team uses a crawler called WebVac, for retrieving data from the Web. WebVac crawls depth first, until depth of 7 levels and fetching a maximum number of 10k pages per site. Uses a list of web sites as initial feed, and it executes until all the sites in that list are processes or the month is over.

The full dataset contains more than 260TB of data (in August 2011), organized into subsets of different topics (general thematic, natural disasters, governments, etc.). For this study, only general thematic datasets were considered. Of the more than 7000 million obtained pages, the study choose a random sample to get a subset of 10 million pages for each year, 2009, 2010, 2011, 2012, 2013 and 2014. Overall, the global dataset contains approximately 60 million web pages.

For analyzing the datasets, we have developed a java application able to generate statistics from the data downloaded from the Stanford WebBase project in WARC (Web ARChive) format. This format allows storing multiple web documents into a single, optionally compressed, file. It also includes, for each web document, its URL and the content of the HTTP headers returned by a web server when it was requested.

Our system uses the JWAT library (https://sbforge.org/display/JWAT/JWAT) for reading WARC files in streaming. For each document, we compute statistics based on the metadata of the HTTP headers associated to the document (e.g. content-type of documents, software used by the web server, etc.) and on the document content. For the second, we use the jsoup library (http://jsoup.org), a java HTML parser for modelling the document as a DOM (Document Object Model) tree. The DOM tree is queried for retrieving information about links (number of links of each type, type of linked documents, etc.), web forms, technologies used, etc.

Finally, for computing the most-used words and tags, an index built by using Apache Lucene software (http://lucene.apache.org) was used.

ANALYSIS

Taking the dataset defined in previous section as a starting point, the following subsections discuss the results obtained for the features introduced at the methodology section.

Features at Word Level

Within the scope of web pages, a word may be used mainly as a term or as an HTML tag. This section analyses the words from these two points of view.

Vocabulary

In order to study the vocabulary used on the Web, a word is any alphanumeric string with length larger or equals than one character. For computing them, we remove all the HTML tags of the pages, and used an Apache Lucene Index for the resultant content. Then, we compute the top words for each year. Table 1 shows the 25 most commonly used words in the Web in the period studied. This indicates that the top web page words remains near the same along all the years except for the token corresponding to the current year (different in each case). We can also perceive that the frequency of occurrences of the more common words is increasing. For instance, the "home" word had an occurrence frequency of 54.73% in 2009 and it grew until 63.42% in 2014. Something similar happened with "about" (from 52.74% to 63.42%) of "contact" (from 50.03% to 58.98%). Regarding the current year token, we would like to remark that in 2009, it appeared in the 32,9% of the analysed pages. I grew until 40.8% in 2010 and in the range 43%-46% between 2011 and 2014. This could be an indicator about the number of new pages created in the corresponding year, with respect to the pages that had been created in previous years, but remain in the current year.

All of these indicate a growing number of common words in web pages. From the point of view of search engines, this means an increment in the number of terms that are no so relevant to represent the content of a web page. So, selecting relevant web documents for a given set of terms, will be more difficult.

Table 1. Top web page words

2009	2010	2011	2012	2013	2014
home(54.73%)	home(56.14%)	about(59.05%)	about(61.12%)	about(61.64%)	about(63.42%)
about(52.74%)	about(56.02%)	home(57.13%)	home(57.71%)	home(57.05%)	contact(58.98%)
contact(50.03%)	contact(53.21%)	contact(55.69%)	contact(57.03%)	contact(56.9%)	home(57.41%)
from(50.02%)	from(50.75%)	us(51.08%)	us(52.74%)	us(53.5%)	us(55.65%)
all(48.23%)	all(49.8%)	from(50.99%)	all(52.69%)	all(53.03%)	all(52.5%)
us(44.95%)	us(48.74%)	all(50.97%)	from(51.9%)	from(51.02%)	from(51.53%)
search(44.44%)	search(45.92%)	search(46.97%)	search(48.44%)	**2013(46.79%)**	search(49.09%)
information(42.94%)	information(43.87%)	**2011(45.02%)**	more(45.99%)	search(46.48%)	more(48.12%)
site(41.8%)	site(42.72%)	information(44.77%)	information(45.4%)	more(46.29%)	information(46.06%)
more(40.66%)	more(42.51%)	more(44.54%)	new(44.29%)	information(45.21%)	**2014(46.01%)**
new(40.5%)	new(41.53%)	site(43.2%)	**2012(43.87%)**	new(44.36%)	new(45.06%)
1(38.89%)	**2010(40.8%)**	new(42.65%)	site(43.3%)	1(43.4%)	privacy(44.43%)
you(37.41%)	1(40.18%)	1(41.52%)	1(43.1%)	news(42.34%)	1(44.1%)
privacy(36.4%)	you(38.98%)	you(40.76%)	you(42.03%)	privacy(42.21%)	news(43.38%)
other(35.77%)	privacy(38.89%)	privacy(40.39%)	privacy(41.97%)	you(41.71%)	you(42.55%)
have(35.62%)	news(36.6%)	news(39.02%)	news(40.82%)	site(41.51%)	your(42.18%)
your(34.35%)	other(35.96%)	your(37.09%)	your(38.99%)	your(40.9%)	site(42.03%)
page(34.09%)	your(35.81%)	other(37.02%)	other(37.24%)	our(37.62%)	our(38.45%)
has(33.93%)	have(34.99%)	have(35.41%)	have(36.18%)	policy(36.59%)	policy(38.39%)
news(33.65%)	2(34.02%)	2(34.89%)	2(36.08%)	2(35.96%)	other(37.38%)
2(32.97%)	page(33.77%)	policy(34.28%)	policy(35.6%)	other(35.92%)	have(36.15%)
2009(32.9%)	policy(33.43%)	has(33.58%)	our(35.49%)	have(35.5%)	research(36.04%)
policy(32.09%)	has(33.33%)	may(33.44%)	use(33.77%)	research(34.44%)	2(35.81%)
use(31.76%)	e(31.93%)	our(33.42%)	has(33.68%)	3(33.11%)	use(34.17%)
e(30.97%)	use(31.86%)	page(33.3%)	page(33.23%)	use(33.05%)	has(34.07%)

HTML Tags

Another type of "important" words on the Web are the HTML tags, which create and shape web pages. We create an Apache Lucene Index with only the HTML tags for each document. Then, we compute the top words for each year. Table 2 shows the top 26 HTML tags for each year.

The 26 most used tags are common over the 6 years analysed, except for minimal changes. But although the top tags are essentially the same, we would like to remark the trend of the occurrence frequency for some tags:

- The use of tag "script" grew a 15% from 2009 to 2014, so the use of scripting technologies is clearly increasing, with the difficulties that it has for crawling engines.The use of lists ("li" and "ul" tags) and "div" tag grew near a 38% from 2009 to 2014 and the use of "span" tag grew a 24%.

Table 2. Top web page HTML tags

2009	2010	2011	2012	2013	2014
head(100%)	head(100%)	head(100%)	head(100%)	head(100%)	head(100%)
html(100%)	html(100%)	html(100%)	html(100%)	html(100%)	html(100%)
root(100%)	root(100%)	root(100%)	root(100%)	root(100%)	root(100%)
body(99.57%)	body(99.66%)	body(99.77%)	body(99.84%)	body(99.87%)	body(99.9%)
title(93.93%)	title(93.55%)	title(93.23%)	title(92.61%)	title(92.33%)	title(91.97%)
p(82.52%)	p(82.85%)	p(83.47%)	p(83.46%)	p(83.49%)	p(83.79%)
img(81.53%)	img(81.86%)	img(81.99%)	img(81.62%)	img(81.12%)	**meta(80.96%)**
br(80.13%)	br(78.67%)	**meta(79.39%)**	**meta(79.93%)**	**meta(80.74%)**	img(80.83%)
meta(77.01%)	**meta(78.55%)**	br(77.49%)	div(77.37%)	link(78.94%)	div(78.87%)
div(70.34%)	div(74.05%)	div(75.82%)	link(76.85%)	div(78.31%)	link(78.86%)
link(69.48%)	link(72.81%)	link(75.18%)	br(75.72%)	script(76.85%)	script(78.24%)
script(68.12%)	script(71.57%)	script(73.91%)	script(75.3%)	br(74.14%)	li(72.33%)
tr(62.83%)	form(59.95%)	li(64.02%)	li(67.47%)	li(70.95%)	br(72.02%)
table(62.79%)	input(59.85%)	ul(63.25%)	ul(66.57%)	ul(70.36%)	ul(71.78%)
tbody(62.73%)	li(59.37%)	form(62.47%)	input(64.75%)	input(66.66%)	span(68.51%)
td(62.59%)	ul(58.33%)	input(62.45%)	form(64.61%)	form(66.53%)	input(67.91%)
form(55.78%)	span(58.05%)	span(61.47%)	span(64%)	span(66.23%)	form(67.76%)
input(55.11%)	tr(56.94%)	**h1(58.45%)**	**h1(60.66%)**	**h1(64.27%)**	**h1(66.56%)**
span(54.21%)	**table(56.9%)**	tr(51.6%)	h2(49.19%)	h2(52.68%)	h2(54.78%)
li(53.29%)	tbody(56.83%)	**table(51.54%)**	**table(46.74%)**	strong(43.45%)	strong(42.52%)
ul(51.98%)	td(56.7%)	tbody(51.49%)	tr(46.73%)	tr(42.55%)	h3(42.2%)
h1(47.93%)	**h1(53.12%)**	td(51.4%)	tbody(46.63%)	**table(42.48%)**	**table(37.44%)**
b(43.04%)	h2(43.67%)	h2(46.99%)	td(46.53%)	td(42.45%)	label(37.44%)
strong(37.74%)	strong(40.79%)	strong(41.73%)	strong(42.21%)	tbody(42.4%)	tr(37.43%)
h2(37.61%)	b(39.62%)	h3(36.2%)	h3(38.14%)	h3(40.37%)	td(37.34%)
style(35.54%)	style(37.13%)	b(35.78%)	style(34.34%)	style(34.45%)	tbody(37.33%)

Nevertheless, the use of tables ("table", "tr" and "td" tags) and "tbody" tags decreased a 60% in the same period (from 62% to 37%). This shows a change in the design of web documents, from a tabular representation to create the layout of pages to stylesheets. In addition, it is also interesting to remark that the use of heading tags ("h1", "h2") was increased between a 15% and 20%. The use of forms ("form" tag) grew a 21% in the last 6 years. Between a 55% and a 67% of web pages include a "form" tag. This confirms that the importance of dealing the server-side Hidden Web is growing.

All of these results show the changing trend in the way of developing web pages.

Features at Web Content Level

This section discusses the evolution of the total/useful size of the web pages, the most commonly used languages, picture, video, music formats among others file formats and the most used styles. In addition, this section also analyses certain attributes of the "meta" tag of HTML pages, such as the content type.

Size of the Total/Useful Content

We define the useful content of a web page as its main content, where the information is really placed, without HTML tags, links, images, etc. The useful content is used by search engines to provide the correct web documents to the users. An important fact for search engines and crawlers is the size of the downloaded and stored content, and its relation to the useful content of each page.

The process of extraction of the useful content of the web pages is very complicated. This study follows the approach developed by Pan et al. in (Pan, Qiu, & Yin, 2008). It is based on that the location of the main content is very centralized and has a good hierarchical structure. Pan et al. found that the threshold values of the DOM nodes (W3C DOM IG, 2005) with useful content are obviously different from that of other DOM nodes in the same level. With these values, they have proposed an algorithm that judges the content by several parameters in the nodes (Link Text Density, Link Amount, Link Amount Density and Node Text Length).

Figure 2 shows the obtained results. It is important to note that our study has considered the full content of the pages, unlike other existing studies that truncate the pages to a certain size (Baeza-Yates & Castillo, 2000).

In the year 2009, the average content per page was 31.01 KB, but this number has been increasing in 3 KB per year, until reach 46 KB in 2014. Analysing the results taken for useful content, it is notable that in 2009 the average size of useful content was 6.7 KB, a number that was increasing in subsequent years until reach 7.9 KB in 2014. Regarding the ratio between total and useful content, it was decreasing from 21% in 2009 until 17% in 2014. So, the difference between total content and useful content is increasing.

These results continue to confirm that web documents are growing in size, mainly with common words. In addition, it is likely that these web pages use client-side technologies such as JavaScript to improve the user experience.

Language

In order to identify the language used in each web page, this study uses the "language detector" library (Shuyo, 2010), which is based on Bayesian filters. It has a precision of 0.99 to detect 53 languages.

Table 3 shows the results obtained. The predominant language is English with 88.91% in 2009, decreasing to approximately 86% in 2014. In the study presented by Grefenstette and Nioche (Grefenstette & Nioche, 2000) in the year 2000, the authors have estimated that about 70% of the web pages were written in English. According with the presented study, this figure has increased 27%, although in the last 6 years the use of English language has decreased a bit. This is due to the increment of use of other languages.

Figure 2. Evolution of the content size of a web page and relation with useful content

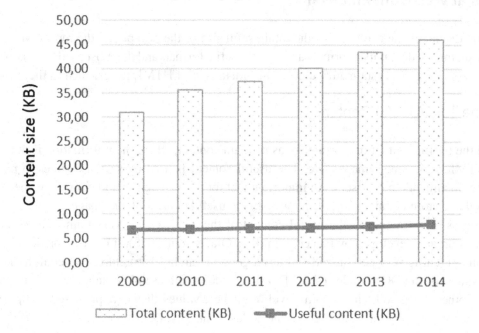

Image File Formats

Figure 3 shows the changes in the use of image file formats. Our study focused on the following formats: GIF (Graphics Interchange Format), JPEG (Joint Photographic Experts Group), PNG (*Portable* Network Graphic), Ico (Icon image file), BMP (Bitmap image format) and TIF (Tagged Image File Format).

We have observed that there is a predominance of the GIF format for images, although it has been slowly decreasing through the years. If we count all the images referenced by the analyzed documents, the 83.58% of the images were of GIF format in 2009, but only a 49.72% of the total of images in 2014. This suppose a very important decrement in the use of this format for images. This decrement has been compensated with the increment in other two relevant image file formats: JPG and PNG. The fraction of JPG images in 2009 was 13.14%, raising until 25.75% in 2014. Something similar, but more impressive, is the growing in use of PNG format, from a 3.27% in 2009 to a 24.53% of the total number of images in 2014.

Table 3. Distribution of languages used on the Web

	2009	**2010**	**2011**	**2012**	**2013**	**2014**
en	88.91%	88.48%	87.92%	87.81%	87.25%	86.75%
unknown	3.19%	3.29%	3.70%	4.05%	3.91%	4.41%
fr	3.15%	3.36%	3.54%	3.34%	3.50%	3.27%
de	1.94%	2.11%	1.84%	2.02%	2.10%	2.23%
es	1.46%	1.28%	1.23%	1.11%	1.18%	1.31%
it	0.46%	0.52%	0.56%	0.54%	0.52%	0.50%
other	0.89%	0.96%	1.21%	1.12%	1.54%	1.53%

Figure 3. Distribution of image file formats on the Web: % of usage of each file format (left), % of pages using each file format (right)

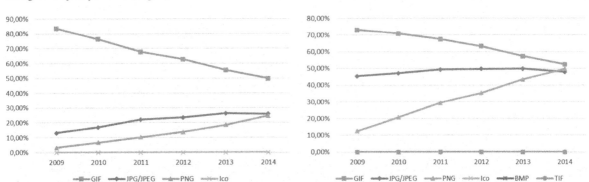

Figure 3 also includes the percentage of pages that use each image file format (on the right). The result is similar to the previously described. In 2009, the 73.11% of pages included some GIF image, but in 2014 only 52.42% of pages contained at least one image of GIF format. By contrast, the number of pages using PNG file format increased from 12.49% to 49.66%. The percentage of pages using at least one JPG file remained more or less the same (between 45% and 50% of pages).

These results indicate that web pages are evolving towards documents with more quality images and less size.

Video File Formats

Figure 4 shows the most used video formats. We analyzed the following video formats: WMV (Windows Media Video), MOV/QT (QuickTime), AVI (Audio Video Interleave) and MPEG (Moving *Picture* Expert Group).

The predominant video formats in 2009 were WMV and MOV/QT, with 45.39% and 44.66% respectively, followed by AVI with a 8.19%. In 2010 the usage of the MOV/QT video format grew a lot, at expenses of the WMV format. In 2011 the difference between this two formats was minimal again, and from 2010 to 2014 the usage of the MOV/QT file format grew again until a 57.16%, decreasing the use of the WMV format until 31.36%. The MOV/QT file format was developed by Apple Computer, and the WMV by Microsoft. This trend could confirm the success of Apple lately. The peak observed in 2010 could be related with some of the new products of apple, the iPad. Regarding other file formats, like AVI, or MPEG, their usage do not vary greatly in the 6 studied years, remaining around 8% and 2% respectively. The AVI format was one of the oldest video formats. It has good quality but it is very heavy. In previous years, it was the most widely used format on the Internet. Today, WMV/MOV/QT has similar quality but with a smaller size. Due to this, AVI has almost disappeared with other smaller formats taking its place.

Regarding the number of pages using video resources, we conclude that videos are not too frequent in the web, except for some specialized web sites not included in this study. Figure 4 shows that WMV was the video format used by the major number of pages, followed by WMV, and there were nearly not changes in the following 6 years of the study.

Figure 4. Distribution of video file formats on the Web: % of usage of each file format (left), % of pages using each file format (right)

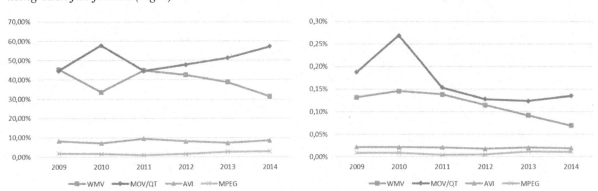

Music File Formats

The music file formats used on the Web have also been analysed. We have considered the following formats: MP3 (MPEG1 - or MPEG2 - Audio Layer III), WAV (Waveform Audio File Format), WMA (Windows Media Audio), ASF (Audio Video Interleaved), MIDI (Musical Instrument Digital Interface).

During the 6 years studied, the distribution of the music file formats has not change notably. Figure 5 shows the obtained results. Focusing on the data obtained in 2014, the most widely used format is MP3 with 91.73%. The next most commonly used music format is WAV with a 5.46%. Other music formats are WMA with 1.66%, and ASF or MIDI, with very insignificant percentages. The limited evolution that has been observed is because the MP3 format has good quality with a relatively small size, and because no new formats have appeared in the recent years that have been able to replace the MP3 format.

Regarding the number of pages using music file formats, occurs something similar that the observed with video formats. Only 0.44% of web pages included a reference to a MP3 file format. We observe that the usage of music file formats in web pages increased a bit from 2009 until 2012 (0.54% to 0.60%), but from 2012 decreased until 0.44% of pages in 2014.

Figure 5. Distribution of music file formats on the Web: % of usage of each file format (left), % of pages using each file format (right)

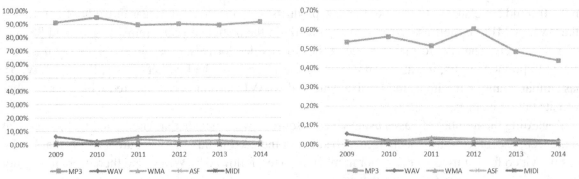

Other Document Types

One point that characterizes web pages is the different types of documents that they contain. Table 8 shows the results for the most relevant file types. For this study we considered documents of types PDF (Portable Document File), XML (eXtensible Markup Language), Txt (text files), Doc (Microsoft Word Document), Ppt (Microsoft PowerPoint presentations) and Ps (PostScript).

Table 4 shows the results obtained. The type of document which appears more often is PDF. In 2014, the 80.94% of all documents types considered were PDF. The next most common type of document is the XML, which grew from 7.46% in 2009 to 11.28% in 2014. The rest of file formats were less than 8% in 2009, and less than 4% in 2014.

Regarding the number of web pages using these document types, 12.87% of web pages used some PDF file in 2009. This percentage grow until 15.82% in 2014. XML files were referenced from 2.65% of the pages, growing until 4.68% in 2014.

In short, the obtained results are logical, since PDF documents, as its initials indicate (Portable Document Format), can be used in any operating system.

Compression File Formats

Figure 6 shows the results obtained for the compression file formats analyzed. In 2009, the most used file format was GZIP with a 55.18%, followed by ZIP with a 32.18%. Along the 6 years-period analysed, the usage of the ZIP format grew until 53.44% and GZIP usage decreased until 42.83%. This trend could justify the situation of power of Windows Operating systems, due to ZIP is a format more commonly used in this operating system.

Table 4. Distribution of other document types on the Web

% of Usage of Document Types		2009	2010	2011	2012	2013	2014
(among the following 6 types)	*Pdf*	76.14%	78.35%	84.40%	86.90%	79.40%	80.94%
	Xml	7.46%	8.54%	5.48%	5.67%	11.42%	11.28%
	Txt	8.15%	6.19%	5.18%	2.75%	3.07%	3.26%
	Doc	5.89%	4.98%	3.57%	3.47%	4.63%	3.39%
	Ppt	1.45%	1.21%	0.84%	0.73%	0.88%	0.69%
	Ps	0.91%	0.73%	0.53%	0.49%	0.60%	0.44%
% of Pages using Each Document Type		2009	2010	2011	2012	2013	2014
	Pdf	12.87%	13.87%	14.35%	14.76%	15.66%	15.82%
	Xml	2.65%	3.23%	3.10%	4.03%	4.35%	4.68%
	Doc	1.40%	1.29%	1.14%	1.08%	0.97%	0.98%
	Txt	1.10%	0.91%	0.80%	0.61%	0.61%	0.67%
	Ppt	0.42%	0.35%	0.32%	0.27%	0.24%	0.21%
	Ps	0.22%	0.20%	0.14%	0.12%	0.11%	0.10%

Figure 6. Distribution of compression file formats on the Web: % of usage of each file format (left), % of pages using each file format (right)

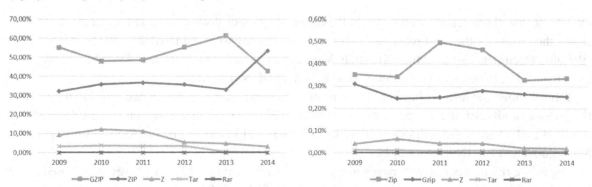

Regarding the number of web pages referencing compressed files, in 2009, only the 0.35% of pages included some file compressed using ZIP and 0.31% GZIP. This results are nearly the same along the 6-year period studied.

Styles

Search engines also consider the style in which certain terms of web page content are written. The fact that a word is highlighted (bold or italic) can indicate that it is more relevant than others. Figure 7 shows a brief survey of commonly used standard styles.

In 2009, the most widely used style is bold, with a 58.30%. But that has decreased until 41,64% in 2014. The use of italics remains around 20% in the 6-years period. The decrease in bold could be due to the increment of the styles of the title sections H2 and H3. Their use was around 7% in 2009 and it grew until around 15% in 2014.

Figure 7 also shows the number of pages in which some of the analysed styles are used. We observe a clear increment in the percentages of pages using styles of the title section. In 2009, a 47.89% of web pages used at least an H1 style, a 37.55% H2 and 27.79% H3. In 2014 the percentages grew to 66.52%, 54.72% and 42.15% respectively. The increment in the use of title sections was previously observed when analysed the top web page HTML tags.

Figure 7. Distribution of usage of styles on the Web: % of usage of each file format (left), % of pages using each file format (right)

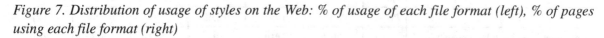

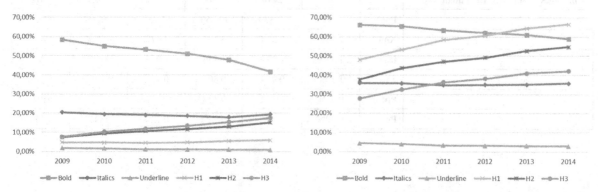

Meta Tags

An important part of the information on the web page content is included in the attributes of the HTML "meta" tags, which are placed at the beginning of the HTML code and provide information to the user, browser, crawlers and search engines. There are several attributes of the "meta" tag, however this study only considers the three most relevant: Keywords, Refresh and Content-type. Table 5 shows the results obtained.

- Keywords: The keywords attribute of the "meta" tag, includes words which describe the content of the page. This study analyses the average number of keywords on web documents. In 2009 the average was 9.60 keywords per web page, in 2011, 8.92 and in 2014 7.91. Over the 6 years the number of keywords has decremented in less than 2.

Attending to these results, search engines must pay special attention to the number of keywords, because as Prieto et al. (Prieto, Álvarez, & Cacheda, 2012) have demonstrated, a method to perform Web Spam includes many keywords and so improves the relevance of the web page. A logical number of words to define the topic of a web page is between 7 and 15. Search engines must use the average number of keywords and penalise those web pages that using a number of keywords bigger than this average, because it is likely that these web pages are trying to improve their ranking by illegal methods.

- Refresh: This attribute indicates the time when the content of the page should be updated. Table 5 shows the results obtained. Around 1% of the pages use the refresh attribute in the 6-years period analysed. Despite the increase in dynamic pages that require continuous updating of their contents, the usage of the attribute "refresh" has not grown. This may be because there are other methods of updating the page content, for the user in a transparent way, using JavaScript functions. Such methods are widely used on pages with AJAX technologies, which update their content without the user noticing.

Table 5. Results of analysing the meta tags of web pages

Average Number of Words in the							
Keywords Meta-Tag		**2009**	**2010**	**2011**	**2012**	**2013**	**2014**
		9.60	9.21	8.92	8.35	8.27	7.91
Refresh Meta Tag		**2009**	**2010**	**2011**	**2012**	**2013**	**2014**
		1.04%	1.30%	1.63%	1.09%	0.99%	1.15%
Used Charsets (Content-Type)		**2009**	**2010**	**2011**	**2012**	**2013**	**2014**
	ISO-8859-1	55.76%	47.59%	38.61%	33.63%	28.66%	24.65%
	UTF-8	33.28%	43.26%	52.90%	59.20%	65.21%	69.44%
	ISO-8859-15	0.38%	0.36%	0.27%	0.18%	0.19%	0.21%
	Windows1252	6.65%	5.30%	4.57%	3.82%	3.12%	2.92%
	Others	3.93%	3.48%	3.66%	3.16%	2.82%	2.77%

- Content-type: This attribute indicates the content type and character set used for encoding the web page. The obtained results are also shown in Table 5. We observe that in 2009 the most used charset was ISO-8859-1. In 2009, the use of ISO-8859-1 represented 55.76% of web pages. Nevertheless, in the following years its use fell until 24.65% in 2014. This decrease occurred by the increment of UTF-8, which in 2009, reached 33.28%, and it was increasing until reach a 69.44% of web documents in 2014. The increment in the use of UTF-8 and the decrement of ISO-8859-1, is due to the need for new types of encoding that allow multilingual support. The use of UTF-8 in web pages allows displaying correctly the web pages in the browsers regardless of the charset used in the computer.

Features at Web Page Level

This section focuses on analysing the characteristics of the Web at web page level. More precisely, it considers the length of the URL, the age of the pages, the compression of the content, the title length of the pages and their similarity, since these are very important characteristics from the point of view of crawlers and search engines.

URL Length

Knowing the length of the URLs is very important because it can improve the development of compression schemes for caching or indexing the Web. For that, this is an aspect very relevant for the crawlers and search engines.

Table 6 shows that the average length in bytes of the URLs on the Global Web has remained the same (between 37 and 39 bytes) during the 6-years period analysed. The most interesting change is that the percentage of URLs which length is greater than 25 bytes has incremented from a 67.83% in 2009 to reach a 76.78% in 2014, although it does not affect to the average length.

Title Length of Web Pages

The title of a web page is one of the most important elements in a web page. The use of descriptive titles is important to the Web usability, since it allows to the web users to know the topic of the web page. To analyse web page titles, its average length was considered, to determine its real importance when describing the content of a web page.

Table 6. Average length of the URLs on the Web

	2009	2010	2011	2012	2013	2014
Average length of URLs (discarding pages without URLs)	37.15	38.27	38.16	38.79	39.34	39.19
% of pages containing some URL with length > 10	98.50%	98.76%	98.81%	98.93%	99.08%	99.16%
% of pages containing some URL with length > 25	67.83%	71.79%	72.19%	74.12%	75.97%	76.78%
% of pages containing some URL with length > 50	16.50%	18.71%	18.39%	18.84%	19.50%	19.39%
% of pages containing some URL with length > 100	1.94%	2.19%	2.03%	2.07%	2.21%	2.09%
% of pages containing some URL with length > 150	0.79%	0.77%	0.79%	0.90%	0.75%	0.60%

Figure 8 shows that in 2009 the average title length was 6.61 words, in 2011 7.03 and 7.22 words in 2014. The value has remained relatively constant at about 7 words. The amount of words in the title has remained relatively constant over the years studied.

Age

It represents the time validity of a web page. To calculate this time the HTTP header "Last-Modified" was used. It can be used to know when a web page has been modified, so it determines when the content downloaded by a crawler is not valid and therefore, this web page must be gathered again.

Table 7 shows the obtained results. First, it is important to note that the number of web pages returning a "Last-Modified" header remains more or less the same in the 6 years, minimally growing from a 33.30% of web pages in 2009 to 38.72% in 2014. So, the results obtained for the evolution of the age of web pages have only considered this percentage of web pages.

In 2009 approximately the 43% of the pages were less than 3 month old. In the next years the age of web pages increased until reach a 70% of web pages with age less than 3 month old in 2014. It is important to note that the increment was mainly for pages with less than 1 month old (35.48% in 2009 and 66.42% in 2014).

The trend of updating the contents faster means that policies of re-crawling and updating indexes have to change, as it is necessary to update contents and indexes so that the user can conduct searches on current contents. Therefore, it is necessary to create a system that allow crawlers to know in a reliable and exact way when a page has changed, improving search engine performance and user experience.

Figure 8. Average title length of web pages

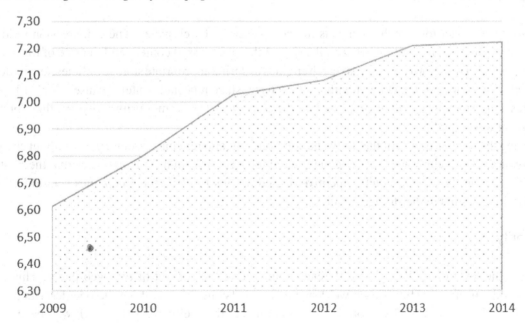

Table 7. Evolution of the Age of web pages

	2009	2010	2011	2012	2013	2014
% pages with LastModified header	33.30%	31.68%	33.37%	34.73%	36.27%	38.72%
% pages with LastModified header and age < 1 month	35.48%	42.09%	46.75%	53.35%	60.15%	66.42%
% pages with LastModified header and age < 3 months	43.83%	49.36%	53.97%	59.01%	66.18%	70.32%

Table 8. Distribution of the similarity of the web pages

	2009	2010	2011	2012	2013	2014
0% - < 10%	0.00%	0.00%	0.00%	0.00%	0.00%	0.00%
10% - < 20%	0.00%	0.00%	0.00%	0.00%	0.00%	0.00%
20% - < 30%	0.00%	0.00%	0.00%	0.00%	0.00%	0.00%
30% - < 40%	0.23%	0.19%	0.38%	0.31%	0.13%	0.19%
40% - < 50%	13.80%	12.78%	19.84%	15.53%	13.65%	12.04%
50% - < 60%	30.12%	31.34%	32.33%	31.03%	24.49%	25.50%
60% - < 70%	26.00%	23.87%	20.41%	22.47%	21.30%	23.46%
70% - < 80%	21.05%	21.37%	17.28%	19.34%	17.66%	19.06%
80% - < 90%	4.21%	5.95%	4.79%	7.33%	17.25%	14.54%
90% - 100%	4.58%	4.49%	4.96%	3.97%	5.51%	5.20%

Compression of the Content

An important aspect for search engines is the compression of web pages. The compression ratio is a value that represents the relation between the size of the compressed content and the size of the content uncompressed. This information helps search engines to define appropriate storage policies, and indicates the level of similarity of the content within a web page, since repeated contents cause a higher level of compression. At a lower level of compression, the content will show more similarity and therefore will often be of lower quality.

During the 6-years period of the study, the compression ratio remained around 0.33, without changes. In summary, the results show that the compression level is quite high. This indicates that the contents of web pages on the Web are quite repetitive. Based on this fact, the search engines should take into account these results in the storage policies.

Similarity

Indicates the level of similarity, or difference, which have the content of two web pages. This study compares the useful content of each web page, using the same approach that the one described in the features at Web content level section. In order to compare the useful content of each web page, a tool implemented by Viliam Holub[3] is used. This tool divides each document in n tokens, each one of them with a weight. After this, it makes a hash of each of the tokens. Finally, with the weight and the hash of each token, the tool creates a hash for each document of each subset, which "summarizes" its contents.

In this study, a dataset per year was considered, which had 10 random subsets of 10,000 web pages. The hash of every page for each year was computed and then the Hamming distance among the document signatures. The end result, shown in Table 8, was obtained as the average of the results of each of the 10 subsets for each year.

Table 8 shows that in 2009, 30% of web pages had between 50% and 60% of similarity, 26% had between 60% and 70% and only 4.21% had a similarity between 80% and 90%. In following years, similarity for values between 40% and 70% decreased, but mainly in last two years, the similarity for values between 80% and 90% has increased from 4.21% in 2009 to 14,54% in 2014 (it reached 17.25% in 2013).

So, we can conclude that the level of similarity in the Web is growing, so search engines have to take this into account for detecting duplicate or similar content to avoid index the same content several times.

Features at Web Site Level

This level explains the main characteristics of a web site, such as number of links and their types (static, dynamic, inlink, outlink), and the technologies used in the client and server side. We place special emphasis on the technologies which are mainly used for the client and server side Hidden Web.

Links

Table 9 shows the results obtained for the links analysis. The number of pages having at least some anchor has remained around 87% during the 6-years period analysed. Nevertheless, the average number of links per pages has grown from 58.63 in 2009 until 107.26 links per page in 2014.

Table 9 also shows results regarding inlinks, outlinks, dynamic and static links, and the kind of path, absolute or relative.

The difference between inlinks and outlinks of a web page is that inlinks point to other pages in the same domain, and outlinks point to pages in other domains. The results obtained indicate that, in 2009, the inlinks represented 62.37% of the total number of links on the Web, and the outlinks 37.63%. The number of inlinks was growing until reach to 66.01% of the total number of links in 2014.

Analysing the type of link path, the relative links dominate the absolute address. In 2009, 61.89% of links were relative versus 38.11%, which were absolute. This result was similar in the next year, although increasing a bit the number of relative links to reach 65.55% in 2014. This result is consistent with the obtained for inlinks/outlinks. The majority of links are intra-domain.

Analysing the results for dynamic and static links, a domination of static links over dynamic links can be observed. In 2009, the static links were 76.34% as opposed to 23.66% for dynamic links, percentages which increased in 2014, reaching 84.50% for static links and 15.50% for dynamic links.

The static link against the dynamic goes slightly against the trend of use of technologies that enable dynamic access to data. This result may be due to the method of coding the URLs, which do not use ?, or that use unknown dynamic extensions. The web sites with a dynamic access to the data offer a better user experience than the static web sites, but with the disadvantage that these technologies makes the access to information by crawlers more complex.

Table 9 also shows the percentage of pages using at least one of the previously described link types. The number of pages referencing at least one link increased, for each type of link, but little. We highlight the growth experimented in the dynamic links. In 2009, the 57.31% of pages contained at least one dynamic link. In 2014, the 65.94% of web pages reference at least one dynamic link.

Table 9. Distribution of different types of links on the Web

		2009	2010	2011	2012	2013	2014
% of Pages with Some Link		86.85%	87.94%	88.17%	88.17%	88.46%	88.17%
Average number of links per page		58.63	69.15	81.19	90.91	94.99	107.26
% of Usage of Each Type of Link		**2009**	**2010**	**2011**	**2012**	**2013**	**2014**
	Inlink	62.37%	60.39%	62.75%	62.20%	63.51%	66.01%
	Outlink	37.63%	39.61%	37.25%	37.80%	36.49%	33.99%
	Relative	61.89%	59.80%	62.10%	61.73%	63.01%	65.55%
	Absolute	38.11%	40.20%	37.90%	38.27%	36.99%	34.45%
	Static	76.34%	77.25%	79.41%	81.40%	83.12%	84.50%
	Dynamic	23.66%	22.75%	20.59%	18.60%	16.88%	15.50%
% of Pages using Each Type of Links		**2009**	**2010**	**2011**	**2012**	**2013**	**2014**
	Inlink	79.14%	80.63%	82.10%	82.43%	82.97%	82.83%
	Outlink	78.77%	80.47%	81.57%	82.21%	82.97%	83.10%
	Relative	77.86%	79.32%	80.83%	81.23%	81.72%	81.67%
	Absolute	80.19%	81.85%	82.76%	83.34%	84.09%	84.09%
	Static	83.73%	85.31%	85.91%	86.27%	86.65%	86.39%
	Dynamic	57.31%	60.77%	62.84%	63.86%	65.69%	65.94%

Server-Side Technologies

Another important information for a crawler is the technology used on the server-side. The results are shown in Table 10. In 2009, the dominant technology was PHP with 24.32% of web pages referencing at least one PHP page, followed by ASP with 22.86%. JSP/JHTML, CGI, SHTML and Perl were referenced in around a 7% of the pages. During the 6-years period analysed, the % of web pages referencing a PHP page grew until 30.94%. The use of ASP remained without changes, and JSP/JHTML, but the rest decreased its number of occurrences.

The usage of the different server-side technologies seems related to the distribution of operating systems, since ASP is a closed-source technology and only works in particular operating systems, and PHP has many open-source interpreters.

Client-Side Technologies

These are those technologies which allow the creation of dynamic web sites and improve the user experience. However, this makes the process of crawling more difficult, creating what is known as client-side Hidden Web.

Table 11 shows the obtained results. The most commonly used technologies are based on JavaScript. Its usage has increased since 2009 with a 60.97% to 75.97% rise in 2014. The second most commonly used technology is Flash, although its presence is much lower (it was present in around 2% of web pages during the period analysed).

Table 10. Distribution of the server-side technologies on the Web

	2009	2010	2011	2012	2013	2014
PHP	24.32%	29.70%	31.91%	32.59%	31.73%	30.94%
ASP	22.86%	24.14%	24.30%	24.65%	24.75%	22.60%
JSP/JHTML	7.92%	8.31%	8.40%	8.57%	8.05%	7.56%
CGI	7.77%	7.57%	6.34%	5.72%	5.06%	4.63%
STHML	7.03%	8.39%	7.33%	7.12%	6.50%	5.50%
Perl	6.95%	6.49%	5.16%	5.03%	4.79%	4.28%
C#	6.83%	8.00%	6.98%	6.83%	6.27%	5.34%
Javaclass	0.03%	0.02%	0.01%	0.01%	0.01%	0.01%
C#	0.03%	0.04%	0.04%	0.04%	0.04%	0.04%
Js	0.01%	0.01%	0.01%	0.01%	0.03%	0.03%
Sh	0.01%	0.01%	0.00%	0.01%	0.01%	0.01%
C++	0.00%	0.00%	0.00%	0.00%	0.00%	0.00%

Table 11. Distribution of the client-side technologies on the Web

	2009	2010	2011	2012	2013	2014
JavaScript	60.97%	66.62%	69.99%	72.11%	74.43%	75.97%
Flash	2.52%	2.98%	2.90%	2.85%	2.34%	2.04%
VbScript	0.08%	0.07%	0.10%	0.08%	0.02%	0.01%
Applets	0.01%	0.01%	0.01%	0.01%	0.01%	0.01%
TclScript	0.00%	0.00%	0.00%	0.00%	0.00%	0.00%
PythonScripts	0.00%	0.00%	0.00%	0.00%	0.00%	0.00%

It is also important to note that since 2009 some languages such as VBScript or Tcl have almost disappeared. These results are mainly due to the widespread use of technologies such as AJAX (Asynchronous JavaScript and XML), and the large number of problems of compatibility and security that Flash is currently experiencing. Based on these results, and on the processing cost of these technologies, a crawling system should work mainly on the processing of JavaScript, since it is the most widely used technology on the client-side for accessing data.

Table 12 shows other results related with client-side technologies that can difficult the task of a crawler:

- The number of meta-HTTP redirects has increased a bit between 2009 and 2011, but it recovered the 2009 value in 2014. Regarding the number of meta-tags used in web pages, its number has increased from 3.5 in average in 2009, to 6.5 in 2014.
- We highlight the growth in the usage of the HTML "link" element, which is used for referencing external resources, like CSS files. It was used in 69.48% of pages in 2009, and it reached 78.86% of pages in 2014.

Table 12. Client-side Hidden Web elements

	2009	2010	2011	2012	2013	2014
% Pages with Meta-Http Redirects	1.04%	1.28%	1.63%	1.09%	0.99%	1.05%
Average Number of Meta Tags used per Page	3.54	3.90	4.53	4.93	5.65	6.53
% Pages with Link Elements	69.48%	72.80%	75.18%	76.85%	78.60%	78.86%
Average Number of Link Elements per Page	2.42	3.11	3.77	4.22	4.85	5.40
% Pages with Object Elements	2.27%	2.52%	2.84%	2.51%	2.22%	1.89%
Average Number of Object Elements per Page	0.03	0.04	0.04	0.03	0.03	0.03
% Pages with Frameset Elements	0.44%	0.34%	0.23%	0.16%	0.13%	0.10%
% Pages with Iframe Elements	7.07%	7.62%	9.92%	11.20%	12.01%	13.46%
Average Number of Iframe Elements per Page	0.12	0.14	0.22	0.23	0.25	0.22
% Pages with Scripts in the Body	55.06%	60.50%	64.14%	65.64%	67.72%	69.40%
% Pages with Scripts out of the Body	56.09%	59.02%	61.92%	64.90%	67.36%	68.64%
Average Number of Scripts in the Body per Page	10.06	12.45	13.09	14.08	16.01	16.56
Average Number of Scripts out of the Body per Page	3.19	4.10	5.13	6.03	7.04	7.74
% Pages with "onXX" Elements	50.05%	52.15%	51.57%	50.10%	50.10%	47.86%
% Pages with "onXX" Elements on Anchors	32.89%	34.55%	33.09%	33.36%	32.96%	31.21%
Average Number of "onXX" Elements per Page	9.61	10.31	9.36	8.85	8.86	9.36
Average Number of "onXX" Elements on Anchors per Page	6.00	6.36	6.28	5.88	6.03	6.71
% Pages with "onClick" Element	30.67%	34.54%	34.56%	35.14%	35.83%	33.95%
% Pages with More than 1 "onClick" Element	21.11%	24.13%	24.38%	24.72%	24.79%	23.47%
Average Number of "onClick" Elements per Page	3.19	4.33	4.61	4.43	4.31	5.13

- The usage of HTML object elements decreased, and the same occurred with framesets, but the number of iframes increased from 7.07% in 2009 to 13.46% in 2014.
- We have also analysed the usage of scripting technologies in different parts of a web page: in the body or in the header. Both in the body or in the header of web pages, the % of pages including scripts have increased: from 55.06% in 2009 to 69.40% in 2014 (in the body), and from 56.09% in 2009 to 68.64 in 2014 (out of the body).
- Inside the body, we also distinguished if the script was on a "onXX" attribute of an HTML tag, and if it was the case for "onClick", the event that is fired when a click is performed on an HTML page. The number of pages using scripts on a "onXX" attribute of a tag has decreased a bit, but the number of pages using scripts on "onClick" attributes has been increased from 30.67% in 2009 to 33,95% in 2014 (reaching peaks of 35% in 2012 and 2013).

All of this confirms that the technologies used in the construction of web sites use scripting languages for improving the accessibility/usability of the web pages.

Web Forms

As explained in the methodology section, the server-side Hidden Web is an important part of the Web. Many websites offer query forms to access the contents of an underlying database. Conventional crawlers cannot access these pages because they do not know how to execute queries on those forms.

In the analysis of the use of web forms, the Web has on average more than 1 web form per web site. This indicates that most web sites use forms to access to certain information, and have, in some cases, more than one. From 2009 to 2014, the number of web pages with more than a web form grew from 55.77% in 2009 to 67.76% in 2014.

We have also classified web forms in two types: authentication forms and data forms. The number of authentication forms grow only a bit (3.71% in 2009 to 4.72% in 2014). The number of pages with data forms, that is, forms that are not for authentication issues, but else are the entry-point to the server-side Hidden Web, have grown from 12.61% in 2009 to 16.72% in 2014.

With these data, crawlers must be prepared for accessing to this type of information, either by automatic query execution based on machine learning, or by establishing some agreement with the creators of information, which enables them to have easier access to data.

Features at Global Web level

This section explains the software used by web servers on the Global Web.

Web Server

On the Global Web the most commonly used web server in 2009 is Apache with 62.52%. The next most widely used web server is Microsoft IIS with 19.87%. Along the 6 years analysed, the Apache web server maintain its level of occurrences, but Microsoft IIS decreases until 14.36% in 2014. During these 6 years, Nginx server increased its presence in a significant way, from a 0.21% in 2009 to 7.32% in 2014. Nginx is a relatively new free, open-source web server (first version was released on 2004), and it is being more used due to its high performance, simple configuration and low resource consumption.

Figure 9 shows the obtained results.

In addition, many of the versions used were not recent. Usually, the system administrators tend to be conservative, so it is likely that they do not want update the web server version quickly, and prefer using older but more stable versions, although the probabilities of security issues is higher.

Exclusion Robots Protocol

The exclusion robots protocol is a mechanism that allows to a web page developer to specify if a web page must be indexed. A web site can define a robots.txt file for specifying a general politic for crawlers, but each page can specify its own preferences by using the robots meta tag. The obtained results for the robots meta tag are shown in table 14.

Table 13. Server-side Hidden Web elements

	2009	2010	2011	2012	2013	2014
% Pages with Forms	55.77%	59.95%	62.46%	64.60%	66.48%	67.76%
% Pages with More than 1 Form	24.56%	27.50%	28.04%	29.77%	31.10%	31.07%
% Pages with More than 2 Forms	10.76%	12.54%	12.25%	13.22%	13.70%	13.49%
% Pages with More than 3 Forms	5.71%	6.47%	6.02%	6.06%	6.09%	6.01%
% Pages with More than 5 Forms	1.80%	2.06%	1.96%	1.85%	1.50%	1.47%
% Pages with Get-Method Forms	33.46%	36.17%	36.71%	37.43%	38.08%	38.07%
% Pages with Post-Method Forms	24.52%	25.99%	25.96%	28.31%	30.06%	31.54%
% Pages with Password Forms	3.71%	4.21%	4.09%	4.24%	4.33%	4.72%
% Pages with More than 1 Password Forms	0.51%	0.76%	0.91%	0.84%	0.67%	0.64%
% Pages with More than 2 Password Forms	0.18%	0.16%	0.16%	0.12%	0.05%	0.02%
% Pages with Data Forms	12.61%	13.85%	14.69%	17.08%	16.99%	16.72%
% Pages with More than 1 Data Form	2.92%	3.28%	2.99%	3.13%	3.29%	3.09%
% Pages with More than 2 Data Forms	0.94%	0.86%	0.89%	0.89%	0.89%	0.78%
% Pages with More than 3 Data Forms	0.38%	0.50%	0.34%	0.26%	0.26%	0.18%
% Pages with More than 5 Data Forms	0.10%	0.18%	0.11%	0.08%	0.13%	0.10%
Average Number of Forms per Page	1.07	1.21	1.21	1.25	1.26	1.27
Average Number of GET Method Forms	0.43	0.49	0.52	0.52	0.52	0.52
Average Number of POST Method Forms	0.43	0.48	0.44	0.47	0.49	0.49
Average Number of Password Forms per Page	0.05	0.05	0.05	0.05	0.05	0.05
Average Number of Data Forms per Page	0.17	0.20	0.20	0.22	0.22	0.22

The number of pages that specify to crawlers that their content must not be indexed has grown from 35% in 2009 to 40% in 2014. This result is also corroborated by the number of pages which indicate in the robots meta tag 'index+follow' or 'all'. This percentage has been reduced from 48.54% in 2009 to 40.62% in 2014. It seems that web page managers are paying more attention to the crawler's policies.

Other interesting result is that values 'noodp' and 'noydir' have grown from 2.75% and 0.51% in 2009, to 7.97% and 4.56%, respectively. 'noodp' is for not allowing to the search engines to use the oficial description of the web page in DMOZ. 'noydir' is equivalent, but only for Yahoo! (i.e., not allowing to Yahoo! to use the description of the web page in the Yahoo! Directory).

These results confirm that the robots meta tag is being more actively used for specifying to search engines how to process web pages.

Figure 9. Web servers used on the Web

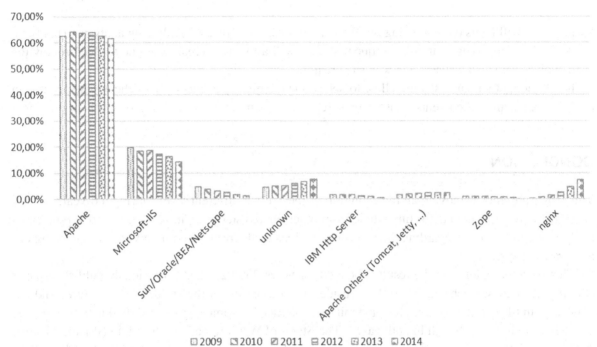

Table 14. Usage of the robots meta tag on web pages

	2009	2010	2011	2012	2013	2014
Follow	37.31%	40.85%	41.88%	38.92%	38.25%	38.49%
Noindex	35.64%	35.60%	36.58%	39.51%	40.38%	40.76%
Index	32.66%	35.12%	36.06%	32.96%	31.89%	30.79%
Nofollow	22.23%	21.81%	22.07%	25.17%	26.00%	25.59%
All	19.32%	15.96%	14.81%	14.47%	12.80%	12.50%
Noarchive	7.52%	7.49%	7.09%	6.32%	6.62%	7.08%
Noodp	2.75%	3.56%	4.04%	5.13%	6.84%	7.97%
	1.32%	0.94%	1.04%	1.03%	1.16%	0.89%
None	0.96%	1.26%	1.07%	0.91%	1.08%	0.85%
Noydir	0.51%	1.29%	2.07%	2.43%	3.42%	4.56%
Index+follow ‖ all	48.54%	47.22%	47.69%	44.70%	41.68%	40.62%

FUTURE RESEARCH DIRECTIONS

Future work will focus on processing the Web and creating new datasets, allowing analysis to continue in the forthcoming years. These subsequent studies will allow to increase the knowledge on how the Web evolves, and also its users and web site creators.

In addition, other studies could allow to determine the quality of the Web, to check whether it is in decline (bad quality of contents, broken links, repeated or similar contents, etc.), or if it is improving.

CONCLUSION

This paper presents a study about the evolution of the Web at different levels during a 6-years period: 2009-2014. What differentiates this article from other related studies is its more detailed approach, its analysis of the evolution regarding time and observations made from the point of view of search engines and crawling systems.

This study complements the results obtained for years 2009-2011 in a previously published paper (Prieto, Álvarez, & Cacheda, 2013), by considering in more detail the Hidden Web features and expanding it until year 2014.There are some minor differences in some results, mainly due to the way the datasets were built. Although in both cases "The Stanford Web Project" was used, in (Prieto, Álvarez, & Cacheda, 2013) web pages were selected randomly, but in this article we selected the first 10 million pages collected by the WebVac crawler for an specific month/year.

After analysing the features of the Web at different levels, and during several years, we can summarise the following conclusions:

- Web page sizes are growing, but not in useful content. The number of common words in web pages have increased.
- The level of similarity of the Web is growing, so search engines have to take this into account for detecting duplicate or similar content to avoid index the same content several times.
- A change in the design of web documents is observed: from a tabular representation to create the layout of pages by using stylesheets.
- Web pages are evolving towards documents with more quality images and less size, raising the usage of PNG format.
- The increment in the use of UTF-8 and the decrement of ISO-8859-1, is due to the need for new types of encoding that allow multilingual support. The use of UTF-8 in web pages allows displaying correctly the web pages in the browsers regardless of the charset used in the computer.
- Regarding the Hidden Web, the usage of scripting technologies is increasing, and the number of web forms too, although not a lot.
- Contents are updated faster. Policies of re-crawling and updating indexes have to change, as it is necessary to update contents and indexes so that the user can conduct searches on current contents.

REFERENCES

Adar, E., Teevan, J., Dumais, S. T., & Elsas, J. L. (2009). The Web Changes Everything: Understanding the Dynamics of Web Content. In *Proceedings of the 2nd ACM International Conference on Web Search and Data Mining, WSDM '09*, Barcelona, Spain. (pp. 282-291). doi:10.1145/1498759.1498837

Baeza-Yates, R., & Castillo, C. (2000). Caracterizando la Web Chilena. In Encuentro Chileno de Ciencias de la Computación. Sociedad Chilena de Ciencias de la Computación.

Baeza-Yates, R., Castillo, C., & Efthimiadis, E. N. (2007). Characterization of National Web Domains. *Journal ACM Transactions on Internet Technology*. 7(2).

Baeza-Yates, R., Castillo, C. & Lopez, V. (2005). Characteristics of the Web of Spain. *Cybermetrics*. 9(1).

Baeza-Yates, R., & Poblete, B. (2006). Dynamics of the Chilean Web Structure. *The International Journal of Computer and Telecommunications Networking*. 50(10), 1464-1473.

Baeza-Yates, R., Saint-Jean, F.,, & Castillo, C. (2002). Web Structure, Dynamics and Page Quality. *String Processing and Information Retrieval: Lecture Notes in Computer Science Series, 2476*, 453–461.

Bergman, M. K. (2001). The Deep Web: Surfacing Hidden Value. *Journal of Electronic Publishing*. 7.

Bharat, K., Chang, B., Henzinger, M. R.,, & Ruhl, M. (2001). Who Links to Whom: Mining Linkage Between Web Sites. *Proceedings of the 2001 IEEE International Conference on Data Mining, ICDM '01,* IEEE Computer Society, San José, California, USA (pp. 51-58). doi:10.1109/ICDM.2001.989500

Björneborn, L., & Ingwersen, P. (2004). Toward a Basic Framework for Webometrics. *Journal of the American Society for Information Science and Technology, 55*(14), 1216–1227. doi:10.1002/asi.20077

Boldi, P., Codenotti, B., Santini, M.,, & Vigna, S. (2002). Structural Properties of the African Web. *Proceedings of the 11st International Conference on World Wide Web, WWW'02*, Honolulu, Hawaii, USA.

Brewington, B.,, & Cybenko, G. (2000). How Dynamic is the Web? *Proceedings of the 9th Conference on the World Wide Web*. (pp. 257-276).

Broder, A., Kumar, R., Maghoul, F., Raghavan, P., Rajagopalan, S., & Stata, R. et al. (2000). Graph Structure in the Web. Computer Networks. *The International Journal of Computer and Telecommunications Networking, 33*(1-6), 309–320.

Cho, J., & Garcia-Molina, H. (2003a). Estimating Frequency of Change. *Journal ACM Transactions on Internet Technology, 3*(3), 256–290. doi:10.1145/857166.857170

Cho, J., & Garcia-Molina, H. (2003b). Effective Page Refresh Policies for Web Crawlers. *Journal ACM Transactions on Database Systems, 28*(4), 390–426. doi:10.1145/958942.958945

Cho, J., Shivakumar, N., & Garcia-Molina, H. (2000). Finding Replicated Web Collections. In *Proceedings of the ACM SIGMOD International Conference on Management of Data,* Dallas, Texas. (pp. 355-366).

Downey, A. B. (2001). The Structural Cause of File size Distributions. *Proceedings 9th International Symposium on Modeling, Analysis and Simulation of Computer and Telecommunication Systems*, Cincinnati, Ohio. (pp. 361-370).

Efthimiadis, E.,, & Castillo, C. (2004). Charting the Greek Web. *Proceedings of the Conference of the American Society for Information Science and Technology (ASIST)*, Rhode Island, USA.

Fetterly, D., Manasse, M., & Najork, M. (2004). Spam, Damn Spam, and Statistics: Using Statistical Analysis to Locate Spam Web Pages. *Proceedings of the 7th International Workshop on the Web and Databases* WebDB '04, Paris, France. (pp. 1-6).

Fetterly, D., Manasse, M., Najork, M., & Wiener, J. (2003). A Large-Scale Study of the Evolution of Web Pages. *Proceedings of the 12th International Conference on World Wide Web, WWW '03*, Budapest, Hungary. (pp. 669-678). doi:10.1145/775152.775246

Gomes, D., & Silva, M. J. (2005). Characterizing a National Community Web. *Journal ACM Transactions on Internet Technology, 5*(3), 508–531. doi:10.1145/1084772.1084775

Grefenstette, G., & Nioche, J. (2000). Estimation of English and Non-English Language use on the WWW. *Proceedings of Content-Based Multimedia Information Access,* Paris, France. (pp. 237–246).

Gulli, A., & Signorini, A. (2005). The Indexable Web is more than 11.5 Billion Pages. *14th International Conference on World Wide Web, WWW '05* Chiba, Japan. (pp. 902-903).

Gyongyi, Z., & Garcia-Molina, H. (2005). Web Spam Taxonomy. *Proceedings of the First International Workshop on Adversarial Information Retrieval on the Web, AIRWeb 2005.* (pp. 39-47).

Huberman, B. A., & Adamic, L. A. (1999). Internet: Growth Dynamics of the World-Wide Web. *Nature, 401*(6749), 131–131. PMID:10490019

Kumar, J. P., & Govindarajulu, P. (2009). Duplicate and Near Duplicate Documents Detection: A Review. *European Journal of Scientific Research, 32*, 514–527.

Lewandowski, D. (2008). A Three-year Study on the Freshness of Web Search Engine Databases. *Journal of Information Science, 34*(6), 817–831. doi:10.1177/0165551508089396

Miranda, J., & Gomes, D. (2009). How Are Web Characteristics Evolving? *Proceedings of the 20th ACM Conference on Hypertext and Hypermedia, HT '09,* Torino, Italy. (pp. 369-370). doi:10.1145/1557914.1557993

Modesto, M., Pereira, A., Ziviani, N., Castillo, C., & Baeza-Yates, R. (2005). Um Novo Retrato da Web Brasileira. *Proceedings of XXXII SEMISH,* São Leopoldo, Brazil. (pp. 2005-2017).

Ntoulas, A., Cho, J., & Olston, C. (2004). What's New on the Web?: The Evolution of the Web from a Search Engine Perspective. *Proceedings of the 13th International Conference on World Wide Web, WWW '04,* New York, NY. (pp. 1-12). doi:10.1145/988672.988674

Ntoulas, A., & Manasse, M. (2006). Detecting Spam Web Pages Through Content Analysis. In *Proceedings of the World Wide Web conference, WWW '06,* Edinburgh, UK. (pp. 83-92). doi:10.1145/1135777.1135794

Olston, C., & Pandey, S. (2008). Recrawl Scheduling Based on Information Longevity. *Proceedings of the 17th International Conference on World Wide Web, WWW '08,* Beijing, China. (pp. 437-446). doi:10.1145/1367497.1367557

Page, L., Brin, S., Motwani, R., & Winograd, T. (1998). *The Pagerank Citation Ranking: Bringing Order to the Web*. Stanford Digital Library.

Pan, D., Qiu, S., & Yin, D. (2008). Web Page Content Extraction Method Based on Link Density and Statistic. *Proceedings of the 4th International Conference on Wireless Communications, Networking and Mobile Computing, WiCOM '08,* Dalian, China. (pp. 1-4). doi:10.1109/WiCom.2008.2664

Prieto, V., Álvarez, M., & Cacheda, F. (2012). Analysis and Detection of Web Spam by Means of Web Content. *Proceedings of the 5th Information Retrieval Facility Conference, IRFC '12*, Vienna, Austria. doi:10.1007/978-3-642-31274-8_4

Prieto, V., Álvarez, M., & Cacheda, F. (2013). The Evolution of the Web. *Proceedings of the 2013 International Conference on Systems, Control and Informatics, SCI 2013* Venice, Italy. (pp. 95-104).

Raghavan, S., & Garcia-Molina, H. (2001). Crawling the Hidden Web. *Proceedings of the 27th International Conference on Very Large Data Bases, VLDB '01* San Francisco, CA. (pp. 129-138).

Rubin, A. D., & Geer, D. E. Jr. (1998). A Survey of Web Security. *The Computer Journal*, *31*(9), 34–41. doi:10.1109/2.708448

Sanguanpong, S., Piamsa-nga, P., Keretho, S., Poovarawan, Y., & Warangrit, S. (2000). Measuring and Analysis of the Thai World Wide Web. *Proceeding of the Asia Pacific Advance Network*. (pp. 225-230).

Serrano, M. A., Maguitman, A., Boguñá, M., Fortunato, S. & Vespignani, A. (2007). Decoding the Structure of the WWW: A Comparative Analysis of Web Crawls. *Journal ACM Transactions on the Web*, 1(2).

Shestakov, D. (2011b). Databases on the Web: National Web Domain Survey. *Proceedings of the 15th Symposium on International Database Engineering & Applications, IDEAS '11*, Lisbon, Portugal. (pp. 179-184). doi:10.1145/2076623.2076646

Shestakov, D. (2011a). Sampling the National Deep Web. *Proceedings of the 22nd International Conference on Database and Expert Systems Applications, DEXA'11*. (pp. 331-340). Toulouse, France. doi:10.1007/978-3-642-23088-2_24

Shuyo, N. (2010). Language Detection Library for Java. Retrieved from http://code.google.com/p/language-detection/

Suel, T., & Yuan, J. (2001). Compressing the Graph Structure of the Web. *Proceedings of the Data Compression Conference, DCC '01*, Snowbird, Utah. (pp. 213-213). doi:10.1109/DCC.2001.917152

Thelwall, M., & Wilkinson, D. (2003). Graph Structure in Three National Academic Webs: Power Laws with Anomalies. *Journal of the American Society for Information Science and Technology*, *54*(8), 706–712. doi:10.1002/asi.10267

W3C DOM IG. (2005). The Document Object Model. Retrieved from http://www.w3.org/DOM

Wu, B., & Davison, B. D. (2005). Identifying Link Farm Spam Pages. *In 14th International Conference on World Wide Web, WWW '05*, Chiba, Japan. (pp. 820-829). doi:10.1145/1062745.1062762

KEY TERMS AND DEFINITIONS

Client Side Hidden Web: Subset of the Hidden Web that is accessible through client-side scripting languages and session maintenance mechanisms.

Crawling Systems: Programs that are capable of traversing and analyzing the Web in a certain order, by following the links between different pages.

Global Web: There only exists one Web, the so-called Global Web, formed by all web documents can be accessed through the HTTP protocol (the entire Web).

Hidden Data: Web documents contained in the Hidden Web.

Hidden Web: Subset of the Global Web that is not directly connected to the rest through conventional links. Therefore, content of this subset of the Web is out of the reach of conventional crawling systems.

Search Engines: Complex systems that allow, among other things: gathering, storing, managing and granting access to Web information.

Server Side Hidden Web: Subset of the Hidden Web that is mainly accessible through ds.

Spanish Web: Subset of the Global Web including only documents from the .es domain.

ENDNOTES

[1]   http://dbpubs.stanford.edu:8091/~testbed/doc2/WebBase

[2]   http://diglib.stanford.edu:8091/

[3]   http://d3s.mff.cuni.cz/~holub/sw/shash/

Chapter 2
Creating Extended-Form Eventgraphs from Social Media Using Publicly Available Software Tools

Shalin Hai-Jew
Kansas State University, USA

ABSTRACT

This chapter explores the feasibility of exploring surprise and unfolding events through the extraction of strategic data from social media platforms and the Web and Internet to form extended-form eventgraphs. "Extended-form eventgraphs" are conceptualized as those involving multivariate descriptors of events: participants, their respective roles, their interrelationships, their messaging, the timeline, related locations, and other event features and dynamics. What are the current extant methods and tools, then, and how are they applied in sequence, and what is ultimately knowable to sketch out an eventgraph based on social media channels? What sorts of real-world human events, which may not be directly "social" or pre-planned, are observable in online spaces? This chapter offers an initial proof-of-concept of a non-scalable manual-based eventgraphing process with two real-world examples: one of a mainstream tracked event and one of a more silent event. Finally, it offers a simple sense of a possible way forward which may be used in whole or in part. The challenge here involves using publicly available software tools for this information capture (versus self-created programs).

INTRODUCTION

The broad and spreading popularity of social media platforms, mobile devices, and Web 2.0, has meant that much of the conduct of people's lives has gone electronic, social, and broadly observable; the prior affordances have enabled "human sensor networks," the uses of people's digital expressions and multimedia to promote broad awareness of emergent and other phenomena. This awareness may be enhanced with the harnessing of social media platforms as electronic listening posts and humans as sensors to

DOI: 10.4018/978-1-4666-8696-0.ch002

real-world events. One challenge has been to use social media to create extended-form eventgraphs, with multivariate descriptors of events: participants, their respective roles, their interrelationships, their messaging, the timeline, the geolocations, and other event features and dynamics. This eventgraph-based data is potentially applicable to situational awareness, decision-making, and interventions, and it is applicable to various types of research. This data is seen as complementary to other maybe more formal forms of news and informational understandings through information that may not necessarily be seen as initially relevant by mainstream journalists. It is widely believed that law enforcement and governments have high-powered cyber tools to tap public and private (with permission or invitation) channels to create extended-form eventgraphs across a broad spectrum of multivariate information. The public capability is likely orders of magnitude less.

What is knowable about sudden and fluidly changing events using broadly-available software tools and publicly available information? In relation to the event, what are potential leading, coincident, and lagging indicators of that event on social media? Real-world events do not have discrete starts and finishes. They do not have artificial marketing efforts to capture attention. They may not have spokespeople to champion the topic and to maintain specific public interest. The environment is complex—with natural and human-caused events (often working interactively), and with many actors and conflicting interests. First causes or event-catalysts are often unknown at least in the moment, and many causes are hidden, unknown, and even unknowable.

For a number of event types, there is almost always a human nexus. These include natural and human-made events; accidental, intentional, or mixed-cause events; health events; political events, and a number of other types. There are human constituencies for a range of issues. A subset of these events may show up on social media platforms at microblogging messages, uploaded images and videos, and other digital contents. While there have been long debates on whether social media is cathartic (serving as a channel to release or purge tensions and human expressions; de-mobilizing) or reinforcing (serving as a channel to strengthen human expressions and impulses; mobilizing) in terms of human impulses, there is no final consensus but rather a mixed set of findings. The cathartic approach suggests that this channel enables citizens to express their pent-up frustrations and to have those needs at least partially met by government. [The efforts to build up social media connectivity between citizens and e-government build on the idea of e-governance efficacy through electronic connections (Mossberger, Wu, & Crawford, 2013).] The reinforcing approach suggests that particular messages may spark cascading events that may go "viral" and out-of-control. Some have argued that social media may be used as a form of repression—with government surveillance of citizens and "astroturfing" with faked accounts by government agents. A counterview is that social media is an aid to pre-existing social networks to bypass "state repressive measures" in order to foment a temporary revolution (Gawhry, 2012, p. 3). However, people choose to view social media, many events have a human aspect—and a subset of those involve a public-facing side that may be expressed at least in part in social media.

Human attention and attitudes on issues are important to monitor because of people's volitional decision-making—both on individual and group levels. Once people are inspired to individual or mass actions, individually or as part of a group, they may cause mass effects on others' lives and well-being. In some cases, the momentum of events may lead to large-scale changes, such as the over-turning of governments or the starting of wars or the remaking of a nation's boundaries. Collective action events are subject to inertial drag and apathy on the one side (which would tend to lead to mass non-action) and the rousing of high emotion and senses of injustice on the other (which would tend to lead to mass action). The prior dynamics may risk a degree of stereotyping and potential over-simplification.

Social media platforms have attracted a vast "installed base" of users; these have become an integrated part of human lives and interactions. They are a core space where physical and cyber interests mesh, in the so-called cyber-physical confluence. Others have argued that there should not be a digital dualism but an understanding that the physical and digital, the offline and online, are intertwined (Jurgenson, 2011). Shelton, Poorthuis, Graham, and Zook (2014) describe "the complex relationship between the material world and its digital representations" (p. 167). One author recounts some of the recent numbers of participants:

The number of people using Facebook and other social networking sites has grown rapidly. Of the 2.41 billion internet users on June 30, 2012 (Internet World Stats, 2012), 67 percent used social networking in December 2012 (Brenner, 2013), more than a billion of whom are monthly active users of Facebook in December 2012 (Facebook, 2013b), and an average of 618 million of these users accessed it every day in December 2012. In the UK, for example, in March 2013 there were 32.2 million users, 61 percent of the online population (Socialbakers, 2013). The average user creates 70 pieces of information per month (Facebook, 2013a). comScore (2011) showed that in August 2010 Facebook became the largest US web 'property'—more time was spent accessing Facebook than any of the other large US web properties: all Google sites (including Google Search, YouTube, Google News, and Gmail) (and) all Yahoo! Sites. (Oxley, 2013, pp. 9-10)

By mid-2013, the 554,750,000 Twitter users tweeted about 9,100 messages every second, or 58 million per day, a number that is growing rapidly.

(Weimann, 2014, p. 8). Twitter users tend to communicate from a generally geographically fixed area and show "high-locality" (Cuevas, Gonzalez, Cuevas, & Guerrero, 2014). An estimated 75% of Twitter users "perform their activity from a relatively reduced coverage area within a country that covers few hundred km. including few (<5) cities and even smaller ($\leq$ 2) number of regions," the researchers write (Cuevas, Gonzalez, Cuevas, & Guerrero, 2014, p. 401). The outpouring of shared information online is even greater among those who actively "life log" or self-record through sensors and messaging, and then broadcast this information. Two and a half billion people "actively produce content" online, and numerous sensors collect data in digital form (Shelton, Poorthuis, Graham, & Zook, 2014, p. 167). The online shift is not only thought of as a movement of peoples of a shift in an axis of creativity and dynamis. Robertson and Olson (2013) write:

The vast majority of Internet users are no longer in North America, which represents only about 13 percent of the global Internet population and is declining. Two-thirds of all global Internet users are under the age of 35, and 40 percent are under the age of 25. Three out of five new Internet users live in states that are considered either failed or at risk of fragility. "The center for innovation, the drive to create things in this space, the impetus to try to describe it in policy terms, is no longer in Washington, no longer in Ottawa, the UK, or anywhere else. It's shifting slowly but distinctly to the South and to the East," said (Rafal) Rohozinski" (p. 36).

This shift to social media has meant that many have moved from more traditional mediums of mass communication to social media as a news source (Haddow & Haddow, 2014). People today are consuming news through multiple devices and multiple channels. Social media is a "first rough draft of history" which also plays a role in what happens next (Bruno, 2010–2011, p. 12). Professional news organizations are including Tweets and Tweetstreams in their reports; they are mapping events on interactive digital maps. They are eliciting responses from their readership through a variety of means. They are tracking readership behaviors on the back-ends of their sites in order to respond to perceived audience needs.

The demographics of those using particular platforms has shifted to be more global instead of U.S.-based:

By the end of 2013, Instagram had 150 million active monthly users, more than 60 percent of whom were from outside the United States, who shared 55 million pictures each day on average. Flickr offers a web service which allows users to upload photos and videos to its website, and, if desired, to their social network profiles. By March 2013, Flickr counted 87 million registered users and approximately 8 billion photos.(Weimann, 2014, p. 13).

Even while many others have come online, their representation has not been egalitarian, with online presence representing long-standing social inequalities (Shelton, Poorthuis, Graham, & Zook, 2014, p. 169). There has been work on the psychological makeup of those who participate in social media, with research suggesting that those who tend to be more neurotic tend to use Facebook and Twitter (the two largest social networking sites in the world) to feel less lonely and less anxious; that those who are active on Facebook and who have joined a number of groups tend toward extraversion (as a personality trait); that those who are open to experiences tend to use instant messaging (IM-ing) and short messaging services (SMS), that those who rate high in conscientiousness tend to spend less time on Facebook (Hughes, Rowe, Batey, & Lee, 2012, pp. 562 - 653).

In addition to investigating whether personality is influential in determining which site is used for social and informational purposes, it was analysed whether a preference for Facebook or Twitter was associated with differences in personality. Participants were asked to indicate which SNS they preferred to use. One-hundred and ninety-seven preferred to use Facebook, whilst 103 favoured Twitter. In order to assess whether there were significant differences in personality dependant SNS preference, a series of one-way ANOVAs were performed. Significant mean differences were observed in NFC ("need for cognition"), Sociability, Extraversion and Neuroticism. No significant differences were found in the traits of Openness, Agreeableness and Conscientiousness. The results indicate that those who have a preference for Facebook see themselves as higher in Sociability, Extraversion and Neuroticism but lower in NFC (Hughes, Rowe, Batey, & Lee, 2012, p. 565).

There is a self-selection process in terms of which social networking platforms people choose to engage in based on their psychological profile and experienced needs. The types of messaging may be analyzed for personality, intellect, and other features, as well.

Understanding who is sharing messages on social media platforms is critical in multiple ways. If there is dominance of certain populations or peoples from particular regions in discussions, there may well be an outsized focus on one point-of-view which is not reflective of the larger population. There will likely be skew to the data. If there was an event that occurred in one locale, but many of the messages are from a very distant locale, then it may be that the messaging here is second or third hand and maybe less informationally valuable than firsthand and proxemics sourcing.

From this initial exploration, it seems clear that tapping multiple social and formal media channels will be necessary to understand the thinking of various stakeholder groups to the issue. Because of the popular usages of these platforms and the relative ease of capturing and analyzing digital data, governments, corporations, and other entities have shown interest in mining publicly available data from social media sites. One of the common ambitions is to use such technologies to learn of unfolding events. In the so-called Web 2.0 age of the Read-Write Web, social media platforms have proliferated. These include all sorts of interactivity: content sharing (of slideshows, information, photos, videos, audio, and other contents); social networking; microblogging; photologging (photo-sharing in a network community), moblogging (mobile blogging); video blogging (vlogging) and classic text-based blogging; sharing via digital bulletin boards and wikis; the publishing of e-books and journal contents; social tagging; fundraising and other types of peer-to-peer endeavors. While many looked to these technologies to change-up societal power structures, more recently, there have been observations that these technologies only reaffirm existing social power.

One important finding from this work was that a small number of "elite" users were followed by half of all Twitter users. Yahoo! used the list feature to help separate out four categories of elite users: celebrities, media outlets, organizations and corporations, and bloggers.4 Researchers put Twitter users into one of the elite categories based on how frequently they were categorized as such by individual users. For example, a Twitter handle labeled as that of a celebrity by 20,000 other users most likely did in fact belong to a celebrity. What was learned was that 50 percent of all attention was being paid to just 20,000 elite users. This is not to say that those elite users were producing half of all tweets, but rather that half of all the tweets that were read were updates provided by these elite users.("Public Response...", 2012, pp. 23 – 24)

This is not to say that extracted microblogging messages are necessarily accurate, especially in high-stress events, when rumors are rampant. Even if the information is not high-fidelity to the actual world in an objective sense, the information may provide a sense of a "folk model" (non-expert people's inaccurate or incomplete mental models of an event or phenomena) or public understanding, which is expected to be disparate from expert conceptual models. There is value to understanding the perspectives within the public constituencies, particularly in events related to public well-being. Some authors have observed the switching of public discussions from one hashtag label to another, leaving those tracking the discussions liable to be engaging in "fragmented discussions" (Charlwood, Dennis, Gissing, Quick, & Varma, 2012). Others focus on the power of communications enabled by social media, with one writing about "emergent, significant, and often accurate form of public participation and backchannel communication" (Palen, 2008, p. 76). There have been studies on how to discern accurate information from rumors on microblogging sites during crises using machine analysis: researchers observe, "Our analysis shows that the propagation of tweets that correspond to rumors differs from tweets that spread news because rumors tend to be questioned more than news by the Twitter community" (Mendoza, Poblete, & Castillo, 2010, p. 71).

Controversial uses of social media. The information that people willingly release into public is generally considered fair game for data-mining researchers as low-risk, passive, and non-intrusive, and that is released through the end user license agreements (EULAs) for the various social media platforms. For the corporations and organizations that maintain social media platforms, there is a critical public trust factor that they must maintain with those who would share their information. The dissipation of trust may mean a potential mass migration away from the social media platform. This customer or user trust relationship is evolved on the one side by the organization's policies, practices, and communications; the site branding; the site's innovations and rates of changes; the organization's uses of the users' data, and other factors. One case in point was research involving 600,000 Facebook users to see if their moods could be changed based on the types of news sent through their news feeds (whether positive or negative) and how that would affect whether they sent a microblog message (and then whether that was positive or negative). The release of this research created a cyber-firestorm of debate over appropriate and inappropriate uses of people's data and the ethics of such experiments without people's foreknowledge. While big data sets may offer statistically significant results, they do not necessarily make for necessarily relevant findings (Morin, July 2, 2014). Some researchers suggest that focusing on small subsets of big data may be more informative, particularly georeferenced social media which may shed light on "the geographies of a range of social processes and practices" (Shelton, Poorthuis, Graham, & Zook, 2014, p. 167). There are continuing debates on the ethics of using data from social media—from whether researchers need to acquire institutional review board (IRB) oversight for human subjects research for such usages or not. There are debates on whether such uses of data collection and analysis infringes on people's privacy (en masse and singularly). Researchers have described surveillance through the uses of cyber social networks for governance, law enforcement, national security and other applications (Rohan, 2011). Some have asked if Fourth Amendment challenges may exist if U.S. government agencies monitor social media ("Public Response…", 2012, p. 41). Some have asked how social media data may be validated or invalidated (falsified) outside those same social media channels. (In general, it helps to maintain multiple channels of knowability). Such surveillance is used as part of "opposition research" to understand competitors and adversaries. For all the controversies, computational social science draws heavily from social media platform contents.

There is also personally identifiable information (PII) captured and released on the Deep Web, which includes dynamically drawn public records from a range of public data bases. This information is collected as part of government work, and it is released by default in most democracies. This information is not directly within the control of the individual as these include public court records, including property ownership, marriages / divorces / deaths, financial status records, and other data.

A complex problem to sense events. The mapping of a real-world event on social media using extant and publicly available software tools and applications may be a complex problem, something that might even fit under the general definition of a "mess" per Ackoff's definition or a "wicked problem" (Ritchey, 2005, as cited in Ritchey, 2003-2011). One challenge involves the need to create coherence from masses of data. Brenner and Izquierdo (2012) describe a complex series of steps needed to try to detect pre-planned social events (vs. arbitrary or unplanned events) from collaborative photo collections in an automated way. In a complex environment, events occur unannounced, invisible, or even purposefully hidden or ambiguated. To apply human attention and effort to an event, the event itself must be sufficiently relevant and applicable to human endeavor (writ large). The social media platforms' application programming interfaces (API) that enable access to some of the data from its holdings are limited (both in access and in rates of download). The software tools that may be deployed to these ends are also limited in the social media platforms that may be accessed. (Certain events would leave electronic trails in some types of social media platforms only based on the user preferences for certain platforms). The software tools and applications are also limited in terms of data extraction capabilities, data visualization, text analysis (based on stylometry, word clusters, word branches, word frequency counts, and others), geolocation, time-stamping, and other factors. There are also the limits of a "human sensor network" and collective awareness of various events. Much of what is occurring in the world is not directly known by the broader public, and valuable information often involves a few valuable signals (important "tells" to the event) mixed in with a lot of noise. Noise may be added with rumor-sharing, hoaxing, trolling, image photo-shopping, video green-screening, and other methods. Another way that "noise" may be added is the practice of some businesses to use trending hashtags of other events to try to drive traffic to their own businesses; this practice of spammers "free-riding social networking" (Oxley, 2013, p. 107) adds a lot of irrelevant spam to the data capture. Volunteered geographical information is often noisy because of the lack of common formatting used by people who populate the text fields themselves (instead of using precise machine-based information). The presence of trolls and hoaxers and spoof accounts also adds another layer of noise. In Twitter, a highly popular microblogging site, only 1.7% of its Tweets contain "explicit geographic information" (Shelton, Poorthuis, Graham, & Zook, 2014, p. 171), but even with sparse data, there can be a mapping of "the territoriality of the event" (p. 173). The phenomena of purposeful message distortion may also add noise to any collected communications data.

An "event," by definition, is something important that happens, or a planned public or social occasion—to paraphrase; it is finite, with a sense of start and finish. An event may be sparked by any number of things—emotions, ideas, measurable objectives, meanings, and desires. Some events require planning and logistics to achieve. Others may be more spontaneous and less requiring of planning and materiel. Not all planned events materialize or instantiate; many remain as a mere concept or plan. Events that are buoyed by momentum and interest may recur or instantiate as part of a sequence. Some events capture plenty of human attention; others occur without any human awareness. How events are viewed may be quite subjective and depend on the backgrounds and interests of the observers.

Figure 1 illustrates some of the difficulties of indicating when an event is starting up, what its stages are, and when it is ending. It brings up the question of what the event means in a larger time context, much less a social, political, economic, historical, or other context. What are the constituent parts to the event? Is there an event trajectory? In terms of a unit of analysis, is this one event part of a larger sequence or event? Is it possible to identify a spark to the event as a first cause or sparks to multiple causes? How can people know that an event is incipient (and then with what degree of confidence)? How can an event that has passed be evaluated for event-graphing (given that some events won't have been recognized as such until its aftermath and in retrospect)? Is there a way to tell what type of event is coming based on signaling in social media? Is there a way to know what stage of an event one is in as it is unfolding (based on studies of past events)? (The visualization itself suggests that there may be discrete elements that may be seen as events, but in reality, there are many occurrences occurring simultaneously and in flux, and the assigning of "event" labels tends to be challenging.)

This scenario enables the introduction of a range of "knowability tools" on the Internet and Web, by highlighting different sources of data and methods that may be used to reveal different information channels (and how these may overlap and also complement each other) and data extraction and analytical methods. The software tools explored will entail two main functionalities:

1. The extraction of data (textual, multimedia-based, and relational) from social media platforms, and
2. The analysis and visualization of extracted information for analytical depth.

This study involves two major questions, involving both tools and methods:

1. What are the current capabilities of creating social-media and Internet-based (extended-form) eventgraphs of unexpected and evolving real-world events using publicly available apps and software programs (both open-source and commercial)?

Figure 1. The Challenges of Defining an "Event"

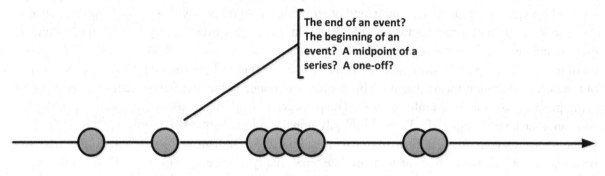

The end of an event? The beginning of an event? A midpoint of a series? A one-off?

The Challenges of Defining an "Event"

2.   What is the optimal method or approach to attain the most relevant information for a particular event?

The major questions are developed with basic sub-questions.

1.   What are the current capabilities of creating social-media and Internet-based (extended-form) eventgraphs of unexpected and evolving real-world events using publicly available apps and software programs (both open-source and commercial)?
      a.   What are the apps and software tools, and what are their capabilities?
      b.   What types of information may be extracted, analyzed, visualized, and presented?
      c.   What is the learning curve in their use?
      d.   What is an "event"?
      e.   What are the components to an "event"? Time and spatiality issues? Participants? Costs? Implications?
      f.   Which components of an event tend to be more stable over time? Which components of an event tend to be more dynamic and fast-changing?
      g.   What is knowable from publicly available social media? (Messaging? Strategic communications? Sentiment analysis? Data provenance? Related tags analysis? Leaders? Cliques? Geolocation?)
      h.   What leads may be generated from an analysis of social media?
      i.   On social media, what are indicators of the onset of an "event"?
      j.   On social media, what are the indicators of the sunsetting of an "event"?
      k.   What is not addressed?
      l.   Where are the informational gaps?
      m.   What are some risks in the usage of this data? (Where can one be misled?)
2.   What is the optimal method or approach to attain the most relevant information for a particular event?
      a.   What are the methodologies (sequencing)?
      b.   What are improvements that may be created with the existing tools?
      c.   What future research may be done to enhance this work?

This approach uses real-world limitations and problem-solving, in terms of attaining real information by using what is available off-the-shelf. This scenario presumes that the information collection will provide a less formal version of events, based on people's sense of lived experiences, and not directly captured by official news versions. With the differential access to formal news media (and the challenges to achieving mainstream media consciousness), those with lesser means may be assumed to go to social media platforms for reaching an audience. This extended-form eventgraphing approach is relevant because it offers different insights on particular unfolding events that may not be attainable otherwise.

REVIEW OF THE LITERATURE

The term "event graph" (with the space in between) has had several evolutions in meanings. The first use of the term "event graph" was apparently made by L. Schruben in 1983 to describe a way to graphically portray Discrete Event Simulation (DES) models of computational systems (p. 957). The graphical depictions complemented and augmented textual descriptors of such designed and structured system processes. Buss and Sanchez (2002) explain: "An Event Graph is a graph (in the formal mathematical sense of being a set of vertices and edges) that captures the event logic of a given model. In an Event Graph the vertices represent the state transition function, while the edges capture the scheduling relationships between events" (p. 732). Another meaning was created by a team of researchers collaborating around a tool that enables the social network graphing of social media platform data. The tool, now in wide use, is Network Overview, Discovery and Exploration for Excel (NodeXL), available off of Microsoft's CodePlex site. Here, an "EventGraph" (note the spelling difference) is "a specific genre of network graph that illustrates the structure of connections among people discussing an event via social media services like Twitter" (Hansen, Smith, & Schneiderman, 2011). Such data captures involve the recording of conversations linked to events on microblogging sites (with the messages labeled by various #hashtags or keywords), content-sharing sites (with photos and videos labeled with certain keywords or tags or audio-to-text transcripted with certain words), scraping of thumbnail images related to accounts, and other information captures. This definition is inclusive of formally created events like conferences (often with formally defined hashtags) as well as spontaneously-occurring ones (which would require the identification of fresh hashtags as well as related keywords). The captures involve backchannel conversations as well as largely public and official ones from microblogging sites. The tool itself enables the capturing of the contents of the related Tweetstreams as well as the uniform resource locator (URL) linking to websites, images, and videos; it also enables the capturing of thumbnail images linked to accounts. Researchers have observed how more comprehensive profiling may be done by cross-referencing related information across different accounts on different "source services." One example of this is the need to cross-identify an individual across multiple social media platforms, especially for those who may wish to remain hidden, which will require deep analysis and inferential analytical work ("Frontiers in Massive Data Analysis," 2013, pp. 36 - 37). Some suggest that actors may be found across platforms by co-membership information or shared attributes. For groups that want to remain "off-radar," they often encounter what is known as the efficiency vs. secrecy trade-off. The more efficiently they want to reach out to a wider group and to recruit and organize others, the less able they are to remain secret or hidden; likewise, the more stealth they want to remain, the less efficiently they can function.

Physical locations have some effect on social ties, with social tie strength decreasing with increasing spatial distance; further, the value of exchanged information tends to diminish the stronger the ties between individuals but is independent of physical distance (Groh, Straub, Eicher, & Grob, 2013, p. 1), which may suggest that those in a tighter cluster may have multiple messages about a topic and potentially shared sources of information (vs. more diverse ones). Geolocation and geotagging information may be extracted to relate messaging with real-world physical locations. This capability involves the capturing of ambient geospatial information (AGI). This involves capturing the "geographic footprints" in social media messaging (Stafanidis, Crooks, & Radzikowski, 2011 / 2013, p. 319). Based on the intuition that people tend to socialize with those in physical proximity, others use social ties to geolocate particular users (Rout, Preotiuc-Pietro, Bontcheva, & Cohn, 2013). Some researchers are using geotagged data from social media platforms to understand a dynamic sense of how people live and interact with the spaces around them based on "geosocial media" (Shelton, Poorthuis, Graham, & Zook, 2014, p. 168).

This process of attaching geographic coordinates to user derived digital content – often referred to as the geoweb – means that big data shadows are intimately connected to the material lived geographies from which they were produced. As such, social media has evolved beyond a simple online repository of conversations, networked interactions, and sites for the consumption of media, and is instead a dynamic record of when and how we move through and act in space, linked to other individuals and actions co-existing with us in those spaces (Shelton, Poorthuis, Graham, & Zook, 2014, p. 167).

In the context of a breaking event, this information may be used to identify geospatial hotspots. Events that are proxemic in time (such as co-occurring or simultaneous events) may also be studied for relatedness. Some researchers have been able to capture locational and classifier data to determine whether a "hyper-local event" (geographically close-in event) is occurring based on Instagram postings (Xie, Xia, Grinberg, Schwartz, & Naaman, 2013). One way to understand whether an event is in the offing involves the relating of occurrences tied to a shared physical location and shared time as well as similarity in messaging (Zhou & Chen, 2014). Often, events may cluster around particular physical locations because of the symbolic power of that locale. For mass political movements, there are locations that have collective meaning or meaning among a subset of the population. There are physical locations where historically resonant occurrences may have happened. Sometimes, history repeats with new layers of meaning for new groups or new generations. Researchers may focus on physical locations and re-compile their data in fresh ways to integrate the knowledge of physical space. Events may be found with overlapping information or shared correlational time-space features.

Cross-entry links are of particular importance, as they reveal semantic relations between entries. Within a particular service such links may become available from the original user community (e.g. retweets or responses in twitter). Additional links can be detected through analysis of the local database entries (e.g. linking entries that refer to the same real-life event, or ones that have comparable content, or using tags). By performing this analysis in our local database we can identify cross-medium links (e.g. linking twitter entries with YouTube videos and Flickr images), which allows us to span the boundaries of source services. Relations between entries are valuable because they reveal relations between the submitters of these entries, allowing us to identify the structure of the underlying social network. The most important relations that form the network are forwarding entries written by other members of the social site, replying to messages, or mentioning of other entries. These are not only very strong indicators of the relations between the submitters, but also indicate information pathways, allowing us to recognize the links through which information is disseminated within different groups, and to identify original sources of the information, and social hubs which disseminate it within their networks (Stafanidis, Crooks, & Radzikowski, 2011 / 2013, p. 323).

Another key affordance of NodeXL is the ability to identify interrelationships between user accounts based on features like follower / following relationships, co-commenting, and other relational connectivity—depicted in data tables and various network graphs (with a selection of almost a dozen different types of layout algorithms). It can identify highly active nodes (individual actors) who have been very busy communicating with others and is deeply connected, what Marc A. Smith calls the "mayor of the hashtag"; it also identifies cliques and clusters of deeply connected and active groups of nodes in an electronic social network. The focus is on conversational linkages (shared keywords, replies-to, mentions, shared hashtags, and other elements) around shared interests and also structural ones around established relationships of follower-following relationships. A contemporary sense of EventGraphs drawn from social media may be viewed in Figure 2.

There is also the capability to create graphs from similar word clustering for related tag (metadata) networks related to digital contents (like images and videos). Depending on the amount of geolocation data captured per each microblogging message or account, there may also be a geographical element to help analysts understand the spatial aspects of an unfolding event. Cheng, Caverlee, and Lee (2013) provide a content-analysis method (honing on evocative locational keywords and location names or toponyms) for probabilistically understanding possible locations within a 100-mile distance of the actual location of the messaging. Ryoo and Moon (2014) suggest that they can infer approximately 60% of Twitter users' locations to within 10 km of accuracy with a South Korean dataset based on the contents of the microblogging messaging; the researchers first build a geographic distribution of Tweeted words and then compare new messages against that set in order to geographically place that user. [A text analysis method may be applied to geolocate wiki documents on Wikipedia as well. Wing and Baldgridge (2011) were able to predict the location of Wikipedia pages "to a median error of 11.8 km and error of 221 km" (p. 963).] A focus on activities in a particular physical location (matched in space and time) may capture some insights about events but may be less precise given that messages unrelated to an event will also be captured. The disambiguation of information will require exploration and the elimination of alternate meanings; likewise, the analysis of network data will require structural pruning in order to focus on the branches that are relevant. Sometimes, such evaluative decisions are made in real-time and on-the-fly, which suggests the need for experience and analytical capabilities—to inform analysts about where to focus for relevance and sense-making. In NodeXL, dynamic filters may be used to roughly show how a network graph describing an event evolved over time. Another way to use this tool to capture time is to label edges by timestamps:

The opacity (or width) of edges can be modified based on the timestamps so that older edges are darker, while newer ones are lighter. This helps capture time in smaller, less dense networks, but does not scale well to large, dense networks (Hansen, Smith, & Schneiderman, 2011, p. 8).

The authors write: "Specialized search engines now make it possible to weed through the 50 million daily tweets to collect messages containing a common string, term, keyword, or "hashtag" (which use the "#" to prefix a topic grouping)" (Hansen, Smith, & Schneiderman, 2011, p. 1). In other words, the tools enable the threading of disparate conversations across space and time to create a summary of the

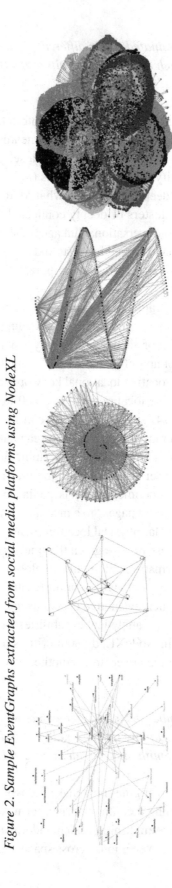

Figure 2. Sample EventGraphs extracted from social media platforms using NodeXL

various conversations going on around a certain event or related topic; another approach enables the understanding of some of the messaging going on geographically (through geolocation data embedded in microblogging messages and multimedia). These researchers offer a broad sense of what information may be captured about an event: its duration, its frequency, its spontaneity, its discussants respective geographical dispersion, and other dimensions (Hansen, Smith, & Schneiderman, 2011, pp. 3 - 4), all captured at web-scale. The setup of a server version of the software enables continuous data capture over time for a comprehensive view once an event has started. In the same way that a network may be captured in high resolution through "many snapshots" (McCulloh & Carley, 2008, p. 15), events may be understood in the same way—through the collection of information from a number of streams. (Some microblogging sites do not allow going back in time for more than a week or so. For-pay services enable capturing of data from specific time periods.) With only approximately 2.5% of the most-viewed videos on YouTube geotagged (Song, et al., 2012, as cited in Song, Zhang, Cao, Tang, Gao, & Li, 2014), researchers are using other methods to "place" where videos were created, in one case based on known locations of author accounts for certain videos and the related videos to those videos—possibly likely geographically proxemics (Song, Zhang, Cao, Tang, Gao, & Li, 2014).

Wilkinson and Thelwall (2012) analyzed nine months of English-language microblogging messages (half a billion short messages) from the United Kingdom, the U.S., India, S. Africa, New Zealand, and Australia, and found that trending keywords involved "festivals or religious events…followed by media events, politics, human interest, and sports," (p. 1631), which may suggest a focus on directly or para-socially experienced events. Another work has more directly alluded to this sense of the use of the Web to understand events, in terms of an EventWeb:

The WWW compellingly demonstrated that a Web of documents is enormously more useful than a database of documents. Based on that experience, a Web of events will clearly provide at least as significant an advantage. In fact, the Web of events or EventWeb is more natural and effective because events are more closely related to each other than are documents. Spatiotemporal relationships among physical events result in significant propagation of their effects and hence are essential in modelling many important concepts and phenomena. Based on these ideas, my research group has been exploring the development of concepts and techniques related to EventWeb. In EventWeb, each node (event) is represented by its basic properties (time, location and type), informational attributes (participants and characteristics of the event) and experiential attributes (text or audio reports, photographs, videos and other sensory information). In Jain, we discussed the structural and causal relationships among the events that create the EventWeb. Events in this Web could be as diverse as an application demands and at the desired granularity. EventWeb is fundamentally a dynamic Web structure that is linked to physical locations and uses familiar natural sensory characteristics. It uses text when needed. EventWeb will link to the current Web because the Web's content (blogs, news sites and so on) frequently describes events and experiences (Jain, 2013, p. 6).

Some analytical methods. There are several general analytical methods that may be used to extract meaning from social media platforms. Electronic social network analysis (e-SNA) draws on various statistical calculations to understand the members of social networks, the structural relationships, member roles and interactions, and other factors; in part, it may be used to identify the most important and influential ("fat") nodes in a network. There are ways to place nodes on a hierarchy of best connected based on its closeness to those in power. Nodes may be identified as "bridging" ones that connect disparate communities, making such nodes critical for the health of social networks in terms of diversity (even if these nodes have a low connectivity or "degree" in the connected social networks). Beyond the individual node characteristics, there are ways to measure the characteristics of the social network at a more global way. One global measure may involve the density of the network or how connected each node is to the others. A geodesic distance measure analyzes the diameter of the social network "graph", from one end to the other. The paths through the network may indicate how information, resources, and other "transmissibles" move through the network. The "hops" or "paths" between any two nodes shows the degree of separation in the network. (The world is thought to be connected by six degrees of separation between any two individuals through friend of a friend or "FOAF" networks, and word-of-mouth is thought to connect people to information, messages, behaviors, and activism.) An "observer effect" is thought to apply to social media, in the sense that people's behaviors change when they are aware that they are observed; this effect is combined with social performance observed in people, which means that what is projected is a designed identity construct. The construct slips at some moments, and data may leak in other ways as well. While some nodes have very public presences, others have gone to ground and electronic silence ("radio silence"). A number of researchers have observed that hidden nodes may be understood by the behaviors of the nodes connected to them (in the same way that a black hole's presence is known based on the behaviors of the objects near it—not least the bending of light). An underlying principle here is homophily or the tendency for people to socialize with others like themselves. Where people might not self-reveal, their associates may shed light on who they perceive the individual to be. In particular, the "ego neighborhood" of "alters" formed by direct ties to the focal node is thought to be revealing. A direct tie on online social media may still indicate weak or thin ties, which are typical of many types of social media platform relationships. In undirected networks, only relationships are indicated with lines (without arrowed line ends), no matter which way the direction exists. In a directed network, the relationships are indicated by lines with arrows on one, the other, or both ends of the line—to indicate the fact of a relationship and its direction. Some nodes can have self-relationships, indicated by a self-loop. Some network graphs include numbers on the lines to indicate the strength of the relationship. Social network graph visualizations are usually depicted as node-link diagrams. There are various innovations on social graphs, such as "interaction graphs" that suggest links if and only if there have been documented and actual volitional interactions to create the relationship (Wilson, Sala, Puttaswamy, & Zhao, 2012), instead of mere followership, for example.

Advancements in data visualization techniques have informed the depictions of structural relationships in social network graphs, such as through motif simplification to maximize limited screen space. "Motifs" are subgraph patterns of relationships (sometimes called "modeling units") between nodes (represented as all possible combinations of types of structures such as dyads, triads, and so on all the way to the highest cluster number of nodes in a subgraph for a network). Motifs may be represented by glyphs or small pictographs that highlight critical aspects of that structural relationship in a kind of visual data reduction and simplification. Motif censuses consist of machine-counts of the various types of identified structures, to illuminate the types of relationships in a particular electronic (or non-electronic) social network; motif census counts describe part of the topology of a network by showcasing common network structures or subnetworks. The researchers describe:

Well-designed glyphs have several benefits: they (1) require less screen space and layout effort, (2) are easier to understand in the context of the network, (3) can reveal otherwise hidden relationships, and (4) preserve as much underlying information as possible.(Dunn & Schneiderman, 2013, p. 3247)

In NodeXL, the system captures three "frequently occurring and high-payoff motifs": fans of nodes with a single neighbor, connectors linking a set of anchor nodes, and cliques of dense completely connected nodes. The authors explain:

A fan motif consists of a head node connected to leaf nodes with no other neighbors. As there may be hundreds of leaves, replacing all the leaves and their links to the head with a fan glyph can dramatically reduce the network size.

A D-connector motif consists of functionally equivalent span nodes that solely link a set of D anchor nodes. Replacing span nodes and their links with a connector glyph can aid in connectivity comparisons.

A D-clique motif consists of a set of D member nodes in which each pair is connected by at least one link. Cliques are common in biologic or similarity networks, where swapping for a clique glyph can highlight subgroup ties.(Dunn & Schneiderman, 2013, p. 3249).

Researchers have developed various models about how to create potential variance in understanding the potential roles of particular nodes depending on certain suspected connections between nodes to model uncertainty. These modeled factors include issues of node centrality in a network in a context with some confirmed associations and some suspected ones (Koban, 2014, p. 27):

Using a universal likelihood assessment for suspected associations is useful because, it shows the relative impact of removing a specified percentage edges. In targeting applications, the ultimate goal is to accurately identify the most important individuals in a network. By analyzing varying levels of edge likelihood, ULRA identifies what levels of uncertainty would result in a change to the top ranked individuals. When models are based primarily on confirmed associations, it is expected that suspected edges will have little to no effect on the top ranked individuals. However, if models include a large proportion of suspected edges, then different levels of edge likelihood may produce different rankings of the most important individuals. (Koban, 2014, p. 29)

A Variable Likelihood Replication Analysis (VLRA) is yet another technique which enables the identification of nodes closest to all other nodes and those with the power of bridging (but is less effective in terms of degree and eigenvector centrality) (Koban, 2014, p. 34). Recent research has focused on ways to assess the validity of various types of social network analysis methods.

Researchers are not only interested in analyzing the structural social relationships in a social network but to identify out the most influential social actors in that context and to understand their capabilities and relationships. They are looking to identify the most relevant interrelationships. They are pursuing predictive patterns in social networks to anticipate where a particular network may be moving. Some researchers explain the importance of compressing a social network representation while maintaining predictive accuracy—or in other words identifying the important parts of a network and its dynamics by pruning or removing the less important parts but still retaining the ability to use those elements to predict events for a more parsimonious model (Singh & Getoor, 2007, p. 1). A social network compression then results in simplifying networks to the relevant parties—actors, relations, events, and other elements—to still protect predictivity in specific contexts. Pruning networks may be done on a number of factors. One group systematically pruned networks based on descriptors of particular nodes:

Figure 3. An electronic social network graph with motifs represented as glyphs (in NodeXL)

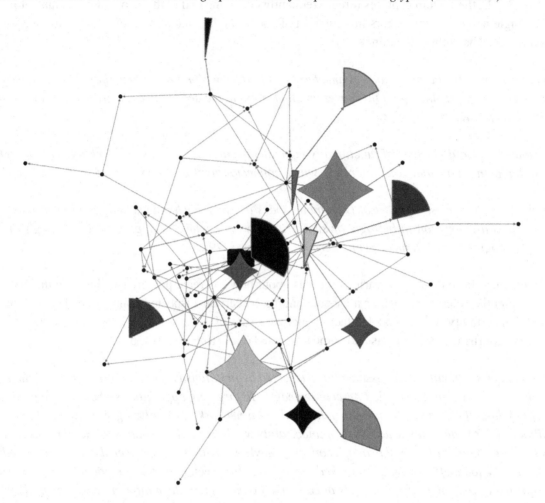

Pruning on position, we achieve an accuracy of 72.3% with a compression of 94%. In this case, we removed all actors except for the chairs of the company boards. Pruning on tenure, we achieve an accuracy of 70.29% with a compression of 95%, and pruning on age, we achieve an accuracy of 69.2% with a compression of 99%. In this case, we kept only the older executives. These accuracies are all better than the baseline prediction accuracy of 61% achieved by simply choosing the most common exchange (Singh & Getoor, 2007, p. 9).

The methodical approach to assess the effectiveness of different types of pruning is informative—so as to not immediately exclude data out-of-hand as it may be unclear early on what may be relevant. What seems a smarter proposition is to maintain the entire dataset but query by filtering (and not by data deletion). In theory, it would be ideal to be able to not only anticipate potential events but to be able to classify forthcoming events and to affect some features or even outcomes of that event. Close observations of changes occurring in social networks may provide inferences about network dynamics; they may provide predictive insights: Such inferences are insights that are not explicitly presented in the original data.

Changes in observed social networks may signal an underlying change within an organization, and may even predict significant events or behaviors. The breakdown of a team's effectiveness, the emergence of informal leaders, or the preparation of an attack by a clandestine network may all be associated with changes in the patterns of interactions between group members. The ability to systematically, statistically, effectively and efficiently detect these changes has the potential to enable the anticipation of change, provide early warning of change, and enable faster response to change. By applying statistical process control techniques to social networks we can detect changes in these networks (McCulloh & Carley, 2008, p. iii).

One approach used to understand potential events from microblogging messages is a statistical approach, such as a regression analysis of messaging in relation to real-world events. In one study, researchers strove to infer rainfall levels at a given location through a year of Twitter messaging, and in another case, to infer regional influenza-like illness rates and found "close semantic correlation with the target topics and inference" and some understanding of event magnitude or "nowcasting" (Lampos & Cristiannini, 2012, p. 72). Rogers (2013) notes that Twitter has gone through various evolutionary phases, with one of them as a way to follow events (based on a Twitter tagline change in 2009); he suggests the importance of de-banalizing the platform. Real-world events have a lot of moving pieces, and a common theoretical and computational model indicates just how difficult it may be to predict future events. The Abelian sandpile model shows how at critical state it may undergo extreme changes with a minute perturbation. In other words, small events may have outsized effects on events, and surface calms may be highly misleading.

In the current day, the research is non-deterministic, and conclusions have to be held lightly. These efforts are made to reduce uncertainties, if possible, but not to anticipate possible events with any deep certitude. It is important to be able to hold paradoxes and complexity as well—to more accurately understand and represent the world. Premature adherence to a particular point-of-view or interpretation closes off the exploration of possibilities and options. Another observation is that researchers would do well to work backwards and forwards in time—to learn from the past, present, and future—and to be able to break apart events for study. Clearly, this work requires some expertise on the particular events because those insights may inform strategy (planned approaches to the eventgraphing), tactics (applied actions, methods, and tools), and analytics (applied procedures on how to analyze work). [On the same hand, there may be benefit to having analysts look at certain eventgraphs "blind"—without specialist knowledge of the event or social backgrounds-- in order to extract insights that the experts may not see. This may be a kind of what Michalko calls "active thinking" or going beyond what others can see without going around the bend (Michalko, 2006 / 1991, p. 35).]

Active (vs. passive) learning captures. Clearly, such learning does not have to be passive only, passive in the sense that information is drawn whole from pre-existing sources. It would make sense to capture information in an actively crowd-sourced way. These may be broad elicitations of responses to particular ideas. They may involve active engagement of ideas with both private and public small-groups. This work may involve actual informal or formal research. The exploration may extend beyond social media. For example, "participatory sensing" involves the use of "sensing, communication, and computational power on mobile devices" to capture geolocational data in the context of large-scale human experiences in built spaces ("Frontiers in Massive Data Analysis," 2013, p. 138).

Further analyses may be conducted on the data linked to EventGraphs based on computer-based sentiment analysis, semantic network analysis, text summarizations, word branching, word frequency counts, and other natural language analysis approaches applied to unstructured data (data that is not prelabeled and already labeled and placed in a dataset). Microblogging communications may be analyzed for moods, such as the application of the "hedonometer" (a measure of pleasure or hedonism) approach to measure the amount of happiness and pleasure in a text corpus (Bliss, Kloumann, Harris, Danforth, & Dodds, 2012). Researchers are still working on how applicable sentiment and lexical analysis may be "in the context of social network analysis where the language tends to be more freeform and informal" (Bermingham, Conway, McInerney, O'Hare, & Smeaton, 2009, p. 2). There has been work on combining sentiment analysis and geolocation to see how closely Tweets of fans mirrored real-world game play during the NBA Playoffs in 2011 (Baucom, Sanjari, Lu, & Chen, 2013). This assumes that there will also be close reading of some of the collected data by people of particular information that is identified as important. This includes close perusals of important images and video. This involves psychological remote readings of leaders and relevant individuals to an event. This may involve a cultural analysis of particular entities and groups.

An extended-form eventgraph. The definition of an "extended-form eventgraph" used in this chapter draws from the latter contemporaneous definition. An extended-form eventgraph consists of a range of qualitative, quantitative, and mixed methods information about a real-world event extracted from social media platforms, the World Wide Web, and the Internet, as well as real-world sources. In a sense, the meaning in this chapter bears little resemblance to the classic definition used in machine states and only a passing resemblance to the EventGraphs concept linked to NodeXL. The idea of an "event" is more ill-defined than in a simulation, with undefined starts and ends (and the possibility of an ill-defined or non-discrete shape to the event being described). By definition, eventgraphs are necessarily multiplex networks, where actors are related by more than more type of tie or relationship. Multiplex networks are not just collecting actors in relationships but actors collected around events and conversations and a range of ties.

Multiplex networks are particularly consequential when they overlap and interact to create processes that cannot be explained by a single network alone. Along these lines, previous research demonstrates that multiplexity is critical to diverse phenomena, such as the mobilization of social movements (Gould, 1991), the consolidation of political power (Padgett and Ansell, 1993), the emergence of trust in economic relationships (Granovetter, 1985), the creation of social bonds within civic networks (Baldassarri and Diani, 2007), and the organization of party coalitions (Grossman and Dominguez, 2009, as cited in Heaney, 2014, pp. 67 - 68).

Interest groups interact and exchange influence through "communication networks," "coalition overlap networks," and "issue overlap networks" (Heaney, 2014, p. 68). Communication networks enable the building of familiarity and trust through information sharing, which increases the sensitivity of the information that may be shared. Such ties enable collaboration around shared social and political interests. Coalition overlap networks "are based on affiliations rather than on direct contacts between groups" and may not interact directly especially if the coalitions are large (Heaney, 2014, p. 68). Issue overlap networks are those that share temporarily common interests.

The drawing of an extended-form eventgraph will ultimately create new understandings and new knowledge; however, the approach itself is about identifying various sources of information, including the identification of what one author calls "information brokers," who share information about an event (Palen, 2008, p. 78). There may be the active cultivation of human sources. If there are existing trustworthy sources, then it makes little sense to exclude them. For any number of issues, there are active individuals and groups collecting information and working on different parts of the social media spaces and Internet. It makes sense to identify credible sources of information. The drawing of an extended-form eventgraph will certain tap both formal commercial mass media as well as social media. Traditional media itself certainly taps social media by including Tweets, Twitpics, Instagram images, Facebook information, and other related contents from social media. Others have noted that based on the so-called "Twitter effect," news cycles are accelerated, and there is pressure to release news right away—for a practically continuous news cycle (Bruno, 2010 – 2011). That speed is part of the microblogging site ethos, to constantly provide status updates.

The extended-form eventgraph may be understood as involving analysis at differing levels, micro, meso, and macro. The "graph" here is more than a social media graph visualization but rather includes a wide range of qualitative, quantitative and mixed-methods information: text corpuses, datasets, images, audio, video, and maps, and others. There is wide latitude to define what an extended-form eventgraph may be, given the rich data streams available. This approach draws both on the available information in the public archive as well as information gleaned from private channels. In this conceptualization, such extended-form eventgraphs are created using a variety of online applications and software tools to extract, visualize, and analyze data. The added capabilities of a NodeXL Graph Server enable continuous captures of eventgraph information on some social media platforms, to enable more dynamic views of evolving events and to increase the amount of relevant data records. (This is not to say that all records will be captured in a dynamic approach. That is not a known capability given the various limitations of software tools, social media platforms and their application programming interfaces—some with rate limiting, and other factors. A static approach offers a slice-in-time look whereas a dynamic one captures more data points and changes-over-time types of information.) The extension of this eventgraph form also extends to the types of events that may be captured, such as events that are unplanned and those that may catch people unawares. Pseudo-events are those that are manufactured ones to capture human attention, with press releases, eye-catching appearances, notable quotes, and other details. Because there is human interest in garnering attention, that sort of event is of low-level difficulty as a target. Electronic artifacts should not be difficult to find. There are identifiable interest groups to explore. A mid-level difficulty target may involve events that should have some natural electronic structures, entities, or digital tracks. The very top-level difficulty targets for this method of extended-form eventgraphing would be those that have no natural stakeholders that would be sharing information about it online. Further, these may be events that people themselves may not be aware of, so even if they were connected online and motivated to share, there may still be no messaging to very little messaging. There is also the contrast between "push" tools that send information out to interested subscribers and the general public, versus "pull" tools, which require some effort to access the particular information. "Push" tools are often used to publicize upcoming events by capturing people's attention and raising their interest. Search engine optimization is a type of "push" tool in terms of the sending out of a message to a broad public by a company. There are clearly identifiable patterns in ramp-ups to particular product or service roll-outs. "Pull" contexts may also require manual (vs. automated) access at critical moments in an unmarked or unannounced event in order to access information.

A chain analysis of the two main research questions. It is important to review why extended-form eventgraphing may have potential value. To review this, a derived form of "chain analysis" (Michalko, 2006/1991, p. 30) is applied, in which a range of questions are asked to parse out the assumptions. The two research questions are as follows.

1. What are the current capabilities of creating social-media and Internet-based (extended-form) eventgraphs of unexpected and evolving real-world events using publicly available apps and software programs (both open-source and commercial)?
2. What is the optimal method or approach to attain the most relevant information for a particular event?

The related chain analysis questions follow:

- Why is it important to understand the current capabilities of created social media-based extended-form eventgraphs?
- Why is it important to understand the capabilities of apps and software programs to extract data from social media platforms and the Internet for extended-form eventgraphs?
- Why are unexpected and evolving real-world events of interest?
- Why is it important to define an optimal method to attain the most relevant information for a particular event?
- What is meant by "optimal"?
- What is meant by "relevant information" for an event?

This chain analysis may continue in much greater depth with questions and subquestions. From this thought experiment, it's clear that the "ask" should be sufficiently aspirational even if it seems ridiculously ambitious or impossible. After all, working from what's possible would not open up possibilities but rather limit them. A currently impossible "ask" may well become possible as various people take on different parts of the challenge to solve. A large "ask" may seem unsolvable from a distance and in whole, but close-up and in segments, the work often becomes much more do-able. At the same time, real-world challenges are discovered based on the methods and the technologies.

Security. The role of effective government is critical is maintaining public order and societal well-being. Monitoring for events that may be disruptive or even violent is one important application of event-graphing today, particularly in the role of law enforcement and disaster preparedness and public health. Researchers have conducted some 60 years of research on how people respond in emergencies. For example, there is a social component in how people tend to respond to an emergency. They often seek social confirmation of warnings before taking protective actions and so lose precious time "milling" ("Public Response…" 2013). Social tools are seen as critical for "digital statecraft" (Stein, 2012). This capability is a necessary one for situational awareness of unfolding events for those in various professional roles, such as emergency management (Smith, Halstead, Esposito, & Schlegelmilch, 2011). There are efforts to collect elusive pieces of information for emerging events, including geolocation information from text message word choices along (without geotags, given their sparseness) (Ikawa, Enoki, & Tatsubori, 2012). The pre-knowledge of impending flash mob activities (and some "flash rob activities" and human social swarming) is a public safety capability ("Flash mobs…" 2011). Communications mediums are powerful spaces with the ability to carry messages to a broad range of people. Messages that are packaged in a popular way may convey "calls to action" that may result in a broad range of mass behaviors. Inspired by fictional stories and visualizations of Slender Man, two young girls were apparently inspired to try to murder their friend. Members of the Anonymous hacker collective have inspired many thousands with the figure of a suited body without a head (to suggest a leaderless organization), images of Guy Fawkes masks, and an ideology of fighting corporate and government injustice. Communications systems inspire multiplier and cascade effects because of its reach and the power of message reverberations through people. People are not only activated to action by ideas and images, but they may also be sparked by charismatic leaders and personalities. There are the classic "true believers" of the Eric Hoffer school of thought and then others who join movements and actions for more mundane reasons. There is the potential for low probability (rare), unprecedented, and high-impact events that may be highly disruptive known as "black swan events" (Taleb, 2010/2007). A number of researchers have worked to strengthen social media as a way to disseminate authoritative information during mass-crisis events by identifying what sort of messaging has value in that context (Freberg, Saling, Vidoloff, & Eosco, 2013). They have also explored ways to enhance the uses of people as sensor networks by proposing prescribed syntaxes such as sequences of hashtags to enable easier machine identification and "the filtering of relevant information and the compartmentalization of information" in preparation for emergency situations (Boyd, 2010, as cited in Oxley, 2013, p. 67). Extended-form eventgraphing may enable some fore-warning and enable prior preparations and other efforts to minimize risk to organizations and the broader public. Various interventions may include counter-messaging, control of physical spaces, the protection of physical spaces and sites, and other efforts.

For first responders, they require a specific type of information collection during an unfolding event. "Knowing the number of people killed and injured, the level of damage at the disaster site, the condition of homes and community infrastructure, and current response efforts provide decision makers with the situational awareness necessary to identify needs and appropriately apply available resources," note G.D. Haddow and K.S. Haddow (2014, p. 9). Social media is seen as an effective tool for the exchange of information during disasters in multiple directions (Tyshchuk & Wallace, 2013) assuming that certain parts of the infrastructure are still intact. Even for very wired and modern cities, a disaster could render cell phone service spotty or non-existent, such as in the case of electrical blackouts, putting into question the effectiveness of social media as a tool for crisis response (Jennex, 2012); such applications depend on the quality of the infrastructure post-event and suggest the need for both cell service and SMS / text-messaging services, and for back-up energy sources. Researchers have looked at the role of information and communication technology (ICT), including social media platforms, to address the challenges of a potential emerging pandemic, particularly in technologically-enabled social distancing to lower infection risk (Hai-Jew, 2014). The idea is the citizens may become force multipliers if they may be properly informed and supported in their preparations and decision-making. The star power of entertainers like Lady Gaga, Ashton Kitcher, Kim Kardashian, and other (who tweeted traffic information to their followers) has been used to warn LA-residents of traffic issues during the 2011 "Carmageddon" event during which road repairs were anticipated to cause mass disruption. Researchers caution about assuming that people will necessarily re-Tweet information to disseminate to their followers even in the event of disasters (Watson & Finn, 2013). There has been a fair amount of research work done on the uses of social media in response to various forms of emergencies, particularly in terms of the role of e-government, but less has been done on eventgraphing based on other types of events and using only commercially-available and non-dedicated tools.

Superficially, various social media platforms such as microblogging sites show spikes in activity during major events, such as disasters (Oxley, 2013, p. 14; Haddow & Haddow, 2014, p. 29). Researchers have been working on ways to identify anomalous bursts in word references in Twitter exchanges and locating these in space and time in order to identify potential events (Abdelhaq, Gertz, & Sengstock, 2013). Social media may be seen as a disaster communications tool book-ended currently by the 2003 SARS (severe acute respiratory syndrome) Epidemic in China up through the 2013 Boston Marathon bombings (Haddow & Haddow, 2014, pp. 58 - 66), with growing human sophistication in engaging these issues from event-to-event. There are ways to observe such "bursty" (or high-volume or trending) events which are typified by intermittent increases in activity; these bursts may show concentrated interest or attention, but does it mean more? Not only do social media offer the promise of early indicators of some types of breaking events but continuing status updates. There are dedicated tools being built to crowdsource information during crises, so that governments may enhance their situational awareness and communications capabilities during emergency response and recovery ("Public Response...", 2013; Haddow & Haddow, 2014). The bridging function of multilingual microbloggers on Twitter enhances cross-lingual understandings and enhance global connectivity (Hale, 2014). In the research literature, there are descriptions of so-called "data spaces," which enable "data co-existence," which is an enablement of searching across highly disparate, disconnected, and non-meta-data'ed sources in a coherent way ("Frontiers in Massive Data Analysis," 2013, p. 42). With the proliferation of many types of available digital data that is unstructured and multi-type, having computerized systems that can query such datasets becomes critical for research.

Anticipation of broad social changes. Several researchers have examined the role of social media in broad social change. Social movement theory encapsulates a number of theories about why mass social mobilization occurs and potentially what formats these changes may take. The various approaches examine dynamics of collective behavior, social inequality and deprivation, rational choice models, political opportunities, cultural differences, social network analysis, and other approaches. A new angle on social change involves the indicators of such change in social media communications. This is not suggest any technological determinism in social movements but that there are complex interactions with media by people during times of social change (Olorunnisola & Martin, 2013, p. 275). There have been studies about which members of an organization handle the public facing side in terms of messaging, and it was found to not necessarily be the direct leaders, based on a social network analytical approach. One research team found that leaders themselves may not have "higher communication-network centrality scores than non-leaders" but that network centrality was associated with media coverage as experts on particular topics (Malinick, Tindall, & Diani, 2013, p. 150). This team examined citation data in terms of media coverage and found the same:

So far, we found that formal leaders were not the most central actors in the movement's communication network, nor were they significantly associated with rates of citation, while the most central actors were actually cited the most (Malinick, Tindall, & Diani, 2013, p. 154).

One researcher combined social revolution research, social network theory, and social media engagements theories (DeFronzo, 1991, Barabasi, 2002, and Roy, 2011) in his model of Mayer's Model on Modern Social Media Influence on Social Revolutions (Mayer, 2011, p. 27). The social revolution model suggests that five elements must co-exist to create an environment ripe for massive social change, including mass frustration in a majority of the population, a discontented dissident elite, a "unifying catalyst" that brings together people from different social classes in support of revolution, a weakened governmental state, and a "permissive environment" created by other nation-states who will not intervene against a revolutionary movement in another society (DeFronzo, 1991, as cited in Mayer 2011). The presence of these five common criteria in social revolutions develops independently over time, culminating in mass mobilization. Mass frustration, dissident elites, unifying motivation, weak government, and a permissive environment factor in social revolutions in varying degrees dependent on the circumstances surrounding the movement. Social structures and ideologies within a population determine the level of relevance (DeFronzo 1989, as cited in Mayer, 2011, p. 13). These five variables are considered interdependent ones, with each affecting the other. In Mayer's model, social media serves as a linking agent between the forces of social revolution and actual events on-ground potentially enabling a mass uprising.

There are underlying understandings that enable researchers to try to anticipate mass social changes. One approach involves the application of social representation theory. A social representation is understood in the present paper **as** a cognitive, symbolic, iconic and affectively laden mental construct with a structure of its own; it is a way of concerted thinking which is shared by the members of reflexive groups (Wagner, Valencia, & Elejabarrieta, 1996, p. 331). A common social representation may be geographical, for example, in terms of collectively-co-created elaborations. This theory posits that collective discourse around issues perceived as salient leads to the creation of social representations, which are thought to help the social group cope with unfamiliar phenomena (which can be threatening). Social representations are built using symbols—like language and imagery. Social representations are conceptualized as having a central care, "the constitutive part of a social representation" (Wagner, Valencia, & Elejabarrieta, 1996, p. 332). Researchers explored whether there were core terms associated with different social representations of war in different societies and found that "stable cores" consisted of emotionally "hot" words proximal to people's lived experiences and that more intellectual and distant "cold" words were not included in the stable cores of social representations (Wagner, Valencia, & Elejabarrieta, 1996, p. 331). This work might suggest that emotions may be a critical factor in how humans identify an issue as salient; emotion appears to be a driver of collective discourse around social representations. Once formed, social representations evoke culturally-bound patterns of thinking and action. A stable core is thought to remain consistent across situations while a periphery is unstable and changing in different contexts (Wagner, Valencia, & Elejabarrieta, 1996, p. 334). One method for exploring social representations involves text analysis of the contents of a stable core vs. an unstable periphery for different societies regarding a particular social construct or social phenomena. Kurt Lewin's force-field theory is applicable to the understanding of social representations. Lewin posited that various competing forces influence a social situation, and how these forces resolve determines the equilibrium state. In terms of social change, the context has to go through three main phases: unfreezing, change, and then re-freezing.

One way that people may analyze societies is to identify dormant (latent) social faultlines (based on one or more attributes, such as demographic features, and based on those, implied differences in culture, history, values, and other factors) and activated ones in which members perceive subgroups based on demographic characteristics. Information does not move in a frictionless way. Whether and how information is considered depends in part on the receptivity of the audience and their space- and culture-based social geographies, based on what Peter Meusberger calls "the knowledge-transfer paradox" (2008). Social psychologists have found that the social categorization of others into particular groups is a central way that people use their perceptions of others to interact and engage (Bodenhausen, Kang, & Peery, 2012). Faultlines, whether latent or activated, may be exploited by messaging or social events or other stressing factors. Researchers have found that groups with "activated faultlines were more likely to form coalitions, have high levels of group conflict, and lower levels of satisfaction and group performance than dormant faultline groups. Furthermore, team identification moderated the effects of activated faultlines on group processes such that a strong workgroup identity decreased the likelihood that activated faultlines led to coalition formation and conflict" (Jehn & Bezrukova, 2010, p. 24). Social group resilience may be strengthened to avoid coalition (subgroupings) formation and conflict with activated faultlines. The framework of group faultlines is sometimes used predictively to anticipate group splits into sub-groups. Researchers have found that equity beliefs, and more particularly the sense of group entitlement, tends to "moderate the relationship between dormant faultlines and activated faultlines; that is, groups with dormant faultlines and with a group personality configuration of two members with strong entitlement beliefs in opposing faultline subgroups will be more likely to have activated faultlines than groups without this group personality configuration" (Jehn & Bezrukova, 2010, p. 27). Underlying the concept of social faultlines is research about social identities and social categorization theory, with social constructs of in-groups and out-groups. When social categories are activated, people are essentially stereotyped as belonging to particular groups, and inferences are made about them based on that grouping (Bodenhausen, Kang, & Peery, 2012). The majority of previous studies in revolutions seek to explain the importance of "social structure, ideology, and culture in creating collective contentious action" (Poulson 2006, 21, as cited in Mayer, 2011, p. 1). When nation-states have long-term large-scale frictions, in political science, these are referred to as enduring rivalries. This form of long-standing competition comes from factors like competing interests (such as predominance, such as access to natural resources, and other features), cultural animosities (such as those stemming from highly divergent world-views), historical animus, political disagreements, and other factors. Cultural-based frictions may create human predispositions to forming differences and experiencing friction.

There are plenty of examples of terror groups (as political agents in a society) on social media that have used Twitter, YouTube, and other social media platforms to narrowcast messages to their constituencies and supporters and funders. Twitter, especially, has been used to live-Tweet militant actions. Narrowcasting "aims messages at specific segments of the public defined by values, preferences, demographic attributes, or subscription." Weimann, 2014, p. 3); broadcasting projects a message to the broad public. Indeed, these communications channels are also used to reach out to a broader base to recruit other support, a kind of remote head-hunting and radicalization (the cultivation of "true believers" through propaganda). This use of new media represents "an increasing continuation of war by other means," to adapt von Clausewitz's famous phrase (Weimann, 2014, p. 15). Charismatic leaders—whether they are appealing through political, religious, or other frameworks—are what some have called entrepreneurs of identity, which provide psychological validation for people by being inclusive and giving them meaning in compelling ways. Those who are more suggestible may be receptive to particular emotional appeals and imagery and may therefore be mobilized to particular political ends through social identity appeals (Seyranian, 2014, p. 468). Various individuals and groups also serve as "influence agents" to affect others' ideas. The expression of identity in public spaces enables the recognition of "persuasion campaign structures and influence operations across social media sites and communities" (Wille, 2012, p. 37).

Table 1 posits three levels of difficulty in terms of event targeting. (The "pull" tools are often required to aggregate, process, visualize, and analyze some of the critical data to understand how events are propagating through social media platforms.)

Figure 4 offers a sense of the narrowing funnel of information that may be available in this process (even with the massive datasets of information that move on a daily basis). A human sensor network is only as effective as what people can observe and describe and are willing to share, no matter how accurate

Table 1. Low-, mid- and high-level difficulty target events for extended-form EventGraphing

Types of Target Events	Low-Level Difficulty Target Event	Mid-Level Difficulty Target Event	High-Level Difficulty Target Event
Definition	(anything that is already tracked, with plenty of pushed information) • Targets that involve stakeholders with interests to push and publicize the event • Targets that are pre-planned • Targets that have pre-existing electronic structures • Targets that have pre-existing electronic surveillants / informants • Targets that have pre-existing discourses	(anything that is partially tracked or is potentially trackable, with pushed and pulled information) • Targets that may or may not have any tie to direct human activities • Targets that have some electronic structures (or the potential for developing electronic structures) • Targets that have some electronic surveillants (or developable electronic surveillants) • Targets that have developable existing discourses	(anything that is not publicly tracked and may be elusive even if one knows to look for it, with a requirement to mostly pull information) • Targets that are not pre-planned • Targets that may or may not be human-caused • Targets without existing human stakeholders assigned to their promotion • Targets without pre-existing electronic structures • Targets without pre-existing electronic surveillants / informants • Targets that lack pre-existing discourses • Low potential for observable "whispers" or other data leakages that could indicate event onset or occurrence
Examples	• Political events • New product roll-outs • Government outreaches • Educational technology advancements (that may be disruptive) • Anything already covered by mass media	• Movements by peoples with little electronic access • Nascent movements which have not reach sufficient critical mass to garner attention • Shifting sentiments on issues not readily articulated by public figures and others • Emergent cool-hunting	• Real-world health events as they are emerging • Natural events outside normal human attention • Events without natural human constituencies and stakeholders

or inaccurate. Human sensors have to be sufficiently close to the information to make the observation. There is built-in ambiguity in communications—whether through written language or imagery or sound or video. There will be information included and excluded. Language is polysemic or many-meaninged. Within the various cultures of microblogs, blogs, social networking sites, and other venues, there are yet other cultural applications that may shape how people share information. There have to be the tripwires in place to capture what people have observed. In this figure, there is a sense of the need for training sensitivity to monitoring electronic streams for certain types of information that may be indicative of events of interest—both in an *a priori* sense and in a discovery sense. For this effort to be effective, the narrowing of the information funnel has to be taken into account—so that people do not make false assumptions about how representative their sample may be. The type of information capturable on social media is already limited; the way people communicate is already ambiguous and open to interpretation; the way software tools may be used to extract data through social media platform APIs is further limited; the types of machine- and human-based analytical capabilities are further limited. Any sort of analysis has to acknowledge these potential skews to the data. In all likelihood, the various steps will require iteration and refinement to disambiguate the information.

Figure 4. Dependencies and delimitations in the event mapping sequence

Complex World

⬇

- **Complexity (context, actors, interaction effects, unpredictability / Godel's undecidability / Taleb's black swan)**

— — — — — — —Observable by People– — — — — — —

Human Sensor Network

- **What people know and want to share broadly speaking...**

⬇

— — —Shared by People / Describable / Capturable by Digital Means— — —
— — — — —Public Channels / Private Channels— — — —

Social Networks

Content Sharing Sites | **Microblogging**

Social Tagging

SMS and TM-ing | **Email Networks**

Blogs and Wikis

- **What is available in the public channel**
- **What is broadly findable**
- **What is accessible through the application programming interfaces (APIs) of various social media platforms**

⬇

— — —Public and Sharable by Social Networking Platforms- — — —

Software and Applications

- **What data is extractable**
- **What data is able to be visualized**
- **What is able to be machine-analyzed coherently**

⬇

— — — — —Capturable and Analyzable by Software — — — —

Human Analysis

- **What research strategies are applied**
- **What background knowledge may be brought to bear in the work**
- **What data is preserved in a meaningful way**
- **What confidence may be applied to the findings**
- **What context is the eventgraph data used in**
- **How is the eventgraph data used**

⬇

— — — — — —Exploitable by Human Analysts— — — — —

Dependencies and Delimitations in the Event Mapping Sequence

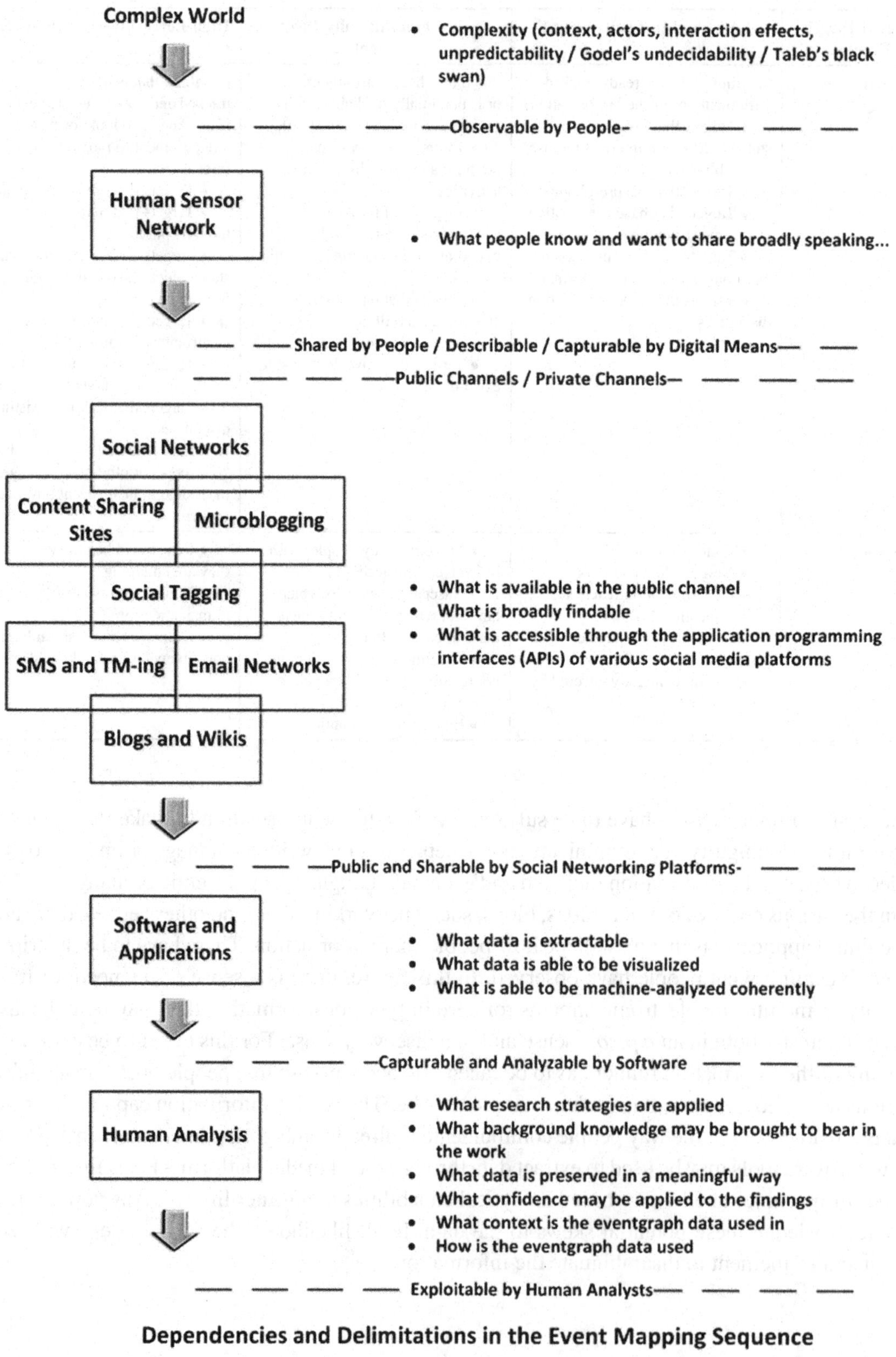

Figure 4 also suggests the importance of knowing the particular social media platform well. Each platform attracts a certain subset of the larger population. They collect different types of information. A microblogging site such as Twitter is seen as more of an "interest network" than an social one, with people clustering around shared interests and conversations than personal relationships (Sonderman, 2012, as cited in Haddow & Haddow, 2014, p. 23). The social networks found on social networking sites are generally assortatively homophilous, with people clustering around others who are similar to themselves, and also who are generally geographically co-located. Another unique feature of the Twitter microblogging site is the relative anonymity enabled on Twitter, resulting in less "social pressure" (Hughes, Rowe, Batey, & Lee, 2012, p. 562). Flickr accepts images and photos, which are digital elements which may be both real-time or lagging or trailing indicators. YouTube captures videos and enables the observing of video networks based on shared topics (according to tagging and other metadata labeling). Some social media sites may be more accessible for analysis than others in the use of third-party data extraction and analysis tools. Some social media platforms will require the use of within-tool search technologies and may not be as amenable to third-party analyses (at least not within a lot of data preparation work). Some rate-limit access to their databases through their application programming interfaces (APIs). There are pre-set limits to how much information any third-party tool will capture also, so even though terms like "big data" and "web-scale data" may be bandied about in relation to social media, it is almost never an $n =$ all, but rather a subset of the data. Instagram and Pinterest carry yet other types of pictorial information. This is so for Vimeo, a video sharing site. There are certain types of information knowable from a slideshow repository. Likewise, a scan of the Internet will result in some types of information but not others. It is important to know what goes silent or invisible in the respective electronic contexts. Also, there are gaps and silences in the software tools used to analyze texts or to draw graphs of relationships based on social media tools.

Even if all information could be gathered, there are gaps in the actual collected information. For example, there may be downsides to the broad and fast proliferation of microblogging communications and other information as well. False rumors (with low informational value if researchers are wanting to understand on-ground realities) may be disseminated and treated as accurate by some. Baseless rumors may contribute to a general sense of chaos in the absence of more direct and authoritative information. (In some situations, rumors may actually be founded and accurate.) Researchers are exploring ways to discern what messaging may indicate about on-ground realities. One researcher is applying an initial naïve Bayes approach for machine-based sentiment analysis where P (sentiment | sentence) $= P$ (sentiment)P(sentence | sentiment) / P(sentence). (Barber, 2010, as cited in Oxley, 2013, p. 78), where the probability of a certain sentiment exists given the presence of a particular sentence (expression) = probability of the sentiment multiplied by the probability of the sentence being present given the sentiment divided by the probability of the sentence being present or expressed.

The Bayes Theorem is application in general because it provides a simple basis for striving to assert what is knowable from the observables. Bayes' theorem is stated mathematically as the following simple form: the probability of A given B equals [the probability of B given A multiplied by the probability of A] divided by the probability of B. This formula enables consideration of known prior probabilities and includes that in the considerations.

Another important aspect is understanding how people intentionally (and unintentionally) use the particular platforms or online spaces. A common assumption of human communications is that they are socially signaling to others in order to achieve particular aims. They are engaging in strategic social performance. Their reputations are built, cultivated, and curated. Messages may be self-censored even as unintended subtexts and data leakage may occur. While people often message to showcase their best angles and work within the limitations of their own egos, something may be lost-in-translation, and something may be leaked beyond the intentions of the communicator. Research studies have found that people's profiles on Facebook can be quite revelatory and may be interpreted with some degree of accuracy by others (Back, Stopfer, Vazire, Gaddis, Schmukle, Egloff, & Gosling, 2010). Still, even if people are messaging in fully candid and transparent ways, there are still gaps between stated intent and actions, gaps between plans and capabilities. Anyone who wants to use messaging to understand forthcoming actions will have to take into account the talk-to-action gap. In other words, what was planned vs. what actually happened in the real world?

Figure 5 highlights some of the general challenges with eventgraphing based on social media platforms. There are challenges with identifying the beginning, mid-point, critical sub-events, and end points of the events. There may not be clear indicators for when researchers should know when to pay attention; they may not even know what to pay attention to. Initially, it may be difficult knowing who the principals are in an event. The prior describes what may be theoretically possible.

Collecting and managing the data for analysis and decision-making. Another important step involves collecting and managing data for findability, analysis, and decision-making. One common method involves the uses of folder structures (with some hosted in the cloud for collaborative work and access). These may be organized in a number of ways—by source type (academic-published, web-based, social media, other), by time period, by target (organization, persons, and others), or a combination of these. The idea is that these complementary types of information will illuminate aspects of the event. Depending on the event, any number of types of information may be seen as relevant. For certain types of events, there will be information that is more salient than other types. There may be directed questions that inform decisions about what information is collected (and what is seen as relevant from what has already been collected).

While it is possible to use a basic folder system to organize information, if an event involves any amount of complexity or time duration, some sort of data management system seems to be the better option. (In the heat of an event, it makes sense to assume near-continuous or continuous data collection.) If there are multiple team members working to graph an event as an extended-form version, it may help to have a system that is hosted off a server for effective submittal of information as well as access to the data.

Some larger-scale projects involve materials collected in a database, with rich ways to query and cross-reference various tables and datasets for analytical value. These may involve both structured and unstructured data.

Still others may house data in a software system. Qualitative and mixed methods software programs enable data collection and analysis will enhance findability, coding, analysis, and the production of reports. Qualitative and mixed methods data analysis tools enable record-keeping of the uploading of information, which may include text or content analyses. The software programs also often enable annotation of various information objects with metadata as well as the writing of research journals. There are also usually machine-based time-stamping of when information is submitted into the system, which may be informative about when information was known—if an audit is needed later. Besides the technology aspect, there are other thought tools that may enhance the analysis of events.

Advanced analytical approaches. There are more complex analytical approaches than social network analysis and text analysis to integrate the disparate streams of information into a coherent event-level approach. These include morphological analysis, association and cross-consistency matrices, and timelines.

Figure 5. Addressing some real-world challenges with creating EventGraphs from social media platforms

- Identifying the Start-Points of Events
- Identifying the Mid-Points of Events
- Identifying Critical Sub-Events
- Identifying the End-Points of Events
  - Social Media Monitoring
  - Experience-Based Tactics and Strategies
  - Cross-Referencing with Real-World Sources and Observations

- Incomplete Data
  - Probing Other Channels
  - Conducting Multiple Data Extractions from Various Platforms
  - Using a Range of Apps and Software Tools
  - Creating Social Media Accounts as Followers

- Noisy Data
  - Filtering Information / Pruning Branches
  - Further Research and Investigations
  - Changing Up Data Extraction Parameters / Focusing In

- Deceptive Data
  - Engagement with Various Entities and Sources
  - Data Vetting, Cross-Referencing, and Triangulation
  - Identity Validatiion on Deep Web Records
  - Further (Extensive) Research, Investigation, and Analysis

- Lack of Stealth
  - Masking of Identity
  - Electronic Identity Backstopping

- Difficulty to Articulate and Present
  - (Re-)Visualization of Datasets with Various Software Tools
  - In-Depth Textual Descriptions
  - Data Provenance

Morphological analysis. One promising tool involves morphological (structural) analysis, which was created by Fritz Zwicky, to engage complex non-quantifiable (or difficult-to-meaningfully-quantify) problems. A grid-box tool (known as a "morphological box" or "Zwicky box") was designed to enhance human decision-making by enabling people to look at a range of possible solutions and to eliminate the illogical or impracticable ones (Ritchey, 2003 - 2011, p. 3). Conceptually, the system does not eliminate any of the governing factors that may affect a complex real-world situation:

The conventional approach here would be to break the system down into parts, isolate the vital parts (dropping the 'trivial' components) for their contributions to the output and solve the simplified system for creating desired models or scenarios. The disadvantage of this method is that real-world scenarios do not behave rationally: more often than not, a simplified model will break down when the contribution of the 'trivial' components becomes significant. Also, importantly, the behaviour of many components will be governed by the states of, and their relations with, other components – ones that may be seen to be minor before the analysis. ("Morphological analysis (problem-solving)," Aug. 7, 2014)

Where causal modeling and simulation may reduce components, morphological analysis uses an approach that filters information instead of omitting it. In that sense, no variables are omitted, so if an obscure variable comes to the fore in an event, it may be brought back into consideration in this form of non-quantified modeling. Out of a universe of facts in a complex world, sometimes, an innocuous variable may play an outsized role in how an event unfolds. In another sense, a small variable may be telling in a narrative; the morphological analysis approach, if applied carefully, would afford the protection of details. The variables included may be analyzed for interaction effects. A variety of possible outcomes may be analyzed in this method. "When we do a morphological analysis, we want to examine the *whole mess* first, stalk out its boundary values and study its possible internal relations – before going on to generate alternative solutions, and then to solve puzzles," explain one researcher (Ritchey, 2003 - 2011, p. 3).

Or the column headings above could be Event Type A, Event Type B, etc. (Morphological analysis is seen as an extended form of typology analysis, so the definitions of event structures may be used to define different event types.) There are many types of morphological boxes. Others have column headings with values or parameters going across the top and paths as rows (without row identifiers in the far-left column). In some creativity contexts, morphological boxes are used to reconceptualize alternatives for attributes to a product ("Tool 13: Morphological box," 2013).

Association matrices. Another intriguing tool involves an association matrix (which may actually be expressed as a graph). Here, elements of events are placed on both the top-level row and the left-most column. The intervening cells are marked if there is an association, and the greater the association, the higher the number in the cell (or the darker the color in a color-based expression of intensity). The intervening cells are left blank if there is no association. Association matrices may be created with either real-world or synthetic data. For the first, the details of an event may be logged into an association matrix to identify patterns of correlations, with strengths of relationships represented by correlation coefficients (which are presented from -1 to + 1) (North, 2012, p. 9). The closer the correlation coefficient is to -1 or 1, the higher the shared variability. With a positive correlation, when one attribute rises, the other attribute also tends to rise (to a degree); when one attribute falls, the other attribute also tends to fall. With a negative correlation, when one variable's attribute rises, the other variable's attribute tends to fall (to a degree); when one attribute falls, the other attribute rises.

Typologies of certain categories of events may be logged into association matrices as well, to identify common features of those events (moving from specific to general, in order to have a tool which moves from general to specific or event categories to categorize specific cases). In the latter case, with synthetic data, projected events may be modeled in an association matrix based on theoretical associations.

Table 2. A morphological box for analyzing events

	Event 1	**Event 2**	**Event 3**	**Event 4**	**Event 5**
Parameter A					
Parameter B					
Parameter C					
Parameter D					
Parameter E					
Parameter F					
Parameter G					

Table 3. An association matrix to log and analyze correlations and connections between variables in an event

	V1	V2	V3	V4	V5	V6	V7	V8
V1	--							
V2		--						
V3			--					
V4				--				
V5					--			
V6						--		
V7							--	
V8								--

Other matrices may be brought into play for enhanced decision-making such as with cross-consistency matrices to see how a decision may line up with competing priorities. Cross-consistency matrices are set up similarly to the association matrix, but the purpose is to look at which priorities align in contrast to others. When fully illuminated, these could also show which options might be antithetical to others. Such tables may also be used to identify contradictory parameter values—where the expression of one is mutually exclusive to the expression of another.

Timelines. Another tool is the timeline. Placing sub-events or occurrences in a timeline may help people see if there are larger temporal patterns. Various timelines may be integrated from various sources for an informationally-deep time-based understanding. One strength of a timeline is that these may contain time-based patterns, which may be informative of potential trends and even future events. (All such information should be held lightly given the limits of the data.) A data visualization that describes events over time (or aspects of events over time) is a streamgraph. This is an area chart that shows—for example—quantitative measures of certain variables over time (like frequency counts of certain terms used in a microblogging stream) over time, for temporal analytics.

Enabling scaling up through distributed teams. There are a number of ways to conceptualize how this extended-form eventgraphing could work. One model based on emergency planning taps highly-skilled distributed teams to digitally map various aspects of a crisis using a variety of social media platforms and methods. It is possible to conceptualize volunteers working together informally around issues of shared interests. The prior interactions enhance the level of trust among the team members. Trainings on a variety of tools, methods, and online social platforms are achieved in a virtual way using real-time video-conferencing tools. It is important to train in the uses of a range of tools in case certain systems are overloaded and go out of use in the moment. Various approaches will have strengths and weaknesses in terms of information accuracy, verifiability, timeliness, and other factors, so multiple approaches may be used to enable complementary chains of information for a fuller view. There may be method and tool tradeoffs as well, such as between automated efficiency vs. accuracy, or manual capture vs. comprehensiveness.

The task force is divided into several teams, each of which focuses on a particular task, including analysis, geolocation, humanitarian aid, media monitoring, reports, satellite imagery, mobile text messaging, translation, verification, and technology support. The teams find, map, verify, curate, and analyze different forms of social media to improve the situational awareness of responding organizations. Volunteers join particular teams but often cross-train in multiple teams. ("Public Response…", 2012, p. 29)

In the research literature, there is a non-profit organization working to maintain a virtual "disaster desk" to provide support in the aftermath of emergencies (Starbird & Palen, 2013). A similar distributed team could be created to enable extended-form eventgraphing. Having a distributed team enables surge capacity and preparedness for unfolding events. The incentivizing of team members may include both direct and indirect benefits. Direct ones include the development of a research skill set on social media platforms and enhanced knowledge of specific events. Indirect ones may include the social networking and travel or other aspects that comes with this distributed work. Such teams may be difficult to coalesce particularly for rare events. The higher the level of expertise required (such as for "big data" analysis and statistical analysis work), the more difficult it would be to seat such a team.

TRACKING A "SUDDEN" AND LIVE EVENT: IN THEORY AND MAYBE IN PRACTICE

The prior section addresses both the extant literature on potential extended-form eventgraphing. This following section addresses how this may look in practice. To maintain a focus on the major and minor questions of this work, they are reviewed again here.

Major Questions

1. What are the current capabilities of creating social-media and Internet-based (extended-form) eventgraphs of unexpected and evolving real-world events using publicly available apps and software programs (both open-source and commercial)?
2. What is the optimal method or approach to attain the most relevant information for a particular event?

Minor Questions

3. What are the current capabilities of creating social-media and Internet-based (extended-form) eventgraphs of unexpected and evolving real-world events using publicly available apps and software programs (both open-source and commercial)?
    a. What are the apps and software tools, and what are their capabilities?
    b. What types of information may be extracted, analyzed, visualized, and presented?
    c. What is the learning curve in their use?
    d. What is an "event"?
    e. What are the components to an "event"? Time and spatiality issues? Participants? Costs? Implications?

  f. Which components of an event tend to be more stable over time? Which components of an event tend to be more dynamic and fast-changing?

  g. What is knowable from publicly available social media? (Messaging? Strategic communications? Sentiment analysis? Its provenance? Related tags analysis? Leaders? Cliques? Geolocation?)

  h. What leads may be generated from an analysis of social media?

  i. On social media, what are indicators of the onset of an "event"?

  j. On social media, what are the indicators of the sunsetting of an "event"?

  k. What is not addressed?

  l. Where are the informational gaps?

  m. What are risks in the usage of this data? (Where can one be misled?)

4. What is the optimal method or approach to attain the most relevant information for a particular event?

  a. What are the methodologies (sequencing)?

  b. What are improvements that may be created with the existing tools?

  c. What future research may be done to enhance this work?

DEFINING THE TARGET

Per the setup of the chapter challenge, various types of events may be conceptualized at different size levels. These may be thought of simply as units of analysis, whether micro, meso, or macro.

Conceptualizations of an unfolding event. There are a range of factors that may be analyzed to understand an unfolding event. These variables may be visualized in a spider chart (spider graph), which may also be referred to as a star chart or a radar chart. Figure 6, "Event Attributes Spider Chart" offers a range of continuums that may be used to describe an event. The various attributes may be divided into four central categories:

1. **The Nature of the Event**: non-disruptive to disruptive (continuum), non-discrete to discrete (definition with clear boundaries), non-public to public, non-serial (one-off) to serial, little change to big change, anti-social to pro-social

2. **The Leadership:** leaderless to leadered, no-expense to high-expense (to organizers)

3. **The Participants:** small population to large population (as a percentage of the relevant population), closed participation to open participation, undefined membership to defined named membership

Table 4. Micro, meso, and macro levels of events

	Micro	Meso	Macro
	Node-level, individual agents Individual account Tweetstreams Experienced level on-ground, subjective experience	Subgraphs, cliques, islands (communities) Small-group dynamics	Social network Large-scale implications Proliferation of messaging Leadership
Event 1			
Event 2			
Event 3			

Figure 6. Event attributes spider chart

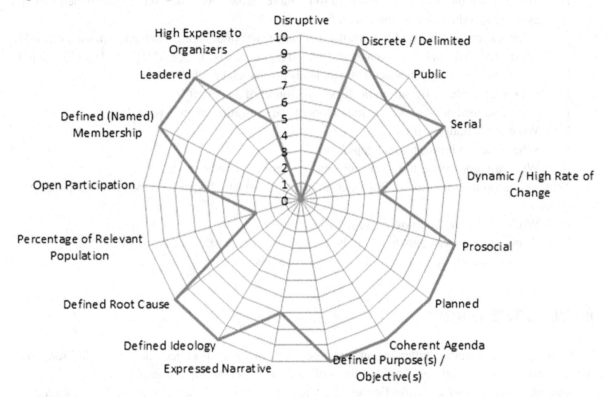

4. **Stated Purpose(s):** unplanned to planned, non-coherent to coherent agenda, no stated purpose to defined purpose [event objective(s)], no stated ideology to a defined ideology, and no defined root cause to defined root cause(s)

A spider chart or a spider graph is understood to have 0 or "non" at the center, with higher gradations as the data points are expressed towards the outer edge of the web. Each event may be understood to have different characteristics as described by the spider chart. For Figure 6, a real-world educational technology conference was used to acquire the data points. Such a spider chart or a similar one could be used to place various events into certain categorizations or types. Such spider charts do not require full information for drawing, and certain axes may be left off if information is not yet known. Or data points may be indicated in particular ways to show the lack of certitude or missing information. Other facets of events may be built onto the existing spider graph as needed.

Depending on the event type, the spider chart itself may have a different shape (in terms of the internal line). Also, depending on the interests of the researcher, the various parameters listed on the outer circle may vary. The variables were set up to address an early conceptualization of the various aspects to an event, but this visualization has not been tested against more than a few types of events.

Pre-event preparation would be an early step to effect extended-form eventgraphing. After all, once an event begins, there may be a wide range of complexity to address. Because of the manual aspects of this information collection, it would help to prior knowledge and training—in order to capture what is needed in a timely way. An individual or a team could "pre-position" for a possible event with some early research, environmental scanning, and other preparations.

Pre-positioning and leads-seeking. In order to have resources ready to track an event, which potentially unknown period of onset, it makes sense to set up methods and tools well prior to the event and to test processes. It may help to begin with some basic conceptualizations. This approach assumes that there is an interchange between the physical and cyber domains. For the sake of argument, it may help to conceive of an event in a general trajectory of multiple stages: pre-, during, and post-event. There may be a pre-event, during which there may be leading signals or indicators for the action to come (or no indicators at all for spontaneous events). There may be prior or precursor or antecedent events. This may be thought of as an alerting phrase, during which there may be signals like certain increases in uses of terms, calls-to-action by political leaders, and other indicators. There may be geo-targeted alerts or messaging that is clustered around a certain geographical location. In most cases, it would make sense that alerts stem from multiple sources. The lead-in period may be best thought of as a time when observers pay attention to whispers and light signals. During the event, it may be thought that there may be "coincident indicators" such as concepts and words and hashtags trending on social media. By the time an event is noticed, and if it has sufficient broad interest, there may be sources from mainstream media. Post-event, there will likely be diminishing messaging and possibly analyses by those in mainstream and alternative media. There may be lagging indicators of the event having occurred. There may be consequents or fallouts to the event (North, 2012, p. 9). There may be a degree of artificiality when naming the onset of an event and its conclusion because events may have continuing related sub-events for quite some time after the apparent close. Any observations about an event is likely provisional unless there are follow-on events. If there is a "first cause" or an "event trigger" (an antecedent event that partially or wholly enables a follow-on event to occur) for an event, that may not be apparent for some time yet.

Figure 7 posits that there are interaction effects between the cyber- and physical- realms.

The creation of a "lead list". A "lead" is a cue or pointer which might be used to indicate a way forward. It would stand to reason to create a lead list of indicators to track a particular event. This may be created well prior to an event and updated as the event unfolds and new information comes in. Or it may be created on-the-fly once there is awareness that a particular event is unfolding. It also helps to continually explore and not stop prematurely. In a sense, researchers are looking for online "listening posts" for certain events. They are looking for geographical locations at which an event may be unfolding. Hashtag sharing is seen to spread spatially but also through lines of community affinities:

We find that distance is the single most important explanation of future hashtag adoption since hashtags are fundamentally local. We also find that community affinities (like culture, language, and common interests) enhance the quality of purely spatial models, indicating the necessity of incorporating non-spatial features into models of global social media spread (Kamath, Caverlee, Cheng, & Sui, 2012, p. 962).

They are also looking for organizations and individuals that may be expert "informants" on particular events and the related issues around those events. For example, one tactic involves choosing to follow social media communications who are not only the most active in relation to an event but also physically proxemics to it—in order to attain the best information about an event (Kumar, Morstatter, Zalarani, & Liu, 2013); the authors term these targeted individuals "geo-topical" users.

Some questions that may be asked in the creation of a "lead list" follow:

- What are some relevant websites to explore? How are website networks set up, and what do they say about inter-relationships and associations?

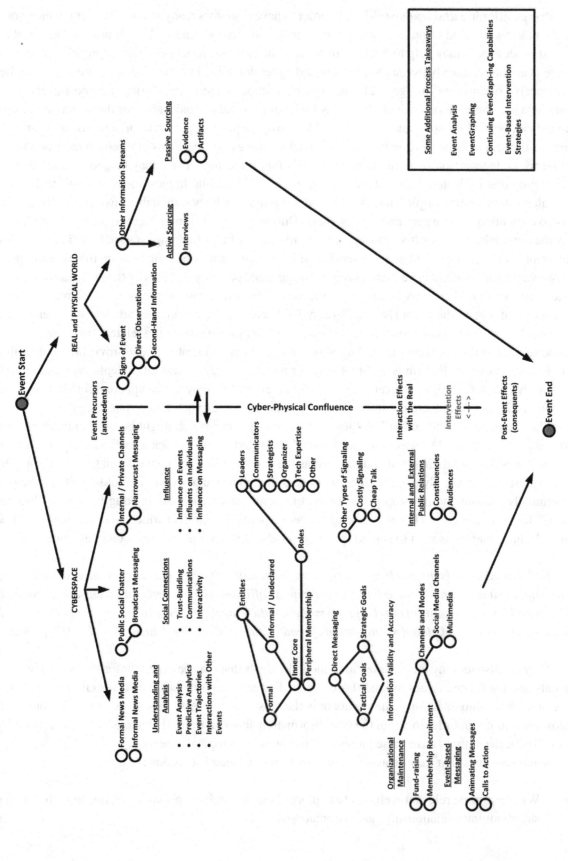

Figure 7. Event flow tracking through social media (an early conceptualization)

- What are some online documents to explore? What are some offline documents to explore?
- What are some relevant repositories and other data collections online? Offline?
- What are some relevant organizations that may have an interest if a particular event occurs?
- Who are some trusted sources related to the target event? Who are some lesser-trusted sources related to the target event? Who are core sources? Who are peripheral ones?
- Which are some social media platforms that are relevant to this issue? Which users and lists and groups on those social media platforms may have information that is relevant to this issue (to be targeted for following)? Which Tweetstreams should be monitored, collected, and analyzed?
- Which are private channels which should be pursued? (on social media, on forums, on microblogging accounts, on content-sharing accounts, on email accounts, and other channels)
- If "snowball" sourcing is used, who else may be of relevance to the issue? Which contacts do others have that they are willing to share?
- What are hashtags that may be used to indicate conversations related to an issue or event? What are hashtags that may be used to indicate images and videos related to an issue or event?
- What are keywords that may be used to indicate conversations related to an issue or event? What are keywords that may be used to indicate images and videos related to an issue or event?

Another important pre-positioning aspect involves listing the available applications and software tools and their respective functionalities. This is a list that will likely evolve based on what is made available to the public through both open-source and commercial channels.

Each of the above tools provides a certain type of information. There are varying degrees of completeness in terms of how much information is captured. There may be different degrees of signal-to-noise ratios (the higher the signals, the better). There may be false positives and false negatives. There may be duplicate information which misleads in terms of message amplification. These respective tools all have their own dedicated range of capabilities and purposes; they are being evoked here for a narrow use-case—that of extended-form eventgraphing. Several of the tools above mention multilingual tools. As a side note, English was found to be the main bridging language on Twitter (Hale, 2014). There are other tools that may be used to directly access various application programming interfaces (APIs) linked to online platforms and repositories to directly download text, images, video, and other digital contents, using command-line codes (Radio, September 12, 2014).

Breadth and depth. In a sense, the extended-form eventgraphing starts out broad to capture as much information as may be relevant. Then, that data is vetted. More interesting information then is probed in depth. For example, an influential node in a social network may become an individual of interest. While the node first appears in the collected data as just a screen name and maybe a list of microblogging messages in a Tweetstream, once it becomes a node of interest, then there are various other tools that may help re-identify the node from the microblogging account and collect related data. Further, there will be ways to create channels for intercommunications (the direct approach) from linked email, telephone, or other accounts.

Of the ideal list, which should be constantly updated, some endeavors may be more effectively actionable than others. In this pre-positioning phase, researchers acclimate to both the tools and the various social media platforms and online environments. They build on their friendships and acquaintanceships with others in the communities of interest based on any groups that may exist around the anticipated event(s). They start to acquire explicit knowledge, intuitions, and tacit knowledge. Researchers could start to build relationships with others who may serve as informants. A large aspect of this work involves

Table 5. Tool functions on social media platforms and other sources

Tool Applications	Tool Functions on Social Media Platforms and Other Sources
Search engines (Google)	**Web-based Research** • Online leads • Website information
Network Overview, Discovery, and Exploration for Excel (NodeXL)	**Data Extraction** • "Mayor of the hashtag" (influential node in a hashtag conversation) identification on Twitter • "Mayor of the keyword" (influential node in a keyword conversation) identification on Twitter • Related tags network on Flickr • User network on Flickr • Video network on YouTube • User network on YouTube • Hyperlink analysis on the Web (using Virtual Observatory on the Study of Online Networks, or VOSON) • Wiki analysis (using Virtual Observatory on the Study of Online Networks, or VOSON) and others **Data Visualization** • Various layout algorithms and other layout options
Maltego Tungsten	**Data Extraction and Data Visualization** • Hyperlink analysis on the Surface Web (http networks) • Data visualization **Information "Transforms"** • De-aliasing of online identities • Identification of subsidiary accounts • Information "transforms" (as "data equivalencies") to associated information types • Uniform resource locators (URLs) to related Internet Protocols (IPs), email addresses, documents, and other data • Physical locations to cyber presences on the Surface Web • IPs to server locations • Twitter identities to PII (personally identifiable information) • Definitions of blogroll inter-relationships between blogs **Geolocation** • Geolocation based on online (and offline) data **Time data** • Rate and frequency data • Time data
NCapture of NVivo 10 (on Windows)	**Data Extraction (Microblogging Sites)** • Tweetstream capture **Website Information Capture** • Website capture
UCINET	**Matrix Creation and Graph Visualization** • Matrices and graphs • Graph visualizations
NVivo	**Qualitative and Mixed Methods Data Management and Text Analysis** • Data management • Text-based data queries (matrix queries, word frequency counts, word branches, word clustering) • Data visualizations
AutoMap and ORA-NetScenes (CASOS)	**Text Analysis** • Sentiment analysis • Autocoding of text for concept analysis • Meta-network analysis and others
Pipl Search	**Verifying Personally Identifiable Information (PII)** • Deep / Hidden Web PII identity search based on access to public records

continued on following page

Table 5. Continued

Tool Applications	Tool Functions on Social Media Platforms and Other Sources
Google Translate	**Disambiguating Terms across Languages** • Translating between languages
Google Chrome (browser)	**Disambiguating Terms across Languages** • High-level language translation on various websites
Google Transliteration	**Transliterating of Text to Text** • Transliterating text to text

building the capacity to "see" what is occurring, and that requires experience and training. The most effective methodologies involve a range of sequences in terms of different applications to the various tools. Based on the research questions asked, particular tools may be applied in particular sequences.

This pre-event work is important to familiarize the researcher or research team with the various features of the tools and their functionalities. For example, software tools and applications may be placed on a 2x2 table which may help in the selection of the "go-to" tools. Such a four-fold table enables the placement of tools into various typologies for both efficiency (speed) and depth (accuracy).

A next step could involve the defining of the social media platform spaces where certain relevant information may be collected, with a basic structure of following an event. At the top of Figure 8, there are the filled-in nodes that may indicate the alerting to the beginning of an event. These could be conceptualized as "algorithmic nudging" to the researcher of potential unfolding events and a reminder to pay attention. To borrow a psychology concept, an event may begin in a "pre-attention" way; however, on electronic social media platforms, information may be captured retroactively in a back-dated sense, so in theory, no time is lost from the lack of instantaneous awareness of the beginning of an event. This approach is sufficiently robust to a cold start if the researcher or research team is aware in sufficient time to capture back-dated information. In other words, the monitoring can feasibly be unblinking. Even if the researcher is a little slow in realizing that an event is in play, it is still possible to regain some footing since past information is capturable (depending on the API enablements by the social media platforms). This prior preparation enables an accelerated start. If researchers are trying to learn the data extraction / harvesting tools, the social media platforms, the underlying issues of the potential events, and such, then they will certainly be caught flat-footed by the potential speed or stealth of real-world events. This adaptivity to unfolding events may be further enhanced by the creation of other resources, like generic lists (of influential nodes, of websites, of informants, and others) that may be filled out on-the-fly.

Setting up semi-automated and fully automated processes. Another aspect of software tool selection may involve the prior setup of macros (sets of computerized instructions that are activated as part of one sequence) for information capture. It would make sense to set up automated processes wherever possible (and to document these accurately). Most macros are set up within software tools and require a

Table 6. A 2x2 table of software features to enhance selection

	Low accuracy	High accuracy
Slow	--	-+
Fast	+-	++

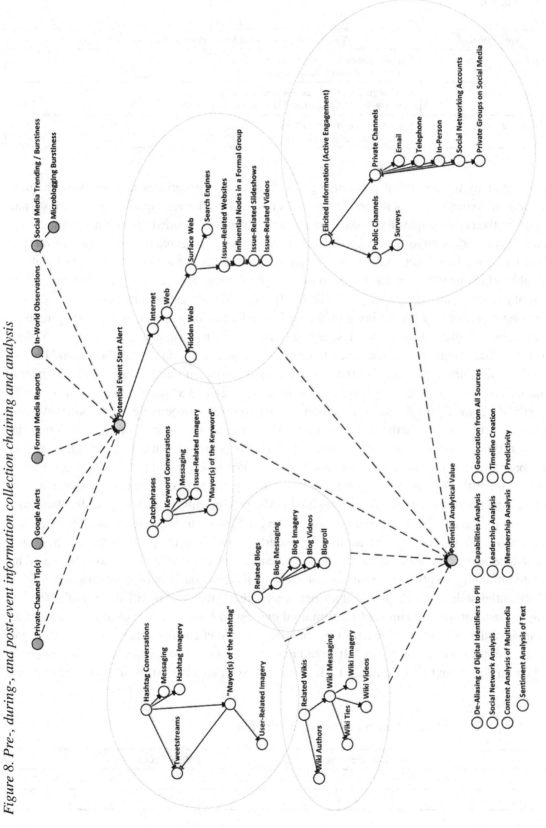

Figure 8. Pre-, during-, and post-event information collection chaining and analysis

user to activate the process. A fully automated process would be pre-set in a computer and might trigger based on any number of factors. They could be trigger based on a certain time or a scan of the environment and the finding of particular terms or some other algorithm.

Deeper targeted event understandings. Depending on the type of event, researchers may want to ask and answer targeted questions. For example, in a socially disruptive event, one typical law enforcement question may involve whether there was a "hidden hand" in the event, even if it seemed ad hoc on the surface. Is there a ringleader, and if so, are there also confederates and collaborators? Who is involved and in what roles? What is the depth of their involvement? Are there "tells" to indicate an influence or psychological operation? If an event is continuing, what is fueling the continuing interest (given that collective action may be difficult to maintain). Some pre-positioning may involve a rich and broad brainstorm of some of these questions. Another form of pre-positioning involves knowledge—the knowledge of history…the knowledge of societies…the knowledge of people—in other words the background knowledge that may inform the analyses of events.

Figure 9 is a conceptualization of what may aid predictivity of understanding where an event is in its stage and where it may be going. This visualization expresses the hypothesis that understandings of the messaging, the leadership, the apparent capabilities, the apparent resources, the popular support and momentum, and the particular fit of the current event to historical patterns, may all be possible indicators of where an event may be headed. These are all variables that may be observed or inferred from social media platforms and information from the broader Internet and Web, with varying degrees of accuracy. These are limited factors, and it would be beneficial to have access to pools of information from other sources as well. The fishbone diagram figure suggests near-term understandings, but it is possible that there may be mid-term and far-term understandings capabilities as well. This diagram addresses a generic event, but it is possible that events of certain types may be better understood using social media and online sources than others. It would be interesting to explore whether sizes of events, speeds of events, and other factors may affect their predictivity. For example, does a larger pool of participants mean more information that may indicate where a social event or even a "movement" is headed? Is a faster-moving event more predictable than a meandering one, or vice versa? Are there ways to anticipate the event's trajectory, its duration, its frequency, its geographical dispersion, its social impacts, its costs-benefits, and other factors?

Table 7 was created to help describe various paths that may be made through social media data and the types of knowledge that may be gained from each path—from left to right—through the materials. This "idea box" was based off a concept that was originally derived from Fritz Zwicky's morphological box (Michalko, 2006/ 1991, pp. 117 – 121).

Users of this table would draw paths from left to right through the table to show various information collection methods. The far left column shows the originating social media site type, the next column the types of information that may be extracted through the site APIs, the data structures of that extracted information, the possible data visualizations from that, and then the type of processed information and analyses possible with the raw data.

Making friends and building destination sites. Understanding particular issues often requires a high level of immersion in a context and learning—to understand the culture, shared values, history, personalities, and codified messaging among related individuals. Ideally, a researcher would be in the inner circle of those discussing and planning relevant events, either as part of a private email chain or private group or dyadic partnership, or some other form. The making of relationships through "friending" and other means in order to create a channel for information may sound utilitarian or even Machiavel-

Figure 9. Extended-Form Eventgraphing contribution to event stage predictivity (a fishbone diagram)

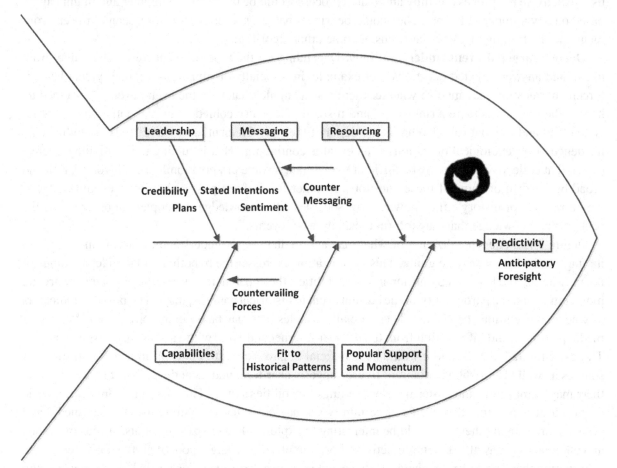

Extended-Form Eventgraphing Contribution to Event Stage Predictivity (A Fishbone Diagram)

lian, but it is actually not an uncommon strategy (online or offline). Acquaintance with others who may be interested in a particular topic may enable the sharing of information through mutual sleuthing. The work of social engineering has been used in physical and cyber spaces as part of offense and defense (Andress & Winterfeld, 2014). Even more, researchers may create destination sites to collect information of interest. These may be wikis, blogs, websites, microblogging accounts, or others. The idea is to make an event as knowable as possible by accessing all relevant streams, in a kind of global inference "attack" by chaining information across platforms. There are likely a number of private channels for groups. An "insider" would be a trusted individual who has standing and credibility in that social group. In this sense, a researcher may be conducting sousveillance, or observation from within (or the recording of an event as a participant). Forewarning and prior knowledge of a wide range of events would benefit people. To that critical-thinking end of thinking about a particular problem or challenge, The Phoenix Checklist used by the U.S. Central Intelligence Agency (CIA) seems like a good place to start (Please see Appendix A).

Table 7. An "idea box" of social media platform sources and possible data extractions

Online Social Media Platform (source)	Informational Material	Data Structure	Visualization	Potential Information Analysis (knowable)
microblogs	User accounts and descriptions Tweetstreams Shared photos Shared videos Hashtag conversations Keyword networks User ego neighborhoods Mayor of the hashtag Mayor of the keyword	Data tables Text lists / text corpuses Matrices Geodata Data sets Databases Heterogeneous data collections Imagery Videos Audio (and others)	Social network graphs Related tags networks Text-based graphs Bubble visualizations Dendrograms Treemaps Word clouds Word trees Geographical maps (and others)	Messaging Terminology Intentions Personalities Event details Sub-events Predictive analytics Geolocation Cultural analytics (and others)
blogs	Text networks User accounts Blog rolls			
wikis	Text networks User accounts			
social networking platforms	User accounts User account imagery User account videos			
video content sharing sites	Video networks User accounts			
photo sharing sites	Related tag networks User accounts Topic-based networks			
photo and video sharing sites	Topic-based network Hashtagged videos Hashtagged imagery			
Surface Web and Internet	Ego neighborhoods in networks / sites User accounts (leading to personally identifiable information / PII)			
deep / hidden web	http networks			
others	others			

TWO TRIAL EXTENDED-FORM EVENTGRAPHING CASES

Two cases were run to operationalize the practice of extended-form eventgraphing. Both cases used real-world data, and both were applied to two original "use cases." The work on both trial cases strives to achieve two aims: (1) a deeper understanding of the effective methods for extended-form eventgraphing and (2) a deeper understanding of the respective and unique events. The first involves general research, and the latter involves applied research.

Figure 10. Ways to pre-position for potential event detection and analysis

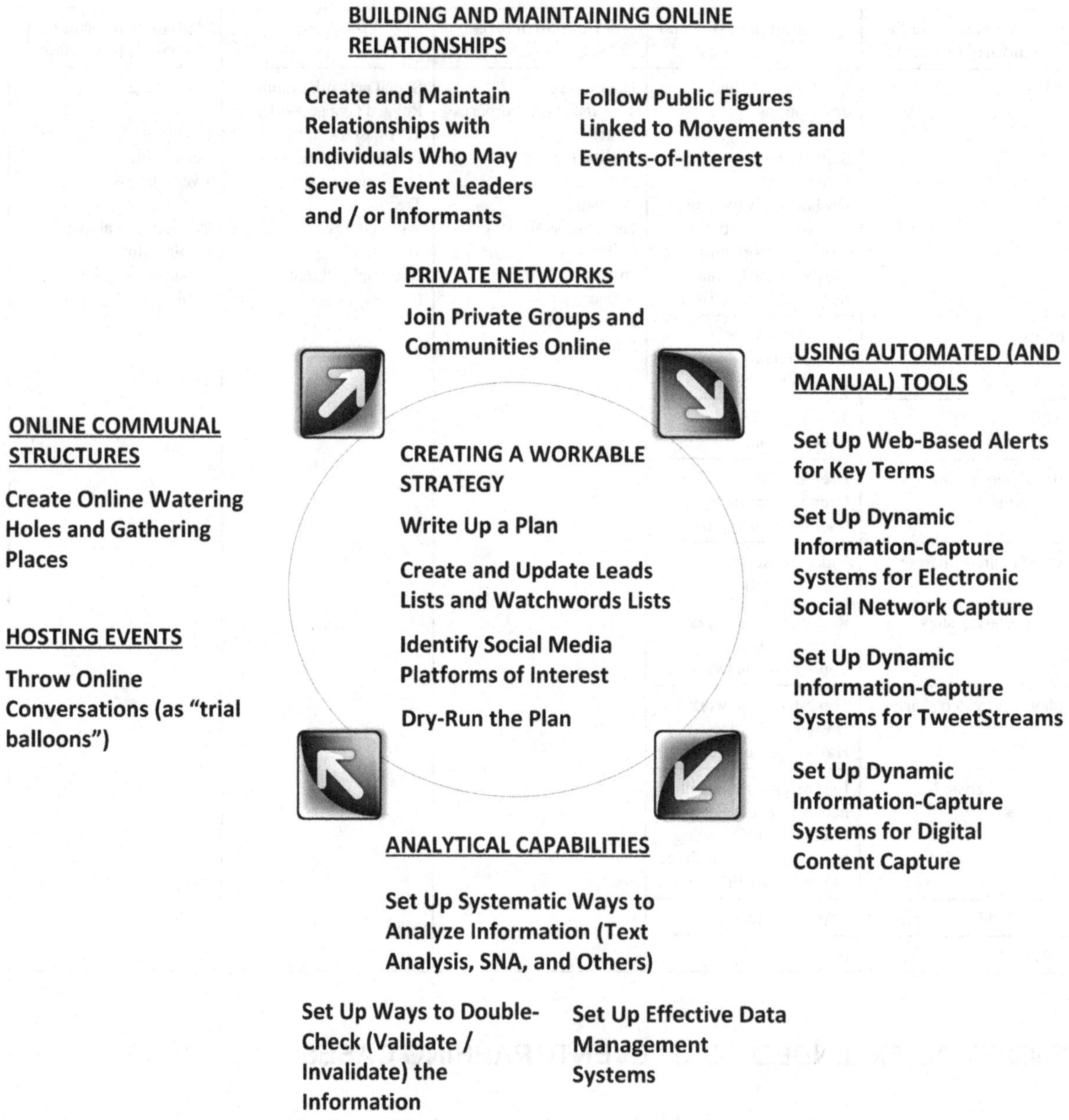

BUILDING AND MAINTAINING ONLINE RELATIONSHIPS

Create and Maintain Relationships with Individuals Who May Serve as Event Leaders and / or Informants

Follow Public Figures Linked to Movements and Events-of-Interest

PRIVATE NETWORKS

Join Private Groups and Communities Online

ONLINE COMMUNAL STRUCTURES

Create Online Watering Holes and Gathering Places

HOSTING EVENTS

Throw Online Conversations (as "trial balloons")

CREATING A WORKABLE STRATEGY

Write Up a Plan

Create and Update Leads Lists and Watchwords Lists

Identify Social Media Platforms of Interest

Dry-Run the Plan

USING AUTOMATED (AND MANUAL) TOOLS

Set Up Web-Based Alerts for Key Terms

Set Up Dynamic Information-Capture Systems for Electronic Social Network Capture

Set Up Dynamic Information-Capture Systems for TweetStreams

Set Up Dynamic Information-Capture Systems for Digital Content Capture

ANALYTICAL CAPABILITIES

Set Up Systematic Ways to Analyze Information (Text Analysis, SNA, and Others)

Set Up Ways to Double-Check (Validate / Invalidate) the Information

Set Up Effective Data Management Systems

Case 1: The August 24, 2014, Earthquake in California

Initially, it was hoped that an initial proof-of-concept would involve a "hidden" event that would be identified and tracked on social media platforms and the Web and Internet. However, on the morning that a first case was to be started, it so happened that there was an earthquake (around 3 a.m. Pacific Standard Time on August 24, 2014) that was all over the news. It seemed valuable to dry-run this concept of extended-form eventgraphing with such an event to test some simpler approaches with a low level difficulty target event before trying for something more difficult. The epicenter was based in American

Canyon, California, but with the quake at seven miles underground, the tremor was felt for hundreds of miles around and throughout Napa Valley and the Bay Area. On the official news, there were reports of electrical outages affecting thousands. Water mains had broken, and gas leaks had led to fires in a mobile home park. There were some fires that had destroyed homes while firefighters worked to bring water trucks to the scene. Reporters themselves were reporting from their own homes and tapping their own social networks for more information. Some initial tips of the event included reports in mainstream media, user-generated (citizen-reporter) videos of the event from home security cameras, Tweeted images and texts, and direct emails with the author. The quake had registered 6.1 on the Richter scale and was sufficiently historically significant—in the sense that this was the most severe quake in the past 25 years in that quake-prone area. The quake was so serious that the governor had declared a state of emergency, and there were early estimates of losses in the range of $1 billion. The following section highlights some of the graphing work done to illuminate angles to the event, albeit without providing in-depth insights per se about the events. A true and deep analysis would require much more effort than provided here.

In Figure 11, five region-based graphs were captured from the Twitter microblogging platform shortly after the earthquake based on reports of areas affected. Some of the graphs are sparse, with only a few groups indicated. A few others have a small number of groups surrounded by a large periphery of isolates, indicating that people are sharing information but that on this topic, they are not necessarily sharing relationally with others responding in discourse. In a sense, this is about individuals sharing information to their universe of followers but without an exchange of information (replies or retweets). The focus on the geographical angle is important because of the advent of what M.W. Wilson calls "everyday cartographers" and their ability to share geographic information about events and occurrences informally using broadly available digital mapping tools (Wilson, 2012, p. 1266).

Another question was set up. Would there be a big difference between #aftershocks and #aftershock, between the plural and the singular? Interestingly, the graphs were quite different in terms of the membership and top communicators (Tweeters), but the number of vertices were fairly close. The graph metrics tables follow for both graphs below. Another option may be to crawl #aftershocks or #aftershock for a combined graph to see how that would look. (If "and" is used with both words, that would result in a more exclusionary set of Tweets that included both hashtags for the singular and the plural, which may be much less likely.) The parameters for both data extractions were set the same, and the data extractions were done in close time proximity to each other. Figure 12 suggests that the software tool does not engage in word stemming (the linking of various word forms into one overarching collection of all related terms) per se.

Another type of data extraction was done on "earthquake" and "quake" as keyword searches and on #earthquake and #quake as Twitter hashtag searches to see how the keyword searches contrasted with the hashtag searches. Generally, keywords are used to capture all the general hashtag conversations going on around a certain topic, and hashtags are used to capture purposive conversations based around the hashtag-marked conversations. In this context, with an unfolding and dramatic emergency event, the hashtagged conversations were much more active and eventful. The #earthquake conversation involved 8,817 nodes (vertices) while the keyword search for "earthquake" only resulted in 162 vertices (1% of the other total). The #quake hashtag search involved 2,578 nodes while "quake" as a keyword search only brought up 234 nodes (9% of the other). It may be that people tend to cluster more relationally in their communications around such traumatizing events. It is helpful to note that such searches on Twitter are not case sensitive (the search renders all inputs in lower-case format). The Twitter API rate-limits access to its data layer, which means that it may slow the actual capture of information depending on how many are accessing its servers at any one time. .

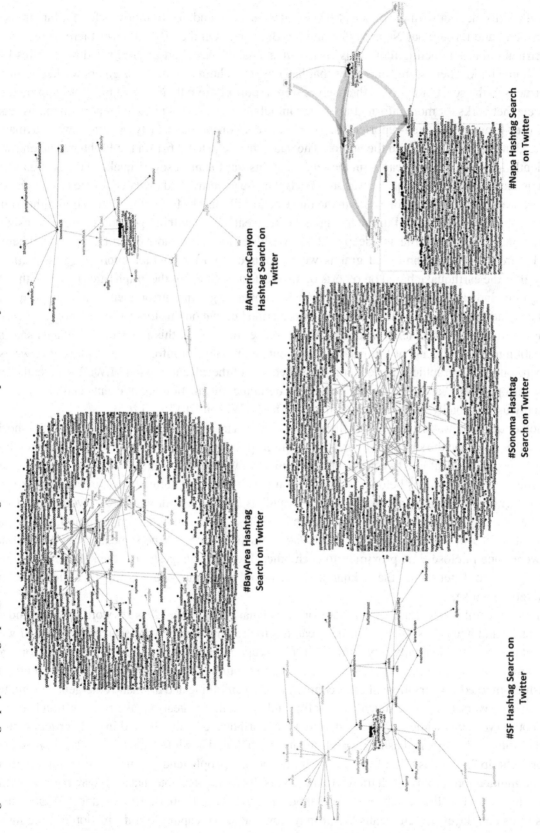

Figure 11. Geography-based graphs related to the August 24, 2014 Earthquake in California, USA

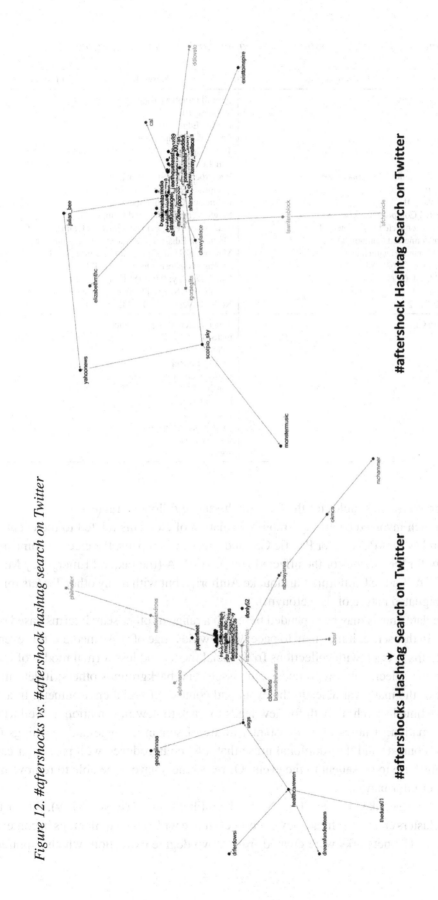

Figure 12. #aftershocks vs. #aftershock search on Twitter

#aftershock Hashtag Search on Twitter

#aftershocks Hashtag Search on Twitter

Table 8. Graph metrics for the #aftershocks and #aftershock twitter hashtag searches

#aftershocks Twitter hashtag search	#aftershock Twitter hashtag search
Overall Graph Metrics: Vertices: 116 Unique Edges: 16 Edges With Duplicates: 0 Total Edges: 16 Self-Loops: 0 Reciprocated Vertex Pair Ratio: 0.0666666666666667 Reciprocated Edge Ratio: 0.125 Connected Components: 101 Single-Vertex Connected Components: 97 Maximum Vertices in a Connected Component: 13 Maximum Edges in a Connected Component: 13 Maximum Geodesic Distance (Diameter): 6 Average Geodesic Distance: 2.640884 Graph Density: 0.00119940029985007 Modularity: Not Applicable NodeXL Version: 1.0.1.332	Overall Graph Metrics: Vertices: 101 Unique Edges: 12 Edges With Duplicates: 0 Total Edges: 12 Self-Loops: 0 Reciprocated Vertex Pair Ratio: 0 Reciprocated Edge Ratio: 0 Connected Components: 90 Single-Vertex Connected Components: 84 Maximum Vertices in a Connected Component: 6 Maximum Edges in a Connected Component: 6 Maximum Geodesic Distance (Diameter): 3 Average Geodesic Distance: 1.147541 Graph Density: 0.00118811881188119 Modularity: Not Applicable NodeXL Version: 1.0.1.332
Top Tweeters in Entire Graph: baronianconsult 83celt mamoosie nbcbayarea cbcnews shellandjeff elizabethkarr drferdowsi yonkersoem40 genxmedia	Top Tweeters in Entire Graph: mattsoleyn yahoonews stratf0rdsangel kenny_wallace ramfire55 bewickwren ohhmurissa ladyshoodjourna wavy_wetback sfgate

The related graph metrics tables for the four graphs above follow in Table 13.

Another approach involved capturing graph information of elements related to the event. In Figure 14, there are searches for #PG&E (for Pacific Gas and Electric Company, the electric company striving to provide energy for the citizens of the affected zone), #FEMA (the Federal Emergency Management Agency), and #CEA (for the California Earthquake Authority, but with many other Tweets mixed in due to the un-disambiguated nature of the acronym).

Clearly, these data crawls may be expanded based on a range of other search terms based on relatedness to the topic. In this sense, it may help to pace with a wide range of mass media if this event is being covered; it also helps to track with collections from social media and less formal modes of information collection. Attention selectively foregrounds some issues and backgrounds others; it determines what has primacy out of the many variables in the event and contextual social environment. In a sense, the work involves continual searching both for new leads to track to new information as well as searching for relevant information. It helps to be constantly aware of semantic range and meanings (or "word senses" based on context) and the additional noise that may be introduced with particular captures. In other words, terms have to be salient to the event. Or researchers have to be able to remove noise from the data for clearer information.

In Figure 15, "Earthquake" Related Tags Network on Flickr (in a Triptych View), this visualization shows the word clusters created by frequency of co-occurrence with other similar tags in contents labeled with "earthquake." The networks were created from a two-degree extraction, which captures the tags

Figure 13. "Earthquake" vs. #earthquake, "quake" vs. #quake: keyword vs. hashtag searches on twitter

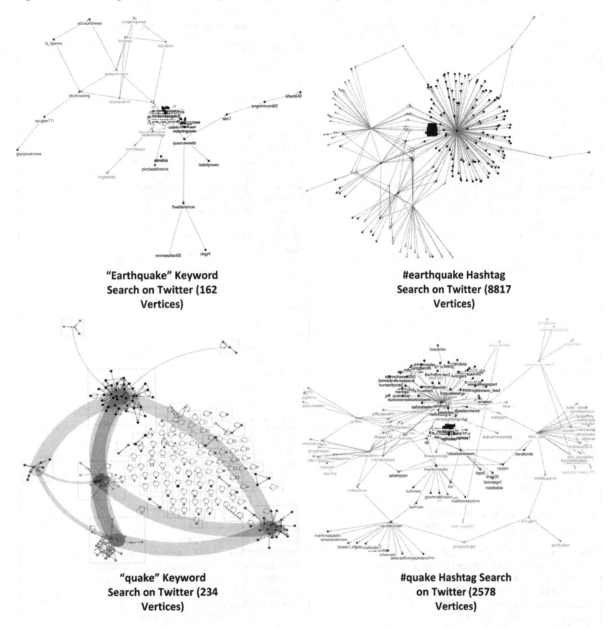

"Earthquake" Keyword Search on Twitter (162 Vertices)

#earthquake Hashtag Search on Twitter (8817 Vertices)

"quake" Keyword Search on Twitter (234 Vertices)

#quake Hashtag Search on Twitter (2578 Vertices)

directly related to the target word but also the neighborhoods for each of those "alters". The various clusters may be identified as having certain purposes, such as regions or camera types or languages. A related tags network taps into the meaning in metadata as captured in folksonomies, the amateur-created tag clouds. In the far-right panel, the scraped images were minimized to ensure that the names of the authors are able to be read.

Additional analyses from extracted network graph information. Behind each of the networks is a range of Tweets or text messaging that is also collected. These text corpuses may be captured and analyzed using text analysis tools, which may show proxemics terms to keywords and word frequency counts

Table 9. "Earthquake" and "quake" keyword searches vs. hashtag searches on twitter

"earthquake" keyword search on Twitter	#earthquake hashtag search on Twitter
Overall Graph Metrics: Vertices: 162 Unique Edges: 29 Edges With Duplicates: 0 Total Edges: 29 Self-Loops: 0 Reciprocated Vertex Pair Ratio: 0 Reciprocated Edge Ratio: 0 Connected Components: 139 Single-Vertex Connected Components: 135 Maximum Vertices in a Connected Component: 19 Maximum Edges in a Connected Component: 24 Maximum Geodesic Distance (Diameter): 8 Average Geodesic Distance: 3.07013 Graph Density: 0.00111187792347213 Modularity: Not Applicable NodeXL Version: 1.0.1.332	Overall Graph Metrics: Vertices: 8817 Unique Edges: 250 Edges With Duplicates: 0 Total Edges: 250 Self-Loops: 0 Reciprocated Vertex Pair Ratio: 0 Reciprocated Edge Ratio: 0 Connected Components: 8611 Single-Vertex Connected Components: 8606 Maximum Vertices in a Connected Component: 203 Maximum Edges in a Connected Component: 246 Maximum Geodesic Distance (Diameter): 7 Average Geodesic Distance: 2.975185 Graph Density: 3.2162336123892E-06 Modularity: Not Applicable NodeXL Version: 1.0.1.332
Top Tweeters in Entire Graph: captain_luv animesh1977 foxnews thefinancepress sandiegonewz fufcall3q thus_spake mercnews hcfradio wcpo	Top Tweeters in Entire Graph: favstar250 flashpresse usradionews mom4everever missb62 rt_racesonoma coopmike48 lorimoreno okcstormwatcher rightnowio_feed
"quake" keyword search on Twitter	#quake hashtag search on Twitter
Overall Graph Metrics: Vertices: 234 Unique Edges: 666 Edges With Duplicates: 113 Total Edges: 779 Self-Loops: 133 Reciprocated Vertex Pair Ratio: 0.135755258126195 Reciprocated Edge Ratio: 0.239057239057239 Connected Components: 97 Single-Vertex Connected Components: 86 Maximum Vertices in a Connected Component: 124 Maximum Edges in a Connected Component: 642 Maximum Geodesic Distance (Diameter): 8 Average Geodesic Distance: 2.732801 Graph Density: 0.0108946847144272 Modularity: Not Applicable NodeXL Version: 1.0.1.332	Overall Graph Metrics: Vertices: 2578 Unique Edges: 156 Edges With Duplicates: 0 Total Edges: 156 Self-Loops: 0 Reciprocated Vertex Pair Ratio: 0 Reciprocated Edge Ratio: 0 Connected Components: 2448 Single-Vertex Connected Components: 2445 Maximum Vertices in a Connected Component: 122 Maximum Edges in a Connected Component: 147 Maximum Geodesic Distance (Diameter): 8 Average Geodesic Distance: 3.808518 Graph Density: 2.34815773478642E-05 Modularity: Not Applicable NodeXL Version: 1.0.1.332
Top Tweeters in Entire Graph: ghulam_rasool1 paijwar tukang_update news24husa h0p_ksks livetns tnsl41 tlw3 tnsl51 washingtonpist	Top Tweeters in Entire Graph: poemtrees davidvidu shawnabner rightnowio_feed moui 7pinkpanther7 housecracka shoq yayayarndiva edwardcalame

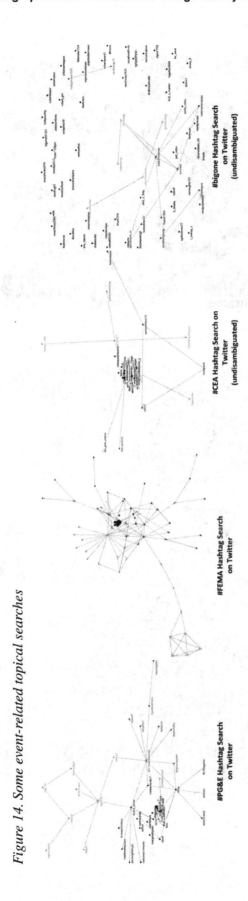

Figure 14. Some event-related topical searches

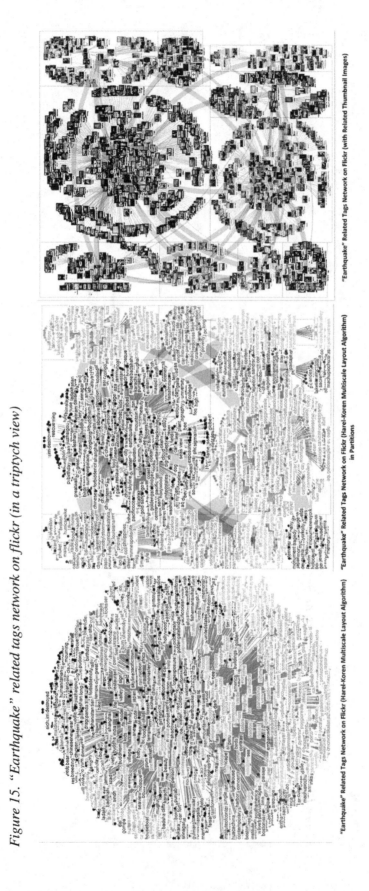

Figure 15. "Earthquake" related tags network on flickr (in a triptych view)

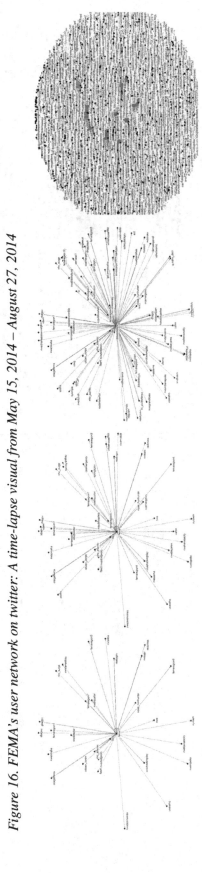

Figure 16. FEMA's user network on twitter: A time-lapse visual from May 15, 2014 – August 27, 2014

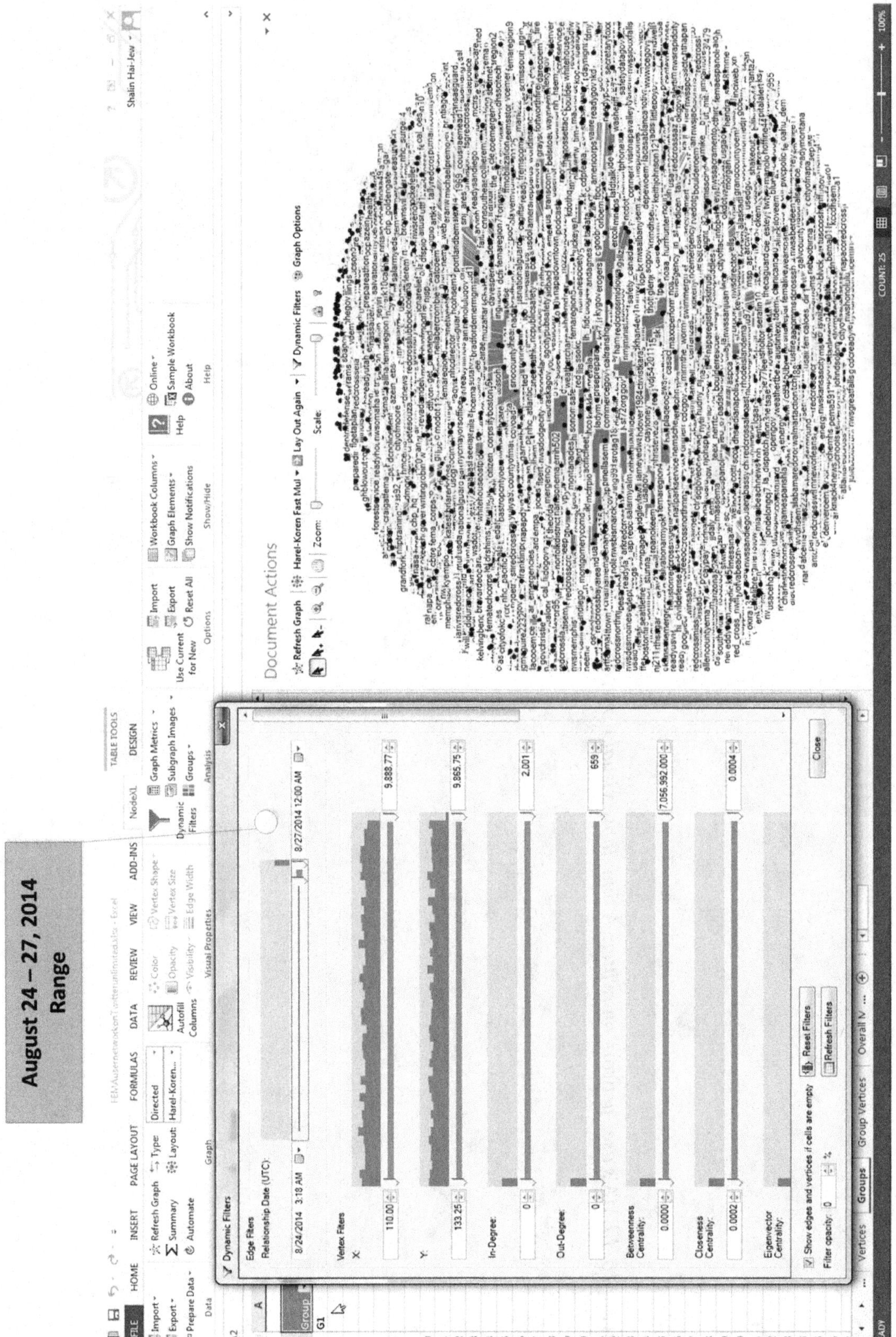

Figure 17. Broad shared communications and network clustering around an event (for the FEMA user network on Twitter)

(to show topics of interest). There are also images collected as well, which may be further analyzed for additional meanings. The activity may be analyzed based on time sequences and time periods. It may be possible also to limit the captures to particular geographical regions to see if patterns may be observed.

The FEMA user network on Twitter was captured and is depicted in a time-lapse visual in Figure 16. This extracted "data" went back from May 15, 2014, and ran the four and a half months through the date of the earthquake on August 24, 2014, and through the morning of the data extraction, August 27. The graphs were drawn at month-intervals and show that the network grew in connectivity and then exploded in connections at the time of the earthquake. Figure 17, "Broad Shared Communications and Network Clustering around an Event (for the FEMA User Network on Twitter)" shows that the giant cluster is not a cumulative collection per se since the dynamic filter to the left was set as the range of Aug. 24 – 27, 2014, and the graph has remained as densely clustered. In other words, the accumulation of links (edges) surrounding the earthquake on August 24 may be understood as a time-proxemic or simultaneity factor in the FEMA network's explosive connectivity.

So far, only one social media platform has been used and actually only one tool (NodeXL). Flickr had a gallery of earthquake aftermath photos curated by Flickr, and YouTube featured a large number of short videos. A generic capture of "earthquake" videos on YouTube was done to show the thumbnail visual component of such data extractions. Figure 18 is presented as a triptych, with all three visualizations created from the same extracted dataset of 499 videos, with 21,342 unique edges, and one group of the five identified focused on the Napa, California, earthquake, just a few days after its occurrence.

Finally, there was a "mild" Level 1 footprint crawl of www.cityofnapa.org with a maximum of 10K nodes using Maltego Tungsten. This could feasibly be used to find various sites and businesses to query about the event. This provides a sense of the electronic presence of businesses around the city of Napa, California.

The complete entity list, as partially depicted in Figure 20, enables in-depth probing for nodes of interest for further research.

Users of interest could have their accounts examined for their ego neighborhoods, the one-degree crawls of their direct ties or "alters". The communications could be analyzed with text visualizations of the most frequent terms. In theory and practice, there would be many other streams of information collected about the event for a full mapping. This chapter only had the space for a limited collection, so only a few selected methods were brought into play. Finally, for a closer sense of how extended-form event-graphing might work, a more "silent" event was tracked and summarized below. The information for Case 1 was captured over a few days. In a real-world situation, it may take much longer to fully see when the event has ended—in this case through aftershocks and maybe through the rebuilding. The definition of the event will determine the sense of when it started, its trajectory, and the conclusion.

Case 2: A More "Silent" Event

The selection of the "silent" event to eventgraph was less serendipitous. In a way, the definition here required the identification of a non-event that might have some presence on social media platforms. This might be seen as a kind of data extraction for leads that may or may not exist for an event that may or may not exist. In the spirit of this endeavor, the author decided to go with a generic term #weekend and "weekend" for a basic trawl of social media to gain a sense of the messaging linked to this neutral term. The assumption is that any communication is shared with such labels because of a sense of some event given the time period. Such terms may have more personal meaning in a narrow-casting way than

Figure 18. A triptych of the "earthquake" video network on YouTube (via NodeXL)

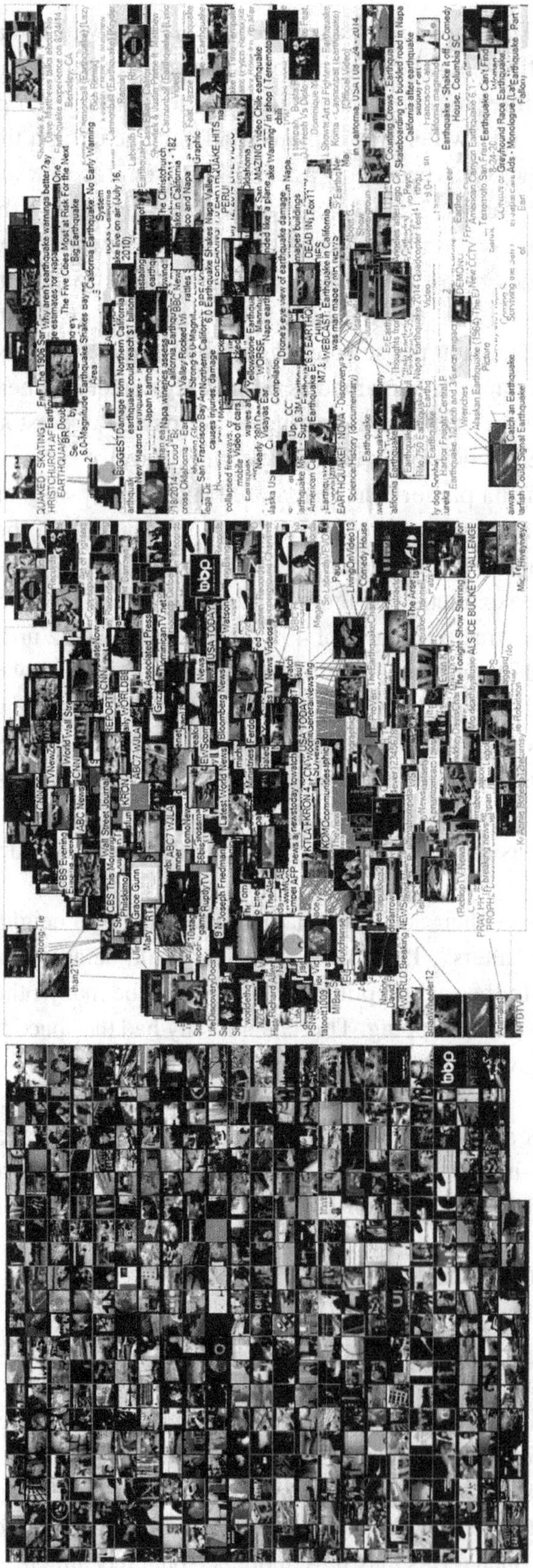

Partitioned Clusters with Video Titles Listed (and Napa Quake at the Bottom Right Corner)

Partitioned Clusters with Author Names

A Grid Layout with Thumbnails of Screengrabs

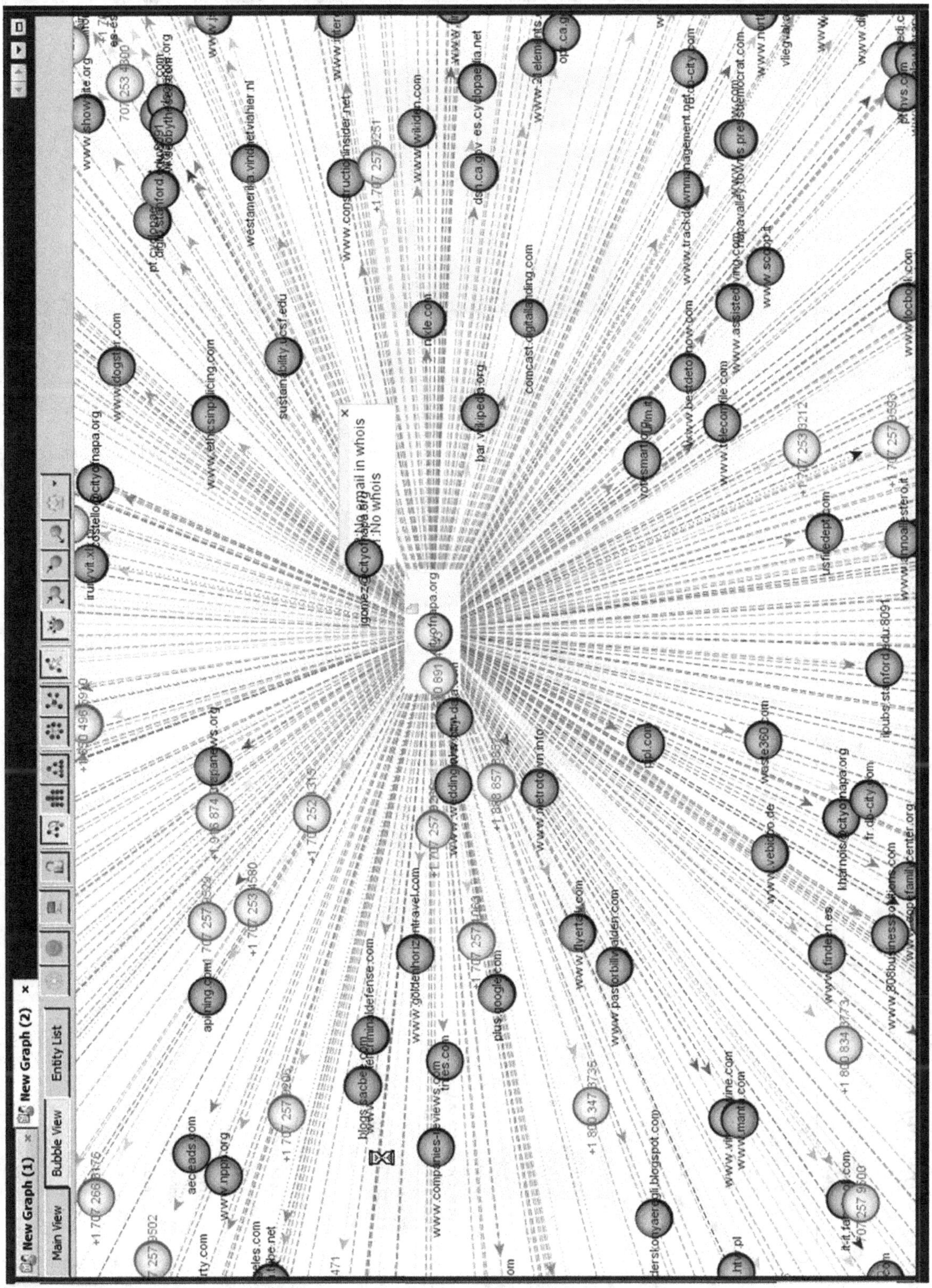

Figure 19. City of Napa.org Links on the Surface Web (Level 1 Footprinting on Maltego Tungsten)

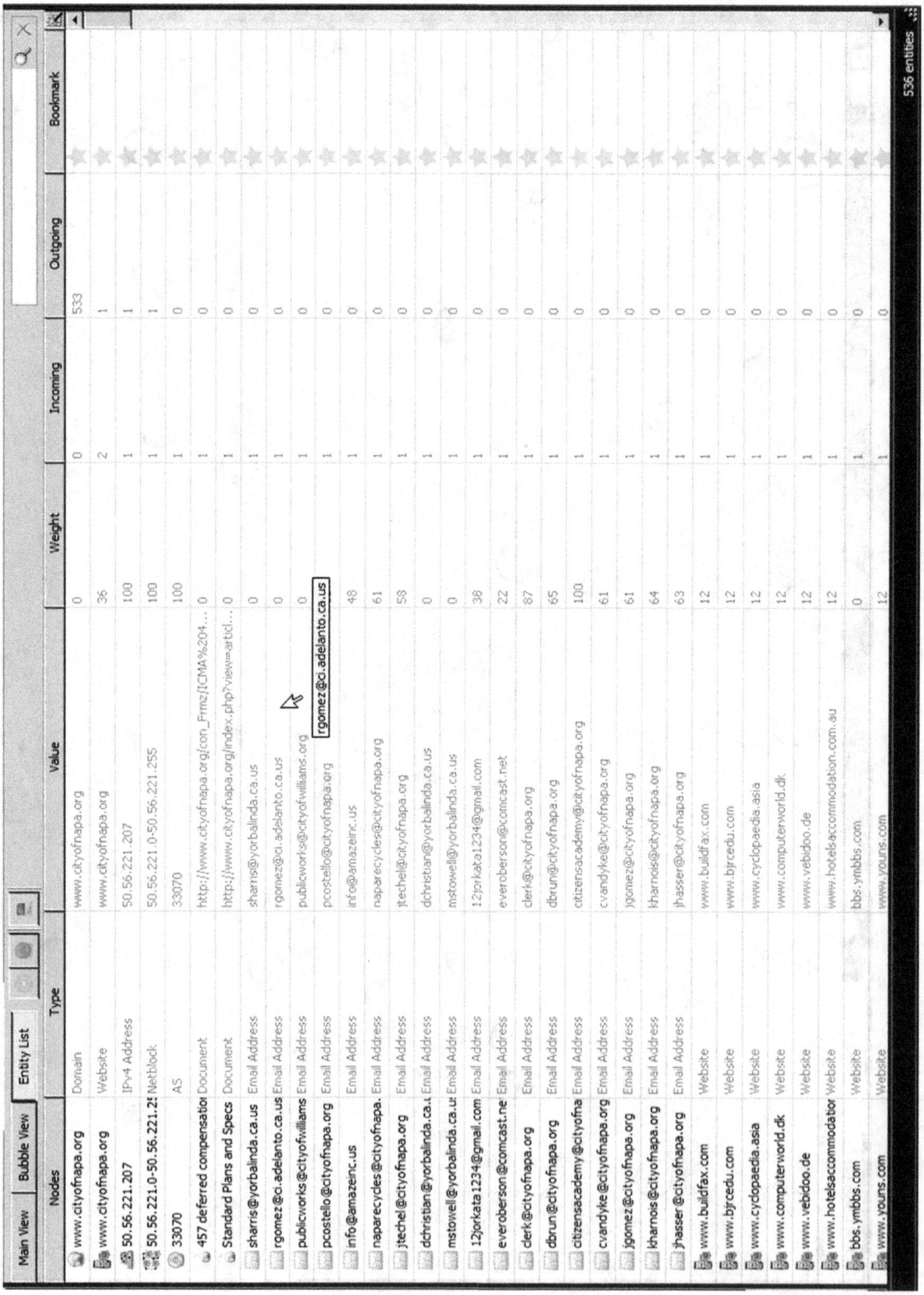

Figure 20. City of Napa.org Links on the Surface Web (Level 1 Footprinting on Maltego Tungsten)

Nodes	Type	Value	Weight	Incoming	Outgoing	Bookmark
www.cityofnapa.org	Domain	www.cityofnapa.org	0	0	533	
www.cityofnapa.org	Website	www.cityofnapa.org	36	2	1	
50.56.221.207	IPv4 Address	50.56.221.207	100	1	1	
50.56.221.0-50.56.221.2!	Netblock	50.56.221.0-50.56.221.255	100	1	1	
33070	AS	33070	100	0	0	
457 deferred compensatio	Document	http://www.cityofnapa.org/con_Frmz/1CMA%204...	0	1	0	
Standard Plans and Specs	Document	http://www.cityofnapa.org/index.php?view=articl...	0	1	0	
sharris@yorbalinda.ca.us	Email Address	sharris@yorbalinda.ca.us	0	1	0	
rgomez@ci.adelanto.ca.us	Email Address	rgomez@ci.adelanto.ca.us	0	1	0	
publicworks@cityofwilliams	Email Address	publicworks@cityofwilliams.org	0	1	0	
pcostello@cityofnapa.org	Email Address	pcostello@cityofnapa.org [rgomez@ci.adelanto.ca.us]	0	1	0	
info@amazeinc.us	Email Address	info@amazeinc.us	48	1	0	
naparecycles@cityofnapa.	Email Address	naparecycles@cityofnapa.org	61	1	0	
jtechel@cityofnapa.org	Email Address	jtechel@cityofnapa.org	58	1	0	
dchristian@yorbalinda.ca.\	Email Address	dchristian@yorbalinda.ca.us	0	1	0	
mstowell@yorbalinda.ca.u:	Email Address	mstowell@yorbalinda.ca.us	0	1	0	
12jorkata1234@gmail.com	Email Address	12jorkata1234@gmail.com	38	1	0	
everoberson@comcast.ne	Email Address	everoberson@comcast.net	22	1	0	
clerk@cityofnapa.org	Email Address	clerk@cityofnapa.org	87	1	0	
dbrun@cityofnapa.org	Email Address	dbrun@cityofnapa.org	65	1	0	
citizensacademy@cityofna	Email Address	citizensacademy@cityofnapa.org	100	1	0	
cvandyke@cityofnapa.org	Email Address	cvandyke@cityofnapa.org	61	1	0	
jgomez2@cityofnapa.org	Email Address	jgomez2@cityofnapa.org	61	1	0	
kharnois@cityofnapa.org	Email Address	kharnois@cityofnapa.org	64	1	0	
jhasser@cityofnapa.org	Email Address	jhasser@cityofnapa.org	63	1	0	
www.buildfax.com	Website	www.buildfax.com	12	1	0	
www.bjrcedu.com	Website	www.bjrcedu.com	12	1	0	
www.cyclopaedia.asia	Website	www.cyclopaedia.asia	12	1	0	
www.computerworld.dk	Website	www.computerworld.dk	12	1	0	
www.vebidoo.de	Website	www.vebidoo.de	12	1	0	
www.hotelsaccommodator	Website	www.hotelsaccommodation.com.au	12	1	0	
bbs.ymbbs.com	Website	bbs.ymbbs.com	0	1	0	
www.youns.com	Website	www.youns.com	12	1	0	

Main View | Bubble View | Entity List

536 entities

in a broadcast sense, although both uses are possible and quite likely. This made for more of a tentative approach since this would possibly result in a dispersed listing of many smaller events instead of something more large-scale and maybe socially relevant. It was thought at the beginning that maybe if there were a larger cluster of discussants around the topic that maybe it would be understood that an event was afoot. Without analyzing the dates of the texts and the messaging in-depth, it would be difficult to determine whether "weekend" is used in an anticipatory way, a retrospective way, or a current way. Likewise, it would require more effort to see if there are time similarities among discussants. It would require more effort to assess if there were shared demographic features (particularly given the noisiness and the sparseness of user-provided geographical data on Twitter accounts).

Figure 21 shows the accounts of those who communicated with "weekend" as a keyword search to the left and #weekend as a hashtag search to the right. Within the dataset are the captured text messages of the public Tweets. On the day of the data extraction, a Tuesday, there was not a lot of messaging about the weekend in either format. Per the sparse links, there were few interactive conversations going on about this. Many of the microbloggers were maybe just sending out the message to their followers without achieving much in the way of a direct response in terms of a return labeled #weekend message.

Figure 22 shows three visualizations of YouTube videos that have been labeled with the word "weekend" in its title or description. The linkages show commentary among the individuals interacting around these video contents.

Figure 23 shows a side-by-side visualization of a related tags network on Flickr. This type of network shows tags that were used to label videos that were identified as "weekend" ones in terms of topics. Five groups of related tags were extracted based on semantic proximity in terms of the metadata labeling. A perusal of the related words may result in a sense of the images and videos that may be depicted in that particular cluster, in a general sense. Even though a formal sentiment analysis was not done on the collected words, many of the words have a positive emotion associated. On the left side, the thumbnail images were not included so that they would not obscure the text. On the right, the images were included because of the informational value of the images as a visual channel.

Some researchers have worked to collate images based on a variety of features, such as their "visual features, geographical coordinates and image taken time" to cluster such digital artifacts (Qian, Liu, Zheng, Du, & Hou, 2013, p. 144). Such means may be applied to tracking events based on both images and video contents because these would identify related contents that may shed light on an event by sharing information from different angles. Another approach may be done in a semi-continuous monitoring method.. For example, if there is an issue that has continuing interest, it may help to track related messages for a long period of time in order to identify bursts of interest (often based on events) and to understand events from those peaks (Kirilenko & Stepchenkova, 2014).

Initial Insights

The original main research questions read:

1. What are the current capabilities of creating social-media and Internet-based (extended-form) eventgraphs of unexpected and evolving real-world events using publicly available apps and software programs (both open-source and commercial)?

2. What is the optimal method or approach to attain the most relevant information for a particular event?

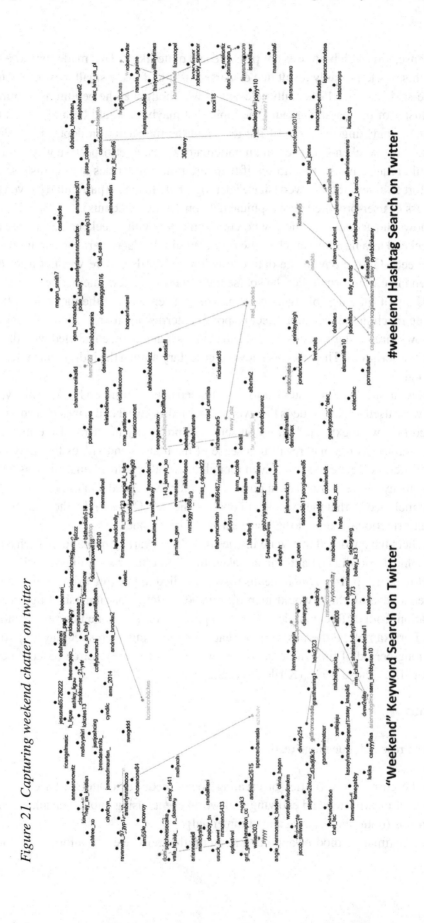

Figure 21. Capturing weekend chatter on twitter

Figure 22. "Weekend" video network on youtube (in three visualizations)

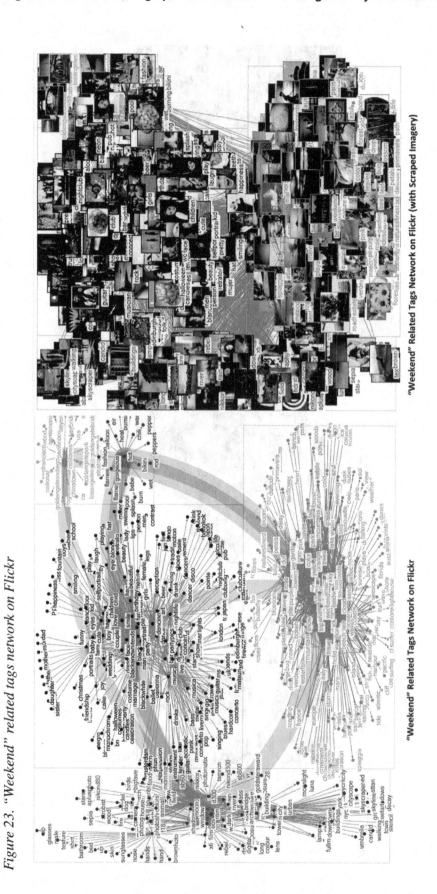

Figure 23. "Weekend" related tags network on Flickr

In light of the initial explorations and limited data extractions, the two questions are only partially explored. Some tentative assertions may be made, such as the benefit of pre-positioning and creating leads lists. It makes sense to train in the various software tools and platforms given their complexity combined with the possible need for adaptive strategies with an unfolding event.

In terms of tracking "silent" events, this seems not to have achieved the level of any proof-of-concept. Case 1 dealt with an event covered to relative media saturation, and the type of information may have seemed more esoteric and less directly useful than that captured through the mass media channels. Case 2 was a small endeavor to look for a potential event in the offing by focusing on the "weekend" as a concept. This endeavor ended without a sense of having achieved any understanding of any elusive event through social media platforms and channels. In this chapter, the strongest aspect seems to be the thinking work and the understanding of the software capabilities applied to this issue. It is hoped that in the future, more than a few tepid cases may be run in order to strengthen understandings.

The work of extended-form eventgraphing clearly works backwards and forwards in time. In other words, methods and tools may be used to capture event data in real time during an unfolding event, but lessons learned from that capture may be applied to future events. Past events may be analyzed using captured and stored data from datasets in order to surface learning (assuming that there is access to that data). As it stands, there are some pretty severe limitations to this approach, with very heavy costs to human attention and effort. This means that this approach is limited in scale, unless more trained people are brought on board and such tools are more widely available.

A few observations about social media platforms. Microblogging sites tend to be much more dynamic than content-based sites (those that host images and / or video). The contrast in dynamism or change over time is especially noticeable in extracted data and metadata. A data extraction on a microblogging site can be quite different based on the time-of-day of the extraction as well as the rate-limiting of the API of the social media platform. Also, in relation to specific topics, microblogging sites can run very hot and popular or very cold, depending on the vagaries of human attention. For social content-sharing sites, the collections tend to be somewhat more stable—at least at the level of related tags networks and video networks, which may be quite stable even over periods of months (depending on the topic). It is possible that the cost of entry is higher—in terms of participants having to take photos, upload them, label them, and so on. While there is potential for insights extracted from a variety of social media platforms, the WWW, and the Internet, a lot of this work will require strategy and smart gleaning.

It is important for researchers to accept and express unknowability where that is observed. Currently, it may seem that the amount of information may only be used for tentative assertions and impressions. Another shortcoming to this approach involves the fact that this cobbles or chains a number of tools that provide different functionalities: social media data extraction, data visualization, multimedia scraping, text analytics, and data management and storage. In some ways, end-to-end systems may be more effective because those may automate connectivity between various tools and functions.

The findings from such work have to be couched in a variety of conditional language to explain what exactly was captured, from what social media platform, and what that data may mean. Many of the findings seem somewhat indirect, such as extrapolated information from related tags networks (which is analysis essentially of metadata). Such information is necessary also because how the data was collected—at the machine and human levels through the various stages—will affect what information is available and also what artifacts there may be in the data. This is a form of seeing through the glass darkly. It is unclear as-yet what the explanatory power may be of extracted data from social media platforms in terms of extended-form event-graphing.

Unique network topologies based on the types of social media platforms. The various social media platforms result in unique network topologies. For example, extracting a hashtag search around a conversation at any one time using NodeXL may extract no nodes to maybe a few thousand nodes (and this is an extraction which covers approximately a week to months' worth of data). Sometimes, there are collections of hashtags with no interactivity—no one interacting around the issue—but people just sort of sending their 140-character maximum messages into the global ether. The collected information may be somewhat informative, but the collected data would likely be always partial. (As yet, there is not a clear way to calculate how much a current data extraction haul is compared to an n=all.) Content-sharing networks that focus on video sharing tend to be much less dynamic, with sometimes the same results even months later, likely because of the effort cost in creating videos, annotating them, and then uploading them. Related tags networks also tend to be fairly stable in part because of the uses of pre-existing available tags for images and videos on some digital content-sharing sites. The APIs for the various social media platforms also can affect what data is collected. Researchers found that whether a basic search or a streaming capture was done on the Twitter API affected the collected data; further, the parameters of the data extraction resulted in varying data. In general, the authors found that the numbers of nodes on the periphery of a network were undercounted, and this undercounting may misrepresent the latent population that may activated into political or other action (González-Bailón, Wang, Rivero, Borge-Holthoefer, & Moreno, 2014, p. 25). The authors summarize:

We find that smaller samples do not offer an accurate picture of peripheral activity; we also find that the bias is greater for the network of mentions, partly because of the higher influence of snowballing in identifying relevant nodes. We discuss the implications of this bias for the study of diffusion dynamics and political communication through social media, and advocate the need for more uniform sampling procedures to study online communication (González-Bailón, Wang, Rivero, Borge-Holthoefer, & Moreno, 2014, p. 16).

Even though tapping into Web 2.0 has brought out optimistic language of empirically-based and web-scale data, often, the available information is much less. This partial access means is that it may be difficult to assess how effective a software extraction tool is in actual practice (in terms of collecting as much data as possible). People have a range of communications tools and platforms through which to interconnect, and one observed relationship on one platform may be highly limited and incomplete. As it stands, researchers may draw information from multiple sources in multiple ways to cross-compare. As in the triangulation of information, confidence levels may rise with the finding of convergent data and may be lessened with the discovery of divergent data. Another strategy has been to see how replicable information extractions may be using competing tools but controlling for all other circumstances of the data extraction. An important issue here is to note be able to communicate the level of confidence or certitude vs. the level of uncertainty for any assertion. In every research context, there are known unknowns, or inherent unresolvable uncertainties. (These uncertainty measures would include factors like the characteristics of the social media platform, the demographics of the participants on the social media platform, socio-economic status factors, the efficacy of the data extraction tools, the scrubbing and handling of the data, the data that was not collectable, and other potential factors.)

FUTURE RESEARCH DIRECTIONS

The novelty of the future means that the study of history can only partially inform current and future events. Situations and events may be so fluid that they belie detailed predictivity (even if some over-arching understanding is possible). And yet, the aim is to understand events prior to their start (based on antecedents), at their start, the critical junctures, the overall trajectory, and their finish. Arrayed against this ambitious tasking is a handful of publicly available off-the-shelf tools and methods. In general, the software tools enable data extraction from select social media platforms with application programming interfaces (APIs) that enable limited data extractions (rarely n=all); data visualizations; text analysis, and other capabilities. The research into various technological ways of mining social media data is promising, and once these functionalities are integrated into commercial tools, the capabilities of extended-form eventgraphing will be much improved. Researchers are working on automated ways to create timelines and mapping from extracted events from Tweetstreams (Marcus, Bernstein, Badar, Karger, Madden, & Miller, 2011a), with some of these tools available in open-source distribution (such as TweeQL). Event-tracking software systems that extract information from microblogging sites may be designed for identifying out sub-events and may enable further event exploration (Marcus, Bernstein, Badar, Karger, Madden, & Miller, 2011b). Currently, though, this approach is often demanding of direct human attention and effort. There are layers of human and technological dependencies.

In terms of research directions, it seems that there are many ways to broaden this work. There may be research on ways to improve data collection methods for a larger "n," different ways to query and probe the collected information, improved analytical techniques, and improved human-machine methods. There may be variations of different sequences for different insights and outcomes. There may be research into ways to validate / invalidate information on social media, particularly if important decisions may be based on the information there. Verification methods to increase confidence in findings will unique strategies based on the particular informational context, such as for mainstream media journalists (Diakopoulos, De Choudhury, & Naaman, 2012; Schifferes & Newman, 2013). There is a lot of potential work in terms of pursuing information about particular types of events, with distinctive and precise chaining sequences. There is room to learn about ways to analyze preserved prior events and extractions of models and understandings from those endeavors. It would help to define approaches in creating scenarios based on known information for a range of predictive possible worlds. There may be challenges set up—such as having teams "eventgraph" elusive knowledge—like the quiet discovery of a zero-day exploit, the moment a social or political group has reached a turning point in ideology or capability, or the moment a research team has achieved a major finding. So much happens in the world in obscurity and silence, whether purposefully or not. It does seem unavoidable that extended-form eventgraphing will involve subjectivity and interpretation at some level.

The research may inform the design of dedicated tools to capture relevant event-based information across a broad swath of social media platforms and online spaces. These tools may also tap below the Surface Web (to the Deep or Hidden Web for dynamically-generated information).

To go further afield, extended-form eventgraphing could be enhanced greatly with the application of "big data" analytical approaches, which could be deployed to create decision-trees based on in-world events (and potential in-world events). For example, what are observed similar word clusters in a data set related to an event, and what do those clusters say about the collective thinking about the event? Do people tend towards consensus or dissensus around particular issues, and what are possible causal factors for those responses? What are possible interaction effects between identified variables to an event (and a potential repeat of that event)? How do people interact socially online around different types of events and information? What forms of expressiveness are there, and what sorts of digital objects are created? In terms of online interactions, which digital objects and messages tend to have the most force, and why? Which variables (from social media and other communications) may be identified as predictors of possible future events, and how predictive are they (and at what confidence levels if using linear regression or neural networks)? These are all relevant research questions which require non-trivial and demanding research and interpretation methods. In analyses involving massive data, there are many levels of analysis which may be applied, in order to zoom in and zoom out from the data, colloquially speaking.

CONCLUSION

The idea of cobbling tools to set up electronic listening posts and sensors for unknown events is not particularly original. The general approach of using the Internet to track the evolution of ideas across peoples and social spaces is already necessarily limited by those who are online and active. The changing realities of online spaces extend to its policies, governance, and practices. These changes suggest that the material practices of extended-form eventgraphing will necessarily change. The approach here offers a temporary, not inexpensive, non-scalable, manual, and very partial and incomplete solution. The extracted information may offer just a degree of explanatory value (and this has not offered any sort of confidence measure for how accurate any of the extracted information may be); however, if while limited, such eventgraphs do offer some insights that may not be attainable in other ways or that may be attainable with somewhat limited costs (vs. having a pollster contacting respondents or having a reporter on-ground). The process described here is rough-cut and may certainly be improved. The software tools ecosystem is in constant flux, and there may well be more powerful and integrative approaches to extended-form eventgraphing. Also, the social media platforms, publicly available tools, and methodologies are likely continually evolving. The targeted events of interest are ever-changing. Given these contextual factors, it is safe to assume that this work is dated before it reaches publication. In other words, there are plenty of ways to improve on this initial work.

There have long been ambitions to capture situational awareness of macro events and movements, larger social changes and shifts, even though historically, the thinking has been that people are generally unaware in the moment. For example, G.W.F. Hegel, in 1820 in the Preface to his *Philosophy of Right*, suggested that insights about a particular time period emerge only in hindsight after the passing of that epoch, or more elegantly: "Only when the dusk starts to fall does the owl of Minerva spread its wings and fly." In the modern speeded-up era, is electronic chatter too piecemeal and close-in to the event to be insightful? Is it too directly experiential and engaged in the throes of the event?

In a world full of professionally managed and packaged pseudo-events, with plenty of attention-getting antics and messaging, it can be hard to re-orient in order to detect events that arrive without fanfare or extant general awareness. It can be difficult to focus on raw instead of processed information. It is challenging to redefine discovery through electronic communications means. It is difficult to find and focus on "whispers" when the world is roiled with "shouts." There is very little in the way of awareness of what nuanced indicators may look like for impending, sudden-emerging, and latent events. There are also indicators that the "spiral of silence"—a phenomenon in which people will not discuss issues about which they think others will not agree—is magnified in social media, putting in question whether controversial or nuanced debates may even occur there (Shahani, Aug. 27, 2014). The more knowable events are online, the more countermeasures there will be against its data leakage. Still, this is an area of untapped potential for understanding relevant occurrences—particularly as methods improve—for this small part of computational social science.

ACKNOWLEDGMENT

I am grateful to the researchers who originated the idea of eventgraphing and evolved it. This chapter would not exist at all if not for the prior ideas.

REFERENCES

Abdelhaq, H., Gertz, M., & Sengstock, C. (2013). Spatio-temporal characteristics of bursty words in Twitter streams. *Proceedings of Sigspatial '13*. Orlando, Florida. doi:10.1145/2525314.2525354

Andress, J., & Winterfeld, S. (2014). Psychological Weapons. Cyber Warfare: Techniques, Tactics, and Tools for Security Practitioners. Amsterdam: Elsevier. doi:10.1016/B978-0-12-416672-1.00008-8

Back, M. D., Stopfer, J. M., Vazire, S., Gaddis, S., Schmukle, S. C., Egloff, B., & Gosling, S. D. (2010). Facebook profiles reflect actual personality, not self-idealization. *Psychological Science*. Retrieve from: http://pss.sagepub.com/content/early/2010/01/28/0956797609360756.short?rss=1&ssource=mfc

Baucom, E., Sanjari, A., Liu, X., & Chen, M. (2013). Mirroring the real world in social media: Twitter, geolocation, and sentiment analysis. Association of Computing Machinery.

Bermingham, A., Conway, M., McInerney, L., O'Hare, N., & Smeaton, A. F. (2009). Combining social network analysis and sentiment analysis to explore the potential for online radicalisation (sic). *Advances in Social Networks Analysis and Mining*. Greece. Retrieve from: http://doras.dcu.ie/4554/3/DCU_aso-nam09.pdf

Bliss, C. A., Kloumann, I. M., Harris, K. D., Danford, C. M., & Dodds, P. S. (2012). Twitter reciprocal reply networks exhibit assortativity with respect to happiness. *Journal of Computational Science*, *3*(5), 388–397. doi:10.1016/j.jocs.2012.05.001

Bodenhausen, G., Kang, S., & Peery, D. (2012). Social categorization and the perception of social groups. In S. Fiske & C. Macrae (Eds.), *The SAGE handbook of social cognition* (pp. 311–330). London: SAGE Publications Ltd.; doi:10.4135/9781446247631.n16

Brenner, M., & Izquierdo, E. (2012). Social event detection and retrieval in collaborative photo collections. *Proceedings of ICMR*. Hong Kong, China. doi:10.1145/2324796.2324823

Bruno, N. (2011). Tweet first, verify later? How real-time information is changing the coverage of worldwide crisis events. *Reuters Institute for the Study of Journalism*. University of Oxford.

Buss, A. H., & Sánchez, P. J. (2002). Building complex models with Legos. *Proceedings of 2002 Winter Simulation Conference*. Charnes.

Charlwood, J., Dennis, A., Gissing, A., Quick, L., & Varma, S. (2012). Use of social media during flood events. *Batemans Bay 2012*. Retrieve from: http://floods.org.au/use-of-social-media-during-flood-events/

Cheng, Z., Caverlee, J., & Lee, K. (2013). A content-driven framework for geolocating microblog users. *ACM Transactions on Intelligent Systems and Technology*: 4(1), Article 2, 2:1 – 2:27.

Cuevas, R., Gonzalez, R., Cuevas, A., & Guerrero, C. (2014). Understanding the locality effect in Twitter: Measurement and analysis. *Personal and Ubiquitous Computing, 18*(2), 397–411. doi:10.1007/s00779-013-0658-y

Diakopoulos, N., De Choudhury, M., & Naaman, M. (2012). Finding and assessing social media information sources in the context of journalism. *Proceedings of CHI 2012, Social Computing: Business & Beyond*. Austin, Texas. doi:10.1145/2207676.2208409

Dunn, C., & Scheiderman, B. (2013). Motif simplification: Improving network visualization readability with fan, connector, and clique glyphs. *Proceedings of CHI 2013: Changing Perspectives*. Paris, France.

Freberg, K., Saling, K., Vidoloff, K. G., & Eosco, G. (2013). Using value modeling to evaluate social media messages: The case of Hurricane Irene. *Public Relations Review, 39*(3), 185–192. doi:10.1016/j.pubrev.2013.02.010

Frontiers in massive data analysis. (2013). *National Research Council of the National Academies*. Washington, D.C.: The National Academies Press.

Gawhry, L. N. (2012). *Assessing the impact of social media on the 25 January 2011 Egyptian Revolution*. Naval Postgraduate Thesis.

Gonzálex-Bailón, S., Wang, N., Rivero, A., Borge-Holthoefer, J., & Moreno, Y. (2014). Assessing the bias in samples of large online networks. *Social Networks, 28*, 16–27. doi:10.1016/j.socnet.2014.01.004

Groh, G., Straub, F., Eicher, J., & Grob, D. (2013). Geographic aspects of tie strength and value of information in social networking. Proceedings of ACM SIGSPATIAL LBSN'13. Orlando, Florida. 1 – 10. doi:10.1145/2536689.2536803

Haddow, G. D., & Haddow, K. S. (2014). *Disaster Communications in a Changing Media World* (2nd ed.). Amsterdam: Elsevier.

Hai-Jew, S. (2014). "ICT4D and its Potential Role in the Detection, Surveillance, and Prevention of Novel Zoonotic Disease Outbreaks for Global, National, and Local Pandemic Prevention." Ch. 7. In C.M. Akrivopoulou and N. Garipidis's Human Rights and the Impact of ICT in the Public Sphere: Participation, Democracy, and Political Autonomy. Hershey: IGI-Global. doi:10.4018/978-1-4666-6248-3.ch007

Hale, S. A. (2014). Global connectivity and multilinguals in the Twitter network. *Proceedings of CHI 2014, One of a CHInd*. Toronto, Ontario, Canada. 833 – 842. doi:10.1145/2556288.2557203

Hansen, D., Smith, M. A., & Schneiderman, B. (2011). EventGraphs: Charting collections of conference connections. *Proceedings of the 44th Hawaii International Conference on System Sciences*. IEEE. 1 – 10.

Heaney, M. T. (2014). Multiplex networks and interest group influence reputation: An exponential random dom graph model. *Social Networks, 36*, 66–81. doi:10.1016/j.socnet.2012.11.003

Hughes, D. J., Rowe, M., Batey, M., & Lee, A. (2012). A tale of two sites: Twitter vs. Facebook and the personality predictors of social media usage. *Computers in Human Behavior, 28*(2), 561–569. doi:10.1016/j.chb.2011.11.001

Ikawa, Y., Enoki, M., & Tatsubori, M. (2012). Location inference using microblog messages. Proceedings of WWW 2012 – SWDM '12 Workshop. Lyon, France. 687 – 690. doi:10.1145/2187980.2188181

Jain, R. (2013). EventWeb: Towards social life networks. *Philosophical Transactions of the Royal Society, 371*(1987), 1–11. doi:10.1098/rsta.2012.0384 PMID:23419853

Jehn, K. A., & Bezrukova, K. (2010). The faultline activation process and the effects of activated faultlines on coalition formation, conflict, and group outcomes. *Organizational Behavior and Human Decision Processes, 112*(1), 24–42. doi:10.1016/j.obhdp.2009.11.008

Jennex, M. E. (2012). Social media—Truly viable for crisis response? *Proceedings of 9*[th] *International ISCRAM. Conference.* Vancouver, Canada. 1 – 5.

Jurgenson, N. (2011). Digital dualism and the fallacy of web objectivity. *Cyborgology. The Society Pages.* Retrieve from: http://thesocietypages.org/cyborgology/2011/09/13/digital-dualism-and-the-fallacy-of-web-objectivity/

Kamath, K.Y., Caverlee, J., Cheng, Z., & Sui, D.Z. (2012). *Spatial influence vs. community influence: Modeling the global spread of social media.*

Kirilenko, A. P., & Stepchenkova, S. O. (2014). Public microblogging on climate change: One year of Twitter worldwide. *Global Environmental Change, 26*, 171–182. doi:10.1016/j.gloenvcha.2014.02.008

Koban, D. D. (2014). Accounting for uncertainty in social network analysis through replication. Thesis. North Carolina State University.

Kumar, S., Morstatter, F., Zalarani, R., & Liu, H. (2013). Whom should I follow? Identifying relevant users during crises. *Proceedings of 24*[th] *ACM Conference on Hypertext and Social Media.* Paris, France. 139 – 147.

Lampos, V. & Cristiannini, N. (2012). Nowcasting events from the Social Web with statistical learning. *ACM Transactions on Intelligent Systems and Technology.* 3 (4), Article 72, pp. 72:1 -72:22.

Malinick, T. E., Tindall, D. B., & Diani, M. (2013). Network centrality and social movement media coverage: A two-mode network analytic approach. *Social Networks, 35*(2), 148–158. doi:10.1016/j.socnet.2011.10.005

Marcus, A., Bernstein, M. S., Badar, O., Karger, D. R., Madden, S., & Miller, R. C. (2011a). Tweets as data: Demonstration of TweeQL and TwitInfo. *Proceedings of SIGMOD '11.* Athens, Greece.

Marcus, A., Bernstein, M. S., Badar, O., Karger, D. R., Madden, S., & Miller, R. C. (2011b). TwitInfo: Aggregating and visualizing microblogs for event exploration. In the proceedings of CHI 2011. Twitter Systems, Vancouver, B.C., Canada. May 7 – 12, 2011.

Mayer, B. L. (2011). *Modern social media and social revolutions.* Master's thesis. U.S. Army Command and General Staff College. 1 – 127.

McCulloh, I.A. & Carley, K.M. (2008). *Social network change detection.* Carnegie Mellon University.

Mendoza, M., Poblete, B., & Castillo, C. (2010). Twitter under crisis: Can we trust what we RT? *Proceedings of 1st Workshop on Social Media Anaalytics.*

Meusburger, P. (2008). The nexus of knowledge and space. *Clashes of Knowledge.* 34 – 90.

Michalko, M. (2006). *Thinkertoys: A Handbook of Creative-Thinking Techniques* Berkeley: The Speed Press.

Morin, R. (2014, July 2). Facebook's experiment causes a lot of fuss for little result. *Pew Research Center.* Retrieve from: http://www.pewresearch.org/fact-tank/2014/07/02/facebooks-experiment-is-just-the-latest-to-manipulate-you-in-the-name-of-research/

Morphological analysis. (2014, Aug. 7). Wikipedia. Retrieve from: http://en.wikipedia.org/wiki/Morphological_analysis_%28problem-solving%29

Mossberger, K., Wu, Y., & Crawford, J. (2013). Connecting citizens and local governments? Social media and interactivity in major U.S. cities. *Government Information Quarterly, 30*(4), 351–358. doi:10.1016/j.giq.2013.05.016

North, M. (2012). *Data Mining for the Masses.* A Global Text Project Book.

Olorunnisola, A. A., & Martin, B. L. (2013). Influences of Media on social movements: Problematizing hyperbolic inferences about impacts. *Telematics and Informatics, 30*(3), 275–288. doi:10.1016/j.tele.2012.02.005

Oxley, A. (2013). *Security Risks in Social Media Technologies: Safe Practices in Public Service Applications.* Oxford: Chandos Publishing. doi:10.1533/9781780633800

Palen, L. (2008). Online social media in crisis events. *EDUCAUSE Quarterly, 3,* 76–78.

Public Response to Alerts and Warnings using Social Media: Report of a Workshop on Current Knowledge and Research Gaps. (2013). *National Research Council of the National Academies.* Washington, D.C.: The National Academies Press.

Qian, X., Liu, X., Zheng, C., Du, Y., & Hou, X. (2013). Tagging photos using users' vocabularies. *Neurocomputing, 111,* 144–153. doi:10.1016/j.neucom.2012.12.021

Radio, E. (2014, Sept. 12). Web Data 101. *Proceedings of Digital Humanities Forum 2014. KU Institute for Digital Research in the Humanities.* University of Kansas. Lawrence, Kansas. https://idrh.ku.edu/dhforum2014

Ritchey, T. (2011). Modelling complex socio-technical systems using morphological analysis. *Swedish Morphological Society.* Retrieve from: http://www.swemorph.com/pdf/it-webart.pdf

Robertson, A., & Olson, S. (2013). *Sensing and shaping emerging conflicts: Report of a joint workshop of the National Academy of Engineering and the United States Institute of Peace: Roundtable on technology, science, and peacebuilding.* Washington, D.C.: The National Academies Press.

Rogers, R. (2013). Debanalizing Twitter: The transformation of an object of study. *Proceedings of Web-Sci'13,* Paris, France. (pp. 356–365).

Rohan, R. J. (2011). *Social networking, counterintelligence, and cyber counterintelligence. Utica College. Treadstone 71.* Whitepaper.

Rout, D., Preotiuc-Pietro, D., Bontcheva, K., & Cohn, T. (2013). Where's @wally? A classification approach to geolocating users based on their social ties. *Proceedings of 24*[th] *ACM Conference on Hypertext and Social Media.* Paris, France. (pp. 11–20).

Ryoo, K., & Moon, S. (2014). Inferring Twitter user locations with 10 km. accuracy. *Proceedings of the WWW '14 Companion,* Seoul, Korea. (pp. 643–648).

Schifferes, S., & Newman, N. (2013). Verifying news on the Social Web: Challenges and prospects. *Proceedings of WWW 2013 Companion,* Rio de Janeiro, Brazil. (pp. 875–878).

Schruben, L. (1983). Simulation modeling with event graphs. *Communications of the ACM, 26*(11), 957–963. doi:10.1145/182.358460

Seyranian, V. (2014). Social identity framing communication strategies for mobilizing social change. *The Leadership Quarterly, 25*(3), 468–486. doi:10.1016/j.leaqua.2013.10.013

Shahani, A. (2014, Aug. 27). Pew study: Facebook, Twitter users held back views on Snowden. *National Public Radio.* Retrieve from: http://www.npr.org/2014/08/27/343623178/pew-study-facebook-twitter-users-held-back-views-on-snowden

Shelton, T., Poorthuis, A., Graham, M., & Zook, M. (2014). Mapping the data shadows of Hurricane Sandy: Uncovering the sociospatial dimensions of big data. *Geoforum, 52,* 167–179. doi:10.1016/j.geoforum.2014.01.006

Singh, L. & Getoor, L. (2007). Increasing the predictive power of affiliation networks. *Bulletin of the IEEE Computer Society Technical Committee on Data Engineering.* (pp. 1–10).

Smith, A., Halstead, B., Esposito, L., & Schlegelmilch, J. (2013). Social media and virtual platforms. New Haven Health System Center Retrieve from: http://yalenewhavenhealth.org/emergency/PDFs/SocialMediaandVirtualPlatforms.pdf

Song, Y., Zhang, Y., Cao, J., tang, J., Gao, X., & Li, J. (2014). A unified geolocation framework for web videos. *ACM Transactions on Intelligent Systems and Technology.* 5(3), Article 49, 49: 1–49: 22.

Stafanidis, A., Crooks, A., & Radzikowski, J. (2013). Harvesting ambient geospatial information from social media feeds. *GeoJournal, 78*(2), 319–338. doi:10.1007/s10708-011-9438-2

Starbird, K., & Palen, L. (2013). Working & sustaining the virtual 'disaster desk.' *Proceedings of CSCW '13.* San Antonio, Texas. 491 – 502.

Stein, R. L. (2012). StateTube: Anthropological reflections on social media and the Israel state. *Anthropological Quarterly, 85*(3), 893–916. doi:10.1353/anq.2012.0045

Taleb, N. N. (2010). *The Black Swam: The Impact of the Highly Improbable* New York: Random House Books

Tool 13: Morphological box." (2013). In *EDIC Ecodesign Manual. Innovation and EcoDesign in the Ceramic Industry*. Retrieve from: http://www.adam-europe.eu/prj/5887/prd/1/4/Tool%2013_Morphological%20box.pdf

Tyshchuk, Y., & Wallace, W. (2013). The use of social media by local government in response to an extreme event. *Proceedings of 10th International ISCRAM Conference*, Baden-Baden, Germany. (pp. 802–811).

Wagner, W., Valencia, J., & Elejabarrieta, F. (1996). Relevance, discourse and the 'hot' stable core of social representations—A structural analysis of word associations. *The British Journal of Social Psychology*, *35*(3), 331–351. doi:10.1111/j.2044-8309.1996.tb01101.x

Watson, H., & Finn, R. L. (2013). Social media and the 2013 UK heat wave. *Proceedings of 11th International ISCRAM Conference,* University Park, Pennsylvania. (pp. 755–759).

Weimann, G. (2014). *New terrorism and new media*. Washington, D.C.: Woodrow Wilson Center for Scholars.

Wille, D. G. (2012). *Every soldier a messenger: Using social media in the contemporary operating environment. Monograph.* School of Advanced Military Studies.

Wilkinson, D., & Thelwall, M. (2012). Trending Twitter topics in English. *Journal of the Association for Information Science and Technology*, *63*(8), 1631–1646http://onlinelibrary.wiley.com/doi/10.1002/asi.22713/pdf. doi:10.1002/asi.22713

Wilson, C., Sala, A., Puttaswamy, K.P.N., & Zhao, B.Y. (2012). Beyond social graphs: User interactions in online social networks and their implications. *ACM Transactions on the Web:* 6(4), Article 17, 17:1–17:31.

Wilson, M. W. (2012). Location-based services, conspicuous mobility, and the location-aware future. *Geoforum*, *43*(6), 1266–1275. doi:10.1016/j.geoforum.2012.03.014

Wing, B. P., & Baldridge, J. (2011). Simple supervised document geolocation with geodesic grids. *Proceedings of 49th Annual Meeting of the Association for Computational Linguistics*, Portland, Oregon. (pp. 955– 964).

Xie, K., Xia, C., Grinberg, N., Schwartz, R., & Naaman, M. (2013). Robust detection of hyper-local events from geotagged social media data. In the proceedings of MDMKDD '13, Chicago, Illinois. (pp. 1–9). doi:10.1145/2501217.2501219

Zhou, X., & Chen, L. (2014). Event detection over twitter social media streams. *The VLDB Journal*, *23*(3), 381–400. doi:10.1007/s00778-013-0320-3

ADDITIONAL READING

Hansen, D. L., Schneiderman, B., & Smith, M. A. (2011). *Analyzing Social Media Networks with NodeXL: Insights from a Connected World*. Boston: Elsevier.

KEY TERMS AND DEFINITIONS

Ad Hoc Event: An unplanned or improvised occurrence.

Animating: Giving life or energy.

Blogroll: A list of cited blogs by a blog author.

Broadcast: The dissemination of information to a wide audience.

Channel: A medium of communication.

Clustering: A grouping of similar things.

Content Analysis: A formal research method in the social sciences for studying texts, multimedia, and other information-bearing artifacts.

Content Networks: Groups of people who interact around multimedia contents such as slideshows, audio, video, imagery and other items.

Content-Sharing Sites: Social media platforms that enable users to share various types of multimedia files (still images, audio, video, slideshows, software, and other types of files).

Correlation Coefficient: A relatedness measure indicating as a number between -1 and +1 and representing the dependence of two variables or two datasets.

Crowd-Sourcing: The act of reaching out to the wider public in order to request information or advice or some other resource.

Dashboard: A dedicated digital panel through which people may interact to acquire certain types of information or services.

Deep Web (Hidden Web): Online content that is not part of the Surface Web and which is not generally accessible using standard search engines.

Discourse: Intercommunications around a particular topic.

Discriminant Analysis: The application of statistical analysis to categorize data into various often-exclusive groups.

Eventgraph: A depiction of an event based on a range of qualitative and quantitative data; "a specific genre of network graph that illustrates the structure of connections among people discussing an event via social media services like Twitter" (Hansen, Smith, & Schneiderman, 2011).

Fissure: A split (as between social groups).

Geolocation: The process of identifying the geolocation of a person or thing through digital information (such as from the Internet).

Hashtags (#): The hash or pound sign used in front of an alphanumeric sequence to indicate topic in shared microblogging conversations or related images or multimedia contents (across various websites and social media platforms).

Hidden Hands: A secret or unknown motivating cause.

Inference: A conclusion arrived at based on reasoning from evidence (for new insights).

Keywords: Selected words or concepts.

Listening Post: A space where electronic communications may be intercepted.

Microblogging: The sharing of brief and frequent text-based posts (and photos and short videos) to a microblogging social media platform.

Monitor: The continuous observation of particular features of the environment through a variety of means and equipment.

Motif census: The machine-counting of all the variations of motifs in a social network.

Motif Structure: The interrelationships between nodes that indicated structured relationships.

Narrowcast: The dissemination of information to a limited or defined audience (vs. the broader public).

Participatory Sensing: The capturing of sensor data from mobile devices used by a population for monitoring and awareness.

Point-of-View (POV): Perspective, worldview, and / or attitude.

Pseudo-Social Event: A created event with manufactured relevance in order to garner attention (extrapolated from Daniel J. Boorstin in *The Image: A Guide to Pseudo-events in America* (1961), as contrasted to a spontaneous event.

Scalable: Able to accommodate larger amounts of information, multiple events, or other types of size or scale.

Sensor: A device that measures a particular property.

Sentiment: Emotion, affect, or feeling; opinion, attitude; evaluation.

Social Event: A generally pre-planned meeting of people around shared interests.

Social Faultline: Potential fissures and points-of-disagreement between social groups.

Social Media Platform: Socio-technical platforms that enable people to create identities and interact through various types of interactivity: content sharing (of slideshows, photos, videos, audio, and other contents); social networking; microblogging; blogging; wikis; e-book and journal publications; tagging; fund-raising and other types of peer-to-peer endeavors.

Social Revolution: A major social re-organization.

Sousveillance: Recorded observation by participants from within an event or organization (vs. surveillance by authority); inverse surveillance from bottom-up.

Streamgraph: A data visualization that captures changes over time (such as of a dynamic event); a stacked area graph.

Toponym: A location or place name, often derived from a topographical or physical landscape feature.

Unsupervised Machine Learning: extraction of data structures from a pre-existing data set; non-predictive machine learning.

Valence (in a Psychological Sense): The direction (positive or negative) and strength of a belief, attitude, or emotion.

APPENDIX A

The Phoenix Checklist

- "Why is it necessary to solve the problem?
- What benefits will you gain by solving the problem?
- What is the unknown?
- What is it you don't yet understand?
- What is the information you have?
- What isn't the problem?
- Is the information sufficient? Or is it insufficient? Or redundant? Or contradictory?
- Should you draw a diagram of the problem? A figure?
- Where are the boundaries of the problem?
- Can you separate the various parts of the problem? Can you write them down? What are the relationships of the parts of the problem?
- What are the constants (things that can't be changed) of the problem?
- Have you seen this problem before?
- Have you seen this problem in a slightly different form?
- Do you know a related problem?
- Try to think of a familiar problem having the same or a similar unknown.
- Suppose you find a problem related to yours that has already been solved. Can you use it? Can you use its method?
- Can you restate your problem? How many different ways can you restate it? More general? More specific? Can the rules be changed?
- What are the best, worst, and most probable cases you can imagine?" (Michalko, 2006/1991, pp. 139 – 140)

Chapter 3
Eavesdropping on Narrowcast Self–talk and Microchats on Twitter

Shalin Hai-Jew
Kansas State University, USA

ABSTRACT

On Twitter, a range of discourse networks may be extracted showing different types of conversational interactions. While the attention is often on what is trending and large-size high-interactive social graphs, many extracted networks are self-loops and small-group discourse networks based on ad hoc narrowcast conversations. In this exploratory study of microblogging messaging on Twitter, the focus is on micro-blogging conversations that result in self-loops (self-to-self conversations, individuals microblogging to themselves) and small-group graphs and motifs (one-to-few or few-to-few conversations). This work proposes and tests hypotheses about the various types of seeding #hashtags and keywords that result in different types of ad hoc microblogging microchat network graphs on Twitter.

INTRODUCTION

The popularization of social media platforms came with widely expressed hopes for global-scale real-time informational awareness and pro-social mass-collaborations. The participation of large swaths of the world's people in crowd-sourcing information and interacting on social media has further enabled the extraction of "big data" for novel research and insights. Twitter, one of the world's largest microblogging sites (with 500 million users as of late 2014), is one of the most popular platforms. On their site, they list 288 million monthly active users, with 500 million Tweets (messages) sent daily. Some 77% of social media accounts are outside the U.S., and the platform has support for 35 languages ("About Twitter," 2015). The U.S. Library of Congress has stepped forward to archive all Tweets ("Library of Congress…" Jan. 22, 2013). The popularization of Twitter, now in its 8th year, is impressive. Many have built this "SMS of the Internet" ("short message service of the Internet") into daily lives, work flows, law enforcement, government planning, marketing, and a range of applications.

DOI: 10.4018/978-1-4666-8696-0.ch003

Messages on Twitter are limited to 140 characters but may include images, video, audio, and URLs (uniform resource locators). In the grammar of the tool, user accounts are listed @name, which may be used in "reply," "retweet," and "mentions". Messages may be favorite-d or "liked". Messaging may be made public or private. Conversations based on particular themes may be labeled with #hashtags, some of which are disambiguated and unique, and others which are generic. In real-world use, hashtags may denote tone or context. They may be used to indicate the particular use of language, as a linguistic marker (#sarcasm, #humor, or #irony); "hashtags are the digital extra-linguistic equivalent of non-verbal expressions that people employ in live interaction when conveying sarcasm" (Kunneman, Liebrecht, van Mulken, & van den Bosch, 2014, p. 1). Other types of related conversations may be identified through the use of keywords, for various keyword-word-sense uses (for multiple theme captures). Interactions around shared information may be understood as Twitter discourse or conversations, what some have termed "conversation-like," because of the constraints of the 140 characters and the designed structure of Twitter. For many, there is challenge tracking interactions and a sense of partial or truncated messaging. There is a sense of missing contextual detail. (The sparse and minimalist approach of Twitter messaging has encouraged a range of spin-off practices, such as thumb-typed "novels" from mobile devices, 140-character tiny Twitter recipes, and other types of brevity.)

Twitter Inc. makes much of its data usable for research and user self-awareness. Publicly-available account information, the messaging, and various types of interactivity may be captured through data extractions through Twitter's application programming interfaces (APIs).

Twitter offers two application programming interfaces (APIs) for collecting tweets: one is the search API, which may be used to retrieve past tweets matching a user specified criteria; the other is the streaming API, which may be used to subscribe to a continuing live stream of new tweets matching a user defined criteria and delivered to the user as soon as they become available. Researchers need not define any specific criteria to receive data from the streaming API. They can receive a (free) 1% sample of everything posted each day, as it is posted (Burnap, Rana, Avis, Williams, Houseley, Edwards, Morgan, & Sloan, 2013, p. 3).

A number of software tools have been created that tap Twitter's APIs. What this means is that, theoretically and practically, every node and network is theoretically highly visible. (This assumes the inclusion of the commercial company and its tools and resources. This company has access to the full databases of Twitter for full data extractions. Publicly available and non-commercial API data extractions are rate-limited and are also content-limited.) There is a lot of information available even given the limits of human attention. With the application of automated data extractions (based on much more expansive machine attention), machine-based text summarization, text frequency counts, and text searches, the capabilities of datamining from the Twitter corpus is enormous and can extend what is knowable.

While some initially saw the brevity requirement of Twitter messages as a negative because of the challenges to conveying complex information, others see the character limits as a barrier-lowering function to encourage people to share (Eyal & Hoover, 2014, p. 70). The ethos of the platform is to provide near-constant status updates to friends, family, and other followers. This sense of over-sharing at the local level may be harnessed as a public good.

Social media accounts on Twitter may be powered by humans, groups, cyborgs (humans and machines), robots, or sensors. For so-called human sensor networks to work, the people within those ad hoc networks have to be constantly capturing and sharing out information, signaling, if you will. By definition, a node in a network may not fully know the larger context, but a node may be at a particular important location at a particular time and may be the one that may capture relevant information that may stream out to others. Sometimes, it is only during an event—based on expert eyes—that information may take on special value, or it may be post-event and in the perspective of historians and analysts that information is seen to be critical. Status updates have relevance. The widespread use of mobile devices has enabled even more Tweeting, with various straight-to-Twitter apps from thumb-typing, voice-to-text, photo and video captures, and other modes of impulse-enhanced quick-sharing.

Compared to some types of social media platforms, the messaging on Twitter is highly volatile, fading in a few hours for most trending issues (which tend to be spiky or bursty and dissipating based on time series analyses). There are different time scales of different types of contents on the Web and Internet (Yang & Leskovec, 2011); for example, by contrast, imagery and videos may be shared on content sharing sites and remain for years. While Twitter messaging has fast entropy, that is not to say that the messages ever fully disappear (even as people turn their attention to other things). The messages are also recorded at the company, and some of this data is made broadly available (while historical data will require access through commercial entities that have commercial access to historical Twitter data). Indeed, there are a number of ways to extract data from Twitter's application programming interfaces (APIs)—with one enabling real-time (synchronic) and dynamic extractions and another enabling the extraction of more static data (such as recent microblogged messages from the past week, social media account relationships, location-based messaging, and others). Data from Twitter may be extracted based on a wide range of queries, such as based on particular accounts, groups, #hashtag or keywords, and others. The information provided is done in a rate-limited fashion, which lowers the speed at which information may be captured. The Twitter API requires white listing for access. The affordances of this Twitter access change in part based on the software used to extract the data, the speed of connectivity via the Internet, and other factors. Social media researchers have been advocating for social media vendors' application programming interfaces (APIs) to release more information about how complete the extracted data is as a percentage of the full set, which is not currently available. There is also a need for comparability across research studies of social media based on standard methodologies and technologies (Black, Mascaro, Gallagher, & Goggins, 2012, p. 229).

To summarize broadly, the research literature includes a wide range of studies on social media. People who are sharing information on various social media platforms are conceptualized as part of a sensor network for nascent and unfolding events (mapped as "eventgraphs"), natural disasters, and other emergencies. There is research on the uses of social media for digital governance and bringing citizens closer to their elected leaders. Some researchers have looked at social media as tools to create social change, including social revolutions. From a security angle, some are researching ways to identify potential astroturfing, fraudulently created and maintained (including social bot) accounts, and other manipulations. Computer scientists and linguists have partnered to create automated sentiment analysis systems to monitor social media in real time. Psychologists have worked on various models for profiling individuals remotely (from a distance) based on their messaging on social media accounts and other online residual digital traces. In both physical and virtual environments, people leave a "behavioral residue" based on their respective personalities (Qiu, Lin, Ramsay, & Yang, 2012, p. 710), even in a context of zero-acquaintance. Using linguistic cues, individuals "could accurately judge the Big Five personality traits of unknown others" (Holleran & Mehl, 2008, as cited in Qiu, Lin, Ramsay, & Yang, 2012, p. 711). Researchers have found that microblogged messages contain "valid linguistic cues to personality". Further, the researchers write:

Our study also identified some novel associations which may indicate the presence of other valid linguistic cues to personality. For example, extraversion was found to be negatively correlated with function words and positively correlated with assent words. Agreeableness was associated with use of fewer exclusive and sexual words (Qiu, Lin, Ramsay, & Yang, 2012, p. 715).

In terms of extracted data about individuals from other social media platforms, researchers found that only a handful of publicly available data points could be insightfully (and even intrusively) revelatory about an individual's personality, with computer programs optimizing cue utilization better than the target individual's family and friends whose subjectivity often led to suboptimal cue use; sometimes, the computer programs employing machine learning interpreted the individual's personality more astutely than even the target individual (Youyou, Kosinski, & Stillwell, 2014, p. 1). This is critical since personality "is a key driver behind people's interactions, behaviors, and emotions" (Youyou, Kosinski, & Stillwell, 2014, p. 1). The particular research study involved the self-ratings from 86,220 volunteers who also had Facebook pages. The survey results were used to measure five personality traits: openness, conscientiousness, extraversion, agreeableness and neuroticism. The measuring of "likes" of an individual was highly revelatory:

With enough information, the computer predictions more closely matched self reports than did those of friends and family. Based on just 10 likes, the computer model outperformed work colleagues. With a sample of 70 likes, it did better than friends or roommates. With 150, better than family members. Spouses stood out as being the toughest to beat but 300 likes was enough for the computer to match how well they knew their own better halves (Schupak, 2015).

Selective and high-concentrated text may be revelatory in ways that may be more telling than if larger amounts of information were brought into the analysis. (Excess information often involves the inclusion of noise, which can mask the signal. For efficiency and parsimony, it is important to identify the indicators that may offer the clearest signals.)

Much of the social media research has been based on Twitter. In 2010, researchers summarized the emerging use of Twitter as "social practice," including the following: "citizen journalism, political activism, maintaining a fan-base, event back-channel, corporate advertising, service marketing, crowd-sourcing, informal social-networking, and ambient sociability" (Gillen & Merchant, 2013, pp. 55 – 56); this research team went on to conduct a "dual auto-ethnography" based on a year of using Twitter as a "social, linguistic practice" (Gillen & Merchant, 2013, p. 48). If email networks are seen as strong tie networks based on one-on-one relationships and reciprocal interactivity in many cases, the ties in Twitter tend to be weak tie networks which do not necessarily build social capital (Stephens & Poorthuis, 2014, p. 1). Do Twitter social networks have a spatial proximity component that may reflect some real-world aspects? Indeed, as with other social media platforms, the online space does reflect some on-ground realities (or socio-spatial relationships):

Takhteyev, Wellman and Gruz (2012) found that 39% of Twitter ties are shorter than 100 km (roughly the size of a metropolitan area), and both national boundaries and language ties are significant in limiting the ties formed on Twitter. Often, the ties that do form across boundaries and long distances replicate airline ties between cities, economic ties, and migration patterns. Additionally, they discovered that ties at distances of up to 1000 km are more frequent than would be expected from random ties, while ties at distances larger than 5000 km are underrepresented. In short, Twitter networks are shaped in part by geographical constraints (Stephens & Poorthuis, 2014, p. 3).

The authors also found that smaller networks were more socially clustered and extended over smaller physical distances; larger networks had less social clustering and were more physically dispersed (Stephens & Poorthuis, 2014, p. 1). Geographical proximity is often a stand-in indicator for shared backgrounds and cultures, and it is one variable in people's homophilous connectivity through social networks. Online networks partially reflect the human relationships in physical space; the "partially" is used as a qualifier here because the electronic networks reflect aspects of real-world relationships, exaggerating some aspects and not others. Interrelationships are not costless, and people create relationships in an assortative or preferential way. This is so even in online networks, even though the apparent cost of a "like" or a "follow" seems minimal. Each communications act online does entail some cost because each decision reflects on the individual and his or her reputation, and each "follow" means receiving a spate of messages that have to be processed (or at minimum ignored)—in a tight attentional economy.

Many who use social media may not be aware of the nature of their social networks, or those with whom they are interacting. This information about who they are interacting with, who they are following, and who is following them, may be latent or hidden. In part, this is because such networks are constantly changing. Information about following-follower relationships, while recorded on the main Twitter page for the account, does not show the actual direct membership or the amount of interactivity; for these types of information, additional tools are needed. The platform itself enables plenty of one-sided relationships with one node subscribing to (following) others without necessarily being followed reciprocally. Said another way, the single node may follow or reply to itself (self-loop), it may follow and interact with a few (small-group), it may follow others who do not reciprocate, or it may be followed by many with whom the single node does not directly reciprocate (single-to-many), or some combination of these relationships.

Likewise, blogs show extreme variability in the choice of topics for posts. It has been suggested that the only macrogoal that is universally relevant to all the blog posts (and, indeed, microblogging updates) is the blogger him- or herself (Puschmann, 2009, as cited in Dayter, 2014, p. 93).

It makes intuitive sense that any individual entity has some interest in what is communicated, no matter what the structure of the information recipient network is. Also, any who microblog is communicating with a possibly unknown audience. For one team, this lack of awareness creates a "context collapse" for information diffusion. One research team writes: "Unlike other forms of social media, only 22% of Twitter relationships are reciprocal. This creates an environment of "context collapse" in which a user has multiple audiences for their tweets, and the user may not be aware of who is in those audiences. As a result of this asymmetric network structure, information diffusion is significantly different on Twitter than in social networking platforms that have symmetric relationships" (Black, Mascaro, Gallagher, & Goggins, 2012, p. 230). A majority of human users of Twitter interact with socialbots on that platform as if they were humans, and they friend such robots from an average acceptance rate of 59.1% to some 80% (Wagner, Mitter, Körner, & Strohmaier, 2012, p. 41). In a sense, Twitter is not a space for intimates but for individuals with public relationships and connecting also with strangers with parasocial relationships.

Influence or "network centrality" on social media. In terms of studies of influence on Twitter, multiple researchers have pointed to the 80-20 rule, also known as the Pareto principle or "the law of the vital few," which suggests that 80% of the effects come from 20% of the causes, or that a few have an outsized effect in most contexts. Online activist campaigns tend to be driven by "a relatively small number of highly-active politically engaged users" (Bastos, Puschmann, & Travitzki, 2013, p. 164). What this means that is the identification of the high-influential nodes (individuals / agents, or groups) in a network will enable a high level of effect if that node may be recruited, turned, or influenced. (Social networks have been a part of sociological analysis for over a hundred years, but the recent use of electronic social network analysis based on the information from social media platforms has been around for only the past few decades.) The research literature is fairly robust in the types of information that may be inferred from structure mining online social networks. One area involves examining how network structures create efficiencies for information sharing. Social media users who are "popular, active, and influential" create "traffic-based shortcuts" that enable efficiencies for information diffusion through networks (Weng, Ratkiewicz, Perra, Goncalves, Castillo, Bonchi, Schifanella, Menczer, & Flammini, 2013, p. 1).

Early meta-scale narratives about electronic social networks were about mass coordination and virality—catalysts (whether messages, people, or events) which could spark informational and reactional (behavioral) cascades with outsized magnifier effects from the technological connectivity. There has been focus on predictive analytics, such as attempting to use as few indicators as possible to attain some analytical insight. In ensuing years, the narrative has changed, and the thinking now is that such virality is actually fairly difficult to spark, and fairly difficult to maintain. In a sense, what goes viral has a lot to do with the network structure of a human network and the early adoption of a meme by high-influence nodes outside of localized and bounded groups that tend to "trap" information; a researcher has identified ways to predict the popularity of #hashtagged messaging within the first 30-50 Tweets to predict the overall trajectory with fairly high accuracy (Weng, June 2013). An underlying concept is that the transmission of ideas between people is not based on a simple contagion (such as some disease models where direct exposure can lead to infection) but on more complex contagion because of human dynamics such as "social reinforcement" and "homophilous" connectivity. The diverse positions of early adopters in the social network is "a strong indicator of larger cascades" (Weng, Menczer, & Ahn, 2014, p.3) and even "long-range diffusion" (p. 4). No matter how popular a trending issue, the general trajectory captures the rise in popularity and then some holding pattern for the popularity and then sunsetting (because of the nature of human attention dynamics and their eventual forgetting). There have been increasing numbers of studies on unique case applications of such research methods and related technologies.

At a macro level, popular graphs may be based on topics of mass interest (entertainment, media stars, popular culture, sports, news, weather events, and other topics); these are phenomena which concentrate human focus and attention with high intensity for a particular period of time. Such events are known as "bursty" or "spiky" ones because they register as activity peaks (on line graphs drawn by monitoring systems using time series analysis). The more typical baseline on microblogging sites would seem to be states of more diffuse focus and attention on the mundane. The norm would seem to be people engaging in their everyday lives, but still signaling via social media based on the culture of near-constant status updates. Some social media platforms were designed to create habituated usage of a particular service in people by triggering the user through external or internal stimuli, encouraging actions, providing variable rewards, and encouraging people to invest in their platforms as part of a four-part cycle (Eyal &

Hoover, 2014, p. 6). One habit-forming aspect of a social media platform involves its delivery of variable rewards (surprises) and the fulfilling of emotional needs (such as for social affirmation), both of which are often provided for by other people interacting on the social media platforms.

In this chapter, the focus will be on the ad hoc and planned conversations on Twitter that are labeled by #hashtags or keywords; the focus will be on the resulting types of small-scale graphs: (1) Twitter users who message in self-loops (self-talk) and (2) those who communicate in small groups about particular topics. The focus will be on some of the quieter talk, which is less visible but much more pervasive than the hyper trending events or messaging. The idea is that value is not only in the popular spaces but on quieter musings and less high-attention conversation spaces. The hypotheses tested include initial ideas of what "seeding" hashtags and what keywords may be used to seed these two types of network patterns. Then, too, there will be initial observations of self-loop and small-group dynamics and possibly what may be knowable from such networks on microblogging ("nanoblogging") sites, like Twitter. Currently, there is little in the way of research in the self-talking-to-self via mediated means.

The research ethics of "eavesdropping" on social media. There has been wide discussion of the ethics of using social media data for research, with some advocating going through the institutional review board (IRB) process for human subjects review and others suggesting that such due diligence is not absolutely necessary. In this case, the information used was all public channel information that is widely publicly available and broadly used in research. Effort was made to avoid linking particular information to an individual person (or any personally identifiable information or "PII"). Most of the information here is provided in a fairly generic way (with many entities not labeled in the visual graphs). This approach may be excessive and ultimately unnecessary especially as more such research is published and contributes to a change in understandings and norms.

Delimitations. This chapter focuses on individual-node self-looped self-talk and also on narrowcast small-group conversations on Twitter. The derived hypotheses are based on two years of social media data extractions and analysis research using Network Overview, Discovery and Exploration for Excel (NodeXL), several years with Maltego Radium / Tungsten / Carbon (albeit only a few months with the Tweet Analyzer "machine"), and several years with NCapture of NVivo 10. In terms of testing out the hypotheses, though, there were only a few actual test runs of data extractions for this exploratory chapter. The hope is that others will advance this preliminary work. A node may have some self-looping on a topic *and* connections to other loops at the same time, so the "self-looping" phenomena is not mutually exclusive to other connections. The type of self-looping that this chapter addresses though suggests a kind of individual-node self-looping related to a particular topical discussion (as indicated by #hashtags or keywords).

REVIEW OF THE LITERATURE

In this time of the Social Web (or Web 2.0), people go online for various instrumental purposes. They socialize, collaborate around shared interests or projects, share knowledge on open-source encyclopedias, share code, promote their careers, fund-raise, buy and sell goods and services, and generally pursue their respective interests. Based on the rational actor approach, people go through a cost-benefit consideration before deciding to engage with social media, and they consider the calculus of cost-benefits every so often in terms of the needs that are being met by their engagement on such sites, or their "social media diet" (Bowman, Westerman, & Claus, 2012, p. 2298). Researchers found that different groups had varying perceptions of the cognitive load required to engage with social networking platforms.

Across conditions, perceived self-efficacy was negatively associated with perceived task load and positively associated with goal attainment, and goal attainment was a significant correlate of increased social media usage. Interpreted, we see that a transparent technology such as Facebook has no cognitive costs associated with its use, while an opaque technology such as Twitter seems to have a salient cognitive cost element. Further, we found that older users of Facebook were more likely to judge the channel as more cognitively demanding and themselves as having lower self-efficacy in using it.

Finally, results indicated that for both Facebook and Twitter, males perceived both channels as more cognitively demanding than females. Theoretical and practical explanations and applications for these findings are presented (Bowman, Westerman, & Claus, 2012, p. 2298).

For some, they decided to step away from their use of social media when the effort to engage was more than they wanted for a "digital detox." In a research project about users who Tweeted that they wanted to step away from microblogging for Lent (in a general sense), one researcher found "hedging patterns" about the withdrawal from Twitter and a general lack of a clear rationale for the stepping away. Complementary interviews were conducted of those planning to step back as a form of self-restriction: "Our interview participants felt they were spending too much time on social media, or it was costing them time that could have been spent doing something else, but their understanding of these trade-offs was vague" (Schoenebeck, 2014, p. 779).

Self-talk on a microblogging site. So why would individuals who are on a wildly public site use that to self-talk (defined broadly)? A simple explanation could be that talking-to-the-self is a part of human communications, an externalization of mental processing and self-organizing through thoughts. This approach would suggest that people bring their physical lives into the cyber realm.

In part, many who use Twitter have habituated to taking their communications to that shared space. This behavior has been popularized as "oversharing"—and for a time was labeled as "TMI" (too much information). Researchers have linked participation on social media sites with a general likelihood to be open to sharing information via polls:

So, if a respondent had a MySpace or a Twitter account, they were more likely to share their opinion via sponsored poll. If the respondent had both a MySpace and Twitter account, they were even more likely. An account on Facebook had no effect on openness to sharing opinion via a poll. In all cases, though, the more social media accounts, the more willingness to share opinions (Jansen, Sobel, & Cook, 2010, p. 3857).

Also, sometimes Tweets are responded to by peers, making the conversation not a self-loop but an actual interaction. In a sense, all Tweets are initially a kind of self-talk unless others also respond, unless the initial communication was a response to someone else.

Another construal may be that going public with a particular goal or approach is a kind of "costly signaling" for the individual. Participation in particular online social networks may well indicate an increased likelihood of acting on expressed opinions (Jansen, Sobel, & Cook, 2010, p. 3853). A public commitment to stay with a diet or an exercise plan or a new year's resolution may be seen as more believable than a private conviction and may indicate improved follow-through. Tweeted expressions of solidarity with a particular political campaign or stance may encourage future political action. For some, Tweeting ideas to the self may be a form of speaking to the universe, to use a common colloquialism.

Another explanation is that such self-talk may be a kind of #selfie to the world, an expression of the communicator's identity and expression of self-worth, a projection of value to the world. Social media sometimes may be seen as a mirror of the self, enhancing self-awareness, and in this space, people are all performing socially and communicating their senses of themselves to others (and back to themselves)—as in a digital mirror (or Narcissus admiring his externalized reflection). In this sense, self-expressions are not only expressions seeking external affirmations from others but possibly also from the self. The messages of media may be reinforcing, supporting the original impetus for the expression, or they may be cathartic, dissipating the emotion and force behind the expressions. There are many roles for talk and self-expression in people's lives.

Another possible understanding is that people go online to achieve a wide range of goals on Twitter, or as one researcher put it, "The interactional goals of Twitter users are notoriously hard to pin down" (Dayter, 2014, p. 93). In terms of mixed intentionality, Tweeting out self-talk on Twitter may be similar to a person talking loudly on himself or herself in a public space (or talking loudly into a cell phone in a public space). Or maybe the analogy is the slipping of #whispers and #secrets through the electronic grapevine, maybe through "drunk-tweeting." There are simultaneous intended audiences. For some, there may be a *frisson* of excitement at the thought that others care and are watching on Twitter.

Further, why would people go to a mass open space to carry on small-group conversations (in 140-characters, no less)? The real-world-to-cyber does not translate so easily because when people meet in small groups socially, the only others who can generally hear them communicating are those who are sufficiently near (and who are reciprocally seeable and hearable). In the real world, such engagements involve near-field communications, of sorts. On Twitter, small group conversations are generally non-private. These social networks are represented then as graphs with small clusters of interactants or small-scale motifs (dyads, triads, and so on).

Another reason could be that the conversations are seen as potentially valuable to a broader public and therefore should be conducted on a public space. Or it may be that the communicators intended the conversations to broaden out and include many, but there were not many others interested in that particular slice-in-time (or that particular period when the social networks were being extracted from Twitter).

Finally, in both the self-loop and the small group contexts, there is a potential for unintended data leakage and unintended sharing because of the technological capability of eavesdropping. While Tweets may feel like fast-changing ephemera, the messages never actually disappear, and they are eminently recoverable; they are part of extensive electronic memory. The data on Twitter may be used to profile accounts, to show inter-relationships, and other types of data mining. The data access affordances of the social media platforms may enable clashes of intentionality and the introduction of malicious use of such information.

The idea of self-talk on a microblogging site (expressed as a "self-loop" in a network analysis graph) aligns with various speech acts. Some go online to post questions, to help themselves ruminate, sometimes as much as trying to crowd-source an answer. Others post concepts in foreign languages in order to practice. One common type of self-talk in social networking spaces is self-praise. Self-praise is a special kind of speech act that is face-enhancing publicly but also potentially empowering internally. One study of self-praise in microblogging among a community of ballet dancers is richly informative:

Self-praise is a speech act that involves uttering a positive statement about oneself, and can thus be seen as a face-enhancing act directed at the speaker. At the same time, it is non-supportive to the hearer, and the assumption in the literature has been so far that self-praise is an interactionally delicate activity.

The present study investigates the pragmatic strategies of self-praise performance in microblogging posts by ballet students. This group of users is seen as a community of practice engaged in the construction of a 'hero' identity, i.e. an image of a professional dancer who possesses necessary physical and sociolinguistic competence. Appropriateness of self-praise is contingent on the community of practice; self-praise centred around ballet-related attributes appears to be the norm in this community. Four attenuation strategies emerged in the data: self-praise plus disclaimer, self-praise plus shift of focus, self-praise plus self-denigration, and self-praise plus reference to hard work. Finally, self-enhancement on Twitter may be performed indirectly, by framing the speech act of self-praise as a third party complaint (Dayter, 2014, p. 91).

Even beyond the intricacies of the research case, generally speaking, on Twitter, bragging is a common speech act. In some cases, at least to the self, it may involve self-heroizing to create courage for a particular risk or activity. However, to the broader audience, bragging may be perceived as a social put-down and may then be annoying. As researchers have noted, some cultures engage much more in bragging as accepted behavior while it is inappropriate in other social contexts. In "bounded" communities, there are shared understandings which may help translate for intentions (Dayter, 2014, p. 93). Bragging through microblogging is not without risk. Individuals are putting an assertion out in the world that may be questioned and challenged by others—in a public sphere. While there is capacity for individuals to self-Tweet and to communicate in small groups, and while there is very much an underpinning of narcissism and ego in the #selfie aspects of social media culture, there is also a countervailing push against excessive self-indulgence. People online may be quite quick in putting down others who may be seen as too self-promoting or dishonest or suspicious. Several recent examples of ego-deflating approaches involve the mention of the "humble brag" (the phenomena of people pretending to be humble while bragging about themselves) and then the "selfie stick," a device used to hold a mobile phone from a sufficient distance to take a photo in order to share and show off. Indeed, there are many types of social regulation and norming of people's behaviors online.

EXPLORING SELF-LOOPED AND NARROW-CAST SMALL-SCALE MESSAGING ON TWITTER

At any one time, there are numerous conversations for whom individuals may engage in as an elicitation to conversation that goes unanswered. At any one time, there are all sorts of self-talk that, collected as a text and / or multimedia corpus, may be revelatory of the individuals (and groups, robots, and "cyborgs") behind particular social media accounts. And finally, at any one time, there are microblogged conversations that are narrowcast among a small group of nodes (in a subcluster); in these messages, the audience is not the broad public but a select small group. This is so even though Twitter is a very open and non-exclusionary structure, with a wide range of enablements and affordances. If the 80-20 rule and power law apply to social media, and there are research accounts that suggest this, then the popular accounts and trending topics make up the bulk of the high-octane messaging on Twitter, but there is a long tail of self-talk and small-group conversations as well.

Light Study Design and Early Graph Samples

This computational experiment is based on the extraction of social networks from Twitter based on the participation of various entities in Twitter discussions based on shared #hashtags or keywords. Figure 1 provides an overview of the general workflow sequence.

A recent site that follows "trending" hashtagged conversations identified <#win> as a trending hashtag. A data extraction was conducted using the freeware tool Network Overview, Discovery, and Exploration for Excel (NodeXL), an add-on to Microsoft Excel. The resulting network of Twitter accounts that had recently communicated using #win in a recent message consisted of 6,892 vertices and 18,605 unique edges, with 1,369 self-loops. There were 364 single-vertex connected components (isolates) in this network. There were also 755 groups. The largest connect component has 5,388 vertices. The maximum number of edges in a connected component was 23,666, indicating the level of interactivity (based on relational ties). The network graph itself had a diameter of 17, the maximum geodesic distance. The average distance between any two nodes of the network was 5.42 nodes for the path. These details may be seen in Table 1.

The data visualization from the underlying data, using the Fruchterman-Reingold Force-Based Layout Algorithm, shows some popular clusters (based on nodes with shared shapes and colors in linked prox-

Figure 1. Process of capturing ad hoc Twitter discourse networks

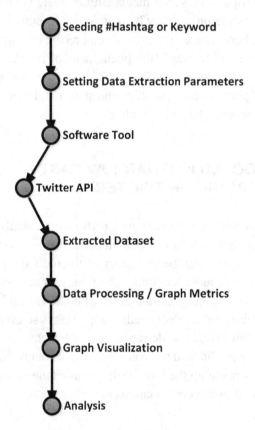

Seeding #Hashtag or Keyword

Setting Data Extraction Parameters

Software Tool

Twitter API

Extracted Dataset

Data Processing / Graph Metrics

Graph Visualization

Analysis

Table 1. Graph metrics table for the #win hashtag discourse network on Twitter

Graph Metric	Value
Graph Type	Directed
Vertices	6892
Unique Edges	18605
Edges With Duplicates	6904
Total Edges	25509
Self-Loops	1369
Reciprocated Vertex Pair Ratio	0.003547847
Reciprocated Edge Ratio	0.007070608
Connected Components	691
Single-Vertex Connected Components	364
Maximum Vertices in a Connected Component	5388
Maximum Edges in a Connected Component	23666
Maximum Geodesic Distance (Diameter)	17
Average Geodesic Distance	5.429962
Graph Density	0.000428823
Modularity	Not Applicable
NodeXL Version	1.0.1.334

imity) and a number of smaller connected components (mostly on the periphery). As a trending term, <#win> resonates across a range of connected networks, small groups, and individual nodes.

Table 2 shows the graph metrics for the #fracking Twitter discourse.

Figure 3 shows a graph visualization of a "network" of those who recently Tweeted #fracking. This network consists of 9,345 vertices, 0 unique edges, a maximum of one vertex in terms of connected components, and a graph density of 0. The number of groups is 9,345 groups, and there is not a link between them. This visualization shows overlapping two-dimensional fields of unrelated nodes (using the Harel-Koren Fast Multiscale layout algorithm) except that these social media accounts all recently (in the past week of the data extraction) communicated using "#fracking."

This work is conceptualized as an exploratory work to better gain insights on the "talking to the self" phenomena on the microblogging site, Twitter, and to understand narrowcast microchats with very small communities. Are there any identifiable patterns? Words that may elicit more such talking-to-self

Figure 2. #win hashtag network graph on twitter (Fruchterman-Reingold force-based layout algorithm)

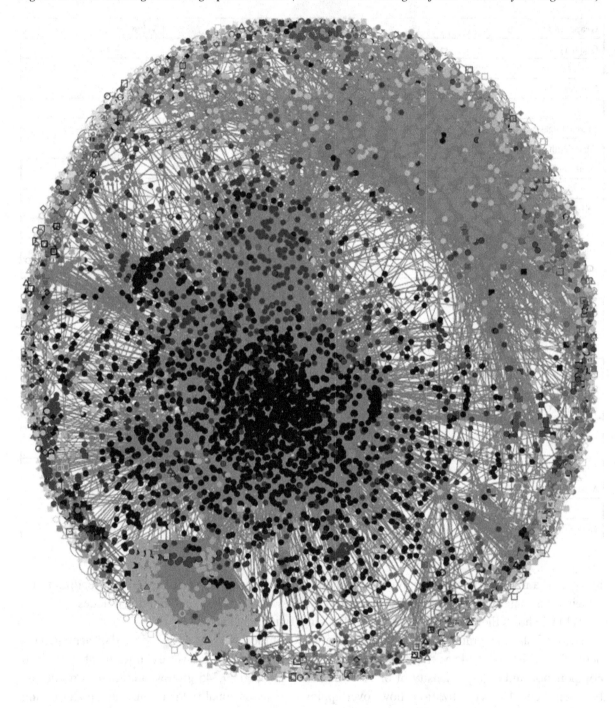

Table 2. Graph metrics table of #fracking network on Twitter

Graph Metric	Value
Graph Type	Directed
Vertices	9345
Unique Edges	0
Edges With Duplicates	0
Total Edges	0
Self-Loops	0
Reciprocated Vertex Pair Ratio	Not Applicable
Reciprocated Edge Ratio	Not Applicable
Connected Components	9345
Single-Vertex Connected Components	9345
Maximum Vertices in a Connected Component	1
Maximum Edges in a Connected Component	0
Maximum Geodesic Distance (Diameter)	Not Applicable
Average Geodesic Distance	Not Applicable
Graph Density	0
Modularity	Not Applicable
NodeXL Version	1.0.1.334

patterns and non-linkage? Larger-size networks without links? Communications-based networks with small clusters of communicators and limited larger clusters? Figure 4 shows just such a network with a few interconnected smaller clusters but a mass of those just Tweeting among themselves or very small motif-based linkages.

Figure 5 shows a different network with a larger predominance of self-loops and small networks.

Different graphs may have different mixed of types of social connections. Another graph visualization that shows the many smaller conversationalists participating in a #hashtag conversation is Figure 6, which shows the lesser-connected components in the large field of small ties below the more condensed larger clusters above. Those nods below show various Twitter accounts with individual entities communicating among themselves.

Another way to seed a data extraction for *ad hoc* discourses on Twitter is to combine hashtags or to offer long phrases. In this example, two hashtags--#sweet #nothing—was used to extract a network on Twitter. This social graph consisted of eight nodes, within which there was only one connected component (consisting of three nodes).

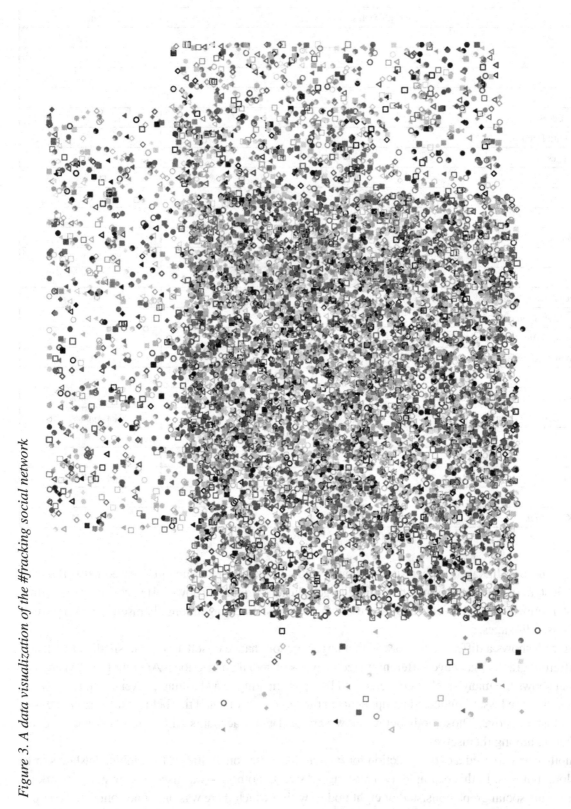

Figure 3. A data visualization of the #ffracking social network

Figure 4. A large cluster of low-node social media accounts (in the red box)

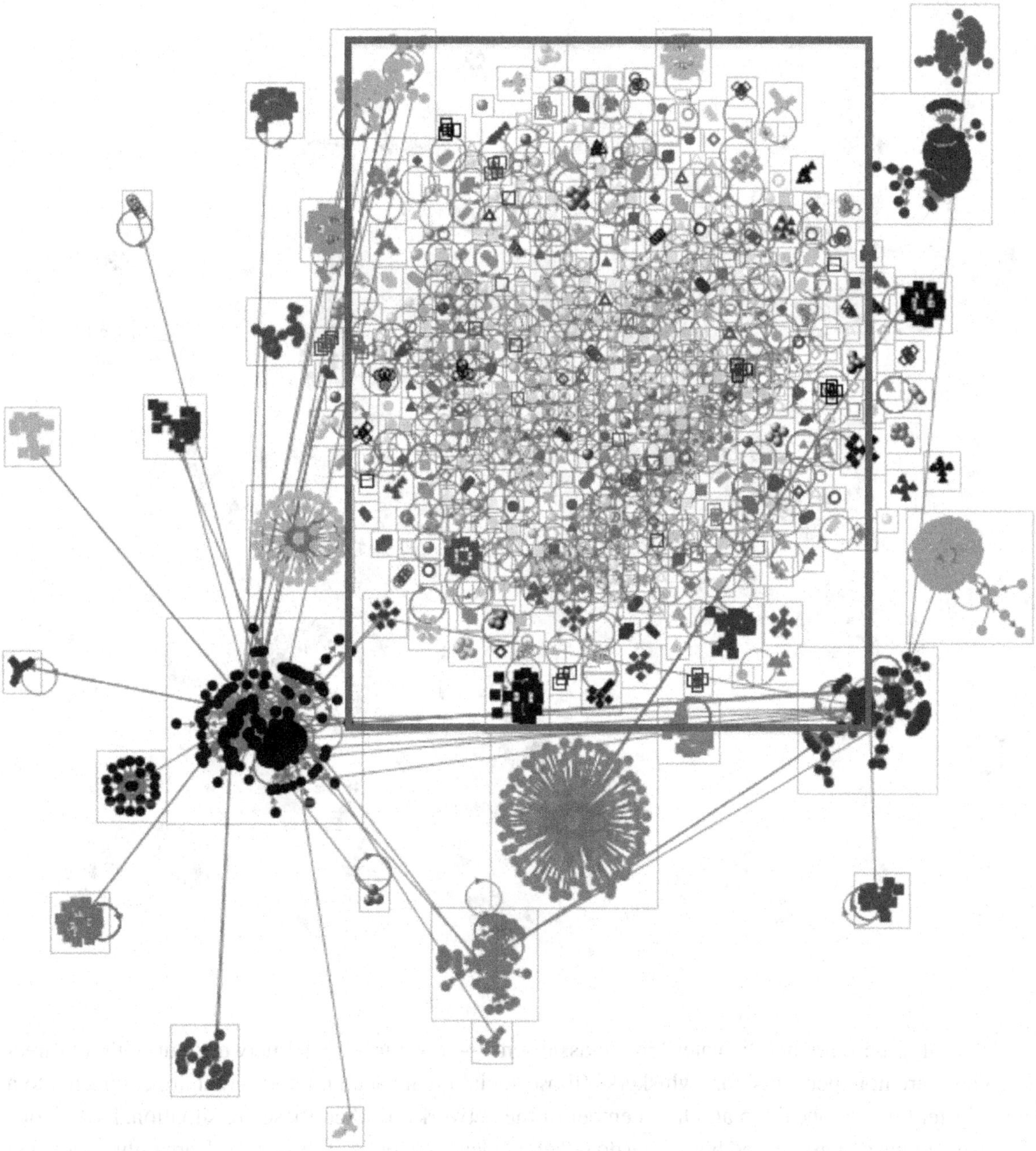

Figure 5. #fair hashtag network on Twitter (basic network)

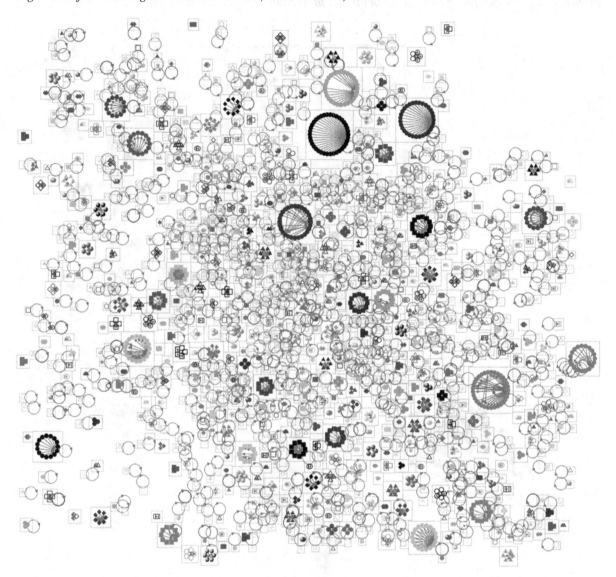

To clarify, these are not "isolates" in a classic sense—those in a social network but without direct ties. These are not "pendants" or "whiskers" (those social media account nodes that are connected to a large cluster by only one tie to another member of the network). Rather, these are situational self-loops of conversations that are started but which do not engender a response or those which are only responded to in small clusters (out of the hundreds of millions of other potential responses). The intuition here is that the particular topic of focus may change the contents of the networks based on the (non)responses of other potential respondents from the social media platform (and beyond on the Web and Internet, depending on the data extraction tool used). This approach builds on micro-level analysis based on the lived experience of microblogging and may shed some light on direct human motivations on why people microblog (at the micro level), including the uses of social media for self-expression (confidence-building through self-talk, expressing commitment to an idea, formulating and sharing commentary, and other

Figure 6. A large scatter of low-node connected components on Twitter graph

common types of self-talk), with the individual interacting with the technology, or with a small group of others, and that smaller degree of reach is often sufficient. One more caveat: the prior graph visualizations provide a visual sense of the social networks; for deeper knowledge, the datasets should be accessed.

While it is not unusual for people to self-express (informally usually) in a variety of venues or to talk among a small group, the ability to eavesdrop on such narrowcast messaging has advanced significantly, and much of this type of information is there for the taking. It is as if a person has said something to himself or herself privately or to a small group near a hot mic. This mic has the ability to raise a close-in narrowcast comment to broad and mass attention; in terms of real-world, captured images, messaging, and video that were shared locally have sometimes been mass-shared and gained a secondary, tertiary and broader-scale life beyond the individual communicator's intent (particularly if the individual hap-

Figure 7. #sweet #nothing hashtag discourse network on Twitter

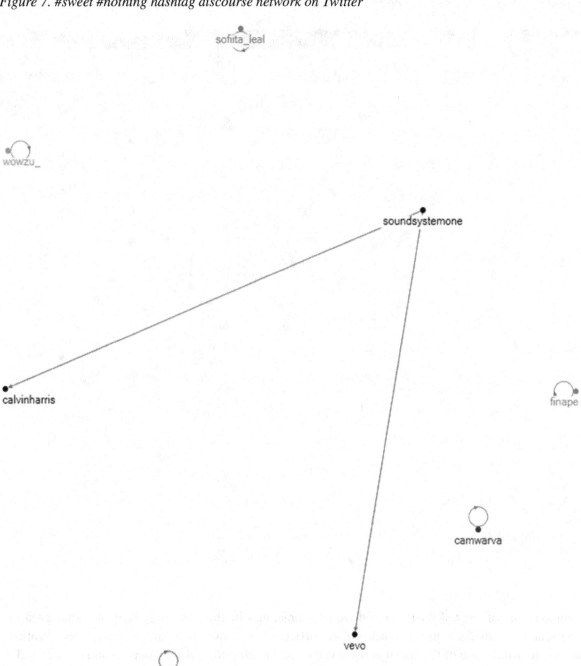

pened to be at a strategic right-place and right-time (at the moment of an unfolding event). In other words, given the scalability of electronic communications, the proximate can easily evolve to become the distal, and vice versa. This broad ability to eavesdrop belies the localness and close-in nature of the data and may point to a different sort of affordance in social media in strengthening people's ability to communicate beyond a broadcast role.

In Figure 8, there is a thread of Tweets suggesting that others are self-pleasuring through #selfies that are not offering a broader benefit to others who are sharing the online space. The integrated Alchemy API sentiment analyzer shows that this aspect of the #selfie ad hoc network on Twitter (accessed through Twitter's streaming API) is trending negative. This data was captured using the Tweet Analyzer "machine" in Maltego Carbon 3.5.3.

Self-loops would manifest differently on Maltego Carbon because this tool actually captures links not only on the particular social media platform but also links out to other parts of the Surface Web. Small group conversations may also manifest differently here as well since this tool captures relationships in a more hierarchical and one-directional way (instead of capturing reciprocity). This is not about taking the "social" out of "social media" but more about understanding the role of the self-loop and small communities within the larger spaces.

This work examines the phenomena of microblogging messages in a narrowcast way, either in a self-loop to the self or to a small group of others in a narrowcast way. In the first sense, this type of blogging is a generic sort of "talking-to-self" / self-talk, and in the latter, this type is a narrowcast microchat to a small audience. People do sometimes talk to themselves in contexts where others are not around, and sometimes, people talk to themselves even when others are around, but no responses are expected. For many, such self-expression is about clarifying ideas and balancing emotions. A more hyperbolic concern may be that such "talking to self" on microblogging sites is yet a further sign of Robert Putnam's observation of people "bowling alone" and not engaging in civic life—the ultimate alone "selfie" while on a social media platform. In terms of the small-group communications shared on open channels, are there concerns of data leakage? Do people forget themselves and slip privy information from a narrowcast context to a broadcast one, based on the "hot mic" properties of Twitter?

How this topic first came to mind was because of several real-world experiences. In 2014, at a conference, I was demonstrating a specific use of Network Overview, Discovery, and Exploration for Excel (NodeXL), and an audience member asked me to graph the network of his university. [The conference was the National Extension Technology Conference at Kansas State University; the presentation was "Hashtag Conversations, Eventgraphs, and User Ego Neighborhoods: Extracting Social Network Data from Twitter." The slideshow is available at the LinkedIn SlideShare site: http://www.slideshare.net/learjk/hashtag-conversationseventgraphsuseregoneighborhoodstwitter-35052887]. We graphed the network in front of a pretty large crowd, and the network showed one node with a self-loop in a directed graph. There were no ties. There was a sense in the room that the individual had imagined a large audience of engaged readers to the account but was shocked to find no followers. That moment evoked one of the training tools for beginning writers—to imagine their "ideal reader" and to write to that reader—even in the actual absence of any readers, at least early on. The externalization of internal conversations can have an effect on the communicator—by encouraging self-disclosure, by encouraging sophistication in honing messages for public consumption, by giving courage for actions, by encouraging the anticipation of a real-world audience (through the development of meta-perspectives), and so on. However, the lack of self-awareness of followership and ad hoc interactive linking around certain topics seems like a negative one-down sort of position to be in, in environments which demand near real-time awareness for most governments and corporations. When I sent the participant the NodeXL file related to the data extraction, he did not respond.

This experience reminded me of a pattern that I had been seeing in the past two years using the NodeXL tool. I would conduct a data extraction of a hashtag or a keyword conversation network, and occasionally, I would extract a network *with no ties*. In other words, the extracted graph showed thousands of social

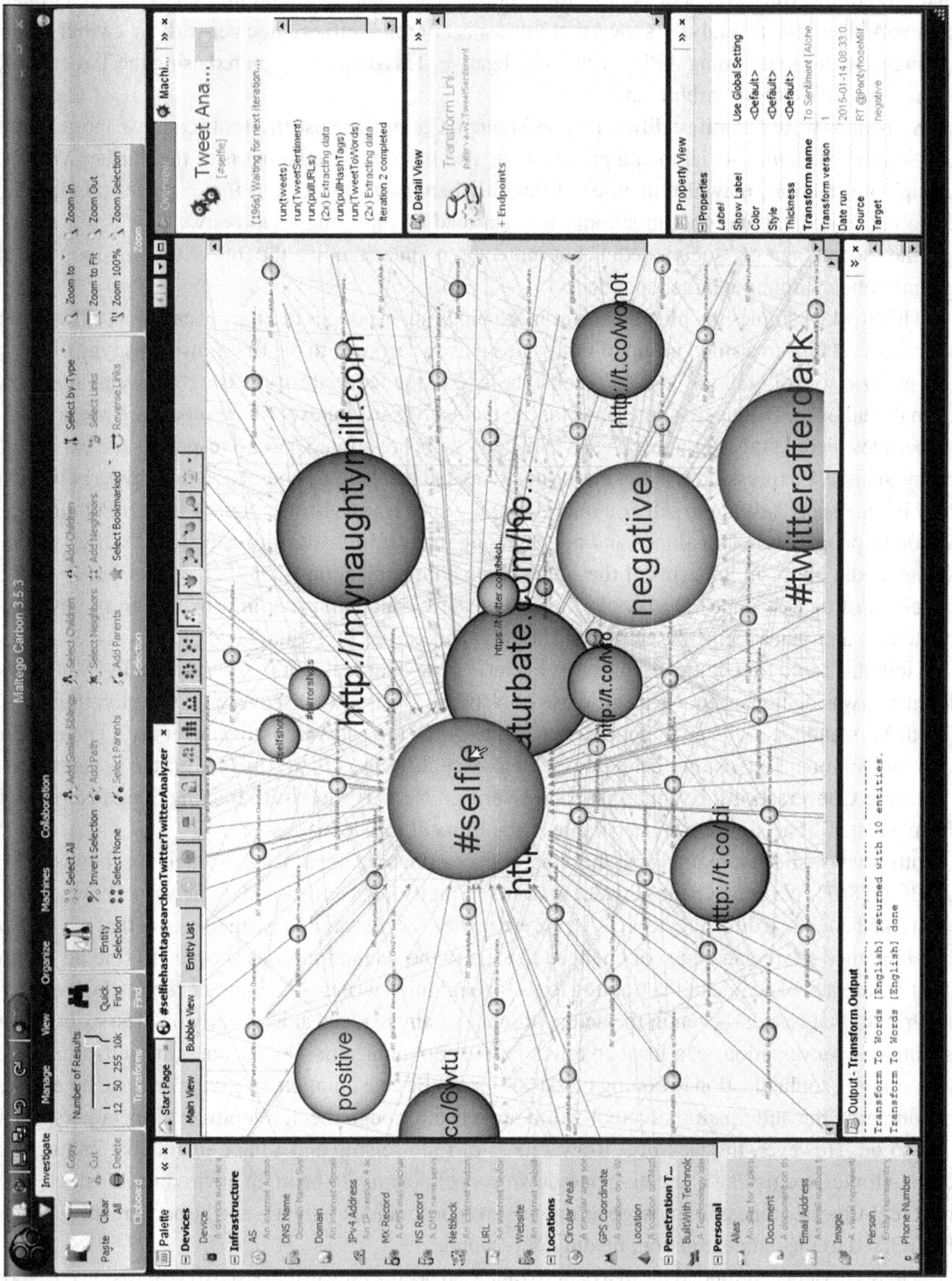

Figure 8. #selfie hashtag network on twitter through Maltego Carbon's Tweet Analyzer "machine"

media accounts that recently (in the past week) expressed a microblogged message on the particular topic, but those accounts did not receive a reply or a retweet or a mention (nothing that would indicate interactions around the message). In some cases, there were potential ways to reason about the lack of links—such as people Tweeting #resolutions for a new year as a promise to themselves—but there were others that did not make particular sense, such as a contentious issue, like #fracking. While the Twitter API only enables some limited data extraction (and rate-limits access during busy times), re-runs of some of these graphs without ties resulted in the same results: plenty of nodes (vertices), but no links (edges). In a sense, the one-node microchat is an extreme of social media, an actor with an audience of one (at least in terms of a particular #hashtag conversation or keyword topic in that particular time slice). This is not to say that the nodes in a particular graph do not necessarily have a large social network; they may. This is not to say that the particular #hashtagged topic does not have a connected community of social media accounts at other time periods. After all, a data extraction with the same parameters at different times can result in highly variant types of network graphs.

Another variation of this narrowcast microchat involves a node communicating with a small group of other nodes, so a social network with maybe the largest connected component as a dozen or so others. The nodes may be individuals who already are familiar with each other and follow each other; they may be self-created nodes to create the impression of a conversation and to try to spark trends; they may be utter strangers who sparked with mutual interest around a particular #hashtagged topic or keyword and were interacting. The irony of small-scale conversations on a microblogging site is that any passerby with Internet access may listen in on these narrowcast conversations. Such eavesdropping capabilities—on public conversations shared on hyper-public social online spaces—is made possible through the application programming interfaces (API) that enable access to some of the available data. The data are harvested using a range of free and open-source software tools to commercial and proprietary ones. For technologies created to build and showcase relationships, what do these technologies say about those connected to themselves and to smaller clusters?

An artifact of the software or an actual phenomena? One of the many strengths of electronic social network analysis (e-SNA) involves the ability to capture not only the proverbial 30,000-foot view of a social network graph but also at the granularity of the node-level, and all points in between: the motif and subgraph (and island) levels and other types of close-in entities and relationships. In terms of a basic network extraction from Twitter based on search terms through the NodeXL tool (Network Overview, Discovery, and Exploration for Excel), a basic network captures the network with links defined as "replied to" or "mentioned" in recent microblogging messages under the "Twitter Search Network" feature. The top limit for all captured Tweets is 18,000, which was the parameter used for all data extractions here. The absence of such links in the tool may suggest that there was no commiseration, no actions interpretable as ties. That would be a naïve and likely erroneous assumption. There are a range of dependencies in capturing this information. The tool used for the data extraction has top limits, as noted earlier. The querying computer used will have different results based on its Internet connectivity speed. While the captured social media accounts are said to be accurate, there is almost always missing information with this type of social media data extraction (few false positives but a much higher likelihood of false negatives, or not so many Type 1 errors but the potential of much higher Type 2 errors); in other words, the information left out may not have been appropriately left out. It is possible that there were ties that were not captured since the NodeXL relies on the Twitter application programming interface (API) which only reports some information and rate-limits access. There is no current way to tell how much of a data sample was extracted and out of how many messages possible (the surest way to know this is to contact Twitter directly for a response, and the company has made such information available to some researchers and some media organizations). It is also not possible to know if the actual captured data was purely random (unlikely because pure randomness is difficult to achieve) or captured based on some machine selectivity (which may be unknown, or if known, not articulated in a publicly accessible way). In other words, the workflow pipeline and its dependencies on various software tools and social media platforms limit and shape the data captured. These various layers of dependencies affect the particular information collected. Beyond the collection issue, "noise" (non-meaningful or irrelevant information) may be introduced through some of the usual challenges of spoofed (non-verified) accounts and all the variations of misinformation common on social media platforms.

These prior data capturing caveats should be kept in mind. However, these dynamics (of self-talk and of small-group communications) have been observed across a range of tools used to capture data and metadata from Twitter (including NodeXL, Maltego Carbon, NCapture of NVivo, and others). Such phenomena also align with intuition and in-world observations about how some people sometimes use microblogging sites—in a push fashion whether or not the demand for that data exists in the near-field relationships or in the larger context in general.

Three Hypotheses

There are three main hypotheses that will be explored in this work. These hypotheses relate to the types of seeding #hashtags and keywords that may create either of three variations of ad hoc discourse-based graphs on Twitter: high-vertex and highly-connected graphs based on popular topics, self-loops, and small-group networks respectively.

Hypothesis 1: Popular and high-attention #hashtag or keyword topics will result in high-node, high-link, and bursty discourse-based microblogging networks on Twitter.

"Bursty" or "spiky" events on Twitter—which is expressed as social networks that include a high number of nodes and relatively high numbers of edges in a short time span—occur based on issues that are seen to be in the public realm and of public interest. These include controversial political issues. These include geographical locations around the world where events are occurring. These are represented by high-influence individuals who "stand in" for particular stances on particular issues.

These are also often professionally manufactured types of interest which are promoted through mass media. The nature of Twitter is a fast-moving cycling of information, with fast entropy, so the topics will evolve. In terms of "trending" topics, there are likely perennials such as commonly used mobile devices used for communicating (like #iphone) or common interests (like #news) or common practice (#openfollow, #followback). So to map high-popularity events on Twitter, it may be helpful to follow high-influence nodes on the microblogging network. It may help to seed search networks using terms that meet the following criteria: in the popular vernacular, addressing an emotional issue, is hotly contested, is fairly simple and broadly understandable, and is supported by high-influence entities. These may include event-based or those based on high-influence individuals.

Hypothesis 2: Self-talk, self-organizing, and self-reporting #hashtag or keyword topics will result in self-looped discourse-based microblogging networks on Twitter.

In the real world, people use self-talk in various ways. They may self-talk to organize their thinking (such as to process tasks), to give themselves courage in pursue a particularly difficult task or endeavor, to self-heroize in order to push beyond perceived barriers. On Twitter, another form of self-looped self-expression may involve self-reporting, such as recording the amounts of caloric intake or fitness information or exercise recording (some of which is automated and Tweeted out through various mobile apps). It may be that such messages tend to be individualistic and are looped back to the individual as a form of encouragement, a positive feedback loop, if you will. To extract such self-looped networks, it may help to use common and generic hashtags or terms that align with general self-talk purposes.

Hypothesis 3: Mundane, personal, and highly original #hashtag or keyword topics will result in small-group discourse-based microblogging networks on Twitter.

People interact with others in small groups based on kinship, friendships, and shared interests. In such groups, messaging is narrowcast—or distributed to the small group (even in semi-public or fully public spaces). The hashtags or keywords that may elicit such small-group graphs may be those that involve particular interests that are "trapped" within small groups and do not make it out to the popular interest. Another way to extract such groups is to use multiple hashtags to focus on the discourses of interest. This helps delimit the focus and accesses subsets of subsets.

Parameters of the data extractions. To test these three hypotheses, NodeXL was used to extract a few social networks per hypothesis to see if such specific types of social network structures may be extracted based on specific hashtags and / or keywords. The researcher assumed that #hashtagged conversations tend to be more connected than keyword ones, which may be pulling from generic conversations which are not even thought of as connected by those engaged in the messaging. In terms of the parameters for the data extractions, the setting was set at 18,000 nodes or the top limit for this type of data extraction on NodeXL. (The tool itself can handle graphs that are upwards of some 300,000 vertices in size, but for Twitter extractions, the tool is set at a maximum of 18,000.) The extracted data was represented in baseline graph metrics tables based on the extracted data. The clustering algorithm used was the Clauset-Newman-Moore. While there are over a dozen layout algorithms available in NodeXL, a few of the most common ones were used in order to increase visual comparability. In virtually all of these visuals, the nodes, links, and clusters are quite viewable, particularly in color. (Different layout algorithms may create very disparate visual senses of particular data. It is well beyond the purview of this work to summarize the graph layout algorithms and resulting layouts in more detail.)

Popular "Trending" Messaging

Hypothesis 1: Popular and high-attention #hashtag or keyword topics will result in high-node, high-link, and bursty discourse-based microblogging networks on Twitter.

A recent event at the time of the chapter's writing was the 2015 Grammy Awards ceremony. To try to create a popular or trending network, #grammy was used to seed an extraction. The resulting graph contained 17,846 vertices and 26,649 edges. Within this graph were 4,498 self-loops, 4,120 connected components, and 2,846 single-vertex connected components (isolates). The maximum number of vertices in a connected component was 9,810, The maximum geodesic distance or graph diameter was 18, and the average geodesic distance was 5.6 hops. In total, there were 4,185 groups.

Figure 10 was created using the Harel-Koren Fast Multiscale Layout Algorithm. To maintain a sort of consistency, the next day, the keyword (not #hashtag) <grammy> was used to conduct a data extraction from Twitter. This data extraction resulted in 18,569 vertices and 19,594 unique edges. There were 5,261 self-loops, 6,221 connected components, and 3,991 single-vertex connected components (isolates). There were 6,276 groups (sub-clusters). The maximum number of vertices in a connected component were 6,923; the maximum edges in a connected component were 10,707. In this network, the maximum geodesic distance or graph diameter was 24 (so wider than the #grammy network). The average geodesic distance was 7.56 hops.

Figure 9. Import from Twitter search network window in NodeXL

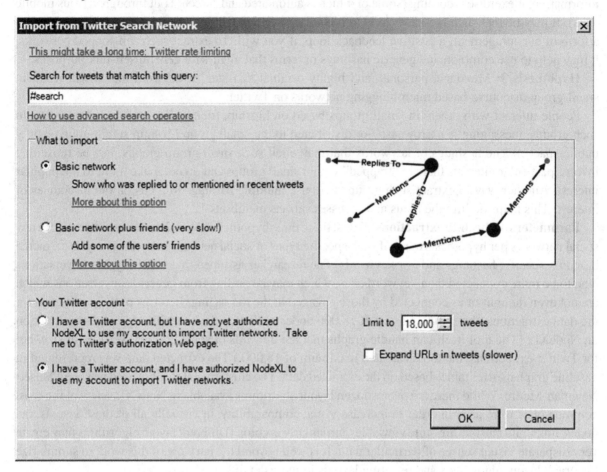

Popular terms then attract a large number of vertices with a fairly high number of linkages. The graph networks may contain a fair amount of diversity of groups and dimensional range from end-to-end. There are clearly isolates, self-loops, and small groups within both of these trending networks, but the main features of these graphs involve large-scale interconnected social networks.

Individualized Self-Looped or Single-Node Messaging

Hypothesis 2: Self-talk, self-organizing, and self-reporting #hashtag or keyword topics will result in self-looped discourse-based microblogging networks on Twitter #run was used as a seeding term to extract a network for self-looped messaging, with the idea that this might be a term used for those describing going on a #run for fitness. Table 5 shows the extracted network, with 9904 vertices and no edges.

This graph then typifies a term that captures a lot of single-loop interest but not much in the way of replies-to, mentions, or retweets.

Figure 12 is graphed based on the Fruchterman-Reingold Force-Based Algorithm. This graph does not show links or ties (lines showing relationships).

Table 3. Graph metrics table for #grammy hashtag network on Twitter (basic network)

Graph Metric	Value
Graph Type	Directed
Vertices	17846
Unique Edges	26649
Edges With Duplicates	2910
Total Edges	29559
Self-Loops	4498
Reciprocated Vertex Pair Ratio	0.005235602
Reciprocated Edge Ratio	0.010416667
Connected Components	4120
Single-Vertex Connected Components	2846
Maximum Vertices in a Connected Component	9810
Maximum Edges in a Connected Component	20438
Maximum Geodesic Distance (Diameter)	18
Average Geodesic Distance	5.642216
Graph Density	7.59651E-05
Modularity	Not Applicable
NodeXL Version	1.0.1.334

Another example involves a network based on #JSON, which may be used by data scientists and technologists, and some others. In this case, there are also no replies or mentions around the particular discussion.

This particular graph shows no groups and no ties. Here, the vertices are labeled with the names of the particular Twitter accounts. In Figure 13, the graph was scaled down to lower the amount of term overlap for readability.

In this section, two hashtagged searches were used because the several keyword ones that were tried resulted in fairly different graph structures.

Figure 10. Graph #grammy hashtag network graph on Twitter (basic network)

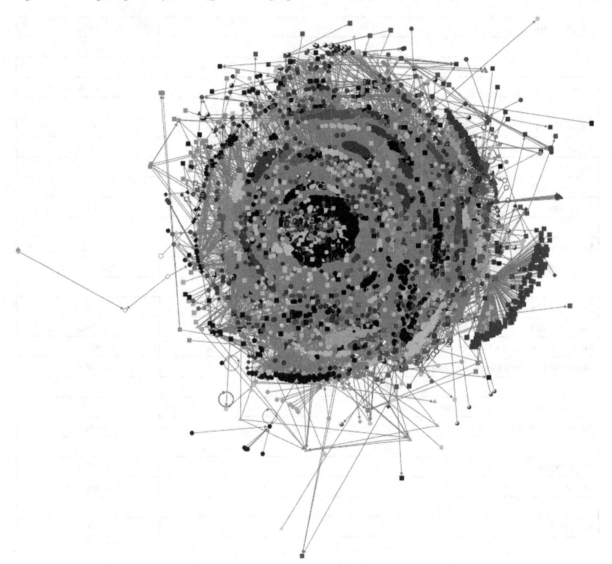

Narrowcast Small-Group Messaging

Hypothesis 3: Mundane, personal, and highly original #hashtag or keyword topics will result in small-group discourse-based microblogging networks on Twitter.

The #hobby hashtag was used to extract a social network based around that discourse on Twitter. The extracted network consisted of 1,928 vertices, with 1,606 unique edges. There were 3,480 self-loops. The largest connected component had 35 vertices. The network itself had a graph diameter (maximum geodesic distance) of five (5). This network comprised 1,413 groups (out of a total network of 1,928 vertices), which gives a sense of the small sizes of the networks. The graph metrics data is at Table 7. This graph is viewable as Figure 14.

Table 4. <grammy> Keyword network on Twitter (basic network)

Graph Metric	Value
Graph Type	Directed
Vertices	18569
Unique Edges	19594
Edges With Duplicates	3232
Total Edges	22826
Self-Loops	5261
Reciprocated Vertex Pair Ratio	0.004737295
Reciprocated Edge Ratio	0.009429919
Connected Components	6221
Single-Vertex Connected Components	3991
Maximum Vertices in a Connected Component	6923
Maximum Edges in a Connected Component	10707
Maximum Geodesic Distance (Diameter)	24
Average Geodesic Distance	7.569505
Graph Density	4.73652E-05
Modularity	Not Applicable
NodeXL Version	1.0.1.334

A keyword search based on <dating> was run on Twitter. This resulted in a social graph with 15,841 nodes, with 14,313 edges. There were 9,491 self-loops in the messaging. In this network, there were 4,706 single-vertex connected components (isolates). The maximum geodesic distance (graph diameter) was 29, and the average geodesic distance was an average of 9 hops between any two nodes in the network. This network had 7,204 groups.

The resulting graph for the dating keyword search is available in Figure 15.

DISCUSSION

The learning from this work was not directly what was expected. To review, the three hypotheses were as follows:

Figure 11. <grammy> keyword network on twitter (basic network)

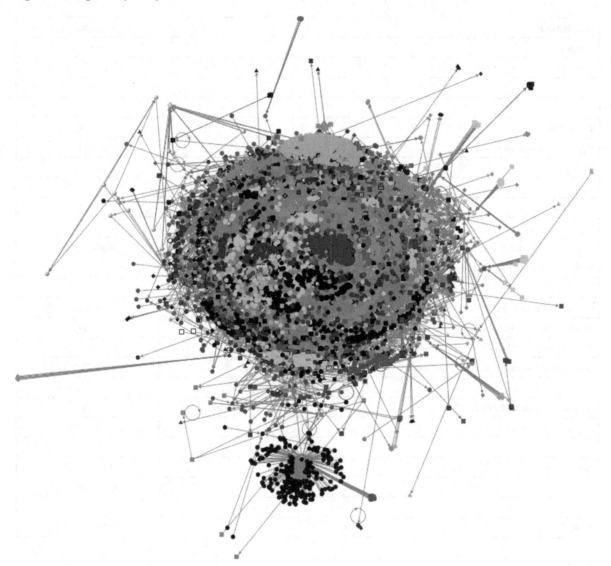

Hypothesis 1: Popular and high-attention #hashtag or keyword topics will result in high-node, high-link, and bursty discourse-based microblogging networks on Twitter.

Hypothesis 2: Self-talk, self-organizing, and self-reporting #hashtag or keyword topics will result in self-looped discourse-based microblogging networks on Twitter.

Hypothesis 3: Mundane, personal, and highly original #hashtag or keyword topics will result in small-group discourse-based microblogging networks on Twitter.

The initial probes did not definitively show whether these hypotheses were true or not. Rather, it may be that these hypotheses are incorrectly formed. Such hypotheses would work better if they addressed predominant mixes and features instead of pure types (pure trending and popular high-connections, pure individualized self-loops, pure graphs of small groups) because these latter ones are rare. The time span

Table 5. Graph metrics table for #run hashtag network on Twitter (basic network)

Graph Metric	Value
Graph Type	Directed
Vertices	9904
Unique Edges	0
Edges With Duplicates	0
Total Edges	0
Self-Loops	0
Reciprocated Vertex Pair Ratio	Not Applicable
Reciprocated Edge Ratio	Not Applicable
Connected Components	9904
Single-Vertex Connected Components	9904
Maximum Vertices in a Connected Component	1
Maximum Edges in a Connected Component	0
Maximum Geodesic Distance (Diameter)	Not Applicable
Average Geodesic Distance	Not Applicable
Graph Density	0
Modularity	Not Applicable
NodeXL Version	1.0.1.334

of the data capture, the size of the graph, and other factors also affect the composition of the networks. In other words, just the seeding #hashtags and keywords are not the singular critical factors for surfacing particular networks; specifically, time and scale are also important.

Time. It is not particularly helpful to just consider #hashtags and keywords without thinking about the particular time period. After all, a particular term may be trending at one moment and dormant in another. Seeding #hashtag terms and keywords cannot be considered independent of the particular moment (or time span) of the data extraction. In other words, a data extraction over the past week will be different than a data extraction covering a year-long period. It may be that there are terms that are always minimally used and non-trending over time, but without access to full datasets, it is difficult to identify which may have these characteristics; further, performance in the past may not indicate necessarily that the same performance will occur in the future. A seeding term, if its used is captured continuously, will likely show differing patterns yet again. These issues with time may be seen in how difficult it may be

Figure 12. #run hashtag network on Twitter

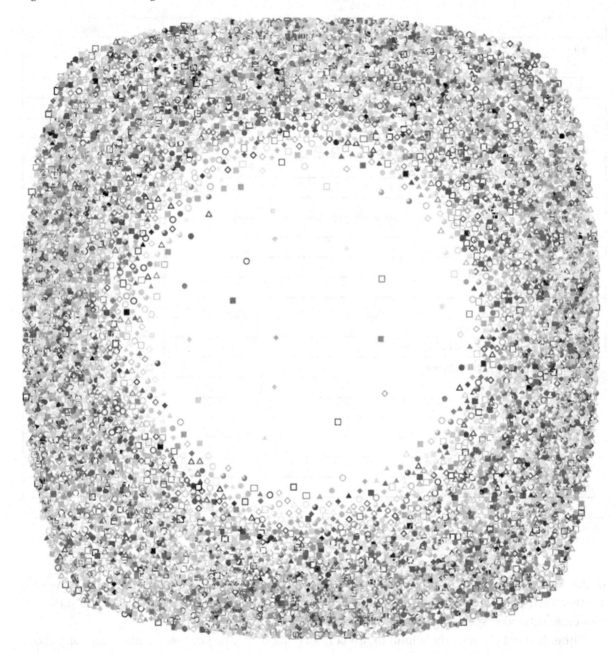

to repeat findings using the same data extraction parameters over time. Sometimes, even simultaneous data extractions with similar parameters on two different machines will result in quite different extracted datasets. The test-retest reliability of slice-in-time extractions of #hashtag and keyword-based Twitter discourse graph networks is not particularly high. In a longer time horizon, terms also change their meanings, and people also change how they use language and terms over time.

Scale. Another challenge involves the issue of size and scale. If a network extraction is wholly un-limited and not rate-limited, would the apparent nature of the social network graph based on the ad hoc

Table 6. Graph metrics for #JSON hashtag network on Twitter (basic network)

Graph Metric	Value
Graph Type	Directed
Vertices	475
Unique Edges	0
Edges With Duplicates	0
Total Edges	0
Self-Loops	0
Reciprocated Vertex Pair Ratio	Not Applicable
Reciprocated Edge Ratio	Not Applicable
Connected Components	475
Single-Vertex Connected Components	475
Maximum Vertices in a Connected Component	1
Maximum Edges in a Connected Component	0
Maximum Geodesic Distance (Diameter)	Not Applicable
Average Geodesic Distance	Not Applicable
Graph Density	0
Modularity	Not Applicable
NodeXL Version	1.0.1.333

Twitter discourse change? Would there be different proportional mixes of popular clusters, single-self-loops, and small groups for a particular social network? In other words, are the resulting graphs a factor of the method of data extraction with the limits from the Twitter API and the limits of the extracting software tool (like NodeXL or Maltego Carbon) or even the human methods of the extractions? Without access to the full dataset, this is impossible to know. It is also still currently not possible to know what the extracted sample size is as a percentage of what is in the full available dataset (available by working with a commercial company, Gnip, for the full set). Understandings, too, of how social media data reflect the actual state of the world are based on a range of interpretations and inferences.

Also, the method of using particular #hashtags or keywords to seed particular graph extractions is painstaking manually. It would be much more efficient to automate the research and see what graphs and graph patterns result and then analyze the resulting hashtags and keywords that empirically result in particular types of social network graphs. Some speculations may be made here from this initial

Figure 13. #JSON hashtag network on Twitter (basic network)

Table 7. Graph metrics table for #hobby hashtag network on Twitter (basic network)

Graph Metric	Value
Graph Type	Directed
Vertices	1928
Unique Edges	1606
Edges With Duplicates	3565
Total Edges	5171
Self-Loops	3480
Reciprocated Vertex Pair Ratio	0.030844156
Reciprocated Edge Ratio	0.05984252
Connected Components	1413
Single-Vertex Connected Components	1179
Maximum Vertices in a Connected Component	35
Maximum Edges in a Connected Component	869
Maximum Geodesic Distance (Diameter)	5
Average Geodesic Distance	1.218111
Graph Density	0.000170917
Modularity	Not Applicable
NodeXL Version	1.0.1.334

work (backstopped by two years of prior exploratory graphing of ad hoc Twitter discourses expressed as networks). One speculation is that while larger graphs will likely result in some larger clusters, some small groups, and some self-loops (functional isolates in that particular conversation), there will be certain terms which tend to be more often "bursty" and popular and others that tend to be less high profile. There will be certain terms that result in certain mixes: 50% large clusters, 10% small groups, and 40% self-loops, for example. Another speculation is that there will be some terms which have never been used in microblogging conversations and have a low chance of future use. Another speculation is that, at scale, there will be virtually no pure networks that are purely large-cluster (and nothing else), self-loops (and nothing else), or small groups (and nothing else). In all likelihood, network graphs from ad hoc discourses on Twitter will be some mix.

Figure 14. #Hobby hashtag network on Twitter (basic network)

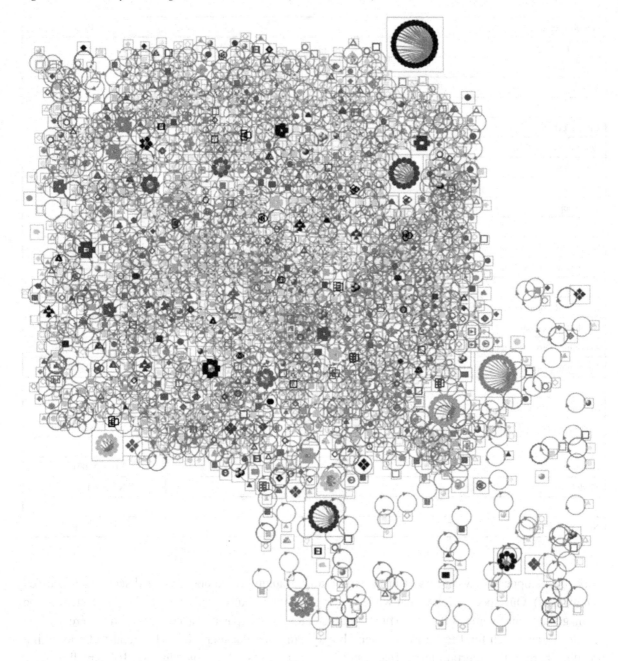

Also, it is clear from these samples that individual self-loops and small groups actually occur in virtually all ad hoc discourse networks on Twitter if it is of sufficient size. So a popular or trending topic will necessarily include these smaller self-looping nodes and small-group connected components. So while this work tried to extract these as stand-alone objects—which they are—having pure graphs of only particular types alone (such as only self-loops or only small groups) is fairly rare. To illustrate this concept, a keyword search for the social network discussing <diet> was extracted from Twitter. This network consists of 11,885 vertices with 9,750 edges. There are 10,825 self-loops (a large number); however,

Table 8. Graph metrics table for <dating> keyword network on Twitter (basic network)

Graph Metric	Value
Graph Type	Directed
Vertices	15841
Unique Edges	14313
Edges With Duplicates	5490
Total Edges	19803
Self-Loops	9491
Reciprocated Vertex Pair Ratio	0.030900041
Reciprocated Edge Ratio	0.059947697
Connected Components	7181
Single-Vertex Connected Components	4706
Maximum Vertices in a Connected Component	2352
Maximum Edges in a Connected Component	3325
Maximum Geodesic Distance (Diameter)	29
Average Geodesic Distance	9.054091
Graph Density	3.9622E-05
Modularity	Not Applicable
NodeXL Version	1.0.1.334

there is also a cluster that is 429 nodes in size (not small, as in a few dozen nodes, but well beyond the Dunbar number of 150). There are a number of single-vertex connected components (4,352 isolates).

A visualization of the graph from the <diet> keyword search is at Figure 16.

This sort of graph configuration captures a sample of each of the three main types of clusters discussed: the fairly large-scale one around an issue, some small groups, and some individualized self-loops.

FUTURE RESEARCH DIRECTIONS

While much of the research on social media platforms has been on the attention-getting viral phenomena, there are quieter topics of interest to reveal how people interact with technologies for self-talk and narrowcasting among smaller groups—even in highly public spaces. Such smaller-scale interactions offer rich research approaches beyond structure mining, such as content mining, social account profiling, survival analysis, and other approaches. In terms of general questions, some of the following would be engaging:

Figure 15. <dating> keyword network on Twitter (basic network)

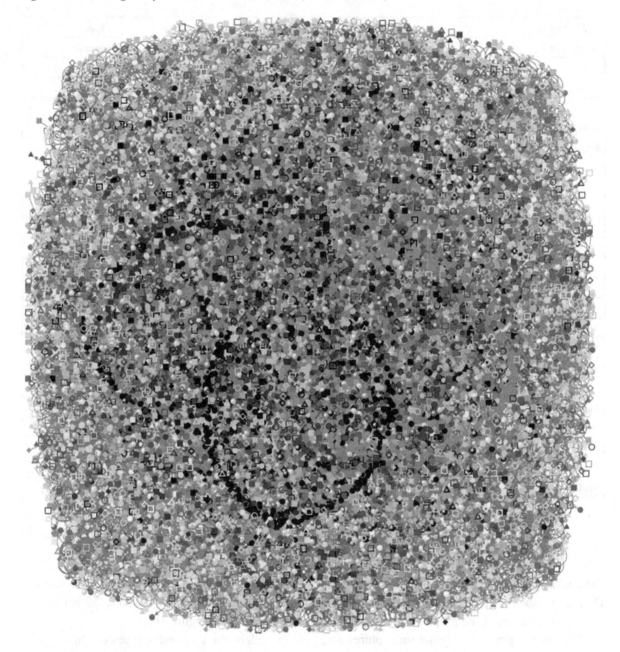

- How aware are individuals and groups of their actual networks and their own communications contents and patterns? What are ways to increase their awareness for more effective messaging on social media platforms?
- What are beneficial ways to tap such information streams manually? In an automated way? In a mixed complementary human-computational way? Which tools are most effective, and why?
- Are there certain terms (hashtags and keywords) that lead to certain types of social networks on Twitter? Are there patterns to these types of terms?

Table 9. Graph metrics table for the <diet> keyword network on Twitter (basic network)

Graph Metric	Value
Graph Type	Directed
Vertices	11885
Unique Edges	9750
Edges With Duplicates	9032
Total Edges	18782
Self-Loops	10825
Reciprocated Vertex Pair Ratio	0.05744888
Reciprocated Edge Ratio	0.108655617
Connected Components	6169
Single-Vertex Connected Components	4352
Maximum Vertices in a Connected Component	429
Maximum Edges in a Connected Component	1174
Maximum Geodesic Distance (Diameter)	16
Average Geodesic Distance	3.576676
Graph Density	4.61338E-05
Modularity	Not Applicable
NodeXL Version	1.0.1.334

- Are there qualitative differences in the kinds of conversations going on in the different types of networks (the large and trending clusters, the individualized self-loops, and the small groups)?

Microblogging self-talk and individualized self-loops. How does an individual's social media presence manifest across multiple social media platforms? How does a social media account of a self-looping individual node change over time? If a sentiment analysis tool were applied to a social media account with a lot of self-looped self-talk, would it be possible to label an account as generally positive, negative, or neutral? Are self-talk topics fairly generic or fairly unique? Do the apparent instrumental uses of such microblogged self-talk evolve and change over time? In terms of survival analysis, how long do these accounts last? What variables encourage such accounts to continue, and what variables encourage such accounts to sunset? What is the structural nature of nodes that self-loop on messaging (or are these all nodes)? The structural nature of small groups (from emergent ad hoc messaging)? Do such ad hoc small groups have weak ties, and if so, what do these ties look like? Or do they have strong ties, and if so, what do these look like?

Figure 16. <diet> keyword network on Twitter

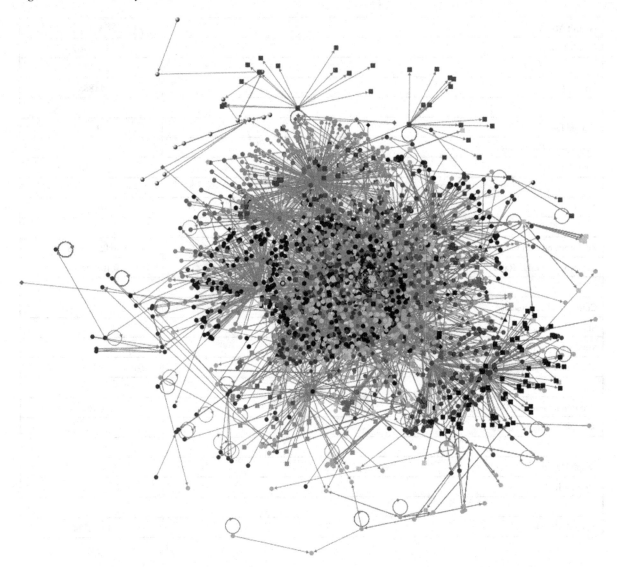

Microblogging small-group messaging. How do small groups' social media presences manifest across multiple social media platforms (or even across the Web and Internet)? What types of instrumental applications are observable from the data? Are there differences in uses and messaging between public-facing groups and private-facing ones on social media, and if so, why?

What sorts of data leakage may be observed through such narrowcast messaging? What is the value of such information? Are there ways to discern bona fide discourses vs. faux ones? Are there qualitative informational differences in messaging between nodes in these various types of social graphs? (For example, are locally relevant topics for individual self-looped conversations and small-group discussions substantively different than topics for large-scale communications and trending events? If so, what are some differences?) What are some methods of batch-processing datasets of shared information from social media accounts for profiling, and how may such tweet corpuses (and related multimedia) be analyzed for informational value? Are there differences between how various groups talk among themselves on different social media platforms? Who are the entities who participate in small-scale conversations on microblogging sites, and what is the nature of the groupness? In terms of ad hoc microblogging conversations, when do small-group conversations occur, and why? In terms of planned microblogging conversations, when do such small-group conversations occur, and why? Are there relationships between small-group conversations and large-scale ones? (For example, do small groups spin-off from large-scale communications in order to pursue a particular side interest or topic? Or for example, do small group conversations sometimes go "viral" and turn into massive conversations? If so, what are some potential triggers?)

This early work describes the pursuit of the un-trending networks. Similar research may be conducted on other social media platforms than microblogging ones, to learn more about what is occurring in the long tail. For efficiency's sake, it may help to automate the approaches for data extraction and analysis.

CONCLUSION

On social media platforms, researchers and the general public have generally focused on trending and popular issues; they have focused on influential nodes with many followers and large connected clusters; they have pursued viral messaging and memes. The focus generally has been on cores and not peripheries, strong links and not weak ones, imminent high-impact events and not lesser ones.

By contrast, this chapter has started an exploration of the smaller-scale types of microblogging, from individual account self-talk to small-group interactions. These types of interactions would likely be in the long tail of the power law graph, but there is unexplored potential in these small-scale and ad hoc (as well as planned) uses of microblogging platforms. What is the value of such eavesdropping on public self-looped conversations and those in small-groups? Such eavesdropping may provide insights on how people use social media in relating to themselves, through various means including electronic self-talk. It may reveal insights on how small-groups form in an ad hoc or planned or mixed way around particular #hashtagged topics or keywords. Research in these phenomena may advance the uses of such platforms as human sensor networks (around both large-scale and small-scale events).

REFERENCES

About Twitter. (n.d.). Retrieved from: https://about.twitter.com/company

Bastos, M. T., Puschmann, C., & Travitzki, R. (2013). Tweeting across hashtags: Overlapping users and the importance of language, topics, and politics. *24th ACM Conference on Hypertext and Social Media*, Paris, France.

Black, A., Mascaro, C., Gallagher, M., & Goggins, S. P. (2012). Twitter Zombie: Architecture for capturing, socially transforming and analyzing the Twittersphere. Proceedings of *GROUP '12*, Sanibel Island, Florida.

Bowman, N. D., Westerman, D. K., & Claus, C. J. (2012). How demanding is social media: Understanding social media diets as a function of perceived costs and benefits—A rational actor perspective. *Computers in Human Behavior*, *28*(6), 2298–2305. doi:10.1016/j.chb.2012.06.037

Burnap, P., Rana, O. F., Avis, N., Williams, M., Housley, W., & Edwards, A. et al. (2013). Detecting tension in online communities with computational Twitter analysis. *Technological Forecasting and Social Change*, 1–13.

Dayter, D. (2014). Self-praise in microblogging. *Journal of Pragmatics*, *61*, 91–102. doi:10.1016/j.pragma.2013.11.021

Eyal, N., & Hoover, R. (2014). *Hooked: How to Build Habit-Forming Products*. New York: Portfolio, Penguin.

Gillen, J., & Merchant, G. (2013). Contact calls: Twitter as a dialogic social and linguistic practice. *Language Sciences*, *35*, 47–58. doi:10.1016/j.langsci.2012.04.015

Hai-Jew, S. (2014). Conducting Surface Web-Based Research with Maltego Carbon. Retrieve from: http://scalar.usc.edu/works/conducting-surface-web-based-research-with-maltego-carbon/index

Hai-Jew, S. (2014). Using NVivo: An Unofficial and Unauthorized Primer. Retrieve from: http://scalar.usc.edu/works/using-nvivo-an-unofficial-and-unauthorized-primer/index

Hai-Jew, S. (2015). Querying Social Media with NodeXL. Retrieve from: http://scalar.usc.edu/works/querying-social-media-with-nodexl/index

Hansen, D. L., Schneiderman, B., & Smith, M. A. (2011). *Analyzing Social Media Networks with NodeXL: Insights from a Connected World*. Amsterdam: Elsevier.

Jansen, B. J., Sobel, K., & Cook, G. (2010). Gen X and Y's attitudes on u sing social media platforms for opinion sharing (Work-in-Progress). Proceedings of *CHI 2010*, Atlanta, Georgia.

Kunneman, F., Liebrecht, C., van Mulken, M., & van den Bosch, A. (2014). Signaling sarcasm: From hyperbole to hashtag. *Information Processing and Management*. Retrieve from: http://www.businessinsider.com/library-of-congress-is-archiving-all-of-americas-tweets-2013-1

Qiu, L., Lin, H., Ramsay, J., & Yang, F. (2012). You are what you tweet: Personality expression and perception on Twitter. *Journal of Research in Personality*, *46*(6), 710–718. doi:10.1016/j.jrp.2012.08.008

Schoenebeck, S. Y. (2014). Giving up Twitter for Lent: How and Why We Take Breaks from Social Media. *SIGCHI Conference on Human Factors in Computing Systems*. Toronto, Ontario, Canada.

Schupak, A. (2015, Jan. 13). Computers know you better than your friends do. *CBS News*. Retrieve from: http://www.cbsnews.com/news/computers-know-you-better-than-your-friends-do/

Stephens, M., & Poorthuis, A. (2014). Follow thy neighbor: Connecting the social and the spatial networks on Twitter. *Computers, Environment and Urban Systems*, 1–9.

Wagner, C., Mitter, S., Körner, C., & Strohmaier, M. (2012). When social bots attack: Modeling susceptibility of users in online social networks. #MSM2012 workshop. Lyon, France.

Weng, L. (2013, June). Virality prediction and community structure in social networks. YouTube. Retrieve from: https://www.youtube.com/watch?v=VVnN5Wm8fcE&feature=youtu.be

Weng, L., Menczer, F., & Ahn, Y.-Y. (2014). *Predicting successful memes using network and community structure* (Pre-publication version). Association for the Advancement of Artificial Intelligence. 1-11.

Weng, L., Ratkiewicz, J., Perra, N., Goncalves, B., Castillo, C., Bonchi, F., et al. (2013). The role of information diffusion in the evolution of social networks. *KDD '13,* Chicago, Illinois.

Yang, J., & Leskovec, J. (2011). Patterns of temporal variation in Online Media. *WSDM '11,* Hong Kong, China. doi:10.1145/1935826.1935863

Youyou, W., Kosinski, M., & Stillwell, D. (2014). *Computer-based personality judgments are more accurate than those made by humans (PNAS Early Edition). 1–5.*

KEY TERMS AND DEFINITIONS

Broadcast: The wide distribution of a message with many potential recipients, often from a concentrated or single point (thought to apply more to traditional media like radio and television).

Burstiness: The sudden spike in an occurrence based on time series analysis.

Content Analysis: Any of a number of systematic ways to analyze data with qualitative and quantitative observations.

Cross-Sectional: A slice in time.

Cyborg: A cybernetic organization, a computer-assisted human or a human-assisted computer social media account.

Electronic Self-Talk: The act of microblogging messages to oneself.

Eventgraph: A network graph based around an occurrence or period in time.

Microblogging: Nanoblogging, the sharing of short messages over a social media platform or online social network.

Microchat: A microblogged conversation.

Narrative: A story.

Narrowcast: A message sent to a small and targeted audience.

Network Analysis: The analysis of interrelationships between entities.

Open Domain: Public.

Self-Loop: The phenomenon of a social media account that is self-referential or replies to its own messages (or somehow relates to itself), with this relationship represented in network analysis as a self-loop (a loop that starts and ends with the same node / entity).

Self-Talk: The act of talking with the self (aloud or silently), often used to describe types of expression involving self-identity and positive self-encouragement Social performance: The behaviors and posturing that people engage in to create an impression on others as a part of impression management Solidarity: Shared or aligned ideas and purpose.

Uniform Resource Locator (URL): A unique Internet address for a website.

Unstructured Data: Information that is not pre-structured or pre-labeled (as in a worksheet or database).

Section 2
Theories, Models, and Practices for Multimedia Design and Deployment

Chapter 4
Leveraging the Design and Development of Multimedia Presentations for Learners

Lijia Lin
East China Normal University, China

Jackie Hee Young Kim
Armstrong State University, USA

Amy Leh
California State University San Bernardino, USA

Danilo M. Baylen
University of West Georgia, USA

ABSTRACT

The chapter addresses how multimedia presentations can be designed effectively for learners. Based on the literature, it defines the related terms and discusses the role of human factors during the design and development process of multimedia. Then, it discusses strategies, such as providing learner control and using visual cueing, to design effective multimedia presentations. In addition, various technologies in creating multimedia-based instruction are described. Finally, the chapter discusses evaluation frameworks, as well as the implications for integrating multimedia into educational practices.

INTRODUCTION

We know the old saying that "A picture is worth a thousand words". And many times we assume that learning from the combination of words and pictures should be better than learning from words alone. That may be the major reason that we have illustrations in the printed textbooks, we have a job aid with static screenshots and text labels to show you how to install a piece of software, or we have a narrated video to get you started for a brand new laptop with a new operating system. Sometimes however, as a teacher, an instructional designer or a developer, you may rely solely on your experience and intuition to design and develop a multimedia presentation without evidence-based guidance. Your target audience may still find the instruction difficult to understand even with the combination of words and pictures. In this chapter, we will define multimedia related concepts and discuss human factors and strategies for effective multimedia design and development in the hope of inspiring both research and practice. To

DOI: 10.4018/978-1-4666-8696-0.ch004

guide educational practices, we will also identify technologies for multimedia design and development, provide evaluation frameworks for effective multimedia products, and discuss implications for integrating multimedia into practices.

Defining Multimedia Presentations as Levers for Learning

In computer-based learning environments such as online learning systems, intelligent tutoring systems, or virtual worlds, information may be presented to learners in a variety of forms, such as on-screen texts, music, narrations, illustrations, diagrams, animations, and videos. The combination of all or some of these media is considered as multimedia. Mayer (2005a) adopted a presentation mode view to define multimedia—"presenting material in verbal and pictorial form" (p. 2). From this broad perspective, multimedia are not limited to computer-based environments. Texts and visualizations in printing format can also be considered as media. Also, a learner is learning from multimedia if the printed texts and visualizations are presented with other technology-based media (e.g., computer-based animations and narrations). As technology advances, multiple forms of information presented on mobile devices may also be categorized as multimedia. For instance, by tapping on the screen of your mobile phone, you learn about how to conduct a knee surgery from the application *Virtual Knee Surgery* that includes audios, visuals and on-screen texts (see: http://www.edheads.org/activities/knee). This type of mobile learning is also in the form of multimedia. In sum, the term *multimedia* in this chapter refers to multiple forms of information presented on a wide range of platforms and these platforms are mostly technology-based.

Multimedia learning, particularly in research, is to describe learning in multimedia environments. It occurs when a learner constructs mental representations via multimedia in his/her working memory by integrating his/her prior knowledge and stores these representations in his/her long-term memory. The rationale for using multimedia presentations to foster learning is that presenting information in multiple formats is aligned with our humans' cognitive architecture (Mayer, 2005b).

Based on our current understanding of human's cognitive architecture, we process incoming information via two channels, one channel dealing with verbal information and the other channel dealing with visual information (Baddeley, 1986; Mayer, 2005b; Paivio, 1986). These two channels do not necessarily process information separately. Information processed in one channel can be converted to the other channel for further processing. For example, when the word "dog" is presented to a learner textually, an individual may process the information via his/her verbal channel. However, he/she can also mentally form a visualization of a dog, therefore converting verbal information to visual information and allowing the visual channel to process. It is also possible that a learner may mentally construct textual descriptions when he/she views an animation that shows the blood flow in the human cardiovascular system. Due to the limited capacity of our working memory (Miller, 1956), each channel can only process a limited amount of information. A learner may experience cognitive overload if too much information is squeezed into one channel at the initial processing stage. For instance, when both animations and on-screen texts are used to explain human cardiovascular system, all of these visual instructional messages may be initially processed through a learner's verbal channel, and his/her limited processing capacity may become a bottle neck for information processing, thus preventing him/her from understanding the incoming instructional messages. However, if animations are visually presented with narrated audio of the instructional explanations, a learner can initially receive and process information via both channels and his/her understanding may be fostered. Therefore, externally presenting instructional messages through multimedia is aligned with our humans' internal cognitive architecture, and multimedia presentations optimize the information processing in our verbal and visual channels.

Exploring Human Factors for Strategic Multimedia Design and Development

Based on decades of studies on the effectiveness of multimedia in education and training, researchers find that there is a diversity of animated visualizations (Ploetzner & Lowe, 2012), which may contribute to the diversity of the efficacy of multimedia (e.g., Mayer, Hegarty, Mayer, & Campbell, 2005; see Höffler & Leutner, 2007; Tversky, Morrison, & Betrancourt, 2002). Hegarty (2004) pointed out that research should investigate "what conditions must be in place for dynamic visualizations to be effective in learning" (p. 344). To inspire research and guide educational practices, it is important to discuss the human factors during the process of designing and developing multimedia presentations.

Learners' prior knowledge is one of the human factors that researchers and practitioners should consider. For example, a primary school child cannot understand a derivative function no matter whether the instruction is multimedia-based or not, because he/she has not even learned algebra. Research in the past decades has supported the claim that the instructional design that enhances novice learners' learning may not be helpful for expert learners, and vice versa (c.f., *expertise reversal effect*, Kalyuga, Ayres, Chandler, & Sweller, 2003; Kalyuga, Rikers, & Paas, 2012). For instance, two recent experiments demonstrated that when learners were instructed to learn soccer play, novice learners benefited more from static and low-speed presentations, whereas expert learners benefited more from animated and high-speed presentations (Khacharem, Zoudji, Spanjers, & Kalyuga, 2014). As learners' existing knowledge plays an important role moderating the effect of instruction, instructional designers should have some knowledge about their target audience's prior knowledge before designing and developing their products. This process is usually referred to as learner analysis in the systematic instructional design process (Dick, Carey, & Carey, 2005). Researchers and practitioners can also focus on designing and developing learning systems that provide adaptive instruction to individual learners (Kalyuga, 2007), as there is evidence showing adaptive computer-based tutoring can produce large learning gains (Sabo, Atkinson, Barrus, Joseph, & Perez, 2013).

Learner motivation is another factor that plays an important role in multimedia-based learning and instruction. Cognitive processes such as selecting information, organizing information in meaningful structures and integrating information with one's prior knowledge, are all influenced by motivation. A highly motivated learner may be willing to spend a considerable amount of time and effort making sense of the presented instructional material, which may lead to enhanced learning and performance. However, a learner lacking motivation may choose to quit learning. The challenge for educational researchers and practitioners is how to motivate learners in multimedia presentations. Traditionally, instructional designers present a problem, ask a question, or present a scenario at the beginning of the instruction to stimulate learners. When this type of motivation techniques is applied to learning in multimedia environments, there is empirical evidence showing that they may be effective. For example, some researchers presented learners with a series of predicting questions and instructed them to predict the function of a mechanical system. They found that this technique enhanced learners' understanding of the mechanical system no matter whether they viewed static or animated visualizations of the system (Hegarty, Kriz, & Cate, 2003). On the other hand, technology per se has a great potential to motivate students in multimedia environments. Multimedia can be used to provide abstract outlines for learners before detailed instruction is delivered, which is served as the function of an advance organizer. Willerman and Mac Harg (1991) utilized a concept map as an advance organizer in an 8th grade science classroom and they found that the students performed better in a science test than their peers who did not use the concept map. Vogel-Walcutt, Guidice, Fiorella, and Nicholson (2013) used video games as advance organizers before a computer-based training that taught learners to complete a military's call for fire task. They found that learner who played the video games showed more interest in learning. In addition to pre-instruction motivators, other technology supported techniques have showed promises. Embedding an animated pedagogical agent in a multimedia presentation is one method that researchers have investigated in the 21st century. An animated pedagogical agent is "a lifelike character that provides instructional information through verbal and nonverbal forms of communication" (Lin, Atkinson, Christopherson, Joseph, & Harrison, 2013, pp.239, see Figure 1 for an example). When the multimedia environment incorporates an agent, learners may consider interacting with the computer as a social event and are motivated to interact with the computer to learn (Atkinson, Mayer & Merrill, 2005). In summary, learner motivation plays an important role in the effectiveness of multimedia presentations, and there are multiple ways to motivate learners in multimedia learning.

It is of note that there are other human factors, such as learners' affect state, metacognition, and self-regulation, which teachers, instructional designers and developers should bear in mind during the design and development process. We recommend conducting a learner analysis (and other related analyses such as needs assessment) at the beginning of a systematic instructional design process so that a clear picture of the target audience can be obtained.

Figure 1. A screen shot of a multimedia environment embedded with an animated agent (Lin, Atkinson, Christopherson, Joseph, & Harrison, 2013)

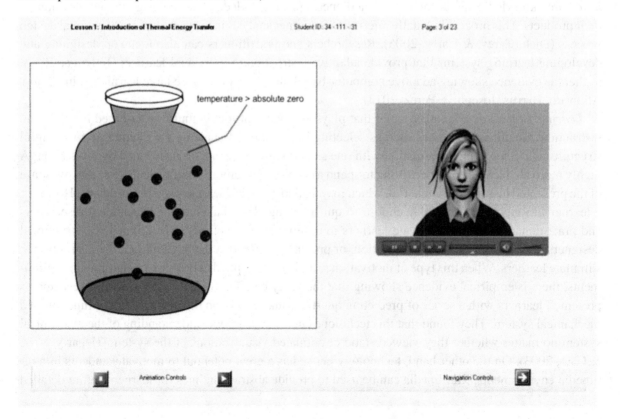

Understanding Strategies for Creating Multimedia Presentations

Based on well-designed scientific studies, researchers have proposed a series of evidence-based principles to guide both research and practice in multimedia presentations (Mayer, 2005c). These principles provide a solid foundation for teachers, instructional designers and developers to understand the strategies for creating multimedia presentations.

Providing learner control is the first strategy we would discuss for creating multimedia. Based on the empirical evidence, Clark and Mayer (2011) summarized it as the *Learner Control Principle*. According to Betrancourt (2005), learner control is to let learners control the pace and/or the direction of a multimedia presentation. This is critical to learning when dynamic visualizations, such as animations and videos, are used to deliver instruction in the learning environments. Due to the transitory nature of an animation, a learner may not fully understand the information contained in the animation when the presentation of the animated information has already finished. Granted with the control (e.g., a playback button or a pause button), a learner can go back to receive the instruction by viewing the animation once again. And he/she can view the animation for the third or even fourth time, if he/she feels that there is a need to do so. The results of some research studies have provided empirical evidence to support this design strategy (Evans, & Gibbons, 2007; Hasler, Kersten, & Sweller, 2007; Mayer, & Chandler, 2001; Mayer, Dow, & Mayer, 2003; Moreno, & Valdez, 2005; Schwan, & Riempp, 2004; Wouters, Tabbers, & Paas, 2007). For instance, Evans and Gibbons (2007) found that using an interactive diagram, in which a learner can control the presentation of texts and segments of animations (see Figure 2), facilitated undergraduate students' deep learning about the mechanism of a bicycle pump. In their case, learners could click the Repeat button to play the segment of animation again, click the Previous button to study the previous segment and the Next button to study the next segment. However, learner control may not be as critical in static visuals as in dynamic visuals, since static visuals are not transient in nature. The study conducted by Boucheix and Schneider (2009) provides some evidence that integrating a series of static graphics without learner control enhanced students' understanding of a mechanical system.

Visual cueing (or "signaling") is another strategy to create effective multimedia presentations for instruction and training. It is a technique to add non-content signaling devices to the learning environments to direct learners' attention to the important information. It is not difficult to imagine a situation that so many elements, such as on-screen texts, narrations, animations, control buttons, navigation links and other elements, are presented to learners in a multimedia environment that learners' attention may be directed to perceptually salient information that may be irrelevant to learning. As a result, instructional designers and developers need to direct learners' attention by utilizing visual cues. Lin and Atkinson (2011) used arrow cueing to point to the important information presented in the animation that showed concepts and processes of rock cycle (see Figure 3), and they found cueing fostered efficiently learning. Nelson, Kim, Foshee and Slack (2014) found that learners experienced lower mental demands in a virtual world, in which sheep objects were cued with symbols (see Figure 4). The current literature shows other empirical evidence to support the use of visual cues as a strategy for creating an effective multimedia presentation (e.g., Lin, Atkinson, Savenye, & Nelson, 2014; see de Koning, Tabbers, Rikers, & Paas, 2009 for a review). The learning principle based on it is referred to as the Signaling Principle (Mayer & Moreno, 2003).

We have described two prominent strategies—providing learner control and visual cueing—for creating effective multimedia presentations. These two strategies are unique for multimedia, but there are other strategies that are worth mentioning. For example, when designing and developing multimedia,

Figure 2. A screen shot of the interactive version of the learning environment (Evans, & Gibbons, 2007)

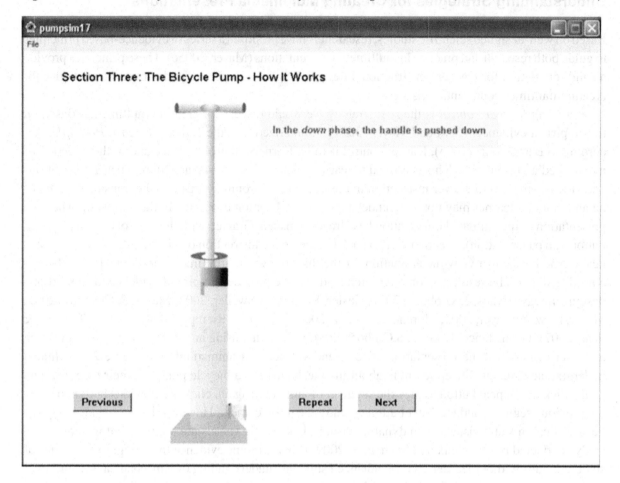

visualizations should be arranged in close proximity to the corresponding texts to enhance the limited attention; graphics accompanied with audio narrations are better than graphics with on-screen texts to optimize learners' information processing in their cognitive system; animations are better to be presented in segments to overcome the transitory nature of animations. These strategies are all based on evidence-based learning principles in the multimedia learning literature (Mayer, 2005c).

Identifying Technologies for Creating Multimedia Presentations

When creating multimedia presentations, we should always keep the aforementioned strategies, providing learner control and utilizing visual cues, in mind and identify appropriate technologies for project development. Media types used in multimedia presentations may include text, images, animations, audio and video; therefore, one may select a variety of hardware and software for the multimedia production. What technologies do we need to consider when creating multimedia presentations? How do we identify appropriate technologies for such presentations?

First, let us look at the technologies available for creating multimedia presentations. Technology advances rapidly. It is much easier to develop a multimedia presentation today than before because many

Figure 3. A screen shot of the learning environment that shows visually cued animations (Lin, & Atkinson, 2011)

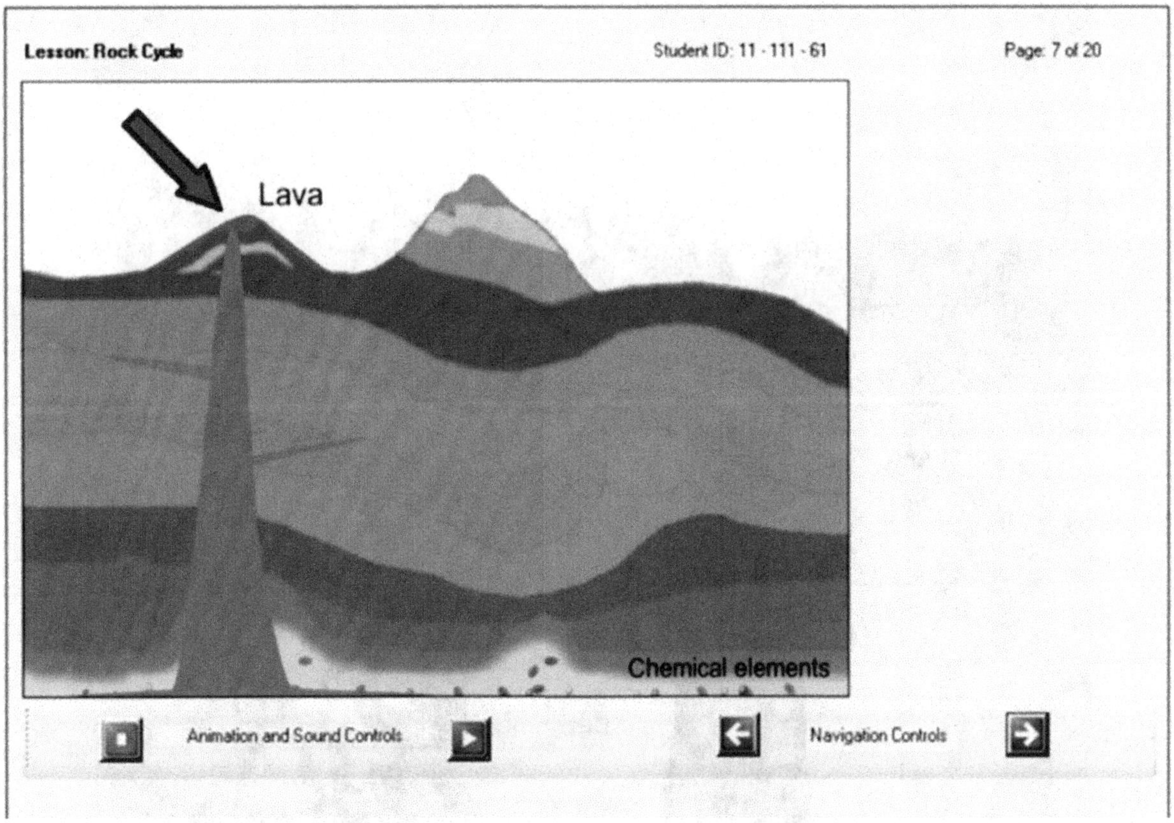

computers come with a built-in microphone and camera, and many multimedia applications are user-friendly at low cost or even free of charge. Hence, it is not difficult to develop a multimedia presentation. However, producing a sophisticated multimedia presentation of high quality may still require money and time that many people cannot afford.

In general, when producing a multimedia presentation, one should use a powerful computer with appropriate hardware and software. Examples of the hardware include, but are not limited to, video cameras, digital cameras, microphones, scanners, storage devices (CDs, DVDs, or/and external hard drives), ports (firewire or/and USB), and monitors. Examples of the software include, but are not limited to, *PowerPoint, Keynote, Prezi, Metta, Mediator, Adobe Captivate, Articulate Presenter, and Camtasia.* For more information concerning multimedia presentation technologies, one may simply conduct an Internet search using keywords, such as, multimedia tools or applications, etc.

How do we identify out of those available technologies the appropriate ones for the multimedia presentation we want to create? One factor to consider is the purpose of the presentation. A presentation with a commercial purpose is expected to be very different from a presentation for education. A sophisticated and highly professional commercial multimedia presentation may help to sell the product. Such a level of sophistication is not required to facilitate student learning in educational multimedia presentations; those presentations may be deemed successful as long as they support student learning.

Figure 4. A screen shot of the virtual world environment that shows a player is interacting with a visually cued sheep (Nelson, Kim, Foshee, & Slack, 2013)

A learning goal is a key factor to consider when identifying technologies for creating multimedia presentations. If the goal of a multimedia presentation is to teach students specific concepts, one may consider using *Metta* that allows instructor to include YouTube videos, pictures, voice recordings, and content from Pinterest, and then to insert a quiz during or at the end of the presentation. Should the purpose of a multimedia presentation be to help learners develop a presentation and to deliver it in front of an audience, one may consider the use of presentation software (e.g., PowerPoint and Keynote), since they are commonly used and widely available.

Another factor for consideration when identifying technologies for creating multimedia presentations is budget. As we mentioned earlier, it is no longer difficult to create multimedia presentations due to the technology advancement and decreasing cost of hardware and software. However, some technologies are still costly, especially the ones for commercial multimedia presentations. Therefore, one should check how much money has been earmarked for the multimedia production before one starts the project. Otherwise, one might run out of money before the project is complete.

The other factor for consideration is the target audience, e.g., culture, age, and gender. Although this factor might not be strictly related to identifying technologies for creating such presentations, it plays a critical role in developing the presentations. For instance, a multimedia presentation for a young learner may involve considerable amount of animations that might not be appropriate in a presentation for adults. For audiences with certain specific backgrounds and cultures, a developer needs to carefully decide the use of colors. A color may mean something positive to one group of people but symbolize the opposite to another. For example, the color of "yellow" symbolizes "Mourning" to Egyptians while means "royalty" to Chinese.

In summary, nowadays everyone should be able to create a multimedia presentation. Factors for consideration when identifying technologies for creating multimedia presentations include, but are not limited to, purpose, goal, and budget. The target audience is also an important factor to consider when developing a multimedia project.

Evaluating the Effectiveness of Multimedia Presentations

Formative evaluation and summative evaluation are two types of evaluation that are commonly used in instructional design and other educational and training practices. Formative evaluation is conducted when the design and development activities are still ongoing. The data collected for this type of evaluation can be quite informal: small-scale interviews with the target audience, interviews with the internal experts, and very small-scale quantitative surveys, etc. It is very useful to improve the ongoing project, as designers and developers can modify their work with relatively low cost of time, money and other resources. It can effectively avoid a project's changes or growth that cannot be controlled as the project progresses ("project creeps"). Summative evaluation is conducted to assess the final project and is usually conducted externally. The data collected for this type of evaluation could be focus group interviews, expert ratings, large-scale attitudinal surveys, and learning outcomes, etc. The results of this type of evaluation are to judge the actual value of the final product—whether it is good or bad. A systematic design and development process for an effective multimedia product definitely needs both formative and summative evaluation. For instance, we, as a team of instructional designers and developers, need to create a multimedia program to teach high school students about thermodynamics for a science course. We have followed the systematic design process: (a) We know that the target students have some knowledge about thermodynamics and they are easily bored in class (learner analysis). We also know that the school would like to have some changes in traditional teaching methods (need analysis). (b) We have formulated a series of instructional goals and objectives according to the standards and consultation with teachers. We have determined the contents and instructional sequence, as well as the interface of the multimedia program. At this stage, a formative evaluation could be conducted by consulting with teachers and interviewing with students to determine (a) whether the contents and instructional sequence are appropriate, (b) whether teachers and students like the program interface. Based on the results of this round of formative evaluation, we modify the content and the program interface if necessary, and then hand the product to the technology staff to let them work on the development. When the developers have a prototype ready, we can run another formative evaluation internally (alpha testing) to test the prototype and provide feedback to the developers. Then, the developers modify the program and we, along with some teachers, run another formative evaluation (beta testing). At the final stage, we submit the multimedia product to the school leaders and teachers and, with their approval, implement the product in class. Based on the collected data from the schools leaders and teachers (interview records, quantitative ratings, etc.), class observations, and students' attitude and learning outcomes, all concerned parties can make a judgment (summative evaluation) about the effectiveness of this multimedia program

Another well-known evaluation model is the Kirkpatrick's four-level model (Kirkpatrick, 1994; Kirkpatrick, & Kirkpatrick, 2006). This model has been so widely used to evaluate training programs in academia and industry that we believe it is still applicable to assess the effectiveness of multimedia presentations. The four levels are *Reaction, Learning, Behavior,* and *Results* and they are listed in order. The first level *Reaction* is to evaluate attitude: how learners perceive about the program—whether they like it or not, whether they feel boring or interesting, satisfied or dissatisfied, competent or incompetent, etc. The second level *Learning* is to evaluate learners' knowledge: how the learners perform on a post-training test (it could be a self-designed test, a standard test or both). The third level *Behavior* is to evaluate the effectiveness of a program on the behavioral level: whether learners have changed their behaviors, how learners apply their knowledge, etc. The fourth and the final level *Results* is to evaluate the effectiveness of a program on an institutional level or on a community level: how the company's sales have changed, how many prospective employees have applied for positions in the company, how many additional students have enrolled, etc. It is often very difficult and costly to conduct the evaluation activities on the third and fourth level, no matter whether it is in the academia or industry. But educational professionals could utilize the Kirkpatrick model to evaluate the effectiveness of multimedia presentations. Using the multimedia program to teach high school students about thermodynamics as an example, Table 1 presents the data sources that we believe could be collected to evaluate the effectiveness of the multimedia program using the Kirkpatrick model.

Implications for Integrating Multimedia Presentations as Best Practice

This section will address: 1) ways of constructing effective learning environments for students' success, 2) pedagogical functionalities of multimedia presentations that can positively impact the successful implementation of technology integration practices, and 3) possible barriers to integrating multimedia presentations.

Multimedia presentations, as a delivery medium in teaching, require pedagogically equipped facilitators who create effective environments for successful learning. Research reports that multimedia presentations impact students' learning in specific contexts where research-based and goal-oriented learning environments promote learning. The prominent learning environment reported was a constructivist-based learning environment using multimedia (Neo & Neo, 2009). It can be seen that students experienced high levels of motivation and self-esteem when doing the multimedia project. More importantly, it enhanced their confidence levels in the newly acquired skills because they realized that they can use the same

Table 1. Use the Kirkpatrick model to evaluate a multimedia program that delivers instruction about thermodynamics to high school students

Kirkpatrick Model	Data Sources
Reaction	Students' satisfaction, perceived confidence and competence, etc.
Learning	Students' scores on an in-class quiz, midterm exam, etc.
Behavior	Observations of applying knowledge in daily life, etc.
Results	Increased enrollment of the course, etc.

skills in future undertakings. A technology-enhanced constructivist learning environment, as suggested by Jonassen (1994, 1999), can be successful in allowing students to engage in meaningful, relevant problem-solving activities, experience active learning, and be more engaged in their learning processes. Another environment that is worth mentioning for is an authentic learning environment (Herrington, Reeves, Oliver, & Woo, 2004). In this environment, students showed increased understanding of the topic and were able to see the relevance of the project to real-life situations. The third environment is a multimedia-assisted, project-based learning environment (Moursund, 1999). This method promotes a learner-centered constructivist model, and helps students develop the pre-service teachers' knowledge and self-efficacy in (a) technology, (b) subject matter, and (c) teaching (Seo, Templeton, & Pellegrino, 2008).

Additionally, we need to pay attention to pedagogical functionalities of multimedia presentations that address many of the contemporary issues in education, such as self-directed learning and evidence-based (data-driven) teaching. A growing body of theoretical and empirical literature supports the view that, when students' perceptions of control in the learning situation increases, so does their motivation to learn (Alderman, 1990; Ames, 1990; Deci & Ryan, 1991). Researchers recently reported a relatively strong relationship between multimedia technologies and self-directed learning (Kim, 2012). Therefore, we can see that learner controlled, multimedia-rich learning environments foster self-directed learning by enabling learners to have control over the pace of their own learning and by being empowered to take charge of their learning trajectories. In terms of data-driven teaching, the assessments in multimedia presentation tools offer more access to instant data than ever before for teachers (Gonzalez-Sanchez, Chavez-Echeagaray, Gibson, & Atkinson, 2013). Multimedia presentation tools strengthen the capacity to access data to improve developmentally appropriate decision-making in instruction, which leads to adaptive learning and personalized learning opportunities.

Although multimedia presentations hold many promises in education, it is important to be aware of some possible barriers to their successful integration and utilization. Steelman (2005) identified technical difficulties with software, hardware, and networks, and teachers lacking uniformed tools, as main hindrances. Time restraints, insufficient teacher training, and tedious administrative requirements, such as keeping up with permission slips, were other difficulties cited. In the course of developing their multimedia projects, the students encountered software glitches and computer malfunctions that led to a great deal of frustration for them. These problems also caused more anxiety when there was no prompt technical support. In addition, it was challenging for the instructor to address the needs of all students because they had different interests and varying degrees of computer skills. Further, teachers need to be able to customize instruction in such a way as to fit the target students' knowledge levels and learning goals. It is critical to understand both the promises and barriers in implementing multimedia presentations as well as making the connection with pedagogy, technology, and content.

CONCLUSION

In this chapter, we have defined the concepts of multimedia and multimedia learning based on the literature. Several factors, such as prior knowledge and motivation, were identified and discussed in the contexts of designing and developing multimedia-based instruction. In discussing these factors, we argued for better understanding of the cognitive mechanisms that contribute to the efficacy of multimedia presentations in helping learners learn. Further, reviewing related research evidence led to identification of effective strategies for creating multimedia that supports learning and instruction. Based on that, we provided principles to guide instructional design and development practices. Finally, we identified and described several technology-based tools and applications that could be used for creating multimedia, along with the frameworks for evaluating multimedia and implications for integrating multimedia into practice.

REFERENCES

Alderman, M. K. (1990). Motivation for at-risk students. *Educational Leadership, 48,* 27–30.

Ames, C. A. (1990). Motivation: What teachers need to know. *Teachers College Record, 91*(3), 409–421.

Atkinson, R. K., Mayer, R. E., & Merrill, M. M. (2005). Fostering social agency in multimedia learning: Examining the impact of an animated agent's voice. *Contemporary Educational Psychology, 30*(1), 117–139. doi:10.1016/j.cedpsych.2004.07.001

Baddeley, A. D. (1986). *Working memory*. New York: Oxford University Press.

Betrancourt, M. (2005). The animation and interactivity principles in multimedia learning. In R. E. Mayer (Ed.), *The Cambridge handbook of multimedia learning* (pp. 287–296). New York: Cambridge University Press. doi:10.1017/CBO9780511816819.019

Boucheix, J., & Schneider, E. (2009). Static and animated presentations in learning dynamic mechanical systems. *Learning and Instruction, 19*(2), 112–127. doi:10.1016/j.learninstruc.2008.03.004

Clark, R. C., & Mayer, R. E. (2011). *E-learning and the science of instruction: Proven guidelines for consumers and designers of multimedia learning*. San Francisco, CA: Pfeiffer. doi:10.1002/9781118255971

de Koning, B. B., Tabbers, H., Rikers, R. M. J. P., & Paas, F. (2009). Towards a framework for attention cueing in instructional animations: Guidelines for research and design. *Educational Psychology Review. 21*(2). 113–140. doi:10.1007/s10648-009-9098-7

Deci, E. L., & Ryan, R. M. (1991). A motivational approach to self: Integration in personality. In R. Dienstbier (Ed.), Nebraska symposium on motivation: Vol. 38, Perspectives on motivation (pp. 237–288). Lincoln: University of Nebraska Press.

Dick, W., Carey, L., & Carey, J. O. (6th Ed.) (2005). *The systematic design of instruction*. Boston: Allyn & Bacon.

Evans, C., & Gibbons, N. J. (2007). The interactivity effect in multimedia learning. *Computers & Education, 49*(4), 1147–1160. doi:10.1016/j.compedu.2006.01.008

Gonzalez-Sanchez, J., Chavez-Echeagaray, M. E., Gibson, D., & Atkinson, R. K. (2013). Multimodal affect recognition in virtual worlds: avatars mirroring user's affect, *Humaine Association Conference on Affective Computing and Intelligent Interaction*, (pp. 724–725). doi:10.1109/ACII.2013.133

Hasler, B. S., Kersten, B., & Sweller, J. (2007). Learner control, cognitive load and instructional animation. *Applied Cognitive Psychology, 21*(6), 713–729. doi:10.1002/acp.1345

Hegarty, M. (2004). Dynamic visualizations and learning: Getting to the difficult questions. *Learning and Instruction, 14*(3), 343–351. doi:10.1016/j.learninstruc.2004.06.007

Hegarty, M., Kriz, S., & Cate, C. (2003). The roles of mental animations and external animations in understanding mechanical systems. *Cognition and Instruction, 21*(4), 325–360. doi:10.1207/s1532690xci2104_1

Herrington, J., Reeves, T. C., Oliver, R., & Woo, Y. (2004). Designing authentic activities in web-based courses. *Journal of Computing in Higher Education, 16*(1), 3–29. doi:10.1007/BF02960280

Höffler, T. N., & Leutner, D. (2007). Instructional animation versus static pictures: A meta-analysis. *Learning and Instruction, 17*(6), 722–738. doi:10.1016/j.learninstruc.2007.09.013

Jonassen, D. H. (1994). Thinking technology: Towards a constructivist design model. *Educational Technology*, 34–37.

Jonassen, D. H. (2nd Ed.). (1999). Designing constructivist learning environments. In C. M. Reigeluth (Ed.), *Instructional theories and models: A new paradigm of instructional theory* (pp. 215–239). Mahwah: Lawrence Erlbaum.

Kalyuga, S. (2007). Expertise reversal effect and its Implications for learner-tailored instruction. *Educational Psychology Review, 19*(4), 509–539. doi:10.1007/s10648-007-9054-3

Kalyuga, S., Ayres, P., Chandler, P., & Sweller, J. (2003). The expertise reversal effect. *Educational Psychologist, 38*(1), 23–31. doi:10.1207/S15326985EP3801_4

Kalyuga, S., Rikers, R., & Paas, F. (2012). Educational implications for expertise reversal effects in learning and performance of complex cognitive and sensorimotor skills. *Educational Psychology Review, 24*(2), 313–337. doi:10.1007/s10648-012-9195-x

Khacharem, A., Zoudji, B., Spanjers, I. A. E., & Kalyuga, S. (2014). Improving learning from animated soccer scenes: Evidence for the expertise reversal effect. *Computers in Human Behavior, 35*, 339–349. doi:10.1016/j.chb.2014.03.021

Kim, J. H. (2012). *Dropping out of high school: The role of 3D Alice programming workshop. Paper presented at Association for Educational Communication and Technology Annual International Convention*. Louisville, KY.

Kirkpatrick, D. L. (1994). *Evaluating training programs*. San Francisco: Berrett-Koehler Publishers, Inc.

Kirkpatrick, D. L., & Kirkpatrick, J. D. (2006). *Evaluating training programs: The four levels*. San Francisco: Berrett-Koehler Publishers.

Lin, L., & Atkinson, R. K. (2011). Using animations and visual cueing to support learning of scientific concepts and processes. *Computers & Education, 56*(3), 650–658. doi:10.1016/j.compedu.2010.10.007

Lin, L., Atkinson, R. K., Christopherson, R. M., Joseph, S. S., & Harrison, C. J. (2013). Animated agents and learning: Does the type of verbal feedback they provide matter? *Computers & Education, 67*, 239–249. doi:10.1016/j.compedu.2013.04.017

Lin, L., Atkinson, R. K., Savenye, W. C., & Nelson, B. C. (2014). The effects of visual cues and self-explanation prompts: Empirical evidence in a multimedia environment. *Interactive Learning Environments*. doi:10.1080/10494820.2014.924531

Mayer, R. E. (2005a). Introduction to multimedia learning. In R. E. Mayer (Ed.), *The Cambridge handbook of multimedia learning* (pp. 1–16). New York: Cambridge University Press. doi:10.1017/CBO9780511816819.002

Mayer, R. E. (2005b). Cognitive theory of multimedia learning. In R. E. Mayer (Ed.), *The Cambridge handbook of multimedia learning* (pp. 31–48). New York: Cambridge University Press. doi:10.1017/CBO9780511816819.004

Mayer, R. E. (2005c). *The Cambridge handbook of multimedia learning*. New York: Cambridge University Press. doi:10.1017/CBO9780511816819

Mayer, R. E., & Chandler, P. (2001). When learning is just a click away: Does simple user interaction foster deeper understanding of multimedia messages? *Journal of Educational Psychology*, *93*(2), 390–397. doi:10.1037/0022-0663.93.2.390

Mayer, R. E., Dow, G. T., & Mayer, S. (2003). Multimedia learning in an interactive self-explaining environment: What works in the design of agent-based microworlds? *Journal of Educational Psychology*, *95*(4), 806–812. doi:10.1037/0022-0663.95.4.806

Mayer, R. E., Hegarty, M., Mayer, S., & Campbell, J. (2005). When static media promote active learning: Annotated illustrations versus narrated animations in multimedia instruction. *Journal of Experimental Psychology. Applied*, *11*(4), 256–265. doi:10.1037/1076-898X.11.4.256 PMID:16393035

Mayer, R. E., & Moreno, R. (2003). Nine ways to reduce cognitive load in multimedia learning. *Educational Psychologist*, *38*(1), 43–52. doi:10.1207/S15326985EP3801_6

Miller, G. A. (1956). The magic number seven, plus or minus two: Some limits on our capacity for processing information. *Psychological Review*, *63*(2), 81–97. doi:10.1037/h0043158 PMID:13310704

Moreno, R., & Valdez, A. (2005). Cognitive load and learning effects of having students organize pictures and words in multimedia environments: The role of student interactivity and feedback. *Educational Technology Research and Development*, *53*(3), 35–45. doi:10.1007/BF02504796

Moursund, D. (1999). *Project-based learning using information technology. International Society for Technology in Education*. Eugene, OR:

Nelson, B. C., Kim, Y., Foshee, C., & Slack, K. (2014). Visual signaling in virtual world-based assessments: The SAVE Science project. *Information Science*, *264*, 32–40. doi:10.1016/j.ins.2013.09.011

Neo, M., & Neo, T.-K. (2009). Engaging students in multimedia-mediated constructivist learning: Students' perceptions. *Journal of Educational Technology & Society*, *12*(2), 254–266.

Paivio, A. (1986). *Mental representations: A dual coding approach*. Oxford: Oxford University Press.

Ploetzner, R., & Lowe, R. (2012). A systematic characterization of expository animations. *Computers in Human Behavior*, *28*(3), 781–794. doi:10.1016/j.chb.2011.12.001

Sabo, K. E., Atkinson, R. K., Barrus, A. L., Joseph, S. S., & Perez, R. S. (2013). Searching for the two sigma advantage: Evaluating algebra intelligent tutors. *Computers in Human Behavior*, *29*(4), 1833–1840. doi:10.1016/j.chb.2013.03.001

Schwan, S., & Riempp, R. (2004). The cognitive benefits of interactive videos: Learning to tie nautical knots. *Learning and Instruction*, *14*(3), 293–305. doi:10.1016/j.learninstruc.2004.06.005

Seo, K. K., Templeton, R., & Pellegrino, D. (2008). Creating a ripple effect: Incorporating multimedia- assisted project-based learning in teacher education. *Theory into Practice*, *47*(3), 259–265. doi:10.1080/00405840802154062

Steelman, J. (2005). Multimedia makes it mark: Benefits and drawbacks of including these projects in your curriculum. *Learning and Leading with Technology*, *33*, 16–19.

Sweller, J., van Merrienboer, J. J. G., & Paas, F. (1998). Cognitive architecture and instructional design. *Educational Psychology Review*, *10*(3), 251–296. doi:10.1023/A:1022193728205

Tversky, B., Morrison, J. B., & Betrancourt, M. (2002). Animation: Can it facilitate? *International Journal of Human-Computer Studies*, *57*(4), 247–262. doi:10.1006/ijhc.2002.1017

Vogel-Walcutt, J. J., Guidice, K. D., Fiorella, L., & Nicholson, D. (2013). Using a video game as an advance organizer: Effects on development of procedural and conceptual knowledge, cognitive load, and casual adoption. *Journal of Online Learning and Teaching*, *9*, 376–392.

Willerman, M., & Mac Harg, R. A. (1991). The concept map as an advance organizer. *Journal of Research in Science Teaching*, *28*(8), 705–711. doi:10.1002/tea.3660280807

Wouters, P., Tabbers, H. K., & Paas, F. (2007). Interactivity in video-based models. *Educational Psychology Review*, *19*(3), 327–342. doi:10.1007/s10648-007-9045-4

KEY TERMS AND DEFINITIONS

Animated Pedagogical Agent: A lifelike character that is incorporated into a multimedia environment to provide verbal and nonverbal forms of communication.

Expertise Reversal Effect: Instructional design that enhances novice learners' learning may not be helpful for expert learners, and vice versa.

Formative Evaluation: Evaluation conducted when instructional design and development are still ongoing.

Learner Control: Let learners control the pace and/or the direction of the instruction.

Multimedia: Presenting verbal and pictorial materials through multiple media.

Multimedia Learning: Learners construct mental representations in multimedia environment in which verbal and pictorial instructional materials are presented.

Summative Evaluation: Evaluation conducted to assess the success of a final project or program when it is completed.

Visual Cueing: A technique to add non-content signaling devices to learning environments to direct learners' attention to the important information.

Chapter 5
Audio for Multi–Media Presentations in E–Learning

Hattie Wiley
National Weather Service, USA

ABSTRACT

Although many advances have changed the way we are able record, distribute, and consume audio enhanced or audio based learning materials, audio can still be either a critical driver or an impeding detriment to learner comprehension and retention. Consequently, this chapter reviews the instructional design implications of audio prior to exploring the impacts advances in audio technology, software, and equipment have on the creation of audio enhanced or audio based multimedia presentations for learning, training, or education.

AUDIO FOR MULTI-MEDIA PRESENTATIONS IN E-LEARNING

As popular as video is, audio will always remain a powerful medium for learning products if only because learners are often not in a position to actually watch content, but may be still be able to listen to it. Think of the daily commute as just one key example—this is prime time for learning that audio can serve well. (Cobb, 2013)

Now it is time to consider the audio aspect of multimedia presentations (particularly for e-learning). Like all things technical, the way we create audio enhanced media has come a long ways over the years. For example, audio enhanced learning has migrated from classroom lecture halls, to records, to books on tape, to CDs, and now to downloadable files sometimes referred to as downloads or podcasts (Handley & Chapman, 2011).

From my own childhood, I recall read along records which quickly became tapes and even stuffed animals. Today, children can press buttons embedded in books, globes, electronic readers, and other objects to learn their early words. Last but not least, of course, mobile devices and computers offer even more ways to access the sounds we all crave.

DOI: 10.4018/978-1-4666-8696-0.ch005

These sounds, from the serene crashing of ocean waves to the obnoxious blaring of emergency alarms, move us. They change us physiologically, psychologically, cognitively and behaviorally (Treasure, 2011) and they can help or hinder our ability to learn (Clark & Mayer, 2011). It is up to us as designers to find the best ways to leverage this *sonic* force in a manner most conducive to our various causes. This chapter examines advances in both theory and technology that allows us to make better use of sound and audio in elearning.

From Theory to Practice (About the Author)

This chapter is written from and for the instructional designer's perspective (although the concepts can be generalized to any multimedia presentation). Instructional design is the art and science of applying a systematic process or work flow to the creation of instructional materials. Instructional design is a field that draws from multiple branches of academic studies including (but not limited to) education, psychology, and writing. Consequently, instructional designers hail from all walks of life.

My career in instructional design actually began with the completion of an MS in Instructional Design and Technology from Emporia State University in 2001, which I have found is somewhat unusual. Oftentimes, pursuit of this type of degree occurs *after* one finds him or herself in the field of training and development. This order of progress, does however, afford me some insight and advantages over many of my colleagues. For one, I find myself naturally considering analysis and theory, **before** course contents, a strategy that can ultimately be a tremendous time, resource, and money saver.

Figure 1. An old gramophone, photo taken by Tania Matvienko courtesy of freeimages.com

With that in mind, you can expect to find both descriptions of theory *and* practice, throughout this chapter. Still, please bear in mind that this chapter is not written as a "how to guide." I urge you instead to take the concepts explored in this chapter and run simple internet searches if you prefer more step-by-step guidance. Developers tend to be extremely active online contributors and so you should be able to locate many free guides and willing gurus rather quickly.

So now, without further ado, (the trumpets), let's begin.

Sound Basics

The better we understand sound, the more effectively we can control it and make use of it. ~ Julian Treasure (2011)

Stop for a moment and listen… Most likely, you are surrounded by sound.

You can hear the hum of your computer, major appliances, or at least white noise now. If you are in an office, you can probably hear your colleagues, a printer or copier, and maybe some music playing. Sound is constant…. even when there is silence. Treasure (2011) makes it a point to emphasize that we have no "ear lids." We are always experiencing sound, even when we sleep. It is a constant presence from the moment we are formed. We even hear sound in the womb.

So What Is Sound?

According to the Encyclopedia Britannica (2015):

Sound, (is) a mechanical disturbance from a state of equilibrium that propagates through an elastic material medium. A purely subjective definition of sound is also possible, as that which is perceived by the ear, but such a definition is not particularly illuminating and is unduly restrictive, for it is useful to speak of sounds that cannot be heard by the human ear, such as those that are produced by dog whistles or by sonar equipment.

In other words, sound is a physical vibration that moves through a medium (usually air), and the spectrum of sound (like light) is much greater than human sensation. Also, sound is something we commonly represent as a wave graphically, which is something to keep in mind when we examine sound editing software.

Types of Sound in ELearning

As illustrated in Figure 2, several types of sounds are commonly used to enhance eLearning including narrations, music, sound effects, ambient sounds, and audio contained within video segments.

The goals of these enhancements vary, but quite often developers employ these strategies in order to increase retention, control moods (context), improve engagement, create a multisensory experience, and/or restore the human element to technology-based training (Bielawski & Metcalf, 2003). (Note: We will examine the specific relevancy of each type of audio within the discussion of design later on in this chapter.) Again, the goals vary and the techniques vary, however they all require audio. So, what is audio?

Figure 2. Types of sounds commonly used to enhance elearning

narration

music & ambient sounds

sound effects

audio contained within video

What is Audio?

Simply stated in this chapter, "audio" refers to the sound (narrations, music, sound effects, ambient sounds, and dialogue) or sound files included in digital training materials.

W3C explains:

The term (audio) commonly refers to a time-based media storage format for sound or music information... Audio recording, also referred as audio codecs, can be uncompressed, lossless compressed, or lossy compressed depending on the desired quality and use cases. Audio codecs can usually contain one audio channel (mono), two audio channels (stereo), or more channels (e.g. "5.1" surround). For example, human voice is recorded using one channel while music uses in general two or more channels. The quality will vary depending on the bitrate, i.e. the number of bits used per unit of playback time (2015).

Did you notice the amount of audio industry specific terminology packed into this statement, which does not even begin to explore file formats! Luckily for eLearning developers, a lot of these details are handled by innovations in our browsers, physical equipment, and eLearning software packages. Still it is up to the eLearning developer to thoroughly analyze each situation carefully and to use audio with great deliberation and care. If not used properly, audio can become a detriment to the learning process (Clark & Mayer, 2011).

Additionally, it is up to the eLearning developer to stay abreast of all the latest innovations in audio! You must consider at least four areas when using audio including instructional design, web technologies, equipment, and software as shown in Figure 3. The rest of this chapter explores each of these areas in greater detail.

Instructional Design Considerations

Fancier tools and innovations will not make a difference if we do not begin with sound instructional design. So, let us begin here.

Advances in audio impact every stage of the instructional design process for eLearning, regardless of which instructional design model one chooses to use. For the sake of simplicity, this chapter will refer to the ADDIE model.

Figure 3. Areas of innovation to consider when using audio in elearning

web technologies

equipment

software

eLearning

Most designers utilize an instructional system that has five elements: analysis, design, development, implementation, and evaluation. This model is commonly referred to as the ADDIE model, after the first letter of each word. ADDIE is used around the world and all other ISD models or approaches use these five elements even though they may be called something else. The ADDIE model or some derivative of it provides designers with the necessary structure for designing any curriculum, regardless of the variables involved. Anything from classroom lecture to distance learning starts and ends with the same fundamentals—the ADDIE model. (Hodell, 2011)

Given the ADDIE model, audio advances and innovations impact the questions asked during analysis, the products drafted during design, the tools used to develop, how training is implemented, and the questions included during evaluation. Next, let's consider each stage.

Analysis

In *ISD From the Ground Up* (2011), Chuck Hodell accurately describes analysis as the "foundation for any instructional design project." It a more common vernacular, it's just information gathering, the key to any successful venture.

This chapter will only focus on those aspects of analysis that are relevant to using audio in eLearning. Specifically, developers should be ready to ask questions regarding:

- Your obligations regarding accessibility (such as transcripts and closed captions)
- The target audiences' ability to access and listen to audio,
- The overall purpose of the training materials,
- And specific task requirements.

The answers to questions on these topics will vary depending upon your circumstance and so it is difficult to provide a formulaic diagnosis of how you should proceed; however they should help guide your decision making when considering whether to include audio based or audio enhanced elements to your training, as well as any non-audio based alternatives.

Audience

Audience or your learner analysis is the first consideration. As with light waves, human beings have a rather limited spectrum for sound and some of us are more limited than others. Furthermore, we require specialized equipment (either headphones or speakers) when experiencing media which includes sound, and an environment that is conducive to listening to media (See Figure 4 and Table 1).

Purpose

Purpose is a close second in as far as areas of consideration are concerned, since audio can be used to impact certain goals more strongly than others. For example, if your goal is a change in behavior, background music and subtle sound effects can provide a lasting impression or mood. If your content is more factual or conceptual, however, such things can be distracting and cause problems with cognitive load.

Ruth Colvin Clark and Richard E. Mayer (2011) explain:

Figure 4. Auditory limitations and needs

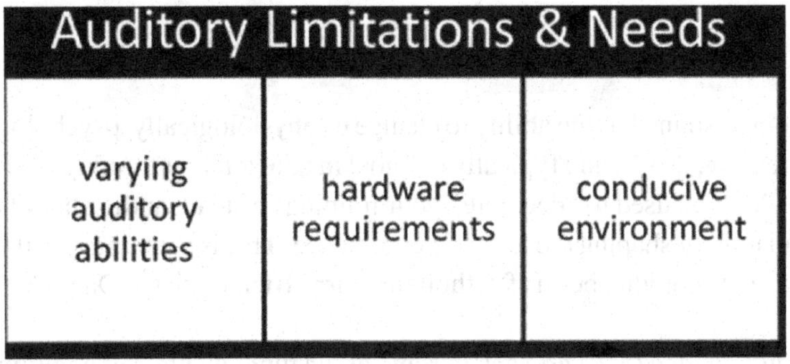

Auditory Limitations & Needs		
varying auditory abilities	hardware requirements	conducive environment

Table 1. Questions to consider

- Are there any hearing impairments to consider?
- Can or will your audience listen to audio based training?
- Can or will your audience listen to audio enhanced training?
- Do they have the proper equipment/location to turn on audio components?

Box 1. A tale of two learners

My husband is a volunteer computer repair person for several non-profit organizations. It's not his primary occupation, however, as you can imagine, he has to stay up to date on his knowledge and skills. He does this by listening to thousands of hours of podcasts on technology. Personally, I hate talk radio, and podcasts do not appear on my "desired" programming list. I'd rather listen to music or if I am going to learn something, a language program and even then, I would want to see the booklet.
So what does this tell me as an instructional designer?

Take time to investigate who your learners are and what their needs entail!

Background music and sounds may overload working memory, so they are most dangerous in situations in which the learner may experience heavy cognitive load, for example, when the material is unfamiliar, when the material is presented at a rapid rate, or when the rate of presentation is not under learner control.

Additionally, there is a significant amount of research that indicates that developers should explain with "visuals with audio narration **or** text but NOT both (Clark, 2010)." This, however, strongly relates to *what* your tasks include (See Table 2).

Task Requirements

Again, typically, developers are looking for a change in knowledge, skills, or behaviors. When those new skills involve the use of computer based applications, simulations may occur. In other words, developers may create mock scenarios and interactive on-screen examples of how to use a particular software. In these cases, the use of audio can reduce onscreen distractions during simulations. Additionally, you may desire to simulate application based sounds. Finally, similar to simulations, the use of audio can assist with making more complex tasks easier to understand (Lee & McLoughlin, 2011) (See Table 3).

Design

As mentioned previously, sound has the ability to change us physiologically, psychologically, cognitively and behaviorally (Treasure, 2011), and typically our goal in education or training is to change or growth! Audio therefore shouldn't be used to "decorate" your training. Instead, audio should be recognized and utilized as a powerful tool for shaping the learning experience. This is something to think critically about during the design stage. It shouldn't be an afterthought. Larry Bielawski and David Metcalf (2003) write:

The key benefits of audio/video (A/V) go back to some of the fundamentals of cognitive learning theory. A few examples follow. Multisensory learning has the added benefit of engaging the learner in addition to greater retention. Audio and video can often convey feelings and the subtle contexts of learning more effectively than other tools. Video is particularly effective when trying to demonstrate a kinetic task such as a tennis serve or proper turning procedure for a bolt assembly. Another use of A/V on the web could

Table 2. Questions to consider

- Are you trying to change behavior, attitudes, skills, or knowledge?
- What are the learner's pre-existing attitudes and mindsets regarding the topic?
- How complex are the concepts?

Table 3. Questions to consider

- How complex are the concepts?
- Do you need more room for visuals on-screen?
- Will anyone complete training via a mobile device?

be for personification. Audio and video can be used to restore the human element to technology-based training. For effective use, consider how A/V media can help you meet learning objectives and accommodate particular learning styles.

Here, Bielawski and Metcalf begin to touch on some of those specifics we mentioned earlier. So now let's consider how narrations, music, sound effects, ambient sounds, and audio contained within video segments can be used to impact learning (See Table 4).

Why use NARRATION?

Clark and Mayer (2011) recommend using audio instead of text in order to leave more screen space for visuals and interactions, improve mobile learning experiences, and add clarity to explanations. But *how*, you might wonder. *How could simply narrating help to clarify content?*

Consider this:

There is no sound more powerful than the human voice. Volcanic eruptions may be louder; music may be more beautiful; a lion's roar more thrilling; surf more soothing – but the human voice is the only sound that can start or stop a war, direct the course of nations, create amazing technologies, bring people together, underpin every aspect of our commercial activities, and of course say "I love you." (Treasure, 2011, p.83)

Communication is not just about word choice. In fact, when speaking, our words only account for a small percent of what people perceive. Instead, human beings are great consumers of tone (volume, speed, pitch, pause, and inflection) and nonverbal signals (Hoogterp, 2014).

For example, try reading the following sentence out loud, emphasizing the bolded words:

I didn't say he stole the money.
I **didn't** say he stole the money.
I didn't **say** he stole the money.
I didn't say **he** stole the money.
I didn't say he **stole** the money.
I didn't say he stole **the** money.
I didn't say he stole the **money**.

Notice that the sentence could have many different meanings based on the emphasis used by the narrator or the personal interpretation of the reader. This is just one example of many situations that could be more deliberately controlled by use of narration.

Table 4. Questions to consider

• Are you trying to change behavior, attitudes, skills, or knowledge?
• What are the learner's pre-existing attitudes and mindsets regarding the topic?
• How complex are the concepts?

Why Use Sound Effects, Music, and Ambient Sounds?

Sound effects, music, and ambient sounds can help put learners in the correct mindset or state for accepting the information you are trying to convey. The movie industry and commercials use this all of the time. Try listening to a movie without the sound track or with a different soundtrack (generally, you can locate examples if you search for "How music impacts movies" on YouTube.) The difference can be quite eye-opening.

From time to time, you may find in conversation or research, studies which indicate that background music is detrimental to learning and should be avoided (Clark & Mayer, 2011). This is a statement that leads back to the goal or purpose of the course. Are your trying to change attitudes/behaviors or are you trying to teach concepts?

Development

If you decide to use audio in your materials, where will it come from? Similar to visuals, there are stock repositories for sounds, but those are primarily music and sound effects. If you want narration, you will either need to record your own or pay a professional to record your narration, which can be quite expensive.

If your decision is to record your own, you will need equipment and either a basic understanding of audio technology or software to handle the process for you. Again, many eLearning development packages have simplified this process, which is something that is explored in greater detail in this chapter later on in the section titled "Advances in Software". Additionally, information on equipment is explored in this section titled "Advances in Equipment" (See Table 5).

Implementation

Somewhere prior to implementation, developers must consider the type of devices, operating systems (OSs), browsers, and audio speakers learners possess. Current advancements have served to increase the variety in all of these areas. Consequently, developers often find themselves publishing multiple versions of their materials. Many of the modern software packages help make this task easier (See Table 6). Details are explored in the sections titled "Advances in Web Technology" and "Advances in Software."

Evaluation

Last but not least, evaluations (course surveys) should contain some reference to the learner's perception on the quality, amount, and appropriateness of the included audio (See Table 7).

Table 5. Questions to consider

- Will you use stock audio?
- Will you outsource your narration or will you record your own?
- Where will you record your audio?
- Do you have the proper equipment required?
- Do you have the software required for processing audio?

Table 6. Questions to consider

• What type of type of devices, operating systems (OSs), browsers, and audio speakers will be used to access your presentations? • How technically saavy are your learners? • What alternatives will you provide?

Table 7. Questions to consider

• Did the delivery format (audio) help you understand the learning materials? • Was the audio presented at a consistently comfortable level? • Would you like more or less audio included in this course?

CONCLUSION

Now that we have examined the basic requirements for incorporating audio in our instructional design strategies, we can explore audio advances in the web technologies, equipment, and software.

Advances in Web Technology

What we choose to use in e-Learning is strongly paralleled to what we *can* do, and advances in web technologies plays a tremendous role in that. Let's avoid the long history and just note that today, Web 3.0 possesses incredible speed and capability for interaction. Consequently, we have an explosion of interactive media enhanced (including audio) social networking based courseware designed for a more mobile generation (Keengwe & Kidd, 2010).

The Dark Side of Web Advances

There is perhaps a downside to all of these advancements (at least for developers). That downside would lie in the diversity of devices, operating systems (OS), monitors, and browsers that have consequently emerged (see Figure 5).

Figure 5. Areas of diversity that may create challenges for audio based or audio enhanced products

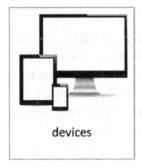

devices

operating systems

monitor sizes

browsers

Unless you are working within a tightly controlled organizational structure, these days it is difficult to tell what type of device, OS, monitor, or even browser, your learner will use to access the training you create. Consequently, if you create audio enhanced training materials, often times you must create a text-based alternative and publish in multiple formats to in order to ensure that the majority of your learners will be able to access your course. For example, if you are embedding audio into HTML, you must first consider if users have browsers installed that are capable of playing HTML5.

HTML5

According to the World Wide Web Consortium (W3C) (2014), the main international standards organization for the World Wide Web, HTML5 "defines the 5th major revision of the core language of the World Wide Web: the Hypertext Markup Language (HTML)."

This organization, however, has no control over companies that create and support browsers or which version of browsers your learners may be using. Given, this is the case, you may need to develop code that will work for older browsers. For example, you may need to roll back to HTML4.

If you are restricted to HTML4, you must rely on an <object> code and browser plugins.

For example something like:

```
<object data="yourfile.midi" type="audio/midi"></object>
```

HTML5 introduced a new standard for embedding audio files called <audio>. This makes embedding audio simpler in one way, and more complicated in another. It's simpler since we are no longer reliant upon browser plugins; however (again) *which* browser, device, or operating system still makes a difference and so with HTML5 code, you may need to include multiple audio file types to ensure that different users have access.

For example, you may need to use something like the following lines to insert audio:

```
<audio controls>
    <source src="yourfile.ogg" type="audio/ogg">
    <source src=" yourfile.mp3" type="audio/mpeg">
```

Your browser does not support the audio element.

```
</audio>
```

The resultant product will first attempt to play as a free, open container format file (**ogg**). If the browser is unable to play that format, it will attempt to play the second line, the **mp3** format. If the second line also fails, the browser will display the third line, "Your browser does not support the audio element."

Still this is all very technical, and many e-Learning developers do not write code. Instead we use authoring software. Examples from these types of software are explored in greater detail in the section titled "Advances in Software."

Cloud Based Services

One final area of consideration in as far as web technologies are concerns is the explosion of cloud based services for audio/video hosting and conversion as well as elearning.

According to the U.S Department of Commerce, National Institute of Standards and Technology's (NIST), "cloud computing is a model for enabling ubiquitous, convenient, on-demand network access to a shared pool of configurable computing resources (e.g., networks, servers, storage, applications and services) that can be rapidly provisioned and released with minimal management effort or service provider interaction."

Cloud-based learning management systems are hosted on the Internet and can be accessed by logging into a service provider's site. Rather than having to install course design and management software, instructional designers can simply use their Internet browsers to upload course content, create new courses, and communicate with learners directly. This is all done through a secure LMS, which also gives designers the ability to store information on the cloud, which can be remotely accessed by other, approved users. (Kaplanis, 2014).

Some providers focus specifically on audio (although often times an audio/video combo) like Audioboo, SoundCloud, DuraCloud, audiobox, and more. These types of cloud based providers often times not only provide a place to store files, but also provide end-users with multiple file formats and sizes for download.

Other providers offer specific eLearning development, hosting, or other types of services. For example, cloud-based learning management systems have become quite popular. In addition to simply hosting media files, these types of services allow organizations to track and deliver social media enhanced online course ware.

Advances in Equipment (End Users and Developers)

With all the advances in technology and the web surely you have realized that audio recording and playback equipment have also come a long way as well! This section will examine the advances in speakers, handheld recorders, microphones, and sound proofing strategies (see Figure 6).

Figure 6. Audio recording and playback equipment

speakers   handheld recorders   microphones   sound proofing

Speakers

It was hit or miss for a while. As an e-learning developer, you couldn't be certain that a learner would have speakers or headphones attached to their computers, but today it has become quite standard. Still it is always a good idea to include a text based option to your audio enhanced materials, either in the form of closed captioning or as transcripts. Additionally, when creating media pieces, I tend to include a note to help set expectations (See Box 2).

Last but not least, as with all things technological, the *quality* of speakers varies greatly. So again, unless you have some control over *what* will use and *how* your learners will access your course, you may be publishing multiple options and triggers such as providing both a low and high quality playback option and delivering varying levels of sound quality.

Handheld Recorders

Although they do not always provide the best sound quality, handheld recorders are still terribly convenient for capturing impromptu interviews with SMEs, recording ambient sound, and more (see Figure 7). The model I happen to use fits easily in the palm of your hand and includes a convenient USB plug in, a rather common feature these days. The other improvement that shouldn't go without mention is the increased capacity for recording time.

Microphones

Again, innovations have yielded a variety of options including built in mics, web cam mics, desktop mics, and all in one headphone (see Figure 8).

Most computers, laptops and tablet pcs as well as Mac products, these days come with built in microphones; however the quality tends to be quite low, they can be tricky to locate or access (physically), and sometimes they just stop working. So, if you plan on using this mic, it is best to see if it is installed, locate it (physically), and make sure the quality meets your needs.

Box 2. Note to help set expectations

▶ **This presentation includes audio. OR ⊗This presentation does not include audio.**

Figure 7. An example of a handheld digital USB recorder

 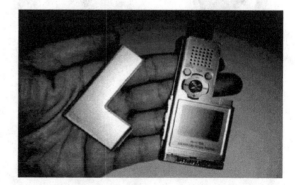

Figure 8. Commonly used types of microphones

built in mic **web cam mic** **desktop** **headphones**

Identifying whether or not your computer even has a microphone is as simple as checking your sound settings for connected input devices. If everything is working properly, you should see your built in microphone listed as an option in your sound>recording or sound>input (for mac users) panel. It may be listed as "integrated", "internal", "built in", or by some other name (see Figure 9).

The tricky part can be *finding the microphone* so that you know where to face when you are recording. You could, of course, read your manual (…you know the one you saved right?) or go online for a digital version of it, or you could just start looking for some tiny holes somewhere along the front face of computer or laptop. It may even be marked "mic" or show a tiny image of a microphone that only an itty bitty child can see.

Even if you do manage to identify that a mic is install and locate it, you may find the quality is too low or that the sound of the computer itself is overriding your voice. If this is the case, consider the following recommendations (from my personal experience) when purchasing a separate microphone.

- First determine your budgetary requirements and then seek out an A/V specialist to discover what is available within your price range.
- Microphones connected through a USB cord produce less electrical noise.
- If you plan on sharing the microphone or have more than one speaker, a desktop microphone may be the wiser option than a headset.
- Desktop microphones are available as omni-directional or uni-directional options. Uni-directional microphones are designed to collect sound waves from only one direction and can help reduce interface from background noise.
- If you see to sets of sound ports on your computer, you might have a second (better) sound card installed. Check with your I.T. department for assistance.
- Last but not least, consider the space you will be working in. You might need to invest in some sound proofing or absorption materials depending on your circumstance.

Soundproofing

Uncontrolled or unwanted noise can reduce the quality of any audio you attempt to record. Sometimes these sound intrude from outside, other times they are the result of "bouncing" sound waves. Think of the how your voice sounds in building with unique architectures.

Figure 9. Sound panel on a PC

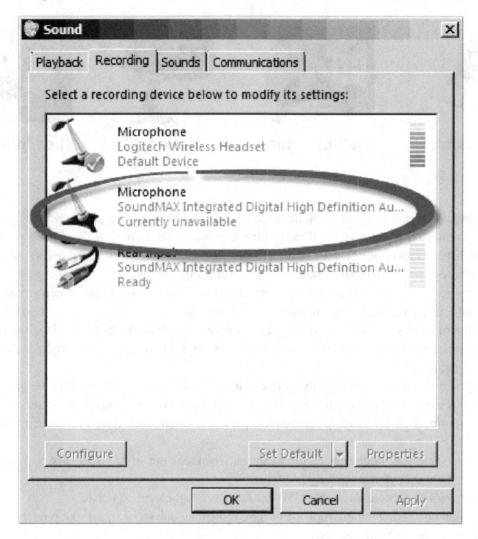

If you find simply want to reduce unwanted sound, you must find a way to block the sound. If the situation is a weird echo or hollow sound, you may need to make your working area smaller or invest in some sound absorption materials.

The science around sound proofing, dampening, and absorption is immense, and you may think that you must immediately invest in an expensive sound booth; however this is not always the case. You may even be able to make your sound booth if this is the solution you desire. Several websites provide instructions on how to accomplish this include those listed below:

- **How to Make Your Own Sound Booth for Better Voice Overs** (http://elearningbrothers.com/how-to-make-your-own-sound-booth-for-better-voice-overs/)
- **Production: How to Build Your Own Homemade Sound Booth** (http://www.steves-digicams.com/knowledge-center/how-tos/becoming-a-professional-photographer/production-how-to-build-your-own-homemade-sound-booth.html#b)

Advances in Software

While professional grade audio editing has come a long way, often times it is more complex than necessary for eLearning development. Instead, software companies have been consistently enhancing our audio editing options within eLearning development packages. Two of the main areas of advancement for audio in eLearning courses include the editing features often found within eLearning software packages and the publishing options.

Editing Features

The main editing features to look for are visual waveform editing, multiple audio adjustment options, closed captions options, and multitrack editing as shown in Figure 10.

Visual Wave Form Editing

If you recall from the beginning of this chapter, "sound is a physical vibration that moves through a medium (usually air). It is something we commonly represent as a wave graphically." This graphic can be extremely helpful when trying to add or remove pieces of your recording, synchronize audio to visual images, identify errors, or make other alterations to what you have recorded.

When I first began authoring in eLearning packages, visual wave form editing was not common. Generally, you had an upload button for audio files and little else. Today, you are often able to see and edit your audio visually. For me, this saves a lot of time when trying to remove unusual elevations or increase sound when a person's voice drops, because I can identify it quickly visually.

Here are some examples of tools that offer this feature:

Figure 11 shows a screen capture from Articulate Presenter's Audio Editor. This tool allows you to cut, copy, paste, add silence, and adjust volume within the time line (or waveform).

TechSmith's Camtasia Studio offers a few additional features including the ability to add and move audio points and fades. These audio points allow users to adjust volume more precisely. See the red circled items in Figure 12.

Figure 10. Useful editing features commonly found in elearning software

visual waveform editing

noise reduction, normalizing, volume adjustment

Welcome to the Written Communications Course.

captions synchronization

multi-track editing

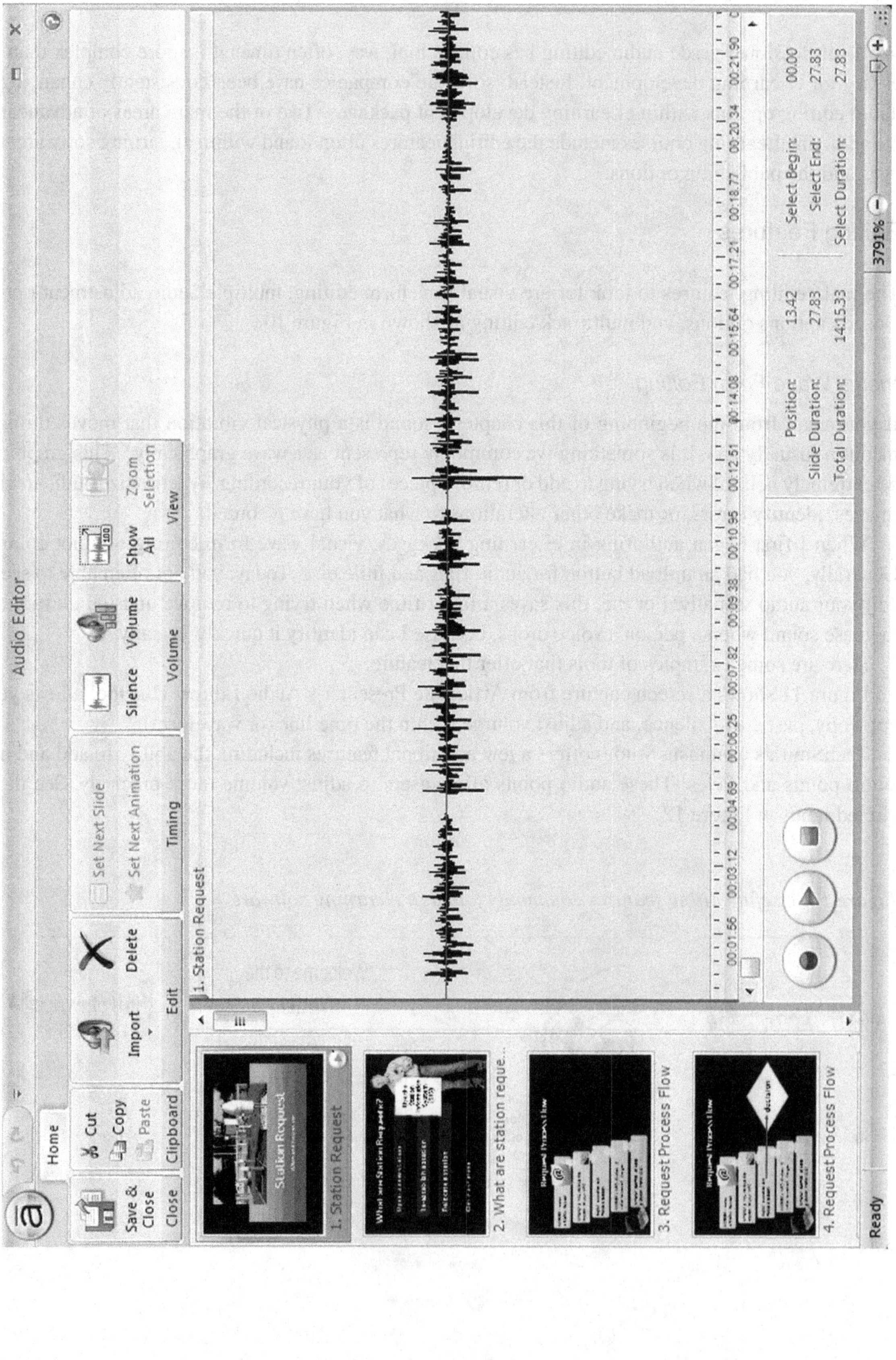

Figure 11. Articulate presenter displaying editable waveform in the audio editor

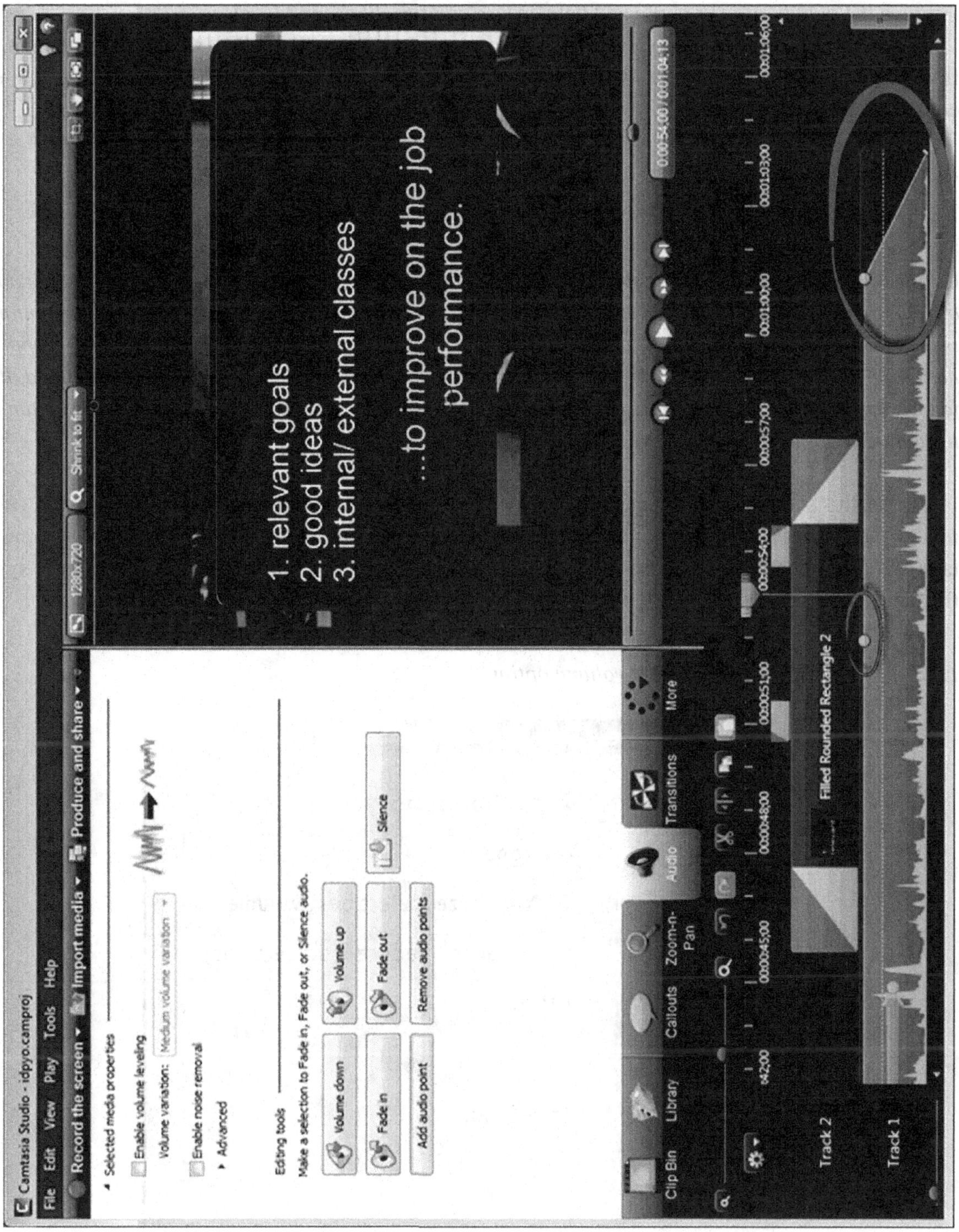

Figure 12. TechSmith camtasia studio displaying audio editing options

Audio Adjustments

You may have notice the noise remove, volume, and volume leveling options above. These features help improve the quality of your audio and help ensure comfortable sound levels.

In the audio world, "volume leveling" is also known as "normalizing" as shown in the screen shot from Adobe Captivate in Figure 13. These types of features adjust radical changes in volume to a more consistent level.

Synchronizing Captions

If you are working with both audio and video, you may want to synchronize onscreen captions.

Captions are text versions of the spoken word presented within multimedia. Captions allow the content of web audio and video to be accessible to those who do not have access to audio. Though captioning is primarily intended for those who cannot hear the audio, it has also been found to help those that can hear audio content, those who may not be fluent in the language in which the audio is presented, those for whom the language spoken is not their primary language, etc. (retrieved from http://webaim.org/techniques/captions/)

Again, this is option that is generally included in eLearning Development software packages. (If you review the images above, you might even be able to spot the buttons for adding captions to the presentations.) Additionally cloud based services such as YouTube also contain their own captioning system that developers can elect to work with when posting their content.

Figure 13. Adobe captivate adjust volume options

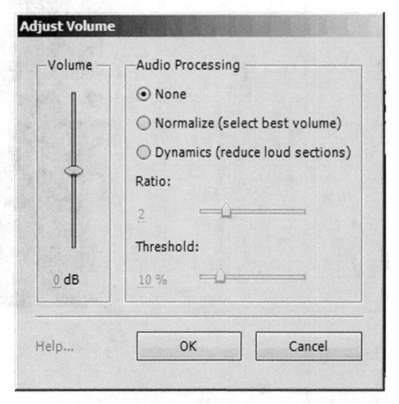

Multitrack Editing

Although ambient sound and background noises can help learners gain a more realistic appreciation for the content you are revealing, you generally will want to have some level of control over that sound. The best way to control ambient sounds, background noises, sound effects, and music is through use of separate audio tracks. At times, packages will actually show you multiple tracks as in the case illustrated by Figure 14.

Other times, packages may offer the option of adding "background music" or sound *on* specific objects. In these cases, although they are not displayed as waveforms, the additional sounds are still maintained on a separate track.

Publishing Options

Last but not least, many of eLearning development packages simplify compression, file formats, packaging, and uploading options (Figure 15).

Production can get complicated, even in the basic overview:

In *Compression for great video and audio*, Ben Waggoner (2010) writes:

The current generation of general-purpose audio codecs using frequency synthesis, notably HE AAC and WMA 10 Pro, can be competitive with speech at much lower bitrates than older codecs, so it isn't always necessary to use a speech codec even for low-bitrate speech. Coupled with the general increase in bandwidth, speech-only codecs are increasingly relegated to mobile devices.

Figure 14. TechSmith camtasia studio displaying multitrack editing

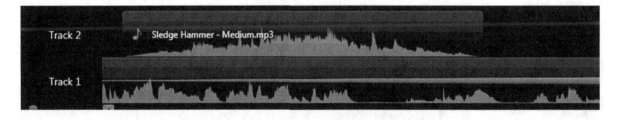

Figure 15. Audio production and publishing options to consider

| compression | file formats | HTML LMS SCORM | cloud based options |

Right... well, I'm going with the eLearning version for preparing audio for publishing. Generally, your tool will give your several options which include laymen's terms like "Web", "LMS", "Their cloud based service", and "custom" or a similar list. Also, these packages have begun to include options for publishing in multiple formats with a single rendering.

For example, the screenshot in Figure 16 shows an example from Articulate Presenter. The resultant product will first attempt to play as an Adobe Flash File (.swf), then as HTML 5, and finally in an IOS format.

Without this type of cascading package feature, you may find that some of your learners are not able to hear the audio and/or see the videos you create.

Figure 16. Publishing options for multiple devices and browsers in articulate presenter

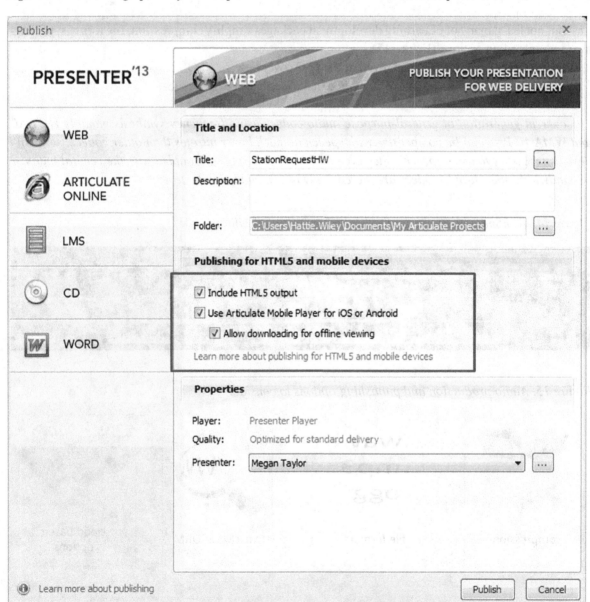

CONCLUSION

Advances in the way we obtain, produce, and play audio makes audio creation a very unique and often times complex industry; however those of us who act as end-users in this field, we find that we now have many options in equipment, software, and cloud based services to help guide us on our path. Still, as instructional designers and project managers, we must first plan then do then act!

Here's a summary of what was included in this chapter:

Sound is a physical vibration that moves through a medium (usually air). It is something we commonly represent as a wave graphically which is something to keep in mind when we examine sound editing software.

Several types of sounds are commonly used to enhance eLearning including narrations, music, sound effects, ambient sounds, and audio contained within video segments.

Audio strategies and supporting technologies have advanced greatly over the years.

REFERENCES

Bair, D., & Dickinson, M. (2011, April 21). *How Much Narration in eLearning? Our Lessons Learned.* Retrieved from: https://www.learningsolutionsmag.com/articles/666/how-much-narration-in-elearning-our-lessons-learned

Bielawski, L., & Metcalf, D. (2003). *Blended elearning: integrating knowledge, performance support, and online learning.* Retrieved from: http://common.books24x7.com/toc.aspx?bookid=4920

Clark, R. C. (2010). *Evidence-based training methods: a guide for training professionals.* Retrieved from: http://common.books24x7.com/toc.aspx?bookid=35123

Clark, R. C., & Mayer, R. E. (3rd Ed.). (2011). *e-learning and the science of instruction: proven guidelines for consumers and designers of multimedia learning.* Retrieved from: http://common.books24x7.com/toc.aspx?bookid=44340

Cobb, J. (2013). *Leading the learning revolution: the expert's guide to capitalizing on the exploding lifelong education market.* Retrieved from: http://common.books24x7.com/toc.aspx?bookid=47761

Driscoll, M. (2nd Ed.). (2002). Web-based training: creating e-learning experiences Retrieved from: http://common.books24x7.com/toc.aspx?bookid=3748

Handley, A., & Chapman, C. C. (2011). *Content rules: how to create killer blogs, podcasts, videos, ebooks, webinars (and more) that engage customers and ignite your business.* Retrieved from: http://common.books24x7.com/toc.aspx?bookid=40621

Hassan, Q. (2011). Demystifying Cloud Computing. *The Journal of Defense Software Engineering, 2011* (Jan/Feb), 16–21. Retrieved from: http://www.crosstalkonline.org/storage/issue-archives/2011/201101/201101-Hassan.pdf

Hodell, C. (3rd Ed.). (2011). *Isd from the ground up: a no-nonsense approach to instructional design* Retrieved from http://common.books24x7.com/toc.aspx?bookid=41948

Hoogterp, B. (2014). *Your perfect presentation: speak in front of any audience anytime anywhere and never be nervous again.* Retrieved from: http://common.books24x7.com/toc.aspx?bookid=65444

Kaplanis, D. (2014). *8 Top Benefits of Using a Cloud Based LMS - eLearning Industry.* Retrieved from http://elearningindustry.com/8-top-benefits-of-using-a-cloud-based-lms

Keengwe, J., & Kidd, T. (2010). Towards Best Practices in Online Learning and Teaching in Higher Education. *MERLOT Journal of Online Learning and Teaching, 6*(2). Retrieved from: http://jolt.merlot.org/vol6no2/keengwe_0610.htm

Lee, Mark J.W. & (eds), Catherine McLoughlin. (2011). *Web 2.0-based e-learning: applying social informatics for tertiary teaching.* Retrieved from: http://common.books24x7.com/toc.aspx?bookid=36761

Morin, E., & Unesco. (2001). *Seven complex lessons in education for the future.* Paris: UNESCO.

sound. (2015). In *Encyclopædia Britannica.* Retrieved from: http://www.britannica.com/EBchecked/topic/555255/sound

(Ed.). Shank, P. (2011). *The online learning idea book: proven ways to enhance technology-based and blended learning, 2.* Retrieved from http://common.books24x7.com/toc.aspx?bookid=44452

The NIST Definition of Cloud Computing". (n.d.). National Institute of Standards and Technology. Retrieved from: http://csrc.nist.gov/publications/nistpubs/800-145/SP800-145.pdf

Purves, D., Augustine, G. J., Fitzpatrick, D., et al. (Eds.). (2nd Ed.). (2001). Neuroscience. Sunderland: Sinauer Associates. Retrieved from: http://www.ncbi.nlm.nih.gov/books/NBK11126/

Treasure, J. (2009, July). The 4 ways sound affects us [Video file]. Retrieved from http://www.ted.com/talks/julian_treasure_the_4_ways_sound_affects_us/transcript?language=en#t-132000

Waggoner, Ben. (2010). *Compression for great video and audio.* Retrieved from http://common.books24x7.com/toc.aspx?bookid=36547

W3C. (2015, January 1). Retrieved from http://www.w3.org/standards/webdesign/audiovideo.html

W3C. (2014, October 28). Retrieved from http://www.w3.org/standards/techs/html#w3c_all

ADDITIONAL READING

Bair, D., & Dickinson, M. (2011, April 21). How Much Narration in eLearning? Our Lessons Learned. Retrieved January 3, 2015, from https://www.learningsolutionsmag.com/articles/666/how-much-narration-in-elearning-our-lessons-learned

Clark, R. C. (2010). *Evidence-Based Training Methods: A Guide for Training Professionals.* Alexandria, VA: ASTD Press.

Clark, R. C., & Mayer, R. E. (2011). *E-Learning and the Science of Instruction: Proven Guidelines for Consumers and Designers of Multimedia Learning* (3rd ed.). San Francisco, CA: John Wiley & Sons.

De Vries, J., & Haskin, S. (2014, August 11). Top Tips for Producing Better eLearning Audio. Retrieved February 13, 2015, from http://www.learningsolutionsmag.com/articles/1484/top-tips-for-producing-better-elearning-audio

Kesher, S. (2010, January 1). Best Practices in eLearning Audio. Retrieved February 13, 2015, from http://snd80.securesites.net/devcon2010/sound80_best_practices.pdf

Kuhlmann, T. (2013, January 1). Audio & Video Tips. Retrieved February 13, 2015, from http://www.articulate.com/rapid-elearning/audio-video-tips/

McLeod, S. A. (2007). Cognitive Psychology. Retrieved from http://www.simplypsychology.org/cognitive.html

Siegel, K. (2013). *TechSmith Camtasia Studio 8: The essentials workbook*. Riva, MD: IconLogic.

Siegel, K. (2013). *Adobe Captivate 7: Beyond the essentials: "skills and drills" learning*. Riva, MD: IconLogic.

Siegel, K. (2013). *Adobe Captivate 7: Adobe Captivate 7: The Essentials: "skills and drills" learning*. Riva, MD: IconLogic.

Treasure, J. "Julian Treasure: The 4 Ways Sound Affects Us." Ted: Ideas Worth Spreading. TED, Oct. 2009. Retrieved February 13, 2015, from http://www.ted.com/talks/julian_treasure_the_4_ways_sound_affects_us?language=en

Waggoner, B., & Waggoner, B. (2010). *Compression for great video and audio: Master tips and common sense*. Burlington, MA: Focal Press.

KEY TERMS AND DEFINITIONS

Audio: The sound (narrations, music, sound effects, ambient sounds, and dialogue) or sound files included in digital training materials.

Audio Equipment: Speakers, handheld recorders, microphones, and sound proofing strategies have shown considerable advancement over the years. First, consider the **diversity** of audio technologies users may use and then use the highest *quality* of audio equipment you can afford.

Cognitive Load: The total amount of mental effort being used by the learner including lost efforts due to extraneous graphics, sounds, and/or music.

Innovations in Web Technology: What we choose to use in e-Learning is strongly paralleled to what we can do, and advances in web technologies plays a tremendous role in that. Although today's technologies allow for greater use of media, it also calls for more diverse delivery of that media. Remember to consider adaptive and responsive design strategies to adjust for user devices, operating systems, monitor sizes, and browser diversity.

Instructional Design Considerations: Advances in audio impact every stage of the instructional design process for eLearning, regardless of which instructional design model one chooses to use. Remember to take time to consider the implications to your instructional design strategy!

Instructional Design: The systematic creation of instructional materials through application of one or more designated instructional design systems such as ADDIE.

SME (Subject Matter Expert): Someone with expert level knowledge or skills in a specified tasks and who acts as an advisor during the creation of training materials for that task.

Software: Today's eLearning packages offer more advance audio editing and publishing options then in the past. Take time to explore these options in your own systems.

Chapter 6
Use of Video to Enhance Education

Brent A. Anders
Kansas University, USA

ABSTRACT

Even with so many different educational tools and evolutions in techniques of instruction (both peda-gogical and andrological approaches), the use of video is one of the most effective means of instructing students. This chapter presents multiple evidence detailing why video can greatly enhance instruction in a multiple of ways to include its use in motivation, explanation (via multi-modalities), and feedback. This chapter will also demonstrate the benefits of using a student-centered/learning-centered instruc-tional video capturing system within the classroom to improve learning for both face-to-face and online learning. Resources and specific examples are provided to demonstrate that video is a fundamental tool that should be used to enhance both the educational process and instructional experience. New uses and video technologies are also addressed for future investigation and incorporation.

CHAPTER OBJECTIVES

- Define the term "video"
- Explain its importance to education
- Show how video can be used to enhance motivation
- Show how video can be used to improve the overall education process
- Show how video can help explain information to students
- Show how video can be used to enhance feedback to students
- Show how video can be used to enhance feedback to instructors
- Describe an instructional video capturing system
- Describe a student-centered instructional video capturing system
- Express the importance of using engagement with video
- Describe video analytics
- Show how video will continue to grow and be used in education

DOI: 10.4018/978-1-4666-8696-0.ch006

INTRODUCTION

It is important to have a shared understanding of what is being referred to when the term video is used. *Video* simply means a recording of visual images that can contain audio (Wetzel, Radtke, Stern, Dickieson, & McLachlan, 1993). With this type of general definition items such as: filmstrips, video-tape recordings, animations, TV broadcasts, DVDs, streaming/on-demand Internet video, and any other type of digital moving image are all considered video. Yet now in the 21st century, video can now have enhanced capabilities in that it can be interactive, can be viewed anytime and anywhere through multiple devices (examples: cellphones, tablets, laptops, desktops, and wearables such as Google glass), can be fully tracked for advanced analytical observations, and can be easily created by anyone with a simple and inexpensive cell phone. Its use, availability, and accessibility are very widespread both for face-to-face and online instruction (University Business white paper, 2013). Yet having video in the classroom (real or virtual) is not the definitive answer to anything. The important aspect to realize is how video can best be used (facilitated) for teaching. Although there has been a large amount of research and debate as to whether or not media itself can influence learning, most notably the Clark (1983) vs. Kozma (1991) scholarly arguments, this chapter will move beyond that and will instead focus on how video can enhance the desire (motivation) to learn and the learning process overall (Desai & Vijayalakshmi, 2015; McCann, 2015). Additionally, this chapter will discuss the value of repurposing video, using video as a means of multi-modality learning, and the power of using a student-centered/learning-centered instructional video capturing system in creating and using video.

MOTIVATION

Motivation is a key concept to grasp in any learning condition and video can assist in attaining it. If a student does not have the desire and is not motivated to learn, then they simply will not focus on the content and therefore the brain will not be able to receive the needed stimuli to even attempt to learn content (Sousa, 2011). The venerable Dr. Woldkowski additionally suggests the use of appropriate video to enhance motivation and student experience (2008). The question then arises as to how to actually motivate a student. By using the effective, popular, and proven ARCS (Keller, 1987; Rigby, 2015; Yau, Cheng, & Ho, 2015) model for motivation, the concept is broken down into four distinct needed conditions to attain full motivation: Attention, Relevancy, Confidence, and Satisfaction. The ARCS (Keller, 1987) model was derived from a culmination of a multiple of other theories, but overall it is grounded in expectancy-value theory, which comes from the works of both E. C. Tolman and K. Lewin. (p. 2). The following is a breakdown and explanation of each of the four ARCS motivational conditions.

Motivation: Attention

It is not enough to just temporarily grab a student's *attention*. If it were, then just yelling at the beginning of a presentation would suffice. What is needed is to properly obtain and hold onto a student's attention for the duration of the instruction. To accomplish this "it is necessary to respond to the sensation-seeking needs of students," as well as to "arouse their knowledge-seeking curiosity," "without overstimulating them" (Keller, 1987, p. 3). Video would be the perfect tool for this. A well crafted video depicting action and/or emotion can be used to spark students' arousal or curiosity for the subject matter.

Motivation: Relevancy

Relevancy is another key factor that must be addressed. In addressing this key factor one must be both explicit and implicit and both immediate and long term. Cleary expressing how what is to be learned is important in the here and now as well as how this will assist in future classes or career applications greatly enhance students' overall motivation (Keller, 1987). In addressing the "so what" or the "why is this important to me" type of questions, students start to see the relevance and the importance of participating and paying attention. Once again video can be a key contributor to addressing this factor by being able to clearly depict relevancy of a particular subject as well as by showing "real life" practitioners applying information learned in the classroom.

Motivation: Confidence

The *Confidence* component in Keller's ARCS model is designed to ensure students feel "that some level of success is possible if effort is exerted" (1987, p. 5). The importance of this component is highlighted in that Keller's Confidence component is very similar to Heider's Attribution Theory (1958). In order for the student to be motivated to learn, they have to attribute their future success in the class to their effort in learning. A video of former students (possibly now working in an applicable field) explicitly stating how their hard work and effort lead them to succeed in class would directly address this critical motivational component.

Motivation: Satisfaction

The final aspect of *Satisfaction*, which Keller (1987) describes as "practices that help make people feel good about their accomplishments. According to reinforcement theory, people should be more motivated if the task and the reward are defined, and an appropriate reinforcement schedule is used" (p. 6). Of course students need to know what they must do in order to pass the class (use of a rubric is highly recommended), but this satisfaction component deals more with actually feeling a sense of accomplishment and pleasure. One way to address this would be to show videos of previous classes' work as well as students talking about their accomplishments in the class. A video of a smiling former student can have a very powerful and motivational effect on new students. The idea that one's work might be selected and shown off to future classes can also be very satisfying. Satisfaction also comes in giving students good actionable feedback on what they have done well and what needs to be improved upon; this also provides an opportunity for reflection (Stavredes, 2011). The push should always be in developing intrinsic motivation and satisfaction of a job well done, but some external rewards and acknowledgments are also beneficial.

A single video or multiple videos can address the components listed. The videos can be presented at the beginning, during, or at the end of the class. The facilitating instructor is the one that must assess the instructional goals and the best path to achieve them.

Figure 1. Visual representation of Keller's ARCS Model of Motivation with the addition of using video components to address each portion of the model

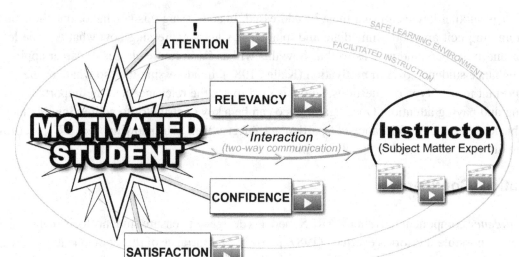

Motivation: More Strategies

Another important strategy that can be applied to each of the motivational components described deals with *interaction* (Keller, 1987). Instruction should always involve two-way communication of some sort. Videos can incorporate questions (example: video pauses and students have to select an answer on the screen for the videos to continue), lead directly to quizzes, or induce prime opportunities for discussion. This makes the use of video not a passive consumption behavior, but a dynamic igniter of motivational arousal and cognitive activation. An instructor could use videos from a multiple of free online sources such as Youtube, TED (Technology, Entertainment, Design), PBS (Public Broadcasting Service), or the BBC (British Broadcasting Corporation), just to name a few. Another option could be to hire professional videographers to create custom content to specifically address any subject matter.

Yet another powerful idea, that should be considered, would be to have the students themselves create the video content. The engagement, application, creativity, motivation, satisfaction, and attention grabbing properties of having students create video content makes this approach very favorable (Keller, 1987). "Having students to produce video not only yields a richer understanding of the subject matter but also promotes active learning and student engagement" (Fung, 2015, p. 237). It is also important to realize that there is no blanket statement with regards to motivation. The course facilitator needs to understand what type of students they have and adjust the motivational framework accordingly. What might work well for younger students might not work well for older, adult students. What might work well for military students might not work well for engineering students. Use the components presented, consider the wants and needs of the students, and experiment with various types and levels of applications.

ENHANCING THE LEARNING PROCESS

In a 2014 survey, conducted by a leading open source video platform, 500 respondents across 300 educational institutions were asked about their thoughts on video, "90% of respondents believe that video improves the learning experience" (State of Video, 2014, p. 12). Yet the power and usefulness of video isn't just in its perceived improvements to learning, there is also neurological evidence (Anderson, Fite, Petrovich, & Hirsch, 2006; Doyle, 2011; Smith, & Gevins, 2004).

Multi-Modalities

"Verbal and visual processing allow students to become more involved in the learning process, and retention increases" (Sousa, 2011). By using multiple modalities such as visuals and audio in a video, as well as multiple sensations through emotions and arousal, learning is enhanced and the information learned can be better retained (Doyle, 2011; Magee, 2011). As a personal example, I can remember that there was a very important president called John F. Kennedy, not because a teacher told me about him, but because I can clearly remember the President's voice and the way he looked in his "Ask not what your country can do for you…" speech video that I watched. In a similar note I really didn't understand or had any real emotional connection to the Cuban missile crises until I watched the movie *Thirteen Days* by New Line Cinema. This movie (video) dramatized the events that lead up to the situation, this in turn made the history (educational content) impactful, understandable, emotional, and very memorable. A great deal of research has documented how emotional arousal greatly enhances long-term memory retention (Richter-Levin, Kehat, & Anunu 2015; Sousa 2011). These two personal examples also illustrate how video can be used to depict content that would be very difficult to show in real life. The Cuban missile crises and President Kennedy's time in office all happened before I was even born, so I couldn't have witnessed it live and in person. But there are many more examples of video use when real life observation is not feasible.

Think of the difficulty that instructors face in trying to get student to understand how small an atom is. A student would find it perplexing to simply imagine something that is typically about 0.0000001 (*or* $1x10^{-7}$) of a millimeter in diameter. Yet through the use of video, an explanation with a moving visual representation makes the information much more salient. Educator Jonathan Bergmann and animator Andrew Park do an excellent job through the freely available educational TED video *Just How Small Is an Atom?* (Bergmann & Park, 2012). There are endless possibilities and so many videos available on the Internet from everything to space travel to recreations of ancient artifacts to voyages through the systems of the body to really see how everything works. Field trips that would be too dangerous or costly can now be replicated in crisp high definition. Traveling all over the world, as well as visiting battle scenes, volcanoes, lion dens, or the inside of a nuclear power plant are all possible through the use of video. Words and pictures are now made much more real, comprehensible, exciting, and experiential through the use of first hand footage, recreation, or animation (Wetzel, Radtke, Stern, Dickieson, & McLachlan, 1993).

Repurposing Video

Another idea to consider when finding videos to use for enhanced instruction is in repurposing video that was originally created for other purposes. Examples of this would be possibilities such as the use of old television shows such as *Friends* or *Seinfeld* but presented in another language to teach that language to students. This type of video repurposing has actually been proven to be both enjoyable and effective within the educational process (Hofschroer, 2012; Lim, 2013). As a personal example I once used a suicide prevention video created specifically for U.S. Army soldiers serving in Afghanistan to help instruct Armenian soldiers on sergeant responsibilities such as the importance of suicide prevention. I took out the original audio of the video and used a voice actress (Nelli Anders, my wife) who could speak Armenian, to translate the content for the intended audience. I added a few text visuals and some regional music and had a fully developed repurposed video. The results were very positive with student-soldiers even clapping after viewing the very personalize, repurposed video. This type of repurposing of video can take additional time, but the type of personalization and impact that can occur will be well worth the allocation of resources. Use of video in this way also correlates with the U.S. Army's Learning Model/Method (ALM), (also referred to as the Army Learning Concept), in that it maximizes the use of technology to make instruction personable, impactful, student-centered, incorporates the operational environment, and utilizes critical thinking skills (United States Army, 2011).

Along with enhancing the explanation of content, video offers the unique capability of being more student-centered and learning-centered. If the content is made available to the student (such as linked within a learning management system), then the student can review the information as many times as they want through audio and/or visual means. An enhanced capability of modern video implementation is the ability to include interactive questions before, during, or after the video so as to require student viewers to apply information observed within the video. "Students in the e-learning environment that were provided interactive video achieved significantly better learning performance and a higher level of learner satisfaction than those in other settings," (Zhang, Zhou, Briggs, & Nunamaker Jr, 2006). It is important to note that creating this interactive component would be beneficial for both online instruction as well as for face-to-face learning (face-to-face implementation could be accomplished via online or through in-class interactions/discussions).

Feedback

Another very important area to address in the learning process deals with feedback. This was quickly mentioned in the previous motivational section dealing with satisfaction, but it should be fully understood with regards to its importance in the educational process and how video can help in its accomplishment. "Feedback about one's learning and behavior significantly contributes to one's sense of control and is vital to intrinsic motivation and improving learning" (Wlodkowski, 2008). The use of video can be a great tool in this regard in that it can provide very clear information to the student as well as personalize the instructional message that much more so as to enhance communication and retention (Arab, Dastfal, & Zareian, 2014; Goldman, Pea, Barron, & Derry, 2014). The Canvas learning management system (LMS) provides an excellent example of this with their *Speed Grader* tool. Within this LMS tool an instructor can easily grade an assignment and then click to launch a built-in video recorder that allows the instructor to visually and verbally comment about the student's strengths and areas to improve (Canvas Instructor Guide, 2014). The student can then view the personalized video feedback as many times as they wish to fully understand and improve. Extending the notion of feedback even further, video can be used to obtain instructor evaluations from students. Obtaining feedback from students in this manner (via video capture) about the instructor as well as the course in general would provide excellent first hand observations and opinions with greater emotion as well as an additional opportunity for the students to reflect on the learned material (Hoare, 2011; Kolb, 1984)

Figure 2. Visual representation of Feedback mechanism with video

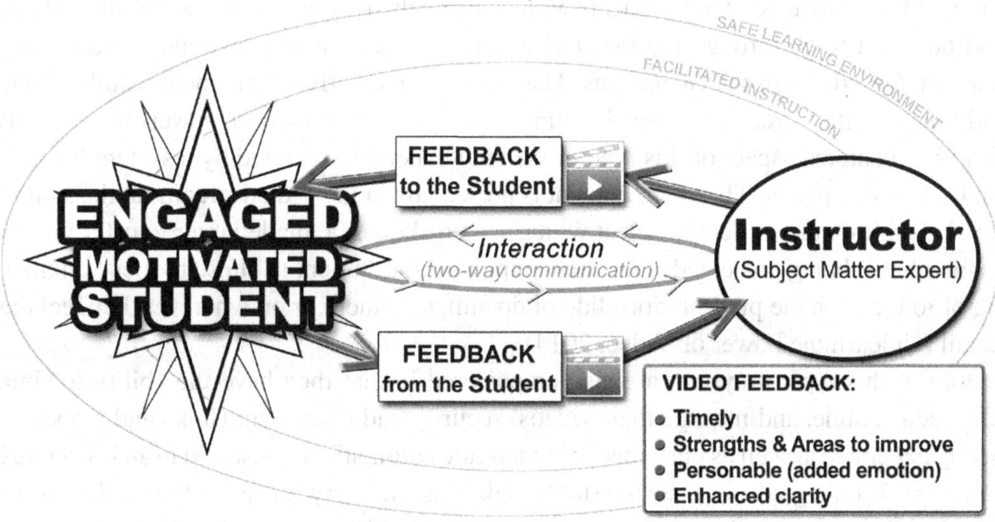

Using A Student-Centered/Learning-Centered

Instructional Video Capturing System

A multiple of instructional capturing systems currently exist that provide for the video capturing of classroom instruction, yet they are all quite varied in their capabilities and focus. It is strongly recommended that a student-centered/learning-centered system be used to maximize the educational process and experience. In this sense, student-centered means that the creation and presentation of the video is done in such a way to be flexible enough to be used in ways that specifically addresses the students' needs and the desired pedagogical/andragogical approach (Hannafin, & Land, 1997; Knowlton, 2000). In a similar manner, learning-centered means the creation and presentation of the content done in such a way to be flexible enough to be used in ways that allow for different learning styles/preferences (such as audio, video, interactive), (Blumberg, 2009). An excellent implementation of this type of student/ learning-centered instructional capturing system is the enterprise video platform Mediasite by Sonic Foundry (Unleash the Power of Video, 2014). Through the Mediasite system, a video can be created either in a classroom through a capture device or within an instructor's office/home via laptop or desktop through specialized software. An instructor will typically have two or more video sources such as: a video of him or her speaking, screen capturing of presentation slides or other action on the computer screen, a document camera, or any other video source. This video can then be enhanced through editing of the content to shorter, more manageable "chunks," adding chapter indexes, meta information, enabling optical character recognition (OCR) for the presentation slides/video, closed captioning, as well as including interactive components such as polling or questions/quiz at the end of the video.

The student/learning-centered video has its greatest impact on the student when a student fully engages with the content. The student can now access this video from anywhere with a laptop/smartphone/tables or wearable device. They can also access the content repeatedly as well as in the speed they wish to view the content (faster or slower). Controlling the video's speak of playback serves as a very powerful tool for international students (who have English as a second language), student's with instructors that speak too fast or are difficult to understand, students with learning difficulties, as well as for students that fully understand but want to go through the material at a faster rate. Students can also search through the content via chapter indexes or via OCR items. The included interactive components (polling, questions/quiz) would then further strengthen their learning experience). Yet another powerful, interactive, and student/learning-centered aspect of this type of viewing experience offered by a system like Mediasite deals with its dynamic player. The video content is presented via individual streams at the same time on the screen. This allows the student to select which screen should be made larger to offer greater detail and focus on what is being presented. This then empowers the student to chose to focus on the instructor talking or to focus on the presentation slide or document camera or on wherever they feel they need greater detail (Unleash the Power of Video, 2014).

Instructors of this type of system are also empowered in that they have the ability to simply and easily edit videos online, and manage their videos' security and placement (links and embed code are automatically generated as well as placement of videos are automatically inserted in an LMS like Canvas or Blackboard if full integration has been established). Another very powerful tool is that of the video analytics. With an instructional video capturing system like Mediasite, full analytics are provided to the owner (the instructor) of the video. Numerical and graphical representations are presented on items such as how many viewers accessed the video, who specifically accessed the video, what parts of the video were most often viewed, when was the content most often accessed, how was the content accessed (browser/device), and other similar type of information (Mediasite Analytics, 2013).

The flexibility of a well developed instructional video capturing system can also allow for diverse and effective pedagogical approaches such as flipping the classroom (Desai & Vijayalakshmi, 2015), (students watch videos at homework and then discuss and/or do assignments in class) and student content development. The Mediasite implementation allows for software distribution of its development tool

Figure 3. Dynamic player example of a student/learning-centered instructional capturing system (Mediasite). Students can click to enlarge any video feed to focus on what is most important to them at that time (instructor talking, slide presentation, or other video source)

that would allow students to create video presentations of their own. The ability to harness the power of video in this way would correlate with the highest order of cognitive process dimensions of Bloom's revised taxonomy: *creation* (Krathwohl, 2002).

SUMMARY

In expressing the extreme amount of continued video use growth, Cisco Systems (major network equipment manufacture) has stated "It would take an individual over 5 million years to watch the amount of video that will cross global IP networks each month in 2018. Every second, nearly a million minutes of video content will cross the network by 2018" (Cisco, 2014). In another example of the value of video use in education, this time on an international level, Australian instructional researchers have stated that "Physics educators at all grade levels will be increasing their use of video and computer technologies in their learning environments. Hence instructors need to consider examples of using these technologies effectively to enhance learning " (Kearny & Treagust, 2001, p. 9). Dr. Kearny and Dr. Treagust's prediction of increased video use has occurred in staggering proportions. When that statement was made in 2001 there was less then 500,000 terabytes of video content on the Internet, as of 2015 there is roughly 50 million terabytes of video online (Cicero, 2012; Cisco, 2014; Scott, 2011). And to state it once again from yet another source "The educational use of video on campus is accelerating rapidly in departments across all disciplines—from arts, humanities, and sciences to professional and vocational curricula" (Kaufman, & Mohan, 2009, p. 2). Additionally, in reading the well known New Media Consortium (2014) Horizon Report on higher education, the wide spread use and acceptance of video technologies is virtually taken as a given.

As technology continues to improve and advance so does video. Tools to create, store, and use video are always evolving along with innovative new techniques and implementations. A developing technology dealing with video that should be reviewed and pursued for additional research is the use of virtual reality. Generally, virtual reality refers to an immersive environment derived from either computer animation and/or actual video to provide completely explorable surroundings. Although this technology has existed for several years and has been proven effective for education (Chang, Chung, & Huang, 2014; Merchant, Goetz, Cifuentes, Keeney-Kennicutt, & Davis, 2014), only now has the technology become accessible in terms of cost and general availability (Betters, 2015; Carson, 2015). The powerful use of video is yet another opportunity to harness the power of video with regards to motivation, impact, explanation/ instruction, emotion, and long term retention.

Video alone however is not the complete answer to improving education. As described within this text, it is through the proper facilitation of video that motivation (ARCS model described) and comprehension can be increased. Additionally, the use of video within the feedback process was described and demonstrated, as a means to improve communication and personalization of the feedback (both from instructor to student and from student to instructor). The use of a student/learning-centered instructional capturing system (such as Mediasite) was also recommended to harness the full power of video (interaction) that is now available through advanced Internet technologies (beneficial for use in face-to-face and online learning). Through improved use of video the overall educational process, instructional experience, and retention will be enhanced, both for the student and the instructor.

REFERENCES

Anderson, D. R., Fite, K. V., Petrovich, N., & Hirsch, J. (2006). Cortical activation while watching video montage: An fMRI study. *Media Psychology, 8*(1), 7–24. doi:10.1207/S1532785XMEP0801_2

Arab, M., Dastfal, S. M., & Zareian, E. (2014). The effect of pairwise video feedback on the learning of elegant eye-hand coordination skill. *Annals of Applied Sport Science, 2*(3), 7–12.

Bergmann, J., & Park, A. (2012). Just how small is an atom? Retrieved from http://ed.ted.com/lessons/just-how-small-is-an-atom

Betters, E. (2015, April 22). Virtual Reality: The VR headsets to buy in 2015, whatever your budget. Retrieved from http://www.pocket-lint.com/news/132945-virtual-reality-the-vr-headsets-to-buy-in-2015-whatever-your-budget

Blumberg, P. (2009). *Developing learner-centered teaching: A practical guide for faculty*. San Francisco, CA: John Wiley & Sons.

Canvas Instructor Guide. (2014). *Canvas instructor guide*, by Instructure. Retrieved from https://guides.instructure.com/m/4212/pdf

Carson, E. (2015, March 4). *The pros and cons of low-cost virtual reality headsets*. Retrieved from http://www.techrepublic.com/article/the-pros-and-cons-of-low-cost-virtual-reality-headsets

Chang, R. C., Chung, L. Y., & Huang, Y. M. (2014). Developing an interactive augmented reality system as a complement to plant education and comparing its effectiveness with video learning. *Interactive Learning Environments*, (ahead-of-print), 1-20.

Cicero, S. (2012, May 30). *Cisco's VNI forecast projects the Internet will be four times as large in four years*. Retrieved from http://newsroom.cisco.com/press-release-content?amp;type=webcontent&articleId=888280

Cisco. (2014). *Cisco visual networking index: Forecast and methodology, 2013 – 2018*, Cisco whitepaper. Retrieved from http://www.cisco.com/c/en/us/solutions/collateral/service-provider/ip-ngn-ip-next-generation-network/white_paper_c11-481360.pdf

Clark, R. E. (1983). Reconsidering research on learning from media. *Review of Educational Research, 53*(4), 445–459. doi:10.3102/00346543053004445

Desai, P., & Vijayalakshmi, M. (2015). Flipped classroom: An efficient pedagogical tool to teach a course for final year computer science and engineering graduate students. *Journal of Engineering Education Transformations*, 306-310.

Doyle, T. (2011). *Learner-centered teaching: Putting the research on learning into practice*. Sterling, VA: Stylus Publishing, LLC.

Fung, H., & Ma, W. W. (2015). Investigating the relationship between students' attitude towards video production project and their generic skills enhancement. In *New Media, Knowledge Practices and Multiliteracies* (pp. 235–248). Heidelberg, NY: Springer Singapore.

Goldman, R., Pea, R., Barron, B., & Derry, S. J. (Eds.). (2014). *Video research in the learning sciences.* New York, NY: Routledge.

Hannafin, M. J., & Land, S. M. (1997). The foundations and assumptions of technology-enhanced student-centered learning environments. *Instructional Science, 25*(3), 167–202. doi:10.1023/A:1002997414652

Heider, F. (1958). *The psychology of interpersonal relations.* New York, NY: John Wiley & Sons. doi:10.1037/10628-000

Hoare, C. (Ed.). (2011). *The Oxford handbook of reciprocal adult development and learning.* New York, NY: Oxford University Press. doi:10.1093/oxfordhb/9780199736300.001.0001

Hofschroer, M. (2012, December 3). *Friends* helps global television audience learn English. Marketwire. Retrieved from http://www.marketwire.com/press-release/friends-helps-global-television-audience-learn-english-1732657.htm

Kaufman, P. B., & Mohan, J. (2009). *Video use and higher education: Options for the future.* Study funded by Copyright Clearance Center and conducted by Intelligent Television in cooperation with New York University. Retrieved from https://library.nyu.edu/about/Video_Use_in_Higher_Education.pdf

Kearney, M., & Treagust, D. (2001). Constructivism as a referent in the design and development of a computer program using interactive digital video to enhance learning in physics. *Australasian Journal of Educational Technology, 17*(1), 64–79.

Keller, J. M. (1987). Development and use of the ARCS model of instructional design. *Journal of Instructional Development, 10*(3), 2–10. doi:10.1007/BF02905780

Knowlton, D. S. (2000). A theoretical framework for the online classroom: A defense and delineation of a student-centered pedagogy. *New Directions for Teaching and Learning, 2000*(84), 5–14. doi:10.1002/tl.841

Kolb, D. (1984). *Experiential learning: Experience as the source of learning and development.* Englewood Cliffs, NJ: Prentice Hall.

Kozma, R. B. (1991). Learning with media. *Review of Educational Research, 61*(2), 179–211. doi:10.3102/00346543061002179

Krathwohl, D. R. (2002). A revision of Bloom's taxonomy: An overview. *Theory into Practice, 41*(4), 212–218. doi:10.1207/s15430421tip4104_2

Lim, L. (2013, January 23). *Friends* will be there for you at Beijing's Central Perk. *National Public Radio.* Retrieved from http://www.npr.org/2013/01/23/170074762/friends-will-be-there-for-you-at-beijings-central-perk

Magee, C. M. (2011). A multi-case study of two studio learning environments: Technology enabled active learning at Massachusetts Institute of Technology and a Reggio Emilia studio at school within school. *INTED2011 Proceedings*, (pp. 4067-4076).

McCann, D. (2015). A flipped classroom using screen-capture video. *The FASEB Journal, 29*, 687–688.

Mediasite Analytics. (2013). *Mediasite analytics*, Mediasite document. Retrieved from http://www. sonicfoundry.com/data-sheet/mediasite-analytics

Merchant, Z., Goetz, E. T., Cifuentes, L., Keeney-Kennicutt, W., & Davis, T. J. (2014). Effectiveness of virtual reality-based instruction on students' learning outcomes in K-12 and higher education: A meta-analysis. *Computers & Education, 70*, 29–40. doi:10.1016/j.compedu.2013.07.033

New Media Consortium. (2014). *Horizon report: 2014 higher education*. Retrieved from http://cdn.nmc. org/media/2014-nmc-horizon-report-he-EN-SC.pdf

Richter-Levin, G., Kehat, O., & Anunu, R. (2015). Emotional tagging and long-term memory formation. In *Synaptic Tagging and Capture* (pp. 215–229). Heidelberg, NY: Springer Singapore.

Rigby, K. T. (2015). Real-time computer-based simulation as an intervention in aerodynamics education. *Journal of Aviation/Aerospace Education & Research, 24*(2), 1–20.

Scott, J. (2011, June 1). The rise of online video will break the Internet. *Reel SEO*. Retrieved from http:// www.reelseo.com/rise-online-video-break-internet

Smith, M. E., & Gevins, A. (2004). Attention and brain activity while watching television: Components of viewer engagement. *Media Psychology, 6*(3), 285–305. doi:10.1207/s1532785xmep0603_3

Sousa, D. A. (2011). *How the brain learns*. Thousand Oaks, CA: Corwin Press.

State of Video. (2014). *The state of video in education 2014*, Kultura report. Retrieved from http://site. kaltura.com/Education_Survey_Thank_You.html?aliId=93189612

Stavredes, T. (2011). *Effective online teaching: Foundations and strategies for student success*. San Fransisco, CA: Jossey-Bass.

United States Army. (2011). *The U.S. Army learning concept for 2015: Training and Doctrine Command Pamphlet 525-8-2*. Retrieved from http://wwwtradoc.army.mil/tpubs/pams/tp525-8-2.pdf

University Business. (2013). *Academic video at a tipping point: Preparing your campus for the future*, (white paper). Retrieved from http://www.sonicfoundry.com/white-paper/academic-video-tipping-point-preparing-your-campus-future

Unleash the Power of Video. (2014). *Unleash the power of video in the enterprise: A guide to building a solid video strategy*. Retrieved from http://www.sonicfoundry.com/white-paper/unleash-power-video-enterprise-guide-building-solid-video-strategy

Wetzel, C. D., Radtke, P. H., Stern, H. W., Dickieson, J., & McLachlan, J. C. (1993). *Review of the effectiveness of video media in instruction, No. NPRDC-TR-93-4*. San Diego, CA: Navy Personnel Research And Development Center.

Woldkowski, R. J. (2008). *Enhancing adult motivation to learn: A comprehensive guide for teaching all adults*. San Francisco, CA: Jossey-Bass.

Yau, H. K., Cheng, A. L. F., & Ho, M. W. M. (2015). Identify the motivational factors to affect the higher education students to learn using technology. *TOJET, 14*(2).

Zhang, D., Zhou, L., Briggs, R. O., & Nunamaker, J. F. Jr. (2006). Instructional video in e-learning: Assessing the impact of interactive video on learning effectiveness. *Information & Management, 43*(1), 15–27. doi:10.1016/j.im.2005.01.004

KEY TERMS AND DEFINITIONS:

Andragogy: Methods and techniques specially used to instruct adult learners.

Instructional Video Capturing System: Device and/or software based system that allows for the audio/video recording of instruction. Enhanced systems also include automatic recording via schedule, full video management by the instructor, and full student control of video playback (example: Mediasite).

Learning Management System (LMS): Online instructional system that organizes educational content (text, images, audio, video, and possible interactive components), typically behind a password protected area that allows for the teaching, grading, and general administration of students (examples include: Canvas, Blackboard, and Moodle).

Learning-Centered: Creation and presentation of the content done in such a way to be flexible enough to be used in ways that allow for different learning styles/preferences.

Media: Communication modes used to provide information (typical examples include: audio, video, images).

Pedagogy: Methods and techniques used to instruct students (originally defined as pertaining to children's learning, but modern use typically applies to all students).

Student-Centered: Creation and presentation of the content done in such a way to be flexible enough to be used in ways that specifically address students' needs.

Video: A recording of visual images (stationary or moving) that can contain audio.

Video Analytics: Numerical and graphical representations presented on items such as how many viewers accessed the video, who specifically accessed the video (if integrated with a student ID system typical of most LMSs), what parts of the video were most often viewed, when was the content most often accessed, how was the content accessed (browser/device), and other similar types of information.

Virtual Reality: An immersive environment derived from either computer animation and/or actual video to provide completely explorable surroundings (full or near 360 degree viewable).

Section 3
Enhanced Technological Tools for Multimedia Designs

Chapter 7
Static Text–Based Data Visualizations:
An Overview and a Sampler

Shalin Hai-Jew
Kansas State University, USA

ABSTRACT

Data visualizations have enhanced human understandings of various types of quantitative data for many years. Of late, text-based data visualizations have been used informally and formally on the WWW and Internet as well as for research. This chapter describes this phenomenon of text-based data visualizations by describing how many of the most common ones are created, where the underlying textual datasets are extracted from, how text-based data visualizations are analyzed, and the limits of such graphical depictions. While this work does not provide a comprehensive view of static (non-dynamic) text-based data visualizations, many of the most common ones are introduced. These visualizations are created using a variety of common commercial and open-source tools including Microsoft Excel, Google Books Ngram Viewer, Microsoft Visio, NVivo 10, Maltego Tungsten, CASOS AutoMap and ORA NetScenes, FreeMind, Wordle, UCINET and NetDraw, and Tableau Public. It is assumed that readers have a basic knowledge of machine-based text analysis.

INTRODUCTION

In the present age, researchers have access to more text-based data than ever. These include core textual data from digitized texts, documents, articles, and other formalized writing (which has gone through professional vetting and editing). There is also metadata describing other data (in multimedia, textual, and other forms); these may include tags on multimedia objects, bibliographies, publication abstracts, and other metadata. There are informal sources of textual data, such as private collections of personal papers, journals, and letters, known as gray literature. There is elicited information, such as through online surveys and "dropbox" sites on the Web. Then, too, there are (four) zettabytes of user-generated data on the World Wide Web (as of 2013): these are on social media platforms (blogs, wikis, microblogs, and

DOI: 10.4018/978-1-4666-8696-0.ch007

others), data repositories, pastebins, websites, learning management systems, and other online venues. There are intranets and reams of email data. There are automated (if not fully accurate) translations of voice-to-text from video and audio files. What this means is that there are plenty of textual sources of information (whether "born textual" or rendered textual) that may be explored for research (literature reviews, domain-analyses on the Web, survey and interview analyses, microblogging Tweetstream analyses, and others).

With so much "big data" available, machine-analysis of various texts often has to be applied in order to enhance what is knowable and communicable. Large-scale mining and analysis of this volume of data highlights the challenges of data veracity and its "velocity" or rate of change over time (Plate, 2013, n.p.). Core to these text analyses are text-based data visualizations which communicate insights about the text: patterns, anomalies, themes, and other insights, in a human-interpretable way. This work provides an overview of some basic types of machine-based text analyses and some common types of static (non-dynamic) text-based data visualizations, along with some basic approaches to their interpretation. It is important to define "text-based" in this context. For this context, "text-based" will include the two central meanings: (1) underlying text corpuses which inform the data visualization and (2) the expression of concepts which are expressed through symbolic textual means. The first type would include visualizations that are closer to the original raw text and are often machine-drawn; the second type is in a sense more processed and abstracted from the underlying data (and may be more abstract) and are often manually drawn. The first type of visualization will tend to be drawn based on machine algorithms. The latter is a form of graphic ideation and will tend to be drawn based on trained human conventions of illustration and diagramming.

A REVIEW OF THE LITERATURE

Language is a core element of culture, and words carry critical concepts. Language is a central element of human socializing and inter-communications. It is the core vehicle for the dissemination and communication of research and of popular understandings of the world. Language is polysemic or many-meaninged; based on its interpretation, it may convey a range of ideas and impressions. Messaging may be understood whether the initial communicator consciously or unconsciously intended to share particular information; meaning is not necessarily dependent on the conscious intentions of those wielding the language. The centrality of language in the human experience in part explains the power of machine-based text analysis. As a data source, language is often rendered into textual form for analysis (whether the original data was a video, audio, image, or other multimedia type).

The textual data analyzed in most data analytics software programs are considered "unstructured" because they do not fit into databases in pre-labeled data cells. The raw textual data is heterogeneous, or it comes in many forms. They are high-dimensional, consisting of a large number of variables or facets. The data may be noisy, with extraneous words which are not particularly meaningful for a particular query or research question. (The "noise" here would suggest that there are distractors that may lower the signal-to-noise ratio, which would raise the probability of coming to erroneous conclusions from the dataset. There would be increased false positives and false negatives mixed in with the accurate signals. Information unreliability may be partially off-set by having large amounts of data available for wider sampling but then being able to de-noise that set by honing in on the relevant signals.) The textual data is inherently ambiguous, in part because language itself is multi-meaninged and defined in part by context, but text analysis decontextualizes information (in some processes) in order to convert textual data into statistical counts. In social media, with people's self-provisioned information and so much posing (or "social performance"), human subjectivity has to be taken into consideration when considering such data. It makes sense to have some standardized ways to assess the reliability of data. *Figure 1:* Categories of Data Trustworthiness (derived from Admiralty Ratings) is a visualization of one such standard known as "admiralty ratings," with the following standards: "confirmed (100%), probably true (80%), possibly true (60%), doubtful (40%), improbable (20%), misinformation, deception, and cannot be judged (50%)" (Prunckun, 2010, p. 30). The 50% for "cannot be judged" may be understood as not better than chance in a binary true / false system.

The provenance or origin of the original "raw" data may be undefined or ill-defined, and further, it may not even be verifiable (such as information from social media platforms with unverified "natural person" accounts [such accounts could be 'bots" or "cyborgs), elusive non-signifying handles, and poor account security]. (In recent years, the larger commercial companies providing social media services have strived to tighten up the regimes for connecting accounts to actual and verified people.) The performances of application programming interfaces (APIs) linked to social media platforms and then the software created by developers to access those data streams may affect the quality of the extracted information.

Contemporary data analysis tools enable a range of functions. Many enable the archival of a variety of digital and multimedia files in one dataset, which may then be coded and analyzed. Words may be disambiguated based on the contextual words around them (in co-occurrence vectors or within certain sized offsets or "windows" highlighting certain n-grams of text) and the statistical probability that it would have one meaning over another, or based on examples (other similar word usages in context). Some have suggested that words found in texts tend more towards polysemy (being multi-meaninged) than monosemy (being single-meaninged). Words themselves may be decontextualized and then indexed or counted, clustered with similar words, and mapped on word trees with proxemics other words or phrases. While the raw data is often unstructured, intermediate form data and visualizations which are part of the sequence of text analysis may be semi-structured or structured (Tan, 1999, n.p.). The identification of extant and descriptive patterns in data is based on unsupervised machine learning ("Frontiers in Massive Data Analysis," 2012, pp. 102 – 103). ("Supervised learning" refers to predictive modeling in the machine learning literature.)

In information science, the "bag of words" approach refers to the treatment of textual documents (or datasets) as non-contextualized and disaggregated textual elements which belong to particular sets. In this approach, natural language units are broken down into "tokens" (meaningful base elements of language) that are then used by computers for various types of text-based analysis. A commonly-cited observation of language is known as Zipf's law, based on empirical observations of natural language text corpuses. It suggests that only a small portion of a text corpus consists of words that frequently occur;

Figure 1. Categories of data trustworthiness (derived from Admiralty Ratings)

Confirmed (100%)	Probably True (805)	Possibly True (60%)	Doubtful (40%)	Improbable (20%)	Misinformation	Deception	Cannot be Judged (50%)

rather, a large portion of words appear infrequently in a kind of "long tail." The law states that in natural language corpuses, "the frequency of any word is inversely proportional to its rank in the frequency table" in a power law probability distribution ("Zipf's law," June 18, 2014).

Various systems have been made to "tag" parts-of-speech, semantic terms, sentiment, proper nouns, and other specific details from large-scale corpora. Based on real-world examples, "collocations" in various languages may be identified out. ("Collocations" are recurrent word combinations or strings that are often unique to particular languages. Externally, collocations may be considered "arbitrary" and generally unpredictable—unless they have been pre-identified based on insider knowledge of conventional usage and tagged to certain meanings. Collocations do not generally transfer across languages or cultures. Some text analysis systems apply significance lists of potential collocations to enhance machine-based understandings of particular phrasing.) Words, as nominal data, may be categorized as "the lowest level of measurement" (Prunckun, 2010, p. 108), which highlights the simplicity of non-ranking sorts of mutually exclusive grouping. Computers may be trained into how to code information and will learn how to "autocode" on the guidance of the human coder (by emulating the human researcher's choices as a training set). Matrix coding queries may be applied to textual data to find strategic "mentions" of particular words. These queries may be used to identify salient word uses in particular text documents or text corpuses. Given the awareness of common errors in data cleaning and processing (such as the inclusion of repeated information, for example), many software programs have been programmed with "error-trapping subroutines".

Humans are able to intuitively cluster documents from imputed similarity. A range of algorithms have been designed to more mechanistically identify similarities and to apply those to texts. Text elements may be coded based on human-created files to tag textual data; other machine systems use raw data as a training set to hone machine learning of what words, phrases, and symbols, are in a text or text corpus and to create self-organizing maps. Synonyms are clustered for semantic meaning. Meaning-ful words (semantics) are separated out from structure-based words (syntactics). There are a breadth of definitions for the concept of semantical relatedness between words and phrases. Synonyms reflect definitional likeness; antonyms refer to words with definitional opposites; hyponyms refer to words or phrases whose semantic field is a subset of that of another word, known as its hypernym or hyperonym; meronyms refer to words that refer to a part of something but is used to refer to the whole; holonyms refer to words that refer to a whole but is used to refer to a part of that whole, and so on. Texts (and textual datasets) may be compared for word similarities based on synonym sets and overall topical relatedness. Frequency counts of unique keyword sets may be used to consider how similar or dissimilar comparable texts may be. Semantic-based similarity is focused on textual meanings, based on the number and strength of relationships among all words (in a matrix-based analysis). Documents may also be compared based on statistical similarities (Thomas, Pennock, Fiegel, Wise, Pottier, Schur, Lantrip, & Crow, 1995, p. 3).

Beyond generalized sets of tagged words, there are particular sets used in certain domains. This type of analytical computing is sensitive to the sequence of applications of filters and other data cleaning, because each step has the potential of changing up the dataset that is passed on to the next process; it is important not to lose relevant data along the way that would skew results. The findings from these textual queries may be visualized in a variety of ways.

As-such, text analyses involve a fair amount of discovery; they are approached with some pre-determined questions but optimally also with open-mindedness about what may be found. For some researchers, the text analysis comes during an early stage in the work and may be used for hypothesis generation. Machine-based text analyses (which generally provide a gist or essence) do not preclude human close reading of the unprocessed texts; however, the slower human information processing renders impossible the close reading of all elements of "big data" datasets. Likewise, text-based analyses and their related text-based visualizations do not preclude the use of the underlying statistical data. In other words, there are multiple channels for information, and the ones that are relevant should all be exploited; one channel should not be used to the exclusion of the others. All said, people play a critical role in the research work even when text analysis technologies are used. Pre-existent knowledge of the textual data and the context of the usage of that data is important for understanding. Said another way, Ware suggests that people tend to be "cognitive cyborgs" (Ware, 2012, p. 376), who closely integrate technology for awareness and problem-solving. One researcher writes:

For data mining to be effective, it is important to include the human in the data exploration process and combine the flexibility, creativity, and general knowledge of the human with the enormous storage capacity and the computational power of today's computers (Keim, 2002, p. 1).

Tools today enable a wide range of types of text and n-gram (contiguous text strings) frequency counts. Machines can sift between semantic (meaning-based) and syntactic (language structure-based) text, with parts-of-speech tagging. Computers may be applied to reduce data, so the core and salient ideas are identified and contextualized in relation to other ideas. Computing machines are capable of measuring the expressed values, emotions, and beliefs, behind expressed messages (by valence measures to capture the direction of the opinion and its strength). These analytical processes may be applied across a wide range of languages and cross-lingually (machine code-switching) as well. These approaches are eminently scalable. These may be dynamically applied as well, such as in the streaming collection of evolving messages from microblogs and their near-real-time analysis to understand trending ideas and sentiments. In other words, machine analysis of texts have been applied for a number of fundamental purposes: (1) coherent information processing of large datasets and emergent (dynamically-created) data for situational awareness; (2) latent information surfacing (finding hidden patterns and relationships that would not be perceptible otherwise); and (3) the visual-based communications of research findings to others. To these ends, various machine- and human-based processing is applied to the texts: descriptive and analytic efforts such as counting (text frequency counts or text indexing), sorting, filtering, relating, co-occurrence identification, proximity identification, clustering, categorization, structuring, data reduction, and summarization; meaning extraction such as coding, and other applications. The data visualizations are part and parcel of the text processing and analytical process.

One of the major affordances of digital visualizations involves the capabilities of people to understand and analyze large datasets. Such visualizations offer an easier point-of-entry through which analysts may investigate the data, through semi-visual means instead of purely abstract and symbolic ones. Studies have found that users tend to prefer visualization systems to textual output (Yuan, Zhang, & Trofimovsky, 2010). Neuroscience researchers looking at memory retrieval suggest that people are better at applying their so-called "where-system" than their "what-system," which some researchers suggest benefits data visualizations for knowledge acquisition and learning (Keller, Gerjets, Scheiter, & Garsoffky, 2006, p. 47).

Visualizations may indicate patterns, trendlines, anomalies, and relationships. Unexpected findings may create disfluencies or dissonant representations—which may help researchers reconsider pre-existing assumptions. In this scenario, the internal mental (or conceptual) model of the researcher is compared with the externalized research findings expressed visually. Insights from text-based data visualizations may indicate important nodes or variables to analyze in more depth. To these ends, a number of tools enable ways for people to interact with the data through visual and textual interfaces. Through these, they may change up the data parameters through filtering (selecting out information that will not be included or displayed in a particular iteration or state). They may change the particular time periods being visualized. They may integrate data from various sources; they may prune out data to enhance focus. They may select different layout algorithms or visualization types to showcase the data. The same dataset may manifest in very different ways depending on the layout algorithms (directions which direct a computer to process the data and output a particular visualization), which enable data to "structure itself" based on data rules. There are benefits to using multiple layouts for the same dataset because different visualizations may spark different insights (Hai-Jew, 2013). They may create a stopwords or delete list in order to remove inconsequential or non-meaning-bearing terms further focus the data extraction and visualization. (Some common extractions include the definite article "the"—which is the most frequently occurring word in natural language documents and accounts for almost 7% of word occurrences—and the preposition "of," which occurs in over 3.5% of words, and the coordinate conjunction "and," which occurs in nearly 3% of words, according to the Brown Corpus of American English text.) Such interactive analytical reasoning may enable new insights. Some researchers suggest that information visualization systems have two core elements: "representation and interaction" (Yi, Kang, Stasko, & Jacko, 2007, p. 1224). Text-based data visualizations offer a way into the data, and that may be a starting point into the research, not necessarily an end point. Some of the intermediate and ultimate states of the analyses are extracted as text-based visualizations. Text-based visualizations may provide one channel—namely visual data mining--for the extraction of research information, among many.

Some real-world applications. Indeed, machine-based text analyses have been used in a wide number of fields. Text mining for natural language processing \draws from a range of fields in order to offer text summaries (the gist of the dataset), text categorization, "top-down" *a priori* query-based information extraction (as well as "bottom-up" knowledge discovery), relationship identification (between words, between documents, between language corpuses, and between communicators), and other functions.

Text mining is a multidisciplinary field, involving information retrieval, text analysis, information extraction, clustering, categorization, visualization, database technology, machine learning, and data mining (Tan, 1999, n.p.).

One common visualization from text mining is a "term map," a two-dimensional figure in which the distance between respective terms is an indication of their relatedness: the closer the proximity, the more intimate the connection. Such term maps are often used in text mining and are a visual expression of results (van Eck & Waltman, 2011).

In the literature, there are a number of different types of "use cases" and user tasks for machine analysis of text. Machine-enabled text analyses play a critical role in intelligence and law enforcement. One well known example involves the analysis of email networks as part of the Enron investigation. There are a number of software tools that enable the visualization of email contents and inter-relationships between email users (Ip, Keung, Cui, Qu, & Shen, 2010). Machine-based text analyses are used in political science to understand the moods of mass populations and on-going social media conversations in all regions of the world. They are used to analyze contents of speeches to understand the intentions of national leaders (Prunckun, 2010, pp. 64 – 67). They are used in marketing to understand what consumers are saying. They are used in the "digital humanities" to understand various classical works, summarize or compare text corpuses, highlight historical time periods, and other analytical purposes. Literary texts are analyzed for insights, with various text-based visualizations including bar charts, word trees, and "newspaper-strip" visualizations (Muralidharan & Hearst, 2012, p. 1958). Machine-based analyses of texts are used to map bibliographic networks (Shen, Ogawa, Teoh, & Ma, 2006) to understand professional research and collaboration tendencies among researchers, the development of innovations across various domains, the productivity of various universities, the state of innovations in nations, and other information. Machine-based text analyses are used in linguistics to understand various languages and their functionalities. They are used to digitally identify the style of various authors (in stylometry or the quantitative-and statistics-based metrics of literary or writing style) and to "fingerprint" (or identify the unique qualities of) and reveal authors who would rather remain anonymous. Text analyses are used to map subject areas and their overlapping edges to achieve a range of aims: to analyze the productivity of universities in terms of their graduates; to understand how professional researchers collaborate (through co-citation bibliographic networks); to rank researchers; to anticipate capabilities of other nations (and organizations), and so on. Computers are used to "read" and "summarize" large-scale online discussions such as in massive open online courses (MOOCs), to enhance human awareness and intercommunications and to direct the responsiveness of the instructor(s). This list is a sparse sampling of the capabilities of the tool. Providing a comprehensive overview is beyond the purview of this work.

Content analysis (of various types of content, often rendered first into textual format) is used to understand cultural groups' social representations. Social representations are a result of personal and collective (and interactive) processes of interactive meaning-making. Text analyses of public and private discourses (and other cultural artifacts) around a particular topic may capture words which are proximal to a particular experience and may reveal the existence of "social representations," or collective ways of thinking about and approaching particular issues. These social representations contain positive or negative psychological valence—attraction or aversion—and these value judgments imbue beliefs and attitudes, which inform (in part) actions and individual and group practices. In this latter sense, social representations (as extracted from text analyses of macro-social discourses—through both formal and informal channels) may be used predictively to understand potential directions of particular events or social trends. According to social representation theory (a collection of related theory from social psychology and sociological social psychology), social representation is understood as "a cognitive, symbolic, iconic and affectively laden mental construct with a structure of its own; it is a way of concerted thinking which is shared by the members of reflexive groups" (Wagner, Valencia, & Elejabarrieta, 1996, p. 331). Such social representations are thought to have an unchanging core, which informs the rest of the representation.

Text analyses may be used to identify core phrases and terms which are referred to with high frequency and which may have salience and power to activate social networks of people into individual or mass action, for example. The authors explain:

We assume, on the one hand, that words pertaining to the core preserve their structural relationship within different contexts because of their necessary and non-negotiable role in defining the object. Peripheral elements, on the other hand, do not preserve their structural relationships within different contexts because their role is to adapt a representation to different situations. Consequently, if we elicit a well-structured social representation in two different contexts, a comparison of the structures of the two should reveal at least two sets of elements: on the one hand, elements which preserve their structure in contrasting contexts, i.e. the **'situationally stable' core,** *and on the other hand, elements which do not preserve their structure in different contexts, i.e. the* **'situationally unstable' periphery** *(Wagner, Valencia, & Elejabarrieta, 1996, p. 334)*

One of the insights from this research related to the human tendency to express ideas and experiences that were more close-in or proxemics to their lived (embodied and emotional) experiences instead of more detached, cooler, or intellectualized observations (Wagner, Valencia, & Elejabarrieta, 1996, p. 342). What creates salience for human communicators are their direct experiences, and the sharing of these experiences contribute to core words in social representations, defined as cognitive, affective, and symbolic structures stemming from common collective experiences. While lived and directly experienced ideas tend to be recorded in the cores of social representations, more intellectual and cooler ideas tend to be captured as peripheral and possibly more context-dependent ideas.

Designing Text-Based Visualizations for End Users

Text-based visualizations clearly have to represent the underlying data. As important, these must convey accurate understandings to a broad range of users with varying capabilities and backgrounds. The visualization constructs must be coherent and clear, and if initial understandings are not immediately apparent, ultimate clarity must be attainable. Text-based data visualizations can take on a wide range of different forms based on the types of layout algorithms used. The software programs used for this work are wide-ranging, and they offer different levels of explanatory depth about the "black box" computations within their programs. Even with thorough explanations of the various research methods and computations, the statistical processes may be confusing to common users, and many may only be able to extract a naïve user view based on the visualization. Beyond the static text-based visualizations alone, there are usually methods that enable user interactions with the data, which enable them to zoom in on particular time periods, geographical locales, branches of a network, word clusters, and even individual nodes or records. Most such interfaces—on dashboards, work benches, microsites, galleries, and apps–allow near-instantaneous changes to the visualizations. Users are able to filter out data or to mix data sets. They are often able to select different types of layout algorithms for different visualizations to achieve different hypothesis testing, analyses, and insights. They are able to retrieve specific information while often still maintaining an overview, for micro and macro levels of analysis. Time-based data may offer historical insights. They may be able to rotate the data visualizations, particularly those that are 3D, in a type of user interaction called "data spinning". They may be able to play animations of the data over time, particularly for trend-line data. Researchers have identified a wide range of informational visualization taxonomies relevant to interaction techniques from the mid-1990s onwards (Yi, Kang, Stasko, & Jacko, 2007, p. 1225), and there has been much progress even since. The gold standard for user-based design involves direct research with live human testing, and for many companies that provide such visualizations online through galleries and other interfaces, they have empirical data from their data analytics from users' real-world engagements.

Human factors in perception, cognition, learning, and memory retention. Some types of information are more readily conveyed in visual representational form than textual ones (Larkin & Simon, 1987, as cited in Keller, Gerjets, Scheiter, & Garsoffky, 2006, p. 45). Some informational forms are more computationally efficient for human use based on their design. Visualizing itself is central to the process of thinking (Gilbert, 2001, p. 15), and it is critical as a "metacognitive skill" for a wide range of science-based learning (Gilbert, 2005). Visual representations may be especially powerful when large amounts of textual data and their interrelationships are being conveyed. Spatial thinking, understanding spatial relationships between objects and the location of objects in space, is a core element in the performance of mathematical, engineering, design, and other tasks. Researchers have found that the use of schematic visual imagery (which encode relationships and functions) was positively correlated with higher mathematical word-problem solving; the use of pictorial images (which encode surface physical features) were negatively correlated with mathematical problem solving (van Garderen, 2006, p. 496). Spatial imagery refers to spatial relationships while visual imagery refers to "the representation of the visual appearance of an object, such as its shape, color, or brightness" (van Garderen, 2006, p. 497), with the first type addressing schematic understandings more than surface ones. The ability to spatially visualize has been found to correlate with math ability (particularly geometry and word problems) (van Garderen, 2006, p. 504).

Generally speaking, the greater the dimensionality of the data, the higher the cognitive load required to process it. Text-based data is high-dimensional, with myriad ways to extract meaning. There are a variety of ways that multi-dimensional data may be visualized (Pastizzo, Erbacher, & Feldman, 2002). In Keim's "Classification of Information Visualization Techniques" figure, the visualization suggests that various types of data match with particular visualization techniques, with hierarchies and graphs matched with geometrically-transformed displays, text/web data with iconic displays and dense pixel displays, and so on. Further, he suggests that particular types of visualized information may be interacted with through a range of techniques: standard, projection, filtering, zoom, distortion, and link&brush (Keim, 2002, p. 2). The chart leaves open the various types of data, the visualization techniques, and the interaction and distortion techniques. The interaction here refers to engaging with the data, and the distortion techniques enable differing re-visualizations of the data (such as exploring the data in drill-down operations while maintaining a high-level overview of the visualized data). Keim suggests that there is a three-step process of visual data exploration: "overview first, zoom and filter, and then details-on demand" (Keim, 2002, p. 2). Michalko, an expert on creativity, suggests that visual thinking is a complement to verbal thinking and is a constantly working process in the human mind (2006 / 1991, p. 184). Some tools enable ways to "freeze frame" a data visualization for analysis and export, which provides a sense of control over data that may be visualized in a number of different ways for new insights and analysis.

Text-based data visualizations are thought to require increase cognitive load to process the information because they require both conceptual and spatial representations of information (Allen, 1998). Various research studies have found that people require a higher cognitive processing load in order to make sense of 3D visualizations as compared to 2D ones, with some finding that 2D ones may be superior in terms of data interpretation (Keller, Gerjets, Scheiter, & Garsoffky, 2006, p. 48). Some researchers even suggest that 3D visualizations. Three-dimensional informational representations are thought to require additional orientation demands (to reveal hidden or visually blocked datapoints or clusters or structures) and increased interactivity for sense-making. It has been argued that the increased cognitive demands may off-set potential benefits (of being able to integrate more complexity in the text-based data visualization). There is some research that shows that there may be some benefits with 3D scatterplots in terms of speed of some types of data extractions that required understanding information from all three depicted dimensions (Wickens, Merwin, & Lin, 1994, as cited in Keller, Gerjets, Scheiter, Garsoffky, 2006, p. 49). However, any speed advantages were lost for the extraction of other types of tasks focused on specific data points (not requiring information integration). Conducting visual rotations mentally is compounded with the difficulty of recognizing certain 2D and 3D objects (Vandenberg & Kuse, 1978). The third dimension (z-axis) is often brought in with multi-dimensional data and "technically complex information visualizations" (Keller, Gerjets, Scheiter, & Garsoffky, 2006, p. 44). The third dimension (3D) usually comes into play with multi-dimensional data; occasionally, it is used to depict the element of time (which is part of dynamic or streaming visualizations, which are generally beyond the scope of this work). One way to justify 3D is to use the concept of the Greek Cross, whose solution requires thinking in three dimensions (Michalko, 2006/1991, p. 143). There are many other dimensions beyond the third one. There are various text analytic systems (types of stream visualizations over time) (Wei, Liu, Song, Pan, Zhou, Qian, Shi, Tan, & Zhang, 2010). Such visualizations go beyond 3D. Indeed, there has long been the use of data cubes and other ways of representing complex dimensionality using even more intricate geometrical shapes and symbolic representations. Theoretically and practically, any of these text-based visualizations may be used with any type of text (even though the data handling and pre-processing, processing, and post-processing may be different based on the research questions and methods).

It is important to note that data visualizations are not only being pursued as a visual modality. Some researchers are exploring the deployment of haptics for data visualization (Roberts & Panëels, 2007). In the same way that multimedia is multisensory, the communications of text-based visualizations are multi-modal and multi-sensory.

The design of text-based data visualizations. Ideally, the best designed text-based data visualizations enhance accurate knowledge acquisition with the least-burdensome cognitive load possible. The best designed visualizations enable performance gains in human understanding and analysis. For the purposes of this chapter, text-based visualizations are 2D and 3D diagrams which are built from core textual (alphanumeric) or symbolic language data. (By contrast, a wide variety of visualizations include some textual labeling and the usage of legends, but the underlying data may be non-textual.) The cognitive theory of multimedia learning (Mayer, 2001) suggests that there are different pathways for textual and visual information processing systems. A text-based visualization may entail "inter-representational queries" (Collins & Carpendale, 2007, p. 1192), which may involve cognitive expense. A judicious tapping of both memory systems in a complementary way may be achieved through proper design with integrations of text and graphics and may lead to "better retention than the use of only one representational code" (Keller, Gerjets, Scheiter, & Garsoffky, 2006, p. 46). "For visual queries to be useful, a problem must *first* be cast in the form of a visual pattern that, if identified, helps solve part of the problem," observes one researcher (Ware, 2012, p. 376). Indeed, data visualizations all follow certain conventions for the conveyance of information in order to properly point human attention to the salient points (through centering, through motion, through highlighting, through text, and other means).

Avoiding negative learning or misperceptions. Another important aspect to design involves heading off potential misunderstandings or confusions about the meaning of the data visualization and the underlying research results. To these ends, it is important to ensure precise rigor in the research work, so the data visualization is built on a solid foundation. It is important to cross-validate data. It is important to pursue lines of falsification to pressure-test the findings. There need to be proper amounts of training data in datasets for the conclusions that are arrived at. The methods for the research should be sound. The data type should be aligned with the proper type of visualization. The confidence level in the findings should be indicated. Often, such work requires iterated checks and double-checks.

Part of the challenge of potentially misleading data in visualizations comes from the communications forms themselves. Some researchers found higher error rates for the reading of tag clouds vs. that of tables across both the "target absent" and "target present" states. The authors used data tables as the baseline for visualization performance (for the speed and accuracy of data extraction). The authors write:

The first experiment concerned the speed and accuracy with which participants could identify the presence or absence of a specified target in an unsorted tag cloud or table. The second experiment also analysed speed and accuracy with tag clouds and tables, but in tasks concerning identification of maximum and minimum attribute values. Tables were faster and more accurate in both tasks (Oosterman & Cockburn, 2010, p. 288).

It is generally good practice to ensure that the visualizations are legible and readable, so there is fidelity to the underlying data in the particular transcoded visualization. It's critical to have the proper contextualization of the text-based visualization, with lead-up and lead-away text. Data visualizations, in other words, serve a communications function, so they must be understandable across a potential broad spectrum of users. Insufficient design considerations (and likely insufficient testing with human users) may well lead to misunderstandings given data complexity and the human tendency to speed through text-based visualizations while engaging the System 1 "fast thinking" instead of the System 2 "slow thinking" (per Daniel Kahneman's *Thinking Fast and Slow*). Some visualizations may lead some to give more credence to the assertions even when the underlying logic is unsound (Beilock, 2010, pp. 42-43). It makes sense that the extracted data tables and even the original raw or semi-processed textual datasets may be made available for further research and exploration, if appropriate. The broad sharing of such data enhances transparency. After all, by the time information is coded into a text-based data visualization, there have already been multiple encodings that have come before it.

Casual and popular-use text-based visualizations. Researchers have mentioned the broad sense that information visualization has crossed over into the public realm and broad usage by casual users (Pousman & Stasko, 2007); for example, a common form of vernacular visualization involves the mapping of tag clouds based on folksonomic user-generated tagging (Viégas & Wattenberg, 2008, p. 49). Tag clouds and folksonomies evolve but stabilize at some point over time (Russell, 2006), with many visualizations offering static slice-in-time views of the tag clouds (whereas time-lapse tag clouds may be informative of changes over time). Another is the use of dynamic word clouds to indicate the semantic evolution of contents at different time intervals (Cui, Wu, Liu, Wei, Zhou, & Qu, 2010), with many such features available on microblogs, blogs, wikis, and websites to enhance user awareness and navigation of the site contents. Word-based trees may be used to enable users to access contextualized blog contents to add more of an understanding of a text hierarchy than a tag cloud alone (Candan, Di Caro, & Sapino, 2008).

Many text-based visualizations present the information all at once, with a simultaneity of textual imagery, instead of sequential revelation in a linear sequence (Gobert, 2005, p. 74), such as in consecu-

Figure 2. Multiple encodings in text-based data visualizations

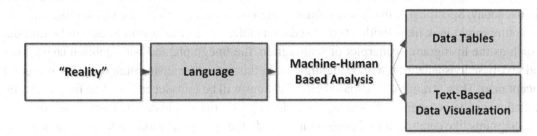

tive slides of a slideshow or pages of a microsite; other visualizations though develop and unfold in time, such as some dynamic streamgraphs with time-series data. Some text-based data visualizations serve a self-expression need as "word art" or "data doodle." For example, Wordles™ may be created as "graphic statements" (with rich typographies, layouts, colors, and differing versions) from personally meaningful documents such as letters, literary texts, political speeches, or thoughts (Viégas, Wattenberg, & Feinberg, 2009, p. 1137). Beyond the dedicated online gallery of Wordles™, these visualizations have been used in a variety of contexts both digital and real-space contexts: slideshows, videos, magazine covers, and cards.] Users of this popular online tool are exercising what the authors call "remixing power" (Viégas, Wattenberg, & Feinberg, 2009, p. 1143). Still others use text-based visualizations as forms of "knowledge media" or informational graphics ("infographics") through the application of inference making. Another term used in this phenomena is "data stories"—data visualizations which suggest a story; one well-known example involves a query to the Google Book Ngram Viewer for both the words "chicken" and "egg" against the tens-of-millions of book text corpus. Such visualizations may offer a sense of simultaneity, with the text-based visualizations offering the data all at once, instead of in a linear sequence (Gobert, 2005, p. 74). Some text-based visualizations are purely aesthetically pleasing, without any text labels within the depicted graph. Text-based visualizations, as informational graphics (of sorts), do involve an aesthetic element—with many bearing visual distinctiveness.

While a naïve interpreter of data visualizations might assume that visualizations are self-explanatory and intuitive, in reality, there are a number of nuances to interpreting various types of data visualizations and many underlying assumptions about the visualization. A histogram may look like just another bar graph unless it is understood that the visualization shows ranges the frequency distribution for an entire set of data with equal intervals. A social network graph conveys more meaning when the different layout algorithms are taken into consideration with the application of core-periphery analysis where relevant and other types of spatial analysis when relevant. Then, too, it's important to understand what sort of word similarity analysis is going on with a particular tool. More sophisticated analysts would almost always go beyond the text-based data visualization to the underlying data and any related datasets in order to understand more about the information. After all, there are no data visualizations that serve as full substitutes for the underlying word dataset. There is always some loss of meaning and potential detail. Optimally, text-based data visualizations address sufficiency of information for a particular targeted and limited question or purpose.

This chapter will contextualize the various visualizations, describe how they were created (and with what datasets and data structures), cite the software tool(s) used in their creation, and provide insights on how to begin to analyze the data (in an applied research scenario). The text-based visualizations will be critiqued for their informational value. There are many dozens of methods for the visualization of an underlying text dataset (or even databases), but this work will highlight some of the most common ones in use today. Specifically, the first text-based data visualization will be one of the closest to what a data structure might look like—with a text-based data table. More classic structures will be introduced next, such as the histogram, scatterplot or scattergram, the linegraph, and bar / column chart. Then, a manual text-based visualization will be highlighted, in this case, a brainstorming diagram or mind map or concept map. Then, a range of text-based visualizations will be introduced based on frequency counts and statistical analyses (treemap diagrams, word clouds, and others), cluster diagrams (various types of affinity diagrams like dendrograms, bubble graphs, and others), and relational data (ring lattice graphs, grids, word trees, related tags networks, hashtag conversations, node-link / vertex-edge diagrams, and others). Then, various matrix visualizations will be introduced, including matrix coding query tables and data matrices. The fairly familiar geographical map will be depicted based on textual data. And finally, a contemporary streamgraph (an area chart showing time-based or even dynamic real-time data) will be depicted. This is often used to represent dynamic data over time albeit in static form. (Some "streamgraphs" are dynamic and full-motion ones as shown in dynamically generated bubble graphs, but this dynamic version will not be shown here.) On the whole, a majority of these are 2D graphs (depicted on a two-dimensional plane, with an x and a y axis); a few will be in 3D (depicted on a three-dimensional plane, with x, y, and z axes).

A new way to explore the Web? One research point of interest has been visual exploration, with multiple research teams considering early design prototypes and interfaces for possible new Web and database search paradigms (beyond the current text one). If the next navigational technique on the Web involves visual exploration, how would it affect people's search strategies and behaviors? Several researchers describe "a new type of information seeking that is high-level and more engaging, by providing the information seeker with interactive visualizations that give graphical overviews and enable query formulation" (Dörk, Williamson, & Carpendale, 2012, p. 13:2). This approach would potentially capture the "social, semantic, and spatial relationships" on the Web (Dörk, Williamson, & Carpendale, 2012, p. 13:2). Given the global nature of the World Wide Web and Internet, it is an important point that international participants in one research context showed preference for image search and navigation to access news articles of the local area.

We analyzed four categories of interaction behavior: zooming and panning, scanning patterns, distraction and reading news summaries. Results show that increasing the ratio of images to text causes more distraction but also leads to more news summaries read. The ratio of text to images also impacted scanning behavior, with participants tending to scan the most prevalent tag type (text or image) first. Preference was split between high and low image ratios, while most participants were comfortable with a more equal mix of text and image tags (Salimian, Brooks, & Reilly, 2013, p. 24).

Online providers of news and other content have captured plenty of data about human usage of online contents and methods of driving traffic, whether it be through increased images or more appealing headlines. There is research on the trending human interests and the fast degradation of interest over time for news.

A Research Angle

Theoretically, text analyses seem to fall into the realm of mixed methods research because the approach taps into methodological pluralism. As in quantitative research, machine-based text analysis relies heavily on statistical means; it relies heavily on computational analysis. Given the pervasiveness of texts, these may be drawn from a variety of quantitative research techniques: experimental research (such as the text analysis of lab notes), pre- and post-research designs, and quasi-experimental research. As in qualitative research, much of the data that is analyzed may come from the world (the "field"), *in vivo* and empirically, with such data manipulated for latent meaning. The texts may come from surveys, focus groups, interviews, Delphi studies, ethnographies, case studies, and other human-intensive interactions. Researchers may integrate any combination of texts (as long as they're ingested in discrete files), across various languages, to query the data. All research paradigms have their enablements and their limitations; only certain types of information may be accessed with any particular approach. The main point here is that text analysis as an applied tool is generally theory agnostic and is more limited by the available texts, the analytical skills of the researcher, the technological limitations of the tool, and the capability of the readers to understand the relevance of the research findings. This text-based content analysis methodology and the various related visualization methods are informed by a range of evolved theories, depending on the research context and the topic domain. As such, they are too many to address here.

The importance of researcher capabilities. How researchers capture the relevant texts, clean their data, mix (or disaggregate) datasets, conduct the text analyses and draw the visualizations (using any number of software tools) will affect the resulting information that is created, the visualizations that are drawn, and ultimately what is knowable from the work. These approaches will determine the ultimate value of the textual and visual information. The actual sequence of text processing in text analysis tools will affect the outcomes, so it helps to be methodical and self-aware in the work. It is critical for researchers to know the textual datasets and the particular subject domain as intimately as possible in order to inform their work and ultimately their interpretations of the text analyses. There is also the importance of creating not only informative data visualizations but those that are aesthetically pleasing, to meet the conventions of data visualizations. Effective researchers should be able to tease out accurate insights from the analyses even if the visualizations themselves are non-alerting to relevance (and most are designed only to highlight or signify obvious points of relevance). Even with one dataset, different researchers or research teams will likely apply different methods and surface different insights (although there will likely be some research findings overlap as well). Researchers' training, intellect, and skillsets all will inform what they find salient. Also, there are particular ways that text queries may be framed and structured given the affordances and enablements of machine-based text querying. For researchers to practice effective text-based research, they will need to know where to look for what information, how to find the relevant information, how to set up proper text queries, and then how to interpret text-based data visualizations. They have to know what may or may not be asserted from the data they have; they have to know how to explore further beyond the information in a particular text corpus or corpuses. Also, the researcher will have to develop a sense for what is relevant in the findings. Optimally, analytical results have to be testable (falsifiable) and able to be recreated by others. This would suggest that extracted datasets should generally be made public, to enable external validation or invalidation of the results.

Some delimitations. The underlying textual data will be drawn from real-world data sets (vs. synthetic or made-up data). Only common off-the-shelf software tools (Excel, Microsoft Visio, NCapture, NVivo 10, Maltego Tungsten 3.4.2, CASOS AutoMap and ORA NetScenes, and UCINET and NetDraw) or open-source ones (FreeMind) or free cloud-based software and services (Tableau Public, Google Books Ngram Viewer, and Wordle) will be used for the original visualizations. These technologies are being used for very limited use cases; they are all capable of a broad range of research applications which are beyond the scope of this chapter. The strengths and weaknesses of the textual visualizations for machine-human analysis will be addressed. Every text-based data visualization obscures some information while highlighting selected others. While such text visualizations may be dynamically captured and rendered, such as off of microblogging sites or other parts of the Web, the text-based visualizations will necessarily be static ones here. The static ones provide a base of understanding that may be generalized to the dynamic versions. One other note: informational visualizations are generally 2D or 3D physical representations of concepts (ideas), data (real or synthetic, or a mix), or rules (such as in theoretical or applied models, or a mix).

COMMON STATIC TEXT-BASED VISUALIZATIONS

Text mining generally involves the work of knowledge discovery from text-based documents, datasets, or text corpuses—or some other mix of textual information. The process of setting up machine analyses of texts is a non-trivial one, with a number of steps required for text refinement and then nuanced machine-based data processing.

To support a more in-depth understanding of text-based visualizations, it may help to have a sense of the sequence of work used to arrive at many of the visualizations built from text databases or corpuses (collections). A very basic work sequence may be described in a semi-linear often-recursive six steps. Prior to the steps, it is assumed that the researcher has a research direction (such as research questions and data discovery interests).

- **Step 1** involves the acquisition of the raw textual data. The popular warning of "garbage in, garbage out" applies here as well. It is critical to have the proper textual inputs for informative outputs. The data should be sourced in a way that its provenance is knowable and that the information is generally trustworthy. If there are questions about the sourcing, then that should be indicated in the data visualization and analysis…and the final presentation. The input-output (I/O) relationship is important in text analysis.
- The **second step** involves text data pre-processing, including its cleaning (getting rid of redundancy in the data, recoding some data for readability, ensuring that all relevant text is included, and other aspects) and other preparations to be machine-processed. This step is often though to require a lot of time, in part because of the complexity of the work and in part because of the criticality of proper processing for answering the specific research questions. Pre-processing coding may be created. Stopwords or delete lists may be created or enhanced.
- The **third step** involves the machine processing of the textual data to extract text frequency tables and other types of data. The time invested in such processing depends on a variety of factors—the sizes of the corpuses, the types of processing, and the access to the proper amount of computational capability. In general, though, this step requires very little time.
- **Step 4** involves post-processing, which involves the analysis of the extracted data tables, machine processing re-runs with new parameters or revised datasets, and visualizations of the data. The idea is that the extracted data has to be sufficiently focused so as not to entail a lot of noise. Excess information should be removed for a clearer result.
- **Step 5** involves human analysis of the data. This step is a critical one because the researcher has to bring his or her expertise to bear (but not allow the expertise to drown out new conceptualizations or insights). If particular data points should be explored, that should be done. If anomalies are identified, those should be explored. Researchers may explore particular nodes, branches, or clusters in a network. For many, text analyses provide beginning points for further research; they are not often considered ends in and of themselves and certainly not stand-alone data. Often, researchers will be integrating the findings from multiple streams of information for a composite and triangulated view. Even if research mostly focuses on textual analysis, that still is bolstered by a range of other information—to help explain and contextualize the results.
- Finally, **Step 6** involves presentation and dissemination of the research findings. This final step may even involve the public release of the research corpuses on websites or on specialized database repositories.

These steps are depicted in *Figure 3:* A Broad Overview of the Process for Machine-Human Text Analysis and Text-Based Visualization (in Six Steps).

What follows are a number of exemplar text-based visualizations broadly organized from simple-to-complex. They are organized as follows. The software used to create the text-based visualization is mentioned in parentheses. Any number of software tools may be used to create various text-based visualizations, but the ones mentioned are some of the more publicly available ones. A mindmap of some of the visualizations that will be shared was drawn using the open-source FreeMind tool, with a central parent node and multiple child nodes.

A text-based outline representation of that same information is included below, with even more details.

TEXT-BASED DATA VISUALIZATIONS LIST

Underlying Data

Text-based table (Microsoft Excel)

Classic Structures

Histogram (Microsoft Excel)
Scatterplot (scattergram) (Microsoft Excel and Visio)
Linegraph (Google Books Ngram Viewer)
Bar / column chart (Microsoft Excel)

Conceptual Visualizations

Brainstorming diagram (mind map or concept map) (FreeMind, Microsoft Visio)

Text-Based Visualizations

2D Cluster map (NVivo 10)
3D Cluster map (NVivo 10)
Ring lattice graph (NVivo 10)
Grid (NodeXL)
Word tree (NVivo 10)
Dendrogram (vertical and horizontal) (NVivo 10)
Treemap diagram (NVivo 10)
2D Bubble graph (Maltego Tungsten)
3D Bubble graph (Maltego Tungsten)
Node-link (vertex-edge) diagram (NVivo 10)
2D and 3D Nodelink graphs (CASOS AutoMap / ORA NetScenes)
Word cloud (Wordle, NVivo 10)
Electronic social network analysis graph (NodeXL)
Related tags network graph (NodeXL or Network Overview, Discovery and Exploration for Excel)

Figure 3. A broad overview of the process for machine-human text analysis and text-based visualization (in six steps)

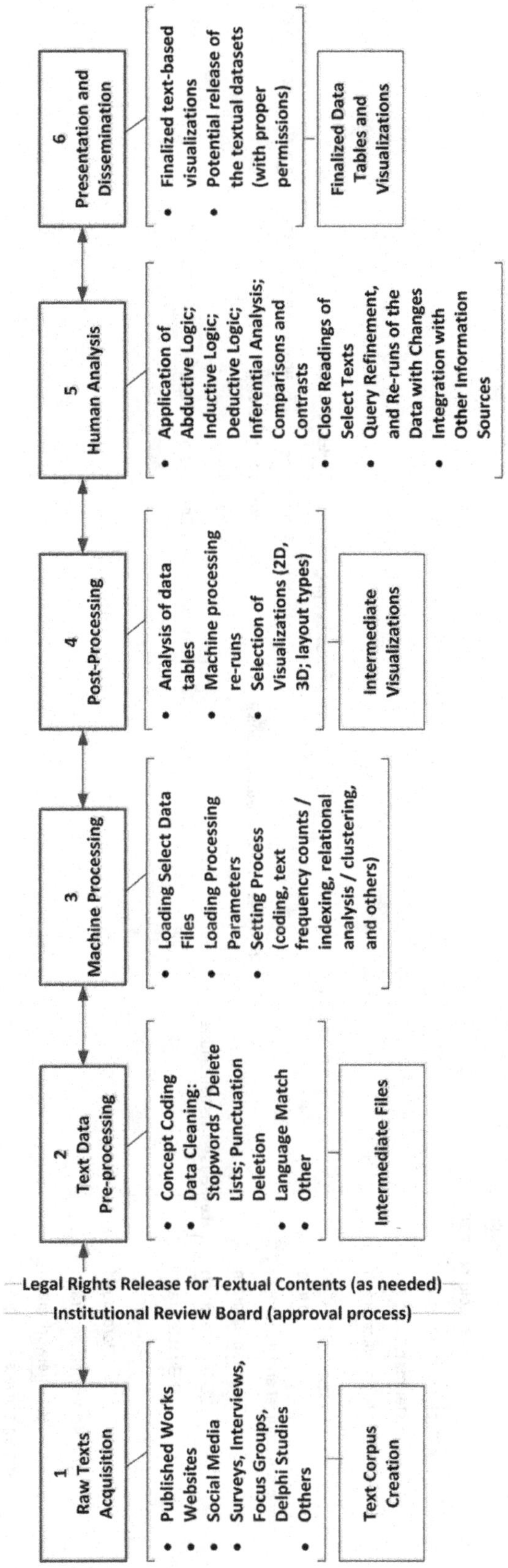

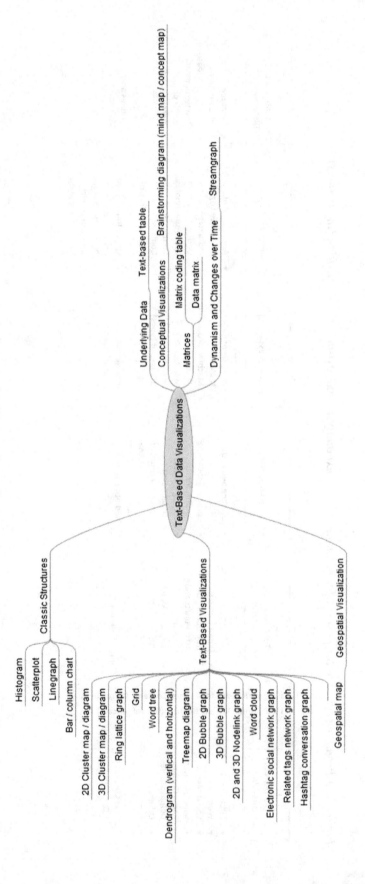

Figure 4. Text-based data visualizations List (as a Mind Map Diagram) (using FreeMind)

Hashtag conversation graph (NodeXL)

Matrices

Matrix coding query table (NVivo 10)
Data matrix (NVivo 10, UCINET and NetDraw)

Geospatial Visualization

Geospatial map (NVivo 10 on a MapQuest structure)

Dynamism and Changes over Time

Streamgraph (Excel / Tableau Public)

UNDERLYING DATA

The data that is used to "draw" text-based data visualizations are virtually all alphanumeric data in tables or worksheets. While the original raw data comes from texts, the data processing turns these into quantitative data and lists of words.

Text-Based Table

Data tables and worksheets are a base form from which visualizations are created. Some tables are intermediate-state ones, such as chi-squared tables (used for similarity analyses between texts based on analyses of occurrences of particular phenomena as contrasted with the expected frequencies based on a random distribution and the probability of whether the real-world results could be arrived at by chance alone—or whether something else could be going on in terms of an effect of a variable, whether visible or invisible, apparent or latent). These are used in a semi-hidden way to arrive at certain statistical findings based on non-parametric data. Some tables are final-state ones which are used to present data in the final form. Tables with manageable amounts of data may be quite readable in the basic form, and most simple spreadsheet software programs enable a range of basic data ordering and visualization functions. There are a wide range of types of text-based tables, and Figure 5 offers a view of some of them based on tools used in this chapter. In the same way that these tables all look quite different, there are a variety of different types of data structures to enable machine-readability of the information and then the various visualizations that are possible. Often, if data is being ported from one system to another for processing or visualizations, the data itself may have to be restructured. It is a competitive advantage to be familiar with a variety of software tools because each one offers some functionality that others may not.

Figure 5. Some Types of Text-Based Data Tables

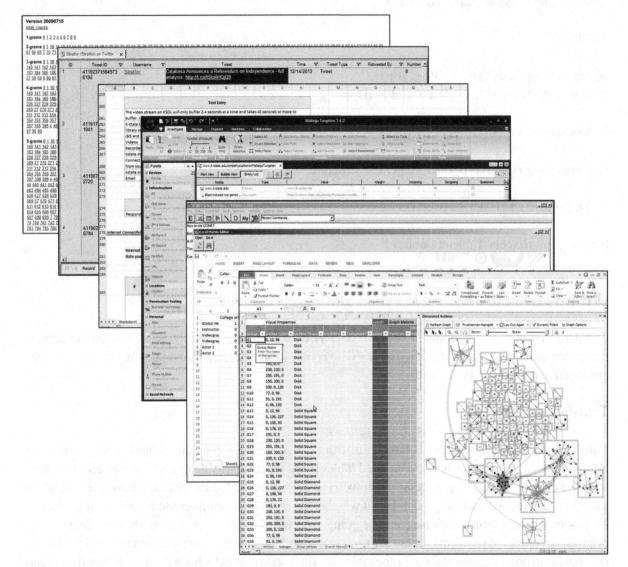

CLASSIC STRUCTURES

One of the more common data visualizations used with textual data is the histogram, which shows an overall distribution curve for a dataset. As such, this is often used with word frequency counts of texts and text corpuses. All datapoints in a set are assigned to particular "bins" or equal-sized categories. A histogram may show normal curves, power curves, bimodal curves, and a range of other data distributions. Histograms work with non-parametric data as long as that data may be translated into frequency counts of contents that fit into certain bins.

Histogram

A Twitterfeed extraction of journalist and activist Glenn Greenwald's account (@ggreenwald) on Twitter resulted in 1,600 downloaded Tweets in the dataset. The official account itself, located at https://twitter.com/ggreenwald had 47,000 recorded Tweets, 172 photos and videos, 949 following, and 376,000± followers, and 60 favorites—at the time of the data extraction. The data was captured using NCapture of NVivo 10 and then output into Excel, with the dataset simplified using a histogram add-in to the software tool. The histogram shows a fair amount of skew, in what appears to be a power law distribution, with a long tail of words beyond the initial bulk. (This may be explained given that the word frequency count was limited to the top 1000 words.) This visualization gives the sense that there is a mass of popular words, which would suggest the importance of reference to the referent data table.

A screenshot of the extracted histogram data (in Excel) is available in Figure 7.

A more coherent complementary visualization in this context of @ggreenwald's Tweetstream would be a word cloud of the top 100 most frequently used terms, as may be seen at Figure 8.

Scatterplot / Scattergram (2D)

Traditionally, scatterplots or scattergrams have been used to identify potential associations or correlations between two variables based on rank, interval, ratio, or ordinal scale data. These visualizations are used to understand associations between variables over time as well. Where these may be used with textual data is with the quantizing of textual datasets, such as word frequency counts, information categorizing, word ranking, and other features. A scatterplot (or scattergram) usually consists of paired samples (of two datasets) that are contrasted to look for the degree of correlation, with positive correlations indicating with a rising line when the presence of one variable means more of the other (read from left to right),

Figure 6. Histogram of word frequencies in @ggreenwald Tweetstream on Twitter (NVivo 10 and Excel)

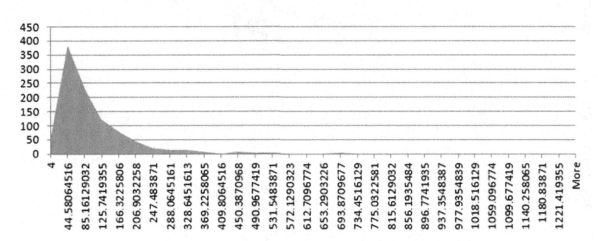

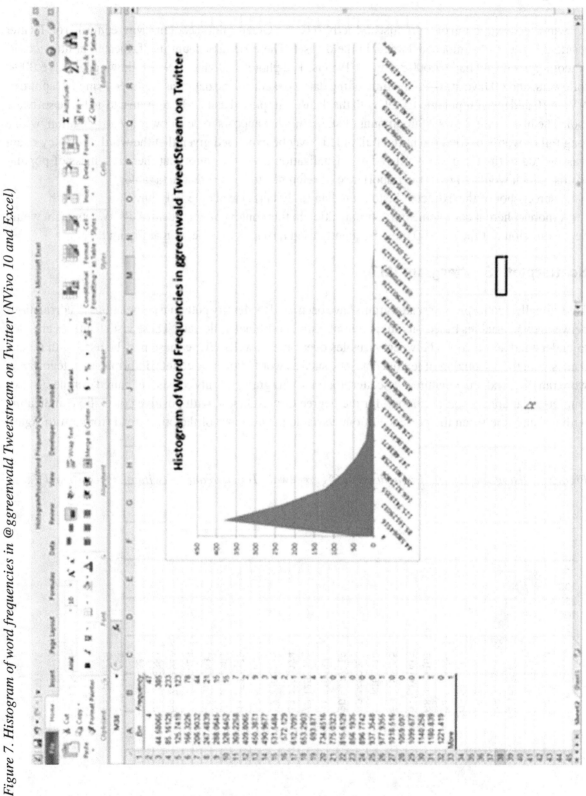

Figure 7. Histogram of word frequencies in @ggreenwald Tweetstream on Twitter (NVivo 10 and Excel)

Figure 8. A word cloud of the top 100 word frequencies in @ggreenwald TweetStream on Twitter (NVivo 10)

negative correlations when the presence of one variable means less of a presence of the other indicated by a falling line, or no correlation (inability to reject the null hypothesis). If there is close fit, a trendline may be drawn to show the correlation. An identity (regression) line may be drawn as a reference against which the two datasets may be compared; two identical datasets will have datapoints that fall exactly on the identity line to indicate a perfect correlational relationship or a "best-fit" scenario. Similar datasets will cluster around the identity line. If it is thought that there may be an independent variable – dependent variable relationship, then the datasets are plotted as follows. The independent variable (or "control parameter") is usually plotted on the x-axis (the horizontal axis); the potential dependent variable is usually plotted on the y-axis (the vertical axis). If there is no consideration of an IV-DV relationship, then each of the two datasets may be plotted at either axis. If there is relatedness, this is seen as a clustering of data points around a particular line in the graph. Two sets of texts may be compared, for example. Two sets of coding (by different coders) may be compared for inter-rater or inter-annotator reliability through coding comparison queries (such as the Cohen's Kappa coefficient, a statistical measure which takes into account the amount of agreement expected to occur through chance alone). There may be a comparison of two datasets over time to see if they converge or diverge. A scatterplot may indicate more complex relationships than simple positive, negative, or non-correlation. The plotting of the data points may show a curvilinear relationship, for example. Non-parametric tests of correlation must be used if data is not normally distributed, and these include tests like Kendal's tau and Spearman's rho (rank correlation), which tend to have lower significance levels, and which are integrated in various text analysis software programs.

To plot a scattergram in a way that is aligned to the data visualization form, the data generally has to be bivariate. One set of data is plotted on the x axis, and the other is posted on the y axis. The patterns or non-patterns found in the scatter inform analysis of possible correlational relationships. Figure 9 shows a quadtych of scattergrams based on a four-part question that was part of an IT satisfaction survey given out to faculty/staff and students. The visualization shows a clear positive correlation between the responses (which are listed on a Likert scale). These numbers were extracted directly from the survey, so there were more numbers of student respondents than faculty ones. If this were listed statistically, that may show a more comparable look at the responses. All said, there is clear sense of general agreement between the data points.

The scattergram was created from one multi-part Likert-scale question that was part of an IT Satisfaction Survey. The basic data structure is bivariate, with one column for faculty/staff and one for students.

A more complex and integrated scattergraph follows below, with faculty/staff responses indicated in red and student responses in blue. These tracked a range of responses to a number of questions and did seem to find correlation, even though it's unclear what potential causes there may be. [It would be too simplistic and misleading to assume that students "follow" their faculty members in assessing various features of information technology (IT) services in a certain way.]

A 3D version would include nodes that have the appearance of geometric shape or roundedness even if the actual axes are just the x and y axes.

Linegraph

A linegraph is generally a 2D chart measuring two variables, with a line or lines representing quantitative measures along both the x and the y axes. *Figure 11*, "A Resulting Linegraph from a "Big Data" Search for Data Visualization Terms Over Time on the Google Books Ngram Viewer," shows the popularity of certain select terms over time, with the lines smoothed (by averaging each data point with the measures to each side). This type of visualization taps into a "shadowed" dataset of pre-extracted n-gram counts over the years (without access to the core textual datasets of scanned or digitized books). In this extraction, only words which appear in more than 40 different books per year are included. In all, this data visualization is based on various "bags of words" in a trendline visualization. This linegraph was used with 12 selected data visualization terms discussed in this chapter: histogram, bar chart, scatterplot, dendrogram, scattergram, brainstorming diagram (mind map / concept map), word cloud, ring lattice graph, cluster map, word tree, linegraph, and treemap. It is possible that other words that could have been included like "graph" or "table" could have been ambiguous—even more so than the included terms.

Figure 12 is a screenshot which highlights an interaction feature of the Google Books Ngram Viewer with "scatterplot" highlighted.

Figure 9. Linked Scattergram of Faculty/Staff and Student Satisfaction on Features of Information Technology Services on Campus (from a 2014 Survey) (Excel)

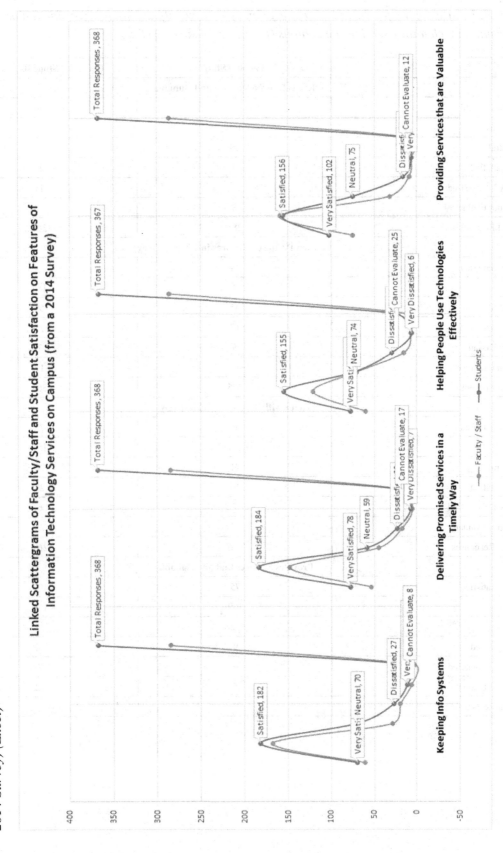

Table 1. Data structure for the linked scattergram of faculty/staff and student satisfaction on features of information technology services on campus (from a 2014 survey) (Excel)

	Faculty/ Staff	Students
Keeps Info Systems Up and Running		
Very Satisfied	61	70
Satisfied	168	182
Neutral	28	70
Dissatisfied	19	27
Very Dissatisfied	6	11
Cannot Evaluate	3	8
Total Responses	285	368
Delivers Promised Services in a Timely Way		
Very Satisfied	54	78
Satisfied	148	184
Neutral	45	59
Dissatisfied	17	23
Very Dissatisfied	5	7
Cannot Evaluate	16	17
Total Responses	285	368
Helps with Technology Effectively		
Very Satisfied	60	78
Satisfied	121	155
Neutral	71	74
Dissatisfied	15	29
Very Dissatisfied	7	6
Cannot Evaluate	12	25
Total Responses	286	367
Provides Services that are Valuable		
Very Satisfied	75	102
Satisfied	159	156
Neutral	32	75
Dissatisfied	9	16
Very Dissatisfied	6	7
Cannot Evaluate	5	12
Total Responses	286	368

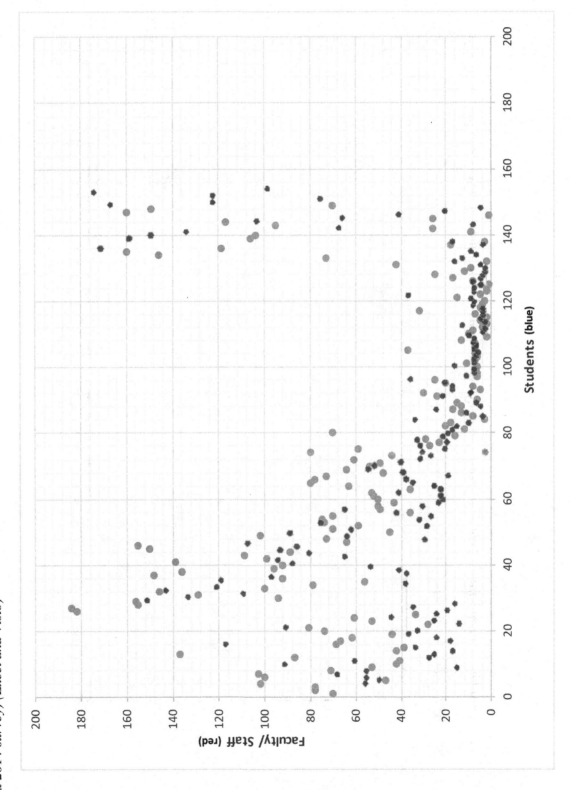

Figure 10. An integrated Scattergram of faculty/staff and student satisfaction on features of information technology services on campus (from a 2014 survey) (Excel and Visio)

Figure 11. A resulting linegraph from a "big data" search for data visualization terms over time on the Google Books Ngram Viewer

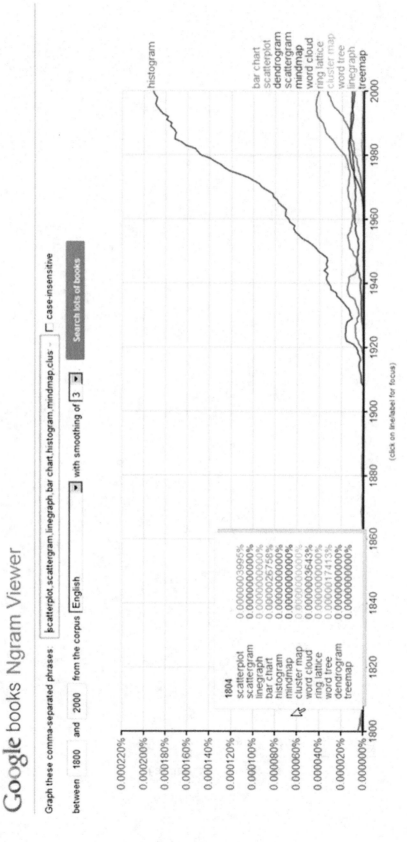

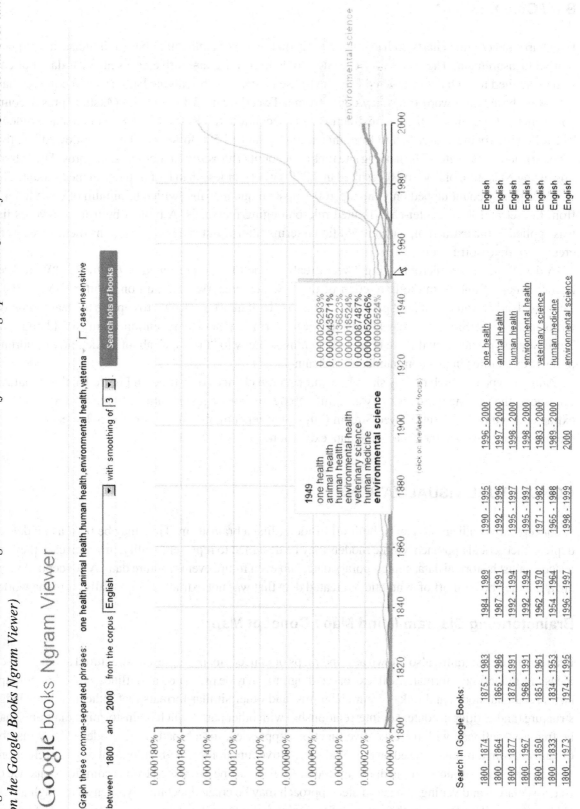

Figure 12. A rollover interaction on the Google Books NGram Viewer (from the linegraph visualization of data visualization terms over time on the Google Books Ngram Viewer)

Bar / Column Chart

Bar charts and column charts both essentially rely on the use of rectangular bars to indicate some quantitative measurement. These are very common tools used for quantitative and statistical data but can also be applied to such data extracted from text-based datasets. The sample bar chart and column chart here were based on a word frequency count from a TweetStream dataset of the @kstate_pres account on Twitter. At the time of the data extraction, this account had 7,841 Tweets, 864 photos and videos, 911 following (being subscribed to from this account), and 17.500 followers (being "followed" on this account), and 14 favorites. The landing site for this account is https://twitter.com/kstate_pres. The extraction, using NCapture of NVivo 10, resulted in 3,220 Tweets, or less than half of those in the account. The word frequency count tapped only the top 1000 most-frequent terms (with a minimum of three letters) from the set of 140-character-each-limited microblogging messages. A typical built-in stopwords list was applied to the extraction, without additional terms filtered out. The visualizations themselves were created in Microsoft Excel.

A data table of the microblogging TweetStream extraction is represented in *Figure 15*, "Word Frequency Query Table from the Extraction of the @kstate_pres TweetStream on Twitter (NVivo 10)". There is clearly a value in at least perusing the data table. It may be valuable to capture the least common terms in the TweetStream. It may help to see which terms are not even mentioned but should be in the TweetStream, particularly if there is an over-arching strategy to "message" about particularly important projects or features in this communications channel.

Another type of bar chart may show how information changes over time. In Figure 16, the visualization shows the varying numbers of Tweets (microblogging messages) month to month. This dataset was extracted from the CI Centre TweetStream (https://twitter.com/cicentre), with 1,473 Tweets extracted, the full TweetStream at the time of the data extraction.

CONCEPTUAL VISUALIZATIONS

A conceptual visualization may be built off of ideas, like a brainstorm. They may be built as models to depict a theoretical approach. Or the models may be designed to represent reality, in which case they are tested against historical data, contemporary data, and even future events / future data. A conceptual visualization may be built off of synthetic or created data that was not extracted empirically from the world.

Brainstorming Diagram (Mind Map / Concept Map)

Brainstorming diagrams, also known as mind maps or concept maps, represent structured and organized ideas in a reductionist format. Such text-based diagrams may be presented as outlines, spatial mindmaps (with relational nodes and links), Venn diagrams, and other similar formats that indicate a knowledge structure (and entities in context or interrelationship with other parts). Such brainstorming diagrams may be free-associational, with the executive function suppressed, for a broad range of ideas. They may be organized from top-down, based on the mind's executive functioning, with individual or group creations of such structures (brainstorming diagram -> data). They may be originated from a complex sequence of free association and vetting. An automated approach may be created technically, such as through a wiki (with automated surfacing of the outline of the uploaded information) or extracted from sets of textual

Figure 13. A bar chart of the top 10 most frequently used terms in the @kstate_pres Tweetstream on Twitter (Excel)

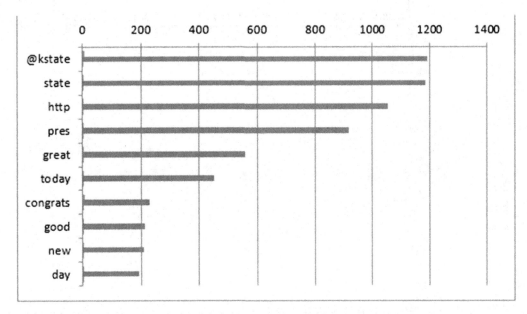

Figure 14. A column chart of the top 30 most frequently used terms in the @kstate_pres Tweetstream on Twitter (Excel)

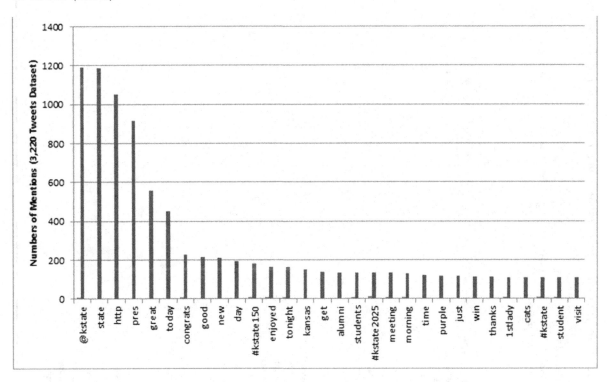

Figure 15. Word frequency query table from the extraction of the @kstate_pres Tweetstream on Twitter (Nvivo 10)

Internals

Name	Nodes	References	Created On	Created By	Modified On	Modified By
Kirk H. Schulz (kstate	0	0	7/10/2014 2:30 PM	SHJ	7/10/2014 2:30 PM	SHJ

Kirk H. Schulz (kstate_pres) o | Word Frequency Query Results ✕

Word	Length	Count	Weighted Percentage (%)
@kstate	7	1192	2.57
state	5	1186	2.56
http	4	1053	2.27
pres	4	917	1.98
great	5	558	1.20
today	5	452	0.97
congrats	8	229	0.49
good	4	214	0.46
new	3	211	0.45
day	3	192	0.41
#kstate150	10	181	0.39
enjoyed	7	165	0.36
tonight	7	163	0.35
kansas	6	151	0.33
get	3	140	0.30
alumni	6	136	0.29
students	8	135	0.29
#kstate2025	11	133	0.29
meeting	7	133	0.29
morning	7	131	0.28
time	4	122	0.26
purple	6	119	0.26
just	4	118	0.25
win	3	115	0.25
thanks	6	113	0.24
1stlady	7	110	0.24
cats	4	110	0.24
#kstate	7	109	0.24
student	7	108	0.23
visit	5	108	0.23
big	3	106	0.23
awesome	7	103	0.22

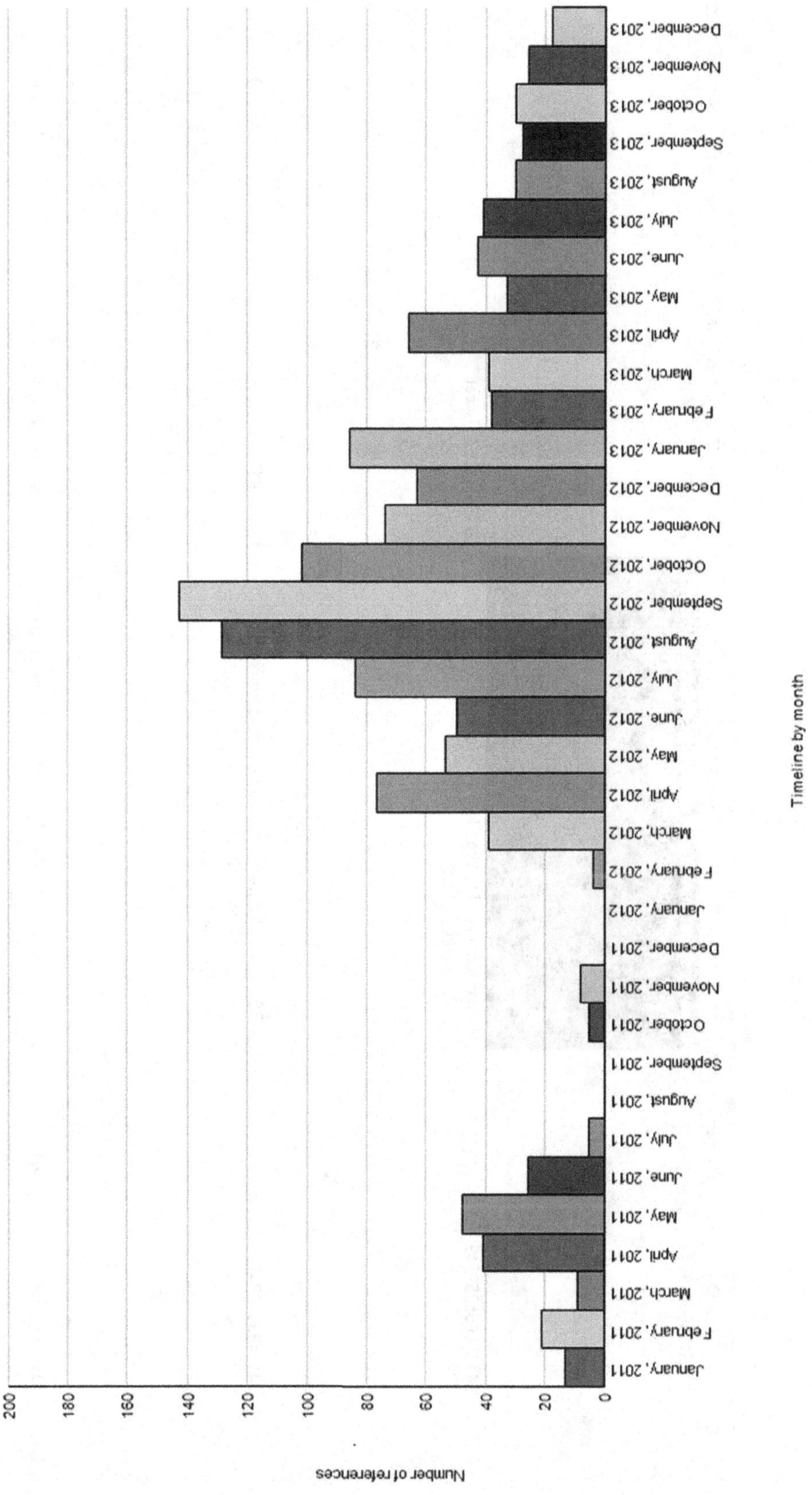

Figure 16. A timeline of cicentre tweetstream on Twitter (Nvivo 10) a screenshot of the underlying data table appears in figure 17

Figure 17. The underlying data table for the cicentre tweetstream on Twitter (Nvivo 10) another type of bar / column chart may be presented as a 3D one

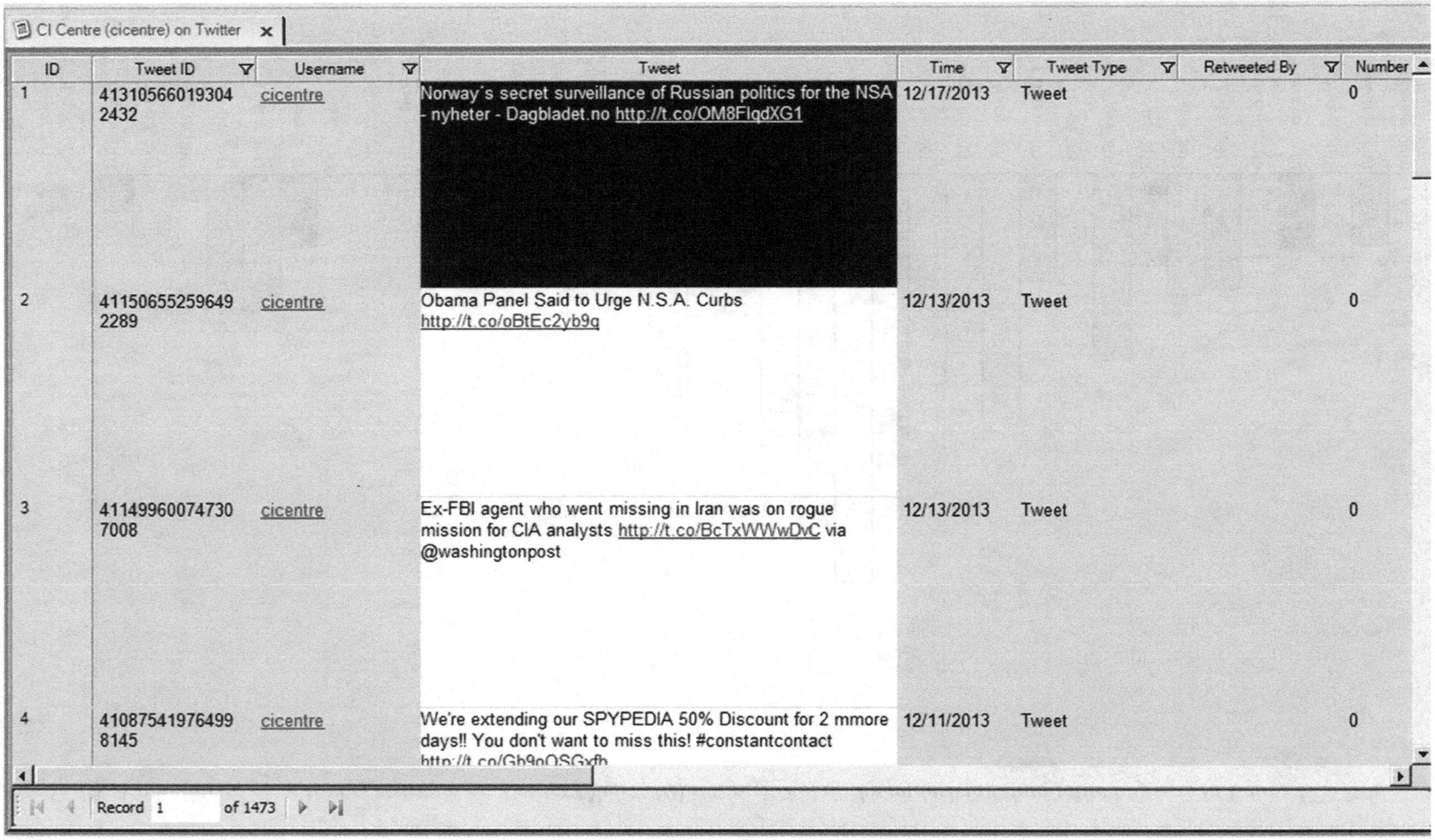

CI Centre (cicentre) on Twitter

ID	Tweet ID	Username	Tweet	Time	Tweet Type	Retweeted By	Number
1	413105660193042432	cicentre	Norway's secret surveillance of Russian politics for the NSA - nyheter - Dagbladet.no http://t.co/OM8FlqdXG1	12/17/2013	Tweet		0
2	411506552596492289	cicentre	Obama Panel Said to Urge N.S.A. Curbs http://t.co/oBtEc2yb9q	12/13/2013	Tweet		0
3	411499600747307008	cicentre	Ex-FBI agent who went missing in Iran was on rogue mission for CIA analysts http://t.co/BcTxWWwDvC via @washingtonpost	12/13/2013	Tweet		0
4	410875419764998145	cicentre	We're extending our SPYPEDIA 50% Discount for 2 mmore days!! You don't want to miss this! #constantcontact http://t.co/Gh9oQSGxfh	12/11/2013	Tweet		0

Record 1 of 1473

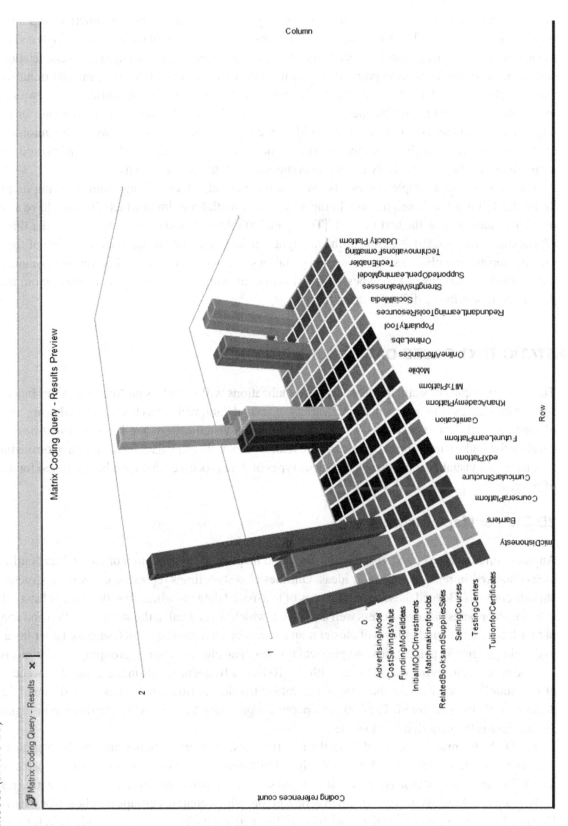

Figure 18. A 3D bar chart resulting from a matrix coding query between "cost" and "technology" nodes for a study into the feasibility of moocs (NVivo 10)

information through machine processing, which may be considered bottom-up functions (data first -> brainstorming diagram). Brainstorming visualizations are a common tool for both individuals and groups to surface internal mental models, as a form of authentic inquiry and learning. Data visualizations are sometimes assigned as writing prompts for learner assignments to elicit personal informational visualizations (Sorapure, 2010). These are created as collaboration-based communications—so development teams may engage with tangible ideas. Outlines are also often used to represent taxonomies or knowledge structures. One common example would be the data structures of wikis (which are automatically extracted from what people contribute as a feature of the wiki software). Another example could be "site maps" that may be automatically created in conjunction with website structures.

Figure 19 offers a simple contrast between some methods of visualizing brainstorming diagrams. To the far left is a text-based outline. In the middle in a spatial mindmap which does not have as much of a linear hierarchy as the text version. [The spatial mindmap is sometimes called a "spider diagram" (Prunckun, 2010, pp. 101 – 102)]. At the far right is a Venn diagram which contains some of the same information albeit without a sense of hierarchy, only a sense of categorization. The various visualizations have differing strengths and weaknesses in terms of conveying particular types of information; further, the aesthetic sensibility differs with each.

STATIC TEXT-BASED DATA VISUALIZATIONS

The main examples of static text-based data visualizations will be in this particular section. Indeed, visualizations are used to represent a wide variety of textual data, which has been captured using a variety of methods and data extractions. As stated earlier, these visualizations are labeled as text-based ones because the underlying original datasets were text. Between that raw data form and the intermediate or finalized data visualizations, there are various types of data processes that have been applied for a range of purposes.

2D Cluster Map / Diagram

Another common type of text visualization are mind maps or semi-structured or hierarchical outlines of ideas clustered in relation to similar ideas. Outlines also sometimes represent knowledge structures in various domains. Beyond these common types of text-based data visualizations, there are at least a dozen or more other types that may be less well known but which are critical in the summarization and analysis of text-based data. Another form of cluster map collects occurrences or events, such as Tweet instances, to certain geographical locations and physical regions. The clusters refer to groupings of various types.

One type of clustering may be seen with the 100 most frequent words in the captured TweetStream of the StateDept account. At the time of the data extraction during a one-week period in early 2014, 3,228 records were captured. The 100 most popular words may be seen in the cluster map in Figure 20. At the right is the underlying data table.

A 2D cluster map was created from the top 100 most frequently used words in the @ggreenwald TweetStream and visualized in Tableau Public. While many of the terms in the clusters posted, a few didn't. This may suggest that using a smaller record set would result in more effective visualization results.

Still another kind of cluster diagram may be a graph, which contains groups (or cliques or islands). In Figure 22, respective groups of nodes with closer ties with each other are represented as circles…within

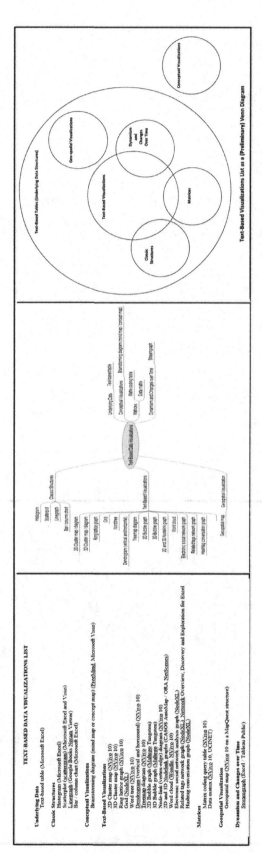

Figure 19. A Triptych of Brainstorming Diagrams: An Outline, A Spatial Mindmap, and A Venn Diagram (Microsoft Word, FreeMind, and Microsoft Visio)

Figure 20. A cluster map and data table of the top 100 words frequency count from the @statedept Tweetstream on Twitter (NVivo 10)

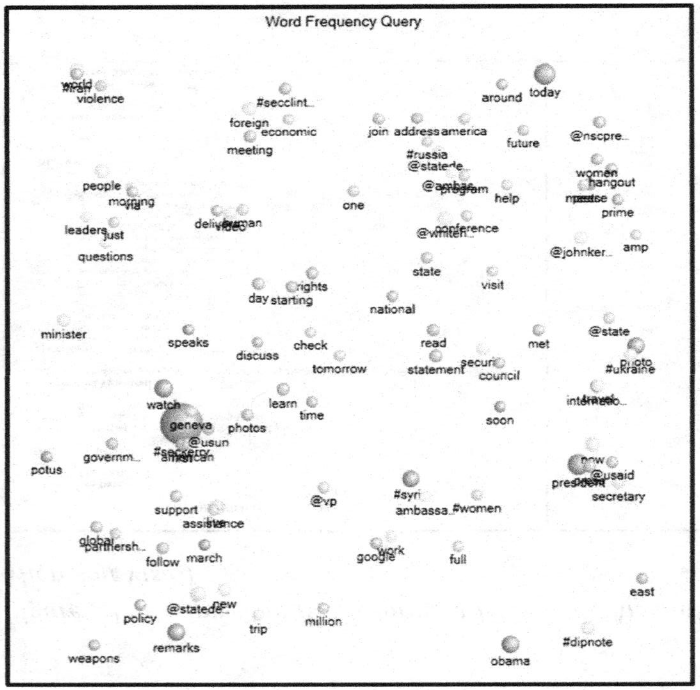

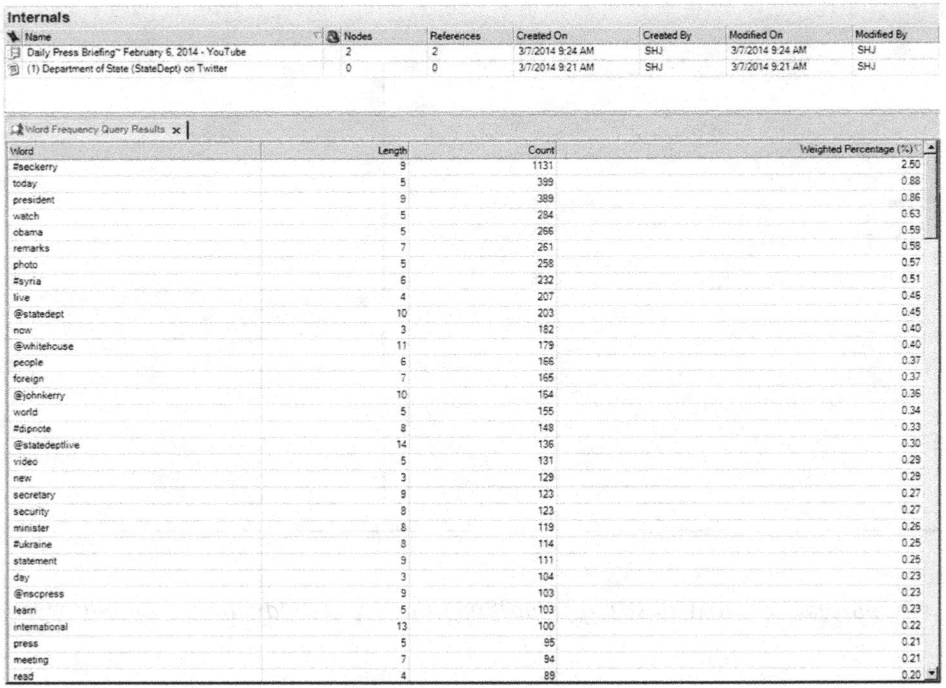

Internals

Name	Nodes	References	Created On	Created By	Modified On	Modified By
Daily Press Briefing" February 6, 2014 - YouTube	2	2	3/7/2014 9:24 AM	SHJ	3/7/2014 9:24 AM	SHJ
(1) Department of State (StateDept) on Twitter	0	0	3/7/2014 9:21 AM	SHJ	3/7/2014 9:21 AM	SHJ

Word Frequency Query Results

Word	Length	Count	Weighted Percentage (%)
#seckerry	9	1131	2.50
today	5	399	0.88
president	9	389	0.86
watch	5	284	0.63
obama	5	266	0.59
remarks	7	261	0.58
photo	5	258	0.57
#syria	6	232	0.51
live	4	207	0.46
@statedept	10	203	0.45
now	3	182	0.40
@whitehouse	11	179	0.40
people	6	166	0.37
foreign	7	165	0.37
@johnkerry	10	164	0.36
world	5	155	0.34
#dipnote	8	148	0.33
@statedeptlive	14	136	0.30
video	5	131	0.29
new	3	129	0.28
secretary	9	123	0.27
security	8	123	0.27
minister	8	119	0.26
#ukraine	8	114	0.25
statement	9	111	0.25
day	3	104	0.23
@nscpress	9	103	0.23
learn	5	103	0.23
international	13	100	0.22
press	5	95	0.21
meeting	7	94	0.21
read	4	89	0.20

Figure 21. A 2D word frequency cluster map of the @ggreenwald Tweetstream on Twitter (Tableau Public)

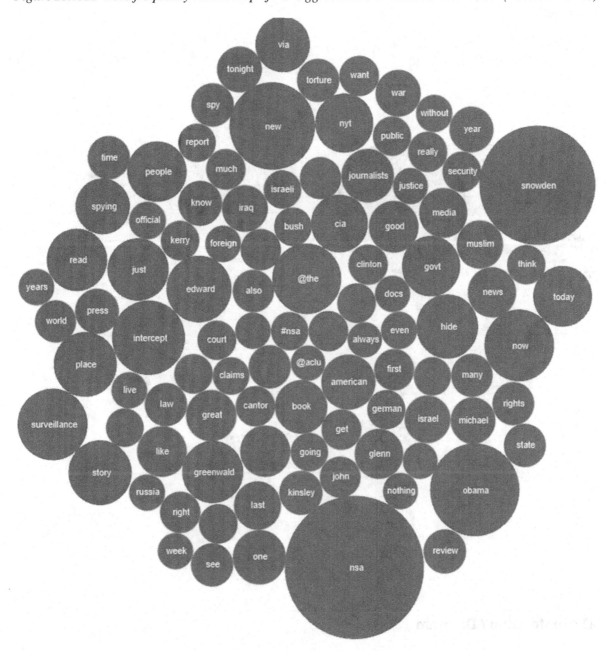

this online discourse-based social network (built around the #legal hashtag). This network consists of 725 vertices, with 1,715 unique edges. There were a total of 2,634 edges, with 919 edges with duplicates and 680 self-loops. The maximum geodesic distance (graph diameter) of the graph is 10, with the average geodesic distance between any two nodes as 4.04. The graph density was 0.00324061726043056, out of a possible full connectivity of every node with each other (as 1).

Using NVivo 10, yet another cluster map is shown in Figure 23. This is a two-dimensional cluster map with apparently mild clustering (indicated by the colors of nodes and the proxemic clustering.

(A 3D version of this cluster map is available at Figures 41 and 42.)

Figure 22. Clusters represented as circles in a #legal hashtag discourse-based social network on Twitter (NodeXL)

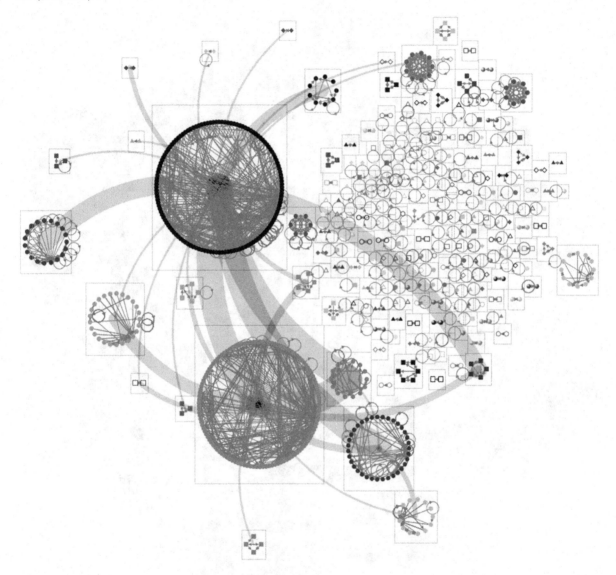

3D Cluster Map / Diagram

A three-dimensional cluster map also shows related clusters of words, user accounts, or other entities. The third dimension often may not represent additional information, only perceptual depth (with a two-dimensional visualization that creates the illusion of depth). *Figure 24,* "A 3D Cluster Diagram of the @bartongellman User Network on Twitter (NodeXL)," creates the look of three dimensions, with clustering by color and proximity. This network graph is comprised of 9,995 vertices, with 13,034 unique edges (and no self-loops or edges with duplicates). The maximum geodesic distance (diameter) is 4, with the average geodesic distance between any two nodes as 3.8.

Figure 23. A 2D cluster map of the hersheykisses user account @tweetstream on Twitter (NVivo 10)

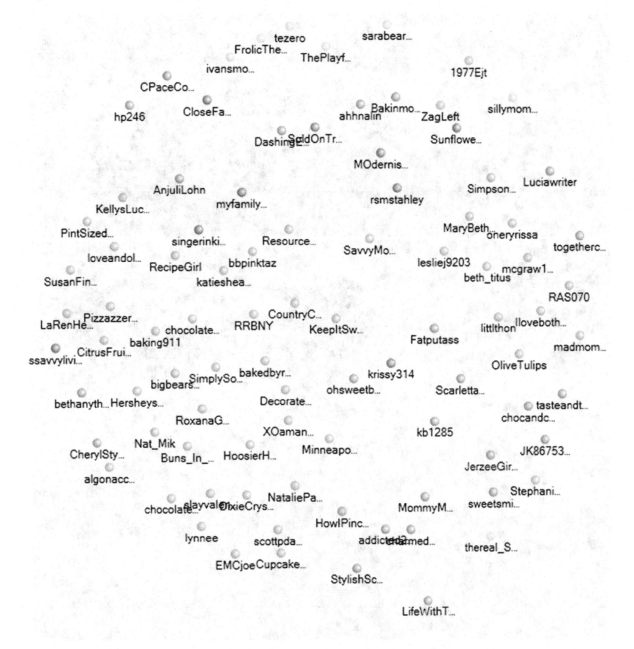

Figure 25 shows a top 100 words 3D cluster diagram from a literature review conducted for a modified e-Delphi study. Two views are shown to convey the sense of dimensional spatiality.

Ring Lattice Graph

A ring lattice graph generally shows the nodes on the ring, and links as lines connecting the nodes inside the circle. This type of visualization, when used with textual data, has words as the nodes and relatedness or similarity or proximity as the link (depending on the type of textual analysis). To work with this

Figure 24. A 3D cluster diagram of the @bartongellman user network on Twitter (NodeXL)

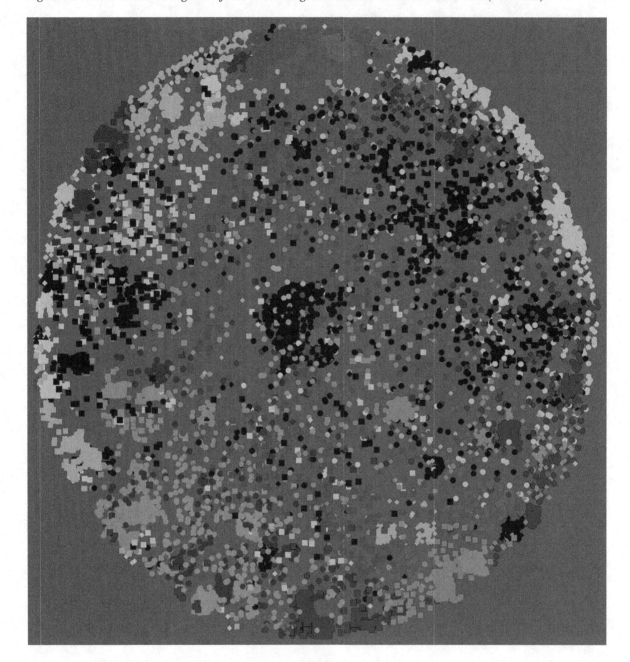

structure, the data clearly cannot be too dense, or else the ring lattice graph becomes unreadable. Also, if there are too many links, that density may make the lattice graph unreadable as well (unless the graph itself is interactive, in which case particular nodes and links may be examined piecemeal). As a data visualization, this type of graph can be used to highlight particular points in an engaging visual way.

Figure 26 was based on the user account @HersheysKisses and its TweetStream on Twitter, with an extraction of 1,224 records of microblogging messages. The software tool used for this visualization was NVivo 10, and the data extraction tool was NCapture.

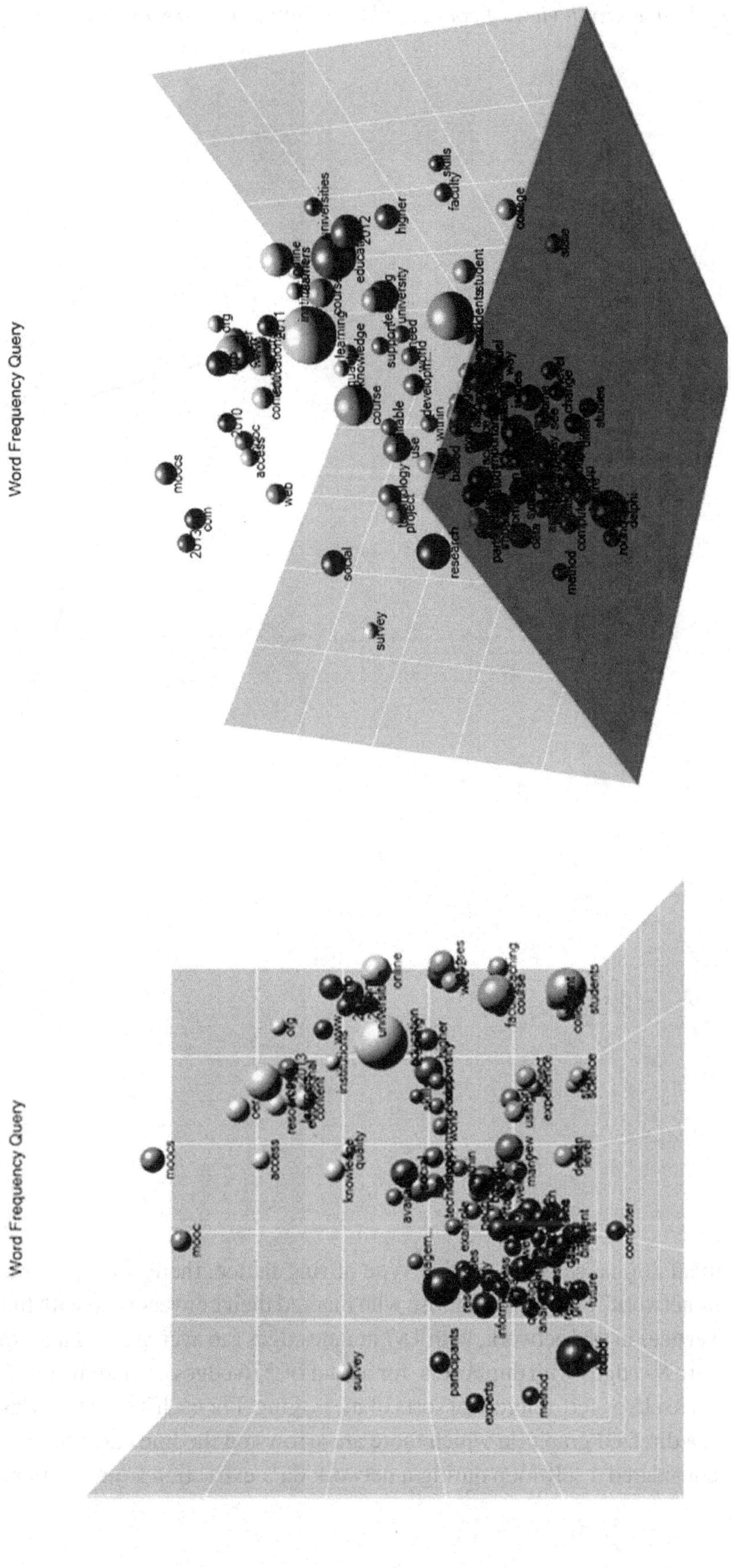

Figure 25. A top 100 words 3D cluster diagram created from contents in a literature review frequency with rotation (NVivo 10)

Word Frequency Query

Word Frequency Query

Figure 26. A ring lattice graph view of connected terms in the @HersheysKisses TweetStream on Twitter (NVivo 10)

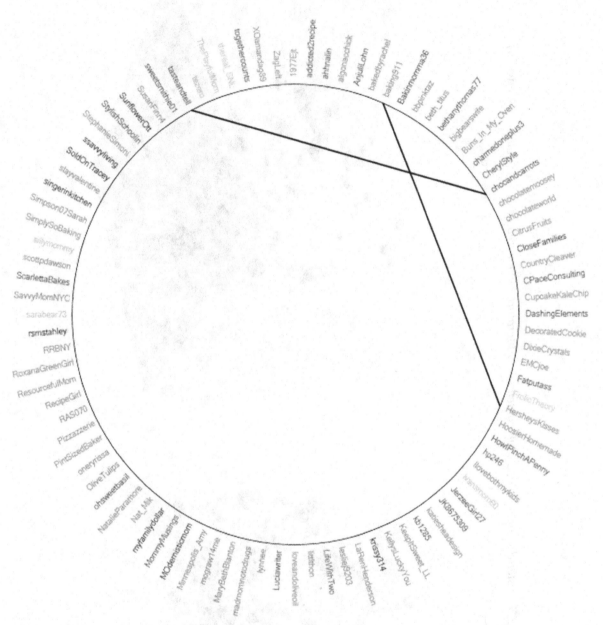

To provide an additional sense of another type of ring lattice, there was an extraction of an ad hoc "communications network" on Twitter of those who marked their conversation with the hashtag #sleeper. There were 116 vertices in this network, with 187 unique edges (an average of at least one link per vertex; however, there were 89 edges with duplicates, for a total of 276 edges). There were 67 self-loops, which connect a vertex to itself, or self-referential sorts of messaging. For each Tweet that was not a "replies-to" or "mentions," in a directed graph (in which there are arrows on the line ends indicating relationships), that message is considered a self-loop during a network data extraction from Twitter (Smith, "NodeXL describes the networks you create…," March 9, 2012). This is not a large network, with a diameter or geodesic distance of 6; there is fairly high connectivity, with an average geodesic distance of 2.5 (two and a half hops between any two nodes in this network. Almost half of the nodes (.43) were part of a reciprocated vertex pair. In terms of reciprocated edges (relationships), about 60% of the nodes were part of this group. The graph density, representing how many connectors there are from all the total numbers of links possible of every node with all other nodes in the network, the density was 0.0129, or around 1%.

To include textual labels on the vertexes of a ring lattice graph, it helps if the resulting data itself is sparse. Figure 28: A Ring Lattice Graph of the Amelia_Earhart Ego Neighborhood on Twitter (NodeXL

Figure 27. A ring lattice graph of the Twitter accounts that cited the #sleeper hashtag during a week in 2014 on Twitter (NodeXL 1.0.1.328)

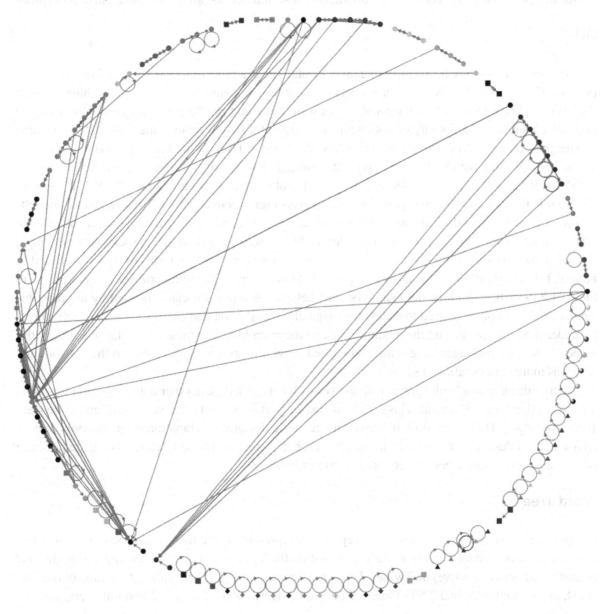

1.0.1.328) shows the ego neighborhood of the Amelia_Earhart user account on Twitter, with a 1 degree data extraction (just direct "alters" connected to the focal node, Amelia_Earhart). This identified 96 vertices and 96 edges, with only one self-loop. (A one-degree data crawl of a network would not capture transitivity or any of the potential connections between any of the "alters" in the network. This only captures direct ties to the principal node.) Because of the centrality of the focal node, the maximum geodesic distance of this network is only 2, and the average geodesic distance from one node to the other is 1.96 (or essentially 2).

Yet another form of the ring lattice (based on the circle layout algorithm) may be used in a way that also highlights peripheral clusters. Figure 29 was created based on the pipl_com ego neighborhood on Twitter, with 75 vertices, 59 unique edges, and 68 edges with duplicates. The maximum geodesic distance or diameter of this graph is 2 (with an average geodesic distance of 1.95). Given that this was a one-degree mapping of the pipl_com ego neighborhood, these numbers are all within the realm of the typical.

Grid

A grid is another structure for representing textual data. The example used here resulted from a two-step process. The first step involved a data extraction of the user accounts that recently microblogged with the hashtag phrase #Syria. Those account names were listed and run for their user networks (1 degree out), which shows a community of communicators around a shared topic along with their respective ego neighborhoods (alters). *Figure 30*, "Ego Neighborhood of Users Who Recently Tweeted #Syria on Twitter in a Grid Layout (NodeXL)," was created from a network with 21,836 vertices (unique nodes), with 22,779 edges. There were 68,185 edges with duplicates, for a total edge count of 90,964. There were 25,250 self-loops in this directed graph, which suggests user accounts with self-referential ties or self-Tweets. The average geodesic distance between nodes was 4.67, and the maximum geodesic distance or graph diameter was 9. Sixty-seven groups or dense clusters were identified in this social network graph. This visualization shows the diversity of this electronic social network in terms of those interested in #Syria. The density of the data makes it impossible to draw out a grid with vertex names connected to these 21,836 vertices, and the ties cannot be seen behind the nodes. Researchers wanting to probe this network more deeply will need to access the original .xl workbook and its various worksheets to better understand the entities and the relationships and the microblogging messaging (the actual verbatim Tweets, when the messages were sent, who replied to who, who was more central in the network and who was more peripheral), and so on.

To provide an example of a graph with the vertex labels included, another data extraction was done around another term: #innocent. This one identified 215 vertices in this "conversation," and there were 16 unique edges. There were no self-loops. The geodesic distance or graph diameter was only 3, with an average geodesic distance of 1.25 hops. The graph density was 0.00034, which shows the presence of very few ties in this discourse network shown in *Figure 31*.

Word Tree

A word tree is used when a particular concept that it represents is the focus of interest or inquiry. For this visualization, a data extraction was conducted on the TweetStream of @microaggressive (https://twitter.com/microaggressive) on Twitter. The extraction acquired 2,557 records. At the time of the data crawl, the account itself had 2,593 Tweets, 9 photos / videos, 1066 following, 2,866 followers, and 411

Figure 28. A ring lattice graph of the Amelia_Earhart Ego neighborhood on Twitter (NodeXL 1.0.1.328)

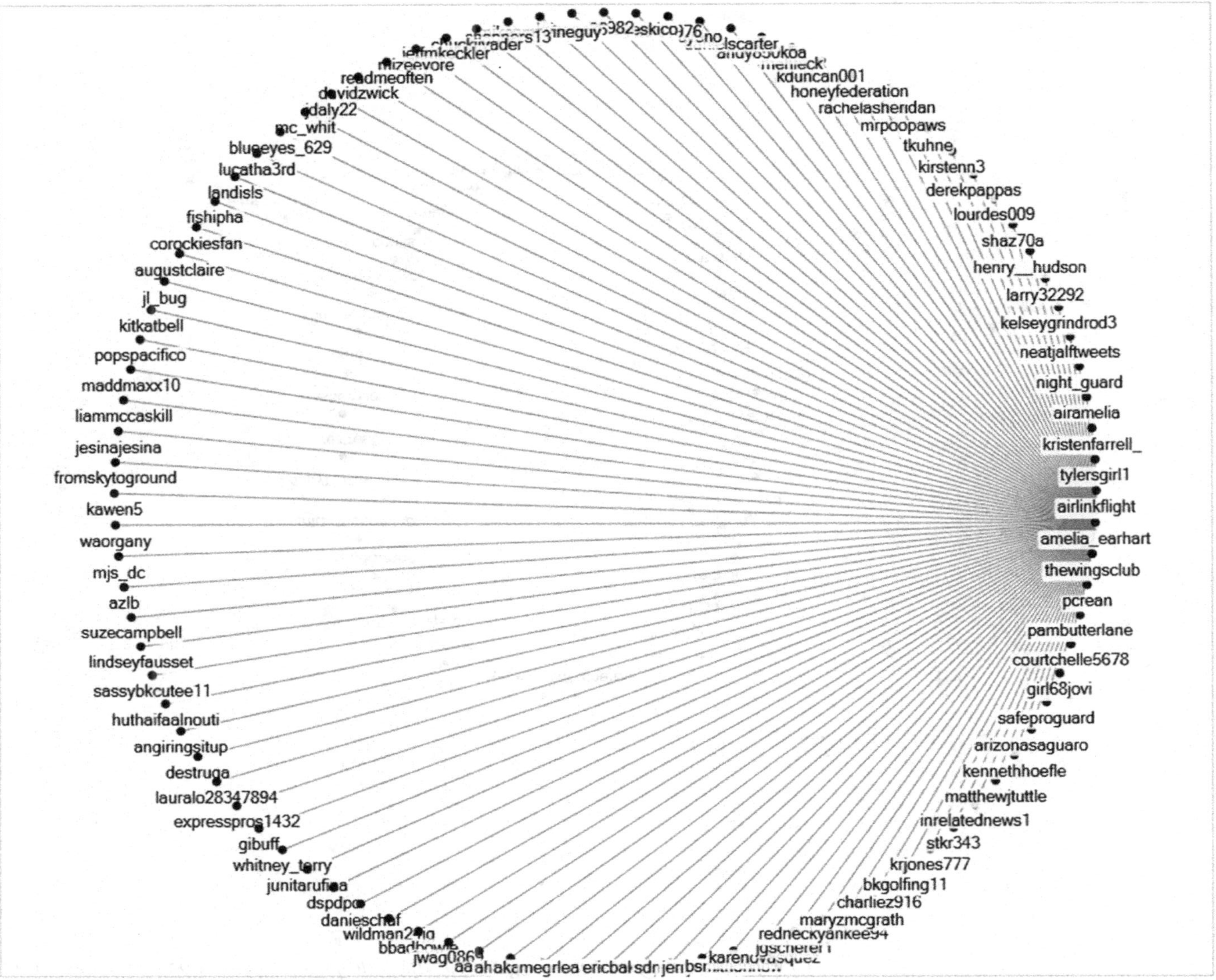

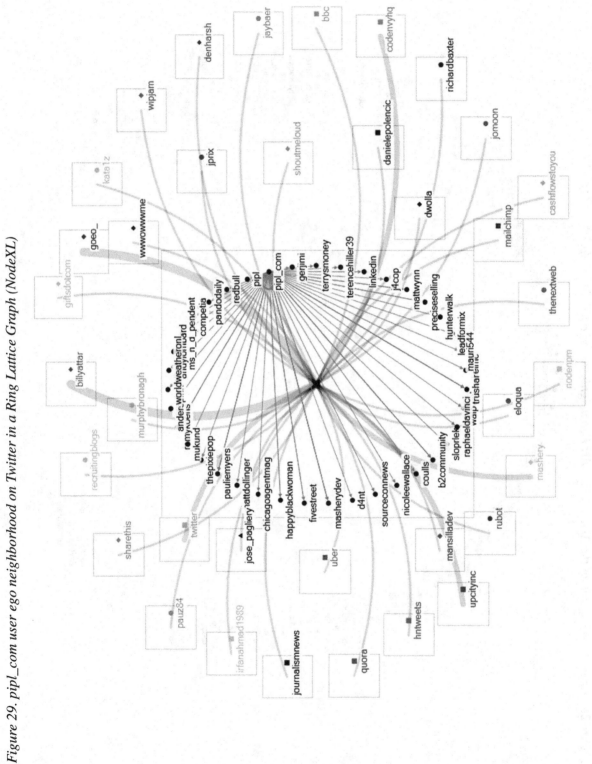

Figure 29. pipl_com user ego neighborhood on Twitter in a Ring Lattice Graph (NodeXL)

Figure 30. Ego neighborhood of users who recently Tweeted #Syria on Twitter in a grid layout (NodeXL)

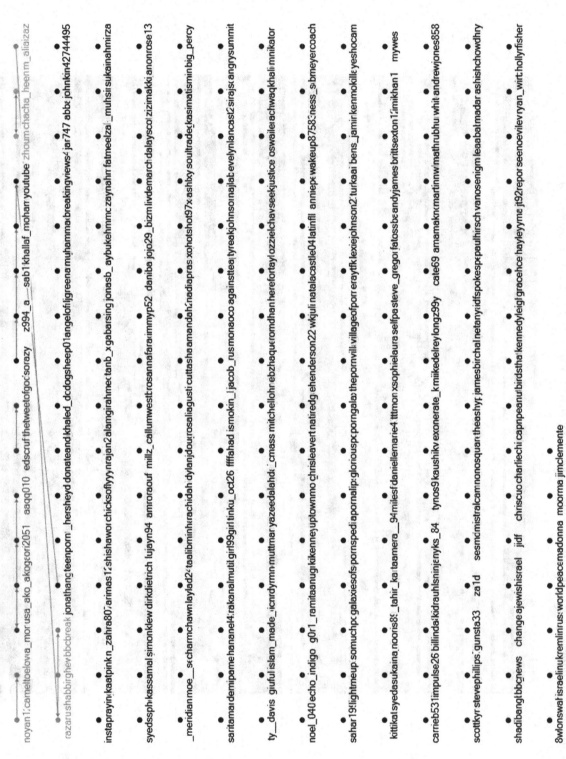

Figure 31. #innocent hashtag search on Twitter with results in a grid layout format and vertex names included (NodeXL)

favorites. The text search query from all sources in the dataset in NVivo 10 was for "female" to try to acquire typical micro-aggressions used against females. From this, a word tree was created, with "girl" as the most common synonym to "female" used in this Tweet set. Within the software, the word tree is interactive. That means if a user clicks on any of the branches to the left or the right of "girl," he or she can see the linking branch to acquire a more complete sense of the term. (A word tree works like a non-quantitative stem-and-leaf plot, with the core word serving as the stem, and with leafing on both sides with usually 5 or more words to either side). Essentially, the word tree is a data reduction with information stacked visually. The words are acquired proxemically and contiguously to the key term in "vectors" to show the role of the key word.

Dendrogram (Vertical or Horizontal)

A dendrogram or "tree drawing" depicts similarity or relatedness between words in a text corpus. The tree metaphor applies to the entire graph, with each branch labeled a "clade," and each terminal end of the clade as a "leaf." There are varying numbers of leaves possible for each branch: a one leaf-ed branch is called "simplicifolious" or single-leafed; a two-leafed branch is bifolious; a three-leafed as trifolious… and so on. Spatiality plays an important role in the interpretation of the contents of a dendrogram. The greater the vertical height of the branches, the greater the differences between the word clusters. The horizontal distance is not relevant in terms of suggesting distance but is just an artifact of layout. In lexomic analysis (the search for patterns in textual corpora), vertical dendrograms may be read from top to bottom (from broad categories downwards or from specific groupings upwards). Isolated branches that branch off at a high level are understood as anomalous to the other words in the text corpus. Those words in certain proxemically linked leaves or linked branches have some measure of similarity. The horizontal orientation of a vertical dendrogram is not relevant in terms of relatedness interpretations, and some actually suggest viewing a vertical dendrogram as a mobile which may be rotated horizontally without changing the meaning as long as the vertical height and subgroup organization are stable (Drout & Smith, 2012, p. 7). Other types of text-based dendrograms may be those that represent ontologies or taxonomic relationships albeit with a similar geometric grammar. Many such dendrograms are machine-extracted, but manual ones (that are conceptual or fairly simpler) may also be created as well.

Figure 35 shows a zoomed-out view of a vertical dendrogram of the @HersheyKisses extracted TweetStream on Twitter.

A Treemap Diagram

A text-based treemap diagram depicts frequency counts of "strings" of terms, phrases, or names on a 2D map, with the higher frequency terms placed on rectangular shapes that are linked size-wise to the count. Oftentimes, the larger-sized parcels begin at the top left, and the smaller counts appear at the bottom right. The underlying data is usually in a table format of a column of words and their frequency count in a column to the right. Such a diagram is used for a quick overview of the most popular terms… as well as the "long tail" of the less popular ones. This visualization does not include all terms in the frequency count (unless there is an artificial delimiting of the most popular terms), so researchers will usually also look at the data table. For this data visualization, 1,000 of the most frequent words found in a collection of literature about e-Delphi studies was collected.

Figure 37 provides a screenshot of the data table underlying the treemap structure in Figure 36.

Figure 32. A (branching) word tree from a text search query in NVivo 10 for "female" in the @microaggressive TweetStream in Twitter

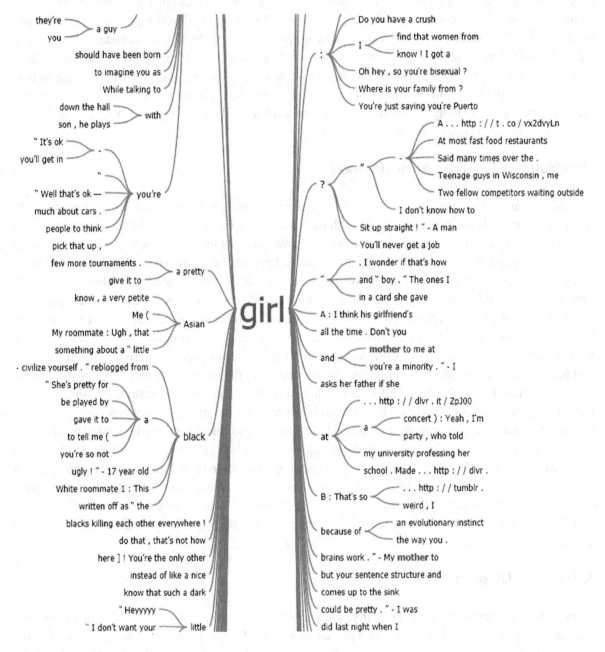

2D Bubble Graph

A two-dimensional (2D) bubble graph represents relational data, with clusters or entities as "bubbles" or circles that are placed in relation to each other and connected by links or edges. These are a form of node-link diagram. *Figure 38* is the result of a data crawl that started with an alias and connected that alias to a range of websites, accounts, online documents, and other elements. The visualization

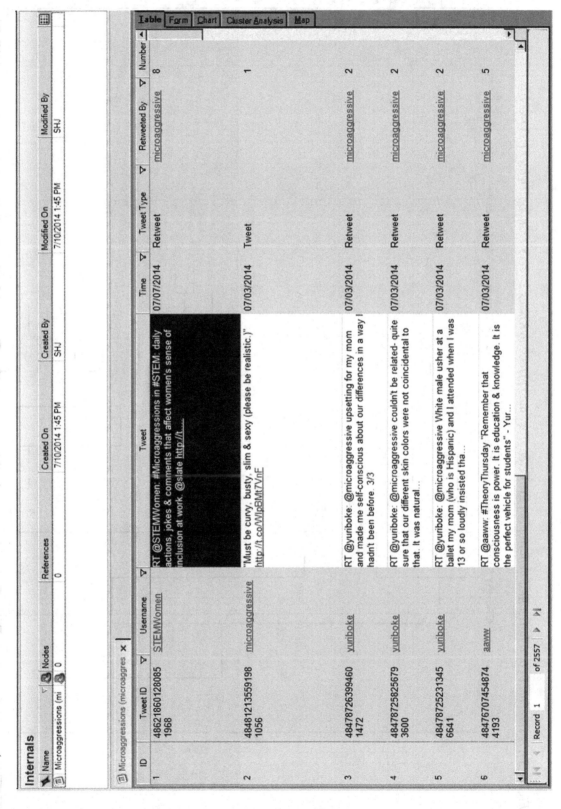

Figure 33. A table of data captured (using NCapture) from the TweetStream @microaggressive of the Microaggression Project (created in NVivo 10)

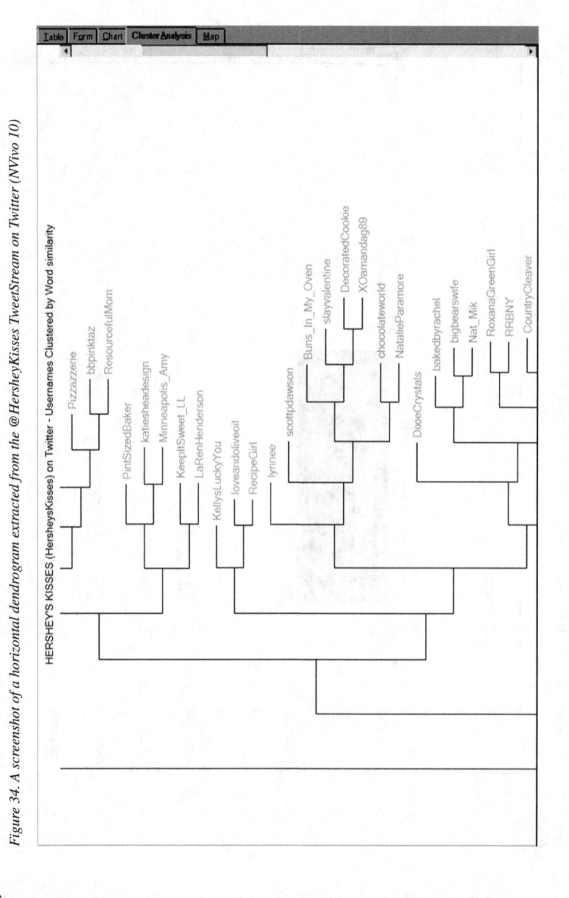

Figure 34. A screenshot of a horizontal dendrogram extracted from the @HersheyKisses TweetStream on Twitter (NVivo 10)

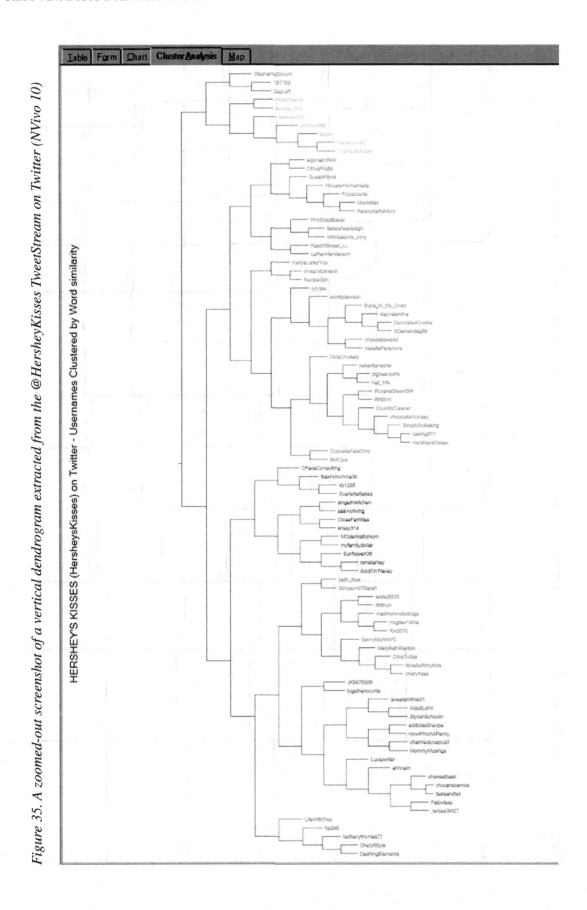

Figure 35. A zoomed-out screenshot of a vertical dendrogram extracted from the @HersheyKisses TweetStream on Twitter (NVivo 10)

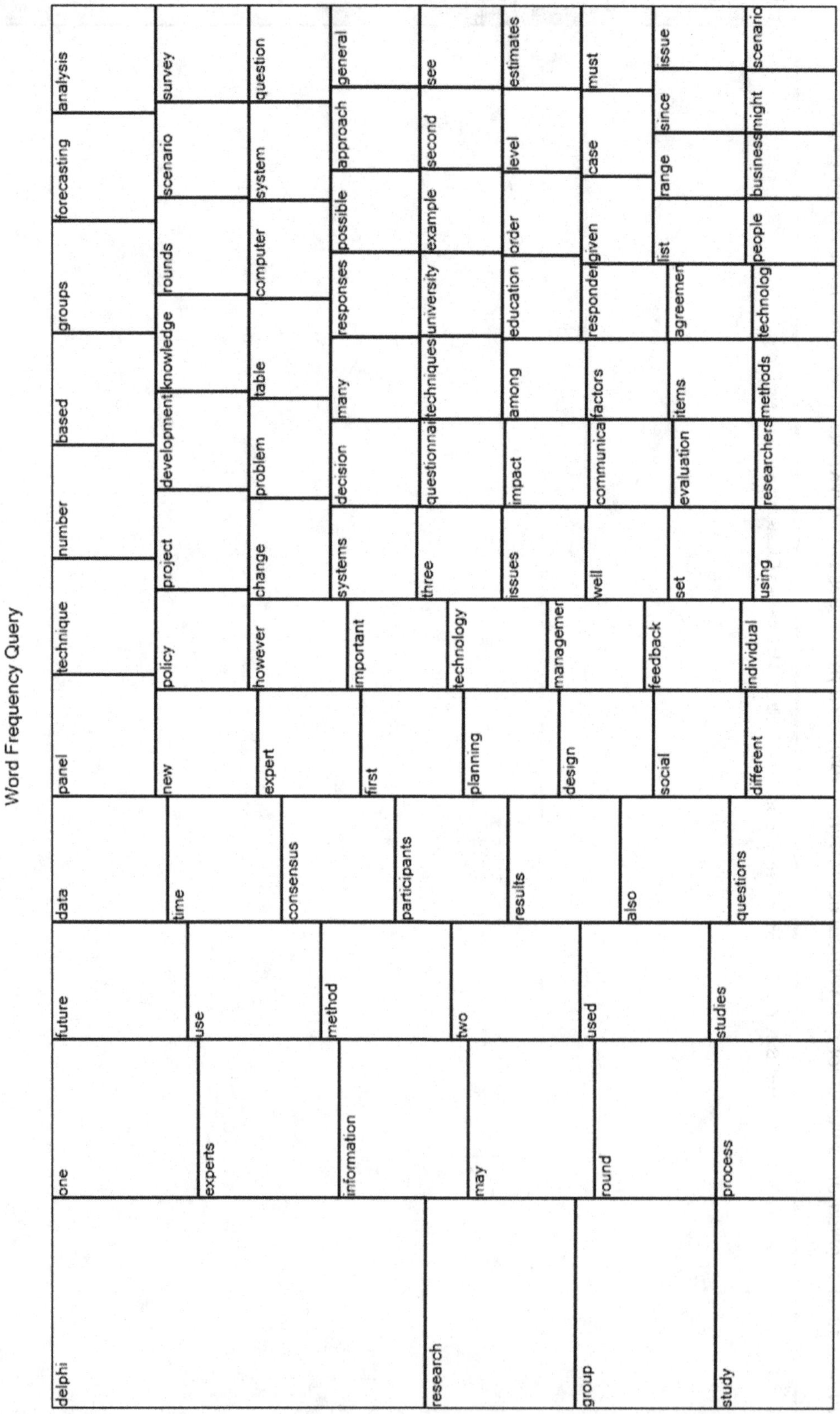

Figure 36. A treemap diagram of a word frequency count from a literature review of research into the Delphi research methodology (created in NVivo 10)

Word Frequency Query

Figure 37. A word frequency count from a literature review of research into the Delphi research methodology (created in NVivo 10)

Word	Length	Count	Weighted Percentage (%)
delphi	6	5212	1.45
research	8	2065	0.57
group	5	1921	0.53
study	5	1638	0.45
one	3	1519	0.42
experts	7	1482	0.41
information	11	1333	0.37
may	3	1294	0.36
round	5	1251	0.35
process	7	1221	0.34
future	6	1053	0.29
use	3	1048	0.29
method	6	1004	0.28
two	3	1002	0.28
used	4	986	0.27
studies	7	969	0.27
data	4	961	0.27
time	4	942	0.26
consensus	9	941	0.26
participants	12	931	0.26
results	7	909	0.25
also	4	903	0.25
questions	9	858	0.24
panel	5	826	0.23
technique	9	793	0.22
number	6	775	0.22
based	5	765	0.21
groups	6	762	0.21
forecasting	11	739	0.21
analysis	8	738	0.20
new	3	723	0.20
expert	6	716	0.20
first	5	710	0.20

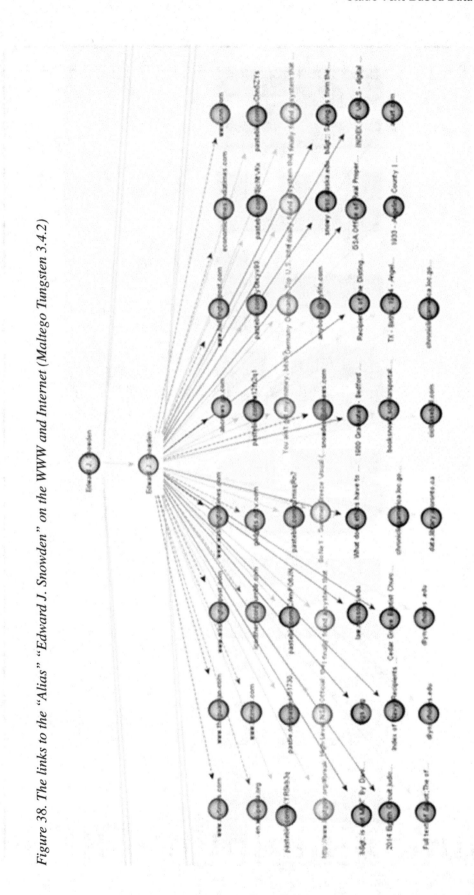

Figure 38. The links to the "Alias" "Edward J. Snowden" on the WWW and Internet (Maltego Tungsten 3.4.2)

represents a multi-modal type of network graph because the entities (nodes) are of various types. This bubble graph visualization is a hierarchical one with the focal node listed at the top and the connected nodes listed below.

A deeper data crawl involves a Level 1 domain crawl for the .edu domain. A zoomed-out view is viewable in Figure 39.

Figure 40 shows an "entity list," or the data table underlying the data visualizations. The entity list, reports, and other elements may be exported from Maltego Tungsten for more probing analytics.

Figure 39. A level 1 domain analysis of the .edu domain on the web (Maltego Tungsten 3.4.2))

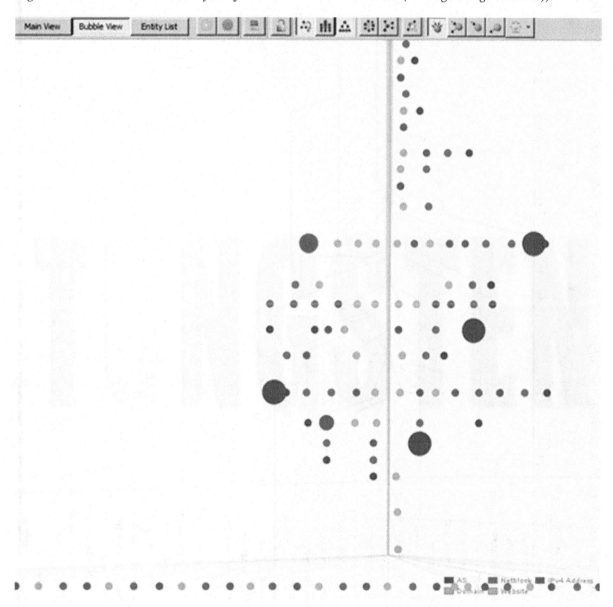

Figure 40. The entity list table underlying the "alias" data extraction for "Edward J. Snowden" (Maltego Tungsten 3.4.2)

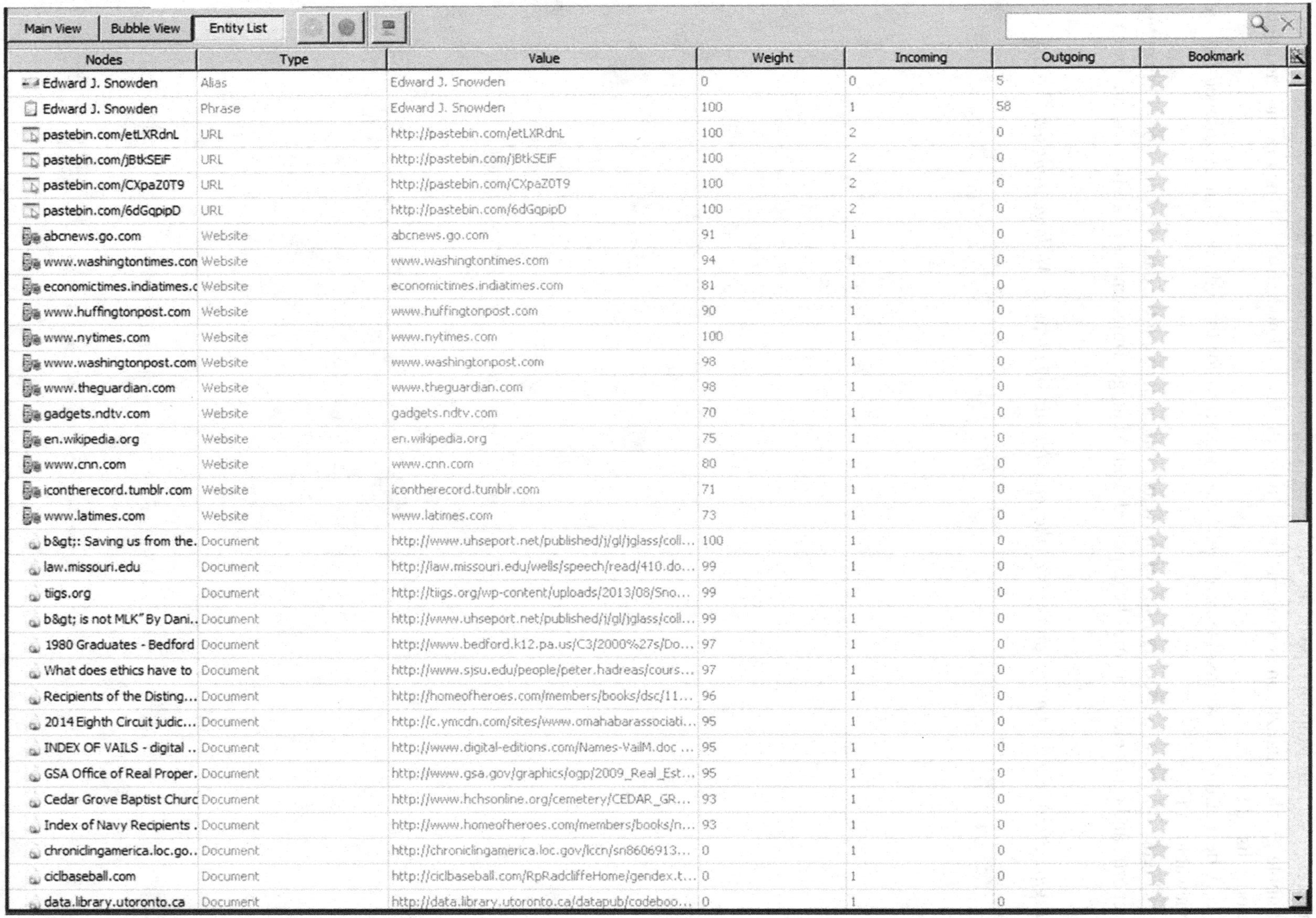

| Main View | Bubble View | **Entity List** |

Nodes	Type	Value	Weight	Incoming	Outgoing	Bookmark
Edward J. Snowden	Alias	Edward J. Snowden	0	0	5	
Edward J. Snowden	Phrase	Edward J. Snowden	100	1	58	
pastebin.com/etLXRdnL	URL	http://pastebin.com/etLXRdnL	100	2	0	
pastebin.com/jBtkSEiF	URL	http://pastebin.com/jBtkSEiF	100	2	0	
pastebin.com/CXpaZ0T9	URL	http://pastebin.com/CXpaZ0T9	100	2	0	
pastebin.com/6dGapipD	URL	http://pastebin.com/6dGapipD	100	2	0	
abcnews.go.com	Website	abcnews.go.com	91	1	0	
www.washingtontimes.com	Website	www.washingtontimes.com	94	1	0	
economictimes.indiatimes.c	Website	economictimes.indiatimes.com	81	1	0	
www.huffingtonpost.com	Website	www.huffingtonpost.com	90	1	0	
www.nytimes.com	Website	www.nytimes.com	100	1	0	
www.washingtonpost.com	Website	www.washingtonpost.com	98	1	0	
www.theguardian.com	Website	www.theguardian.com	98	1	0	
gadgets.ndtv.com	Website	gadgets.ndtv.com	70	1	0	
en.wikipedia.org	Website	en.wikipedia.org	75	1	0	
www.cnn.com	Website	www.cnn.com	80	1	0	
icontherecord.tumblr.com	Website	icontherecord.tumblr.com	71	1	0	
www.latimes.com	Website	www.latimes.com	73	1	0	
b>: Saving us from the.	Document	http://www.uhseport.net/[published]/tjql/jqlass/coll...	100	1	0	
law.missouri.edu	Document	http://law.missouri.edu/wells/speech/read/410.do...	99	1	0	
tjigs.org	Document	http://tjigs.org/wp-content/uploads/2013/08/Sno...	99	1	0	
b>: is not MLK" By Dani..	Document	http://www.uhseport.net/[published]/tjql/jqlass/coll...	99	1	0	
1980 Graduates - Bedford	Document	http://www.bedford.k12.pa.us/C3/2000%27s/Do...	97	1	0	
What does ethics have to	Document	http://www.sjsu.edu/people/peter.hadreas/cours...	97	1	0	
Recipients of the Disting...	Document	http://homeofheroes.com/members/books/dsc/11...	96	1	0	
2014 Eighth Circuit Judic...	Document	http://c.ymcdn.com/sites/www.omahabarassociati...	95	1	0	
INDEX OF VAILS - digital ..	Document	http://www.digital-editions.com/Names-VailM.doc	95	1	0	
GSA Office of Real Proper..	Document	http://www.gsa.gov/graphics/ogp/2009_Real_Est...	95	1	0	
Cedar Grove Baptist Churc	Document	http://www.hchsonline.org/cemetery/CEDAR_GR...	93	1	0	
Index of Navy Recipients .	Document	http://www.homeofheroes.com/members/books/n...	93	1	0	
chronidingamerica.loc.go...	Document	http://chronidingamerica.loc.gov/lccn/sn8606913...	0	1	0	
ccibaseball.com	Document	http://ccibaseball.com/RtpRadcliffeHome/gendex.t...	0	1	0	
data.library.utoronto.ca	Document	http://data.library.utoronto.ca/datapub/codeboo...	0	1	0	

3D Bubble Graph

A three-dimensional bubble graph then plots data points along all three axes: x, y, and z. The placement of the respective data points on all three axes carry potential meaning, and the proximity of the nodes to each other (calculated based on pairwise distances), their individual sizes, and their labels, all matter as well. The next few bubble graphs (both 3D and 2D) were created from an extraction of the HersheyKisses user account on Twitter. This extraction pulled 1,224 records of Tweets from the @TweetStream on Twitter. A word frequency count was run on the contents of the microblogging messages. The sizes of the labeled nodes indicate their frequency count (with a larger size indicating a higher frequency count). The more closely the terms were clustered with others, the more related they are; conversely, the more physically distant two nodes are from each other, the more unrelated the terms are.

In other words, the added dimensionality of a bubble graph indicates richer ranges of data. Figure 41: provides a sense of the challenges of conveying 3D space on a 2D screen. The inclusion of the shaded background and grid lines on the background are used to try to indicate depth and z-axis. The interactivity functions—zooming in and out of the floating nodes—and the ability to re-orient all enhance the quality of information in such visualizations.

Figure 42 shows a more zoomed-in view of the 3D visualization, which looks much flatter and two-dimensional.

Finally, Figure 23 (presented earlier) depicts a two-dimensional version of the same graph. By contrast, there does seem to be a sense of some loss of dimensionality. In this visualization, also done in NVivo 10, there is more of a sense of a center-periphery dynamic possibly. Or it may be that there is no over-arching order but only free-floating concepts with local relevance in terms of proximity but no over-arching order.

Some bubblegraphs show much more clustering. This word frequency count, Figure 43, shows 10 different clusters of related words by both proximity and color.

Node-Link Diagram (Vertex-Edge Diagram)

The core elements of a node-link diagram (also a vertex-edge diagram) consist of a node (indicated with a closed geometric shape, icon, or glyph usually) and a link (indicated by a line, without arrows on the end in undirected graphs, and with arrows on the line ends indicating directionality in directed graphs). Essentially, node-link diagrams indicate entities and interrelationships between those entities. Entities themselves may be single individuals or groups; they may be websites, email accounts, online documents; they may be any number of people or objects or events. There are a wide number of variation in looks and feels of node-link diagrams, and they may be represented in two or three dimensions or even higher dimensionality (such as motion as a fourth dimension). Lines may be elaborated on by thickness, labels, or other elements as well. Node-link diagrams may be depicted manually (hand-drawn on Microsoft Visio), or they may be drawn using data in a number of data visualization tools. Bi-modal or two-mode node-link diagrams are those in which the nodes are not of one type of thing but may include two types, such as people (actors) and events (occurrences). Node-link diagrams may be multi-modal or include a wide variety of types of entities.

The first example in Figure 44 shows a more classic associational sociogram or social network graph, with the nodes representing various social entities known as "alters" that are direct ties to the focal node at the center. The center-periphery dynamic applies in this graph in the sense that those clustered around

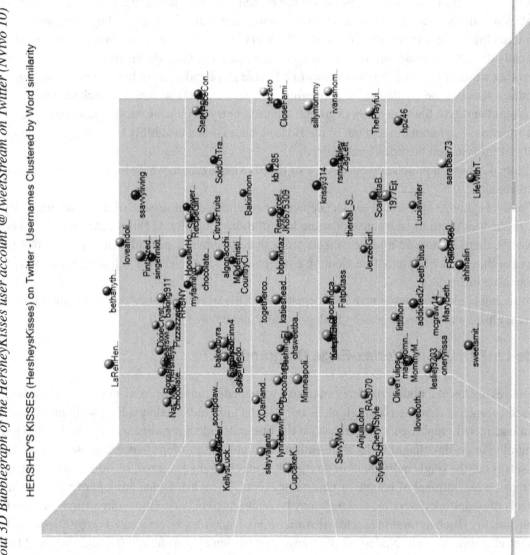

Figure 41. A zoomed-out 3D Bubblegraph of the HersheyKisses user account @TweetStream on Twitter (NVivo 10)

HERSHEY'S KISSES (HersheysKisses) on Twitter - Usernames Clustered by Word similarity

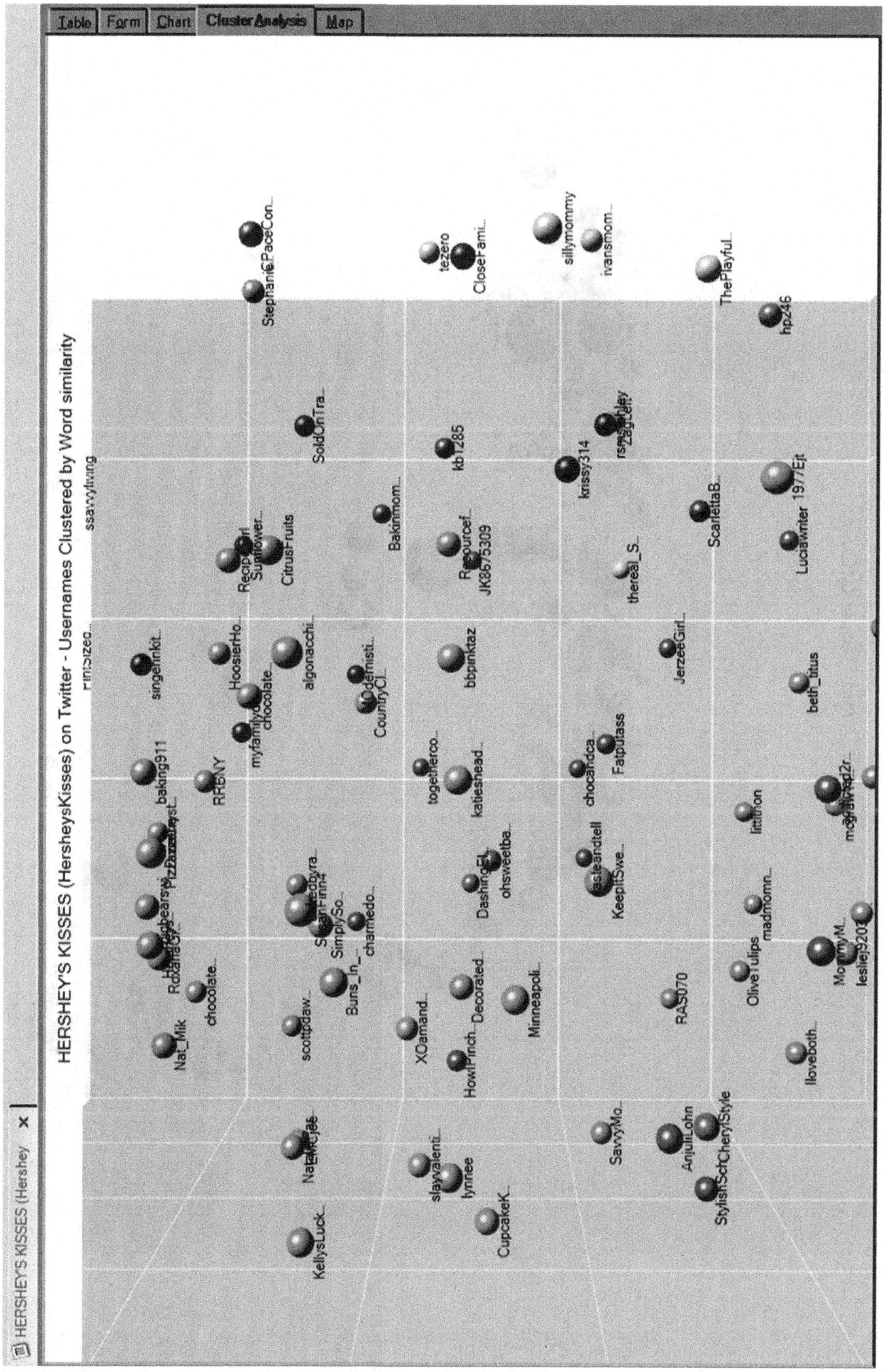

Figure 42. A zoomed-in 3D Bubblegraph of the @HersheyKisses user account TweetStream on Twitter (NVivo 10)

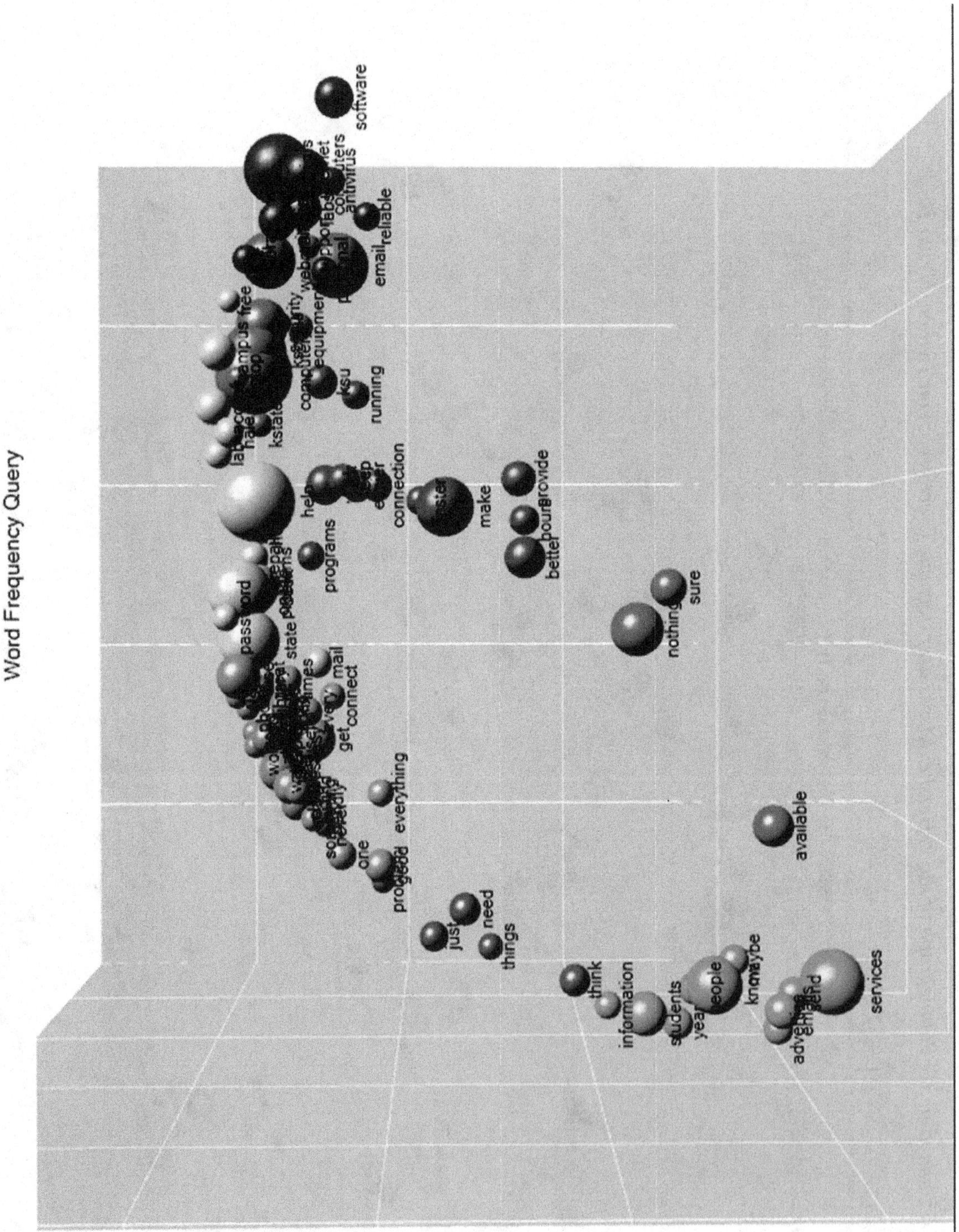

Figure 43. A zoomed-in 3D bubblegraph of keywords found in a survey (NVivo 10)

Word Frequency Query

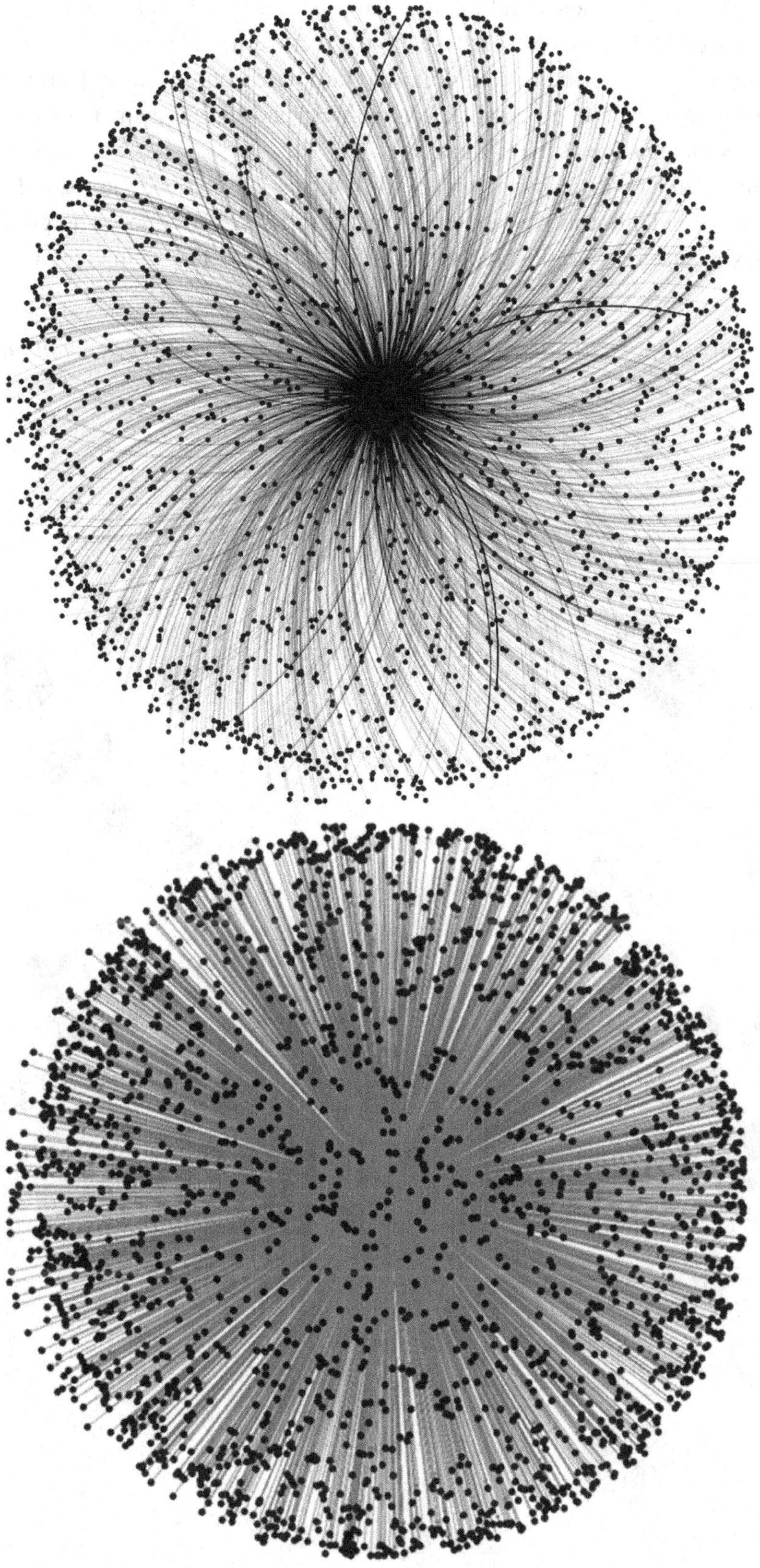

Figure 44. Two views of the ego neighborhood of an affiliation network with a center-periphery dynamic (NodeXL and Graph ML)

the center have more engagements and interactions with the focal node. Those on the periphery are part of the social network but are not as "close" to the focal node. This node-link diagram is visualized in two ways. The left one is a simple node-link diagram based on the Harel Koren Multi-scale Layout algorithm; the right one is the same graph drawn with Graph ML and is interactive in its online version (with vertex labels that resolve as users zoom in).

Another example of a two-dimensional node-link network graph is depicted in Figure 45, a view of the @TravelGov ego neighborhood, with 9,427 vertices and 7,599 edges. The graph has 28,257 total edges, with 20,658 edges wit duplicates and 6,995 self-loops. The diameter or maximum geodesic

Figure 45. Ego neighborhood of alters belonging to the @TravelGov user account on Twitter (NodeXL)

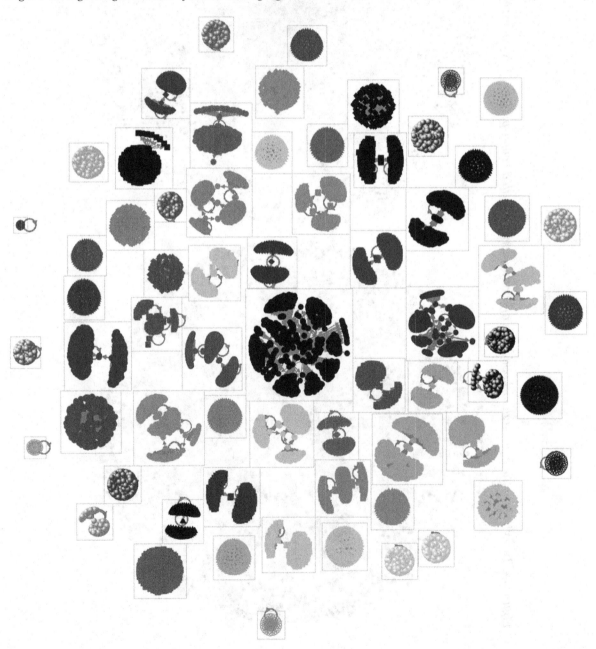

distance in the graph is 6, with the average distance between nodes as 3.97. In this visualization, only the clusters were highlighted, and the links themselves were made invisible, so the actual connections between various clusters is not viewable. Such "filtering" of visual effects is an option.

UCINET 6.461 and the accompanying NetDraw 2.127 were used to create the following star diagram with 302 nodes. This was drawn using machine-generated "synthetic" data. The resulting visualization is suggestive of motion and is also based around a central focal node. Figure 46 is the only visualization which is based on synthetic machine-generated data.

Figure 47 shows three manually created node-link diagrams that have varying degrees of conceptualization. The far-left visualization explains the dynamics of an ego neighborhood; the middle one shows a conceptualization of an open-source multi-modal model; the far right visualization explains other associational concepts related to node-link diagrams. The two far-right panes contain explanatory data pull-outs.

A "Twitter Digger" extraction along with other "transforms" was done for the hashtag conversation #sanctions for Figure 48.

The 2D node-link diagram for Figure 49 shows a ring lattice graph with the nodes as words on the edges of the circle and deep ties that fill in the circle. This visualization came from a top-50-words word frequency extraction of the 2,262 Tweet extraction dataset from the TweetStream of MOOCNews user account on Twitter.

2D and 3D Node-Link Text Network Graphs

A machine-extracted meta-ontology was conducted on a dataset consisting of the text contents of a blog which ran for eight years. A meta-ontology is an extraction of concepts that may be used to help structure the underlying textual dataset. To the left is a zoomed-out view of the resulting clustered text (with related concepts based on proximity and frequency of use), and to the right is a 3D visualization, for a side-by-side contrastive look in *Figure 50*. Those who would use this for research would do well to thin the network…and to zoom in for deeper insights. (Machine-based meta-ontologies tend to capture all potential concepts for an overflow of data. Human-created pre-definitions of main concepts may be more conducive to a useful extraction, or a sequence of human-machine-human-machine sorting may result in a more usable dataset.) Meta-ontologies may be all of a type, or they may capture a range of categories of information, such as "agent, organization, location, task, event, knowledge, resource, and belief, in AutoMap. The outputs of such text processing may be used for content or thematic analysis at a basic level, and they may be applied for a much wider range of analytical tasks (which are beyond the scope of this chapter).

Word Cloud

The word cloud is a data visualization that may be the result of an extreme data reduction. Figure 51, "Word Cloud of the Instructional Design Open Studio (IDOS) Blog on Wordle™" was the result of condensing literally thousands of pages of single-spaced text that was the result of 8.5 years of blogging on the Instructional Design Open Studio blog (2006 – mid-2014).

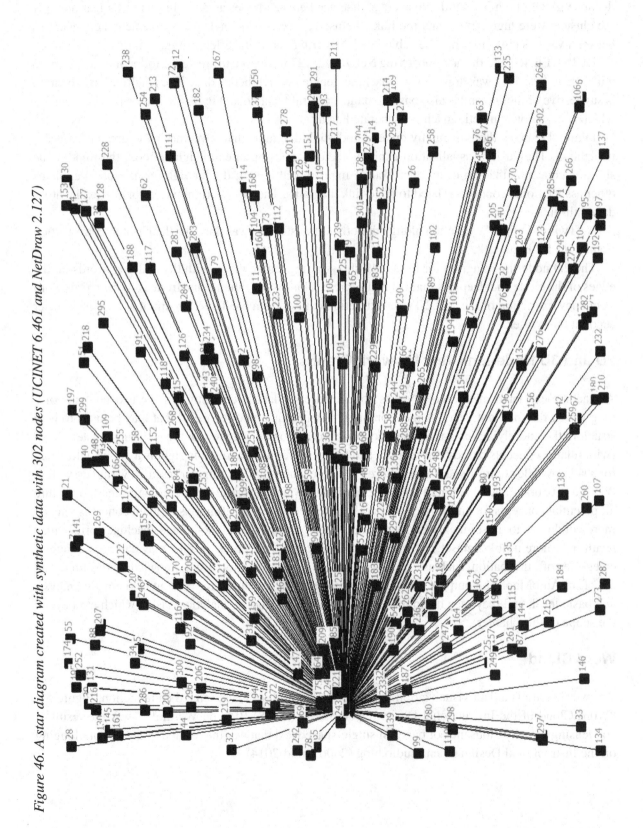

Figure 46. A star diagram created with synthetic data with 302 nodes (UCINET 6.461 and NetDraw 2.127)

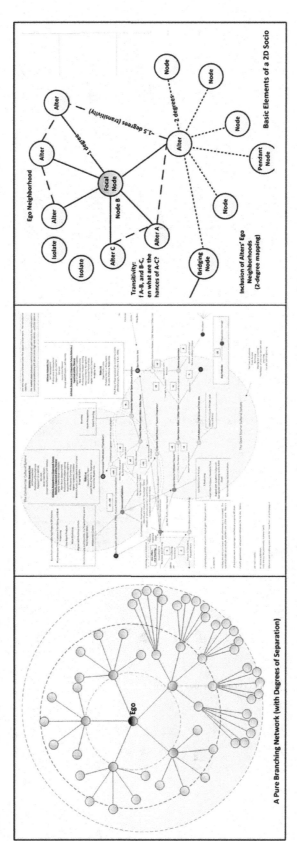

Figure 47. Some hand-drawn node-link diagrams in Microsoft Visio

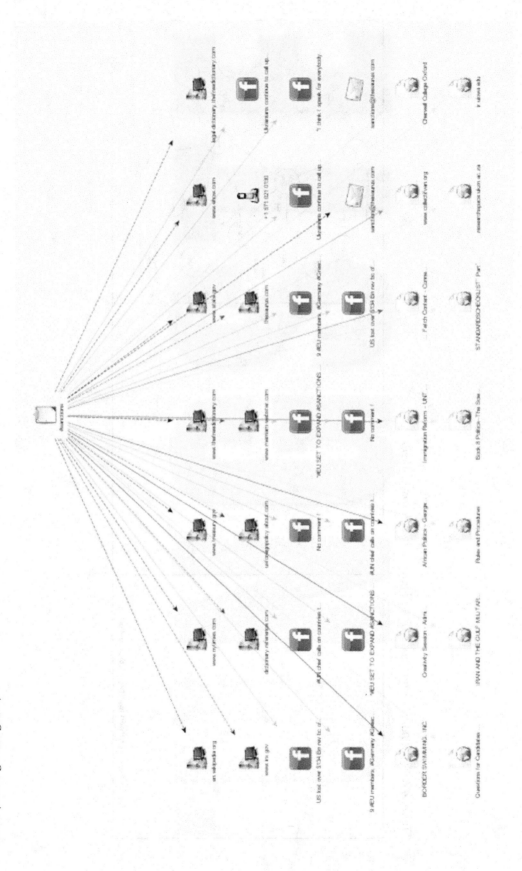

Figure 48. A twitter digger and other transforms data extraction for a #sanctions hashtag conversation on Twitter and Related Links on the Web (Maltego Tungsten)

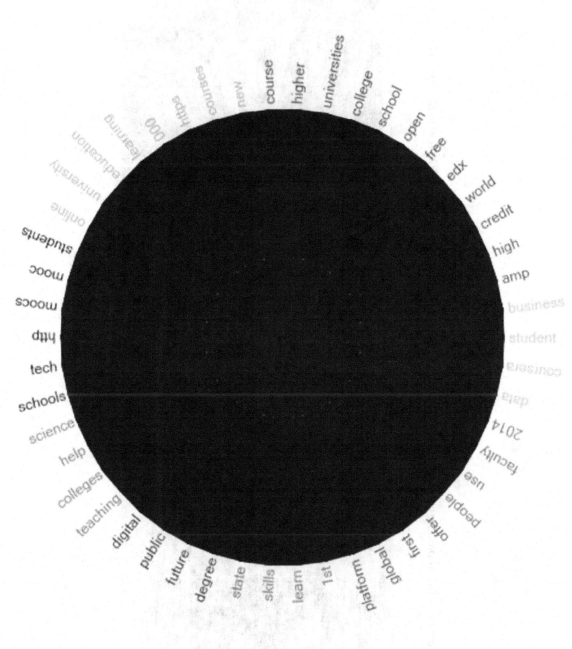

Figure 49. A ring lattice graph (form of a node-link diagram) of the MOOCNews TweetStream on Twitter (NCapture and NVivo 10)

Figure 50. An extracted meta ontology from an active blog with 2D to the left and a zoomed-in 3D view to the right (CASOS AutoMap / ORA NetScenes)

Figure 51. Word cloud of the instructional design open studio (IDOS) blog on Wordle™

The growing popularity of static text-based data visualizations has come about in part from their popularization on online sites like news sites, blogs, and websites, to summarize contents and highlight popular concepts and themes. Tag clouds, word-based visualizations where selected tags are positioned in a "cloud," and depicted with visual elements like font type, sizes, and colors, summarize the most popular contents user-tagged in folksonomies across the Web and Internet.

For an example of another word cloud from a different software tool, the author conducted a data extraction of the @CNN account on Twitter. At the time of the crawl at https://twitter.com/CNN, the account had 45,600 Tweets, 1,503 photos / videos, 957 following, 13.3 million followers, and 638 favorites. Based on statistics like these, this is a destination site. Using NCapture, the most recent 3,189 messages were extracted and displayed in NVivo 10.

Figure 52. A word cloud from the @CNN TweetStream on Twitter (NVivo 10)

Electronic Social Network Analysis (e-SNA) Graph

Electronic social network analysis (e-SNA) refers to the application of social network analysis on electronic spaces: social media platforms (social networking sites, content-sharing sites, wikis, blogs, microblogs, websites, and others) and email systems. There has already been a long history of social network analysis in fields like sociology, but the application of social network analysis to electronic communications is a fairly recent phenomena. Essentially, the nodes in such graphs are individuals (user accounts), and the links are various types of relatedness, both extrinsic and intrinsic. Extrinsic relatedness on various platforms may include the following: following, follower relationships on microblogging sites; subscriptions to certain accounts; co-membership in particular groups (which may suggest shared interests), and others. Intrinsic relatedness may include the following: participation in a shared hashtag (#) conversation; using a similar keyword in a microblogging message; commenting; replies; re-tweets; co-tagging of multimedia contents; reply videos; and similar tagging of contents. A typical rationale for the power of e-SNA is that this data is based on actual behaviors in the real-world instead of self-claimed and generally unsubstantiated assertions. A wide range of social networks may be extracted from the various social media platforms based on the affordances by the companies that own those platforms and the tools used to extract and visualize the networks. The underlying datasets usually contain user accounts, relatedness, scraped textual messages or tags, digital imagery (if available), and links. In undirected graphs, relationships are noted only if they exist or not (indicated with a line or an absence of a line between nodes). In directed graphs, relationships are directional, with arrows on one or both ends of a relationship (is the relationship one directional or bidirectional?). Line weights may indicate the depth of the relationship in terms of interchanges. Node sizes may be indicated by numbers of in-coming relationships (in-degree) as balanced against outgoing relationships (out-degree), or an overall degree measure. Nodes may be analyzed for their connectivity to other nodes in power, their influence and centrality in the network, and a range of other types of structural power. The overall social graph itself may be analyzed to understand the nature of the social community within that network, the types of relationships within it, the types of messages and other transmissible contents moving through the network, and the nature of the respective subgraphs (motifs) and nodes within it. Dynamic network analysis may reveal how the social network has formed, how it evolves over time, and how it eventually ends. Beyond this simple overview, there are myriad other types of analyses that may be conducted on such electronic social networks. Figure #, A Sampler Grid of Social Network Analysis Graphs Extracted from Social Media Platforms (with NodeXL), shows some 16 social graphs extracted from various social media sites and various types of network layouts. All are variations on node-link diagrams. Suffice it to say that each graph has unique data extraction parameters and resulting datasets. Each would have a particular plausible use case scenario in which valuable research information would be extracted, based on the dataset and the visualization(s). One of the main takeaways from Figure 53 should be the wide variances possible in how information may be structured and the resulting "morphological designs" possible based on the layout algorithms. All of these are from one tool, Network Overview, Discovery and Exploration for Excel (or NodeXL). There would be even greater variety if the visualizations from a range of other tools were included.

In Figure 54, the quadtych shows how the force-based Fruchterman-Reingold layout algorithm revisualizes a dataset over a number of iterations during which increasing amounts of repellence are applied between the nodes. The far left-image shows the original visualization of the dataset, and each one thereafter is two iterations more of the force-based algorithm. The algorithm may be applied to a

Figure 53. A sampler grid of social network analysis graphs extracted from social media platforms (with NodeXL)

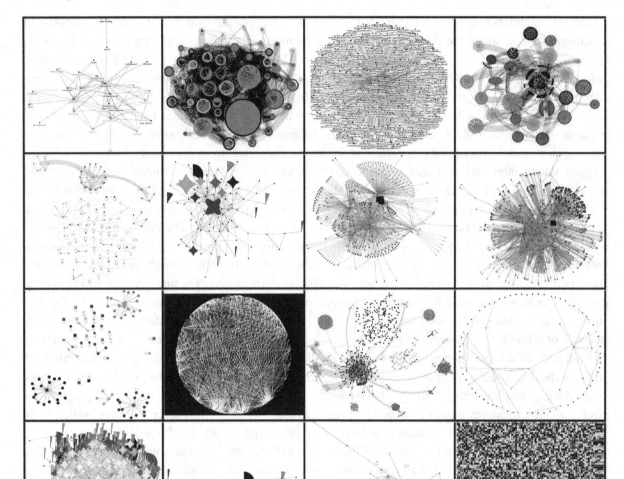

high degree, with many of the nodes all pressed into an outer circle based on the virtual "centrifugal" force of the layout algorithm. As may be visually ascertained, there is increased dispersion in space as the nodes are pushed outwards. (As a side note, many network graphs may be re-drawn iteratively without changing the core meanings of the network graph. The general connectivity remains the same even as the overall look-and-feel of the graph may change slightly. Many types of network graphs are not reliant on the x and y axes. They may be stood on one end or the other without changing essential network topographical features.)

Figure 55 was created as a two-degree crawl. The first degree consisted of all those who recently had "Iraq" as a keyword in a microblogging Tweet. The second degree consists of the ego neighborhoods of all the user accounts that were netted in the first extraction. This method explains why 205,099 vertices (nodes) were captured, with 272,112 unique edges. The maximum geodesic stance for this graph was

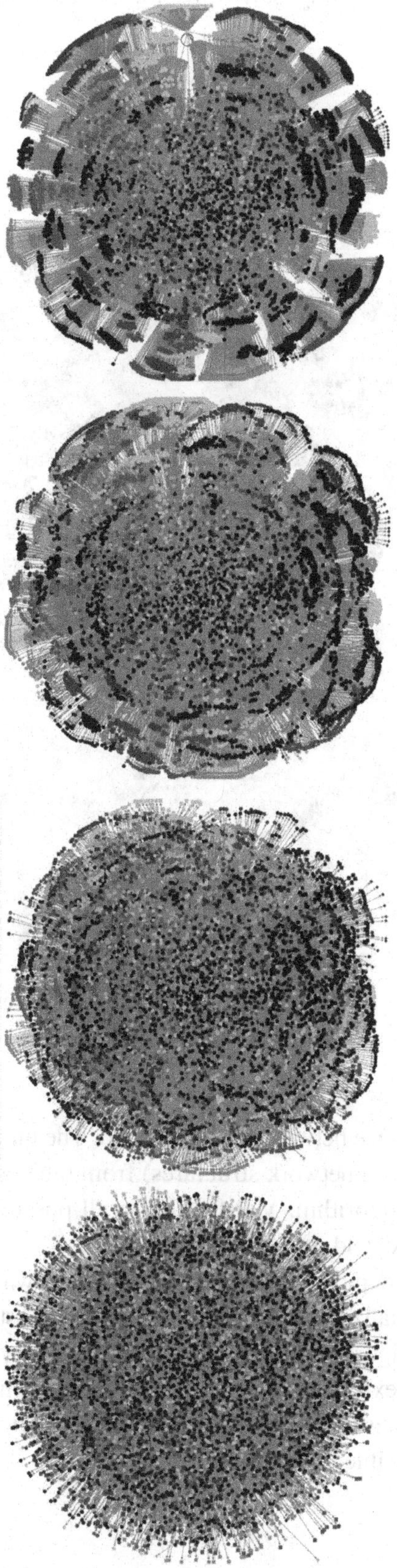

Figure 54. A quadtrych of ego neighborhoods of BlackhatEvents' alters on Twitter: Two-Iterations per panel of the force-based Fruchterman-Reingold layout algorithm (NodeXL)

Figure 55. Conversations around "Iraq" keyword in a layout using motifs to indicate network graph local structures (NodeXL)

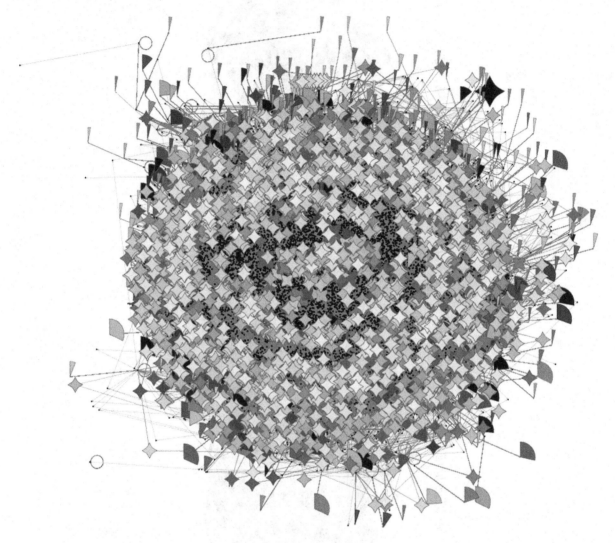

11, and the average geodesic stance between nodes was 4.6. The unique visualization here was achieved with an extraction of motifs (local network structures) from the network and then visualized using the Fruchterman Reingold layout algorithm. Motifs refer to all possible structured relationships between nodes: dyadic, triadic, quadratic, and so on.

The underlying data may be depicted in a number of different ways by computers based on the layout algorithm directions. Some visualizations offer a sense of imposed structure, like ring lattices, like grids, and like the Sugiyama layout algorithm (based on a line). Other layout algorithms are more apparently free-form and less apparently externally pre-structured. Those who would use data visualizations to conduct some research or analysis may iterate a dataset across various types of visualizations to extract the most information value possible.

Figure 56. A string of motifs laid out on a Sugiyama line (NodeXL)

Related Tags Network Graph

One type of textual metadata extraction that may be done involves analyzing user-generated (non-professionally labeled) tags of multimedia contents on content-sharing sites, like Flickr, which hosts images and videos. Related tags networks capture clusters of terms which co-occur in proximity to provide a sense of how the multimedia contributors conceptualize the contents. From these clusters, researchers may also infer various groupings of related contents. Inferences may be tested in part against a broad sampling of scraped images depicted as thumbnails from the various accounts. In lieu of the shaped vertices, the scraped images may be used. Related tags network graphs may be analyzed at multiple units of analysis. The overall network may be analyzed for its general clusters and contents. Researchers may surface anomalies by reviewing the data visualization. They may consider what clusters may be missing. At the cluster level, the various tags may be analyzed for patterns as well as anomalies. If there are gaps that the researcher thinks is missing from the data, he or she may contribute multimedia contents with tags to see if the related tags metadata extractions may be changed up. The analysis of related tags networks show that word associations may not be conscious by those doing the tagging. Meaning does not have to be purposively or consciously made to be valid. The related tags network for "Seattle" involved 907 vertices, with 4,671 unique edges. There were no self-loops. The geodesic distance or diameter of this content-based network graph was 4, and the average geodesic distance a node would have to travel to connect with any other node was 3.19 hops. Connectivity between the photo and video contents on Flickr are based on implicit measures of relatedness, including commenting on photos and videos, being in the same collection, classification under the same tag, being co-flagged for "interestingness", and tags "grouped into clusters based on co-occurrence across photos or common use across users" (Rodrigues & Milic-Frayling, 2011, p. 207). Explicit relatedness in Flickr would involve factors like users being part of the same Flickr groups and formally adding others as contacts. *Figure 57*, "A Related Tags Network for "Seattle" in Flickr (NodeXL)," was laid out using the Harel-Koren Fast Multiscale and partitions for easier readability. NodeXL refers to an open-source software add-on to Excel (in Windows machines) called Network Overview, Discovery and Exploration for Excel; this is available for download from the Microsoft CodePlex site.

To provide a sense of what images may look like in a related tags network, Figure 58, "A Related Tags Network for "Panda" in Flickr with Scraped Imagery at the Vertices (NodeXL)," shows a visualization with the scraped imagery included. Finally, it is possible to visually and manually (or use machine analysis) to conduct a kind of non-statistical principal component analysis in order to summarize the contents of each partitioned group, to understand the main components of each group in this network of related tags (centered around one word or term). This related tags network had 926 vertices (nodes), with 3,343 unique edges. There were no edges with duplicates and no self-loops. The maximum geodesic distance or graph diameter was 4, and the average geodesic distance between any two nodes was 3.25. The graph density was 0.0039, suggesting that many opportunities for connectivity have not been explored or pursued.

Hashtag Conversation Graph

A #hashtag conversation refers to the online discussions that occur between individuals and groups that tag their conversations with the same label. Hashtags are used to create some form of coherence around a certain topic or related topics. Unique hashtags are used to label messages related to particular events, to create eventgraphs (social network graphs of those participating in the conference or the conversations around the conference). The example here of a hashtag conversation graph captures not only the microblogging Tweets communicated but the communicants and the interrelationships between them (in terms of responding to Tweets, re-Tweeting, as well as the follower / following relationships that may exist among the nodes in this network). In *Figure 59*, "#3Dprinting Hashtag Search on Twitter (NodeXL)," the particular visualization did not include the names of the various accounts in the vertices, but it could. Figure # captures the graph from a hashtag search of "#3Dprinting" from Twitter using NodeXL 1.0.1.331. The Twitter API terms enables extraction of Tweets only for up to the prior seven days, so this graph contains information from July 8, 2014, and the prior week. There were 674 vertices captured, with 9,748 edges (links or connections among these vertices). The average geodesic distance in this network was 2.6 hops, and the maximum geodesic distance (diameter) was 7. The graph density was 0.02, which is not unusual given the size of the graph. In terms of groups of users or clusters, three were identified. Further research into the graph would require going into the graph metrics and the actual data tables and revisualizations with the Twitter user accounts mentioned. The vertices of this graph were grouped by cluster using the Clauset-Newman-Moore cluster algorithm, and the graph itself was laid out using the Fruchterman-Reingold force-based layout algorithm. This visualization viscerally evokes the energy and potential beauty of such data depictions.

Matrix Coding Query Table

A matrix coding query table offers a way for researchers to achieve a many-to-many type of textual comparison by placing documents, textual nodes, interviews, and any sort of textual data on a matrix (with rows and columns of data) in order to identify where there may be texts that show overlapping contents. The selected contents may be within-type (nodes with nodes, documents with documents) or cross-type (research documents with nodes). The cross-tabulation may provide leads in terms of which documents to probe for particular ideas. This high-level view may also be suggestive of potential patterns or themes that may be explored further. *Figure 60*, "A Screenshot of a Portion of Matrix Coding Query Table (NVivo 10)," shows the inclusion of some research documents based on a search of massive open online course (MOOCs) platforms (Coursera, edX, and Udacity) cross-referenced with coding data based on "big data" and student tracking analytics on MOOCs. This resulting table from a matrix coding query shows a low amount of overlapping information between these sources.

As a side note, matrix diagrams may be simple binary ones, with a 1 to indicate presence of a relationship and a 0 to indicate non-presence. Or, the matrix diagram may indicate degree of connectedness, with higher numbers indicating higher relatedness, and 0 indicating no relatedness.

Figure 57. A related tags network for "Seattle" in Flickr (NodeXL)

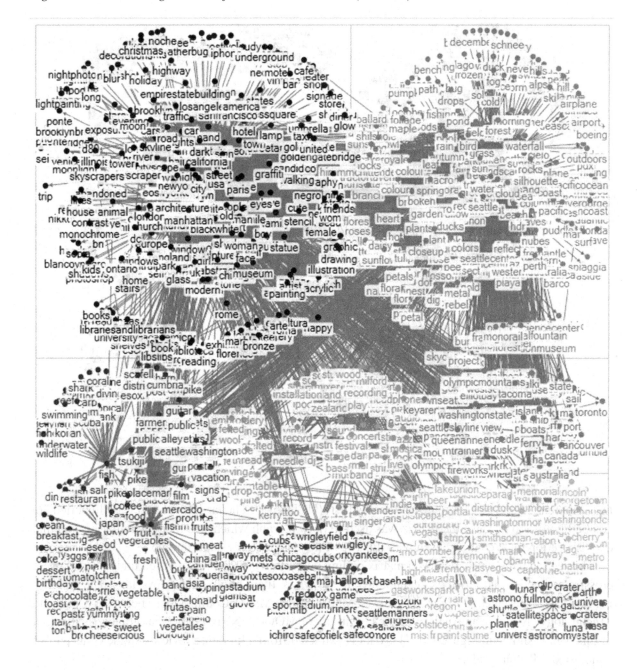

Data Matrices

Data matrices may be used as stand-alone data visualizations, or they may be used as the underlying data structures for data visualizations like graphs. The first data matrix below was used to depict a network graph, and the latter was used for analytical purposes only. An associational matrix connects people with people (is there a relationship or not?), or people with events or endeavors (in a two-mode or bi-modal graph), such as the one depicted in Figure 61, *"Sample Associational Matrix of an "Intro to Public Health"*

Figure 58. A related tags network for "Panda" in Flickr with scraped imagery at the vertices (NodeXL)

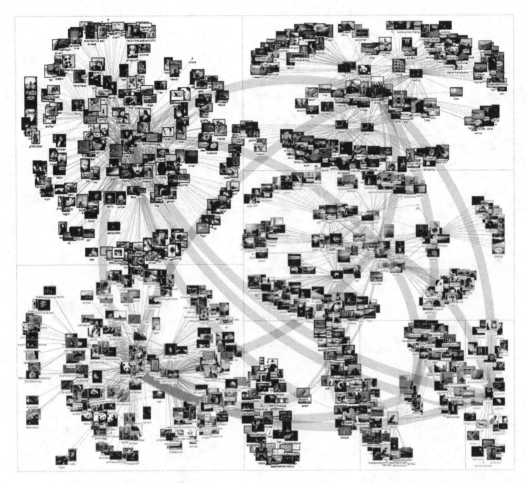

Development Team (with a Liquified Records List) (UCINET)". The far-left column was "liquefied" in Adobe Photoshop because the matrix was used to draw a graph which was then anonymized, and that data protection must continue even with this use of the data matrix as an example.

The second data matrix depicts a matrix coding query in which the nodes listed under "Cost" were cross-referenced to those listed "Technology" to see where there might be data overlaps. The underlying figure is represented in *Figure 62:* A Data Matrix from a Matrix Coding Query between "Cost" and "Technology" Nodes in an Analysis of the Feasibility of MOOCs (NVivo 10). A bar graph visualization of this data is shown in Figure 18). This data is extracted from a literature review conducted as part of a modified e-Delphi study.

Figure 59. #3Dprinting hashtag search on Twitter (NodeXL)

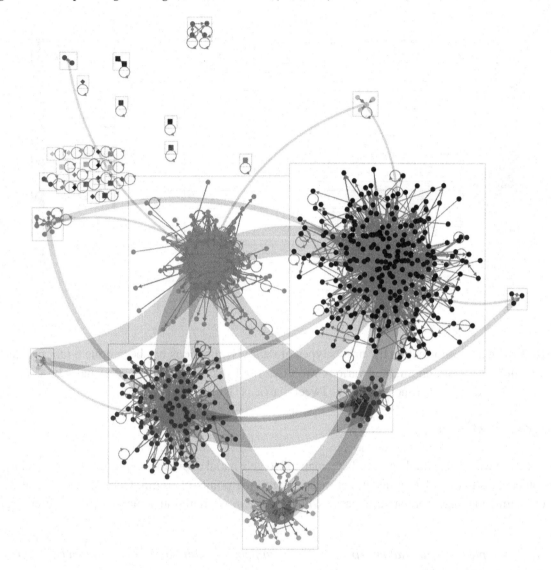

GEOSPATIAL VISUALIZATION

As contrasted to more classic terrestrial datasets, text-based visualizations may be mapped to more traditional physical maps that represent physical locations. Textual data often contains geographical or geospatial elements. Literary texts may have their plotlines mapped to physical locations (particularly over time). Hashtag conversations may be mapped to physical locales. Terms may be located to certain locales and certain times. The metadata linked to multimedia shared on content-sharing social media platforms often include geotagged information (such as "exchangeable image file format" EXIF data with digital photos). The types of spatially referenced information available in various text sets may require some additional work to extract. The geospatial data may be of varying quality (from specialized geographic information to semantic ones—related to spatiality).

Figure 60. A screenshot of a portion of matrix coding query table (NVivo 10)

Matrix Coding Query - Results

	F : LimitedGeneralizability	G : Longitudinal	H : Massification	I : Privacy	J : Scalability	K : StudentTrackingAnal...
1 : SEAJournalIssue1_fi...	0	0	0	0	0	0
2 : p28-cooper	0	0	0	0	0	1
3 : p27-younos	0	0	0	0	0	0
4 : Kim-ThumbnailExtra...	0	0	0	0	0	0
5 : C130109C	0	0	0	0	0	0
6 : C120719Y	0	0	1	0	0	0
7 : 6-come-the-revolutio...	0	0	0	0	0	0
8 : 15-online-education-...	0	0	1	0	0	0
9 : 1209.2166	0	0	0	0	0	1
10 : 120723 - edu	0	0	1	0	0	1
11 : 072312	0	0	1	0	0	0
12 : 06272250	0	0	2	0	1	0
13 : Recent Developme...	0	0	0	0	0	0
14 : p136-malan	0	0	1	0	0	0
15 : E%3A%5CResearc...	0	0	0	0	0	0
16 : D Skiba MOOC 010...	0	0	0	0	0	1
17 : C121001P	0	0	0	0	0	0
18 : 705-3256-1-PB	0	0	1	0	0	0
19 : 06487339	0	0	0	0	1	0
20 : 2012-Leonor-Barroc...	0	0	0	0	0	0
21 : CHER2012Final	0	0	0	0	0	0
22 : Cross-CHI2013-Typ...	0	0	0	0	0	0
23 : EEE6065	0	0	0	0	0	0
24 : guo-sigcse-preprint...	0	0	0	0	0	0
25 : HICSS-final-draft	0	0	0	0	0	0
26 : JCSC28_6	0	0	0	0	0	0
27 : Udacity-y-el-futuro-...	0	0	0	0	0	0

Node Matrix | Chart

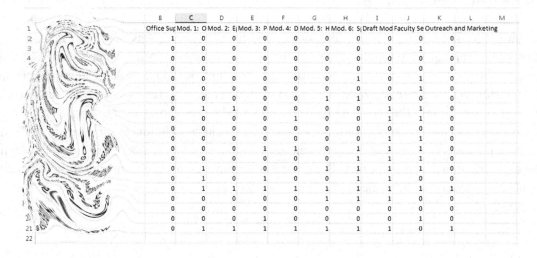

Mapping textual information to various types of data visualizations has been done a fair amount in the literature. One work highlighted various ways that the Bible may be mapped visually based on the characters' bloodlines, timelines, and even Tweet matrices (Kim & Park, 2013).

Geographical Map

One common way that textual data has been mapped to geospatial depictions representing physical locations on earth is in the relating of Twitter messaging to the points-of-origin. Geospatial data linked to microblogging messages is relatively sparse, with only one in a hundred such messages on Twitter tagged

Figure 61. sample associational matrix of an "intro to public health" development team (with a liquified records list) (UCINET)

	B	C	D	E	F	G	H	I	J	K	L	M
1	Office Sup	Mod. 1: O	Mod. 2: E	Mod. 3: P	Mod. 4: D	Mod. 5: H	Mod. 6: S	Draft Mod	Faculty Se	Outreach and Marketing		
2	1	0	0	0	0	0	0	0	0	0		
3	0	0	0	0	0	0	0	0	1	0		
4	0	0	0	0	0	0	0	0	0	0		
	0	0	0	0	0	0	0	0	0	0		
	0	0	0	0	0	0	1	0	1	0		
	0	0	0	0	0	0	0	0	1	0		
	0	0	0	0	0	1	1	0	0	0		
	0	1	1	0	0	0	0	1	1	0		
	0	0	0	0	1	0	0	1	1	0		
	0	0	0	0	0	0	0	0	0	0		
	0	0	0	0	0	0	0	1	1	0		
	0	0	0	1	1	0	1	1	1	0		
	0	0	0	0	0	0	1	1	1	0		
	0	1	0	0	0	1	1	1	1	0		
	0	1	0	1	0	0	1	1	0	0		
	0	1	1	1	1	1	1	1	1	1		
	0	0	0	0	0	1	1	1	0	0		
	0	0	0	0	0	0	0	0	0	0		
20	0	0	0	1	0	0	0	0	1	0		
21	0	1	1	1	1	1	1	1	0	1		
22												

with locational information. Much of that data in the Location column is semantic only and some not even geospatial (with labels such as "Mars" or "outerspace" and other user-created descriptors of spatial locations). Figure 63, "The Geospatial Mapping of Extracted Tweets from the AlprqAsari Account on Twitter (NVivo 10)" shows some of the locations of Tweets to the @AlprqAsari account's TweetStream.

Other tools, like Tableau Public (which has a layout function for data that acts like a pivot diagram) and ArcMaps, provide richer overlays of geospatial data to enhance such mapping with additional information for a more complete "mosaic" (Prunckun, 2010, p. 185) depending on the requirements of the researcher.

Another example follows with a social graph of those with Twitter accounts who participated in a #ThingsTimHowardCouldSave (lauding an American goalie who participated in the 2014 World Cup). These microblogging messages were linked to creatively edited images that showed the famous goalie engaging in a variety of creative saves of things like the Earth from global warming, Eve from biting into the apple in the Garden of Eden, and so on. This #hashtag conversation identified 148 vertices (user accounts), 0 edges (no relationships), and a graph density of 0. In other words, people were sharing in the meme of #ThingsTimHowardCouldSave, but they were broadcasting to their own followers more than engaging with each other. Figure 64: #ThingsTimHowardCouldSave Hashtag Discussion with Vertexes Represented by Locations (Created in NodeXL) shows the locations of the various accounts that

Figure 62. A data matrix from a matrix coding query between "cost" and "technology" nodes in an analysis of the feasibility of MOOCs (NVivo 10)

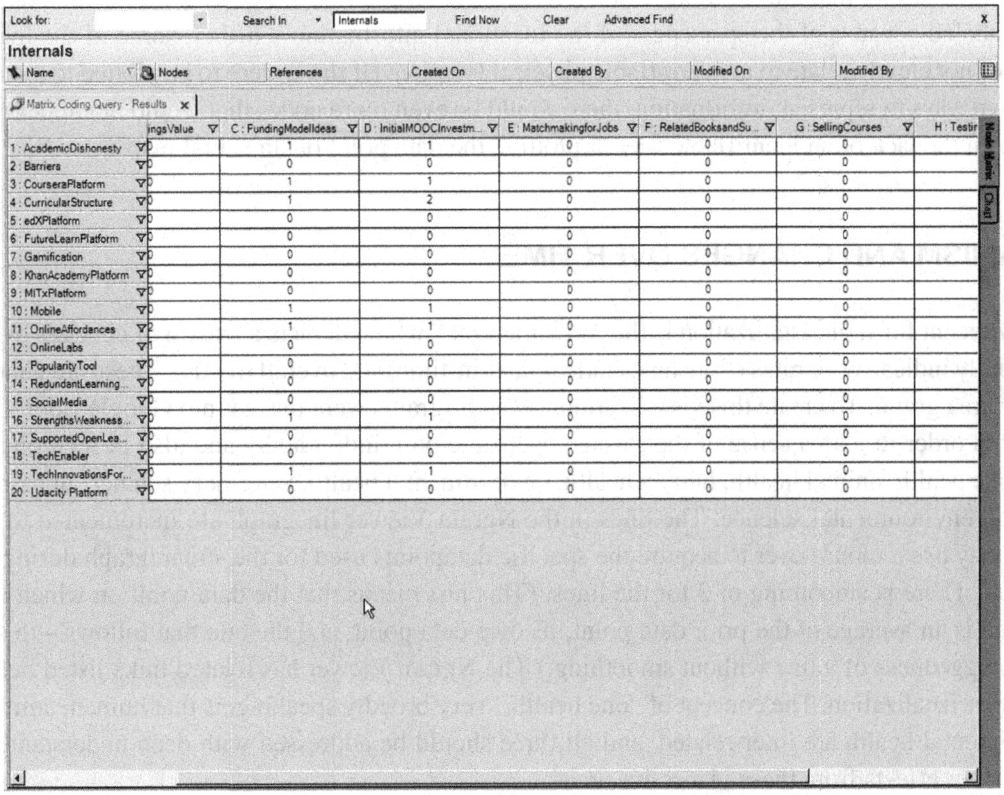

	ingsValue	C : FundingModelIdeas	D : InitialMOOCInvestm..	E : MatchmakingforJobs	F : RelatedBooksandSu..	G : SellingCourses	H : Testir
1 : AcademicDishonesty		1	1	0	0	0	
2 : Barriers		0	0	0	0	0	
3 : CourseraPlatform		1	1	0	0	0	
4 : CurricularStructure		1	2	0	0	0	
5 : edXPlatform		0	0	0	0	0	
6 : FutureLearnPlatform		0	0	0	0	0	
7 : Gamification		0	0	0	0	0	
8 : KhanAcademyPlatform		0	0	0	0	0	
9 : MITxPlatform		0	0	0	0	0	
10 : Mobile		1	1	0	0	0	
11 : OnlineAffordances		1	1	0	0	0	
12 : OnlineLabs		0	0	0	0	0	
13 : PopularityTool		0	0	0	0	0	
14 : RedundantLearning ..		0	0	0	0	0	
15 : SocialMedia		0	0	0	0	0	
16 : StrengthsWeakness ..		1	1	0	0	0	
17 : SupportedOpenLea..		0	0	0	0	0	
18 : TechEnabler		0	0	0	0	0	
19 : TechInnovationsFor..		1	1	0	0	0	
20 : Udacity Platform		0	0	0	0	0	

Figure 63. The geospatial mapping of extracted Tweets from the AlprqAsari account on Twitter (NVivo 10)

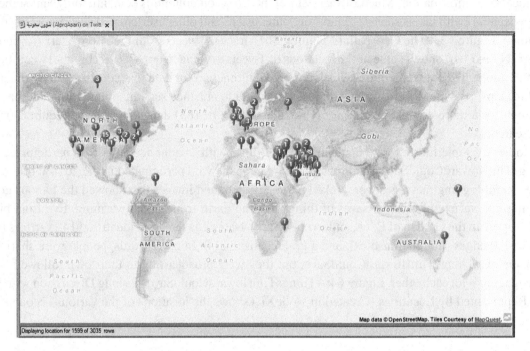

engaged in this conversation, and these are quite global, in part reflecting global fandom for soccer. This visualization shows that the locations were offered where available, but quite a few of the nodes were left unlabeled because of the sparseness of the locational information. Further, some of the locational data does not clearly relate to an identifiable physical location. (If these were to be plotted to a map with all known ways to represent information, there would be even more nodes that would not appear on that map given the lack of an identifiable way of plotting the data point on an actual map.)

DYNAMISM AND CHANGES OVER TIME

A fairly recent form of visualization is the "streamgraph," which depicts a stream of changes over time (potentially indicative of rates of change, static points-in-time, and overall trends). These are generally a form of area graph. To create this visualization, seven bi-grams were placed into Google Books Ngram Viewer in order to gain a sense of their usage over time both individually and also in relation to each other: one health, animal health, human health, environmental health, veterinary science, human medicine, and environmental science. The lines in the Ngram Viewer linegraph are incremented to a year. A user may use a mouse over to acquire the specific datapoints used for the streamgraph during any of the years. There is smoothing of 3 for the lines. (This just means that the data point on which the line is plotted is an average of the prior data point, its own data point, and the one that follows—to smooth out the jaggedness of a line without smoothing.) The Ngram Viewer has related links listed below the linegraph visualization. The concept of "one health," very broadly speaking, is that human, animal, and environmental health are inter-related, and all three should be addressed with deep understandings of the spillover effects from these respective areas.

Figure 64. #ThingsTimHowardCouldSave hashtag discussion with vertexes represented by locations (created in NodeXL)

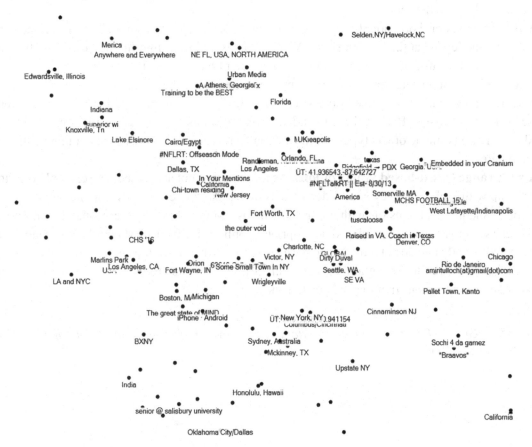

Streamgraph (Area Chart)

The data was then extracted from the "big data" extraction from Google Books Ngram Viewer at 20-year increments. That data was input into an Excel file as over-time data. The Ngram frequency counts are so small because each occurrence of the term is placed in the numerator, but the denominator is all the other words in the text corpuses for the year.

Depending on the visualization tool and the skill of the individual handling the data, there are more eye-catching streamgraphs that may be created.

Streamgraph (Dynamic and Changing Over Time)

Given the varying terminology, "streamgraph" has also been used to indicate data visualizations that describe dynamic and changing data over time. In that spirit, *Figure 68* depicts a Level 1 data crawl of the www.weather.gov site and its interrelationships over a 10,000 node search. The experience of this mapping involves nodes virtually exploding onto the screen as Maltego Tungsten maps out the links between this site and literally hundreds of other connections in structural relationships on the public

Web. This visualization captures a sense of a "stream graph" as the information is being captured live in time. The arrows pointing out from the focal node at the center give a sense of a radial diagram, with radii emanating from the center.

A 10,000-node crawl of a popular site can result in a wide range of different types of online data, as indicated by the legend at the bottom right. What results is a kind of multimodal graph, with a mix of various types of information. Users can filter out particular types of information down to specific nodes for more exploration. Further data extractions may be made using the "transforms" feature.

A variety of visualizations based on text corpuses have been highlighted here, but these were by no means comprehensive. Rather, these included a general sampling of visual structures used for text-based information (among others types of information). The conventions of visual communication were depicted here.

A wide range of text-based visualizations. As for what was not addressed, one example is a "topigraphy" map with high frequency counts depicted as high mountain elevations from an aerial view with chloropleth shading and lines (as with topography maps). Many of these other visualizations are from proprietary systems. Some are displayed on proprietary online or off-line dashboards. Some are dynamically created. Another angle not directly addressed here in any depth was the angle of "big data" analytics (except for the Google Books Ngram Viewer example). Beyond such tools, there are many other types of text-based visualizations that may be created and visualized.

Figure 65. A Google Books Ngram Viewer data run of seven bigrams related to one health (Google Books Ngram Viewer)

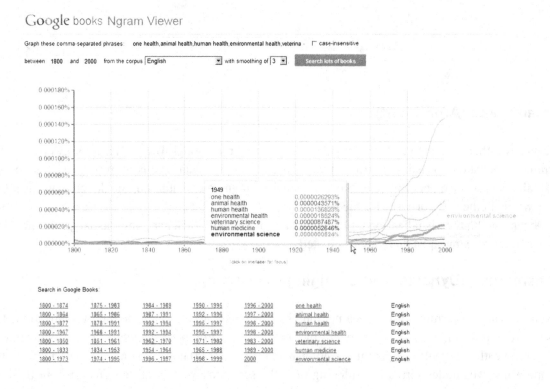

Figure 66. The extracted dataset input into Excel for the data visualization

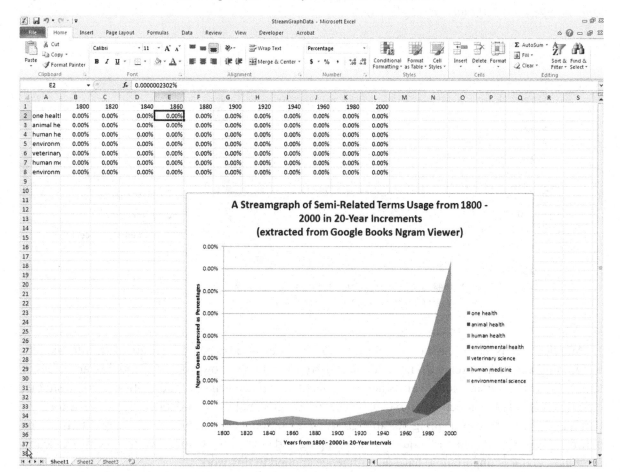

DISCUSSION

Earlier in this chapter, it was asserted that text-based visualizations are used for the following three main objectives: (1) coherent information processing of large datasets and emergent (dynamically-created) data for situational awareness; (2) latent information surfacing (finding hidden patterns and relationships that would not be perceptible otherwise); and (3) the visual-based communications of research findings to others. It is important to keep these objectives in mind during every stage of the work.

This may be a good time to bring in some points that have been referred to indirectly prior. There are a wide range of different types of static text-based data visualizations, and the underlying information that they refer to must be structured a particular way for accurate usage of the forms. Categorical data should not be treated like frequency data. Parametric analyses should not be applied to non-parametric or categorical data. (The software programs themselves will present data that is input into it even if it may not actually make sense. There is not absolute fool-proofing of these software programs against mis-use.)

Figure 67. A streamgraph of semi-related terms usage from 1800 – 2000 in 20-year increments (extracted from Google Books Ngram Viewer (Excel)

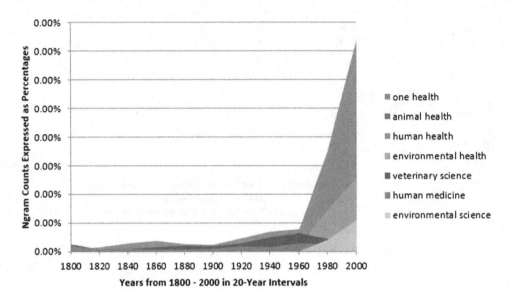

Another point is that researchers and information designers need to be selective about the information, by focusing in on what's relevant. Data do not all have value for their own sake. Oftentimes, an excess of data will introduce confusion. (This is not to say that a broad capturing of information is not desirable, only that it should be broken out into chunks for presentation and more in-depth analysis.) The temptation may be to capture everything possible given computational capability, but that may not always be optimal. Virtually all data will require some prepping and "cleaning" before they may be processed in machines, and it is important to have due diligence applied to this work.

The design of text-based data visualizations has to include consideration of data coherence and aesthetics. This means that those creating such visualizations should consider how users might interpret the data and even set baseline understandings for users to know before using the visualizations (if possible). There are understood rules for visual, auditory, animation, haptic, and other ways of communicating text-based data. There are expectations for how data measures are expressed, how data objects are labeled, how relationships are depicted, and how overviews are provided. Beyond the mainstream conventions, there are further assumptions that are unique to particular domains and research areas. It helps to know how human visual perception and close-on thinking function—such as paying attention to larger objects, color, and motion, such as inferring relationships between proxemics objects, and reading meaning into objects that may actually be unrelated because of a need to sense-make. Also, the analysis of textual visualizations will call on both left and right brain functions—the analytical, mathematical, reasoning, symbolic and verbal side, along with the holistic, intuitive, synthesizing, pattern-recognizing, and visual side (Michalko, 2006/1991, p. 36).

Ethically, they need to consider all the possible uses of the information that they are releasing even if they do not have direct control over its usage. It would be important to control for unintended meanings or inaccurate points. If anything, it's critical to show that much information is encapsulated in data visualizations. The surface simplicity is hiding a lot of underlying complexity. The design of data visualizations should avoid data lossiness. Figure 70 shows how many cells of data may resolve to no

Figure 68. A screen capture of the exploding BubbleGraph capturing live connections to www.weather. gov as a kind of StreamGraph (Maltego Tungsten 3.4.2)

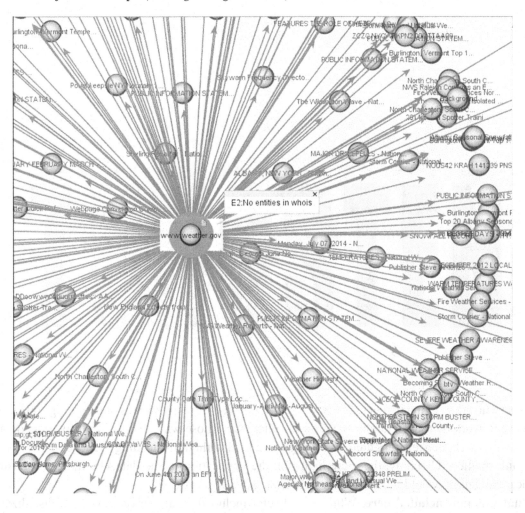

label because of the crowdedness of the dataset. (A heat treemap shows greater frequencies in the uses of the words to the left of the treempap diagram. To the middle section and the right are the terms that make up the diverse "long tail" of the word frequency counts. The unseen words will show if a user mouses over the cells.

The bubblegraph in *Figure 71:* A BubbleGraph of the @JohnKerry TweetStream (from Tableau Public) reveals even fewer text-labeled nodes than in Figure 70. This example shows just how design can affect not only the overall look-and-feel of the visualization but the amount of information that may be conveyed in a stand-alone way. Both visualizations in Figures 70 and 71 came from the same dataset and were processed in the same software tool. A lot of words that do not appear in the visualization but are accessible on the data table, which would suggest that it's a good practice to study the data in the originating dataset along with the reductionist text-based visualizations. (As an aside, a bubblegraph was also referred to as a "cartogram" in another source. The terminology is all over the map in terms of the labeling of data visualizations.)

Figure 69. A screen capture of the BubbleGraph capturing live connections to www.weather.gov as a kind of StreamGraph (Maltego Tungsten 3.4.2)

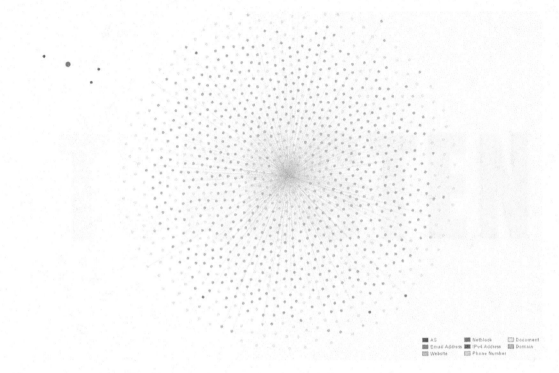

Those who are working in dynamic data systems, with fast-moving streams of incoming and outgoing text, have to work that much harder to preserve coherence. Those who deal with multivariate data also will have many challenges to lighten users' cognitive load without misleading them about the meaning of the information. Certainly, the more high-risk the application of the data, the more responsibility producers and users would have to ensure data accuracy and clarity.

What was not included here. While this chapter included a number of text-based visualizations, there were still others that were not depicted here. A common type could be a radar chart (also known as a "spider" or "star" chart) which shows descriptive attribute data about a particular thing or phenomena. Such an image would be conceptual and would represent underlying descriptive information (usually textual). A "fishbone diagram" could be used to show different "forces" acting on a phenomena or event in a visualization that represents underlying concepts (expressed in words). There are quite a few text-based data visualizations used for predictive analytics which were not included. Visualizations related to discriminant analysis, logistic regression, and neural networks were not included (but could offer plenty of insight and support to research work); the visualizations for this type of data would be various scattercharts, cluster visualizations, and node-links in the neural network branching sense. This work could have included even more complex levels of data dimensionality. Their omission was not purposeful, but the limits of a chapter (even a very extensive one) requires that some elements be omitted. The visualizations included here were offered in the spirit of sparking creative approaches, not to offer any sense of limiting possibilities.

Figure 70. A heat treemap of the @JohnKerry Twitter account TweetStream extracted with NCapture and visualized with Tableau Public

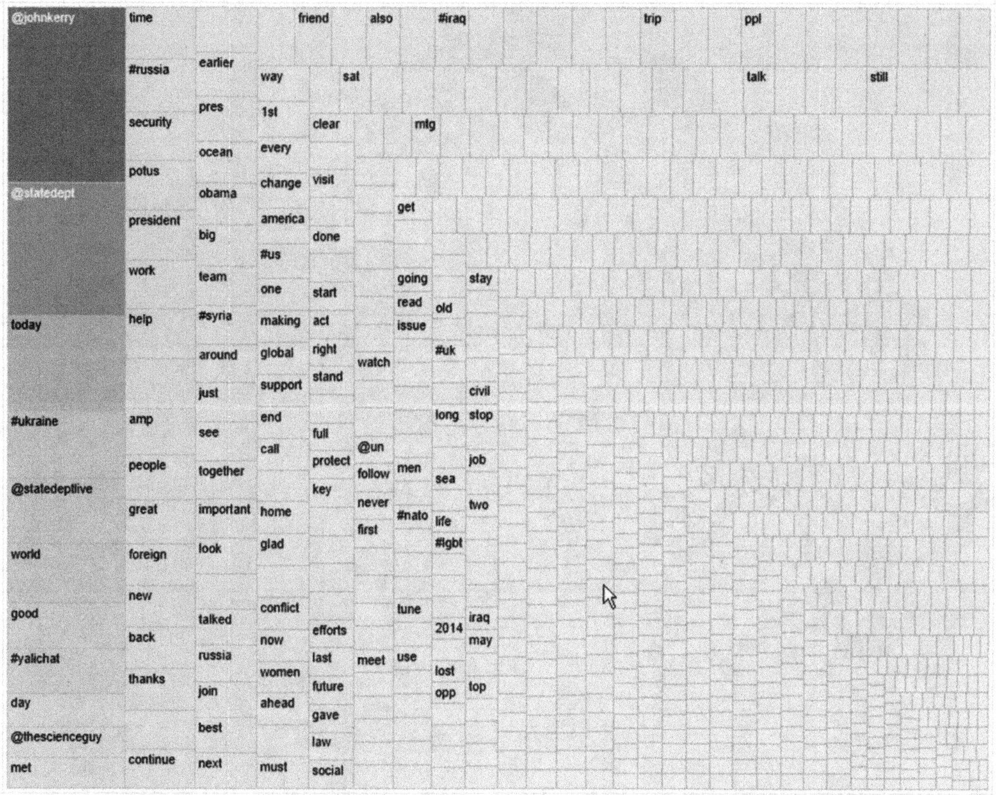

FUTURE RESEARCH DIRECTIONS

Research work in data visualizations (including text-based ones), in text analyses methods, in human-computer interactions, and other related areas are continuing at a healthy clip. It is anticipated that there will be continuing advancements in these areas.

It is hoped that many who apply such technologies to text analyses will report on their learning to encourage the usage of these and other related tools. The work of applied analysis offers a wide range of potential insights.

CONCLUSION

Finally, those who already have wide experiences with data visualizations based on research may have found some of the visualizations fairly intuitive. Text-based data visualizations, both static and dynamic, are an important part of publications, presentations, websites, social media platforms, and other communications contexts.

This is an early work on text-based data visualizations, with only a basic sampler of some of the more common text-based data visualizations that are creatable using widely available data-processing

Figure 71. A BubbleGraph of the @JohnKerry TweetStream (from Tableau Public)

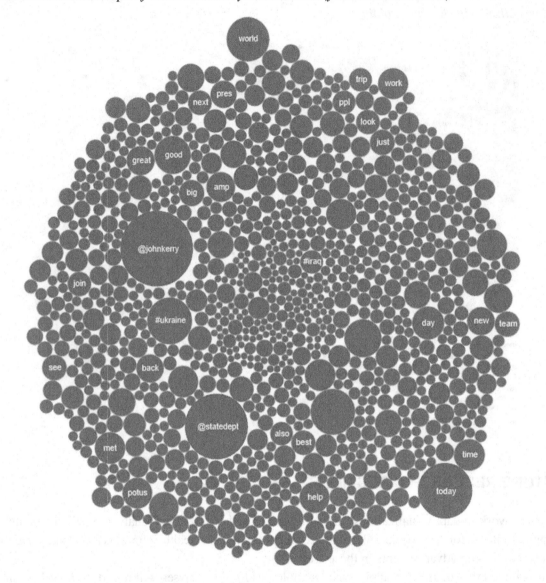

and visualization software tools. In this work, readers were familiarized with some basic samples of such visualizations and some basic ways to analyze such data at a superficial level. It is hoped that there would be greater usage of text analyses and text-based visualizations to convey information as well as a greater public sophistication and application of critical thinking in analyzing such visualizations, which are deceivingly simplistic on a surface level.

ACKNOWLEDGMENT

Thanks to Interlibrary Loan staff at K-State for their high-level of efficiency in tracking down several publications that were important to the evolution of this work. I am grateful to the makers of the various software tools that were used to create this chapter. Without these functionalities and clear documentation for their application, this work would not be possible. Thanks to the Information Technology Assistance Center (iTAC) and Kansas State University (K-State) for the space and affordances to pursue some of this work.

REFERENCES

Allen, B. L. (1998). Visualization and Cognitive Abilities. In Pauline Atherton Cochrane; Eric H. Johnson (Eds.) (1998) *Visualizing Subject Access for 21st Century Information Resources*

Beilock, S. (2010). *Choke: What the Secrets of the Brain Reveal about Getting it Right When You Have To*. New York: Free Press.

Candan, K. S., Di Caro, L., & Sapino, M. L. (2008). Creating tag hierarchies for effective navigation in social media. In the proceedings of SSM '08, Napa Valley, California. (pp. 75–82). doi:10.1145/1458583.1458597

Collins, C., & Carpendale, S. (2007). VisLink: Revealing relationships amongst visualizations. *IEEE Transactions on Visualization and Computer Graphics, 13*(6), 1192–1199. doi:10.1109/TVCG.2007.70521 PMID:17968064

Cui, W., Wu, Y., Liu, S., Wei, F., Zhou, M. X., & Qu, H. (2010). Context preserving dynamic word cloud visualization. In the proceedings of the *IEEE Pacific Visualization Symposium*, Taipei, Taiwan. doi:10.1109/PACIFICVIS.2010.5429600

Dörk, M., Williamson, C., & Carpendale, S. (2012). Navigating tomorrow's web: From searching and browsing to visual exploration. ACM Transactions on the Web: 6(3). *Article, 12*, 13–26.

Drout, M., & Smith, L. (2012). How to Read a Dendrogram. Retrieved from http://wheatoncollege.edu/lexomics/files/2012/08/How-to-Read-a-Dendrogram-Web-Ready.pdf

"Frontiers in Massive Data Analysis." (2013). National Research Council of The National Academies. Washington, D.C.: The National Academies Press.

Gilbert, J. K. (2005). Visualization: A metacognitive skill in science and science education. Visualization in Science Education. (pp. 9–27). Springer.

Gobert, J. D. (2005). Leveraging technology and cognitive theory on visualization to promote students' science. Ch. 5. In John K. Gilbert's, Visualization in Science Education: (pp. 73–90).

Hai-Jew, S. (2013, Aug. 2). Data visualization: Drawing with data, with concepts, and with rules. *Summer Institute on Distance Learning and Instructional Technology (SIDLIT) 2013*. Retrieved from http://www.k-state.edu/ID/DataVisualization/mobile_pages/DataVisualization.html

Ip, D., Keung, K. L. K., Cui, W., Qu, H., & Shen, H. (2010). A visual approach to text corpora comparison. In the proceedings of the *first international workshop on Intelligent Visual Interfaces for Text Analysis (IVITA) '10*, Hong Kong. doi:10.1145/2002353.2002361

Keim, D. A. (2002). Information visualization and visual data mining. *IEEE Transactions on Visualization and Computer Graphics*, *8*(1), 1–8. doi:10.1109/2945.981847

Keller, T., Gerjets, P., Scheiter, K., & Garsoffky, B. (2006). Information visualizations for knowledge acquisition: The impact of dimensionality and color coding. *Computers in Human Behavior*, *22*(1), 43–65. doi:10.1016/j.chb.2005.01.006

Kim, H. & Park, J.W. (2013). Topics on Bible visualization: Content, structure, citation. In the proceedings of *SIGGRAPH Asia 2013*, Hong Kong.

Michalko, M. (2nd Ed.). (2006). *Thinkertoys: A Handbook of Creative-Thinking Techniques* Berkeley: The Speed Press.

Muralidharan, A., & Hearst, M. A. (2012). A sensemaking environment for literature study. In the proceedings of *CHI 2012*. Austin, Texas. doi:10.1145/2212776.2223735

Oosterman, J., & Cockburn, A. (2010). An empirical comparison of tag clouds and tables. In the proceedings of *OZCHI 2010*. Brisbane, Australia. doi:10.1145/1952222.1952284

Pastizzo, M. J., Erbacher, R. F., & Feldman, L. B. (2002). Multidimensional data visualization. *Behavior Research Methods, Instruments, & Computers*, *34*(2), 158–162. doi:10.3758/BF03195437 PMID:12109006

Plate, B. (2013). Big data opportunities and challenges for IR, text mining and NLP. In the proceedings of Unstructured NLP. San Francisco, California.

Pousman, Z. & Stasko, J.T. (2007). Casual information visualization: Depictions of data in everyday life. *IEEE Transactspi ions on Visualization and Computer Graphics:* 13(6), 1145–1152.

Prunckun, H. (2010). *Handbook of Scientific Methods of Inquiry for Intelligence Analysis*. Lanham: The Scarecrow Press, Inc.

Roberts, J. C., & Panëels, S. (2007). Where are we with haptic visualization? In the proceedings of the *Second Joint EuroHaptics Conference and Symposium on Haptic Interfaces for Virtual Environment and Teleoperator Systems (WHC'07)*. doi:10.1109/WHC.2007.126

Rodrigues, E. M., & Milic-Frayling, N. (2011). Flickr: Linking people, photos, and tags. In L. Derek (Ed.), *Hansen, Ben Schneiderman, & Marc A. Smith's Analyzing Social Media Networks with NodeXL: Insights from a Connected World*. Amsterdam: Elsevier. doi:10.1016/B978-0-12-382229-1.00013-8

Russell, T. (2006). Cloudalicious: Folksonomy over time. In the proceedings of *JCDL '06*, Chapel Hill, North Carolina.

Salimian, M. H., Brooks, S., & Reilly, D. (2013). Examining the impact of regional familiarity and design characteristics on use of a map-based news visualization. MAPINTERACT., Orlando, Florida. doi:10.1145/2534931.2534943

Shen, Z., Ogawa, M., Teoh, S. T., & Ma, K.-L. (2006). BiblioViz: A system for visualizing bibliography information. Australian Computer Society. Asia-Pacific Symposium on Information Visualization (APVIS2006), Tokyo, Japan. *Conferences in Research and Practice in in Information Technology: 60.*

Smith, M. A. (2012, Mar. 9). NodeXL describes the networks you create: Graph Summary in v. 2013. Retrieved from http://www.connectedaction.net/2012/03/09/nodexl-describes-the-networks-you-create-graph-summary-in-v-203/

Sorapure, M. (2010). Information visualization, Web 2.0, and the teaching of writing. *Computers and Composition, 27*(1), 59–70. doi:10.1016/j.compcom.2009.12.003

Tan, A.-H. (1999). Text mining: The state of the art and the challenges. In proceedings of the PAKDD 1999 Workshop on Knowledge Discovery from Advanced Databases. Retrieved from http://www3.ntu.edu.sg/sce/labs/erlab/publications/papers/asahtan/tm_pakdd99.pdf

Thomas, J., Pennock, K., Fiegel, T., Wise, J., Pottier, M., Schur, A., et al. (1995, May). The visual analysis of textual information: Browsing large document sets. In the proceedings of the *DL '95 Conference,* Washington, DC. Retrieved from http://www.osti.gov/scitech/servlets/purl/71681

Van Eck, N. J., & Waltman, L. (2011). Text mining and visualization using VOSviewer. ISSI Newsletter, 7(3):50-54. Retrieved from http://arxiv.org/ftp/arxiv/papers/1109/1109.2058.pdf

Van Garderen, D. (2006). Spatial visualization, visual imagery, and mathematical problem solving of students with varying abilities. *Journal of Learning Disabilities, 39*(6), 496–506. doi:10.1177/002221 94060390060201 PMID:17165617

Vandenberg, S. G., & Kuse, A. R. (1978). Mental rotations, a group test of three-dimensional spatial visualization. *Perceptual and Motor Skills, 47*(2), 599–604. doi:10.2466/pms.1978.47.2.599 PMID:724398

Viégas, F.B. & Wattenberg, M. (2008). Tag clouds and the case for vernacular visualization. *Forum Timelines.* 49 – 52.

Viégas, F.B., Wattenberg, M., & Feinberg, J. (2009). Participatory visualization with Wordle. In the proceedings of IEEE Transactions on Visualization and Computer Graphics, 15(6), (pp. 1137 – 1144).

Wagner, W., Valencia, J., & Elejabarrieta, F. (1996). Relevance, discourse and the 'hot' stable core of social representations—A structural analysis of word associations. *The British Journal of Social Psychology, 35*(3), 331–351. doi:10.1111/j.2044-8309.1996.tb01101.x

Ware, C. (2012). Visual thinking processes. Ch. 11. In Ware's Information Visualization: Perception for Design. Elsevier. 375 – 423.

Wei, F., Liu, S., Song, Y., Pan, S., Zhou, M. X., Qian, W., et al. (2010). TIARA: A visual exploratory text analytic system. In the proceedings of *Knowledge Discovery and Datamining (KDD) '10.* Washington, D.C. doi:10.1145/1835804.1835827

Yi, J. S., Kang, Y. A., Stasko, J. T., & Jacko, J. A. (2007). Toward a deeper understanding of the role of interaction in information visualization. *IEEE Transactions on Visualization and Computer Graphics, 13*(6), 1224–1231. doi:10.1109/TVCG.2007.70515 PMID:17968068

Yuan, X., Zhang, X., & Trifmovsky, A. (2010). Testing visualization on the use of information systems. In the proceedings of *Information Interaction in Context Symposium (IIiX) 2010*, New Brunswick, New Jersey, USA. doi:10.1145/1840784.1840840

Zipf's law. (2014, June 18). *Wikipedia*. Retrieved from http://en.wikipedia.org/wiki/Zipf%27s_law

ADDITIONAL READING

Hansen, D. L., Schneiderman, B., & Smith, M. A. (2011). *Analyzing Social Media Networks with NodeXL: Insights from a Connected World*. Amsterdam: Elsevier.

The NodeXL Graph Gallery. (n.d.). Retrieved from http://nodexlgraphgallery.org/Pages/Default.aspx

KEY TERMS AND DEFINITIONS

2D: Two-dimensional space represented on the x and y axes.

3D: Three-dimensional space represented on the x, y, and z axes.

Affinity Diagram: A form of cluster diagram.

Alerting: Signifying the importance of attention or vigilance towards something relevant.

Application Programming Interface (API): Tools and resources in an operating system (such as a social media platform) that enable access to some of the system's select data and functionalities through specialized software applications.

Autocoding: Automated machine-based coding of data (in either a machine-learning / unsupervised way based on human-emulation or a fully-automated way based on rules).

Brainstorming Diagram (Mind Map / Concept Map): A text visualization which captures a brainstorming outline or spatial organizational structure of a concept map (an idea-based structure).

Cluster: The grouping of words and phrases based on some similarity measure.

Collocation: The "arbitrary" patterned juxtaposition of words and word combinations often unique to particular languages; the recurring placement of words in close proximity as institutionalized phrases.

Corpus: A collection of written texts of any kind (sometimes based around a particular subject).

Data Cube: A 3D data representation, often indicating time series data.

Data Matrix: A table of related data (such as bigrams).

Data Visualization: A 2D or 3D physical representation created from data.

Data Spinning: The rotation of data points in 3D space (on the x, y, and z axes) in either an automated (passive) or user-determined (active) way.

Decomposition: The decontextualization of language by breaking up the text and corpuses into atomistic parts (like words and phrases as n-grams).

Dendrogram: A tree diagram ("tree drawing") showing branching hierarchical clustering around related words and phrases.

Disambiguation: Removing ambiguity to arrive at an accurate definition or meaning.

Facet: A specific angle or dimension of a multi-dimensional phenomenon.

Fidelity: Accuracy of a depiction or model or reproduction to the original, exactitude.

Granularity: Scale of detail; a particular unit of analysis.

Graph: A diagram showing relationships between variables (and descriptive quantities).

Hashtag: A string of text preceded by a # hashtag or pound sign to indicate multimedia contents or messages related to a specific topic (used on social media sites); a kind of machine labeling.

Heatmap: A 2D treemap with values represented by color intensities (higher intensities represent greater frequencies) similar to a chloropleth map (which is shaded or patterned based on a particular statistical measure).

Histogram: A graph of a frequency distribution [with regular widths of class intervals on the x-axis (horizontal) and frequencies on the y axis (vertical)] ; the total area of the histogram is equal to the number of data and shows the overall distribution curve of the data.

Isomorphism: Equivalency of form, the fidelity of a depiction to the original.

Latent: Hidden, non-obvious, undiscovered, concealed, not manifest.

Motif: A subgraph of a patterned relationship in a network (often captured in network motif censuses).

Natural Language Processing (NLP): The study of computing and human languages, drawing from computer science, linguistics, and artificial intelligence (with wide practical applications in discourse analysis, machine translation, optical character recognition, sentiment analysis, and information retrieval).

N-Gram: A contiguous sequence of n (number of) words (in a sequential string) in a text document or corpus, what one researcher has called a "short range sequential" pattern.

Parse: Syntactic analysis; to analyze a text by breaking it up into its various structural parts (such as parts of speech).

Part-of-Speech: The category defining the syntactic role of a word.

Provenance: The origin and "chain of custody" of a dataset (with implications for its informational value and validity).

Pruning: The selective deletion of particular branches and clusters in a graph in order to shape a data visualization.

Scatterplot (Scatter Diagram, Scattergraph): A 2D or 3D depiction that maps data points based values for two variables for a dataset to aid in the search for correlations (whether positive or negative or null), a visual depiction of a linear regression.

Semantic: Meaning-bearing words, phrases (contiguous word strings), and symbols.

Spatial Imagery: A visual depiction or representation that indicates the spatial relationships between parts of an object or scene, or the location of objects in physical space.

Stemming (of Words): The act of reducing or simplifying inflected words to their root form (for a defined basic meaning).

Stopwords (Delete) List: A list of terms and phrases which are filtered out of a dataset of text; a delete list.

Stream Graph: A stacked area graph based around a central axis indicating word or term frequency (and other phenomena) over time (with time usually indicated on the x-axis).

Structure Mining: The analysis of interrelationships to create new understandings.

Structured Text Data: Data that is pre-labeled and organized in a fixed field as part of a record.

Stylometry: The quantitative- and statistics-based analyses of writing to identify authorship and produce insights about particular texts and text corpuses (such as those from particular genres).

Syntactic: Related to the structure of language through words and phrases.

Tag Cloud: A visual diagram of user-generated tags (folksonomy) describing contents on the Web and Internet.

Term Map: A word-based visualization that uses the physical distance between terms as an indication of their relatedness; may be 2D or 3D.

Text: Formal (and informal) writing based on conventional (and unconventional) forms of written communications.

Text Corpus: A collection of texts, usually as unstructured data.

Text Mining: The exploration of text and text corpuses for information.

Tokenization: The breaking down of writing into meaningful elements called "tokens" for machine analysis of text.

Topigraphy: The visual representation of a topical data structure as a topographical map (a play on the word "topography").

Transcode: Conversion of information from one type of code to another (as from statistical data based on text to a visualization).

Treemap: The display of hierarchical data through nested rectangles (with higher frequencies of data expressed as larger-area rectangles).

Unit of Analysis: The granularity or scale of the entity being studied.

Unstructured Text Data: Text in its original form or in the wild without any *a priori* or fixed data structuring (for a database or other data-processed form).

Visualization: A 2D or 3D physical representation (diagrams, graphs, charts, maps, and other forms) depicting concepts, data, rules, or models.

Visual imagery: The depiction of the outer or surface visual appearance of an object.

Word Art: An artistically rendered visualization based on words or alphanumeric characters.

Word Cloud: A 2D diagram of words, with larger-size words indicating a higher frequency count (and possible importance or centrality in the text document or text corpus).

Word Frequency Count: The number of times a word or phrase appears in a text or text corpus (based on machine count).

Word Tree: A structured or hierarchical diagram consisting of words and phrases.

Chapter 8
Using Microsites as Live Presentation Platforms
(with Three Embedded Real-World Cases)

Shalin Hai-Jew
Kansas State University, USA

ABSTRACT

Live presentations in academic conferences often link to online resources for preview or post-view. Microsites may enhance live and real-time presentations. To examine the human factors and software challenges involved, this chapter offers three real-world partial solutions for interactive microsites that serve multiple purposes. This article focuses on the use of SoftChalk as a core authoring tool to create microsites for live presentations. Three real-world and unique cases (all from 2012) are showcased here: "Using Tableau Public for (Spatial and Trendline) Data Visualization (An Early Exploration and 'TMI' Musing on Data)" at https://softchalkcloud.com/lesson/rtNYCf1K80el9w; "Building and Analyzing Node-Link Diagrams to Understand Social Networks" at https://softchalkcloud.com/lesson/c4d8tSWMCwm39n; and "Building Effective Study Guides for Online Learning and Assessment" at https://softchalkcloud.com/lesson/rFnD0AQX3xRVTa.

INTRODUCTION

In academia and professional contexts, there are requirements for creating live presentations to share information with colleagues. Most live presentations involve some digital residuals, such as links to websites, videos from the presentation, or downloadable slideshows. A new approach involves the uses of microsites (small and targeted-purpose websites) for the lead-up period to a presentation (to raise interest), during the presentation (to offer interactive and rich information), and after the presentation (as post-event reference and as a general resource developed via Web and Internet). These sites may be similar to "digital poster sessions" except that they are designed also for live use, not just for the automated presentation of information without human facilitation (as if often the case with digital poster sessions).

DOI: 10.4018/978-1-4666-8696-0.ch008

THE CHALLENGES OF LIVE PRESENTATIONS AND STRETCHING TIME

The challenges of this professional organization and its membership are similar to others who host live conferences with synchronous events held. The participants of the conference may want to attend multiple synchronous events and are forced to wrangle other ways to benefit from multiple real-time events. For presenters to build presentational microsites that are used in both the F2F presentations and in enriched archived format, they may enable conference-goers to benefit by learning from multiple presenters by using "off-time" to review the presentational multimedia materials. Going beyond the limits of a slide-show means that the conference goers may experience a closer-to-the-live and full-sensory experience than reviewing static or non-interactive traditional presentation materials.

The Rationales for a Microsite

There are a number of straightforward rationales for using a presentational microsite instead of a tradi-tional slideshow or more traditional method of presentation. Critics have long pointed out short-comings of various slideshow tools, which are said to force users to "separate content and analysis" and reduce "concepts to meaningless bullets" and force "strict, unneeded hierarchies"; further, data resolution and visual reasoning are impoverished because information is distributed over time "instead of adjacently over space" (Lanir, Booth, & Findlater, 2008, p. 696). Microsites may be used to mitigate some of these concerns because the work space is not the size of a slide—but of sequential web pages—with a range of non-linear presentation methods and interactive functions. If there is sufficient information and mul-timedia resources, a microsite could be used to encapsulate and present that complexity.

Depth and Variety of Digital Information: The amount of content that may be presented using a microsite is much greater than what may be placed inside a slideshow. A microsite itself may contain multiple slideshows, for example. Information may be presented in a range of ways. Iframes, inline keyframes in interframe HTML compression, may enable the encapsulating of live websites within the presentation; this capability enables the integration of real-time updates to capture the ephemerality of the WWW and Internet. Various multimedia—video, audio, photos and images, diagrams, simulations, and interactive games—may be integrated into a microsite. Web 2.0 technologies like wikis and blogs may be linked into a microsite. Microsites offer a much larger canvas than a slideshow. Alternate non-linear presentation structures may be used, such as image maps or hyperlinked spatial mapping outlines or interactive interfaces. Further, all these elements may be brought together in a coherent and packaged way, with sequencing and navigation. Those who want to be more sophisticated may draw data from live sensors or databases—as part of the presentation. **Counterpoint:** In live presentations, people may use a variety of contents from various sites and offline from their computers. The presenter could create coherence between the objects through their presentation. However, after the presentation, there is no packaged coherent site to visit. There may have been a video or audio capture of the event.

Ease of Build: Modern-day authoring tools are relatively easy to use to create a microsite. Those who regularly build digital contents as part of their daily work may find this just a regular part of a work day. The culture of the WWW and Internet also promotes less formal uses of these spaces as needed. There does not have to be a sense of occasion to the creation of microsites.

Increased Digital Object Lifespan and Reusability: For some conferences, the organizers will publish papers in a related journal, or they will submit vetted papers for archival in repositories. However, for smaller host organizations and colleges, there are no resources for such publishing. Or the repositories have limited indexing and general access. Often, conferences do not include published works. For many practitioners, the rigors and formal structured writing of publishing may be off-putting. Presentational microsites are a much more free-form structure, and their inherent nature enables the expansion of their possible usage on the Web and Internet. Such sites may be used prior to a live event to introduce topics and draw audience members; during the live F2F event for the actual presentation, and after the event—both in the near-term and the long-term for other "use cases". The design challenge for designers is to design presentational microsites in a flexible way that enables its use in a live F2F presentation context and in digital archival format.

The following is a comparison table of some of the basic needs. This table is informed by common expectations of face-to-face presentations and of destination microsites. The challenge assumes that the designer has access to the typical parts of a digital software set for audio, video, diagram, and photo capture and editing; desktop lecture capture tools; animation software; and other pieces of a basic design IT skill set.

The central authoring tool that will be described is SoftChalk, which offers a range of tools for creating interactive games and learning experiences. The tool enables the building of stand-alone objects. However, it also enables the creation of entire web sites, with or without a design overlay, and with or without a navigational table of contents (TOC) / structural outline and named pagination structure. (Live presentations do not usually begin with the dry TOC but usually the first link or landing page.) This authoring tool allows for the tagging of text with various levels of headings—for data hierarchies—which enhance a sense of coherence and structure. This tool enables the integration of various types of media: audio, video, animations, slideshows, various text file types, web links, and other elements. The various integrated Web objects may be labeled with metadata and supplemented with accessibility information.

The activities in this tool include over a dozen different types of interactive Flash objects: Charts, Crossword, DidYouKnow, DragNDrop, Flash Card, Hot Spot, Jigsaw Puzzle, Labeling, Ordering, Photo Album, Seek A Word, Slideshow, Sorting, Tabbed Info, and Timeline. Further, to enhance the experiences for mobile users, all created sites are automatically output with a mobile-friendly version, and there are a half-dozen mobile-friendly activities templates in HTML 5 (which emulate some of the Flash objects, which are not currently accessible on iPads and iPhones). The tool's Iframe functionality enables access

Table 1. A comparison table of the F2F presentation demands and online user demands of a microsite

Face-to-Face (F2F) Presentation Demands of the Microsite	Online User Demands of the Microsite
• Visually engaging • Interactive • Coherence and smooth transitions • Clear sequencing • Easy navigation • Sufficient screen resolution • Low latency in video demonstrations • Non-distracting excess information • Flexibility in terms of presenter pacing • Transitions and live bridging • Visual examples	• Original and valuable contents making it a destination site • Self-explanatory (by being fairly comprehensive and informative; designed against negative learning) • Legal (IP, privacy rights, no libel, no defamation, no slander) • Accessible (alt-texts, transcripts) • Navigable and searchable • Technological file transcoding / distillation; file versioning • Proper labeling with metadata • Mobile-friendly • Low latency or time delay in video playback • A legible print version • Downloadable resources; linked resources • Findable on the WWW and Internet; archivable into the future

to the Web and Internet, for open-source and other types of sites, visuals (2D and simulated 3D), videos and animations, and interactivity. The authoring tool overall enables the uses of composite mixed-media digital objects. This tool also allows the creation of various interactive questions and quizzes.

The microsite may be packaged and output with a range of reusability-based object wrappers (Common Cartridge, CD, SCORM 1.2, SCORM 2004, and others) for easier machine identification and sequencing. Finally, the makers of SoftChalk also have launched a SoftChalk Cloud service, a virtual repository of digital learning objects that may be openly shared by others if released through Creative Commons licensure, or may be archived on the Web but kept private. The public versions may be downloadable from the Web as integrated zipped (highly portable) folders of digital contents that may be hosted on other Web servers, and if the proper rights releases are available, such learning objects may even be editable for greater reusability. These affordances enhance the potential shelf life of the microsites and digital learning objects.

BUILDING PRESENTATIONAL MICROSITES

The structure of this chapter is built around a core question of how to design, develop, and use a presentational microsite. This essential question is a strategic one surrounding the design and development of presentation microsites and then their strategic use in F2F contexts.

At the macro level. Some relevant initial questions at this level could include the following:

- What technologies would be particularly effective for presentational microsites, and why?
- What are some important features to include on presentation micro sites?
- How may such microsites be made appealing prior to a conference? During a conference? After a conference?
- What are ways to add value to the presentational microsite during the F2F presentation? Post presentation?
- What checklist items should appear on a list for evaluating presentational microsites? Why?

At the micro level. This chapter is informed by three specific real-world cases in which microsites were created for both live presentation and Internet archival. These three cases are introduced in granular detail. These sites (partial or pseudo solutions) are live and currently hosted and available. Another angle to this chapter may involve the critique of these designed sites. Some relevant questions could include the following:

- How effective or ineffective were the specific cases? Why?
- How effectively were the different software programs? Elaborate.
- What were the apparent effects of the domain contents on the resulting presentation microsites?
- What strategies were apparent in analyzing the presentational microsites?

Actual reusability. These presentational microsites may be used to draw an audience to a live event, by priming them for the live interactions. During the event, microsites may be used for a variety of presentational and interactive uses. After an event, microsites may be used to not only commemorate the event but reinforce the learning from the event. Further, public microsites enable individuals who did not even participate in the conference from benefitting from the event. In this sense, presentational microsites work as digital poster sessions to advertise and augment a live conference or event. Figure 1, "A Screenshot of the SoftChalk 7 Authoring Tool and its Activities Options," provides a view of the design workspace in SoftChalk.

This work showcases three actual microsites (created using SoftChalk®) used for live academic presentations on three disparate topics. All three presentational microsites were created for multiple usages for higher versatility. They were all used in live F2F presentations as complement to the live speaker, but they were also used as substitute presentations for individuals who did not attend the actual presentation.

THREE MICROSITES FOR RECENT LIVE PRESENTATIONS

Public presentations involve the nexus between researchers, the domain field, and the particular hosting organization. To set the context, the relevant organization is described here in broad terms.

Organizational background. The relevant organization is a professional educational one that has approximately a 500-member list from institutions of higher education and government agencies from both Kansas and Missouri. This organization does not have a membership cost. It hosts a summer confer-

Figure 1. A screenshot of the SoftChalk 7 authoring tool and its activities options

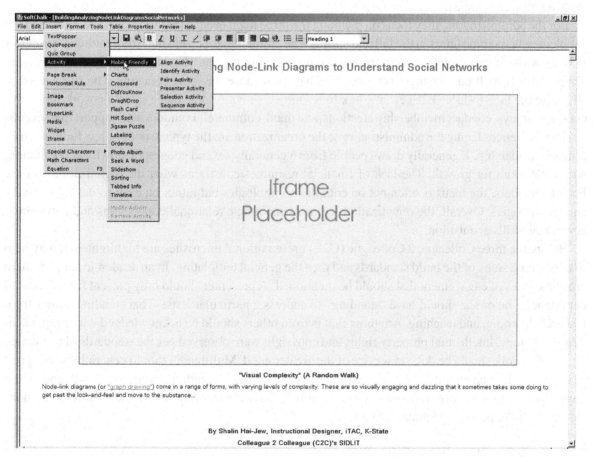

ence for its members along with two smaller symposiums—one in the summer and one in the fall. Those interested in presenting submit proposals for presentations, which are vetted by the leadership in the organization, and a percentage of the submittals are accepted. Those presenters then create a presentation for their 50-minute face-to-face presentations. These are usually held in classrooms or conference rooms (and sometimes, auditoriums). Presenters usually have access to the organization's website (where the descriptions of their presentations are offered) and then digital projectors, computers, and whiteboards in the presentation venues.

The culture of this organization is highly academic in an applied sense. Its members come from the Midwest, particularly Kansas and Missouri. As is characteristic of many in academia, there is a skepticism about commercial vendors and their motives, but such vendors play a critical role in funding the three main events and other endeavors of this group.

This volunteer organization has a long history of supportive camaraderie among its members. Most of its members are practitioners in their various fields. Their preferences for technologies are free, open-source, and widely available. They often pursue so-called "low-hanging fruit" because of the low cost of adoption and the low learning curve. Academic research and publishing are practiced by some of its members, but not typically among the main membership.

The group's members are all working in situations of economic constraints. The professional culture is one of good will and sharing. Its members are very open to helping each other out in a pinch. However, the challenge is that the technologies that the various organizations use are highly divergent, and given the breadth of information technology (IT), the membership are generally all working with a wide range of different technologies.

For the administrators, they focus on planning the three main events, the summer conference, and the supplementary symposiums in the fall and spring. The administrators, who hail from multiple campuses in Kansas, use Internet telephone conferencing tools to communicate. They occasionally meet in person. Their website, built on a Django infrastructure, has been cause for some concerns. The site is used to advertise the face-to-face (F2F) events, link to resources, provide some basic social network functions, conduct surveys, conduct membership elections, and thank commercial vendors who support their events.

The challenges facing the administrators of the organization are the typical ones of low funding and a transient leadership. It generally draws people from a generally set and geographically local population, with little room for growth. The lack of financial resources constrains what the organization can do. For its members, the focus is often not on complex technologies but rather on easy-to-deploy software and technologies. Overall, the organization seems to encourage relational connections and networking above new skills acquisition.

Before the three Colleague 2 Colleague (C2C) presentational microsites are highlighted, it may help to understand some of the build standards and then the general templating. In an academic context, there are some rules of engagement that should be mentioned. A presenter should only present from firsthand experiences: he or she should have "standing" to address a particular issue. That standing comes from research, learning, and teaching. Anything that is from others should be acknowledged with proper academic citations. Intellectual property rights and copyright were observed per the standards of academia.

Finally, work should be done in service of the greater good. Multimedia should generally be designed to align with human cognition, for the optimal learning effects, through the auditory, visual, and tactile channels to engage the working memory and to ultimate have the learning stored into long-term memory (Moreno, 2006, p. 64). The author notes:

Modality: Students learn better from words and graphics when words are spoken rather than printed

Verbal redundancy: Students learn better from graphics and narration than from graphics and redundant narration and text.

Temporal contiguity: Students learn better with concurrent rather than successive corresponding words and graphics.

Spatial contiguity: Students learn better when multiple sources of visual information are integrated rather than separated.

Coherence: Students learn better when extraneous material is excluded rather than included in a lesson.

Multimedia: Students learn better from words and graphics than from words alone.

Personalization: Students learn better when explanations are personalized rather than nonpersonalized.

Guidance: Novice students learn better when given principle-based explanations than they do when asked to infer principles by themselves.

Interactivity: Students learn better by manipulating the materials rather than by passively observing others manipulate the materials.

Reflections: Students learn better when given opportunities to reflect during the meaning-making process. (Moreno, 2006, p. 65)

Some of the above issues (spatial contiguity, coherence, multimedia, interactivity, and reflection) were built into the microsite design; others (modality, verbal redundancy, temporal contiguity, personalization, and guidance) were handled through the live presentational aspects. This quick analysis would suggest that presentational microsites meet various needs in different contexts and in so doing may leave gaps in different use case contexts. Finally, the microsites were informed by some of the conventions of enriched slideshow production, with sequential clicking forward through the contents, but also the ability to scroll down pages; the design of digital learning objects using multimedia conventions; digital galleries and collections; website design, and print article conventions. (A version of the presentation may be printed based on SoftChalk, so the work has to make sense even in print form.)

In terms of the basic templating structure, each microsite started with a table of contents / textual outline (a feature of opt-in styles in SoftChalk). The first page (index) of the site is the landing page which includes the presentation title, the event, the date, the content summary (of what's to follow), and some preliminary information. Also, those mostly began with audience self-introductions. The microsites followed a sequential and developmental sequence unique to the topics. All three microsites involved iframes to external sources, many with downloadable resources. All three involved some degree of interactivity (with questions, discussion points, examples, and simple cases) and multi-sensory experiential learning. (The archived sites themselves could be used by individuals who would be encouraged to consider the interactivity points and ideas themselves.) Finally, each microsite wrapped with contact information and the invitation to discuss and / or even collaborate.

In terms of designing for the live F2F presentation, the visuals were mostly explanatory and descriptive. A few were included for conversational points and design. The presentation sites were not made to show up the presenter but to augment the talk and to encourage the live audience to visit the sites later for additional exploration. The questions that the audience brought up, post-event research, access to new resources post-event, and other factors meant all three microsites were updated after the event. (All three events were downloaded on the laptop in the event the Internet connection failed, which would have resulted in the same online experience except for the access to websites through Iframes.)

All three presentations were hosted in the SoftChalk Cloud and in a mirror site at the university in case of potential inaccessibility of the Cloud. The author took the approach that a presentation involves a short period of presentation to a small group of individuals, with a window of intense attention. For the work to have value, it must be made accessible into the future, and for that purpose, it must be hosted and preserved throughout its life cycle with a trusted source. (Built into the microsites were metadata describing the various objects and textual annotations / alt texting or alternate texting for accessibility.)

Case 1: Spatial and Trendline Data Visualization

Figure 2 shows some of the contextualization of the opening page of this microsite. The first case spotlighted a free and publicly available tool to educators that plots geographical information on a map. The purpose of this presentation was to show some of the academic uses of this tool for people involved in education. Further, this presentation focused on the uses of data visualizations and the elusiveness of extrapolating meanings from the data—to encourage cautious use of data visualizations (with an awareness of the data provenance).

The archived microsite for "Using Tableau Public for (Spatial and Trendline) Data Visualization (An Early Exploration and 'TMI' Musing on Data)" is available here: https://softchalkcloud.com/lesson/rtNYCf1K80el9w (Hai-Jew, 2012). The outline of the presentation is available at the landing page of

Figure 2. The opening screen of the Tableau Public data visualization microsite

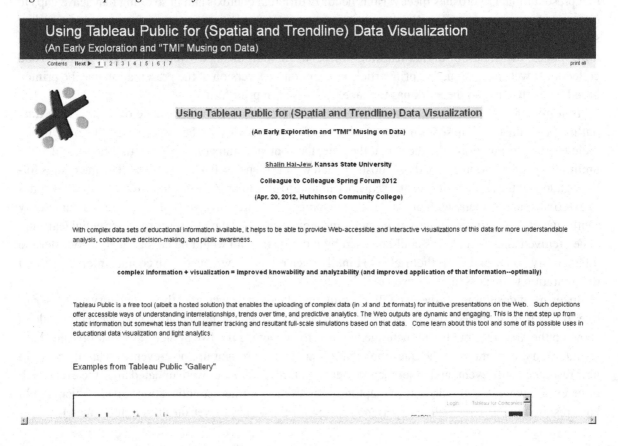

the microsite. The microsite was designed with the assumption that the users were not individuals who dealt with data sets or data visualizations on a regular basis. The presentation started out with some definitions of terminologies and descriptions of the parts of data sets and visualizations. The landing page gave some ideas for how visual analytics add value. A part of the presentation follows in the bulleted list.

How Do Visual Analytics Add Value?

- Is easier to understand (than reams of raw numerical data)
- offers multiple learning channels (visual, textual / symbolic, kinesthetic)
- enables interactivity with changing variable values
- enables some distance to see patterns and relationships

Then, individuals could look at screenshots of some of the open-source galleried data visualizations in Tableau Public. (These were annotated using Microsoft Visio to help readers understand the various views of the dashboard in Tableau Public.)

The next page offered a backgrounder on electronic data and some controversial points on its collection and use. There was a brief "TMI" overview on data collection and the rigorous methods used in academia for valid information. In this section, there was an animation (created in Adobe AfterEffects) showing floating frames coalescing around a particular issue. This animation made the point of the need for information surveillance around certain topics with an ultimate focus on particular aspects of the data. (The timings on the keyframes of this were set for the live talker. A person just viewing the microsite post-conference likely would not have made as much sense of this as those in attendance.) To continue the discussion on data, Nassim Nicholas Taleb's "black swan" argument about the inefficacies of the bell curve assumptions were addressed. The purpose was to help participants question data and its actual relation to reality.

The next page involved the creation of a classic data array or structure for use with spatializing data visualization tools. Participants could see a 2D image of an annotated Excel file for where information should go, and there were ideas on where academics could find open-source or publicly available data for analysis. Then, there followed the explication of the geographic coordinate system and spatiality, with the quip: "The world is mapped." (It is.) Several vivid images were used to indicate how spatiality is described, using open-source imagery. Then, there was the interactive question: "Why does spatiality matter?" To illustrate this point, a bright red spot was used with the common term: "You are here" as seen on any number of maps. A number of examples of how spatiality matters (from academia and professional realms) were listed. In another section, why spatiality matters for online instructors was added. (The revised microsite included insights from the audience.) To illustrate, the author used a mock data set from a local university. This unique information was not only de-identified but also falsified in order to make the data impossible to be re-identified. The mock data was fully expressed using the software, with multiple views of the data. (This was an interactive dashboard, which enabled some interactive engagement). The next page offered a list of open-source data sets, mostly from the U.S. government.

The next page offered a back-end view of Tableau Public and a slideshow showing how to download it and to start using it. There were step-by-step directions for how to clean data and then to upload and visualize datasets.

The microsite wrapped with a page of Iframes showing more complex spatialized data, such as that of Gapminder, US Geological Survey global visualizations (and their data warehouse), the OIE's WAHID interface with animal disease distribution maps, the US CDC's Arbonet maps, and big data analysis sites.

Case 2: Social Network Visualizations through Node-Link Diagrams

Figure 3 shows the dazzling visual impact of a number of social network diagrams on the visual complexity site, which is set in an Iframe.

"Building and Analyzing Node-Link Diagrams to Understand Social Networks" is available at https://softchalkcloud.com/lesson/c4d8tSWMCwm39n (Hai-Jew, 2012). An outline is available at the landing page of the site. The rationale behind the complexity and fullness of this presentation came from both the nature of social network analysis (SNA) and the need to support the proper intuitions and instincts about this research approach. With data visualizations, especially, viewers may make incorrect assumptions about the data and go unchallenged. To strive for user clarity, the designer worked to show a longer end-to-end explanation of the process of research using social network analysis. In the same way, Analytic Technologies' UCINET and NetDraw, the main software referred to, have a fairly straightforward interface but plenty of complexity beneath (with complex statistical analysis applied to the data). These challenges existed already independent of the presentational approach.

Figure 3. The opening screen of the node-link diagrams microsite

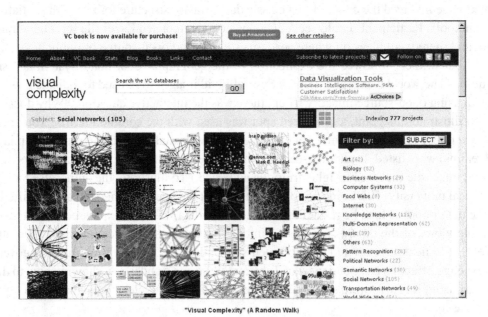

Contextualization and interest. The opening page of this presentation began with an eye-catching graphic, a range of social network visuals from the visual complexity site. In the live presentation, this site was used as a conversation starter to introduce the glitzy world of node-link diagram visualizations in full real-world applications, color, depth, and informativeness. The presenter then went to provide an overview of the presentation and encouraged the audience to describe their own interests in the topic (the ice breaker).

In the next page, the presentation microsite offered a basic introduction to social networks by explaining the constituent parts of the visualization. There were Iframes to live sites to show how such node-link diagrams are used beyond social networks (such as in content analysis, neural networks, and other applications). Then, the presentation was applied to node-link diagrams as applied to social networks. The presentation segued to the basics of social network research, in a basic step-by-step approach. The rationale was to help learners see how researchers arrived at the eye-catching social networks. Not only were these steps spelled out in a numbered list, but there was also a visual 2D workflow to explain the process of social network research. Finally, the point was made that social network analysis is done to both explain and predict. Those are tough standards for any kind of research. (This information was offered to offset the glamour of the visualization with some well grounded facts.)

The next page dealt with how to read sociograms and sociomatrixes. This was all about interpretation. This touched on the micro and macro levels of units of analyses. Further, this addressed how complex information could be mechanistically layered into node-link diagrams (sequences, data overlays, and dynamic displays). The participants were introduced to various types of sociogram visualizations (of which node-link diagrams are one), including dendrograms, block diagrams, and adjacency matrices. Then, some basic types of node-link diagrams were introduced: a regular node-link social network, a ring lattice, and then a two-mode network (involving both entity and event nodes, along with relationships). Further, the presenter showcased the importance of understanding the social context. She addressed the various analytical tools used in social networking software tools to analyze the centrality of a node; draw out patterns; identify structural strengths and weak points in a social network; and offer descriptors about large-scale or remote social networks. She made a point about the history of social network research and showed the influences of subject domains on how this analytical tool was used.

In the next page, the presenter offered some of the sociological thinking behind social networks: the types of relationships; the types of non-kin social networks, the nature of small world networks (and their relevance), and the "transmissible" elements moving through a social network. A "Let's Talk" discussion box at the bottom of the page focused on the audience members' own social networks (professional and personal); the work of designing a virtual work team (and what strategies could be applied); the strategies for how to de-link if something undesirable was moving through the network; and then a strategy for how to insert oneself into a desired social network.

The next few pages were focused on specific domain field applications of social network analysis to enable more in-depth analysis. The next page focused on more in-depth information about the diffusion of innovation (or "contamination") in a social network. This is conceptualized as the movement of transmissible elements through certain parts of the network more susceptible in the transmissible element. Nodes have varying susceptibilities to the element being transmitted, but they are generally influenced by the other nodes in their ego neighborhoods. The aim of many marketing endeavors is to identify accelerators for diffusion in order to target efforts. Diffusion can be positive in some ways but also negative in others (such as groupthink in which ideas are contagious and may lead a group in a wrong direction). This page included a curve showing accelerated diffusion in a network once a certain threshold amount of individuals in the network were "contaminated". For this part of the presentation, the audience considered some phenomena such as "the madness of crowds," marketing "cool hunting" (in search of trend setters), the concept of "going viral," the experience of being infected by an innovation, and the work of profiling a virtual group which may be sparked by a "diffusion of participation."

The next page focused on population health: the spread of some diseases along social lines and the work of disease detectives (epidemiologists) using contact tracing (to find the origins of diseases, if possible) and public health practitioners (working to promote herd immunities and health). The presentation participants focused on the work of social network strategies to disrupt or stop a disease contagion (theoretically). They considered how to prevent infection from an ego or node perspective.

The next section focused on the selectorate theory of power. This concept assumes that leaders tend to work hardest for those to whom they are beholden for their power, labeled here as "essentials." In the next concentric circle out from the center are the influentials, who may affect a leader's power but generally not in a big way. Finally, there are the interchangeables, or the constituents who experience the power of a leader but who have little sway over his / her decision-making. The context of power served as a segue for the discussion of social networking's brokerage roles and the ways that people may use a social structure to enhance their own power base, such as by playing nodes off against each other (as in a "*tertius gaudens*" approach). Other social structures may be analyzed in large social networks through network censuses to better understand social groups. Finally, the software may also be applied to understand network holes which may be exploited. As examples of power and structure, there was an example of web blogs and the polarization between differing groups (based on their language overlap as identified by text analysis tools). Another example involved the analysis of terror groups and their structures, to help those in law enforcement understand how to neutralize these risks. The participatory "Let's Talk!" section in this page involved a discussion around strategies for breaking up social networks. Those in the audience were asked about why the U.S. might fund "Internet in a suitcase" in certain countries—to make connections between certain nodes. The audience was asked about how they would structure and field a discreet cross-functional team. Finally, they were also asked to think about how a community could be encouraged to engage in more civic engagement through social networking.

The final example page was thinly developed and requested that the audience members consider how social network analysis technologies could be applied to academia, in a number of different fields. As a playful touch, there was a sample social network diagram offered that showed the "secret" life of a work group at the presenter's university. The "Let's Talk!" focused on ways to enhance the knowledge in higher education. Further, the presenter asked the group to conceptualize the social network that they were all a part of in the regional professional collegial organization. To introduce a sense of social strategy in the participants' choices, the presenter asked what features they would look for in terms of project partners. And finally, she also asked about academic content analyses to understand their respective academic domains.

The remaining pages involved how to use UCINET. There were several other (open-source) software programs that were introduced for those who may want a less complex tool to use early on (but with manual social network diagramming and not data-driven diagramming). This information was included as a nod to technologists but also to point to less complex tools, given the fairly high learning curve of UCINET.

Given the complexity of the topic, there was an alphabetized listing of terminology. This was augmented by some Iframes of online visualizations of some of the concepts. For the rare few who would be interested in learning more about node-link diagrams and social networks, there were references to various online texts and readings, and downloadable data sets linked to the UCINET technologies.

To emphasize the breadth of this analytical approach, there were links to real-world analyses of social networks and relationships, social network analysis as an investigative tool, content analysis in academia, real-time real-space mappings, and other examples.

Case 3: Building Study Guides

The third real-world case involved the building of digital study guides for online learning. This practice is common in early science-based fields as a type of cognitive scaffolding to support learners in their endeavors. Coupled with the affordances of digital authoring, study guides are now much more information-rich and interactive.

The purpose of the "Building Effective Study Guides for Online Learning and Assessment" was to re-define the retro tool of print study guides (traditionally used to augment books, to repurpose mainstream media for learning purposes, and to explain how lab and study kits should be used) in the new digital age with the many affordances of the technologies.

Figure 4 offers a visual play of a compass to suggest a shared direction-seeking in the development of study guides for the present-day online learning context.

Figure 4. The opening screen of the study guides microsite

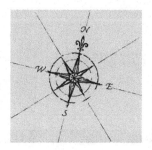

Building Effective Study Guides for Online Learning and Assessment

Contents   Next ▶   1 | 2 | 3 | 4 | 5 | 6   print all

Building Effective Study Guides for Online Learning and Assessment

By Shalin Hai-Jew, Instructional Designer at K-State

Colleague 2 Colleague (C2C) SIDLIT

Aug. 2 - 3, 2012

Study guides are common features of science-based (and some social science) courses. These are information sets created by learners to help them prepare for upcoming exams. If effectively designed (by the faculty member usually) and executed (by the learners) with faculty oversight, such study guides offer effective notes for student learning. They serve as powerful resources to enhance memory. Study guides are effective because they help learners synthesize (sometimes contradictory) information from various information sources and are expressed in the learners' own words to enable instructor evaluation of their actual comprehension. These guides enhance learner citations of research sources. Such digital study guides may integrate text, imagery, URLs, and other resources. These help learners take ownership of the learning and help them express their understandings through their own interpretive lenses. This presentation will include some live examples of study guides and their various strengths and weaknesses. There will be ideas for how to take the "retro" concept of a study guide and re-make study guides into interactive learning resources, with special strengths in intensive, concentrated, or accelerated courses.

"Building Effective Study Guides for Online Learning and Assessment" is available at https://softch-alkcloud.com/lesson/rFnD0AQX3xRVTa (Hai-Jew, 2012). A full outline is available at the top-level (landing page) of the site, per the template.

Figure 5 highlights a navigable structure to access the contents, whether in sequence or piecemeal.

Early on, the audience was introduced to a baseline template for the creation of a study guide. They learned that most contained the following elements: learning objectives; an outline or TOC, basic textual contents, 2D visuals, review questions, a list of vocabulary, a summary, and a references list. The site then included a visual showing when (and how) study guides are used in the learning process: prior to a module, during the module, and post-module.

The presenter asserted that study guides have usefulness today as cognitive scaffolds, given the speed and complexity of subject matters today. Particularly for online learning, study guides may be particularly important to provide that support. The presenter went through various digital object types that may be used in the design of study guides. She highlighted larger-scale tools like digital laboratories, wikis, web logs, knowledge structures, learning / course management systems, and other systems level tools.

The next section summarized the building of study guides and the strategies that inform that work. Some online study guides are co-built with learners as part of their study. Some parts of a study guide may be convergent (focusing on defined "right answers"), and others may be divergent (focusing on

Figure 5. The table of contents for "Building Effective Study Guides..." microsite

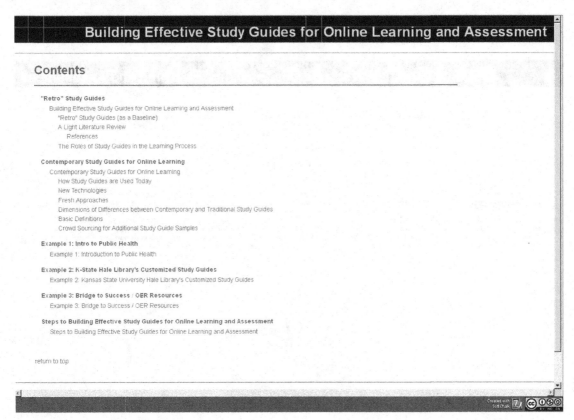

Figure 6. Multiple (and aligned) uses of study guides in the learning process

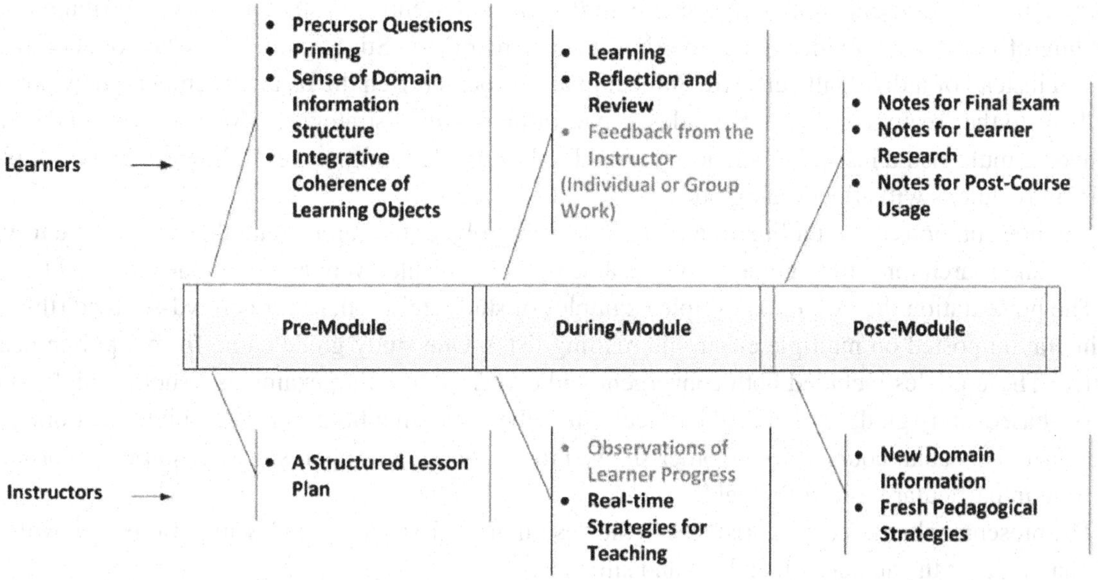

Learners →	• Precursor Questions • Priming • Sense of Domain Information Structure • Integrative Coherence of Learning Objects	• Learning • Reflection and Review • Feedback from the Instructor (Individual or Group Work)	• Notes for Final Exam • Notes for Learner Research • Notes for Post-Course Usage
	Pre-Module	**During-Module**	**Post-Module**
Instructors →	• A Structured Lesson Plan	• Observations of Learner Progress • Real-time Strategies for Teaching	• New Domain Information • Fresh Pedagogical Strategies

innovative approaches). Numerous open-source and open-access resources may be integrated for use in study guides. Besides the range of digital contents that may be used in study guides, those that are hosted on websites may be tracked using site analytics in order to see how they're being used by learners.

The presenter offered a visual highlighting some differences between contemporary vs. traditional study guides.

Figure 7. General features of contemporary vs. traditional study guides

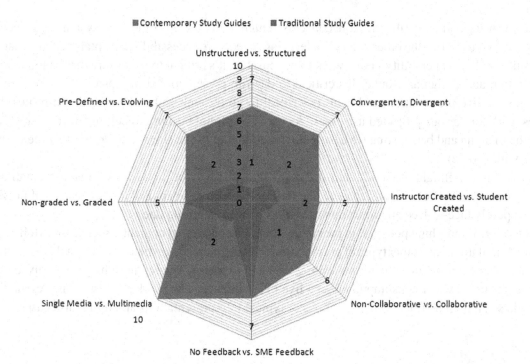

Modern study guides tend to be evolving and less conventionally structured. The learning addressed in modern study guides is both convergent and divergent. Oftentimes, students may contribute to the building of these study guides alongside their faculty members. Study guides may be collaboratively created instead of individually created. Subject matter experts (often the faculty members) may provide feedback to the creators of the study guides as part of the learning strategies. Modern study guides tend to involve multimedia instead of single print media. In some learning contexts, how students complete their study guides will affect their grades.

The presentation offered a link to a popular learning object referatory. The directions were to visit the site and search for "study guides." What came up in the results were a wide range of contents.

The presentation then went to multiple examples of study guides that were crowd-sourced (through an invitation posted on multiple electronic mailing lists). One study guide came from a public health course. These guides included both convergent and divergent learning examples. Another highlighted course-based study guides co-created by faculty members and area librarians at a university library for students in particular courses. Yet another showed the harnessing of open-source resources to promote learning in particular basic skills fields.

The presenter abstracted best practices in the design of modern study guides and offered a download-able handout for the audience members and site visitors

DISCUSSION

This "presentational microsite" approach was designed to start the discussion about how microsites may be built for both live presentations and before-, during-, and after- presentation usage by the larger virtual community. This highlighted some initial ideas for necessary features of the microsites to meet the multiple use cases described here. While building microsites requires more work in the near-term, it has the potential to pay off in the middle- and longer- term by offering informational contents to a wider audience.

Repurposing and reusability are core concepts behind the so-called "ilities" (in systems engineering). (Along with reusability, the other "ilities" in learning objects are accessibility, adaptability, affordability, durability, and interoperability.) For a work to be reusable, it's critical to make sure that its foundational information and design are sound. It's critical to dry-run presentational microsites to make sure they work for the live presentation, and then it's critical to go through and make sure that the sites themselves work for various projected use cases. As with any digital design project, the developer needs to go through alpha and beta testing (to ensure the functionality of the site and to ensure that the usability works with people).

These cases highlight usage of multi-use microsites that may be created for a live presentation but also have another usage in virtual spaces. The findings here may be applied to the creation of presentations in purely face-to-face environments as well as blended learning ones.

These forms have high potential in packaging other presentational contents, such as storytelling, immersive simulations, and other types of presentations. Using microsites in lieu of traditional presentational contents offer a variety of tools for presenting data and experiences, and these may be archived on the Internet for much wider consumption than a live F2F audience. This work suggests that presentational microsites can both be fitted to the dynamics of typical F2F presentations and online use cases.

THE FUTURE

In terms of future research opportunities, because the uses of microsites for live presentations and digital archival are so new, it would be critical to explore which designs are the most effective for various presentational contexts. It would help to gain a sense of the range of the authoring tools that may be used for microsites. If there are variations on the microsite theme, those may prove rich veins of exploration.

CONCLUSION

As for the case itself, there are many ways to answer the questions of how to design presentational microsites. How effectively these microsites work in the live presentation and in the longer-term archival depends in large part on the actual audiences and the short- and medium-term (and even long-term) usage of the digital contents. This article is essential propositional in suggesting that such presentational microsites may be built for amplified value and increased efficient use of presenter / content developer time.

ADDITIONAL INFORMATION SOURCES

SoftChalk: http://softchalk.com/

Multimedia Educational Resource for Learning and Teaching (MERLOT): http://www.merlot.org/merlot/index.htm

REFERENCES

Hai-Jew, S. (2012, July 1). *Building and Analyzing Node-Link Diagrams to Understand Social Networks*. Retrieve from https://softchalkcloud.com/lesson/c4d8tSWMCwm39n

Hai-Jew, S. (2012, June 24). *Building Effective Study Guides for Online Learning and Assessment*. Retrieved from https://softchalkcloud.com/lesson/rFnD0AQX3xRVTa

Hai-Jew, S. (2012, Mar. 3). *Using Tableau Public for (Spatial and Trendline) Data Visualization (An Early Exploration and 'TMI' Musing on Data)*. Retrieved from https://softchalkcloud.com/lesson/rtNYCf1K80el9w

Lanir, J., Booth, K. S., & Findlater, L. (2008). Observer presenters' use of visual aids to inform the design of classroom presentation software. In CHI 2008 Proceedings: Tools for Education, Florence, Italy. (pp. 695–704).

Moreno, R. (2006). Learning in high-tech and multimedia environments. *Current Directions in Psychological Science*, *15*(2), 63–67. http://www.jstor.org/stable/20183078 doi:10.1111/j.0963-7214.2006.00408.x

Schell, G. P., & Burns, M. (2002). Merlot: A repository of e-learning objects for higher education. *E-Service Journal*, *1*(2), 53–64.

KEY TERMS AND DEFINITIONS

Data Analytics: The study of sets of data to extract analytical meaning.

Iframes: Inline keyframes.

Interoperable: The ability to exchange data; the ability to operate in a complementary way through interfaces.

Node-Link Diagram: A linegraph consisting of circles (representing entities) and lines (representing relationships).

Study Guide: An often-ancillary object to enhance students' learning efficacy and performance.

Section 4
Considering Human Needs in Multimedia Presentations

Chapter 9
Promoting Engagement with Online Presentations

Amy Gaimaro
St. John's University, USA

ABSTRACT

Educators delivering online presentations face many challenges when teaching in this modality. Lack of student engagement is one such challenge. Students can study online with lackluster learning experiences when participating in a predominately text-based course. Applying multiple instructional strategies to address students' diverse learning styles can provide students with a more engaged online learning experience. Another challenge many educators face, is the need for support and guidance to facilitate effective online learning. More specifically, educators of the twenty-first century are seeking the know-how to move traditional text-based materials into online, media-rich course content. This chapter will examine some of the challenges of delivering quality online presentations. In conclusion, the author will provide examples of strategies for delivering effective online presentations within the virtual college classroom.

INTRODUCTION

According to the authors of the New Media Consortium Horizon Report: 2014 Higher Education Edition, the integration of online, hybrid, and collaborative learning models will drive changes in higher education over the next one to two years (Johnson, Becker, Estrada, & Freeman, 2014). With higher education institutions developing courses in these modalities of teaching, the need for effective and engaging instructional strategies is in great demand. To further reinforce the importance of delivering quality online presentations, a recent study of more than 2,800 colleges and universities reported 7.1 million students have taken at least one online course during the fall 2012 semester. This represents a 411,757 increase from the previous year. With a reported overall enrollment growth rate of only 1.2% for these institutions; online enrollment grew by 6.1% (Allen & Seaman, 2014). For purposes of this chapter, an online presentation is a form of delivering a lecture or content to students in the online learning environment.

With the increase in students enrolled in fully online learning courses or courses delivered partially online, universities are moving away from the traditional text-based lecture hall style of teaching. Edu-

DOI: 10.4018/978-1-4666-8696-0.ch009

cators are now delivering flipped, blended and online classes. Flipped learning models involve faculty uploading lectures into a virtual environment while students complete work in the classroom. This is considered flipped, because the delivery of lectures and the completion of homework assignments are inverted or flipped. According to the Sloan Consortium's definition of blended learning; a blended or hybrid learning model of instruction contains between 30 and 79 percent of the course content delivered online. Striking a balance of online lectures and activities with face-to-face interactions inside the classroom is often a challenge when designing a blended course. An online course is defined as one in which at least 80 percent of the course content is delivered online (Allen & Seaman, 2014). With the increase use of new teaching models, and in the absence of face-to-face interactions, developing engaging online presentation materials is both relevant and timely. According to Miller (2011), educators now have a vast and emergent body of course-relevant content which can expand student learning opportunities outside those provided in the conventional classroom. Today's educators face many challenges while teaching in the twenty-first century; most instructors are digital immigrants who are now teaching digital natives. A digital native is defined as someone who grew up with the use of computers, video games and the Internet (Prensky, 2001). While digital immigrants are not native speakers of the digital language; however, they can adapt to their environment. Today's students have changed from prior generations of students with the use of technology in their everyday lives. "Students have a need-to-know, short-term, goal-oriented world view that contrasts with professors' value of life-long learning for learning's sake" (Lane, Hunt & Farris, 2011, p. 105). The implications can be profound, resulting in a disconnection between the educator and the learner. The role of faculty development today, as it relates to teaching the twenty-first century learner, has never been so relevant in bridging the teaching and learning gaps that exist in higher education today.

Online learning allows students the flexibility to learn at a more convenient time, access a variety of educational content and engage in conversations with their instructor and peers. Online learning can take place within flipped, blended or fully online courses. However, students can study in the virtual world with lackluster learning experiences when viewing predominantly text-based course materials. Why is text-based content so prevalent? Text is the most economical means to represent ideas with widely available software tools (Henry, 2009). Applying a variety of educational content and instructional strategies to address students' diverse learning styles can provide students with a more compelling online learning experience. Providing diverse educational content requires more time and commitment on the part of the faculty member. To develop a collection of diverse learning content and to employ a range of learning strategies in the virtual world, faculty require support and guidance of instructional designers and technologists to facilitate a more effective online learning experience. Educators of the twenty-first century require more advanced technology skills to move traditional text-based materials into media-rich course content.

ENGAGING THE TWENTY-FIRST CENTURY LEARNER

Teaching the twenty-first century student of today may challenge educators at higher education institutions. Who are these twenty-first century learners and why should it matter? According to Diana Oblinger, Vice President for EDUCAUSE (as cited by Rogers, Runyon, Starrett, & Von Holzen, 2006), students of the twenty-first century are also known as "Net-generation" learners, "Millennial students," "Generation-Y," and "Digital-natives." Most educators who are teaching these students are digital immigrants. A digital immigrant did not type book reports on a computer, use electronic math games for education, learn his or her ABCs on a personal computer, search the Internet for resources, or prepare PowerPoint presentations during his or her developing years as a student. Rogers et al. (2006) described a twenty-first century learner as someone born after 1982 who mainly learns through interactions with technology. These students are multi-taskers, rely heavily on technology for spelling and grammar checks, perform quick mathematical calculations, often prefer chatting using abbreviations throughout their conversations, and demonstrate the extensive use of gaming for engagement.

Discussing the millennial student in relation to other generations is important to gain a clearer perspective on their interactions (Junco & Mastrodicasa, 2007). Table 1 provides an overview of four generations of individuals who may be interacting inside today's classroom (Junco & Mastrodicasa, 2007, p. 4). "Whether you believe the characteristics commonly attributed to the Millennial Generation or not, it is clear that the manner in which students are motivated to engage in higher education has been changing and will continue to change rapidly" (Crone & MacKay, 2007, p. 18). This is a challenge for the twenty-first century educator because many educators are digital immigrants who did not grow up with using technology for learning. Why should educators be concerned with the millennial student of today? The answer is clear—because learning is the focal point of academic institutions.

According to Tapscott and Williams (2010), there are disturbing signs at higher education institutions, such as reductions in endowments (due to the financial crisis), increases in tuition costs leaving students with large student loan debt, and students choosing alternative methods of education. With that said, today is a time of increased opportunities on the college campus. This can also lead to opportunities for educators to find new ways to engage these learners and step outside the traditional methods of teaching. "Change is required in two vast and interwoven domains that permeate the deep structures and operating model of the university: (1) the value created for the main customers of the university (the students); and (2) the model of production for how that value is created" (Tapscott & Williams, 2010, p. 18). Technology can provide a new model of production for how that value is created. With the twenty-first century learner interacting more with technology, specifically the Internet, educators can respond to these methods by thinking "outside the box" and participating in available programs to promote new

Table 1. Overview of Four Generations

	1925-1942 Silent Generation	1943-1960 Boomers	1961-1981 Generation X	1982 – Now Millennial
Peer Personality	Loyal Collaborative Personal sacrifice Patriotic Conformity Respect for authority Civic Pride	Optimistic Competitive Individualistic Reject authority Return to religious value	Independent Skeptical Latchkey kids Shun traditional value Nihilism	Special Sheltered Confident Conventional Team-Oriented Achieving Pressured
Defining Events	WWI & II Great Depression New Deal	Vietnam War Watergate Women's Rights Reagan recession Civil Rights Movement Television	Challenger accident MTV Computers Video Games Persian Gulf War	Columbine shootings September 11 attacks Oklahoma City bombing
Attended College	1943-1960	1961-1978	1979-1999	2000 - Now

methods of teaching outside the traditional "chalk and talk" approach, or "a talk or lecture illustrated by a blackboard" ("Chalk talk," n.d., p. 1). Often times, this method of teaching is referred to in a critical manner. However, many educators are finding this teacher-centered approach to be the only style of teaching they know or to which they are accustomed. According to Crone and MacKay (2007), today's students do not respond favorably to straight lectures or teacher-centered PowerPoint presentations. A student-centered approach, with faculty members taking on more of a mentor role, where students can collaborate through technological means can be a new approach taken by the traditional faculty member. This approach can be implemented in both the in-classroom and virtual learning environments. New programs offered at educational institutions, including faculty support programs and faculty mentors through communities of practice, can promote change among the teaching styles of today's faculty.

Learning Styles and Multimedia Learning

While today's twenty-first century learners grew up in a world surrounded with technology, we should ask ourselves if we can successfully teach with a traditional "one-size-fits-all" approach. Can educators teach their courses in a similar way as they taught twenty years ago? This assumes learners have not changed the way they learn and interact with technology. Taking one sole approach to teaching implies all students learn the same way. "An appropriate balance must be determined thoughtfully with attention to beliefs, theories, and research rather than efficiency" (Guild, 2001, para. 7). Educators need to make the necessary choices about selecting what should be uniform for all learners and what should be diverse. So taking into account students' diverse learning styles can enhance the teaching and learning experience that takes place inside and outside the classroom. To illustrate this point, let's say an instructor assigns a book to read and asks students to self-select a project to complete a summary of the book. Now let's say students were given the option to complete the summary of the book by completing one of the following projects; a written report, multimedia presentation or a video digital story. Can we be certain all students will complete the same type of project? Should educators present their teaching content in strictly one format? "Individuals have such unique patterns for learning new and difficult information that it is hard to judge accurately how to teach anything academically challenging without first identifying how each student learns" (Griggs & Dunn, 2000, p. 19). "Sameness is always easier to accommodate than difference and education practices often have been developed to consciously promote the same education for all students" (Guild, 2001, para. 7). This section of the chapter will discuss student learning styles and cognitive constructivist theory of multimedia.

What are learning styles? "Learning styles are traits that refer to how individuals approach learning tasks and process information" (Morrison, Ross, Kalman & Kemp, 2013, p. 54). Learning style preferences of both educators and students play a role in course design. Educators taking into account their own individual preference can influence the design of courses that takes place online. "The diversity of the field arises from various theoretical foundations and definitions and, therefore, presents some challenges to understanding and implementation" (Wilson, 2012, p. 68) .While there has been research written to support learning styles (Griggs & Dunn, 2000; Honigsfeld & Shiering, 2004); there has also been research that challenges the validity of learning styles (Wilson, 2012; Sparks, 2006). One thing we can acknowledge; people do not learn the same way. There are three main cognitive learning styles; visual, auditory and kinesthetic. Learning style theory suggests when designing courses for online learning, it is important to keep in mind that learners have different preferences. With appropriate planning, educators can offer content in a variety of formats.

The characteristics of a visual learner involve the preference to learn by pictures and charts. Visual learners tend to remember content by reading text and watching lectures. The online environment can easily present visual content effectively through the use of text and graphics. And while the visual learner prefers text, pictures and charts; the auditory learner remembers information by listening to lectures and has an aptitude for music. Videos or video screen capture tools with spoken words or music can meet the preferences of the auditory learner. Kinesthetic learners like to be hands-on with learning and are often strong in science and math. They prefer to demonstrate a concept as compared to explaining the concept in written format or verbally. Interacting with videos or creating videos can be an effective strategy to employ for the kinesthetic learner.

To understand more about why we take the time to plan and design online multimedia presentations, let's look at recent theory that has emerged utilizing learning style theory, constructivist theory and cognitive theory of multimedia learning. Mayer & Moreno (2003) define multimedia learning as learning from words and pictures, and they define multimedia instruction as presenting words and pictures that are intended to nurture student learning. Bull (2009) developed cognitive constructivist theory of multimedia (CCTM). It is defined as creating purposeful interactive faculty-made digital learning content that engages and motivates learners (Bull, 2013). CCMT is a supporting theory of the cognitive theory of multimedia learning (CTM). CCTM design is the integration of multimedia (text, image, animation, graphic, video and audio) in a systematic design structure of visual thinking combining verbal and non-verbal communication to minimize cognitive overload of the learner's memory (Bull, 2013).

According to Bull (2013), in designing interactive digital learning materials, the learner utilizes visual and verbal information processing systems to engage in learning. All auditory information received during this process of learning goes to the verbal system and all graphics, pictures and animations goes to the visual system. This means that educators in designing interactive digital materials should create a balance between verbal and visual repository systems of the learner to fully engage them in the learning process. (p. 615)

Possessing an awareness of diverse student learning styles and multimedia learning can promote educators to effectively plan materials in order to strike the balance for delivering digital course materials while implementing instructional strategies to engage students in the online environment. Why should we be concerned with cognitive overload? As educators, our ultimate goal is to have our students learn and retain knowledge. Offering a variety of formats can help ensure the needs of learners are effectively met.

Role of Faculty Development

Where can educators find the needed support and development at today's higher education institution? While K-12 educators enter their roles with formal training and education as to how to effectively teach in a classroom, most higher education faculty members have little, to no formal training in the area of learning theories. "The growth of online education programs is one of the most pressing and rapidly changing issues faced by faculty members and administration in higher education" (Herman, 2012, p. 87). Professors rely on quality professional development offerings with respect to teaching and technology. Higher education institutions are faced with the challenges of offering quality online preparation for faculty (Herman, 2012). With all the talk about digital natives or millennials, professors are faced with the challenges of effectively delivering their content to today's students. Add the layer of a virtual environment, and we now have two challenges; lack of formal training in learning theories and inexperience with a virtual learning environment. Whether professors are looking to flip their classroom, teach blended or fully online, effectively integrating technology becomes both a challenge and opportunity. Change is inevitable. Institutional change has been researched by many within diverse sectors of business and not-for-profit organizations. According to Gilley, Dixon, & Gilley, (2008), successful implementation of change has been identified as leading to innovation, and consequently, increased competitiveness. Higher education institutions are competing more for new and transfer enrollments because borders are no longer within a defined geographic region. Leaders at colleges and universities are asking new questions about their student bodies. The traditional student is now attending classes with the non-traditional student. What allows an institution to stand out during an open house session? Is the institution reaching out the new millennial student? According to Elam, Stratton, & Gibson (2007), millennial students are accustomed to computers and cell phones that have allowed them to be masters at multitasking. Is the institution keeping up with this type of student? Parents are committing significant dollars for higher education, and an old outdated institution with few learning offerings is falling short of today's student and parent expectations.

Because online education is becoming more prevalent in higher education, and institutions need to remain nimble in order to remain strong and viable in the face of growing financial and enrollment pressures, adequate faculty support needs to be addressed (Herman, 2012). Faculty development professionals are often sought out by faculty in order to gain the necessary support to incorporate technology effectively into their teaching. What about the faculty members who do not seek out faculty development staff? Higher education administrations are seeking new and innovative ways to offer faculty development programs in order to reach both the full-time and part-time professor. Another challenge to faculty development occurs when an institution does not have a formal requirement for professional development. As a result, participation in such programs may not be as high. This is why a strong dedicated team of faculty development and support professionals, who are in touch with the teaching community in higher education, is critical to providing quality teaching and diverse learning opportunities for students. In the fall of 2012, the proportion of higher education students taking at least one online course is at an all-time high of 33.5 percent (Allen & Seaman, 2014). With these numbers continuing to rise, a demand for quality faculty development programs exists within higher education. While this poses both a challenge and opportunity, engaging faculty in diverse opportunities for training is fundamental to acceptance and participation.

One of the primary roles of faculty development professionals is to stay current on the trends and research of technology integration inside and outside the classroom. With the increase in online offerings at universities, no longer is learning restricted to the classroom walls on campus. Learning now takes place outside of the classroom with the increased use of courses delivered in flipped, blended and online formats. A growing trend is delivering quality faculty development programs using online modalities to emulate best practices. With demands on existing budgets, seeking a network of talent within the institution can expand the reach of faculty development. Communities of practice can be an effective way to access and develop faculty in higher education. Communities of practice or learning networks, are established when groups of individuals want to share their passion and frequently get together to engage to further support their practice (Teeter et al., 2011).

Providing the necessary support for faculty can determine whether a faculty member will move forward with more advanced integration of technology, or take the next step to develop personalized online presentations. It's far easier and quicker to find someone else's content on the Web than to create a personalized online presentation. What are some of the alternatives to personalize presentations? Some alternatives include posting a presentation file used in the classroom, typing text-only notes or finding existing open educational resources (OERs). OERs can be highly effective in an online classroom. However, the challenge of researching the appropriate content to match the unique course objectives can be difficult. Many educators have their own resources, so the issue of converting the format to a media-rich learning object requires proper training, development and support.

Personalization and Its Importance in Online Courses

Why should we be concerned with adding a personal touch to online learning? According to Kelly (2009), learning research shows that students learn better when there is an emotional connection to the content or to other people. A lack of personalization within online course materials can contribute to the feeling of isolation among students and causing students to lose interest. It is even more important to engage our learners online since we cannot pick up on visual cues as we do often when teaching in a face-to-face environment. Who is on the other side of the computer during an online lecture? A student may ask this question. All too often professors will take the teacher-centered approach and post their PowerPoint files to the virtual learning space. Simply taking face-to-face courses and transferring the content to a learning management system will not provide a quality learning experience. What can lack is the instructor's use of personalization within the course. There are many ways instructors can personalize an online course; some examples include delivering personalized welcome announcements, designing ice-breaker activities, posting a biographical sketch and sending ongoing personal feedback to students. While these are all effective activities to integrate within an online environment, providing instructor-created online presentations can make a significant impact on the perceived quality of the course. Personalizing online presentations benefit students by allowing students to feel more connected to the instructor and promoting a sense of social presence. According to Johnson et al. (2014), the use of voice and video tools is shown to improve the quality of online courses. After all, our goal as educators should be to deliver a quality online course, not to deliver a quality face-to-face course online. Whether teaching takes place inside or outside the physical classroom, all learning requires engagement (Clark & Mayer, 2011).

STRATEGIES AND SOLUTIONS FOR EFFECTIVE ONLINE PRESENTATIONS

Today, online instructors have many choices to implement multimedia into their courses. "Increased bandwidth and techniques such as streaming media files and podcasts have enhanced the feasibility of integrating audio in online learning environments" (Calandra, Barron, Thompson-Sellers, 2008, p. 589). While simply asking students their preferences may seem straight-forward and relatively simple to accomplish, many students may not possess self-awareness of their learning style. There are easy and accessible online tools that students and educators can access to gain a better understanding of their own preferred learning style. These quizzes can be embed into a learning management system and can spur an online discussion about the results. Students are sometimes surprised by the results and enjoy sharing with one another. This is an example of an online ice-breaker activity. The results can initiate a lively online discussion while faculty can take note of the results. This assumes students possess the awareness of how they learn.

There are many tools, some free and some available at a cost, that can support both professors and students in creating effective online presentations. I include students intentionally because creating effective online presentations by students will be discussed a little later on as an engaging teaching strategy. Sound instructional design should offer diverse online learning opportunities and allow students to consume content in a variety of formats. In addition, professors taking the time to learn more about their own learning styles during faculty development can initiate the dialogue for support and development of diverse strategies in their own classroom. Allowing for a variety of course content will not only address diverse learning styles, but will also address accessibility of course content. Before we address strategies to accommodate each of the three learning styles, it's important to understand that it may not be possible to create individual lessons for every learning style. Beginning with the overall course view, and allowing a variety of content throughout the semester, can be a good place to start. I describe strategies and examples to address the visual, auditory and kinesthetic style learner. The level of difficulty increases when preparing online presentations that address the visual, auditory and kinesthetic learner.

The strategies presented will discuss examples of online presentations from the basic through more advanced interactive online presentations. Let's begin by addressing the visual learner. Preparing an online presentation that speaks to the visual learner can be relatively easy to create and cost-effective. Allowing students to read text and view graphics can aid in remembering information. Effective online presentations include images, graphs, and charts to help illustrate and reinforce concepts. According to Vik (2004), some of the most common pitfalls when writing presentations that specifically focus on text include:

- too many words on a slide
- backgrounds that are too busy or inappropriate
- text and background colors are too similar in color
- too many bells and whistles (animation and sounds)
- too many slides
- lack of overall presentation organization

While these recommended tips apply to classroom lecture presentations, they also can apply to creating online presentations. Visual learners thrive on reading and visual cues from presentations. With a relatively low-level of technology competency, educators can easily develop presentations to accommodate the visual learner. Such productivity software may include applications like PowerPoint or Keynote. Free online tools include Prezi, Google Docs and Slide Rocket. Researching the features, costs and institutional support should be conducted prior to adoption of such tools.

Engaging the auditory learner requires more technical skills to produce online presentations. The auditory learner prefers listening to lectures. An online presentation can be in an audio format, such as a podcast or can integrate both visual and auditory elements with screen capture and audio combined. Educators can produce quality online presentations using productivity software such as PowerPoint presentation graphics program. More advanced software can produce effective online presentations. Such commercial applications like Camtasia Studio® and Adobe Captivate®. However, there are free alternatives that can easily be found by completing a simple Web search of free video screen capture tools. Free products have their advantages and disadvantages. The obvious advantage is the cost, while the disadvantages may include of lack of university support, discontinued versions of products and possible unwanted advertising and watermarks on the video site. Developing an online presentation with audio requires more planning than a simple text-based presentation. If you simply record your voice while reading text, then this may not result in an effective learning experience for your students. It is recommended to write a script that will accompany the presentation content. Writing a script can help improve the quality of online lectures. By preparing a written script, time is saved by not making recording mistakes. Make your scripts a bit personal and not so formal. Add your own personal style. In addition, having a script can keep you more organized and allow you to stick to a set time frame for your lecture. All too often, faculty members may record a two-hour lecture and believe this is a sound pedagogical practice. Consuming a two-hour lecture can result in disengagement and boredom. Chunking lectures into more meaningful and manageable units can pace the delivery. Shortening lectures to no more than fifteen minutes each can allow students to maintain their level of focus during the lecture. I recommend indicating to the student, in an explicit manner, the length of time for each online presentation. This allows the student to manage their time accordingly. A large lecture file is can be edited down to smaller segments with today's software. Examples of meaningful units can include topic, chapter or learning objective. With practice and appropriate pacing, students can benefit by having the ability to clearly follow along with your lecture through the use of audio and visual content. Some tips for recording lectures include:

- a quiet location to remove any unwanted background noise
- use of a headset to maintain sound quality throughout the lecture
- a well-planned written script to follow

Scripts are critical to the success of your screencast. I recommend faculty not "fly by the seat of their pants" when recording their audio for presentations. I have tried this myself with limited success. While I have been screencasting for over five years now, I continue to find a script critical to the success of my online presentation. Scripts help reduce the amount of time I spend recording the presentation. Figure 1 summarizes scripting and narration tips recommended to anyone who plans to write a script prior to recording their presentations ("Screencasting Best Practices," n.d.). Whether a purchased tool or a free tool is used to create screencasts with audio, posting the online presentations can be easily done with the use of a free video streaming site. The most popular free video streaming sites are YouTube® and Vimeo®.

A student-centered strategy to engage the kinesthetic learner is a student-created presentation. The instructor asks students to create their own online presentations and share them with the class through a file upload or posting to a Web site. This usually requires the most advanced level of planning and technical proficiency. Just like educators posting online presentations to free video streaming sites, students can also use this approach to sharing online presentations. Students can easily provide the Web address to share their work with the class. This requires providing explicit instructions to the students and additional support for students. Clear instructional guidance can lead to a more independent learner. I have successfully implemented this student-centered approach to online presentations. No longer is the student the passive learner in this situation. Students are researching tools and taking ownership in their work. As digital natives, they can easily find a tool to accomplish such tasks. Another student-centered online presentation strategy involves adding a form of interactivity on the part of the student. All too often, students "check out" during online presentations because they find themselves in a passive mode of learning. Creating online presentations, using more advanced tools, can allow faculty to integrate

Figure 1. Scripting and Narration Tips

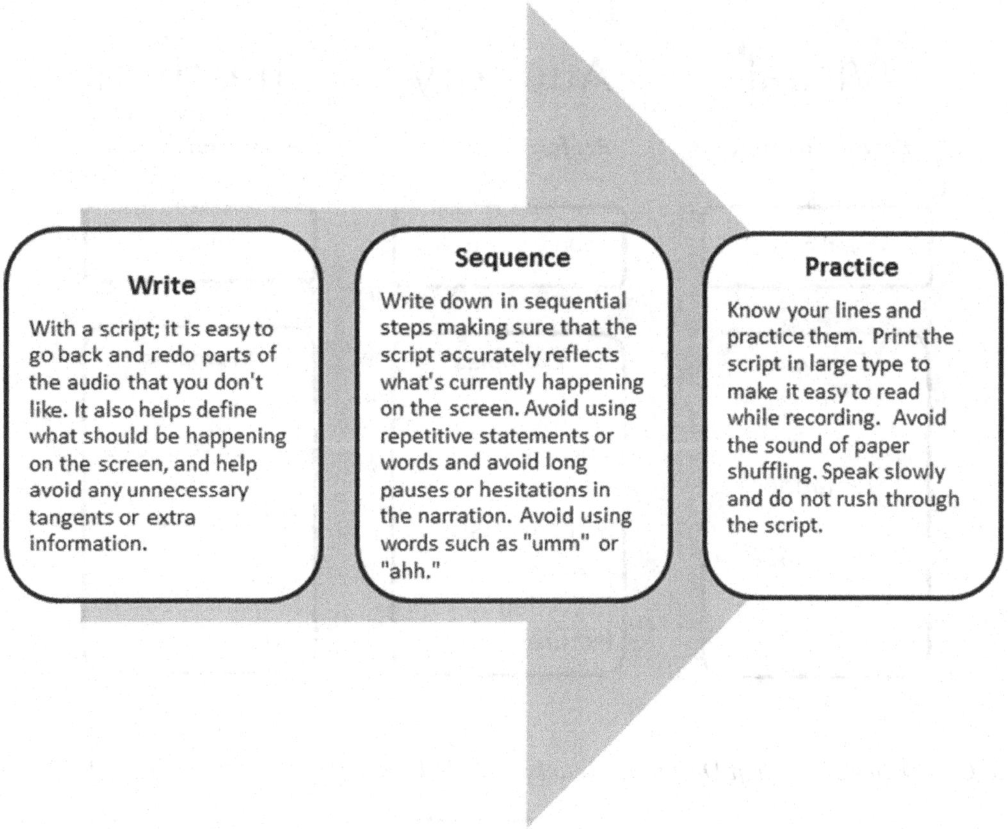

Write

With a script; it is easy to go back and redo parts of the audio that you don't like. It also helps define what should be happening on the screen, and help avoid any unnecessary tangents or extra information.

Sequence

Write down in sequential steps making sure that the script accurately reflects what's currently happening on the screen. Avoid using repetitive statements or words and avoid long pauses or hesitations in the narration. Avoid using words such as "umm" or "ahh."

Practice

Know your lines and practice them. Print the script in large type to make it easy to read while recording. Avoid the sound of paper shuffling. Speak slowly and do not rush through the script.

quizzes or surveys within the online presentation. Quizzes can be used for self-assessment; meaning not graded by the instructor or integrated within the learning management system grade center. Surveys can also be used to aggregate student responses. Whether you are employing quizzes or surveys, the focus for kinesthetic learners is the actual act of doing. Engaging the learner further can take place with some simple strategies to follow after students view the segment:

- ask students to complete a quick online quiz
- post a question or series of question to the online discussion board for class interactions
- ask students to blog about their reaction to the lecture while including some guiding questions

Figure 2 illustrates examples of online presentations and learning styles. While reading from left to right, the level of difficulty increases, with text and graphics being the easiest way to create an online presentation through the most difficult hands-on (kinesthetic) approaches.

As discussed earlier in this chapter, CCTM takes into account a variety of learning styles within its theory. Bull (2013) found several benefits of using CCTM in designing teacher-made interactive digital learning materials. Figure 3 summarizes some of these benefits.

In summary, creating interactive online presentations can promote asynchronous delivery of online learning, provide an environment whereby faculty can flip their classes, allow students to understand

Figure 2. Online Presentation Examples by Learning Style with Increasing Difficulty

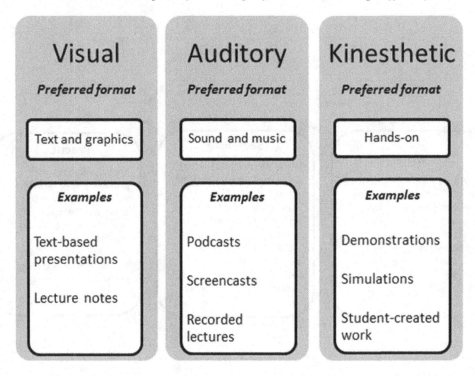

Figure 3. CCTM Benefits When Designing Teacher-Made Interactive Digital Learning Environments

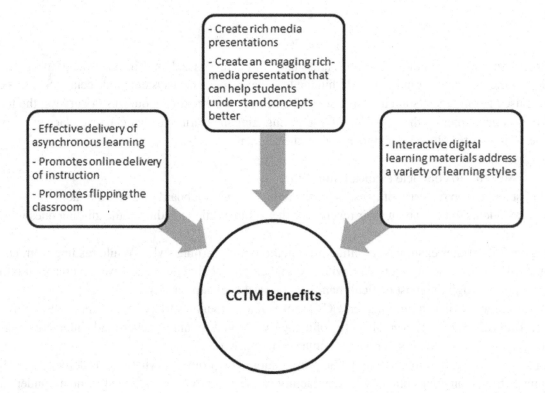

concepts better; all while addressing a variety of learning styles. Faculty who teach flipped, blended or fully online require appropriate planning and faculty development through university administration or through communities of practice with their peers. Faculty not only require the skills to master the technology, but need to gain a deeper understanding of the students on the other side of the computer and how they learn. Engagement can be enhanced by providing effective teaching strategies and developing quality content for online presentations. The "one-size fits all" approach is not recommended when developing online presentations.

A VISION OF ONLINE PRESENTATIONS

So what is the future of virtual learning environments and online presentations? From the studies cited throughout this chapter, online education is not going away anytime soon. In fact, it has been keeping a steady pace with enrollment figures within higher education. According to Johnson et al. (2014), voice and video tools have been increasing in both practice and quality. With faculty use of videos to deliver online presentations, students will be able to capture human gestures that will not be captured through text-only content; specifically voice and body language. Throughout this chapter, I incorporated themes of engagement for today's learners including; learner theories, faculty development and teaching with technology strategies. Universities and colleges are challenged with delivering effective technology integration, robust faculty development and flexible student support. As stated earlier in the chapter, while the controversy exists on the validity of learning styles, we cannot ignore the fact that we all learn differently. With more recent theories emerging like CCTM, developers of online presentations can better understand the implications of integrating multimedia effectively. When planning for the new semester, offering multiple strategies and formats of online presentations can reach a diverse audience and help ensure engagement throughout the course without the "one-size fits all" approach. With more teaching and learning taking place in virtual environments, educators should seek effective ways to reach their students and promote engagement and share best practices through learning communities at their campus.

REFERENCES

Allen, I. E., & Seaman, J. (2014). *Grade change: Tracking online education in the United States, 2014.* Babson Survey Research Group and Quahog Research Group, LLC.

Bull, P. (2009). Cognitive constructivist theory of multimedia design: A theoretical analysis of instructional design for multimedia learning. In G. Siemens & C. Fulford (Eds.), *Proceedings of World Conference on educational multimedia, hypermedia and telecommunications 2009* (pp. 735–740). http://www.editlib.org/p/31581

Bull, P. H. (2013). Cognitive constructivist theory of multimedia: Designing teacher-made interactive digital. *Creative Education, 4*(9), 614-619. Retrieved from http://0-search.proquest.com.liucat.lib.liu.edu/docview/1448245192?accountid=12142

Calandra, B., Barron, A. E., & Thompson-Sellers, I. (2008). Audio use in E-Learning: What, why, when and how? *International Journal on E-Learning, 7*(4).

Chalk talk. (n.d.). In Merriam-Webster online dictionary. Retrieved from http://www.merriam-webster.com/dictionary/chalk%20talk

Clark, R. C., & Mayer, R. E. (3rd Ed.). (2011). *E-Learning and the science of instruction: Proven guidelines for consumers and designers of multimedia learning* San Francisco, CA: John Wiley & Sons. doi:10.1002/9781118255971

Crone, I., & MacKay, K. (2007). Motivating today's college students. *Peer Review, 9*(1), 18–21.

Elam, C., Stratton, T., & Gibson, D. (2007). Welcoming a new generation to college: The millennial students. *Journal of College Admission, 195,* 20–25.

Gilley, A., Dixon, P., & Gilley, J. W. (2008). Characteristics of leadership effectiveness: Implementing change and driving innovation in organizations. *Human Resource Development Quarterly, 19*(2), 153–169. doi:10.1002/hrdq.1232

Griggs, S. A., & Dunn, R. S. (2000). Practical approaches to using learning styles in higher education: The how-to steps. In R. Dunn & S. A. Griggs (Eds.), *Practical Approaches to Using Learning Styles in Higher Education* (pp. 19–33). Westport, CT: Greenwood Press.

Guild, P. B. (2001). Diversity, learning style and culture. *New Horizons for Learning.* Retrieved at http://education.jhu.edu/PD/newhorizons/strategies/topics/Learning%20Styles/diversity.html

Henry, P. (2009). Online Presentation Strategies for Visual Learners. *Proceedings of The European Conference On E-Learning,* 743-749.

Herman, J. H. (2012). Faculty development programs: The frequency and variety of professional development programs. *Journal of Asynchronous Learning Networks, 16*(5).

Honigsfeld, A., & Schiering, M. (2004). Diverse approaches to the diversity of learning styles in teacher education. *Educational Psychology, 24*(4), 487–507. doi:10.1080/0144341042000228861

Johnson, L., Becker, S., Estrada, V., & Freeman, A. (2014). *The NMC horizon report: 2014 higher education edition.* Austin: New Media Consortium.

Junco, R., & Mastrodicasa, J. (2007). Connecting to the net generation: What higher education professionals need to know about today's college students. *National Association of Student Personnel Administrators.* Retrieved from http://blog.reyjunco.com/pdf/NetGenerationProof.pdf

Kelly, R. (2009). A learner-centered emotionally engaging approach to online learning. In *Faculty Focus Special Report: Faculty Development in Distance Education: Issues, Trends and Tips.* Madison, Wisconsin: Magna Publications.

Lane, P., Hunt, J., & Farris, J. (2011). Innovate teaching to engage and challenge twenty-first century entrepreneurship students: An interdisciplinary approach. *Journal of Entrepreneurship Education, 14,* 105–123. Retrieved from http://0-search.proquest.com.liucat.lib.liu.edu/docview/885241325?accountid=12142

Mayer, R. E., & Moreno, R. (2003). Nine Ways to Reduce Cognitive Load in Multimedia Learning. *Educational Psychologist, 38*(1), 43–52. doi:10.1207/S15326985EP3801_6

Miller, M. V. (2011). A system for integrating online multimedia into college curriculum. *Journal of Online Learning and Teaching*, 7(2), 294.

Morrison, G. R., Ross, S. M., Kalman, H. W., & Kemp, J. E. (7th ed.). (2013). *Designing effective instruction* Hoboken, NJ: John Wiley & Sons, Inc.

Prensky, M. (2001). Digital natives, digital immigrants. *On the Horizon*, 9(5), 1–6. Retrieved from http://www.marcprensky.com/writing/Prensky%20-%20Digital%20Natives,%20Digital%20Immigrants%20-%20Part1.pdf doi:10.1108/10748120110424816

Rogers, M., Runyon, D., Starrett, D., & Von Holzen, R. (2006). Teaching the 21st century learner. *22nd Annual Conference on Distance Teaching and Learning*. Retrieved from http://umstrategicplan.wikispaces.com/file/view/teaching_21sC_Learner.pdf

Screencasting Best Practices. (n.d.). Retrieved from http://www.screencast.com/help/tutorial.aspx?id=403&

Sparks, R. L. (2006). Learning styles-Making too many 'wrong mistakes': A response to Castro and Peck. *Foreign Language Annals*, 39(3), 520–528. doi:10.1111/j.1944-9720.2006.tb02903.x

Tapscott, D., & Williams, A. D. (2010). Innovating the 21st century university. *EDUCAUSE Review*. Retrieved from http://www.educause.edu/er

Teeter, C., Fenton, N., Nicholson, K., Flynn, T., Kim, J., & McKay, M. et al. (2011). *Using communities of practice to foster faculty development in higher education. Collected Essays on Learning and Teaching*. CELT.

Vik, G. N. (2004). Breaking bad habits: Teaching effective PowerPoint use to working graduate students. *Business Communication Quarterly*, 67(2), 225–228. doi:10.1177/1080569904672012

Wilson, M. L. (2012). Learning styles, instructional strategies, and the question of matching: A literature review. *International Journal of Education*, 4(3), 67–87. Retrieved from http://0-search.proquest.com.liucat.lib.liu.edu/docview/1323309431?accountid=12142 doi:10.5296/ije.v4i3.1785

KEY TERMS AND DEFINITIONS

Auditory Learning Style: A learning style in which a person learns through listening.

Blending Learning Model: A learning modality that delivers 30 – 79% of content online. Also known as: Hybrid.

Chalk Talk: a talk or lecture illustrated by a blackboard.

Cognitive Constructivist Theory of Multimedia (CCTM): A theory creating purposeful interactive faculty-made digital learning content that engages and motivates learners. It is a supporting theory of the cognitive theory of multimedia learning (CTM).

Flipped Learning: A style of teaching where students learn new content online by watching video lectures, usually outside of the classroom, and homework is now done in class with teachers offering more personalized direction and interaction with students, instead of lecturing.

Kinesthetic Learning Style: A learning style in which learning takes place by the student carrying out a physical activity, rather than listening to a lecture or watching a demonstration.

Learning Styles: Traits that refer to how individuals approach learning tasks and process information.

Multimedia: The use of text, sound, video, computer graphics and animation for expressing ideas.

Online Learning: Where courses are delivered over the Internet that delivers 80% or more of the content online. Also known as: E-learning.

Online Presentations: Consisting of screen capture videos or videos that deliver content online. Also known as: online lectures.

Twenty-First Century Learner: According to Rogers et al. (2006) a twenty-first century learner is someone born after 1982 who mainly learns through interactions with technology. Also known as: Millennial students, net-generation learners, generation-Y and digital natives.

Video Screen Capture Tools: A digital recording of computer screen output usually containing audio. Also known as: Screencasting.

Visual Learning Style: A learning style in which learning takes place best through visual information.

Chapter 10
Evaluation of Situations Causing Split of Attention in Multimedia Learning Environments via Eye-Tracking Method

Duygu Mutlu-Bayraktar
Istanbul University, Turkey

Servet Bayram
Marmara University, Turkey

ABSTRACT

In this chapter, situations that can cause split of attention in multimedia environments were determined via eye tracking method. Fixation numbers, heat maps and area of interest of learners were analyzed. As a result of these analyses, design suggestions were determined for multimedia environments to provide focusing attention to content without split attention effect. Visual and auditory resources should be provided simultaneously. Visual information should be supported with auditory expression instead of texts. Images such as videos, pictures and texts should not be presented on the same screen. Texts provided with pictures should be presented via integration to each other instead of separate presentation of text and picture. Texts provided with videos should be presented via integration to each other instead of separate presentation of text and video. Images should be given via marking important points on images to increase attention.

1. INTRODUCTION

In learning environments, many studies revealed that learners showed higher learning performances in the environments with audio-based animations than in static environments (Plass, Heidig, Hayward, Homer and Um, 2013; Lin, Hung and Chang, 2013; van Genuchten, Scheiter and Schüler, 2012; Kühl, Scheiter, Gerjets, & Edelmann, 2011). In the studies performed by Huff, Bauhoff and Schwan (2012), Cierniak, Scheiter and Gerjets (2009), Liu, Lai, and Chuang, (2012), they found out when text and pictures were

DOI: 10.4018/978-1-4666-8696-0.ch010

not integrated together, applied test scores of people learning with split attention effect decreased. On the other hand, simultaneous presentation and presence of semantic harmony between them should be considered when animation and narration is used together (Širanović, 2007; Mayer, 2009).

In multimedia, presentation of texts visually rather than aurally prevents split of attention (Bayram and Mutlu-Bayraktar, 2012; Schmidt-Weigand, Kohnert and Glowalla, 2009; Seufert, Schutze and Brunken, 2009). It was highlighted that learners needed more expressive education and guidance to manage split attention situations better (Agostinho, Tindall-Ford and Roodenrys, 2013). In addition to these, it is emphasized that preparation of effective presentations in multimedia has positive effects on prevention of cognitive load, focusing of attention correctly and emotional and perceptual processes such as motivation and these effects are reflected on perception and transfer performances (Plass et al., 2013; Moreno & Park, 2010; Plass, Moreno and Brünken, 2010).

1.1. Split Attention Effect

Attention is loudly and clearly to embrace one of objects or thoughts appeared simultaneously in the mind. When it comes to attention, it is understood to give up others in order to deal more effectively with some things (James, 1983). Attention is defined as concentration of mental effort on sensory or mental events by Solso, Maclin and Maclin (2008).

Diversification of stimulants while providing information to learners is effective in terms of attracting attention. However, attention is divided while providing these stimulants and mental efforts of individuals can be directed to different parts (Mayer, 2001).

People can learn better in the environments that words and pictures are integrated and provided close to each other physically and formally. In the environments which information is provided from multiple sources, split attention effect does not arise in the case of that sources are quite clear and they are integrated without any need for further explanation (Ayres and Sweller, 2005). Extra information that is not integrated with other sources decreases learning performance of student and constitutes unnecessary memory space. In Web-based education, more effective results are obtained when verbal and visual information is provided together. Presentation of this information close to each other without separation prevents split of attention (Sweller, 2004).

While learners are studying information from multi-source presentations, giving information as integrated provides learners to understand better. Information that is not presented in accordance with this principle causes split of learner's attention for two different tasks. For instance, it is thought that trying to read text results in split into two different tasks while animation is operating (Sorden, 2005). In addition, learners watching visual contents have to simultaneously combine number of features such as perception-oriented style, form or direction with movements of objects moving from one place to another on screen. It is stated that movements and changes in objects draw attention and prevent to focus on actual content (Hillstrom and Chai, 2006). Besides these, it is emphasized that preparation of effective presentations in multimedia, prevention of cognitive load and accurate focusing positively affect learners' emotional and perceptional progresses such as motivation and it is reflected on cognition and transfer performances with this effect (Plass et al., 2013; Moreno and Park, 2010; Plass, Moreno and Brünken, 2010).

In presentations that texts and pictures are provided together, it is known that giving text below picture as an explanation is enough, but it is thought that more effective results can be obtained when text is integrated to picture. In this case, picture and text is put into information process. In presentations that animation and expression is provided together, simultaneous presentation and semantic harmony between them should be considered (Širanović, 2007; Mayer, 2009). The first study about split attention was carried out for geometry education by Tarmizi and Sweller (1988). In the study, samples were described via two types of geometric forms. Performances of problem-solving strategies with the samples that were provided with geometric shapes integrated directly with information and the samples that information was given below shape with stages were compared. In the second environment which shape and text were provided separately, it was found that attention of learners was divided between shape and text and they needed to make more effort due to cognitive load when compared to other environment.

Eye tracking method which is one of the innovations used to put forward the principles considered for prevention of split attention effect in multimedia learning designs having text and picture combination provides to obtain more precise results from studies. In recent studies, it is emphasized that eye tracking method should be used to provide findings based on more precise evidences (Liu, Lai and Chuang, 2011). It appears that eye tracking method is quite effective especially in multimedia learning environments that visual and verbal information is provided together (Yang, Chang, Chien, Chien, and Tseng, 2013; Molina, Redondo, Lacave, and Ortega, 2013; Alkan, 2013). In many studies based on multimedia learning environment theory, data are based only on test results and comments remain incomplete in terms of cognitive processes. Especially in studies carried out about attention, lack of eye tracking data causes not to obtain clear results. Comments about design according to only expression of individual or test results are not enough to explain cognitive processes. Therefore, eye-tracking method is used in the studies aiming to examine multimedia learning environments (Mason, Tornatora and Pluchino, 2013; Bayram and Mutlu-Bayraktar, 2012; Liu, Lai and Chuang, 2011). For this purpose, results have been strengthened via eye tracking method within the scope of the study.

1.2. Eye-Tracking Method

Eye tracking method provides eye movement data about focused areas while people following content on screen, objects that they ignore and they are disturbed (Underwood and Radach, 1998; Russell, 2005). Eye tracking measurements are quite valuable in terms of supporting and verifying the results previously produced in multimedia studies. Moreover, eye movements deeply provide qualitative and quantitative data about processing information by users. This method helps to find individual differences via tracking eye movements and to interact with source provided (Liu, Lai ve Chuang, 2011).

1.3. History of Eye Tracking

When we look at the history of eye tracking methods, studies about examination of eye movements were performed via direct observations in the 1800s. Then, eye movements were tracked on an aluminum indicator using a kind of contact lens. The first eye tracking more convenient than other methods was developed via a principal based on use of beam reflected from eye and recorded as a film. Buswell examined eye movements about reading and viewing picture in his two different studies (Buswell, 1922; 1937). New studies about eye tracking were carried out in the 1950s and 1960s. Experiments were carried out especially about attention and related issues (Yarbus, 1967).

In the 1970s, new researches especially about 'reading' were performed in studies about eye tracking (Rayner, 1998). In the study about eye tracking carried out during problem solving process by Hunziker (1970), visual problem solving displayed on glass plate was filmed.

Researches that were performed in the 1980s and 1990s and were thought to provide a base for recent eye tracking studies presented new findings about eye tracking method (Posner, 1980; Deubel and Schneider, 1996; Hoffman, 1998). In the 2000s, studies performed with measurements giving better results with developing technology prove or reject findings of studies previously carried out (Liu, Lai and Chuang, 2011; Russell, 2005). With this method, it is one of the most effective methods to perform usability tests of items such as user interface, menu, graphic (Bazar, 2009; Byrne, Anderson, Douglass, & Matessa, 1999) and web sites (Tüzün, Akıncı, Kurtoğlu, Atal, & Pala, (2013), Faraday, 2001; Goldberg, Stimson, Lewenstein, Scott, & Wichansky, 2002). Upon reviewing previous studies, it is seen that measurements of eye movement variables used to measure and define individual's cognitive activity are used most commonly (Mutlu-Bayraktar & Bayram, 2013, Yang et al., 2013; Jarodzka, Van Gog, Dorr, Scheiter, & Gerjets, 2013).

Screening path of eye, duration spent for looking at various images, focusing areas of visual attention and number of winks are obtained with eye tracking method.

1.4. Eye Tracking Systems and Data Obtained

Eye movements are related to cognitive operations in the brain, so that it provides to obtain information about these operations and processes via observing and interpreting eye movements (Biedert, Buscher and Dengel, 2009). It is quite important that experimental environments prepared with this method measuring cognitive processes should be natural and they should be in a way that participants will not feel like they are in experimental environment. Simple-to-use eye-tracking device located away from should be preferred to the device mounted on head (Namahn, 2000). Within the scope of this study, it was integrated under the monitor in Human-Computer Interaction laboratory and unnoticed eye tracking device was used.

Definitions of some terms used for eye tracking data were listed below (Jacob and Karn, 2003):

Fixation: Fixing eye, looking at object or areas generally with 2-degree distribution threshold and minimum 100-200 ms duration.
Gaze Duration: The duration that eye looks at a certain point via keeping on.
Scan Path: Roaming pattern of fixed gaze on screen (See Figure 1).

Area of interest: Attractive picture or visual environmental area that researcher specifies (See Figure 2).
Heat map: The screens are rated with colors on heat maps according to gaze duration and number (See Figure 3).

In addition to these data, images are obtained from video records saved by cameras found in HCI laboratory. It provides important information via enabling to observe individuals' reactions and behaviors in video and via being an information store including visual and audio sides.

Eye tracking method provides eye movement data about areas paid attention, subjects ignored and irritating things when people follow content on screen (Underwood and Radach, 1998; Russell, 2005). Eye tracking measurements are quite valuable in terms of support and confirmation of the results produced in previous multimedia environment studies. Moreover, eye movements deeply provide qualitative and quantitative data about processing of information by users. This method helps about finding individual differences and interacting with presented source via tracking eye movements (Liu, Lai and Chuang, 2011).

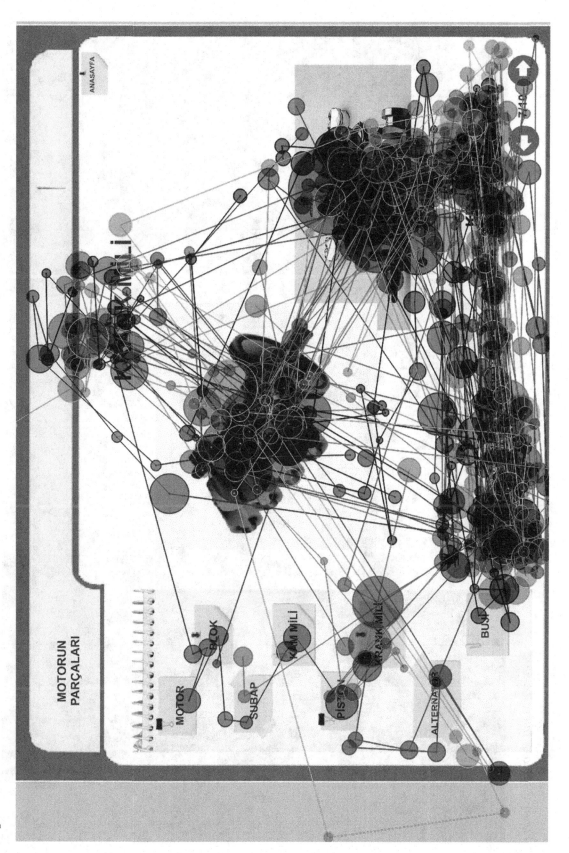

Figure 1. Scan Path Data

Figure 2. Area of Interest Data

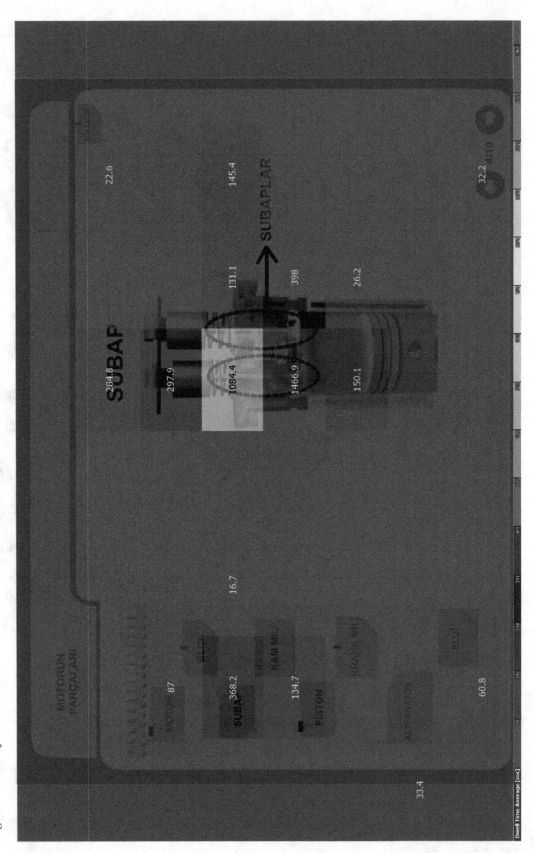

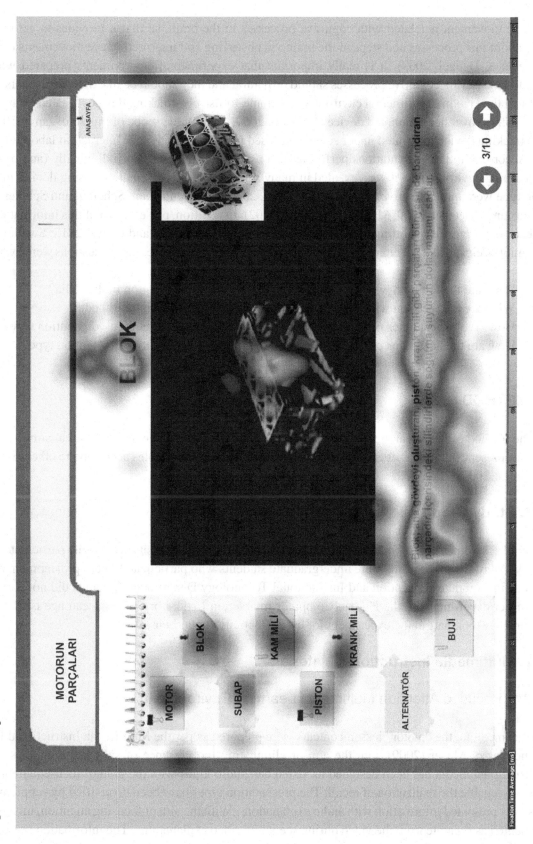

Figure 3. Heat Map Data

Eye movement is related with cognitive processes in the brain, so that it provides to get information about this processes and steps in the brain via observing and interpreting eye movements (Biedert, Buscher & Dengel, 2009). It is really important that experimental environments prepared with this method measuring cognitive processes should be natural and they should be like that participants should not feel they are in experimental environment. Simple-to-use eye-tracking devices located away should be preferred over head-mounted device (Namahn, 2000). Within the scope of this study, an unobtrusive eye tracking device integrated under screen was used in Human-Computer Interaction laboratory.

According to the presentations performed via using information types individually (audio, visual) in learning environments, it was revealed in many studies that the presentations using double information type were more effective (Mayer and Moreno, 2013; Van Genuchten, Scheiter, and Schüler, 2012; Florax and Ploetzner, 2009; Mayer and Moreno, 2002). In addition, presentation of this information near to each other prevents splitting of attention (Crooks, Inan, Cheon, Ari and Flores, 2012; Sweller, 2004, Schmidt-Weigand and Scheiter, 2011). For this purpose, the following research questions were examined.

1. What are the areas on which learners focus more in focused attention multimedia?
2. What are the areas on which learners focus more in split attention multimedia?
3. How are the heat maps of learners during the use of multimedia in focused attention type?
4. How are the heat maps of learners during the use of multimedia in split attention type?

2. METHOD

In the method of the research was survey model. Survey models are the researches that aim to describe past or present situation as it exists and are performed with larger samples according to other researches (Karasar, 2007).

2.1. Study Group

Overall, 27 women and 20 men, total 47 students from Marmara University voluntarily participated in the study. All of the participants were undergraduate students who participated in the project management course in Computer Education and Instructional Technology Department. Students did not participate in earlier experiments in the Human Computer Interaction Laboratory. Their mean age is 21.5. They voluntarily took part in the experiment for extra 10 points about their exam.

2.2. Multimedia Instructional Materials

2.2.1. Focused Attention Multimedia Learning Environment

In this medium, the "motor" lesson contents were prepared as per the Multimedia Instructional Design Principles of Mayer (2009) with the aim of eliminating the presence of split attention causes. This instructional media has been designed as visual and audio kinds with the goal of focused attention, in order to enable the realization of recall. The presentation types have been diversified by supplementing visually presented information with audio explanations. With the aim of focusing attention, images were presented as separate from the video during scenes of video explanations. The information presented in

Figure 4. Screenshot of a Presentation from Focused Attention Multimedia

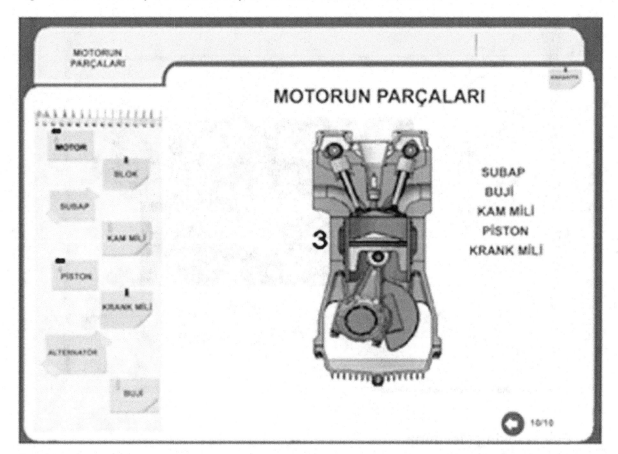

images was thus presented with the objective of offering the explanation in audio and enabling focusing on the image and the explanation. The information presented in the images were supplemented with audio and presented in progression. The texts relevant to the images were presented in an integrated manner to the explained images. The material was designed to allow the self-pacing of the student. The students were presented with operation instructions for perusing the material (See Figure 4).

2.2.2. Split Attention Multimedia Learning Environment

In this medium, the "motor" lesson contents were prepared in audio presentation according to the possibility of the occurrence of split attention effect. Images and texts were added into the scenes containing information presented in the videos. The audio information was prepared to present different sections than those presented as texts. The text descriptions of the images were presented spatially distanced from the images themselves. The application's preparation allowed the student's self-pacing. The students were presented with operation instructions for perusing the material (See Figure 5).

Figure 5. Screenshot of a Presentation from Split Attention Multimedia

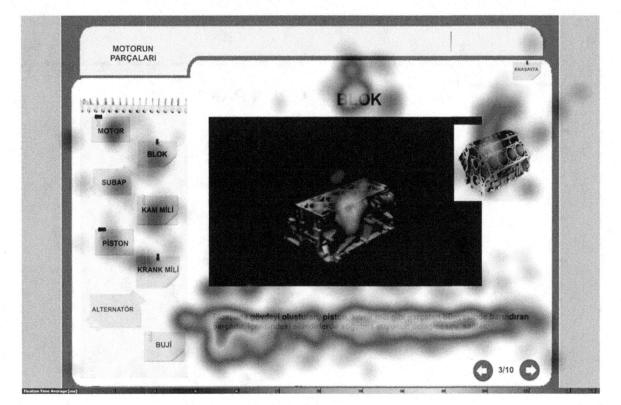

2.3. Eye Tracking Measures

Eye tracking data can provide valuable information about the attention processes of the learners. The participants studied these materials and they were tested individually at the Marmara University Human Computer Interaction Laboratory. It will be completed.

In this study, SMI Experiment and Begaze 2.4 programs were used for measuring eye-movement data. After calibration, participants were presented with multimedia learning environments.

2.4. Tools Used During Eye Tracking

The experiments were carried out in Human-Computer Interaction Laboratory used in Computer and Education Technologies Department of Atatürk Education Faculty of Marmara University. Units used in the laboratory:

2.4.1. Cameras

In the test room, one remotely controlled dome camera serving to observe all movements of user, where camera looks at is not understood due to translucent plastic cover on it and one mobile camera serving to show keyboard use (See Figure 6).

Figure 6. Cameras

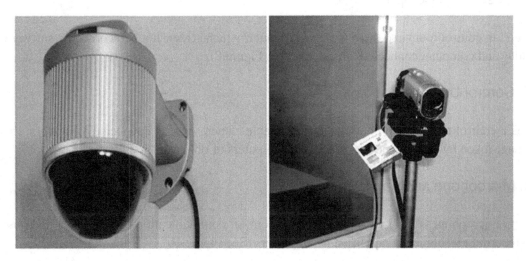

2.4.2. Eye Tracking Device and Test Computer

There is an eye-tracking device that gives information about where, how long and how many times user looks at the screen and simultaneously records eye movements during test process. It is connected to a test computer which is linked to the device and user will perform the experiment and to another computer which is found in observer's room and records screenshots of user (See Figure 7).

Figure 7. Eye-Tracking Device and Test Computer

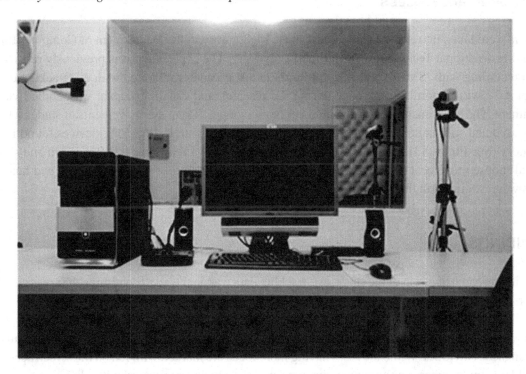

2.4.3. Observer's Computer

It is found in control room and there is also a computer which screenshot is recorded by software such as Noldus and computer connected to cameras (See Figure 8).

2.4.4. Control Unit

There is a control unite which controls 360° pivotable cameras and is connected to monitor showing both image taken by camera and screenshots of computers of observer (See Figure 9).

2.4.5. Microphone and Amplifier

There are microphones in test room and control room for communication between user and observer. Audio recording resolution is amplified by amplifiers (See Figure 10).

2.4.6. Sound Isolation

It should be performed to be protected from harmful effects of noise and to create proper use conditions via isolating test room from unwanted sounds during test.

2.4.7. One-Way Mirror

Observers follow behaviors of users via one-way mirror that separates test room and control room.

2.5. Experiment Process

Learners were taken into experiment process in HCI laboratory in the Department of Computer Education and Instructional Technology of Marmara University. The experiment was previously recorded as screen recording with 'SMI Experiment' program in test computer mounted with eye tracking device. This process was performed only once during the research and each participant was studied via this experiment. The experiment was started after calibration of eye. Then, eye movements of students studying focused and split multimedia environments were recorded with eye tracking devices found in HCI laboratory (See Figure 13). The records which were recorded via Experiment 2.4 program and showed eye and mouse movements were analyzed via Be Gaze 2.4 program. Fixation, duration and heat map values were examined in the analyses.

3. FINDINGS

In the first research question of the study, eye-tracking data was analyzed to determine the areas on which learners focused more in multimedia designed according to focused attention.

While fixation numbers were detected via eye-tracking device, the duration between stage opening and moving to other page was accepted as beginning. Fixation numbers were detected during the duration between these two times. While the areas having more focus are marked with red on the screen according to total focusing numbers on the screen, the areas with less focus are marked with blue.

Figure 8. Observer's Computer

Figure 9. Control Unit

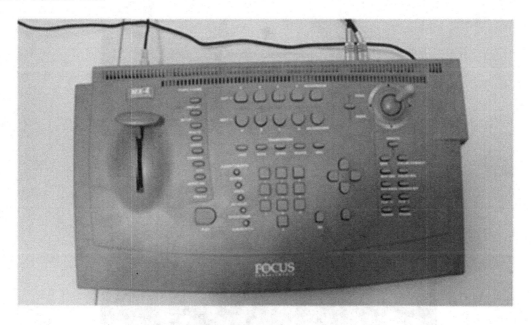

Figure 10. Microphone and Amplifier

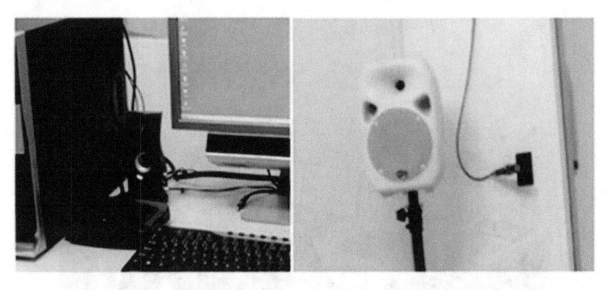

Figure 11. Experiment Process

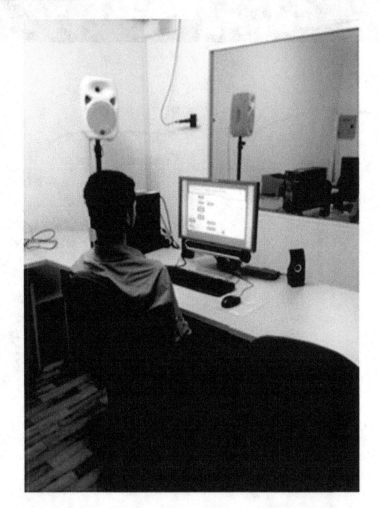

Figure 12. Color Transition for Fixation Number

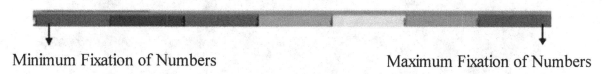

Minimum Fixation of Numbers   Maximum Fixation of Numbers

On the screen which names of motor parts were presented as integrated into picture and video, it was aimed that students focused on both of them without any split of attention between text and picture. When eye tracking data was evaluated, it was seen that students mainly focused on pictures, then on texts and menu buttons (See Figure 13).

On another focused multimedia screen that audio expression and video were used, it was aimed to make fixation on actually described part in the video via images. So that it was aimed to prevent split of focuses of learners on other objects in the video. When eye tracking data of this screen is evaluated, it is found that learners focus more on the object described in the video. Then, they focus on name of the object and menu buttons (See Figure 14).

In the second research question of the study, Eye-tracking data was analyzed to determine the areas that learners focused more in multimedia designed according to split attention. When eye tracking data obtained for the screen used for video, text and audio expression is evaluated in multimedia learning environments which emergence of split attention effect is possible and motor and its parts are described, it is seen that learners focus more on texts and fixation numbers are more in texts than in picture or video. It is seen that learners' attentions are split between picture and video and use of texts as well as audio expression makes focusing difficult. This situation affected learner performance as a result of emergence of effect of extremeness (See Figure 15).

When eye tracking data belonging to the screens that names of motor parts in picture or video are presented without integration into pictures is evaluated in multimedia learning environments which emergence of split attention effect is possible, it is seen that attentions of learners are split between picture and text. It is found that they focus more on texts then on picture and buttons according to fixation numbers (See Figure 16).

In the next research question of the study, eye-tracking data was analyzed to determine heat map during use of multimedia in focused attention type by learners. Another analysis type for processing the data obtained from eye tracking is heat maps. The screens are rated with colors on heat maps according to gaze duration and number. After opening screen, the most focused area on interface for related objects can be detected. While heat map images on the screens were being obtained, the duration between stage opening and moving to other page was accepted as beginning. Heat maps were established with constant gazes during the duration between these two times.

While the areas having more focus are marked with red on the screen, the areas with less focus are marked with blue. Color transition for heat maps are presented in Figure 17.

On the image in focused attention multimedia, it was aimed that learners focused on both the text and picture without attention split on the screens which texts containing names of motor parts were integrated into the picture. When heat maps are evaluated according to eye tracking data, it is seen that learners focus more on pictures then on texts and menu buttons (See Figure 18).

In focused attention multimedia, it was tried to perform focusing via marking on actually described part in video. Therefore, it was aimed to prevent attentions of learners to split into other objects in video.

Figure 13. Fixation Numbers Belonging to the Screen in which Texts were Integrated to Pictures in Focused Attention Multimedia

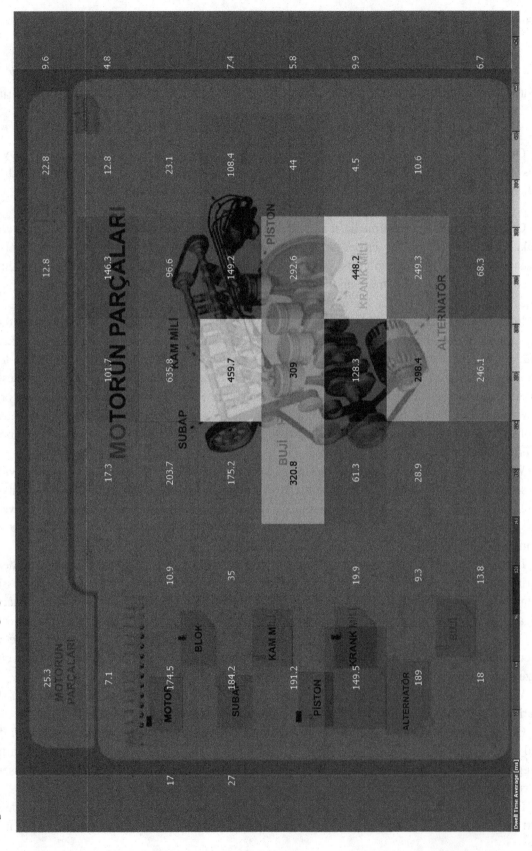

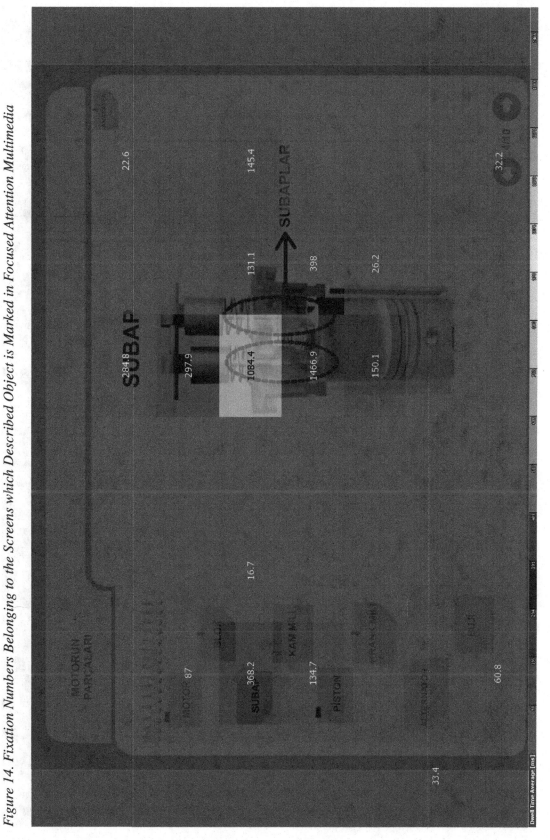

Figure 14. Fixation Numbers Belonging to the Screens which Described Object is Marked in Focused Attention Multimedia

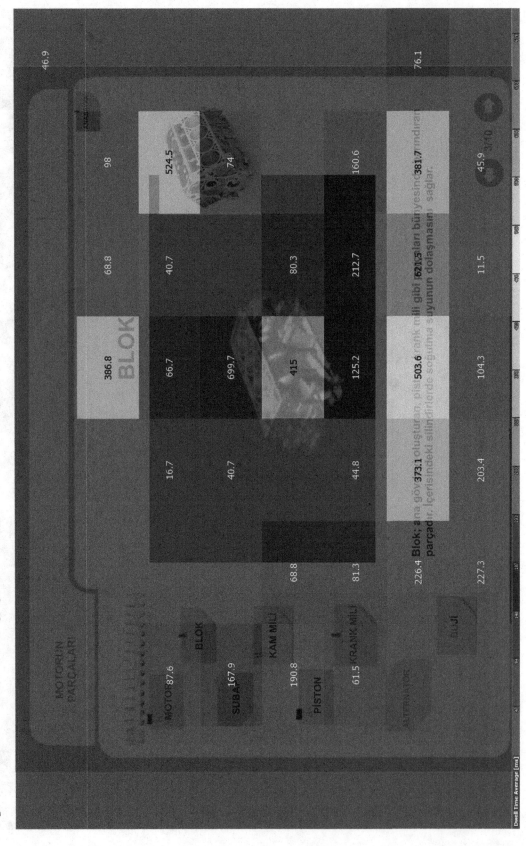

Figure 15. Fixation Numbers Belonging to the Screen which Video, Text and Audio Expressions are Present in Split Attention Multimedia

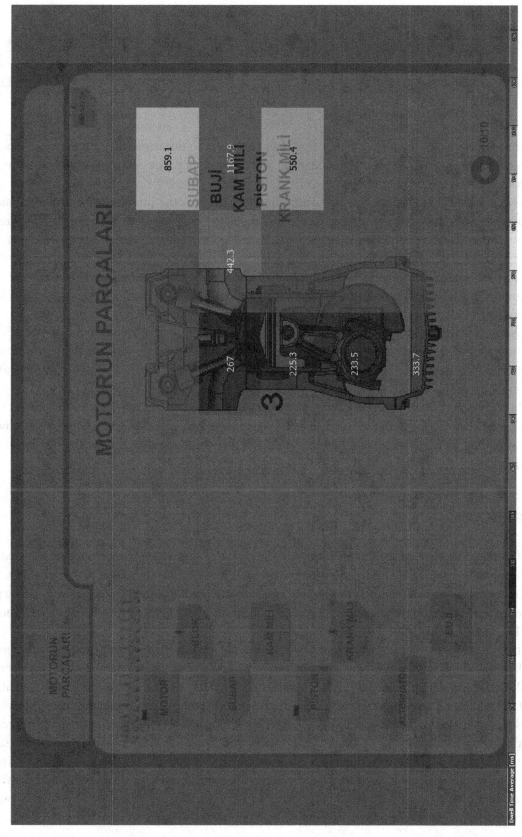

Figure 16. Fixation Numbers Belonging to the Screen in which Texts are Separately Presented from Video in Split Attention Multimedia

Figure 17. Color Transition for Heat Map

Minumum Duration   Maximum Duration

When the heat maps about the eye tracking data belonging to this screen are examined, it is seen that learners focus more on the object marked in the video. Then, they focus on name of the object and menu buttons (See Figure 19).

Eye tracking data was analyzed to determine heat maps in the progress of use of multimedia by students in split attention type. When heat map about eye tracking data obtained for the screen that video, text and audio expression were used was examined in multimedia learning environments which emergence of split attention effect is possible, it is seen that learners focus more on texts than on picture or video. It is seen that learners' attentions are split between picture and video and use of texts as well as audio expression makes focusing difficult. This situation affected learner performance as a result of emergence of effect of extremeness (Figure 20).

When heat map belonging the screens that are presented as names of motor parts in picture or video are not integrated into pictures is evaluated in multimedia learning environments which emergence of split attention effect is possible, it is seen that attentions of learners are split between picture and text. It is found that learners focus more on texts, then on picture and buttons (See Figure 21).

In focused attention multimedia, the part was marked in the video to increase focusing on motor part being described with the video. This marking was not performed in split attention multimedia. In this situation, focusing is dispersed on the video and it is not focused on the part being described (See Figure 22).

4. RESULTS

Use of different sources such as picture, text and audio in learning environments enriches education environments. Especially online learning environments as tools assisting rapid development and spread of knowledge support learning. In developing online learning environments, interactive learning process is generated between content and learners. Environments used aim to provide configuration of knowledge via keeping students active during learning process.

In e-learning environments, many studies revealed that learners showed higher learning performances in the environments with audio-based animations, also text and pictures were integrated together (Plass, et al., 2013; Lin, Hung and Chang, 2013; van Genuchten, Scheiter and Schüler, 2012; Liu, et al., 2012; Huff, Bauhoff and Schwan, 2012; Kühl, et al., 2011). On the other hand, simultaneous presentation and presence of semantic harmony between them should be considered when animation and expression is used together (Širanović, 2007; Mayer, 2009). In this study, it was similarly found out that restoration performances of learners were higher in the environments with presentation of integrated visual and verbal presentation type information than in the environments without this integration. On the other hand, simultaneous presentation and presence of semantic harmony between them should be considered when animation and expression is used together (Širanović, 2007; Mayer, 2009).

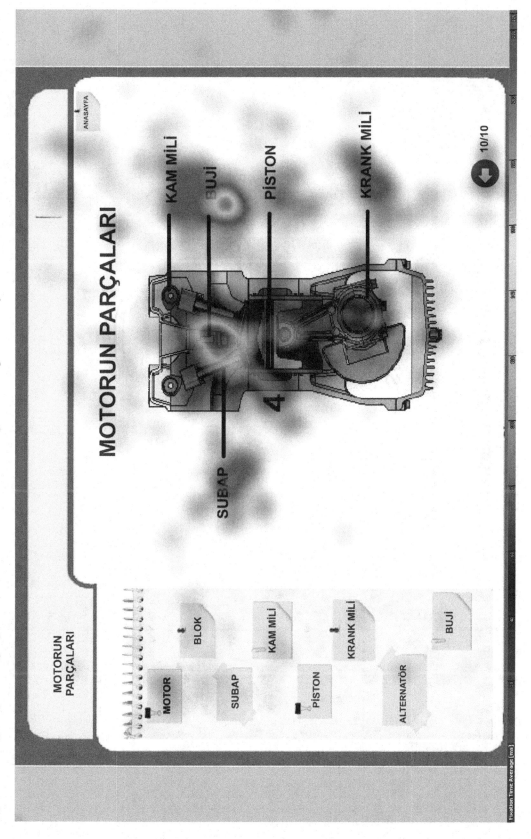

Figure 18. Heap maps belonging to the screens which texts are integrated into pictures in focused attention multimedia

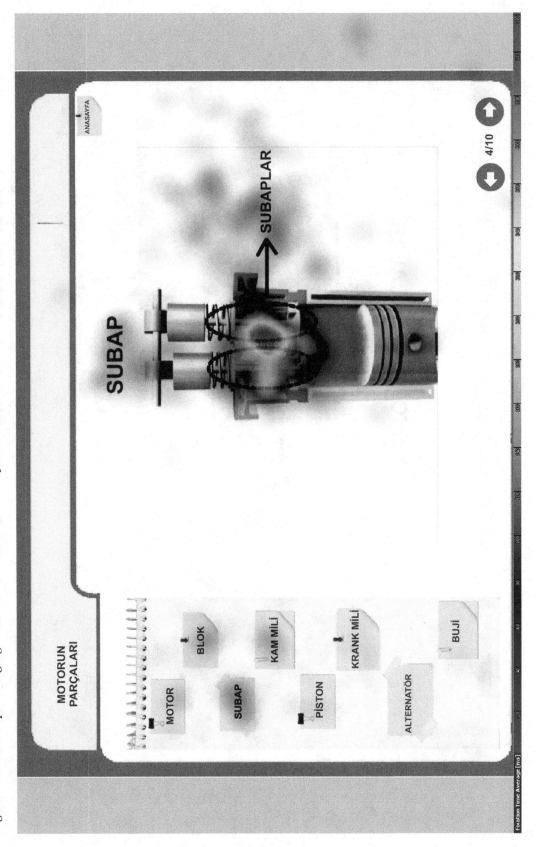

Figure 19. Heat Map Belonging to the Screen in which the Object is Marked in Focused Attention Multimedia

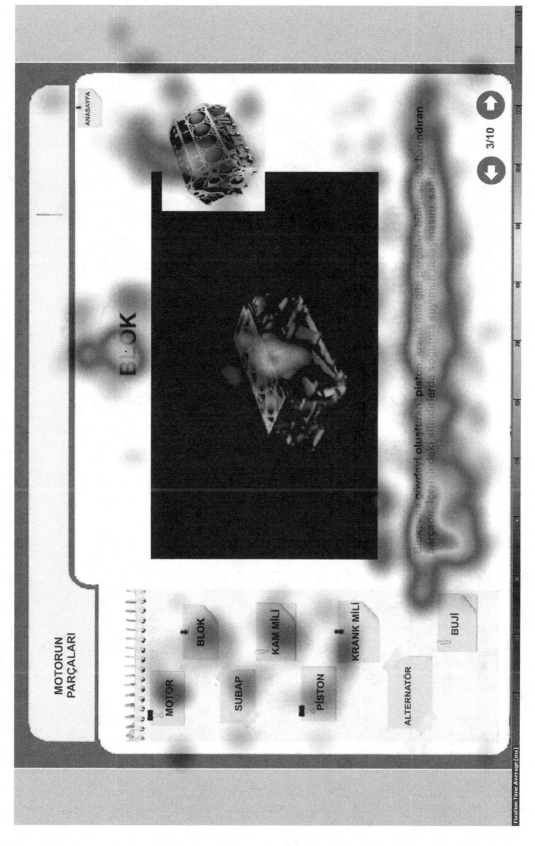

Figure 20. Heat map belonging to the screen that video, picture and audio expressions are present in split attention multimedia

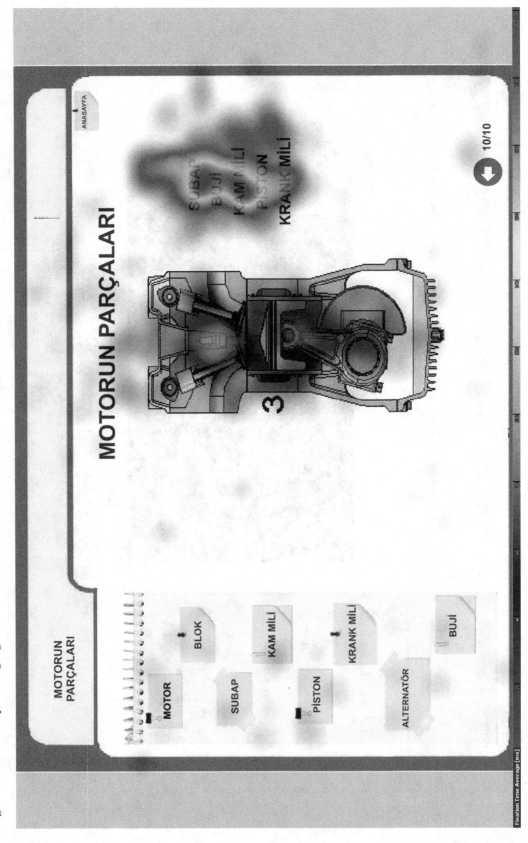

Figure 21. Heat Map belonging to the Screen that Texts and Pictures are Separately Presented in Split Attention Multimedia

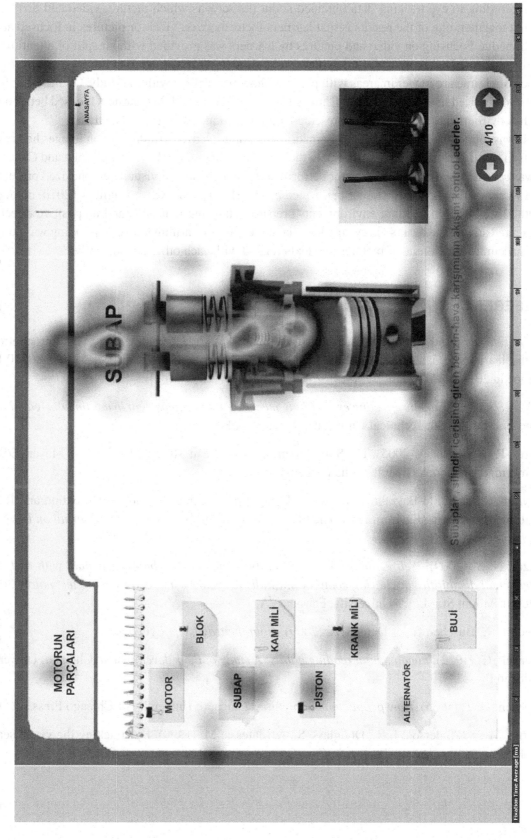

Figure 22. Heat Map Belonging to the Screen that is Presented without Marking the Object in Split Attention Multimedia

According to eye tracking data obtained about the screens which picture, video and texts are presented together, one of the results is that learners focus more on video or pictures in focused attention multimedia. Focusing on video and pictures by learners was provided without split of attention. In the study performed by Yang et al. (2013), the results showing that average fixation time and average data processing time are longer in areas with pictures show parallelism with the study. On the other hand, in the study carried out by Liu, Lai and Chuang (2011), they revealed that learners focused better on video in the environments that texts were presented with narration, rather than visually.

It was found that markings made to aim drawing attention to a certain point on images had contributions to recall performances of learners. In the study carried out by Chen, Wang, Chen and Chen (2014), it was seen that learners showed better performances with the use of visually emphasized presentations and visual markings. In two studies performed by Ozcelik, Arslan-Ari, & Cagiltay, (2010) color coding method was used in learning environments prepared via using markings and its positive effects were presented among the results via eye tracking data. Increase in learning with color-coding was performed with accurate positioning of pictures and texts related with each other concurrently.

REFERENCES

Agostinho, S., Tindall-Ford, S., & Roodenrys, K. (2013). Adaptive diagrams: Handing control over to the learner to manage split-attention online. *Computers & Education*, *64*, 52–62. doi:10.1016/j.compedu.2013.01.007

Alkan, S. (2013). *Factors effecting eye tracking measures and achievement in multimedia learning* (PhD Thesis). Middle East Technical University, Ankara, Turkey.

Ayres, P. ve Sweller, J. (2005). The Split-Attention Principle in Multimedia. In R. E. Mayer (Ed.)., The Cambridge Handbook of Multimedia Learning.

Bayram, S., & Mutlu-Bayraktar, D. (2012). Using Eye Tracking to Study on Attention and Recall in Multimedia Learning Environments: The Effects of Design in Learning. *World Journal on Educational Technology*, *4*(2), 81–98.

Bazar, N. S. (2009). *Web usability or accessibility: Comparisons between people with and without intellectual disabilities in viewing complex naturalistic scenes using eye-tracking technology.* (Master Thesis). Mount St. Mary's University, Fairfax, VA.

Biedert, R., Buscher, G., & Dengel, A. (2009). *Hauptbeitrag / The Eyebook.*

Buswell, G. (1922). *Fundamental reading habits: A study of their development.* Chicago: University of Chicago Press.

Buswell, G. T. (1935). *How people look at pictures.* Chicago: University of Chicago Press.

Byrne, M. D., Anderson, J. R., Douglass, S., & Matessa, M. (1999). Eye tracking the visual search of click-down menus. *Human Factors in Computing Systems: Proceedings of CHI '99.*

Chen, M.-P., Wang, L.-C., Chen, H.-J., & Chen, Y.-C. (2014). Effects of type of multimedia strategy on learning of Chinese characters for non-native novices. *Computers & Education*, *70*, 41–52. doi:10.1016/j.compedu.2013.07.042

Cierniak, G., Scheiter, K., & Gerjets, P. (2009). Explaining the split-attention effect: Is the reduction of extraneous cognitive load accompanied by an increase in germane cognitive load? *Computers in Human Behavior*, *25*(2), 315–324. doi:10.1016/j.chb.2008.12.020

Crooks, S., Inan, F., Cheon, J., Ari, F., & Flores, R. (2012). Modality and cueing in multimedia learning: Examining cognitive and perceptual explanations for the modality effect. *Computers in Human Behavior*, *28*(3), 1063–1071. doi:10.1016/j.chb.2012.01.010

Deubel, H., & Schneider, W. (1996). Saccade target selection and object recognition: Evidence for a common attentional mechanism. *Vision Research*, *36*(12), 1827–1837. doi:10.1016/0042-6989(95)00294-4 PMID:8759451

Florax, M., & Ploetzner, R. (2010). What contributes to the split-attention effect? The role of text segmentation, picture labelling, and spatial proximity. *Learning and Instruction*, *20*(3), 216–224. doi:10.1016/j.learninstruc.2009.02.021

Goldberg, J. H., Stimson, M. J., Lewenstein, M., Scott, N., & Wichansky, A. (2002). Eye tracking in web search tasks: Design implications. *In Proceedings of the Eye Tracking and Related Applications Symposium*, 51-59. doi:10.1145/507072.507082

Hillstrom, A. P., & Chai, Y. C. (2006). Factors that guide or distrupt attentive visual processing. *Computers in Human Behavior*, *22*(4), 648–656. doi:10.1016/j.chb.2005.12.003

Hoffman, J. E. (1998). *Visual attention and eye movements*. Hove, UK: Psychology Press.

Huff, M., Bauhoff, V., & Schwan, S. (2012). Effects of split attention revisited: A new display technology for troubleshooting tasks. *Computers in Human Behavior*, *28*(4), 1254–1261. doi:10.1016/j.chb.2012.02.008

Hunziker, H. W. (1970). Visuelle Informationsaufnahme und Intelligenz: Eine Untersuchung über die Augenfixationen beim Problemlösen. Schweizerische Zeitschrift für Psychologie und ihre Anwendungen. Retrieved from http://www.learning-systems.ch/multimedia/forsch1e.htm

Jacob, R. J. K., & Karn, K. S. (2003). Eye tracking in human-computer interaction and usability research: Ready to deliver the promises. In J. Hyona, R. Radach, & H. Deubel (Eds.), *The mind's eye: cognitive and applied aspects of eye movement research* (pp. 573–603). Oxford, UK: Elsevier Science. doi:10.1016/B978-044451020-4/50031-1

James, W. (1983). *The Principles of Psychology*. Cambridge, MA: Harvard University Press.

Jarodzka, H., Van Gog, T., Dorr, M., Scheiter, K., & Gerjets, P. (2013). Learning to see: Guiding students' attention via a Model's eye movements fosters learning. *Learning and Instruction*, *25*, 62–70. doi:10.1016/j.learninstruc.2012.11.004

Karasar, N. (2007). *Bilimsel Araştırma Yöntemi. 17. Baskı*. Ankara: Nobel Yayın Dağıtım.

Kühl, T., Scheiter, K., Gerjets, P., & Edelmann, J. (2011). The influence of text modality on learning with static and dynamic visualizations. *Computers in Human Behavior, 27*(1), 29–35. doi:10.1016/j.chb.2010.05.008

Lin, C. F., Hung, Y. H., & Chang, R. I. (2013). Analyzing the Effects of Different Multimedia Materials on Learning System. *Journal of Computer Trends and Technology, 4*(5), 2145–2150.

Liu, H. C., Lai, M. L., & Chuang, H. H. (2011). Using eye-tracking technology to investigate the redundant effect of multimedia web pages on viewers' cognitive processes. *Computers in Human Behavior, Vol, 27*(6), 2410–2417. doi:10.1016/j.chb.2011.06.012

Mason, L., Tornatora, M. C., & Pluchino, P. (2013). Do fourth graders integrate text and picture in processing and learning from an illustrated science text? Evidence from eye-movement patterns. *Computers & Education, 60*(1), 95–109. doi:10.1016/j.compedu.2012.07.011

Mayer, R. E. (2009). *Multimedia learning.* New York, USA: Cambridge University Press. doi:10.1017/CBO9780511811678

Mayer, R. E., & Moreno, R. (2002). Aids to computer-based multimedia learning. *Learning and Instruction, 12*(1), 107–119. doi:10.1016/S0959-4752(01)00018-4

Mayer, R. E., & Moreno, R. (2010). Techniques that reduce extraneous cognitive load and manage intrinsic cognitive load during multimedia learning. In J. L. Plass, R. Moreno, R. Brünken, (Ed.), Cognitive load theory (s.131-153). New York: Cambridge University Press.

Molina, A. I., Redondo, M. A., Lacave, C., & Ortega, M. (2013). Assessing the effectiveness of new devices for accessing learning materials: An empirical analysis based on eye tracking and learner subjective perception. *Computers in Human Behavior.*

Moreno, R., & Park, B. (2010). Cognitive load theory: Historical development and relation to other theories. In J. L. Plass, R. Moreno, & R. Brünken (Eds.), *Cognitive Load Theory.* Cambridge: Cambridge University Press. doi:10.1017/CBO9780511844744.003

Mutlu-Bayraktar, D., & Bayram, S. (2013). Using Eye Tracking to Investigate the Relationship Between Attention and Change Blindness. *World Journal on Educational Technology, 5*(2), 257–265.

NAMAHN. (2000). *Using eye-tracking for usability test.* Brussels: NAMAHN.

Ozcelik, E., Arslan-Ari, I., & Cagiltay, K. (2010). Why does Signaling Enhance Multimedia Learning? Evidence from Eye Movements. *Computers in Human Behavior, 26*(1), 110–117. doi:10.1016/j.chb.2009.09.001

Plass, J. L., Heidig, S., Hayward, E. O., Homer, B. D., & Um, E. J. (2013). Emotional Design in Multimedia Learning: Effects of Shape and Color on Affect and Learning. *Learning and Instruction*; Advanced Online Publication. doi:10.1016/j.learninstruc

Plass, J. L., Moreno, R., & Brünken, R. (2010). Cognitive Load Theory. New York: Cambridge. doi:10.1017/CBO9780511844744

Posner, M. I. (1980). Orienting of attention. *The Quarterly Journal of Experimental Psychology, 32*(1), 3–25. doi:10.1080/00335558008248231 PMID:7367577

Rayner, K. (1998). Eye movements in reading and information processing: 20 years of research. *Psychological Bulletin, 124*(3), 372–422. doi:10.1037/0033-2909.124.3.372 PMID:9849112

Russell, M. (2005). Using eye-tracking data to understand first impressions of a website. *Usability News, 7*(1), 1–14.

Schmidt-Weigand, F., Kohnert, A., & Glowalla, U. (2009). A closer look at split visual attention in system- and self-paced instruction in multimedia learning. *Learning and Instruction, 1*, 11.

Schmidt-Weigand, F., & Scheiter, K. (2011). The role of spatial descriptions in learning from multimedia. *Computers in Human Behavior, 27*(1), 22–28. doi:10.1016/j.chb.2010.05.007

Seufert, T., Schütze, M., & Brünken, R. (2009). Memory characteristics and modality in multimedia learning: An aptitude treatment interaction study. *Learning and Instruction, 19*(1), 28–42. doi:10.1016/j.learninstruc.2008.01.002

Širanović, Z. (2007). *Guidelines for designing multimedia learning materials*. Varaždin: University of Zagreb.

Solso, R. L., Maclin, M. K., & Maclin, O. H. (2008). Cognitive Psychology, Bacon, USA: Pearson.

Sorden, S. D. (2005). A Cognitive Approach to Instructional Design for Multimedia Learning. *Informing Science Journal, V*, 8.

Sweller, J. (2004). Instructional design consequences of an analogy between evolution by natural selection and human cognitive architecture. *Instructional Science, 32*(1/2), 9–31. doi:10.1023/B:TRUC.0000021808.72598.4d

Tarmizi, R., & Sweller, J. (1988). Guidance during mathematical problem solving. *Journal of Educational Psychology, 80*(4), 424–436. doi:10.1037/0022-0663.80.4.424

Tüzün, H., Akıncı, A., Kurtoğlu, M., Atal, D., & Pala, F. K. (2013). A Study on the Usability of a University Registrar's Office. *The Turkish Online Journal of Educational Technology, 12*(2).

Underwood, G., & Radach, R. (1998). Eye guidance and visual information processing: Reading, visual search, picture perception and driving. In G. Underwood (Ed.), *Eye guidance in reading and scene perception* (pp. 1–28). Oxford, England: Elsevier Science Ltd. doi:10.1016/B978-008043361-5/50002-X

van Genuchten, E., Scheiter, K., & Schüler, A. (2012). Examining learning from text and pictures for different task types: Does the multimedia effect differ for conceptual, causal, and procedural tasks? *Computers in Human Behavior, 28*(6), 2209–2218. doi:10.1016/j.chb.2012.06.028

Yang, F. Y., Chang, C. Y., Chien, W. R., Chien, Y. T., & Tseng, Y. H. (2013). Tracking learners' visual attention during a multimedia presentation in a real classroom. *Computers & Education, Vol, 62*, 208–220. doi:10.1016/j.compedu.2012.10.009

Yarbus, A. L. (1967). *Eye Movements and Vision*. New York: Plenum. doi:10.1007/978-1-4899-5379-7

ADDITIONAL READING

Bayram, S., & Mutlu Bayraktar, D. (2012). Using Eye Tracking to Study on Attention and Recall in Multimedia Learning Environments: The Effects of Design in Learning. *World Journal on Educational Technology*, *4*(2), 81–98.

Chang, T. W., Kinshuk, , Chen, N.-S., & Yu, P.-T. (2012). The effects of presentation method and information density on visual search ability and working memory load. *Computers & Education*, *58*(2), 721–731. doi:10.1016/j.compedu.2011.09.022

Florax, M., & Ploetzner, R. (2010). What contributes to the split-attention effect? The role of text segmentation, picture labelling, and spatial proximity. *Learning and Instruction*, *20*(3), 216–224. doi:10.1016/j.learninstruc.2009.02.021

Jacob, R. J. K., & Karn, K. S. (2003). Eye tracking in human-computer interaction and usability research: Ready to deliver the promises. In J. Hyona, R. Radach, & H. Deubel (Eds.), *The mind's eye: cognitive and applied aspects of eye movement research* (pp. 573–603). Oxford, UK: Elsevier Science. doi:10.1016/B978-044451020-4/50031-1

Jamet, E., Gavota, M., & Quaireau, C. (2008). Attention guiding in multimedia learning. *Learning and Instruction*, *18*(2), 135–145. doi:10.1016/j.learninstruc.2007.01.011

Liu, H. C., Lai, M. L., & Chuang, H. H. (2011). Using eye-tracking technology to investigate the redundant effect of multimedia web pages on viewers' cognitive processes. *Computers in Human Behavior*, *Vol*, 27(6), 2410–2417. doi:10.1016/j.chb.2011.06.012

Mason, L., Tornatora, M. C., & Pluchino, P. (2013). Do fourth graders integrate text and picture in processing and learning from an illustrated science text? Evidence from eye-movement patterns. *Computers & Education*, *60*(1), 95–109. doi:10.1016/j.compedu.2012.07.011

Molina, A. I., Redondo, M. A., Lacave, C., & Ortega, M. (2013). *Assessing the effectiveness of new devices for accessing learning materials: An empirical analysis based on eye tracking and learner subjective perception. Computers in Human Behavior*. Basımda.

Mutlu-Bayraktar, D., & Altun, A. (2012). The effect of multimedia design types on learners' recall performances with varying short term memory spans. *Multimedia Tools and Applications*. doi:10.1007/s11042-012-1257-z

Ozcelik, E., Karakus, T., Kursun, E., & Cagiltay, K. (2009). An eye-tracking study of how color coding affects multimedia learning. *Computers & Education*, *53*(2), 445–453. doi:10.1016/j.compedu.2009.03.002

Rehder, B., & Hoffman, A. B. (2005). Eye-tracking and selective attention in category learning. *Cognitive Psychology*, *51*(1), 1–41. doi:10.1016/j.cogpsych.2004.11.001 PMID:16039934

Schüler, A., Scheiter, K., & Gerjets, P. (2013). Is spoken text always better? Investigating the modality and redundancy effect with longer text presentation. *Computers in Human Behavior*, *29*(4), 1590–1601. doi:10.1016/j.chb.2013.01.047

Schüler, A., Scheiter, K., Rummer, K., & Gerjets, P. (2012). Explaining the modality effect in multimedia learning: Is it due to a lack of temporal contiguity with written text and pictures? *Learning and Instruction*, *22*(2), 92–102. doi:10.1016/j.learninstruc.2011.08.001

Tchoubar, T. (2014). Effective Use of Multimedia Explanations in Open E-learning Environment Fosters Student Success. *International Journal of Information and Education Technology*, *4*(1), 63–66. doi:10.7763/IJIET.2014.V4.370

Yang, F. Y., Chang, C. Y., Chien, W. R., Chien, Y. T., & Tseng, Y. H. (2013). Tracking learners' visual attention during a multimedia presentation in a real classroom. *Computers & Education*, *62*, 208–220. doi:10.1016/j.compedu.2012.10.009

KEY TERMS AND DEFINITIONS

Attention: The nervous system function that provides selecting only in need stimuli.

Eye-Tracking Method: It's a eye movements data collection method used for while individuals follow the content on-screen where pay attention to the areas, which elements are ignored, to determine what they are uncomfortable.

Focused Attention: It is the concentration of attention on a specific part of the information.

Multimedia: It's a media where words (as textual and narrative) and images (photographs, animations or videos) as they are used together. It's an environment which text, image, audio, animation, video or a combination of these used together.

Multimedia Learning: For the presentation of certain learning content text, graphics, animation, photography, video and audio of the different symbol systems complement each other in a way that is integrated.

Split Attention: Attention is divided between two simultaneous inputs.

Section 5
Digital Visualizations for Learning and Knowing

Chapter 11
Conducting Semantic-Based Network Analyses from Social Media Data:
Extracted Insights about the Data Leakage Movement

Shalin Hai-Jew
Kansas State University, USA

ABSTRACT

*Network analysis is widely used to mine social media. This involves both the study of structural metadata (information about information) and the related contents (the textual messaging, the related imagery, videos, URLs, and others). A semantic-based network analysis relies on the analysis of relationships between words and phrases (as meaningful concepts), and this approach may be applied effectively to social media data to extract insights. To gain a sense of how this might work, a trending topic of the day was chosen (namely, the free-information and data leakage movement) to see what might be illuminated using this semantic-based network analysis, an open-source technology, NodeXL, and access to multiple social media platforms. Three types of networks are extracted: (1) **conversations** (#hashtag microblogging networks on Twitter; #eventgraphs on Twitter; and keyword searches on Twitter; (2) **contents** (video networks on YouTube, related tags networks on Flickr, and article networks on Wikipedia; and (3) **user** accounts on Twitter, YouTube, Flickr, and Wikipedia.*

INTRODUCTION

Electronic social network analysis (e-SNA) has been applied to a broad range of data from the social web. The analytical approaches tend to work on two axes: (1) the structural approach at the macro, meso, and micro levels, and (2) the content-analysis-based approach. To generalize, the structural approach may highlight the following: clusters within a network, broad-scale types of motif and subgraph relationships in a network (a motif census), and general network membership. The content approach enables the

DOI: 10.4018/978-1-4666-8696-0.ch011

study of conversation gists (as in group labels of Tweets), the identification of individual accounts (at the various levels of the network graph), the study of individual messages or groups of messages, and so on. There is also a kind of middle-space, which enables the study of network graphs with an overlay of various types of text for a semantic-based network analysis (of social media data).

In this approach, the related text and verbiage are an integral part of the visual-based data analysis. To contextualize the concept of semantic meaning in a social media context, it helps to consider the semantic meanings of names (even non-sensical ones) in their various cultural contexts; the meanings in hashtags (even those that are abbreviated and stand in for certain coded meanings); the meanings in metadata like tags for multimedia contents; and then regular semantic meanings in language. [This is not to be confused with semantic network analysis which involves the study of semantic relations between concepts—often through the automated extraction of such relationships from a text or text corpus or through the application of a pre-structured "thesaurus" / concept map of terms applied to a text or text corpus. Such semantic networks are created as a form of data reduction or data summarization. These are virtually always used with stop words lists. Semantic networks may be formed based on various types of word-based relatedness, such as synonymy, antonymy, meronymy, hyperonymy, and others.] A semantic network or frame network also results in data represented in text-labeled graphs, but the theories and methods are different than this approach. The structure of the network graphs extracted from social media platforms comes from how relationships are enabled and defined on the social media platform. The extracted word-based labels are then applied]

To gain a sense of the affordances of semantic-based network analysis of social media data, a trending issue of the day was analyzed across four social media platforms (Twitter, YouTube, Flickr, and Wikipedia) in order to gain some insights on how this could function. The topic is the activist-based "data leakage" movement which pits activists against government and corporations in the interests of free information and citizen freedom. While there are a number of rationales to support the activity that this movement would suggest, the activism involves collecting sensitive information and releasing that for broad public access and usage. One of the subtexts to his movement suggests that governments the world over have too much power and access to citizens' and non-citizens' private lives. To combat this over-reach, activists advocate hacktivist actions such as compromising computer networks and systems to gather information to notify the broader public; they advocate the leaking of data through sites dedicated to such purposes. They also advocate insider attacks, such as that exemplified by Edward J. Snowden's widely-covered absconding with over a million highly sensitive and classified files from the National Security Agency (NSA); he was thought to have leaked nothing less than "the blueprints to its global surveillance system" (Harris, 2014, p. 212). There has been plenty of mystique and cloak-and-dagger in the backstory for how the files got leaked to journalists (Harding, 2014). The release of Laura Poitras' film *Citizenfour,* the continuing interviews of Snowden in person and remotely, and the revelations of U.S. intelligence capabilities at the NSA by various publications around the world, have kept the issue of his leaks in the public eye. [In a sense, these revelations have borne out the prescience of what law professor and Creative Commons licensure creator Lawrence Lessig noted years ago in *Code: And Other Laws of Cyberspace* (1999), in which he noted the high levels of control and surveillance that may be achieved with code in cyberspace by dint of the technologies.] This topic was selected because of its broad interest to the public and its technology links. The issue is hotly debated on public platforms like microblogging sites (and other social media platforms), which will leave explorable trails for research. There are a number of keywords which may be used for various searches on online encyclopedia sites and content-sharing sites. This data leakage issue offers a lot of "seed" words that may be used for the purposes of this chapter (to see how semantic-based network analysis may be applied to data extracted from social media).

This "data leakage" issue is still a nascent and evolving one, and the historical implications are only just becoming apparent (and the interpretations currently vary greatly based on the differing stakeholders and subjective interests regarding the topic). It is hoped that a wide range of verbiage will be used here to surface insights and understandings; even the selection of particular terminology will show differing points-of-view. This issue captures some of the *zeitgeist* of the age, with its implications for people's lived lives and privacy.

Finally, the Network Overview, Discovery, and Exploration for Excel (NodeXL) tool will be used for the data extractions and graph visualizations. NodeXL is a free and open-source add-in to Microsoft Excel, and it is available off of the Microsoft CodePlex site. (**Note**: The visuals are processed at the highest dots per inch for print publishing, but because of the nuances in color and some of the limits in book processing, the social network graphs look better and are more legible in electronic format.)

REVIEW OF THE LITERATURE

There are individual personalities and entities understood to embody certain issues, and in the case of the "data leakage" movement, it might be the Anonymous hacktivist collective (founded in 2003); Julian Assange, founder of WikiLeaks (2006), and Edward J. Snowden, who went from low-key contractor for the National Security Agency (NSA) to global public consciousness in May 2013. Of these, arguably, the most polarizing would be Snowden, who has been labeled a "traitor," a "whistleblower," and a "hero" for absconding with a giant trove of classified documents from NSA servers and distributing them to a number of journalists and apparently others. Multiple narratives are at play in the push for data leakage.

A simplified representation of stances regarding the data leakage movement may be described by defining the two polar ends of the argument. At the one end are the activists who want more free data and less government control over intellectual property (IP) and less access to private data about citizens. At the other end are those in government, law enforcement, and business, who suggest that IP laws and practices protect innovations which are critical to the economy and job market, government access to big data and government secrecy are necessary to its functions, and that citizen privacy is protected still (given that the collected metadata is not accessed or seen with human eyes without legal cover and cause). Figure 2 provides a highly simplified continuum of stances regarding data leakage. At the left end is the activist stance suggesting that data leakage is a way to right social wrongs and protect citizen rights; at the right end is the conservative stance suggesting that data leakage as national and corporate security compromise that harms the *polis*. Between these two extreme points are many points in-between.

Data leakage as civil disobedience and social activism. Writ large, the activist viewpoint is several-fold, with multiple threads. One thread is that information wants to be free, an idea of technology activists that originated well back in the 1980s (Google Books Ngram Viewer). A core idea here is that government protection of intellectual property (IP) restrains the use of that same information in the public domain. Another related concept involves government secrecy, particularly military and intelligence-based, which is seen to impinge on people's human rights to information.

Another thread in the data leakage movement is also anti-government powers. The idea is that government surveillance (in the name of national security and law enforcement) restricts people's inherent

Figure 1. "Data leak" linegraph on the Google Books Ngram Viewer

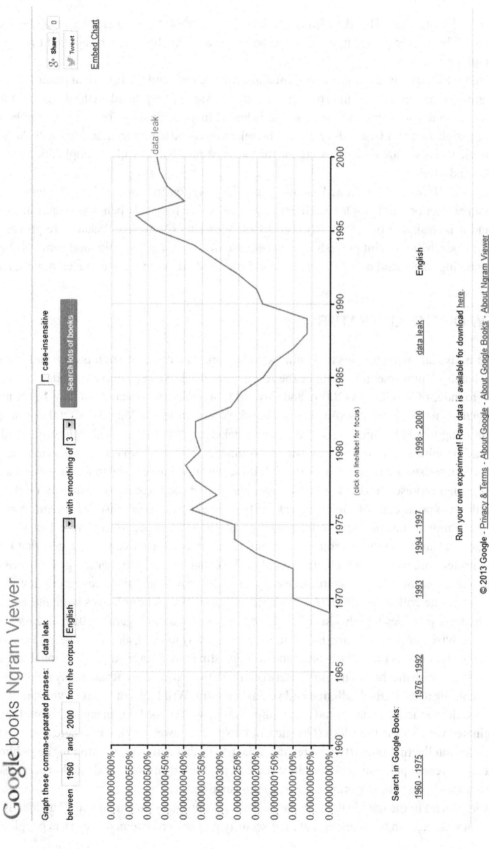

Figure 2. Simplified continuum of stances re: data leakage

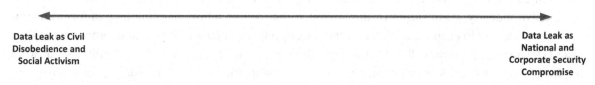

Data Leak as Civil
Disobedience and
Social Activism

Data Leak as
National and
Corporate Security
Compromise

privacy rights and restricts people's degrees of freedom in making decisions about their own lives. In a time of recent multiple hot wars, the U.S. government is seen as remaining on war footing and over-reaching in its capabilities of collecting and analyzing data. The popular literature has included books describing the U.S. with words like "fortress," "dragnet," and "emergency." Some activists suggest that Americans' Fourth Amendment rights against unreasonable search and seizure

To minimize government reach, activists are encouraging the leaking of information of government wrongdoing in order to raise public awareness in order to encourage rollbacks on government power. The broad electronic communications-based "knowability" of government and private industry enables a panopticon sort of awareness of people and their private facts. An aggressive information collections posture by government intelligence agencies are creating an environment of oppressive surveillance (Greenwald, 2014). The U.S. war footing post 9/11 has led to the instituting of a security state that makes "domestic spying" the new normal, with mass collection of a majority of American's electronic (phone, email, and other) records (Risen, 2006); the application of government secrecy has been used to hide government mis-use of funds from the Fourth Estate (journalism) and to compromise democratic ideals (Risen, 2014). Multiple journalists have advocated increased government transparency in order to enable better informed policy-making (Harris, 2014). This big data knowledge enables "surveillance as social sorting" (which involves identifying people and "assessing risks and assigning worth") and ultimately nothing less than "digital discrimination" (Lyon, 2003). Such decision-making based on probabilities and correlations stand to affect others' job prospects, access to credit, access to housing, healthcare, and other life aspects. In the data realm, there is a "big data divide" between the sorters and those being sorted (Andrejevic, 2014, p. 1683), and the correlations found in big data may lead to decisions being made in a "black box" way without underlying understandings about why certain variables may be correlated. Predictive "actuarial assumptions" may be applied in biasing ways (Gandy, 1993, 2005, p. 2, as cited in Andrejevic, 2014, p. 1677). People's lives could be guided by an "automated calculus" that forecloses on opportunities (Andrejevic, 2014, p. 1677). Projecting the future based on past patterns is problematic because the past itself is historically contingent on a range of factors, and predictive analytics are often highly inaccurate given the world's complexity. As it stands currently, there are thousands of data points linked to each individual, and individuals may be profiled in deeply revealing ways. It is difficult to know what may be "knowable" by datamining in the future. Two sophisticated observers write:

For the purposes of cybersecurity, the bottom line is that digital identity is a balance between protecting and sharing information. Limiting acquired information is not only good for privacy, it can prevent others from gaining information for more sophisticated authentication fraud. At the same time, each system has incentives to maximize the amount of data it collects, as well as use that data for its own goals (Singer & Friedman, 2014, p. 34).

This thread of the narrative is that activist must protect citizen rights against intrusive government and intrusive industry. [One subset of this thread is the idea of whistleblowing to minimize government corruption and to keep leadership accountable, as a formal channel for righting others' wrongs or abuses (Devine & Maassarani, 2011).] Another sub-thread involves the risks of the "military-industrial complex," which is considered a colluding vested interest that hypes risks in order to access taxpayer funds. In this view, a range of efforts to counter the influence of this complex is justified. The idea of the data leak is to empower citizens and create some sort of power parity and to reduce the advantage of big government and special interests.

A number of dedicated "leak" sites have been created by activists to enable the broad-scale leaking of information which is often cursorily viewed and dispersed on the Web and Internet. (Some leaked information is packaged and propagandized to take certain stances on government policies.) Another approach has been the classic insider attack, in which an insider with access upgrades privilege and absconds with the information, which is then leaked to journalists, who are used as the vetting agents for what ultimately goes public. In both observed cases, these have been big data dumps with limited to no initial vetting by the leakers.

Governmentally-achieved long memory, without any forgetting, has long been stated as a goal by intelligence agencies, who have aspired to create end-to-end life histories of people from the beginning. Counter to this stance is the so-called "right to be forgotten". Human independence and self-hood comes from some degree of experimentation, goes the argument, and a long digital memory may not only squelch experimentation but be used inappropriately against an individual at a later date, say, for political purposes. Anything that may be done to disrupt the collection and storage of people's information should be done, at least in the extreme view. In terms of this argument for data leakage as acts of social justice, this is a fairly contested view.

Terminology for data extractions: From this stance, there are a number of terms that may be used to probe social media accounts: whistleblowing, WikiLeaks, Thomas Andrews Drake, William Binney, Edward J. Snowden, Julian Assange, Laura Poitras, *Citizenfour,* and others

Data leakage as national and corporate security compromise. Another thread to this issue is about national security and the need for a broad range of investigative tools. The outline of this argument is that every nation state is in an "arms race" with other nation-states in stockpiling cyber exploits and skill sets, in order to secure the cyber domain against threats and also in using that domain to achieve national security and other state interests. In this context, there are advanced persistent threats (APTs) or moneyed and skilled nation-states and criminal entities working to compromise others' systems for their own advantage. The thinking is that dominance is the ultimately least-risky and least-expensive approach because it means increased capabilities in learning of others' capabilities and protected information, a broad reach, necessary stealth, and the ability to actively degrade others' abilities. In this view, the critical infrastructure of a country—its economy, its intellectual property, its physical infrastructure, and others—and its leadership and peoples are all elements which may be compromised by "bad actors" in cyberspace. How a nation competes in that cyber space is partially determined by some partially external factors, such as the state of the field (a form of technological determinism) and the threat environment. The space is understood in an adversarial way, with nation-states to individual entities all engaging in hand-to-hand competition and sometimes direct combat:

Security isn't just the notion of being free from danger, as it is commonly conceived, but is associated with the presence of an adversary...Things may break and mistakes may be made, but a cyber problem only becomes a cybersecurity issue if an adversary seeks to gain something from the activity, whether to obtain private information, undermine the system, or prevent its legitimate use (Singer & Friedman, 2014, p. 34).

Yet, if hardened targets are hardened by the expensive and complex skills and tools, the broader public itself, the so-called 85%, are less protected and as "soft targets" will likely be attacked and compromised in terms of retributive action by excessive actions of capable nation-states. To create a more resilient 85%, the thinking is that there are critical public-private partnerships to secure the elements that ensure the healthy proceedings of a country and the well-being of all. In this view, all data collection is done under cover of law and is necessary given the nano-seconds speed of computing and the risk environment. The public need-to-know is balanced against protecting sensitive data against leak to adversaries, who may gather information for inference attacks. The threat model posed by adversaries is formidable. In cyberspace, there has been the long-term challenge of attribution ("who is responsible?"), which has to be accurately achieved in order to hold others accountable or to exact deterrence and retribution (Harris, 2014).

If the Internet were a wheel, the rim at the edge would contain all the network 'endpoints': desktop computers, iPads, smartphones. The hub would be the servers and services on the network that drive its use: the machines providing access to Netflix, Gmail, eBay, Amazon, and millions more. The spokes that link the center to the edge are the network itself, a fantastically complex set of global data centers, network interconnection points, business arrangements, fiber-optics, undersea cables, and massive routers that direct global traffic...In the chaos of the Internet, digital surveillance can productively take place at all three places (Anderson, 2013, p. 99).

From this viewpoint, the Snowden leaks are criminal, and they compromised national security. The argument goes that he had official ways to actually report his concerns as a whistleblower. A national security lawyer specializing in security clearance legal cases was asked what he would do if he were Snowden's attorney. He suggested that the main legal course of action that Snowden could take would be challenging the classification status of the information leaked; as it stands, if he were brought to trial, he could receive 10 years for each of the sensitive documents he leaked, with a potential sentence well beyond his natural lifetime (Zaid, 2014). All three branches of the federal government signed off on the constitutionality of the surveillance that Snowden was fighting, Zaid said. He added that there are ways to get information out in the public for a policy debate without directly causing harm to the U.S. by leaking its critical documents. What about a whistleblowing defense?

For one thing, there is no exception to any of the statutory provisions for which he would he will no doubt be charged that speaks to whistleblowing. There are or is whistleblower protection to some extent in the national security field. It is so weak that quite honestly as much as I am always called a whistleblower lawyer I ignore it. It's frankly legally irrelevant as far as I'm concerned (Zaid, 2014).

A number of others have commented that what was leaked went well beyond protest of a particular program but involved the distribution of sensitive data, possibly directly to a foreign government.

The advocacy of hacking to reveal protected information approach is not only illegal but turns the idea of Internet freedom on its head because of hacktivism (hacker + activism) intruding on others' usage of the Internet as a public good:

An interesting issue for hacktivism moving forward, however, turns the notion of Internet freedom of expression on its head. Many see hacktivism as a new form of civil disobedience that echoes back to past generations of activists, whether it be Thoreau's essays in the 1840s or the Chicago Eight's use of TV in 1968, just now on a new medium. Others note that the tactics, like denial of service or altered websites, involve some attack on the other party's use of the Internet, effectively undermining their freedom of speech (Singer & Friedman, 2014, p. 80).

An organizational view. Regardless, for those managing cybersecurity—which includes the protection of information—the point is to not spring a data leak. Data leaks are not unusual. For businesses with 250 employees or more, 80 – 90% of these businesses have experienced data leaks in 2010, according to a news article in *Computer Fraud & Security.* Insiders pose a large threat because of their enhanced knowledge and privileged access; in 60% of convicted inside attacks, there were "clear behavioral 'red flags'" (McCormick, 2008, p. 56) and motives such as employee disgruntlement, anger, or profit-seeking. Yet, the majority of data leaks are accidental (McCormick, 2008, p. 57). The higher the "misuseability" score on data and capabilities, the higher the levels of individual vetting and protections emplaced. In terms of defense, the current strategy applies a mix of policy, practices, and technological controls. Newer strategies involve the "masking" of data through methods like substitution and encryption (Mansfield-Devine, 2014, pp. 17 – 21). The work of protecting data is manifold, with poor designs in software or hardware enabling potential leaks. For example, the capturing of hidden information in a Microsoft Word file may be exploited (Byers, 2004). Human gullibility—those vulnerable to social engineering—provides a large channel for data compromise. The "security" of technology systems is a system-level feature; it depends on every component working properly to avoid mis-use and exploitation.

To prevent the seeding topic from becoming incoherent, however, a basic illustration of potential leak dynamics will be offered from a technology and semi-law enforcement point-of-view based on a sampling of the academic research literature. Data may be exfiltrated from systems from the inside-out or the outside-out. Data may be extracted while at rest (in storage) or in transit or while in creation. The X's represent points at which a data leakage may be identified and potentially tracked back to perpetrators. For example, the point at which data is exploited may be a way to identify those who've absconded with the data; online markets for stolen credit card data, for example, are widely known to be penetrated spaces with the presence of law enforcement (Glenny).

Terminology for data extractions: So some select terminology for the data extractions follow. National Security Agency (NSA), Michael Hayden, information security (infosec), data leakage, defense in depth, cybersecurity, insider risk, and Data Leakage Prevention (DLP), and others

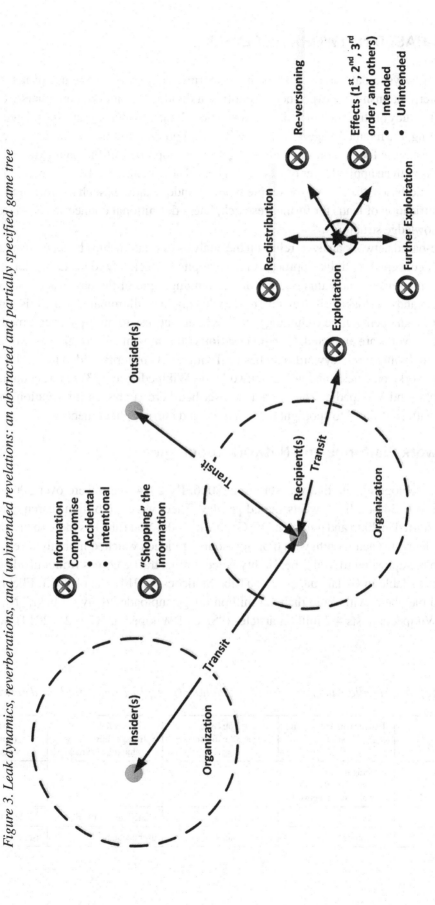

Figure 3. Leak dynamics, reverberations, and (un)intended revelations: an abstracted and partially specified game tree

SEMANTIC-BASED NETWORK ANALYSIS

One of the main ways to datamine social media platforms today involves the use of network analysis, the study of interrelationships between nodes (entities, individuals, contents, and others). This approach involves both the study of structural metadata (information about information) and the related contents (the textual messaging, the related imagery, videos, URLs, and others). In this current use case, a semantic-based network analysis focuses on the underlying network topology of the data extracted from social media platforms with an applied layer of words as labels. The semantic analysis here is considered more of a non-linguistic-based "folk" one, for simple types of understandings such as word sense disambiguation, the identification of leads for further research, latent definitional connections and storylines, and ontological knowledge structures.

A semantic-based network analysis relies on the analysis of relationships between words and phrases (as meaningful concepts), and this approach may be applied effectively to social media data to extract insights. To gain a sense of how this might work, a trending topic of the day was chosen (namely, the free-information and data leakage movement) to see what might be illuminated using this semantic-based network analysis, an open-source technology, NodeXL, and access to multiple social media platforms. Three types of networks are extracted: (1) **conversations** (#hashtag microblogging networks on Twitter; #eventgraphs on Twitter; and keyword searches on Twitter; (2) **contents** (video networks on YouTube, related tags networks on Flickr, and article networks on Wikipedia; and (3) **user** accounts on Twitter, YouTube, Flickr, and Wikipedia. The approach described here coalesces information from different social media platform "silos" to spotlight one complex and current phenomenon.

Social Network Platforms and Network Topologies

Twitter is a microblogging site that was started in 2006. By 2014, there were over 500 million users; in 2012, there were 340 million Tweets shared per day. There were 1.6 billion search queries per day. YouTube was started in 2005 and purchased by Google in 2006. YouTube has more than a billion unique users visiting their site each month, with 6 billion hours of videos watched monthly; every minute, 100 hours of video are uploaded to YouTube. Eighty percent of its traffic comes from outside the U.S., and this service is available in 61 languages ("YouTube Statistics," 2014). As of 2013, Flickr had 87 million registered members, with more than 3.5 million images uploaded daily ("Flickr," Nov. 25, 2014). The English Wikipedia hosts 4.7 million articles ("Size of Wikipedia," Oct. 21, 2014), with 800 new

Table 1. Types of social media data extractions for graphing (to explore semantic-based network analysis)

	Twitter (microblogging site)	YouTube (video-sharing service)	Flickr (image- and video-sharing service)	Wikipedia (open-source encyclopedia)
1. Conversations	#hashtag networks #eventgraph networks keyword search networks			
2. Contents		video networks	related tags networks	article networks
3. Users	@accounts	user accounts	user accounts	user accounts

articles daily (Wikipedia:Statistics, Nov. 25, 2014). Wikipedia was started in 2001, and its contents in the English version are created by 3.77 million unvetted volunteers (Wilkinson & Huberman, 2008).

The speed-of-change or dynamism of contents on a social media site depend in part on the understood usage of the platform. For example, microblogging content on Twitter can be highly dynamic particularly if an issue is trending. Tapping in 140-character messages on mobile devices and snapping photos to share may be quite simple. By contrast, data on YouTube, Flickr, and Wikipedia may be much slower to change because of the cost of creating video contents for YouTube, and imagery and videos for Flickr, and cited and vetted articles for Wikipedia. Not only do contents change, but so do user accounts and user relationships. A contemporary author described the fragility of in-world relationships:

What's more, our friend networks are remarkably unstable themselves. A study by a Dutch sociologist who tracked about a thousand people of all ages found that on average, we lose half of our close network members every seven years. To think that half of the people currently on your 'most dialed' list will fade out of your life in less than a decade is frightening indeed" (Flora, 2013, p. 55).

Indeed, the churn on social networks is much faster, with most online "friendships" lasting about three years, and people going through cycles of collecting followers and then pruning some. Some researchers suggest that the idea of "friend" has changed so much in the present day as to be unrecognizable. The larger the social network, the less attention given to each individual member in that network, even with automated tools serving as stand-ins for attention.

The application of network analysis also varies between the different social media services. An essential network topology consists of nodes (entities) and links (relationships). An entity on Twitter may be a user account; an entity on YouTube may be a user account or a video artifact; an entity on Flickr may be a user account or a tag; an entity on Wikipedia may be an article or a user account. The definition of links may also vary based on the various accounts and types of data extractions. On Twitter, a link or relationship may be based on replies-to, re-tweeting, or followership. On YouTube, a link may be a comment around videos or following relationship. On Flickr, a link may be based on co-membership I a group, replies, or following; a tags relationship may be based on co-occurrence. On Wikipedia, relationships are often based on co-linking of articles between article pages (as knowledge structures) or user pages on the site, which show co-authorship teams focusing on particular articles and topics). There may also be relationships based on the co-editing of articles (as represented on the history pages), and so on.

These social media services are summarized to give a sense of the basic affordances of the platform and also a sense of the numbers. For all the "big data" potential here, it is important to note that certain platforms attract a subset of the population. A minority portion of the online populations are robots and sensors. For research purposes, a lot of qualifiers will have to be applied in terms of generalizing from the data (Ares, Nov. 29, 2014).

1. Conversations

A hashtag conversation refers to the various short messages that are sent with the label of a hashtag to indicate its topicality. This sort of data extraction enables the mapping of interrelationships between the various user accounts who are "discussants." Their frequency of interactions, contents of their messages (like linked other hashtags), time zones, are all capturable.

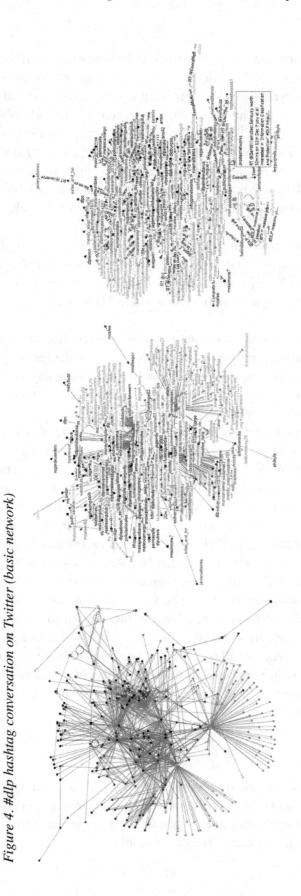

Figure 4. #dlp hashtag conversation on Twitter (basic network)

#HASHTAG CONVERSATIONS ON TWITTER

The hashtag network from "#dlp" resulted in a network graph comprising 455 vertices, 655 edges, and 131 groups. To the far left of this triptych in Figure 4 is the visual graph structure; in the middle are labeled vertices; at the right are labeled vertices and edges (with the actual Tweets). The interactive graph in the NodeXL graph pane enables the highlighting of particular messages in a pop-up. This graph is multilingual.

The graph in Figure 5: "'#snowden' Hashtag Search on Twitter (Basic Network)" contains 4,523 vertices (individual accounts engaging in this online microblogging conversation) and 6,001 unique edges, showing interactivity between some of those having the conversation. In this network, there were 902 groups using the Wakita-Tsurumi clustering algorithm; this fairly high number of groups suggests a diversity of clusters engaging in the conversation (vs. a monolithic few clusters, for example). It is possible to redraw the network maps to show the most active conversationalists in the group, the most influential (highest degree, highest in-degree), the best connected (the highest betweenness centrality), and to highlight conversation contents (Tweets), and other features.

In Figure 6, the #nationalsecurity hashtag graph involves 445 vertices, 399 edges, and 177 clusters. The graphs on the left are the same as the ones on the right except without the vertex labeling.

In Figure 7, two standalone hashtags (#cyber and #policy) were used to delimit the data extraction to messages that mentioned both, given the implied "and" operator. This graph contains ten vertices and eight edges, in two groups.

#EVENTGRAPH ON TWITTER (BOTH KEYWORD AND HASHTAG SEARCHES)

An eventgraph is a type of network visualization that is based on shared conversations and digital resources labeled by a particular hashtag (#) indicating an event (such as a conference, a demonstration, or some other time-delimited occurrence). These are a subset of a general hashtag (#) conversation. Because there is not a direct hashtagged "event" that is linked to the data leakage movement, the rollout of the *Citizenfour* film in October 2014 was used as the event.

Figure 8 shows a grid-based graph around a keyword search on Twitter. A "keyword" search focuses on occurrences of the term in various microblogged messages. This data extraction showed 7,920 vertices of accounts that included this disambiguated word in its message, but there were no edges or links. In a sense, those controlling these accounts were possibly discussing this idea with their own networks but not in a way that resulted in intercommunications. These may be broadcast (to a large group) or microcast (to a small and more intimate group) sort of messages. The graph indicates some of the lead-up buzz to the film's release. Keyword searches in general tend to show less connectivity than #hashtagged conversation searches.

However, a more recent keyword search of "citizenfour" found 4,453 vertices and 6,022 edges, so it may be that the initial lack of connectivity in the keyword search was because it was conducted prior to the film's release when there may have been less substantive information to engage with friends and acquaintances. In terms of grouping, Figure 9 shows 942 groups, which may suggest a fairly dispersed community of communicators instead of dominant clusters. The data visualization using the Fruchterman-Reingold force-based layout algorithm shows just a few main clusters (for the graph without words). For the graph with words, the Harel-Koren Fast Multiscale layout was used because of the clearer sense of clustering.

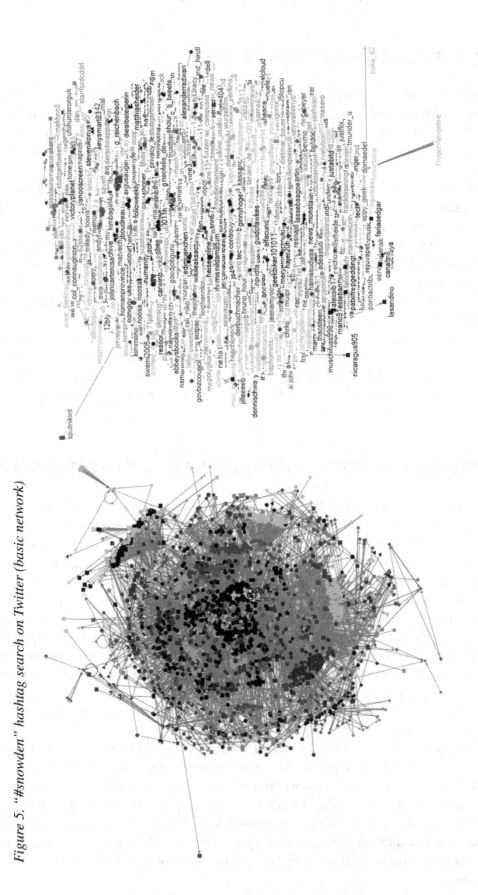

Figure 5. "#snowden" hashtag search on Twitter (basic network)

Figure 6. #nationalsecurity hashtag search on Twitter (basic network)

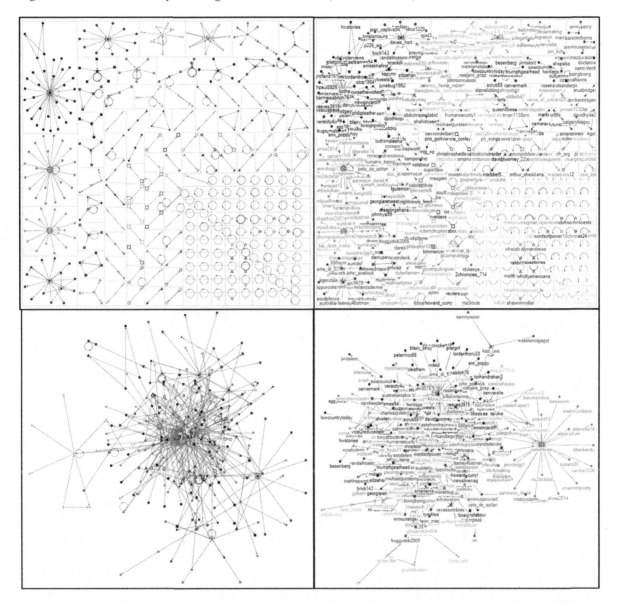

To see what a #hashtag search would surface in terms of changing dynamics, a hashtag data extraction was conducted approximately a month after the film's release as well. This latter extraction captures conversations between those who are purposefully wanting to share in the particular labeled conversational thread. The #citizenfour hashtag data extraction resulted in 1127 vertices and 1386 unique edges, with 311 groups. In Figure 10, on the left, is the resulting graph (using the Harel-Koren Multiscale layout algorithm). To the right is the same layout with the names of the various microblogging accounts as labels; these names show individuals, publicists, and media accounts (various stakeholders to the topic). It would make sense though that after the release there would be potentially more connectivity around the term.

Figure 7. #cyber #policy hashtag search on Twitter (basic network)

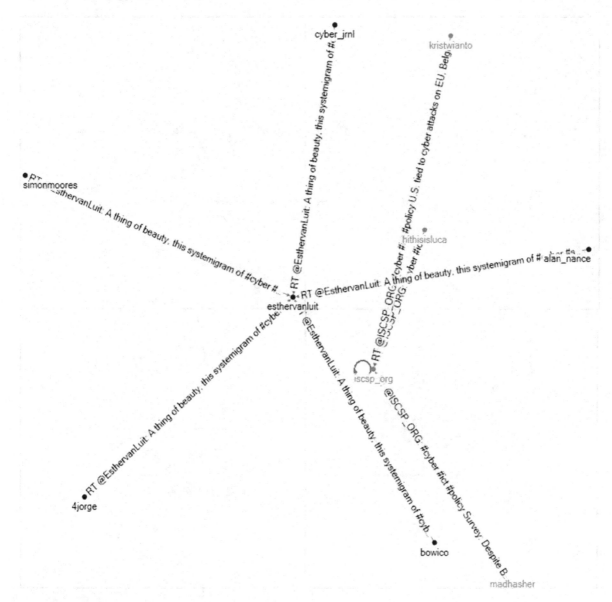

KEYWORD SEARCHES ON TWITTER

Figure 11 shows a keyword search for "cybersecurity" on Twitter. This has 10,576 vertices, 12,246 unique edges, and 3759 groups. The deep clustering of vertex names may be better explored in the Excel worksheets and tables; if a visualization is preferred, the NodeXL graph pane enables interactive exploration with the ability to highlight particular subgraphs, zoom in/ out, pan, and otherwise engage the data.

In Figure 12, a keyword search of "DARPA" resulted in the extraction of 2,665 vertices, 2,887 unique edges, and 1,184 groups.

Figure 8. Citizenfour keyword search on twitter at the lead-up to the film's rollout

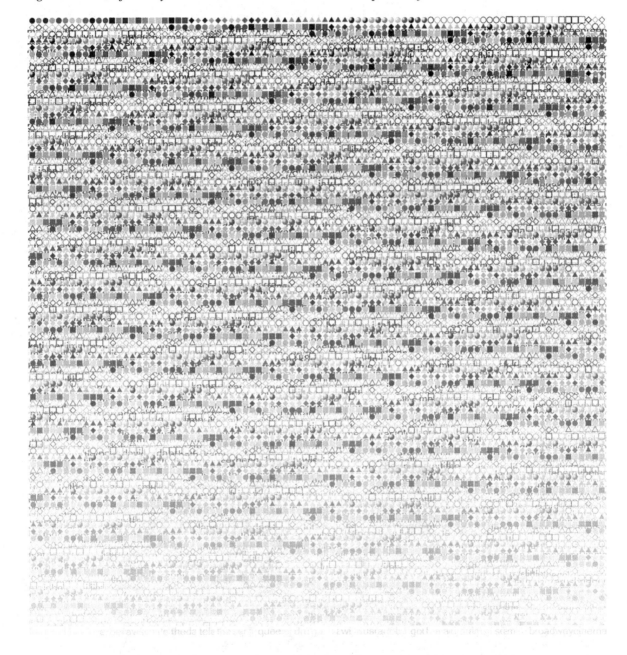

2. Contents

The "contents" of a social media platform may be textual messages, articles, images, video, URLs, or some combination of these. The extraction of these contents are usually in textual format (vs. the videos, for example) and thumbnail images (usually from the respective user accounts). In lieu of extraction of the multimedia files, which are large, such contents are usually represented by titles.

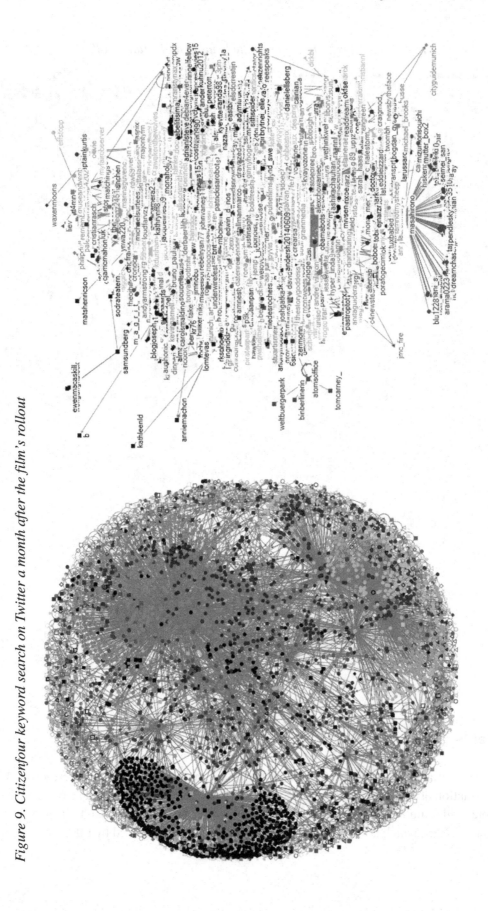

Figure 9. Citizenfour keyword search on Twitter a month after the film's rollout

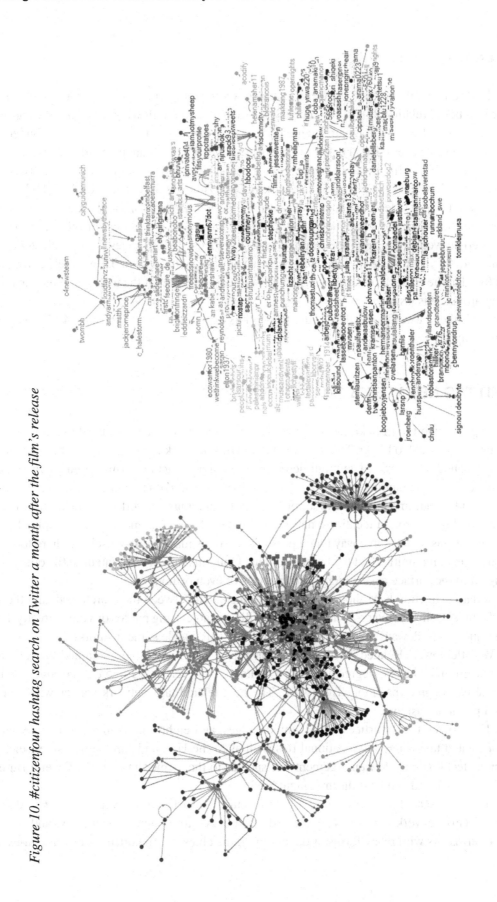

Figure 10. #citizenfour hashtag search on Twitter a month after the film's release

Video Networks On Youtube

The typical video network structures involve a number of clustered videos based around certain topics and a wide number of relational links between those videos. For the following extractions, relationships (edges) were described as the following: "pair of videos that have the same category; pair of videos commented on by the same user (slower), pair of videos responded to with another video by the same user (slower)" and no artificial limits on the numbers of videos were applied (in the NodeXL software tool).

In Figure 13, "'Cybersecurity' Video Network on YouTube (with Video Title Labels)," the titles have been applied to the video contents. A cursory and inferential read of the titles provide a sense of the purposes for the sharing of the videos, whether for educational or political or other purposes. The extracted video network from YouTube resulted in 472 vertices, 27,986 edges, and six clusters.

In Figure 14, "'Cybersecurity' Video Network on YouTube (with Author Title Labels)," the authors have been listed at the respective vertices, which give a sense of some of the user accounts that are used in engaging around this issue.

In Figure 15, the "Edward Snowden" video network is depicted with 470 vertices, 40,214 edges, and three main groups.

RELATED TAG NETWORKS ON FLICKR

A "related tags" network on Flickr clusters tags that co-occur with other tags used to label image and video resources uploaded to Flickr. The intuition behind this network is that this type of metadata, when relationally graphed, may reveal latent public opinion about a particular term. To understand the data though will require understanding that the tags are "folk" (non-expert) ones, and they are related to a range of image and video multimedia. The extraction of such related tags networks on Flickr show common some common clusters around locations, nature, and types of digital cameras, for example. There are some other intuitions: in the same way that a person's opinions may be subconscious, there too may be latent opinions in communities and the broader public. Opinions may remain latent until some in-world event brings it to the surface as an emergent consensus or even orthodoxy.

The first data extraction here shows a purposeful mismatch between the search term and the social media platform. A "whistleblower" is not necessarily illustratable using photos or video directly, but this method of "querying sideways" (with the mismatch) may still enable some insights.

The "'Whistleblower' Related Tags Network on Flickr" (in Figure 16) contained 28 vertices, 27 links, and one group in the one-degree network; it contained 436 vertices, 1,435 unique edges, and eight groups in the two-degree (partitioned) network. The next related tags network was crawled to enable some actual potential insights.

Figure 17 involves 1,191 vertices, 3,441 unique edges, and eight groups in a two-degree network. In terms of related tags, there are locational ties such as to the U.S. and some universities, electronic ties to various technologies, law enforcement ties such as to the former head of the Federal Bureau of Investigations (FBI), and some un-disambiguated references.

The "Snowden" related tags network on Flickr (Figure 18) surfaced 489 vertices, 1,063 edges, and eight groups. This network map shows dispersed references—to a band, to Germany, and some disambiguated terms. As with many forms of data mining, the clues may be diffuse or even non-existent.

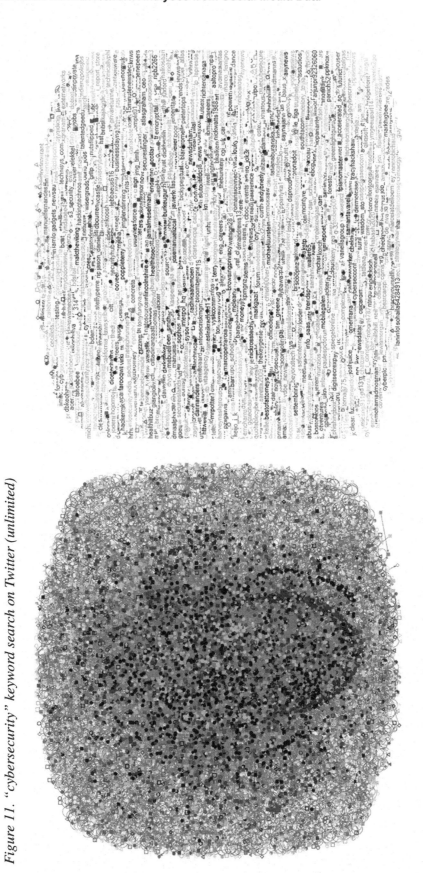

Figure 11. "cybersecurity" keyword search on Twitter (unlimited)

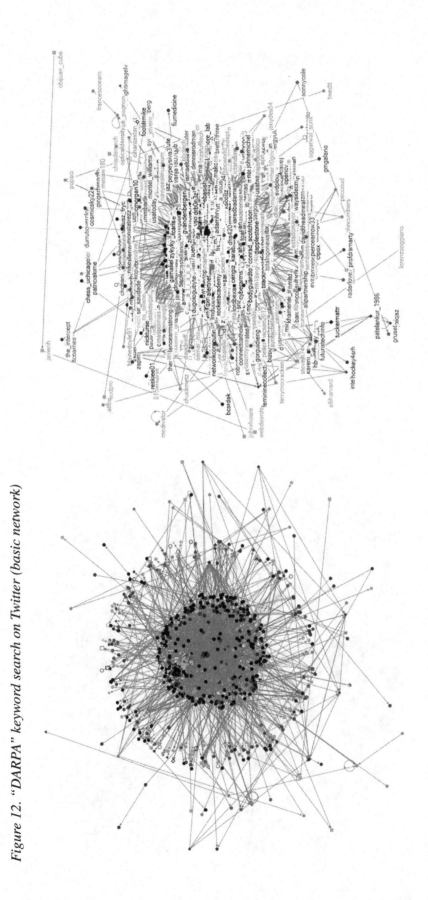

Figure 12. "DARPA" keyword search on Twitter (basic network)

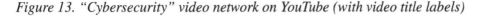

Figure 13. "Cybersecurity" video network on YouTube (with video title labels)

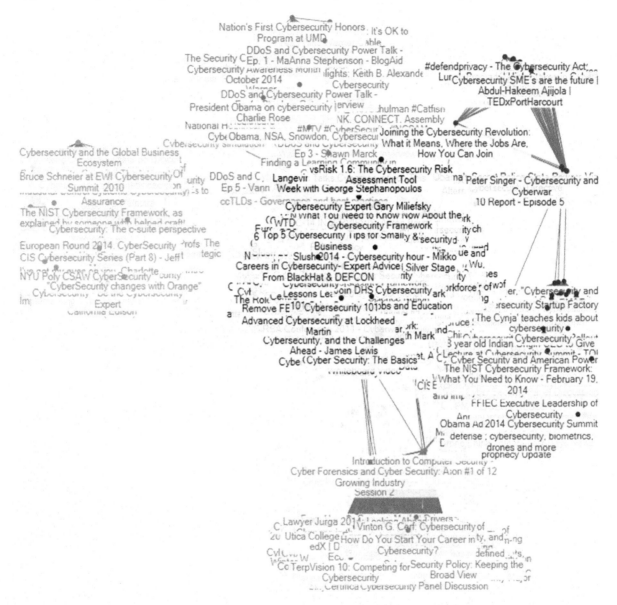

A one-degree "Cyber" related tags network on Flickr (Figure 19) resulted in 63 vertices, 62 edges, and one group. The approach of using a related tags network may be too diffuse for analytical depth in this context because of the abstractions of cyber vs. the photo-graphable and video-graphable materiality of the contents on Flickr and the related tags to those material objects.

CONTENT ARTICLE NETWORKS ON WIKIPEDIA

The creation of a "wiki" ("quick" in Hawaiian) was first created in 1995 by Ward Cunningham to enable shared editing and collaboration tasks (Leuf & Cunningham, 2001). The technological enablements were to make the wiki structure openly editable, with pages evolving over time into its own organic structure,

Figure 14. "Cybersecurity" video network on YouTube (with author title labels)

and every edit and posting available for perusal, for a deep transparency. This structure has meant that various types of analyses may be applied to wiki structures to understand how people interact around the creation of shared informational contents. The open-source encyclopedia Wikipedia is built on the open-source MediaWiki substructure. Article networks on Wikipedia enable the mapping of ontological knowledge structures by showing the human-created connections between information at varying units of analysis—from the article level to the category levels. This is explained by one research team: "In particular, Wikipedia articles form a network of semantically related terms, while the categories are organized in a taxonomy-like structure called Wikipedia Category Graph (WCG)" (Zesch & Gurevych, 2007, p. 2). Wikipedia enables the mapping of user interactions around co-editing shared articles, with

Figure 15. "Edward Snowden" video network on YouTube

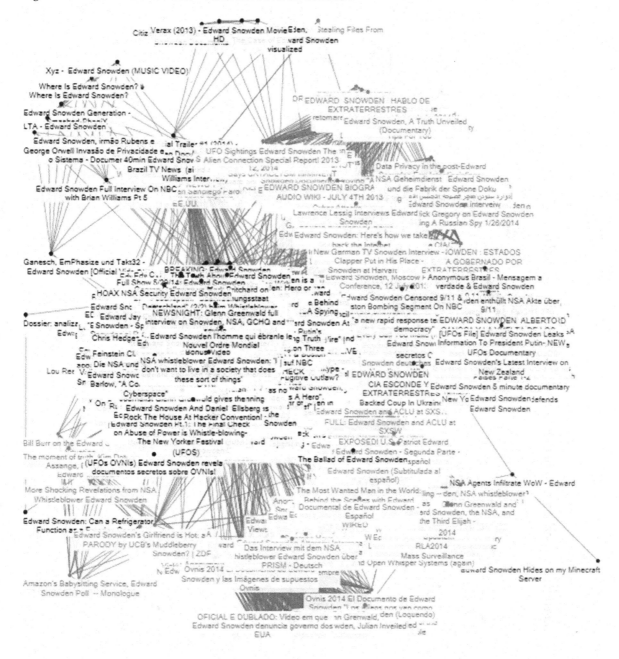

bi-partite networks (those including users and contents). The two-modal aspect of the data extractions are summarized as "the articles network" and "the contributors network".(Korfiatis, Poulos, & Bokos, 2006, p. 256), or actors and contents.

Wikipedia is seen as contributing to the social construction of collective memory based on wrangling over contested understandings and interpretations: "…discourses give access to the examination of collective belief systems, patterns of thought and argumentation structures. This connects to the understanding of discourses as a form of social cognition" (Pentzold, 2009, p. 261) and the creation of

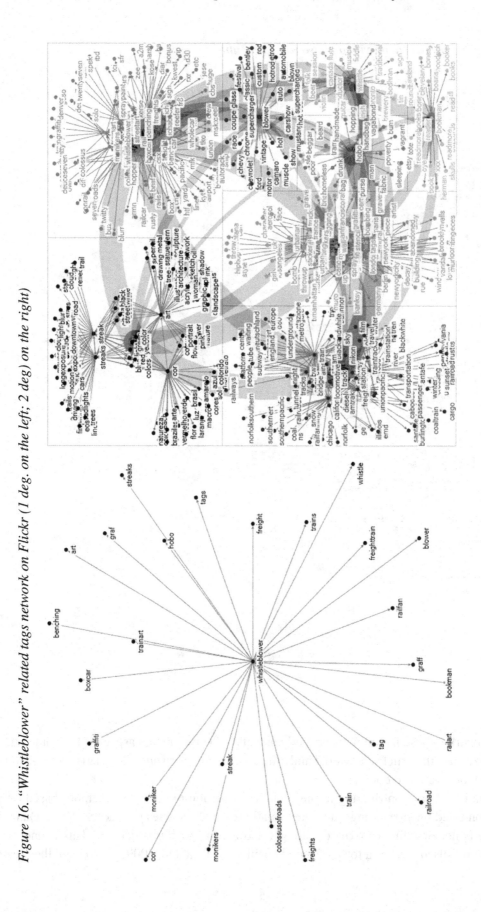

Figure 16. "Whistleblower" related tags network on Flickr (1 deg. on the left; 2 deg) on the right)

Figure 17. "NSA" related tags network on Flickr (2 deg)

a kind of "global brain" around certain topics (Holloway, Bozicevic, & Bőrner, 2007, p. 30). Quality standards for articles are co-created through crowd-sourced peer revisions of articles on Wikipedia. In terms of machine-based ways to assess quality, researchers have looked at basic metrics such as article length or word count (Blumenstock, 2008). Others have examined the reputational quality of editors, based in part on the survivability of their work against others' edits:

Figure 18. "Snowden" related tags network on Flickr (2 deg.)

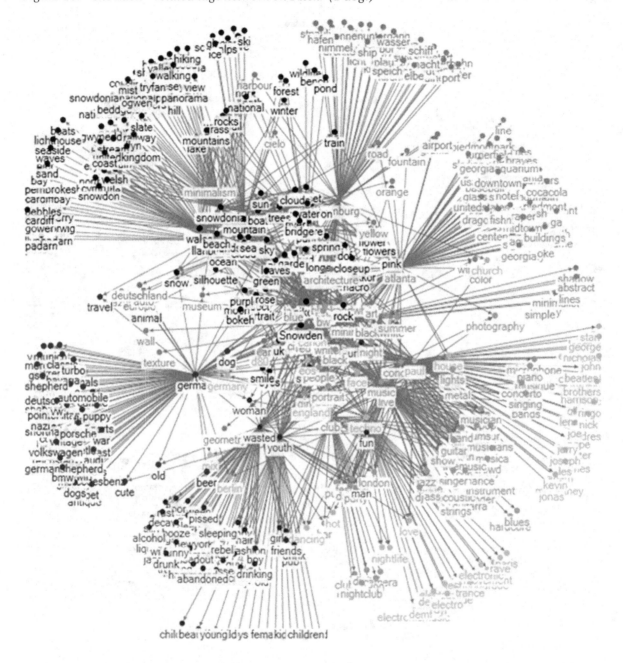

Our results show that our notion of reputation has good predictive value: changes performed by low-reputation authors have a significantly larger than average probability of having poor quality, as judged by human observers, and of being later undone, as measured by our algorithms (Adler & de Alfaro, 2007, p. 261).

Figure 19. "Cyber" related tags network on Flickr (1 deg.)

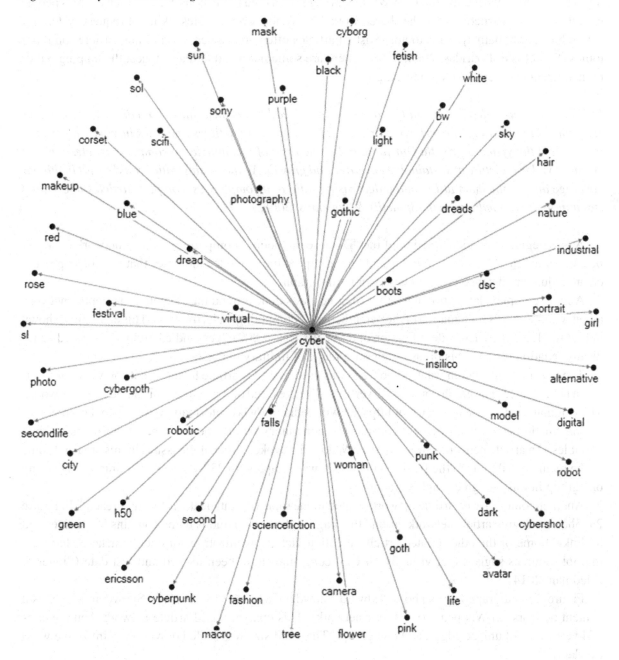

The numbers of edits and the numbers of distinct editors on an article had effects on article quality, with quality describe as "accuracy, neutrality, completeness, and style" and pagerank (Wilkinson & Huberman, 2008, p. 8). Not only do those who contribute to Wikipedia have influence on the contents, there is also communally-arrived-at practices based on debated norms, which "become codified in the shared communal practices and hard-coded into the wiki algorithms over time" (Müller-Birn, Dobusch, & Herbsleb, 2013). Volunteer members serve on a committee to decide whether or not automated agents may run accounts on Wikipedia for managing various aspects like editing, spelling, and information sharing. The human-contribution focus on Wikipedia suggests a kind of virtuous cycle, which enables people to collaborate constructively for the shared work. The system even enables a kind of request system for new information; namely, links to non-existent articles often precede creation of new articles on those topics (Spinellis & Louridas, 2008, p. 68). There are some metrics that may suggest the tapping out of human talent and goodwill to contribute:

In Wikipedia more depth eventually translates into breadth, because the Wikipedia style guidelines recommend the splitting of overly long articles. The evolution of articles and links in Wikipedia allows us to model the system's growth. Our finding that the ratio of incomplete vs. complete articles remains constant yields a picture of sustainable coverage and growth. An increasing ratio would result in thinner coverage and diminishing utility and a decreasing ratio of incomplete vs. complete articles to eventual stagnation of Wikipedia growth (Spinellis & Louridas, 2008, p. 71).

A one-degree network extraction of the "Defense_in_depth_(computing)" article network on Wikipedia resulted in 26 vertices, 25 links, and one-group. Some of the technologies that may be applied to create redundant defense-in-depth is shown in this graph.

A more complex data extraction, at two degrees, was done around the "Defense_in_depth" network albeit without the disambiguation of the parenthetical "(computing)" clarification. This extraction, shown in Figure 21, resulted in the identification of 8,066 vertices, 9,809 edges, and 23 groups. The word-sense disambiguation here for this phrase suggests a range of military understandings.

The slogan "information wants to be free" was used as a seed article to analyze its network on Wikipedia in Figure 22. The graph contains 72 vertices, 73 edges, and one-group (in this one-degree network). The original seed article is located at http://en.wikipedia.org/wiki/Information_wants_to_be_free.

Information security (infosec) is a core tenet for computer systems, and this concept subsumes multiple variables. An article network extraction from Wikipedia evokes some of the issues in this area and some of the main contributors to the field. Figure 23 shows a graph with 238 vertices, 237 unique edges, and one group in this 1-degree graph extraction.

Another content-based article network related to the topic of "data leak" is "Data_breach". In Figure 24, 5he one-degree article network around this page with a synonymous name contains 88 vertices and 89 links. Some of the other related articles mention victim organizations of data breaches. That said, multiple sources suggest that virtually all U.S. companies have been hacked and lost data (Singer & Friedman, 2014).

Figure 25 is a graph that is about "Edward Snowden" and not "by" Edward Snowden, so this is a content network on Wikipedia (vs. a user network). This content-based article network then contains 474 vertices, 473 unique edges, and one group. (The word size was scaled down to minimize the word overlap.)

The one-degree "Julian_Assange" article network (Figure 26) consists of 189 vertices, 188 unique edges, and one group.

"Chelsea_Manning Article Network on Wikipedia (1 deg.)," Figure 27, is comprised of 228 vertices, 227 edges, and one group.

Figure 28 is comprised of 139 vertices, 138 edges, and one group.

"William_Binney_(U.S._intelligence_official) Article Network on Wikipedia (1 deg.)," Figure 29, is made up of 66 vertices, 65 unique edges, and one group.

Figure 20. "Defense_in_depth_(computing)" article network on Wikipedia (1 deg.)

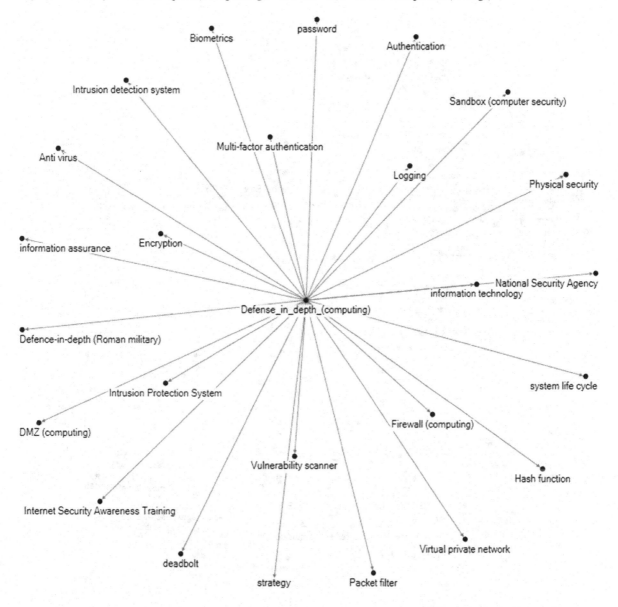

Figure 30 contains 87 vertices, 86 unique edges, and one cluster or group. One approach to extracting understandings from the graph is to find anomalous ties that may provide informational value for a researcher.

Figure 31 shows the focal page link to 117 vertices, and 116 unique edges, in one cluster or group. Such entries are about the individual but also about his or her representation of issues based on his or her social role. Deeper understandings may only be obtained through reading through the various connections, but the network map of related article titles in Wikipedia offers a sense of gist and some leads to follow.

"National_Security_Agency Article Network on Wikipedia," Figure 32, contains 454 vertices, 453 unique edges, and one group. An article network on Wikipedia shows the other pages on Wikipedia

Figure 21. "Defense_in_depth" article network on Wikipedia (2 deg)

that are directly linked to the focal page. With the increasing size of this encyclopedia, there are more opportunities for enriched understandings and clarity with increasing depth of information.

In Figure 33, "James_R_Clapper Article Network on Wikipedia (1 deg.)," the network graph contained 148 vertices, 147 unique edges, and one group. In the "grammar" of this online encyclopedia, page titles have to be disambiguated. For individuals, this may mean that middle initials are critical to include. There may also be the inclusion of parenthetical information to further elaborate on the page title meaning and page contents.

Figure 22. Information_wants_to_be_free article network on Wikipedia (1 deg.)

An article network may be seeded by an organization as an entity or "self". In Figure 34, "WikiLeaks Article Network on Wikipedia (1 deg.)," the resulting graph contained 289 vertices and 288 unique edges, all in one group.

3. Users

A user network on a social media platform is an account which usually represents a person or a group. In virtually all social media platforms, there are also robot accounts (automated agents, sensor-based accounts) and some cyborg accounts (automation-enhanced human accounts, or human-enhanced automated accounts).

Figure 23. Information_security article network on Wikipedia (1 deg.)

@ USER NETWORK SEARCHES ON TWITTER

The "@occupy_www" account on Twitter attracts a wide range of posters on a variety of Internet-based activism.

Figure 35 shows a one-degree network for the @occupy_www account on Twitter, with its 67 vertices, 62 edges, and one group. A glance at recent hashtagged communications offer a wide selection of activist movements.

Figure 24. Data_breach article network on Wikipedia (1 deg.)

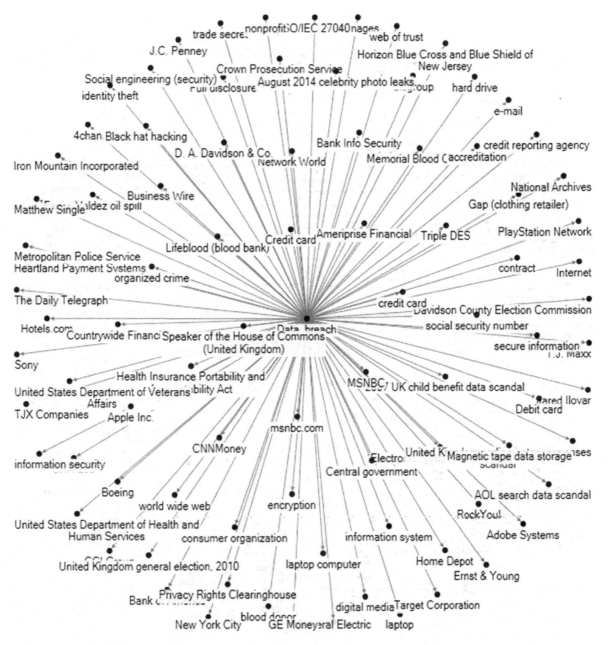

A one-degree extraction of the "ego neighborhood" of the @youranonnews account (linked to the Anonymous hacker collective) was explored on Twitter. The exploration of the user account resulted in Figure 36, which contains 130 vertices, 91 edges, and one group (of direct ties to @youranonnews). The Twitter landing page for this account is available at https://twitter.com/youranonnews.

Figure 25. Edward_Snowden article network on Wikipedia (1 deg)

User Networks On Youtube

User accounts on YouTube are those run by entities or individuals, and through which topical channels are created and run. Their networks are those with direct ties—of interactivity.

After a half-dozen tries to capture user networks on YouTube, it became clear that a number of account holders had chosen to set their privacy at sufficient levels to restrict the extraction of their networks.

Figure 26. Julian_Assange article network on Wikipedia (1 deg)

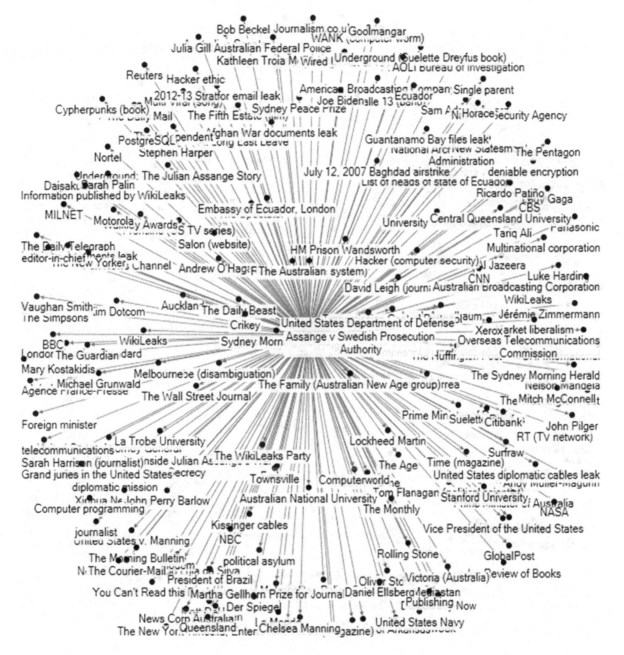

Finally, the NBC News (https://www.youtube.com/user/NBCNews) account on YouTube was extracted. A one-degree extraction of the NBCNews user network resulted in the identification of 8 vertices, 7 edges, and one group. Several of the nodes seem to be accounts related to the parent company of NBC. In a directed network, these links might be seen as self-loops. The graph in Figure 37 had node sizes set based on betweenness centrality. Given that the searched-for network is at the core of this network, its node size is clearly larger to show its connective function.

Figure 27. Chelsea_Manning article network on Wikipedia (1 deg)

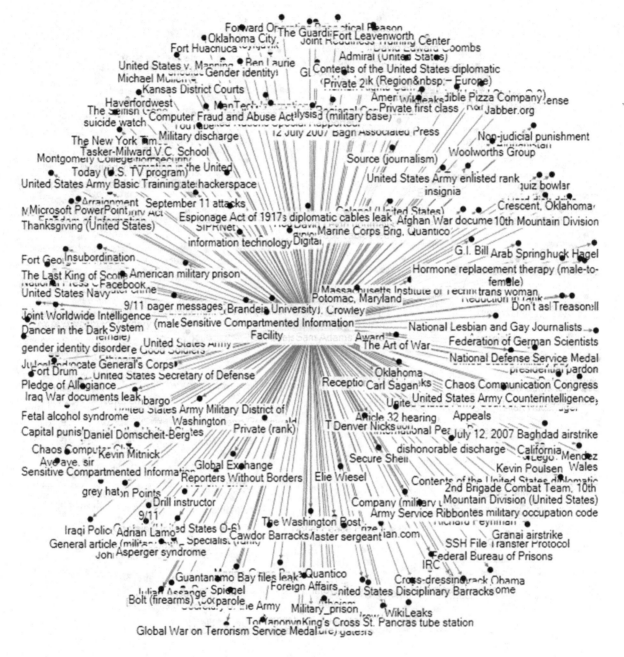

A 1.5 degree network extraction of the NBCNews user network on YouTube resulted in connectivity between accounts that appear corporately related (in Figure 38). This network has eight vertices, eight links, and two groups.

Figure 39 resulted in a graph with 208 vertices, 241 unique edges, and four groups.

Figure 28. Thomas_Andrews_Drake article network on Wikipedia (1 deg)

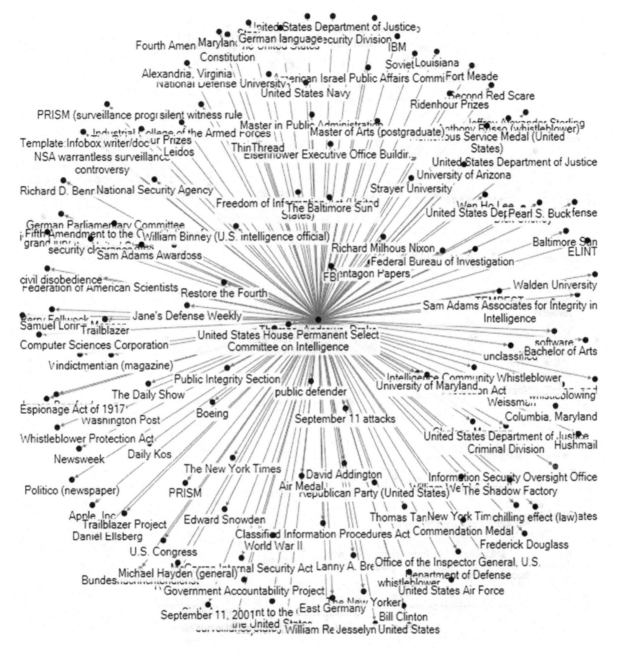

USER NETWORKS ON FLICKR

User networks on Flickr may be extracted with vertices extracted for the following: either "contact of the user" or "person who commented on the user's photos (slower)," or both. Quite a few accounts were located, and attempts were made to extract the user networks, but many holders of such accounts also declined to share their data.

Figure 29. William_Binney_(U.S._intelligence_official) article network on Wikipedia (1 deg.)

In Figure 40, the SamsungTomorrow photostream was extracted on Flickr. The graph itself contained 224 vertices, 190 edges, and one group. SamsungTomorrow was finally arrived at after searching through a variety of seed words, and as such, it really likely has little direct tie to the issue of "data leakage" as initially conceptualized.

Figure 30. Laura_Poitras article network on Wikipedia (1 deg.)

USER ARTICLE NETWORKS ON WIKIPEDIA

User article networks on Wikipedia are those accounts—run by people or approved 'bots—and their respective links with other users and article-contents.

One account that was pulled from the cryptography article history page was for User:Omnipaedista. This network (shown in Figure 41) includes 34 vertices and 33 edges. The article network contains ties to other users as well as article accounts. There are also ties to multimedia. The landing page for this

Figure 31. Michael_Hayden_(general) article network on Wikipedia (1 deg.)

account on Wikipedia is the following: http://en.wikipedia.org/wiki/User:Omnipaedista. Note that the user account is labeled different than an account about a particular person, group, or entity.

The extraction of the "User:Monkbot" user article network on Wikipedia is available in Figure 42. This account was also found as a contributor to the cryptography article on Wikipedia. This graph involves 19 vertices, 18 edges, and one group. The landing page for this account is http://en.wikipedia.

Figure 32. National_Security_Agency "article network" on Wikipedia (1 deg.)

org/wiki/User:Monkbot. The vertices show clear links to itself and clear identifiers for its identity as a legitimized robot on Wikipedia. Often, pages that have been updated by robots do not show in the networks; specifically, here, the tie to the "Cryptography" page (http://en.wikipedia.org/w/index.php?ti tle=Cryptography&action=history) is not seen in the extracted network as an article. (This is based on how MediaWiki was set to handle the changes by robots.)

Figure 33. James_R. Clapper "article network" on Wikipedia (1 deg)

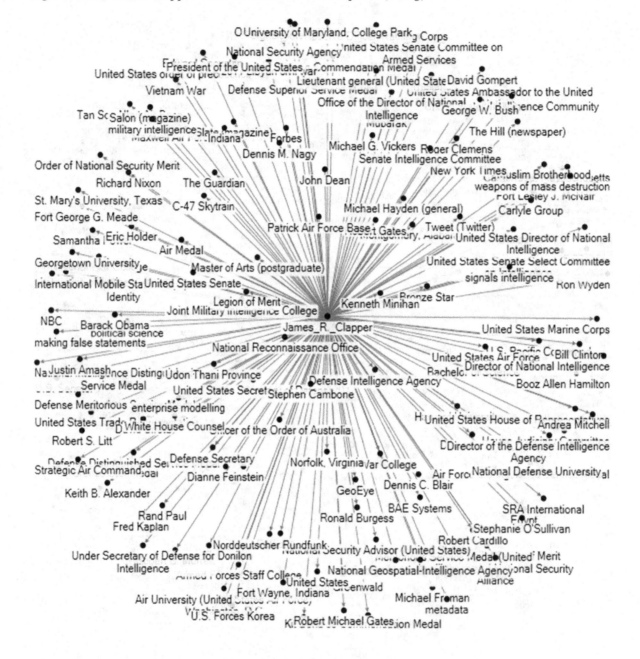

A REVIEW OF SOME OF THE PRACTICES APPLIED TO THE SEMANTIC-BASED NETWORK ANALYSIS

In this work, very few (if any) definitive conclusions were drawn; rather, the focus was on exploratory method and information types extractable from four major social media platforms. It may help to review some of the ways information may be extracted from these semantic-based networks from social media.

Figure 34. WikiLeaks "article network" on Wikipedia (1 deg)

Figure 43 shows three paths: a target proximity search, a selected path search, and a target periphery search for leads from an article network in Wikipedia. The target-proximity and target-periphery searches are based on the center-periphery / core-periphery analytics approach to some types of graphs. Centripetal forces (pulling inward to the center) pull in nodes closer to the focal node if there are a lot of interactions (a lot of relational types of behaviors); centrifugal forces (pulling outward) apply to the nodes with fewer interactions with the focal node in the center, resulting in nodes with more remote relationships being

Figure 35. @occupy_www user network on Twitter (basic network plus friends and followers)

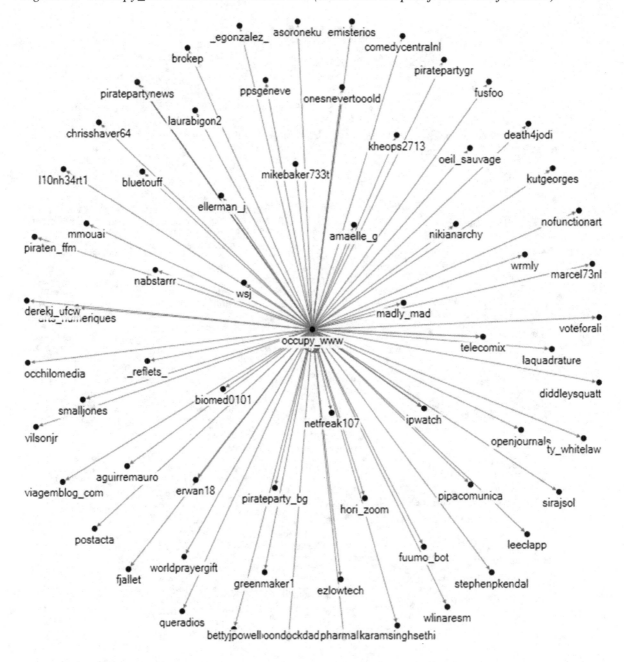

pulled to the periphery. The graph here involves an assumption of Euclidean space and proximity, with those articles closest to the target as being more related than those farthest away and on the periphery.

In a related tags network on Flickr (Figure 44), some of the same ideas may apply to the analysis… by analyzing which tags are most proxemically close to the target or focal tag but also those on the periphery, particularly in a one-degree network search. Identifying anomalous words may also provide leads and insights.

Figure 36. YourAnonNews user account on Twitter (basic network and friends and followers)

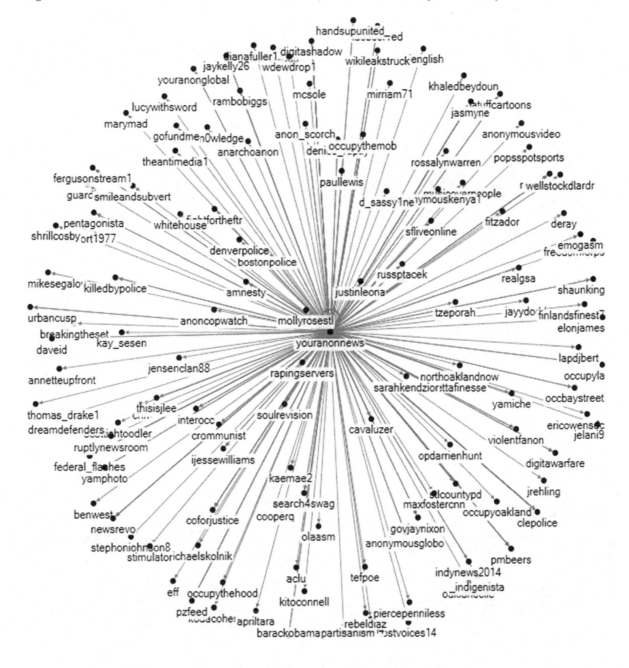

In a Twitter hashtag conversation network, such as Figure 45, the types of groups or clusters may be of interest because they may indicate different interest groups or those clustering around differing conversational angles. Bridging nodes that connect the various groups may be of interest because of their inherent structural power (in connecting groups that would not otherwise be bridged). Motif censuses may be conducted to analyze smaller subgraphs to understand potential power and communicational dynamics. The various types of accounts within a conversation network may be indicative of stakeholders and interests. The types of messaging being shared around the #hashtagged conversation may also be revealing of conversational gist.

Figure 37. "NBCNews" user network on YouTube (1 deg.)

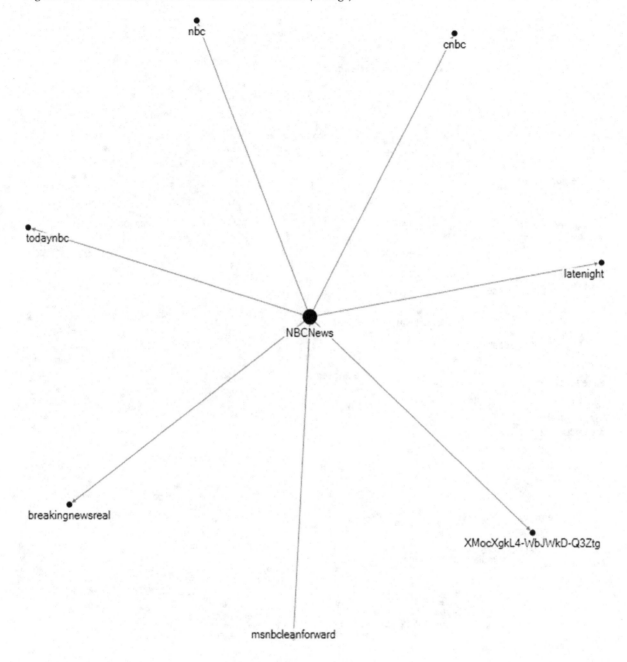

There is a rich body of literature about social networks that go back to the early days of the start of sociology over a hundred years ago. Since those early days, there has been a lot of research on how people socially organize, communicate, friend- and unfriend-, build and dissolve alliances, collaborate and interact. In this present age, computer-supported research may contribute greatly to such understandings.

Figure 38. "NBCNews" user network on YouTube (1.5 deg.)

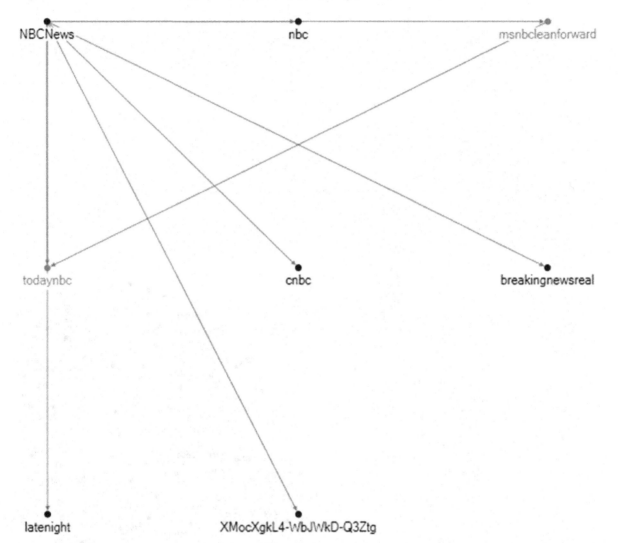

FUTURE RESEARCH DIRECTIONS

This chapter addressed ways to apply semantic-based network analysis to data extracted from social media platforms, namely, Twitter, YouTube, Flickr, and Wikipedia. The types of information gathered were based on conversations, contents, and users, as indicated by Table 1. This approach is presented as a way to add social dimensionality to an issue, given how many use social media for social performances and social signaling. The work presented here is not that unusual. It merely shows the application of one software tool (NodeXL) applied to four platforms for a variety of data extractions and graph visualizations, which may be analyzed spatially and semantically.

This approach requires a depth of knowledge about network analysis, the respective social media platforms, the NodeXL tool, and methods for extracting meaning from words. In a dynamic environment, any of these aspects will be in a state of change, so it is important to double-check information

Figure 39. "BuzzFeed" user network on YouTube (2 deg.)

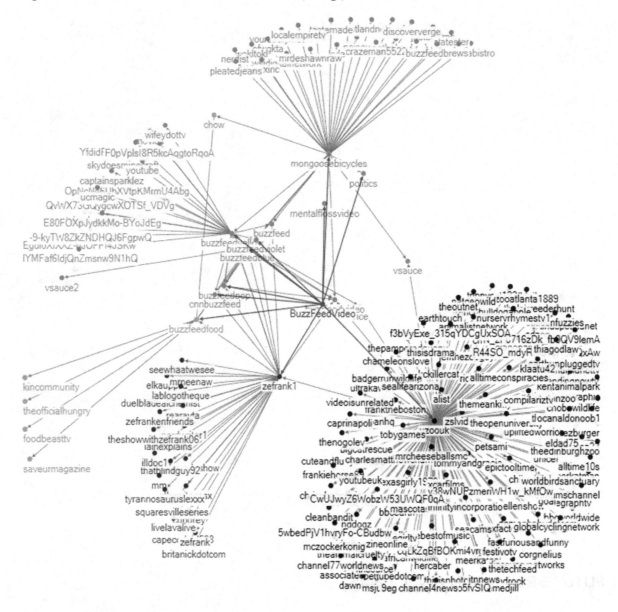

before making any assertions. The search terms themselves are based on human selection, and they are multi-meaninged. The information gathered is also likely quite incomplete and also of a social type, what Henk Eijkman called "non-foundational learning" in a Web 2.0-enabled network-centric learning space. The author has described this growing type of data:

Whereas Web 1.0 practices in higher education revolve primarily around the (global) dissemination of information by individual (and "authoritative") academic authors to individual learners, Web 2.0 opens a whole new world of social interconnectivity in which academics, experienced professionals and students alike can now much more easily network with each other for life-like collaborative knowledge construction (Eijkman, 2007, p. 97).

Figure 40. SamsungTomorow photostream on Flickr (1 deg.)

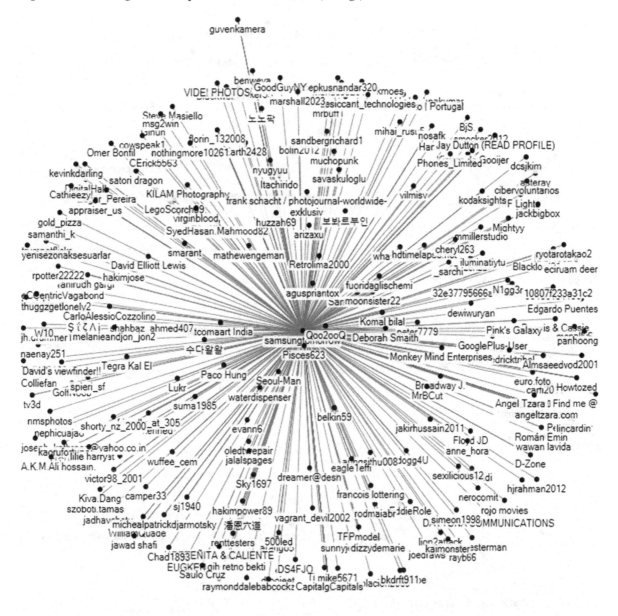

Additional research may be achieved on a number of other social media platforms. A wide range of other topics may be pursued using this method. The complementary analysis of content messaging would be helpful to extract concepts, multimedia, URLs, and sentiment direction and strength.

CONCLUSION

Semantic-based network analysis based on data from social media sites enables the analysis of online social phenomena and public thinking on particular issues. This approach enables the identification of various social media accounts engaged in particular recent conversations and some of the roles and

Figure 41. "User:Omnipaedista" user article network on Wikipedia (1 deg.)

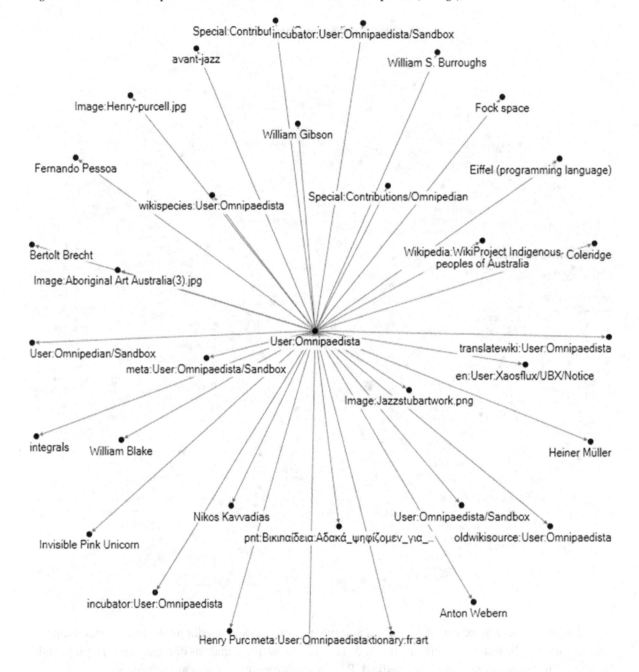

relationships based on messaging and other interactions; it enables the capturing of recent messaging contents; it enables the identification of concept connections based on metadata like tagging of digital contents and titles of videos. This method may be applied to understand evolving social networks and publicly debated issues. Complementary types of analyses involve accessing the various Excel worksheets of extracted data, and in particular, the graph metrics table, groups table, and the extracted messaging. Other software tools may be used to extract other types of data to enhance the analysis. The network maps or graphs may also be interacted with based on different labeling, dynamic filtering, and zooming in- and out- and panning.

Figure 42. "User:Monkbot" user article network on Wikipedia (1 deg.)

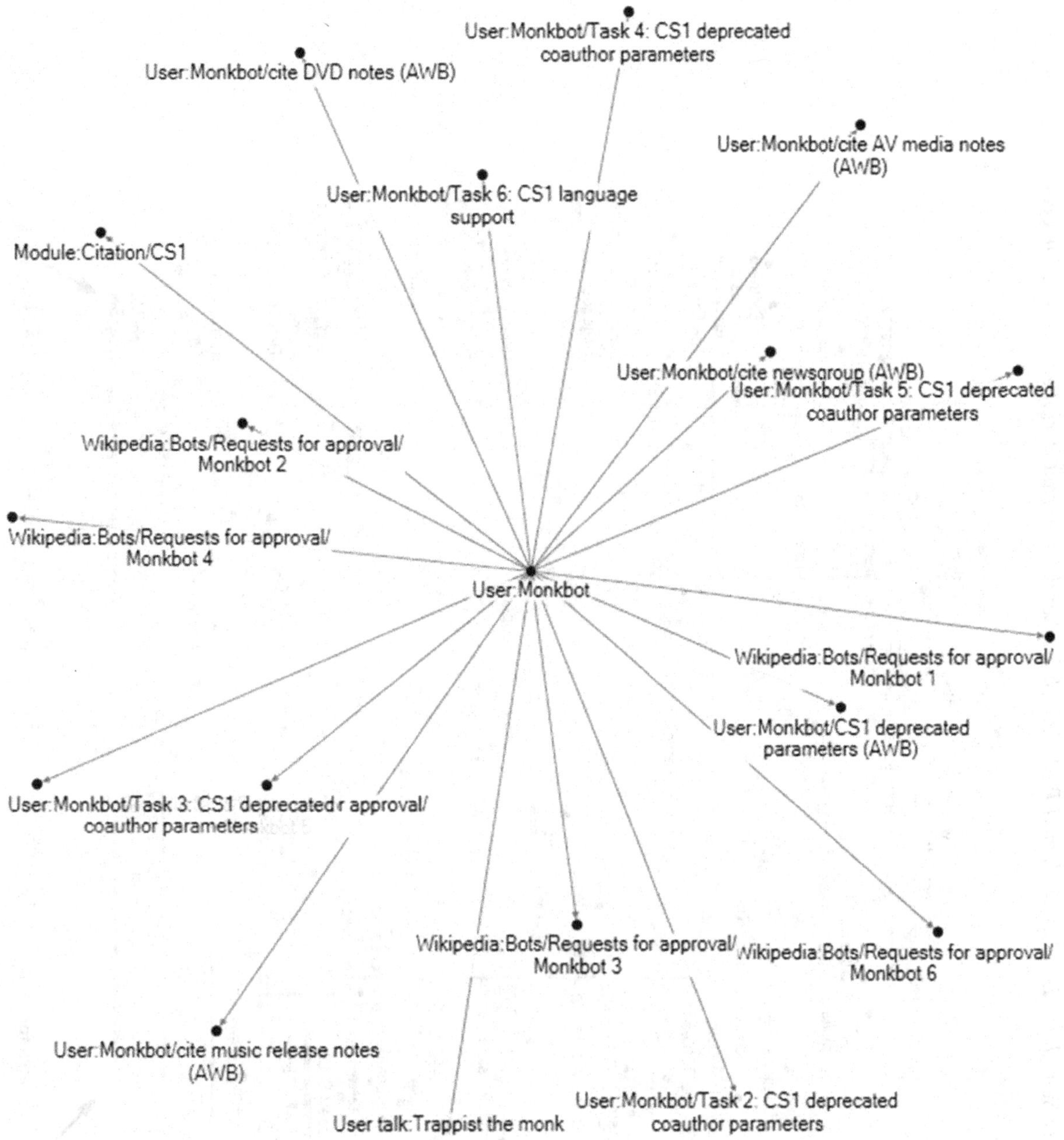

User:Monkbot/Task 4: CS1 deprecated coauthor parameters

User:Monkbot/cite DVD notes (AWB)

User:Monkbot/cite AV media notes (AWB)

User:Monkbot/Task 6: CS1 language support

Module:Citation/CS1

User:Monkbot/cite newsgroup (AWB)
User:Monkbot/Task 5: CS1 deprecated coauthor parameters

Wikipedia:Bots/Requests for approval/ Monkbot 2

Wikipedia:Bots/Requests for approval/ Monkbot 4

User:Monkbot

Wikipedia:Bots/Requests for approval/ Monkbot 1

User:Monkbot/CS1 deprecated parameters (AWB)

User:Monkbot/Task 3: CS1 deprecated r approval/ coauthor parameters

Wikipedia:Bots/Requests for approval/ Monkbot 3

Wikipedia:Bots/Requests for approval/ Monkbot 6

User:Monkbot/cite music release notes (AWB)

User talk:Trappist the monk

User:Monkbot/Task 2: CS1 deprecated coauthor parameters

This chapter addressed a limited use case revolving around the phenomenon of "data leakage" as a contested present-day social movement. The methods here, enabled by NodeXL and the various social media platforms, may be applied to a range of other topics and contexts. The software tool itself has a wide range of capabilities not addressed here. The data extracted using NodeXL may be analyzed using other software and data visualization tools.

Figure 43. A Target Proximity Search for Leads; a Selected Path Search for Leads; a Target Periphery Search for Leads

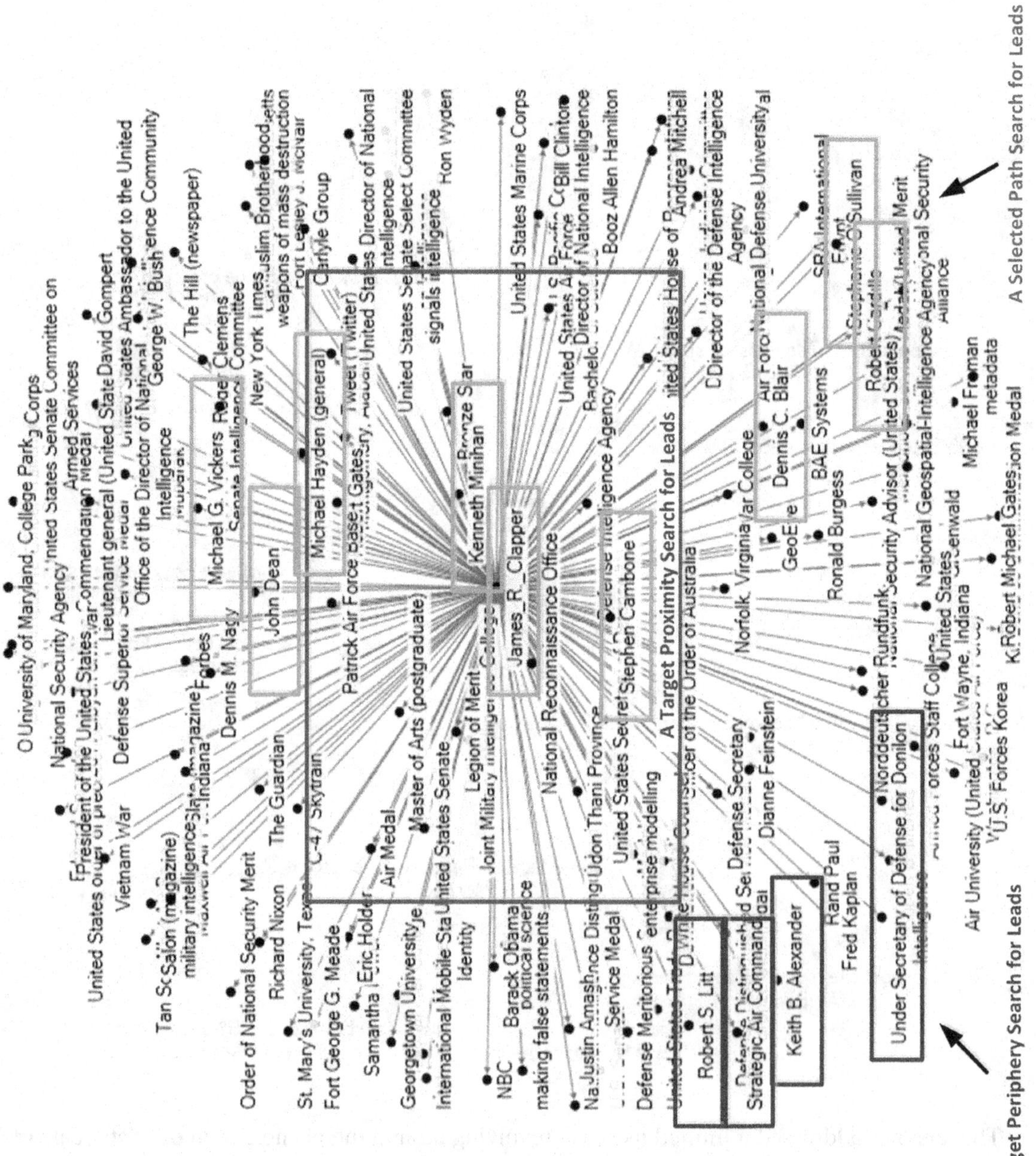

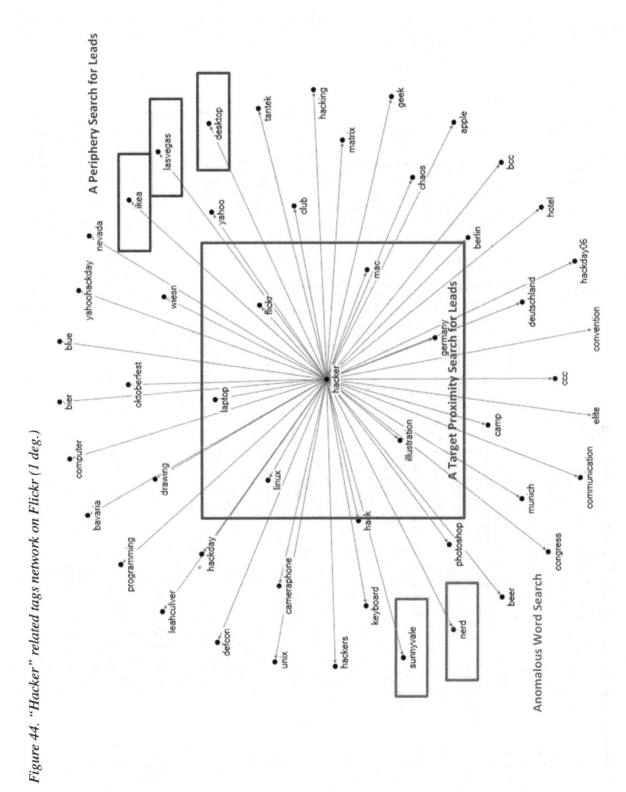

Figure 44. "Hacker" related tags network on Flickr (1 deg.)

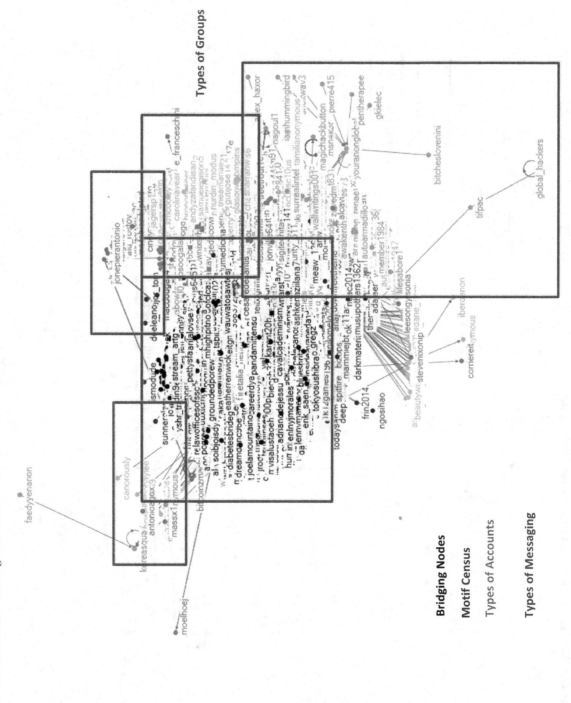

Figure 45. A #hacker hashtag search network on Twitter basic network

Bridging Nodes

Motif Census

Types of Accounts

Types of Messaging

REFERENCES

Adler, B. T., & de Alfaro, L. (2007). A content-driven reputation system for the Wikipedia. In *WWW 2007* (pp. 261–270). Track E-Applications. doi:10.1145/1242572.1242608

Anderson, N. (2013). *The Internet Police: How Crime Went Online, and the Cops Followed*. New York: W.W. Norton & Company.

Andrejevic, M. (2014). The big data divide. *International Journal of Communication*, 8, 1673–1689.

Ares, K. (2014, Nov. 29). Social media data does not reveal true human behaviour. *Tech Analyst*. Retrieved from http://www.techanalyst.co/social-media-data-does-not-reveal-true-human-behaviour/14462/

Blumenstock, J. E. (2008). Size matters: Word count as a measure of quality on Wikipedia (Poster Paper). In the proceedings of *WWW 2008*. Beijing, China.

Byers, S. (2004). Information leakage caused by hidden data in published documents. *IEEE Security and Privacy*, 2(2), 23–27. doi:10.1109/MSECP.2004.1281241

Devine, T., & Maassarani, T. F. (2011). *The Corporate Whistleblower's Survival Guide: A Handbook for Committing the Truth*. San Francisco: Berrett-Koehler Publishers, Inc.

Eijkman, H. (2007). Web 2.0 as a non-foundational network-centric learning space. *Campus-Wide Information Systems*, 25(2), 93–104. doi:10.1108/10650740810866567

Flickr. (2014, Nov. 25). Retrieved from http://en.wikipedia.org/wiki/Flickr

Flora, C. (2013). *Friendfluence: The Surprising Ways Friends Make Us Who We Are*. New York: Doubleday.

Glenny, M. (2011). *DarkMarket: Cyberthieves, Cybercops, and You*. New York: Alfred A. Knopf.

Greenwald, G. (2014). *No Place to Hide: Edward Snowden, the NSA, and the U.S. Surveillance State*. New York: Metropolitan Books.

Harding, L. (2014). *The Snowden Files: The Inside Story of the World's Most Wanted Man*. New York: Vintage Books.

Harris, S. (2014). *War: The Rise of the Military-Internet Complex*. New York: Houghton Mifflin Harcourt Publishing.

Holloway, T., Bozicevic, M., & Börner, K. (2007). Analyzing and visualizing the semantic coverage of Wikipedia and its authors. *Complexity. Interscience*, 12(3), 30–40.

Korfiatis, N. T., Poulos, M., & Bokos, G. (2006). Evaluating authoritative sources using social networks: An insight from Wikipedia. *Online Information Review*, 30(3), 252–262. doi:10.1108/14684520610675780

Leuf, B., & Cunningham, W. (2001). *The wiki way: Quick collaboration on the Web*. Boston, Massachusetts: Addison-Wesley.

Lyon, D. (2003). *Surveillance as social sorting: Privacy, risk, and digital discrimination*. New York: Routledge.

Mansfield-Devine, S. (2014). Masking sensitive data. *Network Security*, *2014*(10), 17–21. doi:10.1016/S1353-4858(14)70104-7

McCormick, M. (2008). Data theft: A prototypical insider threat.. In S.J. Stolfo, S.M. Bellovin, S. Hersh-kop, A., Keromytis, S. Sinclair, & S.W. Smith, (Eds.), Advances in Information Security. SpringerLink. 53 – 67. doi:10.1007/978-0-387-77322-3_4

Müller-Birn, C., Dobusch, L., & Herbsleb, J. D. (2013). Work-to-rule: The emergence of algorithmic governance in Wikipedia. In the proceedings of *C&T '13*. Munich, Germany. (pp. 80–89).

Pentzold, C. (2009). Fixing the floating gap: The online encyclopedia Wikipedia as a global memory place. *Memory Studies*, *2*(255), 255–272. doi:10.1177/1750698008102055

Risen, J. (2006). *State of War: The Secret History of the CIA and the Bush Administration*. New York: Free Press.

Risen, J. (2014). *Pay Any Price: Greed, Power, and Endless War*. New York: Houghton Mifflin.

Singer, P. W., & Friedman, A. (2014). *Cybersecurity and Cyberwar: What Everyone Needs to Know*. Oxford: Oxford University Press.

Size of Wikipedia. (2014, Oct. 21). http://en.wikipedia.org/wiki/Wikipedia:Size_of_Wikipedia

Spinellis, D., & Louridas, P. (2008). The collaborative organization of knowledge. *Communications of the ACM*, *51*(8), 68–71. doi:10.1145/1378704.1378720

Wikipedia. Statistics. (2014, Nov. 25). Retrieved from http://en.wikipedia.org/wiki/Wikipedia:Statistics

Wilkinson, D. M., & Huberman, B. A. (2008). Assessing the value of cooperation in Wikipedia. *First Monday*. http://firstmonday.org/article/view/1763/1643

YouTube Statistics. (2014). Retrieved from https://www.youtube.com/yt/press/statistics.html

Zaid, M. (2013, June 24). A Legal Perspective on the Snowden Case. Spycast. International Spy Museum. Retrieved from http://www.spymuseum.org/multimedia/spycast/episode/a-legal-perspective-on-the-snowden-case/

Zesch, T., & Gurevych, I. (2007). *Analysis of the Wikipedia Category Graph for NLP Applications*. *TextGraphs-2: Graph-Based Algorithms for Natural Language Processing. 1 – 8*. Association for Computational Linguistics.

ADDITIONAL READING

Lessig, L. (1999). *Code: And Other Laws of Cyberspace*. New York: Basic Books.

KEY TERMS AND DEFINITIONS

Add-On (Plug-In): Software that adds functionality to another tool (like a browser or spreadsheet software program).

Civil Liberties: Human-based freedoms based on human rights and also citizenship.

Center-Periphery (Core-Periphery) Dynamic: A model of analysis which involves data that is spatially placed with some data in the center and others on the outside periphery (often with implications of both centrifugal force and centripetal force at play).

Credential: The objects that are uniquely related to unique people's identities and enables their accesses to services, resources, and information.

Cybersecurity: Protection against unauthorized access to data, services, credentials, and other cyber-related resources.

Data Leakage: The loss of sensitive data, with an implied sense of unauthorized mis-use.

Defense In Depth: An information security term which refers to the application of redundant systems in order to detect and mitigate risks of intrusion or other technology system compromises.

Euclidean Distance: Ordinary distance.

Fraud: Criminal deception or machinations often for financial gain.

Hyponymy: An "umbrella term" containing a subset of items which fit within the term.

Insider Threat: The risk stemming from disgruntled employees at an organization.

Mediawiki: A free and open-source wiki tool.

Meronymy: A term which represents an object that is a part or member of a larger category.

Microblogging: The sharing of short text messages and URLs through a microblogging site.

Monetize: To turn something (like information) into money.

Node-Link Diagram: A graph drawing consisting of entities (represented as vertices) and relationships (represented as lines or edges or arcs).

Open-Source: Software or informational contents that are made freely available and sometimes fully editable by users based on intellectual property release licensure.

Robot: An automated agent that is designed for particular functions and objectives.

Semantics: The study of meanings in language (as a branch of linguistics).

Sensor: A device that detects and measures a particular property in an environment.

Social Media Platform: An online service that enables people to inter-communicate and to share digital contents.

Subgraph: A type of interconnected concentration of nodes in a social network graph.

Surveillance: Close observation.

Whistleblower: An individual who reports on illegal activity that he or she has witnessed.

Chapter 12
Grounding Cyber:
Querying Social Media Platforms, the Web, and Internet for Geolocational Information

Shalin Hai-Jew
Kansas State University, USA

ABSTRACT

Tying "cyber" entities, spaces, and events to real-world physical spaces is a critical step in de-mythifying cyberspace. This chapter introduces Maltego Tungsten™, a penetration testing tool, as one method to extract geolocational information from social media platforms, the Web, and the Internet—in order to relate online accounts, emails, aliases, and online-discussed events to specific physical spaces. This tool may be used for general research or applied "oppo" (opposition) or "doxing" (documenting) research of targets. This also discusses how the geolocational information may be further used to extract deeper understandings. Also, Network Overview, Discovery, and Exploration for Excel (NodeXL) is applied for some geolocational information extractions.

INTRODUCTION

Contrary to common sense, the popular Western narrative about the WWW and Internet in popular culture has long romanticized the online connectivity. In cyberpunk literature, cyberspace was hallucinatory, magical, and other-worldly, with its denizens pumped up with a kind of supernatural awareness and capability. Back in the day, people would start websites and sell "passports" and citizenship to virtual countries, without any physical equivalency. Early writing suggested that people could experiment with any number of alternate selves without repercussion (an early form of "what happens online stays online"). There was a rhetoric of disembodiment and weightlessness in human representations by email handles initially and later 3D digital avatars in immersive virtual spaces. There was a sense of anonymity, with people hiding in the onslaught of bits and bytes, and this fostered a sense that there was no traceability back to their real-world selves. Virtual communities promised cross-border good will and helpfulness in a new global village with support available 24/7 (Holeton, 1998). People could learn from others in a seamless electronic way. The "cyber" trope was used by some to engage in flights

DOI: 10.4018/978-1-4666-8696-0.ch012

of fancy and to suspend their own critical thinking and hard-earned knowledge of the real world, and this assumption of otherness in that space left many vulnerable to poor decision-making (such as losing massive sums to "Nigerian princes" and those "seeking business partners." Many were functioning at a level of imaginative abstraction that was not particularly warranted by the technology, essentially a rudimentary communications network of computers connected over existing phone lines initially. There were mass endeavors reifying cyber and imbuing it with a sense of magical realism. Over time, though, a healthy disillusionment has set in, which has enabled more rational understandings and conversations of real-world phenomena manifesting online.

This new rationality has not hindered the breadth of creative mental linkages to "cyber"—as indicated by a related tags network of "cyber" in Flickr (at two degrees). [A related tags network refers to a clustering of co-occurring folk-tags used to label online contents. This related tags network graph enables the sense of which words are related in collective people's sensibilities as a somewhat indirect method, since this uses metadata.] This visualization shows a range of evocations from the term cyber based on uploaded photos and videos that were tagged with the term "cyber". This graph, laid out using the Harel-Koren Fast Multi-scale layout algorithm, shows the penetration of the concept of cyber as used in the tagging of multimedia on the Flickr content-sharing social media platform. The references include a technology section but also go well beyond that domain.

A #cyber hashtag conversation was captured recently as well, which engaged a number of discussants on the microblogging site Twitter. [A "hashtag conversation" on a microblogging site captures the conversations labeled with a particular #hashtag, which is an alphanumeric label prefaced by a #hash to indicate the relatedness of the contents to a larger discussion.] The concept of cyberspace very much a part of the popular parlance even decades after sci-fi writer William Gibson used it in 1984 in a novel. In Figure 2, there are clusters of conversationalists (fittingly, individuals, groups; humans, 'bots, and cyborgs) engaging this hashtag to label their conversations. The dataset behind the visual includes a verbatim Tweetstream dataset, which may be further analyzed (by machine analysis and / or close human reading) for content analysis.

A keyword search for "cyber" on Twitter showed a number of discussants. [A "keyword search" refers to the collating of all messages which contain the particular keyword and / or stemmed versions of that keyword. This type of extraction collects messaging in which the keyword may be a part—but not necessarily a central part—in the way a #hashtag search may collect conversations purposefully labeled with a particular hashtag.] The user names on the accounts possibly indicative of various interests regarding cyberspace, such as security, news, analytics, law, and other issues in Figure 3. The "keyword" search highlights Tweets with all mentions of "cyber" (not necessarily those linked to a hashtag) and so shows fewer connections between user accounts on Twitter.

Finally, a search of YouTube found a robust "cyber" video network with a wide range of video titles expressed in the vertices of the network in Figure 4. The titles suggest a range of topics for these videos: cyberpunk fiction, conferences, technologies, and contested social spaces like cyberespionage and cyber activism (such as through the Anonymous hacker collective).

Now, several decades in, those in cyberspace are starting to come around to seeing the Web and Internet in more realistic terms: as a communications mechanism grounded in a physical structure of wires, undersea cables, and wired and wireless access points very much in the physical realm (Blum, 2012). They understand communications as pulses of light. They better see the Web and Net as places of human markets and interactions—for high-minded and less high-minded endeavors. They lost some sense of the mystique of the faraway and exotic and maybe gained a sense of the similarities between people.

Figure 1. "Cyber" related tags network on Flickr (2 degrees)

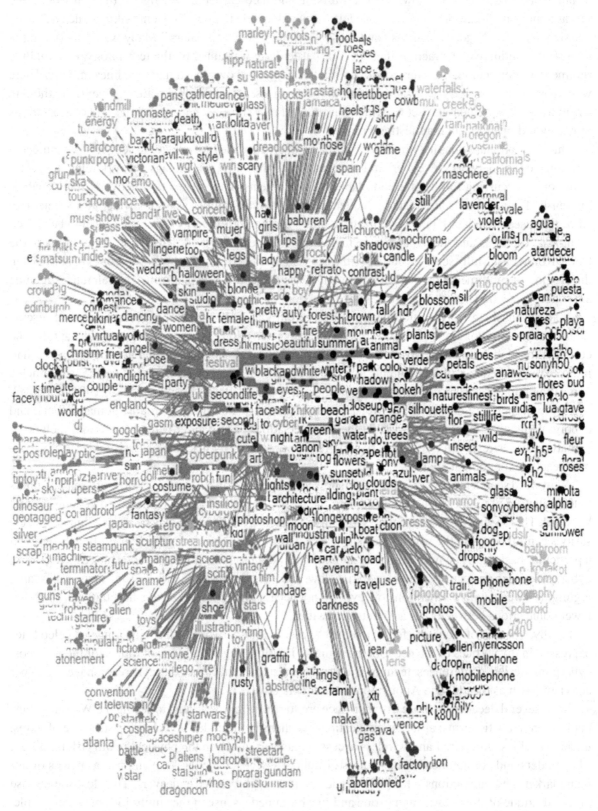

Figure 2. #cyber hashtag search on Twitter (18,000 Tweet limit)

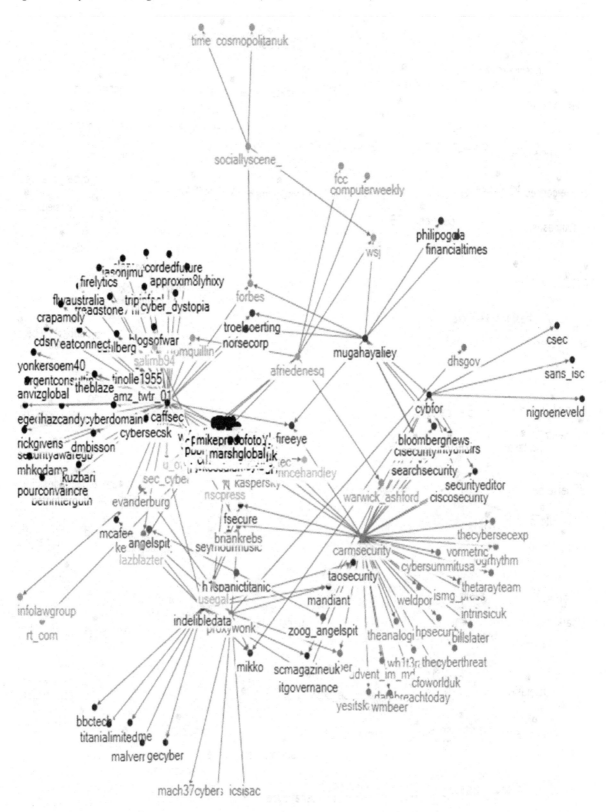

Figure 3. "Cyber" keyword search on Twitter (18,000 Tweet limit)

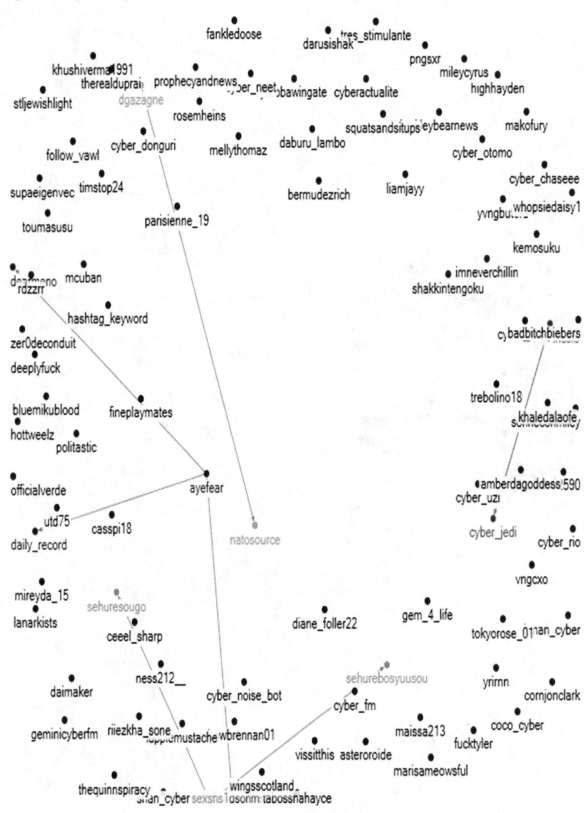

Figure 4. "Cyber" video network on YouTube

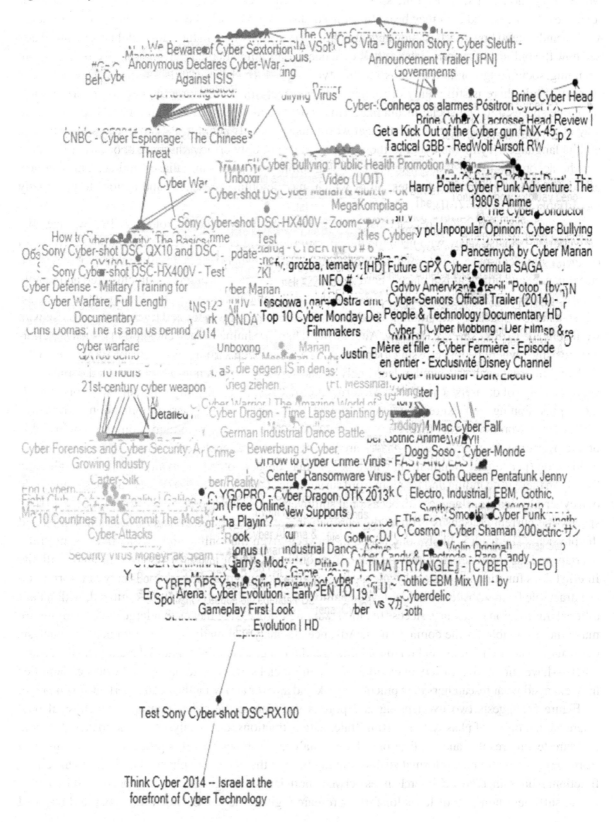

More savvy modern users of online spaces are seeing them as potential attack vectors in which their identities, finances, and data may be compromised (Jakobsson, 2012). People who are going online do well to understand how much is knowable about them post-Snowden, in the data and the metadata. They see how the online spaces mirror back their own deep patterning--in their personalities, self-expression, spending, socializing, communications, and lifestyles—all of which leave "tells" online (whether intended or not). While there is still plenty of imagination and fantastical creativity applied to understandings of online spaces, relating social media platform accounts and websites to actual physical spaces is one way of grounding cyber realities to the real world: its spaces, its peoples, its geographies, its cultures, and its languages. Tying the cyber to the real may raise not only critical thinking about what is online but the accountability of those who are engaging online by de-aliasing aliases and account handles, and defining understructures to sites, all of which may tie online presences and actions to personally identifiable information (PII).

In some ways, while cyberspace seems ephemeral and transitory, it may be considered a "leverage-able chokepoint" because many who need to engage with the world and their respective publics have to go online. In physical space, a geographical chokepoint is one in which a group is vulnerable to observation, surveillance, and attack; it is a place where people wanting to pass through end up clustered and unable to pass through with speed or stealth. To extend the geographical metaphor of a chokepoint, cyberspace is also a narrow space of vulnerability because of the electronic presences and trackability of those who would engage in this "space" (Hai-Jew, Aug. 2014). There are human-made chokepoints, such as at border crossings, where people crossing them are placed under deep scrutiny for security. Exposure on the Web and Internet enables a similar deep analysis and scrutiny using a number of tools and comparison against a range of datasets. The Web and Internet are spaces for virtually all of human endeavors: socializing, provisioning, self-expression, entertainment, learning, research, mass mobilization, commerce, and others. It would be highly difficult (some would say "impossible") to remain anonymous or invisible online over time. In a sense, online spaces are part of the "digital enclosure," which serves as a kind of panopticon (per Jeremy Bentham) in which people may observe others from any number of angles and for whom there is no hiding and freedom from surveillance (Andrejevic, 2007). If academics used to talk of a cyber-physical confluence with occasional spillovers, suggesting some overlap of online and offline spaces, the current consensus is on a "digital dualism" or an enmeshed engagement of the virtual and the physical. The truth is likely somewhere in between given that online and offline lives do not fully overlap, and the inferences that may be made from online to offline and vice versa are limited. Still, the Internet does function like a global-scale database (with the right querying tools). Plenty of information is extractable from websites with low-level technical skills. All the data is already digitized, without additional digitization necessary. Access to cloud computer processing means that large-scale analyses are much more possible for the common user. Advances in analytical methods—through network analysis (a form of structure mining) and relational linkage, the integration of geospatial data, text analysis, and others—have enhanced a variety of explorations in the social sciences and beyond. The new capabilities have changed what researchers may practically ask and answer and what they can assert and even prove.

Figure 5 suggests two overlapping and porous swimlanes: the cyber one and the physical one. There are a number of phases: the starting state, data extractions, data analyses, further data extraction, pressure-testing results, and applications. This visualization shows how this process of extracting data from the cyber realm may inform decision-making both in the cyber and physical realms. In this cross-functional diagram, there are interchanges between both lanes throughout the entire process. It is critical to run sufficient numbers of leads for further research, given the gap between the cyber and physical

Figure 5. Cyber-physical confluence and digital dualism depicted in a cross-functional (swimlane) diagram

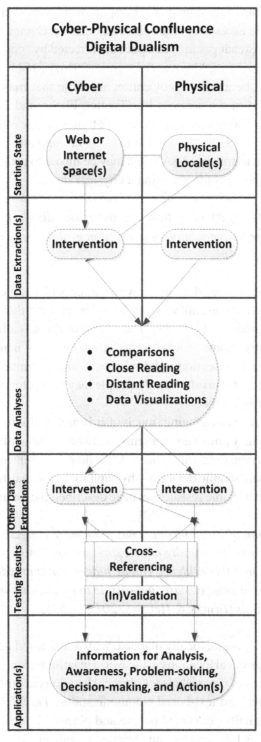

Cyber-Physical Confluence and Digital Dualism Depicted in a Cross-Functional (Swimlane) Diagram

realms. This does also show that there has to be effort in the extractions, the analyses (particularly for disambiguation). If anything, the suggestion that cyberspace had resulted in "the end of geography" was premature and probably a little excessive. After all, frictionless exchange of information has not been fully actualized. Cross-border exchanges in cyberspace are affected by "countries' social, economic, and cultural attributes" (Garcia-Gavilanes, Mejova, & Quercia, 2014, p. 1511).

The types of data that will be used for geolocation are those that may be considered "lightweight content items" posted to social media services like Twitter, Flickr, and Facebook (Naaman, 2011, p. 54). The regular updating to various accounts or various topics enables the forming of what Naaman calls "social awareness streams" (SAS) of data that may cohere into an apparent story or some degree of sense-making over time. Such streams of SAS data may be linked to geographic information systems, and their analysis may reveal how people are using a physical space:

These applications include boundary definition and detection (district); computation of attractions (landmarks); derivation and recommendation of paths; and evaluation of activities, interests and temporal trends (Naaman, 2011, p. 54).

Georeferenced and spatio-temporal data may reveal patterns of people's lives and "expose activities and interests of local communities, allowing us to understand the dynamics and patterns of urban and geographic activity" (Naaman, 2011, p. 57). The advent of the so-called geospatial web (geoweb) raises privacy concerns because "some of its representational forms – namely geo-tagged images and self-authored texts – facilitate identification and disclosure with more immediacy and less abstraction" (Elwood & Leszczynski, 2011, p. 6); in other words, people may be disclosing their location in real-time, real-space and broadcasting this to others.

While social media data are ever-changing, much of it is archived into posterity and accessible for querying. Such extracted data may power human sensor networks (the human groups that provide information for particular purposes) and the phenomenon of "participatory sensing" (the purposeful contribution of sensory information from mobile devices)—by capitalizing in real-time human awareness of the world and their engagement in it. Some researchers have described the nature of such social media data:

Digital evidence, especially that of social media, tends to be more capacious, more difficult to destroy, easily modified, easily duplicated, potentially more expressive and more readily available than traditional forms of evidence. Much of this evidence can be hidden (or embedded) from the naked eye, can be hard to locate and capture, or can be nearly impossible to obtain without legal intervention such as court orders and search warrants (Brunty & Helenek, 2012, p. 54).

Likewise, the world itself is geographically mapped, with a structured geographic coordinate system indicators pointing to precise physical locations in the world in latitude, longitude, and elevation. There is also a whole other "folk" system of place labels for physical locations in unstructured data like literature, text or multimedia geo-tagging, and text-based communications. The Web is in part a "geo-Web," an interlocking connection of digitally-connected people and places who interact in cyber- and physical-spaces simultaneously. Their mobile devices and enriched mobile apps enable real-time spatial awareness and connectivity with others. Geospatial information is commonplace (think Google Streetview), and there are a wide range of digital map representations for travel and weather. In a sense, all physical space is at least partially imaginary and interpretive. The act of mapping—and the inherent selectivity in the features of the maps—also suggest the social construction of such cartographic visualizations.

Table 1. Basic unstructured and structured references to physical space

Unstructured References to Physical Space	Structured References to Physical Space
Place names	ZIPcodes (Zone Improvement Plan codes)
City, state; city, province	Area codes / dialing codes
Textual descriptors (such as phrases referring to locations or places	Latitude, longitude, elevation or altitude or sea level
in relation to other locations)	x, y, and z coordinates (earth-centered, earth-fixed or ECEF) or
"Folk" (amateur, non-professional) descriptors or tags	(earth-centered rotational or ECR) system

Transforms. One other concept is important to set the context here: transforms. A "transform" within the main tool used here suggests that one type of digital information may be changed into another type of information, and with sufficient numbers of changes, one information type may be ultimately "located" to physical space information. In the same way, it is helpful to consider how a timestamp (or a pattern of time stamps) may be transformed to geography—based on time zones and the earth's rotation, people's circadian rhythms and times of highest activity (daytime). Time and space are intimately interrelated. Also, many relate predominant languages to certain geographies and cultures (although this leads to a much broader-scale and potentially inaccurate assumption, given the world's intermixed communities and diasporas as well as their broad mobility). Some researchers do warn against erroneously conflate language and location (Jakobsson, 2012, p. 14).

The tools that will be described here include publicly available ones, some commercial-based and others free and open-source. The main software tool used to probe the social media platforms and the Web and Internet is Maltego Tungsten™, a penetration-testing tool with multi-use capabilities. [A "penetration testing" tool enables organizations to test their own defenses by understanding where vulnerabilities exist in their own networks. Penetration testing tools enable individuals to conduct surveillance of their own and others' networks as a precursor to a simulated or actual attack that aims to compromise the system.] This tool enables the collection of publicly available information from the Internet and WWW.

Another tool used will be Network Overview, Discovery, and Exploration for Excel (NodeXL), which enables the extraction of information from a number of social media platforms through their application programming interfaces (APIs), which enable access to rate-limited data extractions from their respective platforms. In these cases, researchers also often need to maintain email-verified accounts on the various platforms in order to be "whitelisted" to access the data.

In this particular "use case," this tool and a few others will be used to extract publicly available online data which may be used for geolocation. As such, this is an example of the use of open-source intelligence (OSINT) to expand what is publicly knowable through data sharing and both intended and unintended data leakage. Awareness of such capabilities—of moving from the physical to the cyber and back to the physical through geolocation and geoparsing—is an important aspect of digital literacy. Geolocation refers to the identification of the geographical area of information from the Web or Internet; further, this may refer to the location of electronic devices like cell phones, MAC addresses, and other computing devices connected to a network. Geoparsing refers to the identification of structured locational data linked to unstructured data, such as an informal description of a place. Expressed in a data-fied way, this approach uses space as a "unique identifier" in a column of data, and this enables pivoting various types of information based on physical spatiality.

REVIEW OF THE LITERATURE

People have historically had an intimate relationship with many of the physical spaces around them. They have experienced deep sentiments for birthplaces and other spaces with personal significance. Collectively, certain public spaces like public squares and government buildings have special meanings and symbolic relevance for people. A "place" goes well beyond physical boundaries; rather, place is created based on social and political institutions, culture, human interactions, languages, shared norms and attitudes, and peoples—in a particular space and time—and with a range of evocations (Clare, 2012). Places and their respective meanings are co-created by people.

Human geography is formal study built on the more permanent features of physical space (both built and natural spaces) and generally stable population features (demographics, cultures, languages, social identities, and ethnicities). The study generally focuses on the macro level of broadscale understandings such as cultural (including symbolic), historic, and emotional meanings attributed to place.

The experiences of lived lives enable people to imagine new possibilities. Based on "the trilogy lived-known-knowable," people create a sense of the socially co-created "beyonds" far past terrestrial space and into what they imagine as possible (Claval, 2004, p. 321). The author explains: "Human beings take also into account their own experience, interests, tastes and positions; they elaborate through the mixing of social and personal elements, the horizons of expectancy which help them to give a meaning to their lives and to orient their action" (Claval, 2004, p. 328). The importance of social geographies means that this awareness has to be integrated into strategic business decisions and tactical communications (to account for people's perceptions and sensibilities), and even warfare (through the study of "human terrain" for tactical reasons). Through time, the control of territory has been a crucial form of power—whether it meant access to resources or the ability to exploit the land for agricultural purposes or proximity to some desired resource. Geographical spatiality involves a broad reach: "Almost all social science phenomena are, in some respect, spatial in nature and for many social science problems, geography acts as a unifying theme in exploring potential answers" (Torrens, 2010, p. 133).

For people, land and territory play a critical role in lived lives. In a geographical sense, people pour meaning to where they live, work, worship, and play. In all populated regions, there are hotspots for certain types of social and basic life activities. They pattern their lives around particular hotspots: home, work, shopping, and play. Popular travel destinations are a form of geographical border-crossing and social bridging at which peoples may learn about each other through lived proprioceptive experiences. In terms of human friendships, there is a diminishing likelihood of the maintenance of friendship with increasing distance (and the necessary extra effort to maintain the social connections).

When people demonstrate publicly for political and other issues, there are geographical hotspots with potent meanings. When there are territorial disputes—and there are multiple ones on-going in the modern political world—those are one of the main escalating agents in the steps to inter-state war [with policy and regime disputes "still significantly less likely to escalate to war than territorial disputes" (Senese & Vasquez, 2008, p. 95)].

The co-location of individuals and companies (and organizations) working in different fields are seen to beneficial to innovations because of the cross-fertilization of ideas, what was termed "regional advantage" (Saxenian, 1994, 1996). There are regional hubs built up to promote both cross-field and within-field innovations. Proximity enhances both knowledge exchange and collaboration (Ponds, van Oort, & Frenken, 2007). Office buildings are designed to encourage friendly and collegial human interactions to promote idea sharing (think open spaces, glass walls, ping pong tables, and comfortable nook and crannies where people may work). Physical proximity oftentimes matters.

Various research studies have indicated that the online indicators of in-world realities have not shown anything close to a 1:1 relationship. Email networks tend to overestimate the communications of peers with technological savvy but "underestimate communication between the core and the periphery" (Grippa, et al., 2006, as cited in Johnson, Kovács, & Vicsek, 2012, p. 462). In a research study at a bank which involved the comparison of self-reported friendship networks via a sociometric survey and the analysis of a workplace email network, online email networks were found to be less shaped by the "gender, tenure, and hierarchical boundaries" that affected offline social networks (Johnson, Kovács, & Vicsek, 2012, p. 462). The researchers found some relation between the extent to which workplace email patterns coincide with "sociometric measures of the friendship, advice seeking, and communication networks"; more precisely, "email networks are relatively good in predicting the betweenness and degree central-ity of employees, especially in the advice seeking and communication networks" (Johnson, Kovács, & Vicsek, 2012, p. 469). If anything, the prior research should suggest plenty of caution in extrapolating in-world understandings from apparent online ones but also suggest that there is some potential value in this research approach.

Off the grid? Some individuals strive to function online but in a more surreptitious way. It may help to address a few terms first. "Pseudonymity" involves the creation of untraceable long-term anonym-ity, through the exclusive use (holdership) of this pseudonym over time. An "authornym" is a name used for authorship and publishing, which may or may not be the same as the actual source of a work. "Traceability" refers to a phenomena in which at least one intermediary knows the actual identity of an individual; this knowability means that that information is technically accessible and recoverable. (One example of how companies that provide free services create traceability is by having people applying for accounts provide a verified email.) Essentially, a traceable pseudonymity or anonymity is none at all because there is a degree of knowability. The popularization of various software tools is lessening the anonymity space; these tools are making the Internet more nonymous and transparent; any hiding in plain sight will be lessened by the enforcement of inescapable identity and unwilling revelation (Hai-Jew, Aug. 2014). Such tools that enable the harvesting of ambient geographical information increase social transparency online.

In the present age, anonymity is often fleeted and limited. What was informally called "the problem of time" in the sense that datasets may be analyzed with future tools and methods that may extract in-formation more readily that was not thought possible before (Hai-Jew, May 2013). The understandings of how people pattern spatially has informed various ways to automatically geolocate individuals based on sparse online data. Researchers have created algorithms to extrapolate individual locations based on sparse Facebook data about individuals' social networks "that exceeds IP-based geolocation" methods (Backstrom, Sun, & Marlow, 2010, p. 61), given the relation between proxemics geography and social relationships. Another automated method for extracting geolocational information from unlabeled im-ages uploaded to social content-sharing sites involves combining the acquired knowledge of a particular account holder, his or her uploading patterns, his or her geotagging behaviors (for those who've tagged images as well as those who haven't), and "the relationship between the taken-time gap and the geo-graphical distance between two images from the same user" (Liu, Yuan, Cong, & Xu, 2014, p. 1232); this research study was based on 221 million images uploaded to Flickr by 2.5 million users.

Real-world spatiality and inference-making. If an online individual or group account, forthcom-ing event, or other in-world phenomena may be located to a physical location in the physical world, researchers may magnify their depth-of-knowledge about that particular target because of the broad capability of layering a variety of information to a physical location. Social media platforms come in a variety of types: social networking sites or "online social networks" (OSNs), wikis, blogs, microblogs, photo and video content-sharing sites, collaborative work sites, pastebins, data repositories, and others. These sites enable the sharing of a variety of file types: text messages, images, audio files, video files, and other types of multimedia. There are also all sorts of traditional data tied to locations. There is almost always the mapping of "built" structures (buildings, roads, bridges, and so on) as well as natural geographical features of the natural landscape. There is climate and weather information. There are human-written histories. There is demographic data. There are reams of government records related to taxes, law enforcement, property ownership, business data, censuses, and others. Locations are related to particular types of human activities (so if a person or group is tied to a physical location, there may be assumptions made about their activities and possible interests). The mapping of a person's typical presences at different locations over time may indicate lifestyle patterning; a break with patterning for presence in anomalous non-habitual locations may indicate something else. A particular sequence of space-time presences may suggest a particular sequence of actions…and may be suggestive of intentions from the inferred actions. Activity patterns in online spaces may indicate locations, sleeping patterns, and socio-psychological behavior (Jakobsson, 2012, pp. 227 – 230). The overlays of select locational / mapped information may be deeply informative for those using online spaces for research. Concerns about what may be knowable have led to calls for the enforcement of location privacy by labelling geo-location data as "personal data" that may reveal "core biographical" information (Cheung, 2014). The placement of "beacons" in commercial and other spaces enables those carrying mobile devices to opt-in to reveal their locations in order to benefit from potential space-based sales and other perks; citizen concerns about such devices have resulted in the rollback of the deployment of such devices in some cities and sparked continuing public discourse over privacy protections ("Anger over hidden commercialized tracking devices," Oct. 11, 2014).

Co-location may be revelatory in terms of bringing into play interrelated phenomena and data—sometimes directly, sometimes inferentially. If co-location may be established in close proximity between individuals and in real time (as with real-time mobility traces), further understandings may be established. For example, a person's co-location in real-space-time with another may suggest "affinity, inter-communications, or collusion" (Hai-Jew, Aug. 2014). Real-time awareness of a person's location may enable physical interception of various types or purposes, whether benevolent or malevolent. Mobile tracking networks built on the electronic awareness of mobile devices to other mobile devices in their vicinity pose risks to people's physical security and privacy (Jakobsson, 2012, pp. 200 - 201). One geolocation attack may be achieved as follows:

Global tracking networks are able to geolocate others as follows. The individuals in the tracking network know their geographical positions through the use of their own positioning systems. These systems may use GPS systems, or they may be based on other technology such as cellular or WiFi positioning systems. To position others that are not in the tracking network, the tracking network uses the existence of short-range radio broadcasters on the tracked individuals. The communications standards for most of these short-range radios embed unique identifiers into most, if not all, communications. When a member of a tracking network observes radio transmissions, it reports all the identifiers to a centralized system, along with its current location. A centralized collector of the data can then triangulate positions of individuals as they are observed (Jakobsson, 2012, p. 201).

Tracking networks (involving only 10% of the population) can be so continuous and effective that the times when individual users may drop out and be invisible at any period of time in a day is measured in seconds: "At least 95% of the time a user will never go undetected for more than 18 seconds when 10% of the population are in the tracking network. As the tracking network's relative size increases (as a percentage of the population), the mean time between detections, and its associated standard deviation will decrease" (Jakobsson, 2012, p. 211). Even if people are mindful about the locational applications they enable and the device check-ins with the communications systems that enable them, there are limits to how hidden they may remain in the vicinity of any other devices. There is no invisibility cloak against locational detection if a person is using a device and if it is being used in the vicinity of other devices.

The study of geolocation datasets based on location-enabled mobile devices have shown a high degree of human patterning in moving between locations-of-interest, such as home, work, shopping, and other spaces. Generally, research has found a connection between geographical proximity and friendships. The selection of most frequently visited places as a trail of mobility traces are quasi-identifiers of individuals (Gambs, Killijian, & Nuñez del Prado Cortez, 2014). Massachusetts Institute of Technology (MIT) researchers who studied the cell phone records for 1.5 million people found that "for 95 percent of the subjects, just four location data points were enough to link the mobile data to a unique person" (Tucker, 2014, pp. 18 – 19). Researchers have found that even when people choose to go geospatially incognito, by turning off all signaling, they may still be tracked based on the behaviors of their friends and acquaintances (Tucker, 2014, pp. 25 – 26), through a kind of geospatial social network analysis. The author suggests that while people can lower the detectability of their prediction level to others, their efforts do not make them less predictable—because the predictability comes from themselves: "Your life pattern is you. It's what you do, with whom, and where. It's the content that fills the vessel of your existence" (Tucker, 2014, p. 29). Further, through a method of "eigendecomposition" from sensor data (collected from subjects over six years), researchers were able to create a model "that could predict a subject's location with higher than 80 percent accuracy up to eighty weeks in advance" (Tucker, 2014, p. 27) or a year and a half into the future. More than 9 percent of Americans are part of a "geo-social network," with plenty of data leakage from malware in apps and mass data collection by service providers in order to provide the service—such as pings off cell towers (Tucker, 2014, pp. 21 – 22). Mobility traces may be created directly using a number of different mobile applications, phone service provider data, and other sources of mobility information, or they may be inferred from microblogging data or shared imagery and videos with locational data included in EXIF ("exchangeable image file format") data or other data types.

Online social spaces as "attack surfaces". Those in law enforcement suggest that online spaces are a kind of "stalker nirvana" given how much personal data is leaked, including "lat/long" postings (Shipley & Bowker, 2014, p. 332). Those who share information online—through uploading digital contents and messaging—are not often aware of the hidden metadata that may be shared and how that may be used to "cyber-case" people's homes for robberies (Brunty & Helenek, 2012, p. 57). They are not aware of the wealth of understandings that may be inferred from what is shared, particularly when trace information is collected from multiple profiles of the same individual from different social media platforms, or when even single accounts are hacked. Individuals may be narrow-casting to a closed set of friends but find that their private messages have been hacked and distributed—particularly sensitive materials like private photos or financial credentials. The capturing of geolocational data is often framed in the context of adversarial attacks, including opposition ("oppo") research and documenting ("doxing") attacks. Such information may not only have value in adversarial contexts. There are many scenarios in which there may be benefits to adding locational information to a wide range of online information, such as for emergency response or law enforcement. One of the latter examples involves ways to understand and communicate crime patterns mapped on physical space and the effective dispersion of messaging geospatially to citizenry (Lampoltshammer, Kounadi, Sitko, & Hawelka, 2014).

To convey a sense of how various types of online information may be linked to geolocational information, this chapter will include some basic descriptions of data extractions (from websites and social media platforms) using several publicly available software tools. The extraction parameters and sequences will be described briefly because those affect the results of the data extractions.

USING MALTEGO TUNGSTEN™, NODEXL, NCAPTURE AND NVIVO, TO GEOLOCATE

This section highlights a number of data extractions of online data leading to geolocation information. While the extractions were presented as they were conducted, there were a few dozen not summarized here because the results ended without any clear indicator of geolocation data. Where there were challenges, these were mentioned below.

Figure 6 provides an overview of the geoprocessing of both textual and online source data in order to map those contents to physical locations. Two general types of geo-processing are depicted: geocoding or forward geocoding, and geolocation. This shows how the map data may be expressed visually in a variety of visualizations that convey information.

One tool that enables such geolocation is Maltego Tungsten™ (3.4.2), which is a penetration (pen) testing tool which has multi-use applications. One approach in the tool involves the use of "machines"— which are powerful macros that may be used to extract publicly available information from the Surface Web. (The "Hidden Web" or the "Deep Web" refers to contents that are placed on web servers which may be called up dynamically, based on specific requests made by users. This data is not as readily available because they do not have a pre-set stable URL that is indexed by search engines and findable by Web browsers.) The tools enable the mapping of a person's or company's or organization's online presences; web domain footprinting (at varying levels of depth); the resolving of a person to an email address; the resolving of a Twitter identity to linked online information; the geolocating of Twitter information based on a user account; and resolving a URL to network and domain information, among others. The information that is extracted is all publicly available. The data extracted may be in turns insightful but also highly noisy, with a need for informed "pruning" of links for more accuracy and disambiguation (through sparsification). The levels of the crawls may be set on a slider from 12 to 50 to 255 to 10,000 results. There are built-in tools in NVivo 10 to create coherence even with fairly large-scale data extractions; however, it is not clear how much of a set of available information is captured. In addition to the Maltego Tungsten™ "machines," there are also "transforms," which are methods to interchange one kind of online information to other types (thus the name). In the Maltego Tungsten™ palette of such transforms, there are a range of information types: devices, infrastructure, locations, penetration testing, personal, and social network. Within these larger categories are a range of specific detail-types. This tool involves multi-lingual functionality. The results of the various data extractions are set up and presented in data grid / table format, 2D and 3D graphs (structured or dynamic or otherwise). Cumulative reports may also be auto-generated from the extracted data. (The parameters of various data extractions are stored as macros if re-runs are wanted.)

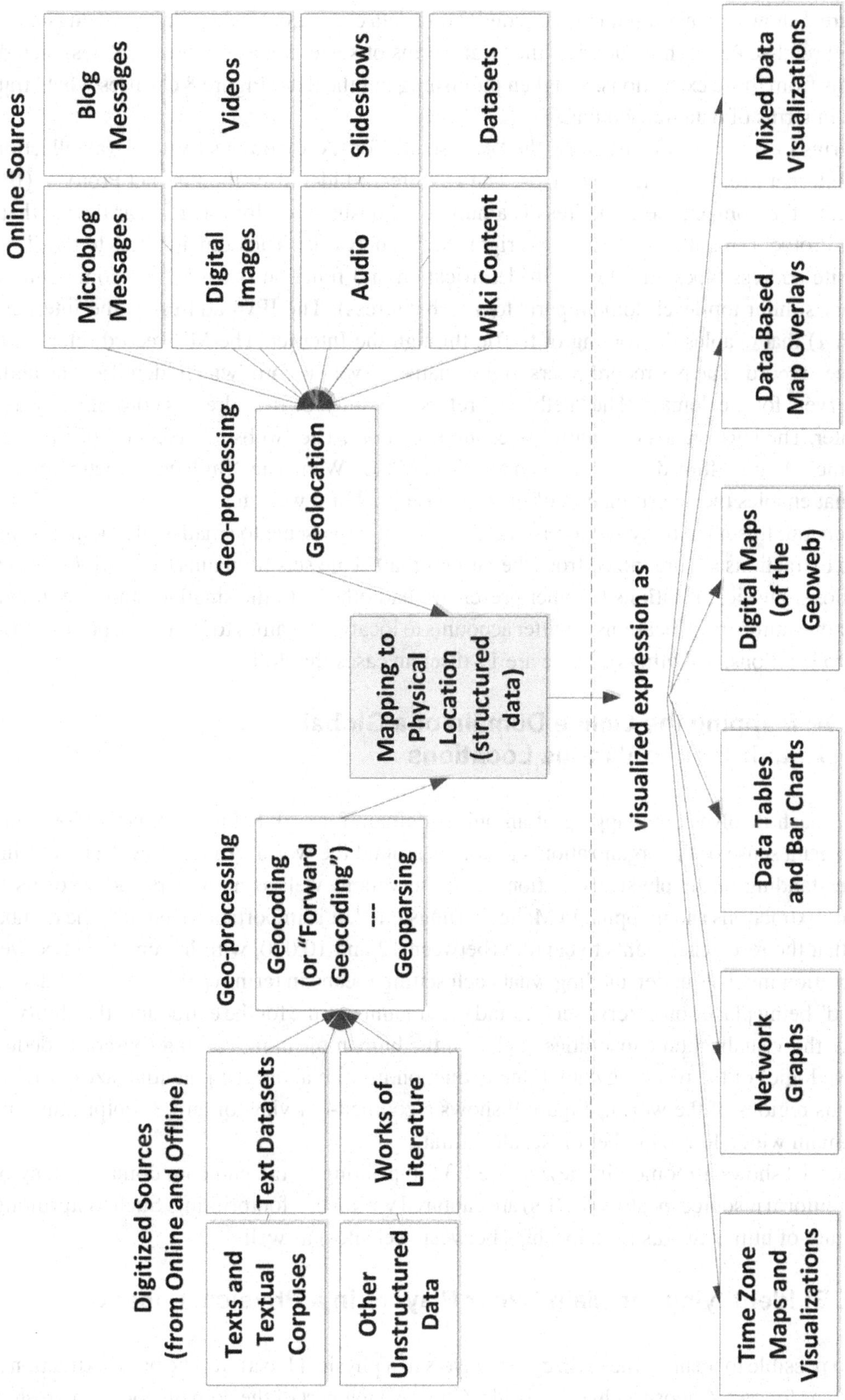

Figure 6. An overview of the geocoding and geolocation work

Figure 7 shows a general sequence of conducting data extractions using Maltego Tungsten™, first by running broad-scale machine queries, then transforms of select nodes on those queries, then data visualizations from those extractions, and then publishing out the data. Figure 8 clarifies what "transforms" achieve in terms of data transcoding.

In terms of Internet infrastructure, the "AS" stands for "Autonomous System" (a collection of connected Internet Protocol routing prefixes. The DNS record identifies the Internet Protocol (IP) address assigned to the domain; the IP address is a numerical designation for a particular device that uses the Internet Protocol (for anyone with access rights to that network). The domain refers to the classification of website address types based on self-identification and function (such as the .com, .edu, .org, .net, and other similar top-level domain parts to a web address). The IPv4 address is the Internet Protocol (version 4) that enables the routing of traffic through the Internet. The MX record refers to the "mail exchange" record. The NS record refers to the "name server" record, which identifies the authoritative name servers for the domain. The "netblock" refers to a range of IP addresses controlled by a particular datacenter. The URL stands for "uniform resource locator". The "website" refers to specific related web pages (including multimedia contents) on the World Wide Web. The "BuiltWith Technology" aspect is a tool that enables the determination of the tools used to build websites.

In general, this main body section is organized from large-scale to small-scale elements. In general, the data extractions are organized from the larger broad-scale sets (domains to locations, http networks to locations, physical locations to cyber presences, and others) to the smaller and more individualized ones (phone numbers to locations, Twitter accounts to locations, names to locations, phrases to locations, aliases to locations, and others). There are 17 discrete cases that follow.

CASE A: Mapping the Online Domain of a Global News Organization to Various Locations

One approach involves the mapping of an online domain for a global news organization (cnn.com) in order to get a sense of the organization's locations around the world. An L3 (Level 3) footprint enables an understanding of the physical locations of its servers as well as an understanding of its URLs. In such data extractions and mapping in Maltego Tungsten™, it is important to indicate the number of data points that the researcher wants to capture (between 12 and 10,000, with increments in between). One consideration involves understanding what each setting means in terms of the amount of data captured, the "load" being placed on Paterva servers and the amount of time for the extraction, the ability to process the data, the visualization capabilities, and then the human meaning-making (based on deductive and inductive logic) of the resulting data. (One deduction may be about the potential sizes of its audiences in various regions of the world.) Figure 9 shows a zoomed-out view of an L3 footprinting of the cnn.com domain with a low "Number of Results" limit.

Figure 10 shows a zoomed-in view of the L3 footprinting of the cnn.com domain. Many of the domain's uniform resource locators (URLs) are captured within this footprinting. Such footprinting enables the capture of http networks (relationships between websites) as well.

CASE B: Identifying the Main Cyber Players in a Physical Location

It is also possible to identify the main cyber players in a physical location. The basic extraction sequence proceeds as follows. Choose a physical locale. Choose what part of the domain you're interested in (such

Figure 7. The general sequence of a web-based data mapping in Maltego Tungsten™ (one conceptualization)

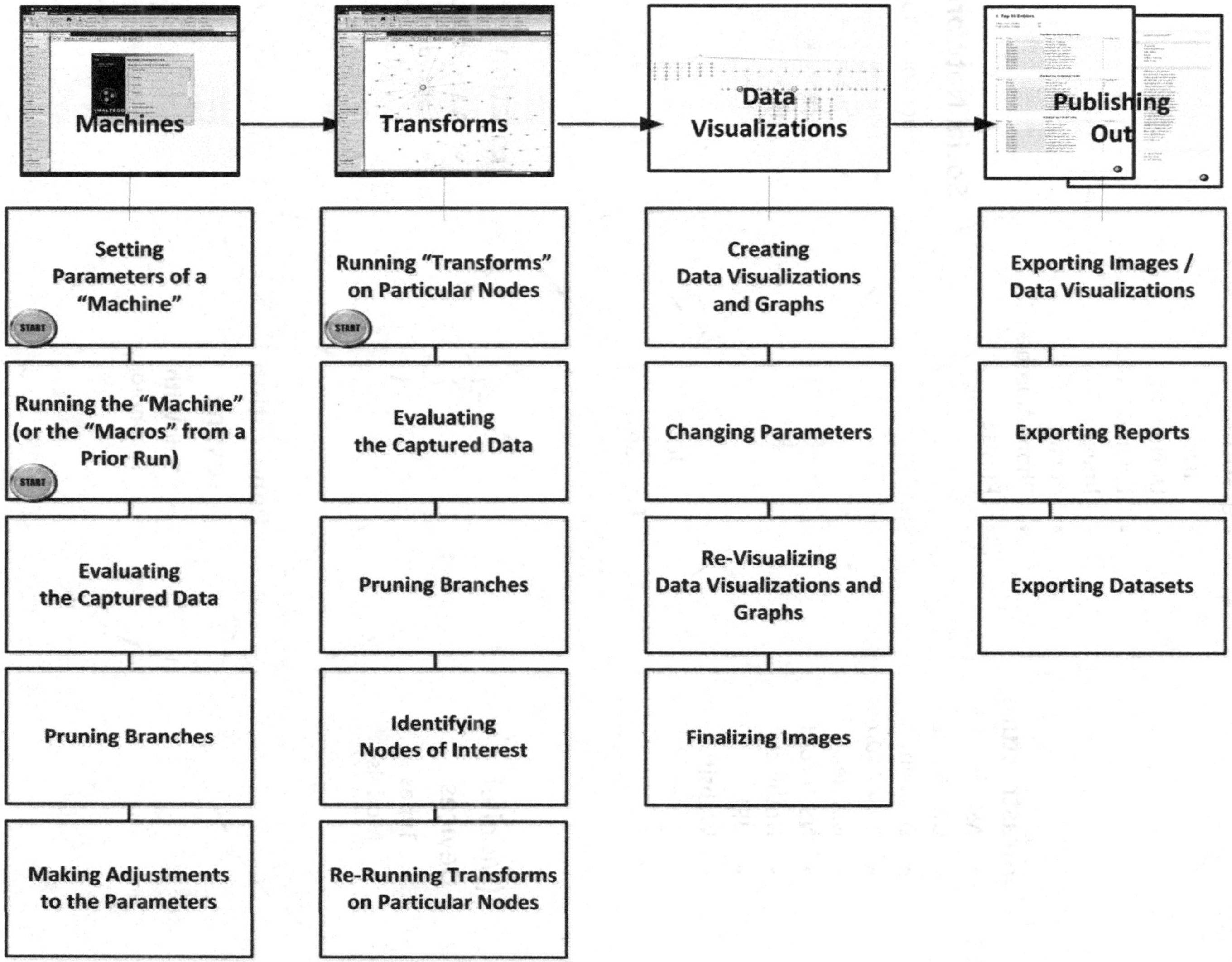

Machines	Transforms	Data Visualizations	Publishing Out
Setting Parameters of a "Machine"	Running "Transforms" on Particular Nodes	Creating Data Visualizations and Graphs	Exporting Images / Data Visualizations
Running the "Machine" (or the "Macros" from a Prior Run)	Evaluating the Captured Data	Changing Parameters	Exporting Reports
Evaluating the Captured Data	Pruning Branches	Re-Visualizing Data Visualizations and Graphs	Exporting Datasets
Pruning Branches	Identifying Nodes of Interest	Finalizing Images	
Making Adjustments to the Parameters	Re-Running Transforms on Particular Nodes		

Figure 8. Some data 'transforms' in Maltego Tungsten™

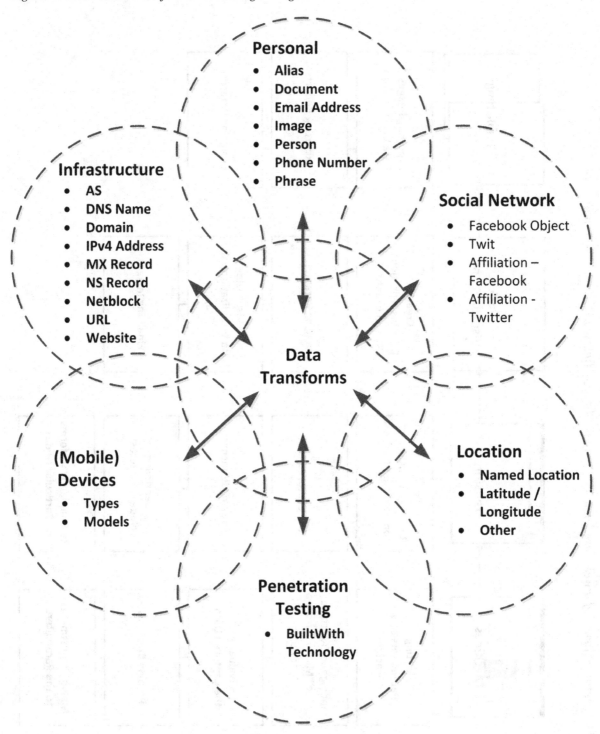

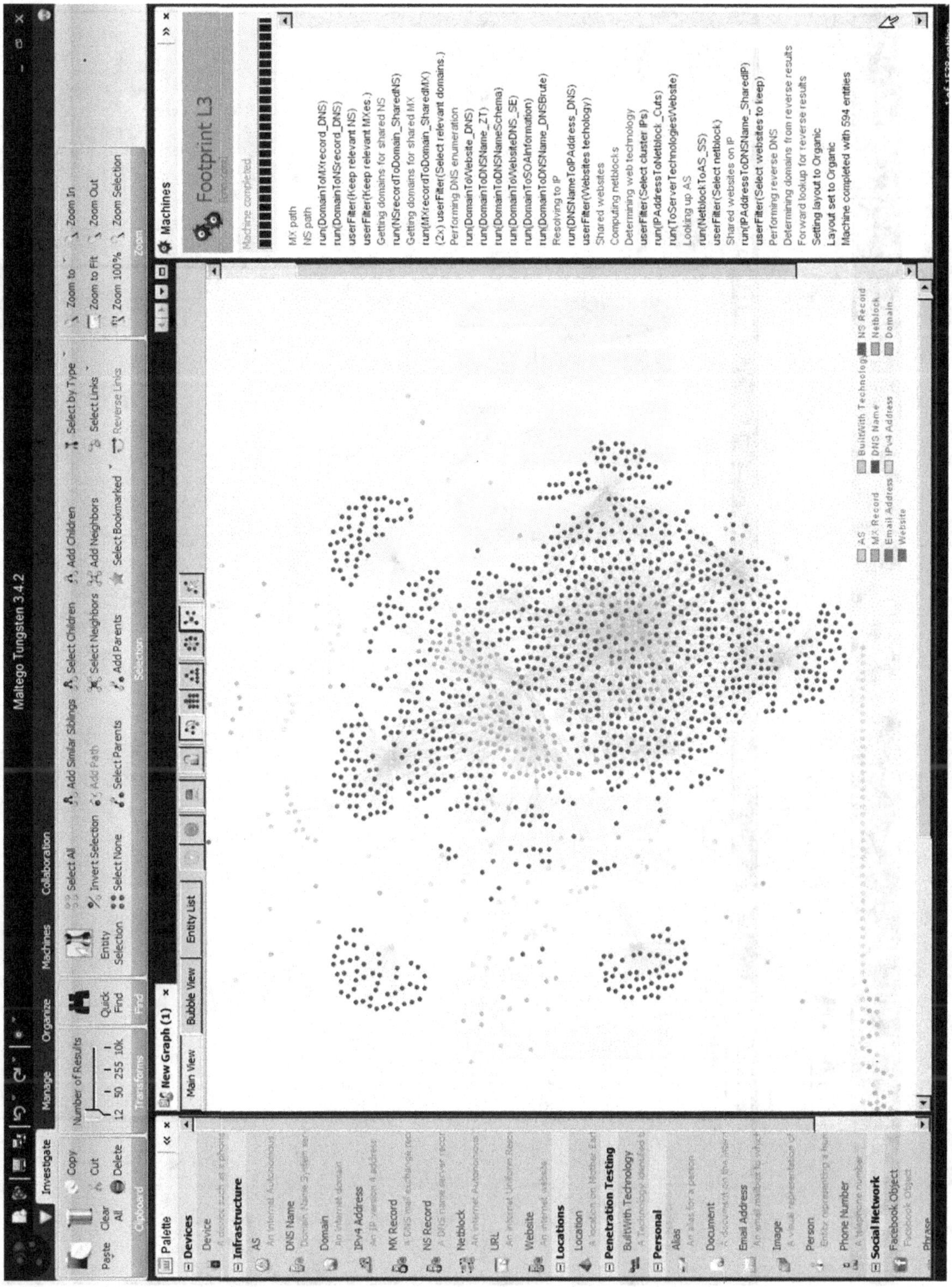

Figure 9. A Level 3 footprinting of cnn.com domain

Figure 10. A zoomed-in view of the CNN.com domain

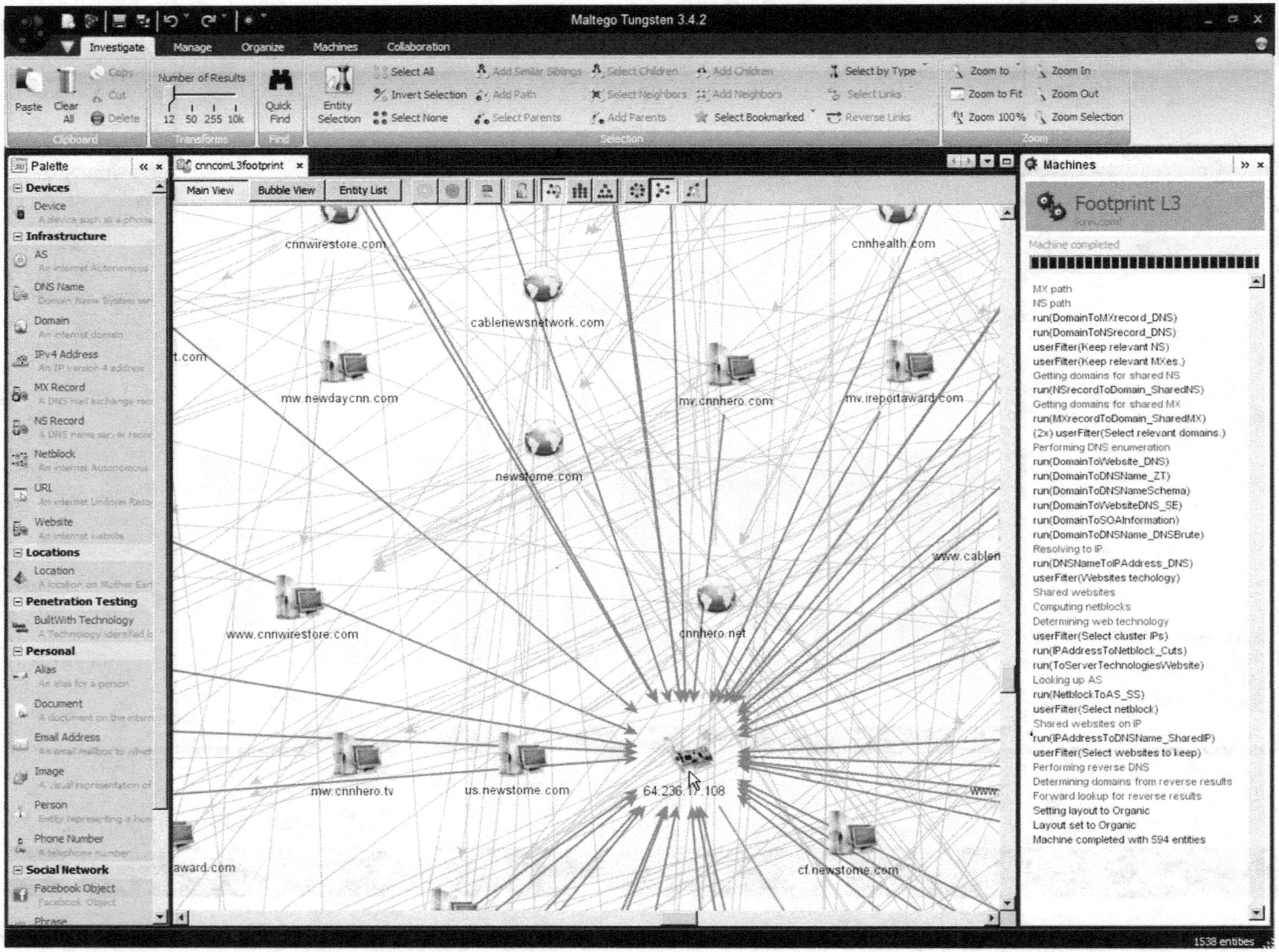

as government or commercial or other). Conduct a Google search of that locale. Identify the relevant domain. In Maltego Tungsten™, select one of the footprinter levels (1 is light and 3 is technical and intensive). Conduct the Web domain footprinting. Respond to the "user filter" queries. Prune the graph as necessary. Visualize and re-visualize the data in various ways. Analyze results. (Hai-Jew, Aug. 2014).

For this example here, the author decided to explore the cyber presence of the capital city belonging to a semi-reclusive nation-state, which was in the headlines at the time of the research and writing: Pyongyang, North Korea. One early lead was "Internet in North Korea" (http://en.wikipedia.org/wiki/Internet_in_North_Korea) to get a sense of the domain, but there was not a domain per se but some information about the IPv4 ranges (said to be 175.45.176.0 – 175.45.179.255) and a main URL: http://www.uriminzokkiri.com/. There were lists of links to about 30 sites tied to this state but not a clear domain. It was decided that a Level 2 footprinting of the prior URL would suffice for a broad sense of related cyber and related "place." Spatially, Pyongyang, North Korea, on Google Maps, is clearly marked in physical space (39.0194° N, 125.7381° E), as seen in Figure 11.

An L2 crawl of www.uniminzokkiri.com/ resulted initially in a very tightly defined technological understructure as seen in Figure 12.

From the initial mapping, other nodes of interest were identified, and "transforms" were run on those nodes for additional links, in Figure 13. Such mapping begins at any number of points-of-interest and fans out through a wide range of connections.

This capture includes some of the 30 websites mentioned in the Wikipedia entry "Internet in North Korea." There is bilingual information—in both English and Korean. The different types of nodes identified may be seen in Figure 14. These include telephone numbers, Web domains, websites, URLs, email addresses, online documents, and others. Each type of node enables different types of knowledge and knowing. Any node may be selected for further exploration—for a kind of node-based snowball research. The emails may be used as ways to contact individuals related to particular sites.

The Built-With feature enables researchers to see what technologies were used to create the understructure of a website or domain as may be seen in Figure 15. This information may be read as the sophistication of both the site (and domain) as well as those behind the particular endeavor.

In Figure 16, there is a zoomed-out view of the cyber presence of North Korea, with an insert image of one of the linked sites promoting tourism.

The data crawl enables the identification of key individuals (by name) whose work underlie the cyber presence. In Figure 17, the three are circled.

These prior figures (Figures # to #) provide a sense of some of the cyber presence linked to North Korea. If there were a more explicit location-based domain, the linkage could be much clearer to the actual physical space of a capital city (which was the original target of this data extraction). Depending on the level of interest, the various nodes could be probed more deeply. As such, this was very much a singular data extraction. To bolster the sense of what may be possible, the author did an additional L2 extraction of http://www.korea-dpr.com/, which revealed a wide network of commercial interests.

Finally, to capture a more comprehensive sense, an L2 domain extraction of the "korea-dpr.com" site was taken, which linked to a wide variety of commercial ventures. The URL http://www.korea-dpr.com/ leads to the official site for foreigners by the Korea Friendship Organization. A half-completed visualization is available at Figure 18. Notice the status bar at the bottom right.

Comparatively, this network is intriguing for the clustering of its structure around particular nodes (as indicated by their size). A wide number of links are related to particular IPv4 addresses. The outsized email addresses may indicate potentially high-powered accounts with links to important decision-makers

Figure 11. Pyongyang, North Korea, based on geographical coordinates on Google Maps

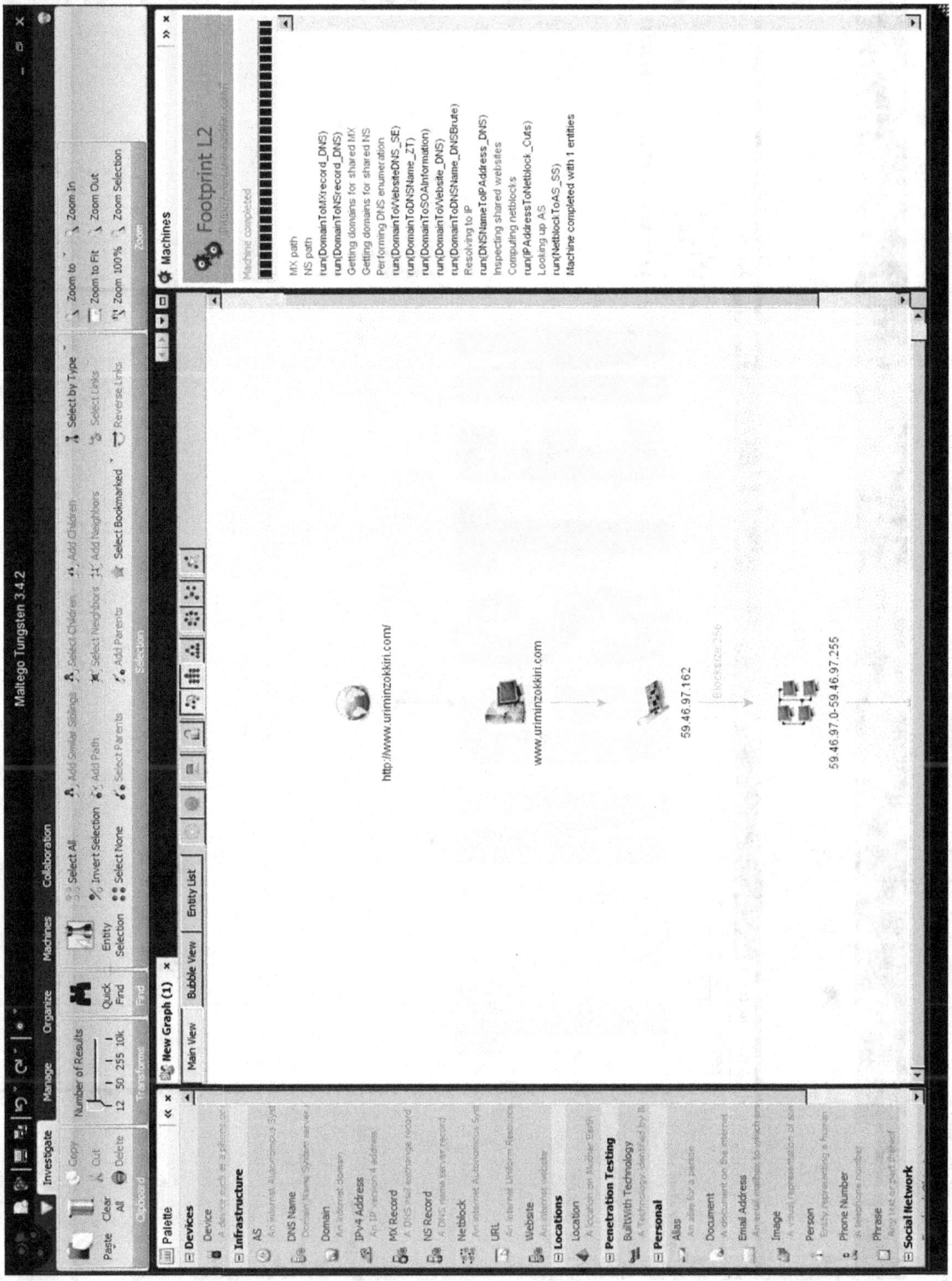

Figure 12. L2 Crawl of www.uniminzokkiri.coml, A Main Site of the North Korean State

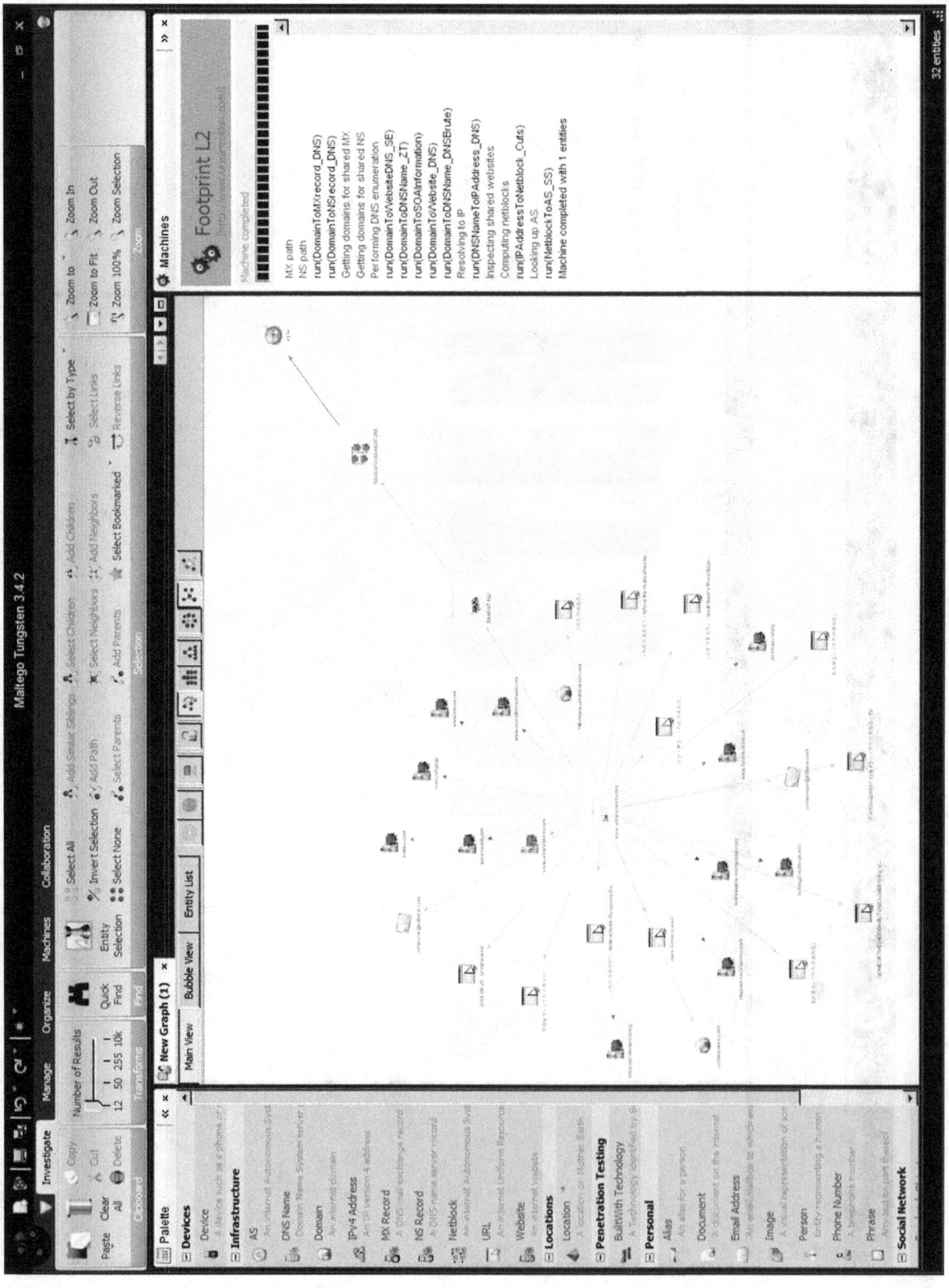

Figure 13. Transforms from another node in the L2 footprinting results of www.uniminzokkiri.com

Figure 14. A greater diversity of information based on the diversity of nodes in the L2 footprinting of www.uniminzokkiri.com

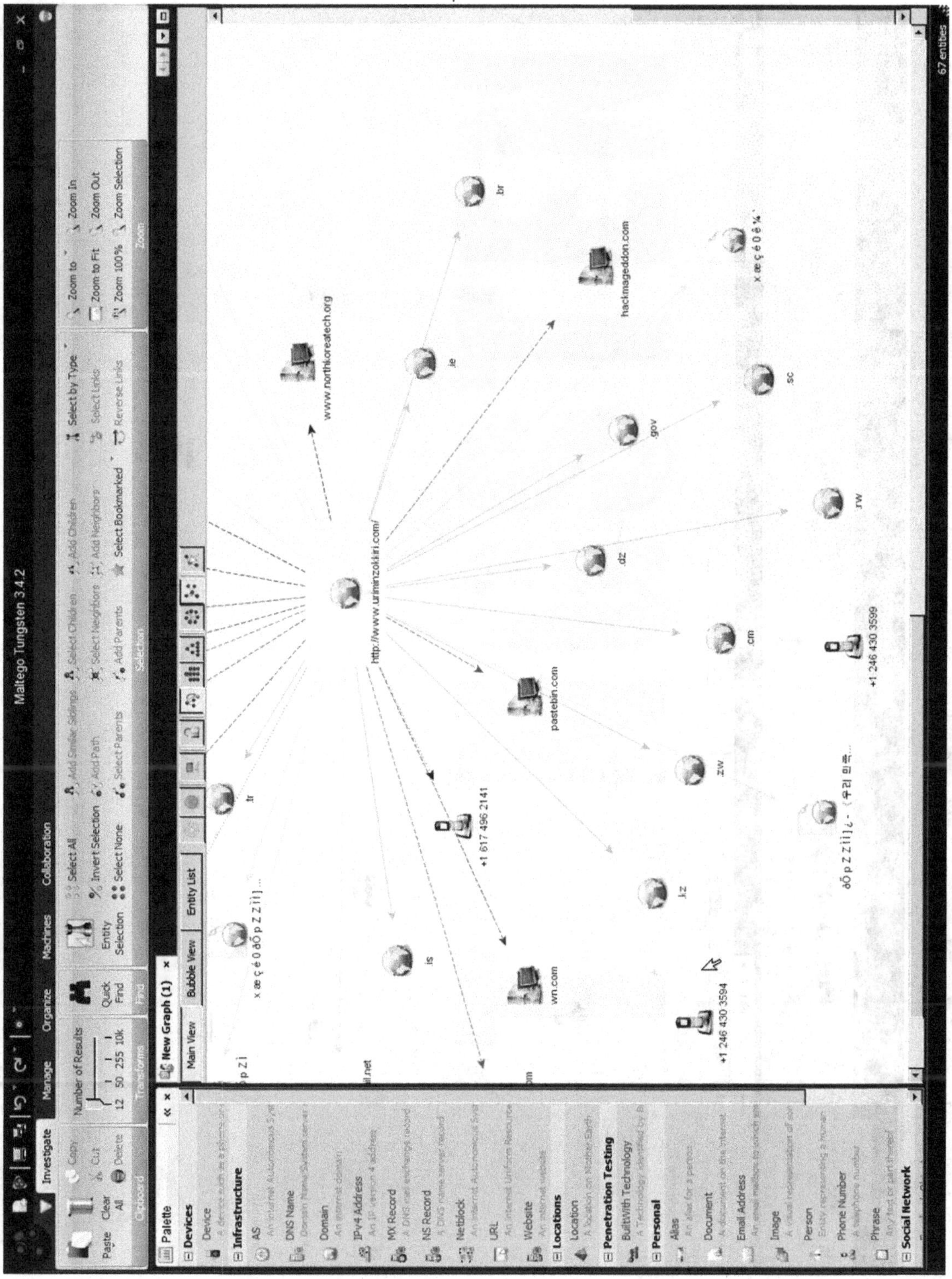

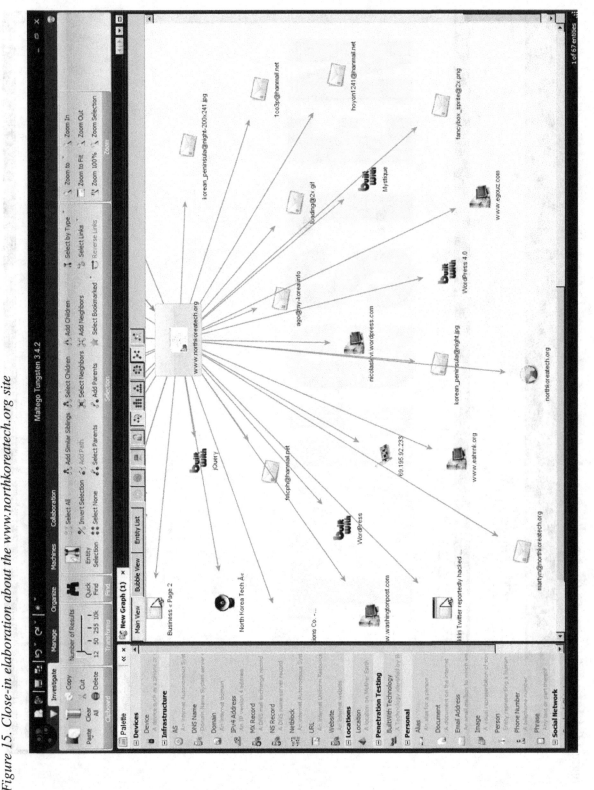

Figure 15. Close-in elaboration about the www.northkoreatech.org site

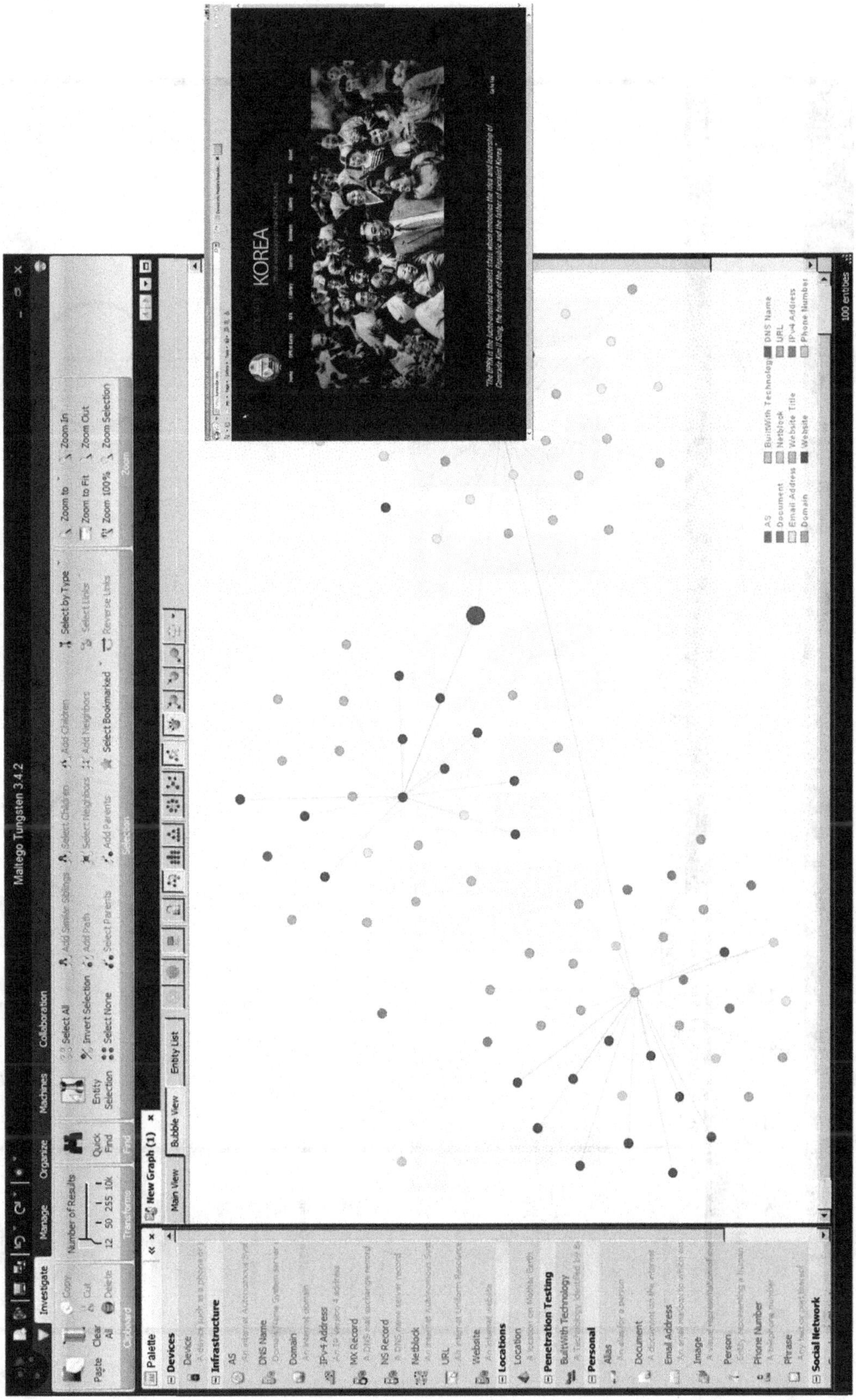

Figure 16. A zoomed-out view of the digital jaunt into part of the North Korea online presence

Figure 17. The identification of key men linked to a site

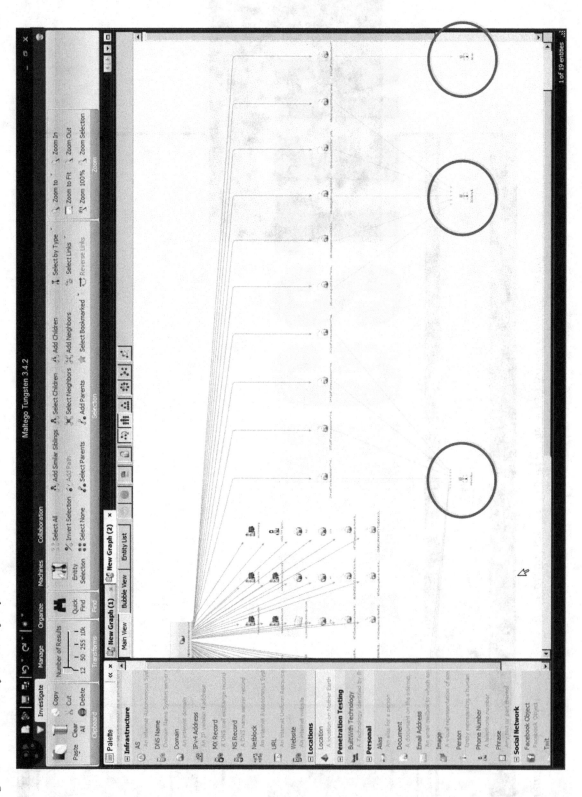

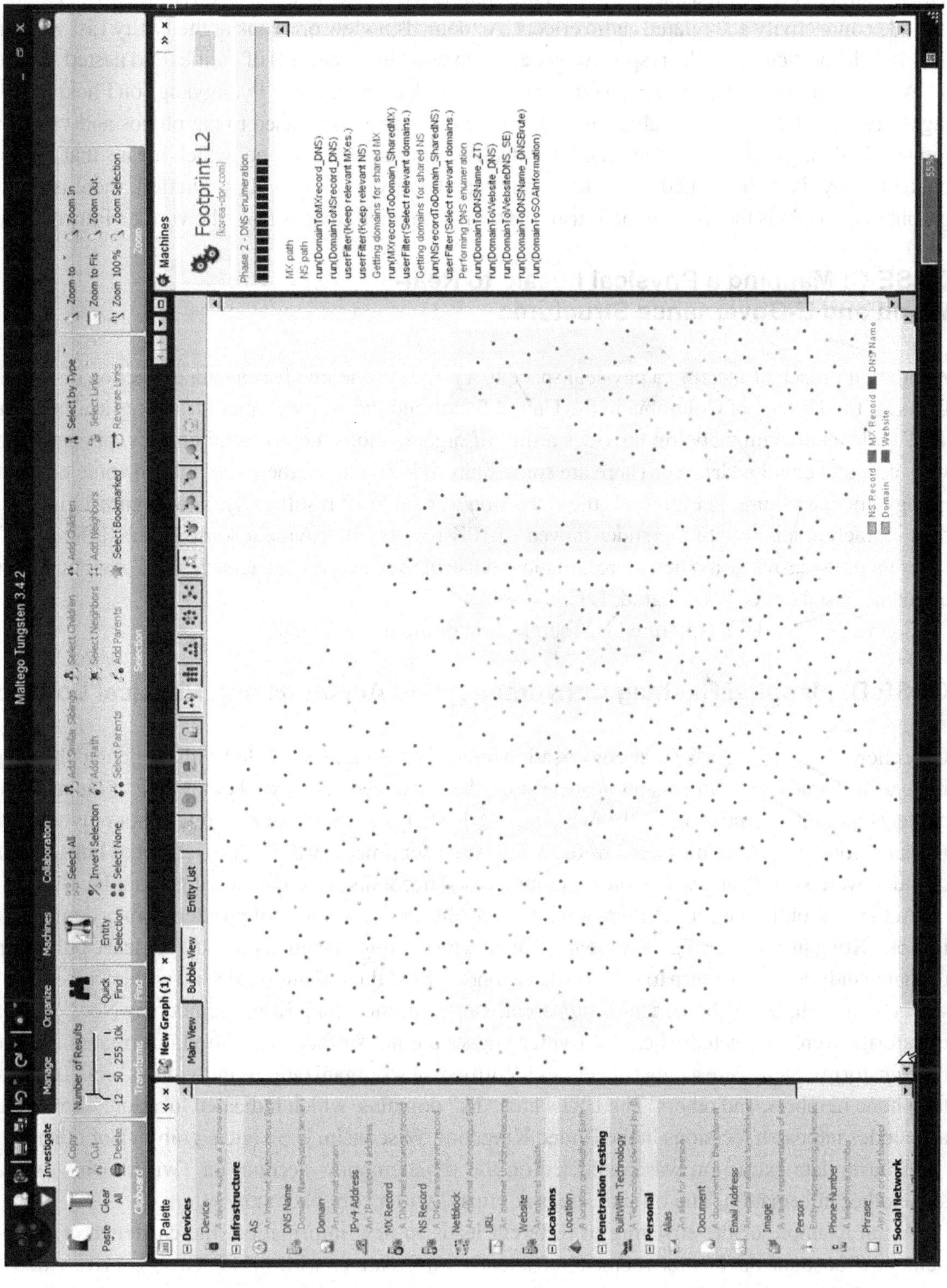

Figure 18. Extensive commercial presence via http://www.korea-dpr.com/

(particularly given the controlled and hierarchical nature of the Internet presence of the various entities). The revealing of the various networks—in the Bubble View—is dynamic and riveting, with explosions of node connectivity and related audio effects. A zoomed-in view or a look at the Entity List will enable a look at the particulars of the respective nodes, even with the thousands of entities and nested structures.

Another angle involves running a related tags network extraction of "Pyongyang" on Flickr. A related tags network (at 2 degrees) enables the viewing of clustered words used to tag photos and videos with the word "Pyongyang" in the tag. The label itself is a disambiguated one, which means that the linked contents may likely be related to North Korea's capital city. In Figure 20, to the left, there is the word graph; to the right is the word graph illustrated with thumbnail images from the various Flickr accounts.

CASE C: Mapping a Physical Locale to Real-World and E-Governance Structures

Another approach of locating a physical space to a physical one involves a data extraction of "dc.us" to focus on the District of Columbia in the United States and the e-governance structures available there.

The dc.us domain mapping provides a mix of organizations, commercial entities, phone numbers, websites, and email addresses. There are some links to individuals; there are links to some of the technology understructure. In Figure 21, the extraction was set to 12 results only; later Figure 22 is the same data extraction albeit with the slider moved to 10K results, to provide a sense of the difference. This latter mapping provides a much more complete sense of the government agencies and other bureaucratic elements based out of Washington, D.C.

Figure 23 provides a structured L2 footprinting of the dc.us domain.

CASE D: Mapping Hashtag Conversations to Accounts and Physical Locations

On a microblogging site, a hashtag conversation refers short messages labeled with particular #hashtags to indicate a shared topic. On content-sharing sites, these may indicate a kind of tagging of the multimedia contents around a certain topic. The mapping of a hashtag conversation may reveal not only which user accounts took part, what messages were shared, what sentiments were expressed, what links to images or video were shared, and where the communicators' accounts were registered geographically.

At the time of the data crawl, there were mass public demonstrations of pro-democracy demonstrators in Hong Kong just prior to a government ultimatum requesting that all demonstrators leave public streets to enable individuals to return to work on that Monday. In Maltego Tungsten™, a Twitter Digger machine was run on the hashtag #hkdemonow (apparently to represent "Hong Kong Democracy Now"). Multiple transforms were conducted when the Twitter Digger did not surface the desired information. Based on the transforms, there were a range of entities identified: news organizations, individuals' email addresses, telephone numbers, and others. The URLs had ".hk" domains, which indicated location. The telephone area codes indicated locations in the United Kingdom; Wisconsin, U.S.; and a grab-bag of other details.

A basic data extraction was conducted on the @hkdemonow account on Twitter, which surfaced some other information. The official site is at https://twitter.com/hkdemonow.

As an example of the stringing of different leads to new information, the existence of the @hkdemonow account on Twitter seemed sufficiently informative, with 3,519 Tweets, 1109 videos and photos, 475 following, 4,890 followers, and 57 favorites on the Twitter account. At the time of the data extractions, the Twitter Digger was not fully functioning in Maltego Tungsten™, so the author went to

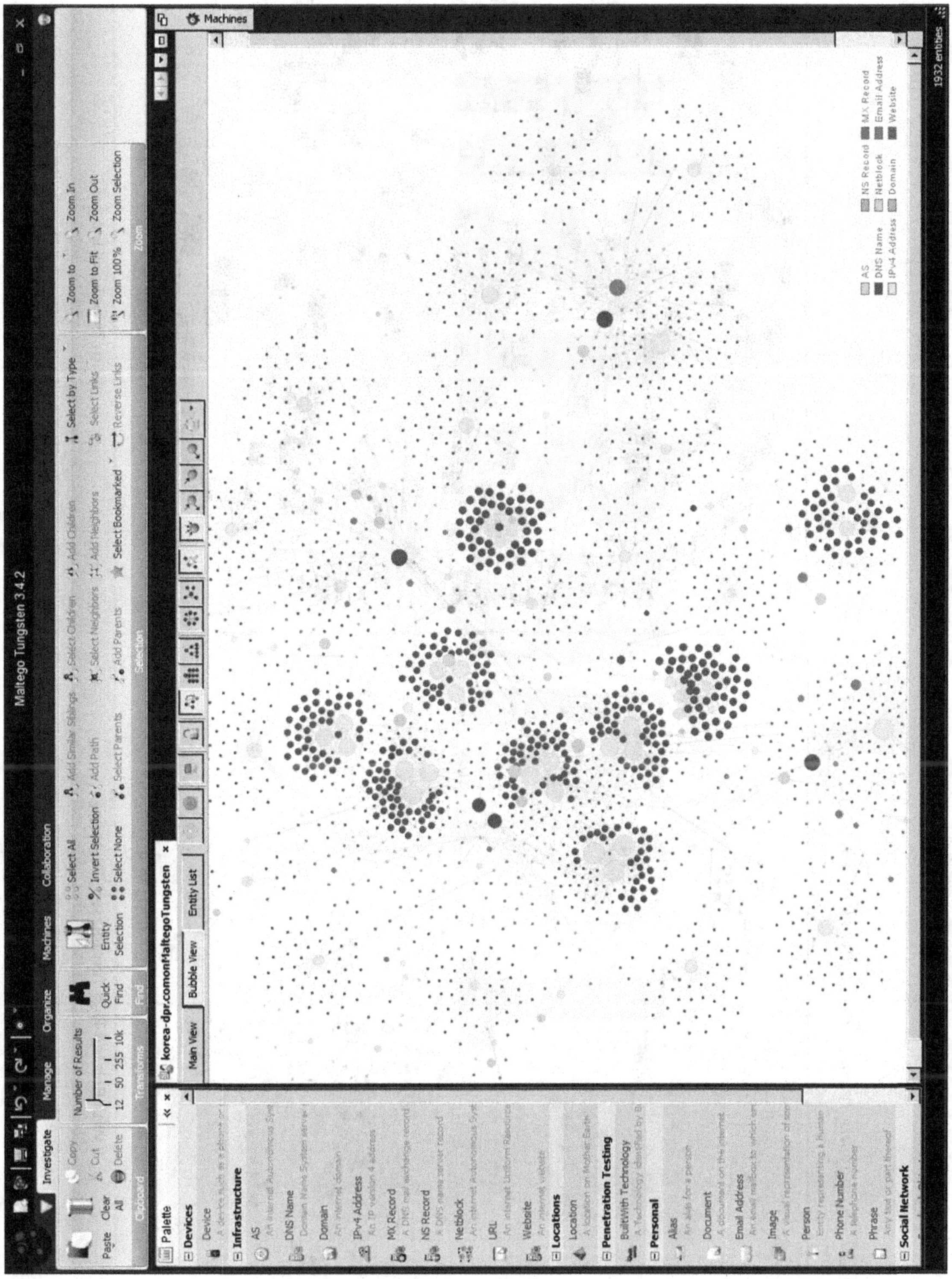

Figure 19. Dominant nodes in an L2 crawl of http://www.korea-dpr.com/ using Maltego Tungsten

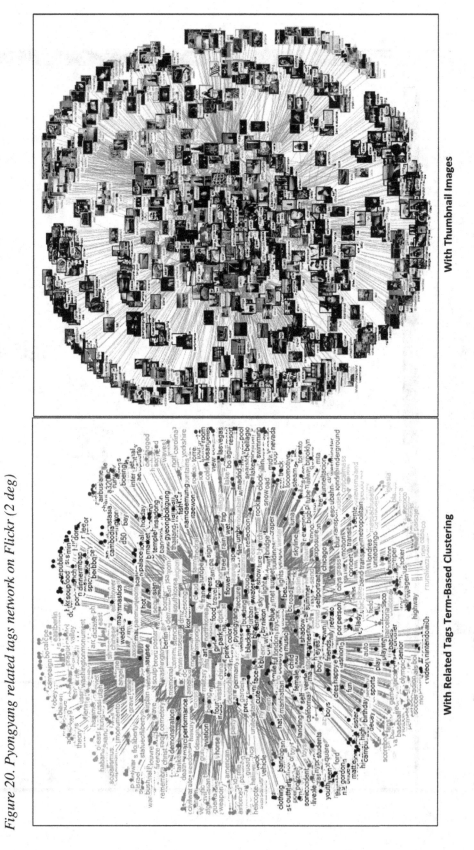

Figure 20. Pyongyang related tags network on Flickr (2 deg)

With Thumbnail Images

With Related Tags Term-Based Clustering

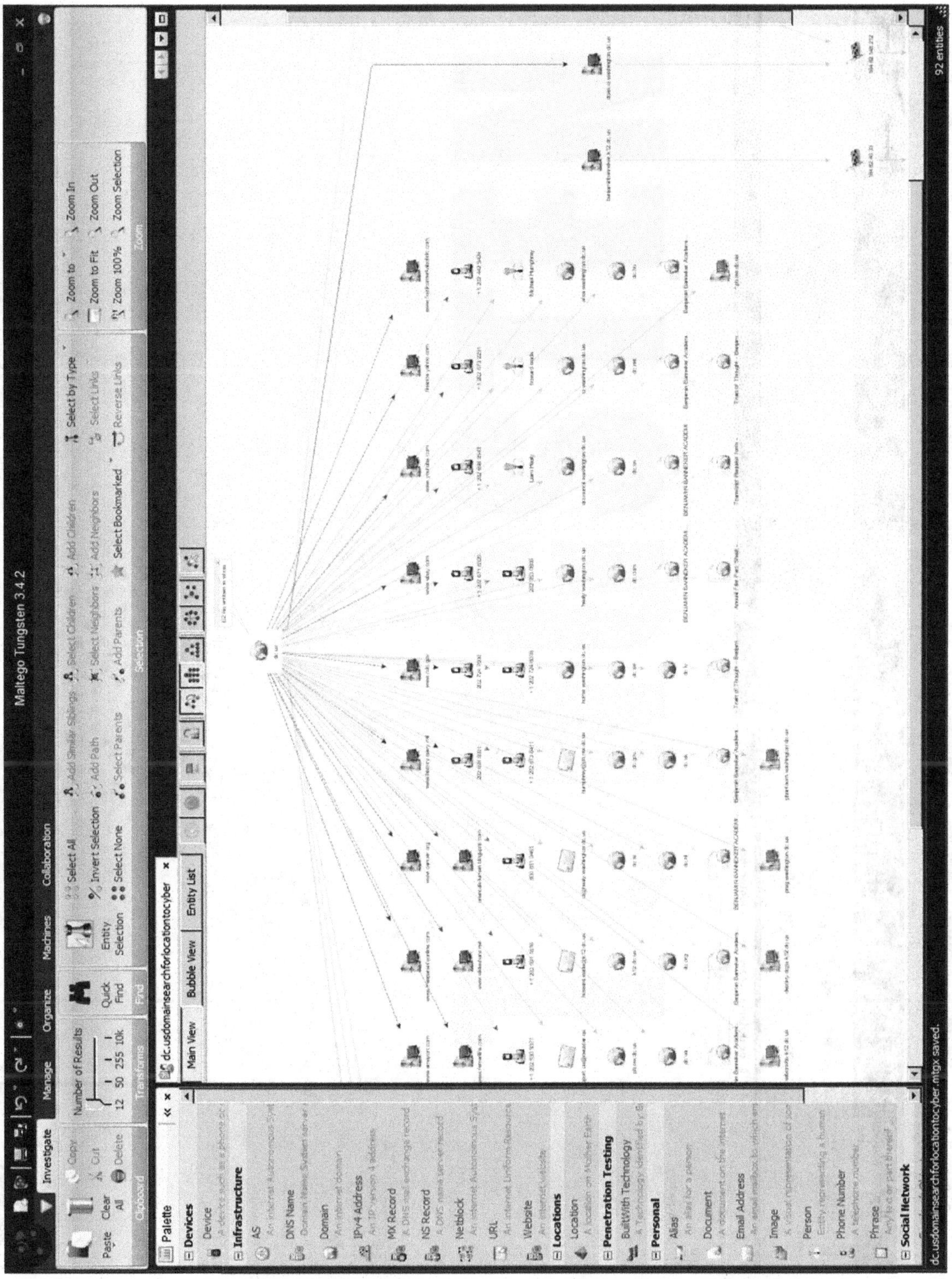

Figure 21. L2 footprinting of the dc.us online network with a 12 entities limit

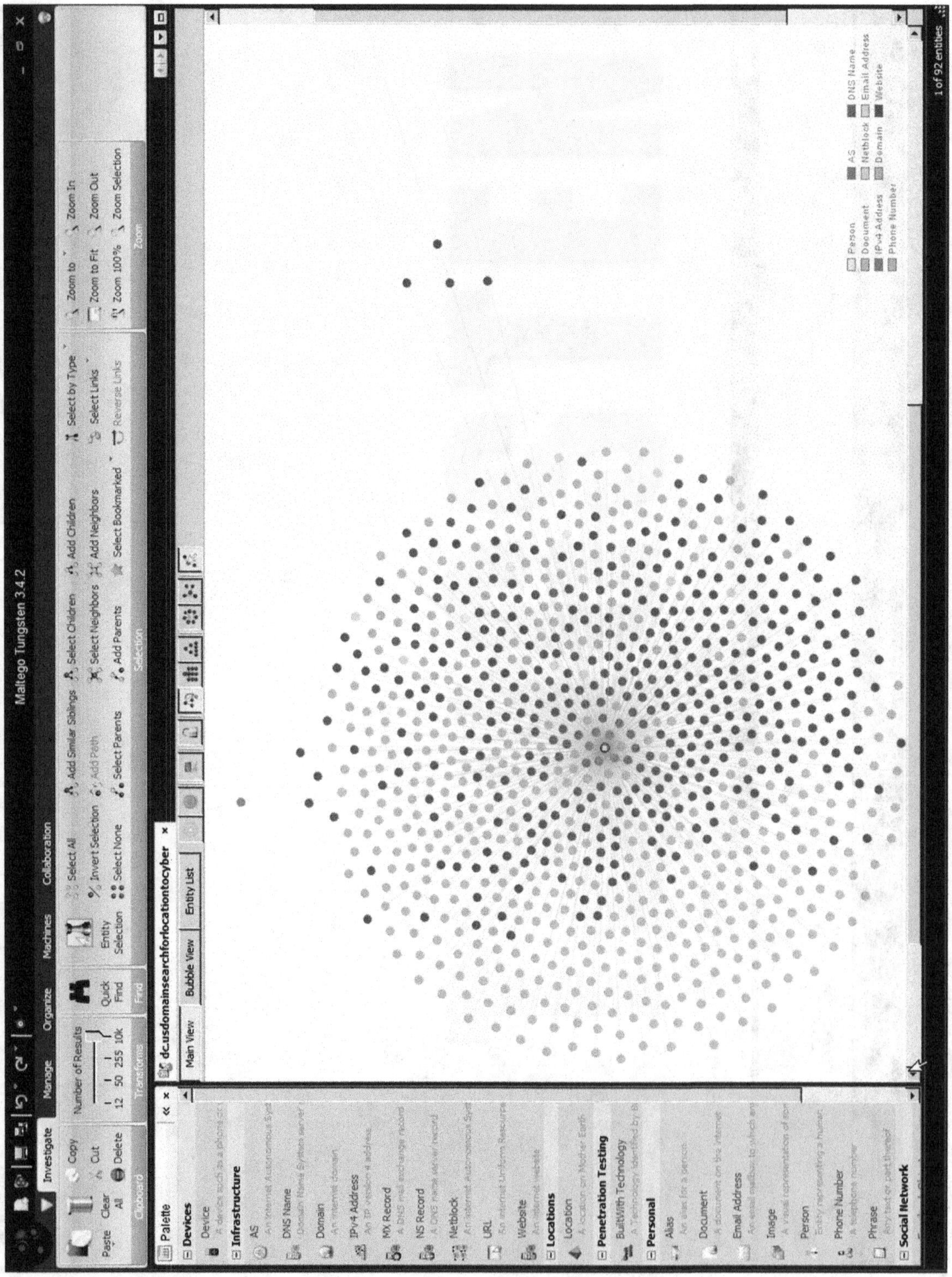

Figure 22. L2 footprinting of the dc.us online network with a 12K limit

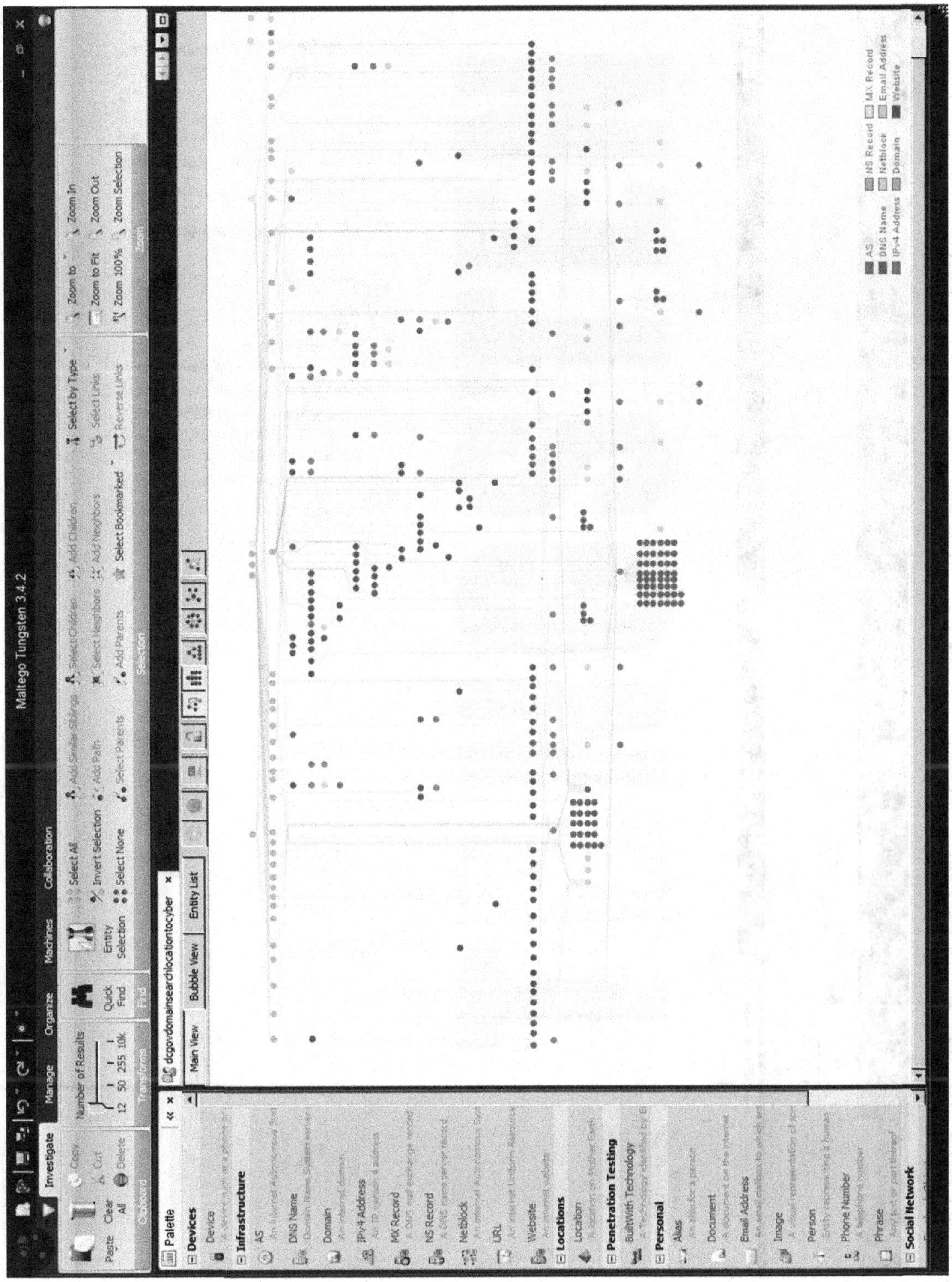

Figure 23. Structured L2 footprinting of the dc.us domain

464

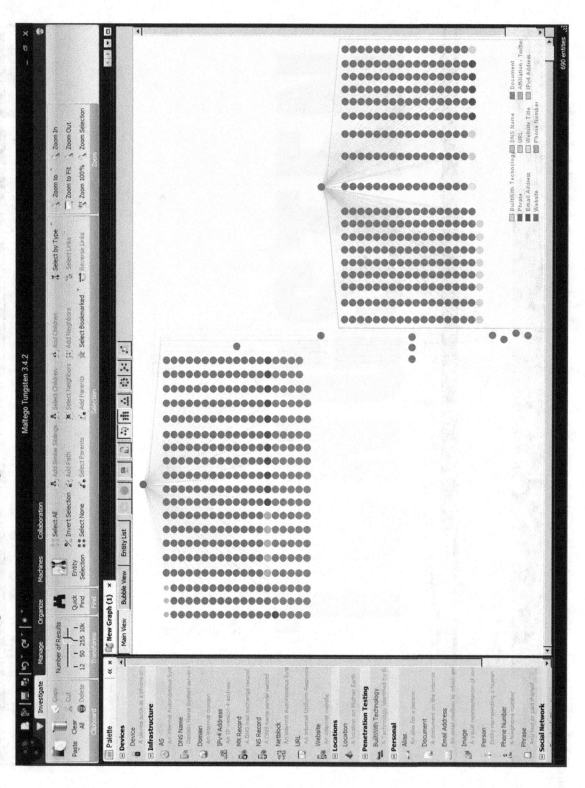

Figure 24. #hkdemonow hashtag search on Twitter and geolocational data

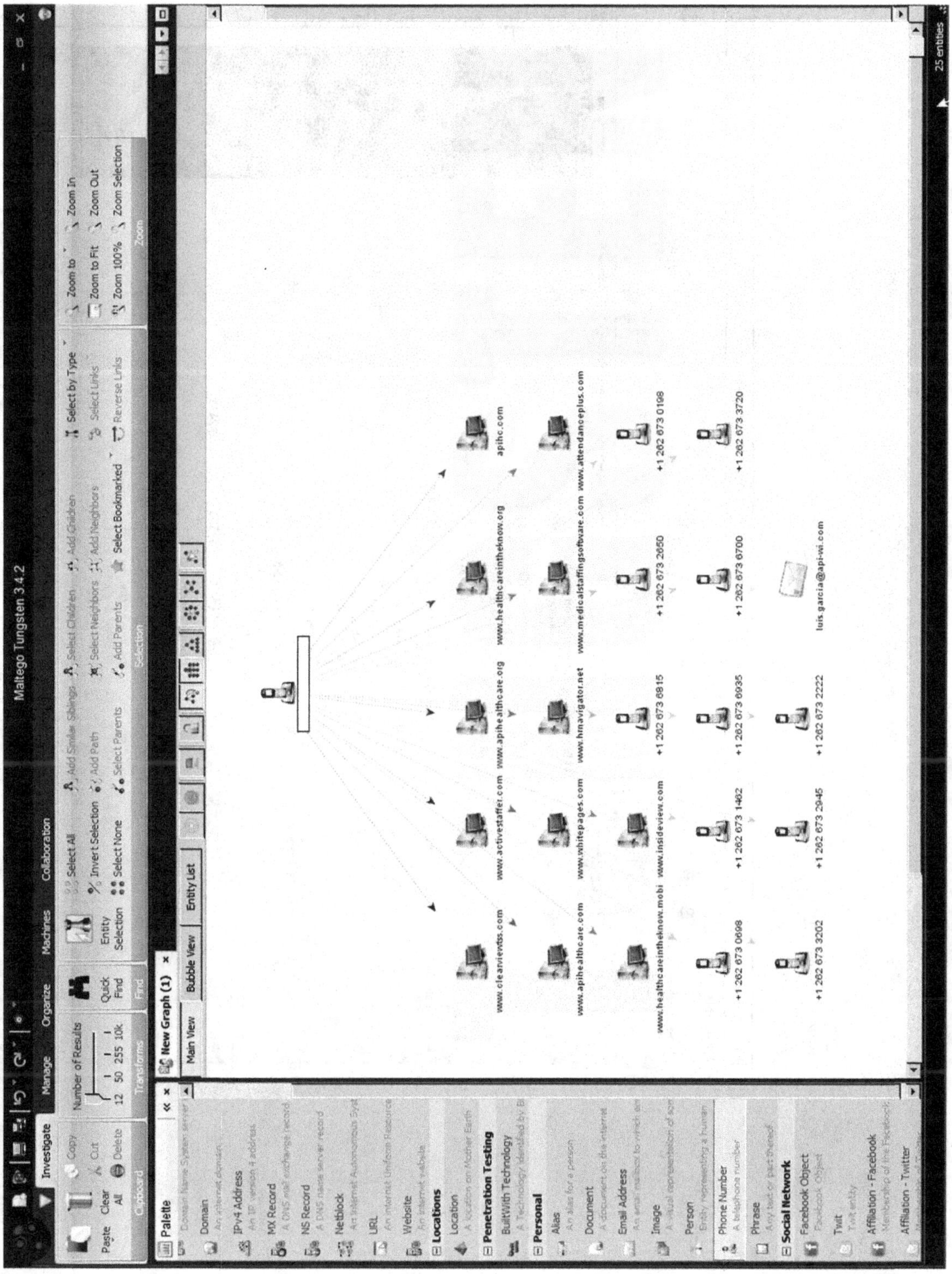

Figure 25. @hkdemonow conversation based around the Twitter account

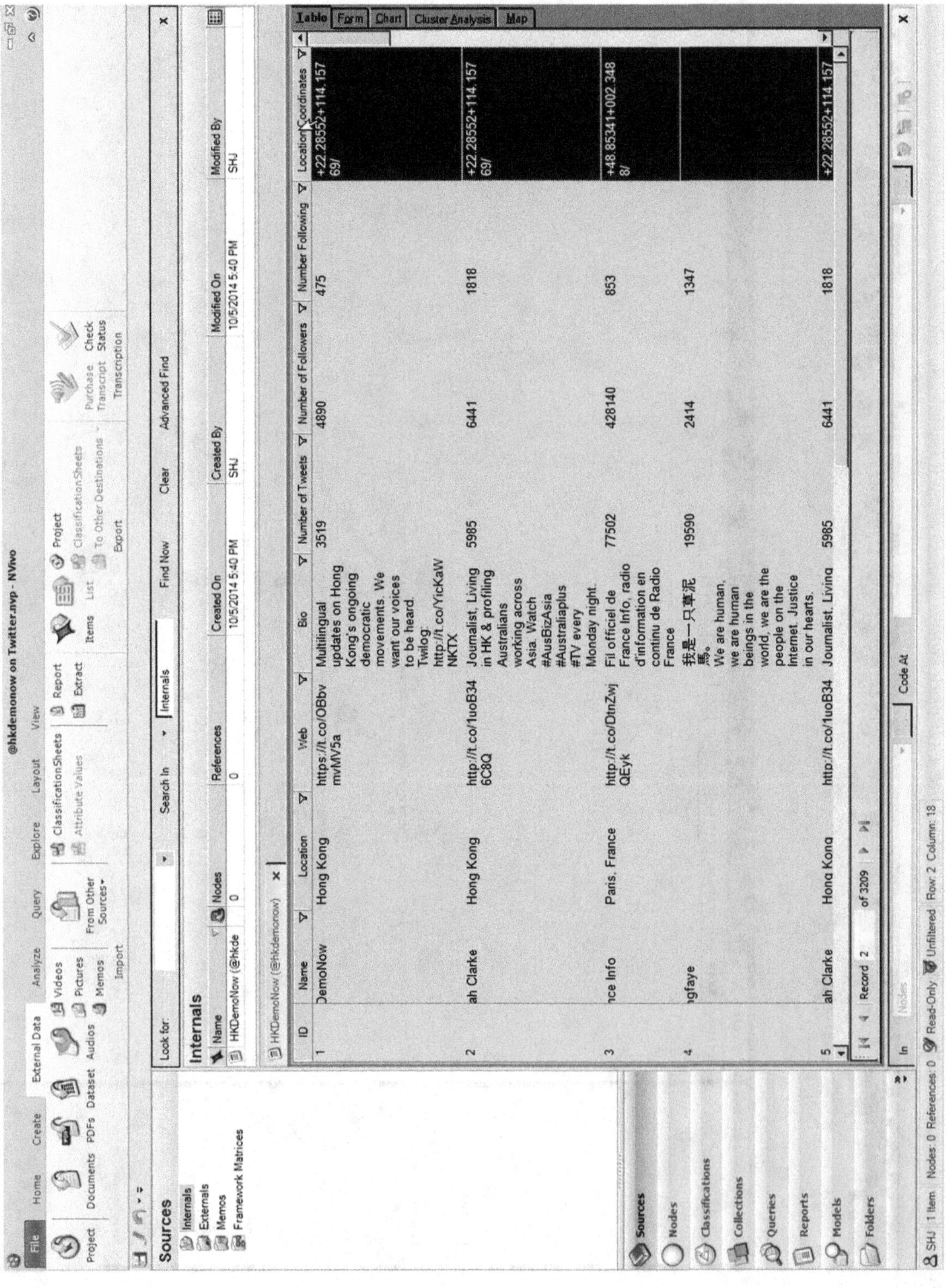

Figure 26. @hkdemonow Tweetstream Data Table (from NCapture of NVivo 10)

NCapture of NVivo 10. Using the browser add-on NCapture, 3,209 Tweets (microblogging messages) were captured from the @hkdemonow account. Figure 26 shows a data table view of the Tweets. The information includes the communicators, the times of the communications, the verbatim messages, URLs to all videos and images related to the captured Tweets, the locations of the Tweets (if that information was included), and so on.

A ring lattice graph of some of the clustered words in the microblogging messages is shown in Figure 27.

A word cloud of the messaging is shown in Figure 28, which provides a fast read of the main semantic terms shared by those sharing messages @hkdemonow. The dominant texts show hashtagged communications that may serve as effective leads to other information.

Figure 29 shows the diminishing messaging being posted to the @hkdemonow, which was an early indicator of the diminishing interest in this demonstration.

In Figure 30, the respective geolocational pins indicate the locations of the accounts of those engaging in the conversation @hkdemonow's Tweetstream. This sparse data would seem to suggest broadscale interest around the world—based on HK's deep trade ties possibly, based also on the social media connectivity (and the low cost of entry to the conversation). This information was extracted from the location column in the extracted dataset and mapped within NVivo 10, with its MapQuest integration. This map shows the available locational data for 2,636 of the 3,209 rows.

As another way to approach this phenomenon of a potential social movement, a Twitter hashtag conversation for #hk (#Hong Kong) was run using yet another software tool, NodeXL. To highlight some of the differences in the types of information that may be collected about the same event, a data extraction was conducted on the #hk (Hong Kong) hashtag on Twitter. This data extraction pulls out information by anyone who is microblogging about anything linked to Hong Kong, but the chances of the messaging being related to the demonstrations were fairly high given the dominance of the issue. A hashtag extraction is not linked to any one account but pulls out those who recently used that hashtag to label a microblogging message. In terms of the Twitter API (which NodeXL was used to query), this would involve messages expressed within the past 5-7 days at the moment of the request and with an 18,000 Tweet limit. In this case, the query resulted in the extracting of 3,033 unique accounts that used the #hk hashtag to label the messaging. The extraction is highly egalitarian; anyone on Twitter who wants to join in that conversation by labeling their message a particular way is free to do so. This extraction did not find any replies between the discussants, so it was unclear what the level of relating (linkage) was. In Figure 31, each vertex was labeled with the location of the communicator—based on "folk" labeling in the geolocation column. The locations may be understood as the places where the users of Twitter registered their account, and it is assumed that the locational data itself is fairly sparse (suggested in multiple publications to be about 1-2% of microblogged messages).

In NodeXL, part of the data capture involves the time period when the message was sent, based on the UTC method. Figure 33 shows the time periods and when the messaging was not very active as well as the times when the messaging spiked. The time periods are coarse-scale ones here. They are noncumulative in terms of the time settings. They do give a sense of some times of message surging. For a fast-moving event, it may help to map time stamps to physical locations (since a majority of people are awake at certain times based on circadian rhythms. The time of most electronic activity may align with particular time zones and locations.

Case D gives a sense of how multiple tools and multiple methods may be used to extracted related data from multiple sources for a more well-rounded view of an event on social media. These data extractions also show how an event in one locale may have repercussions across many regions.

Figure 27. A ring lattice graph of related words in the Tweetset (NVivo 10)

Figure 28. A word cloud of themes from the @hkdemonow Tweetstream (NVivo 10)

CASE E: Mapping a Website to Physical Spaces

Another way to extract geolocational information from online data is to map a website (representing a wide range of entity types, from individuals or organizations to corporations to government entities, and others) to physical spaces. The extraction sequence basically goes as follows: Select a website URL. Footprint it. Or run the URL to Network and Domain "machine." Or run the URL as a "Company

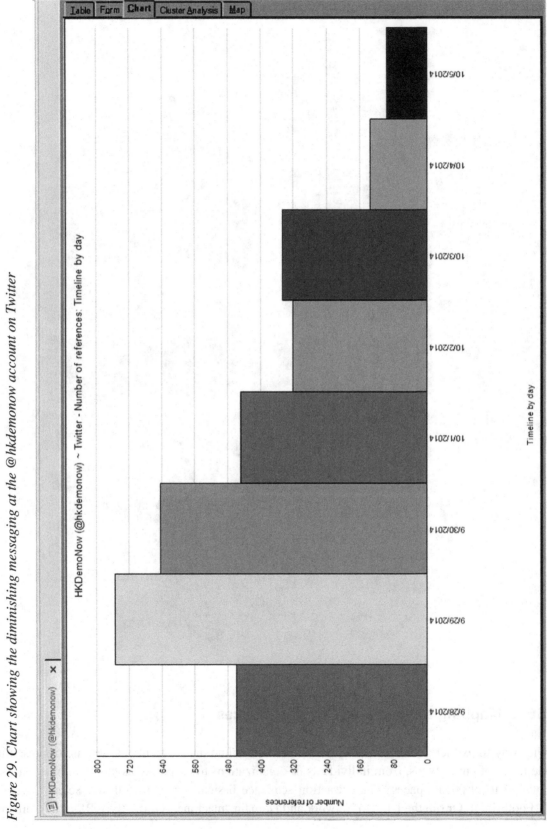

Figure 29. Chart showing the diminishing messaging at the @hkdemonow account on Twitter

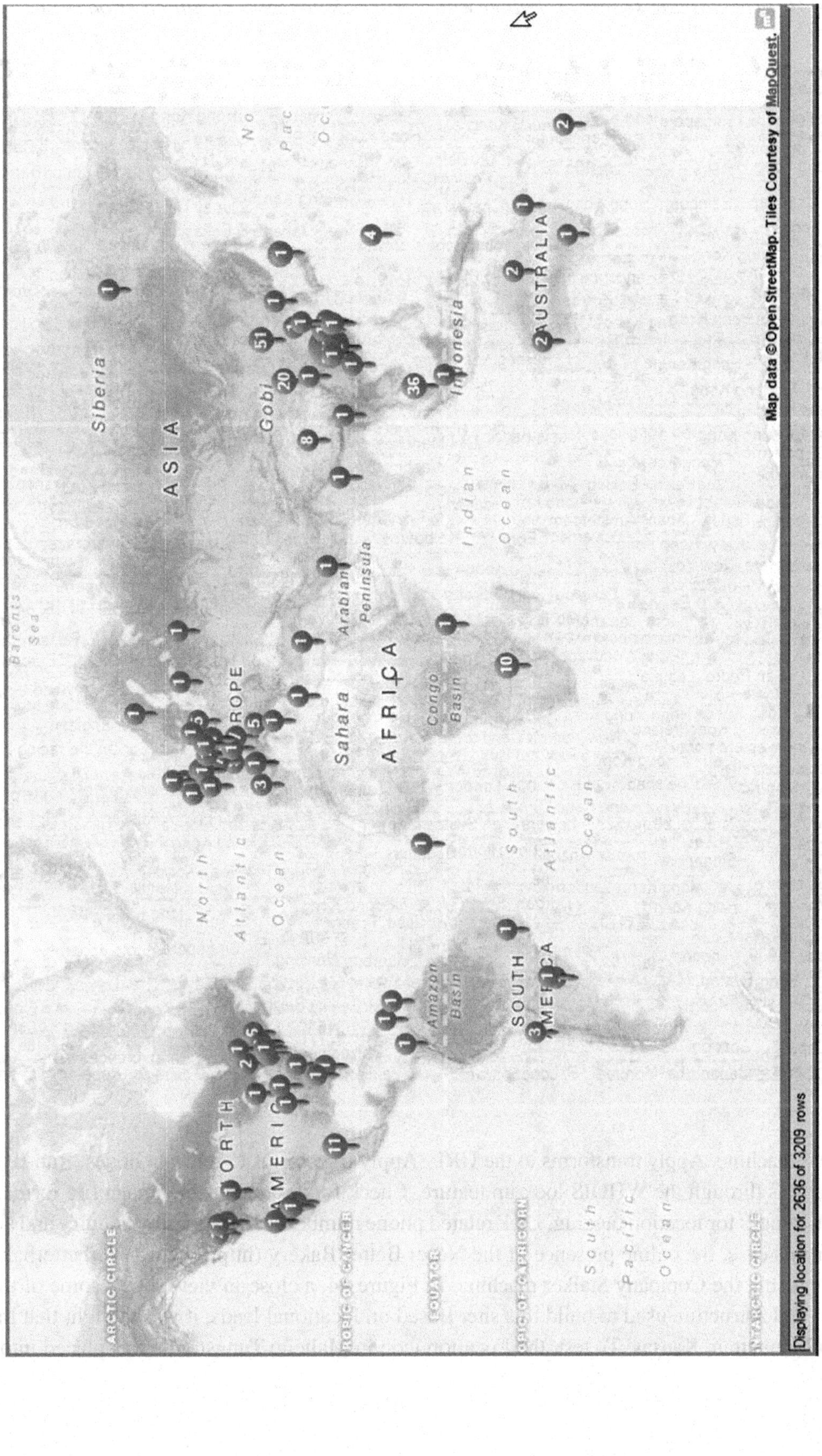

Figure 30. The locational data of the @hkdemonow Tweetstream as visualized by NVivo 10

Figure 31. #HK hashtag search on Twitter with Vertices Relayed as Locations (NodeXL)

Stalker" machine. Apply transforms to the URL. Apply transforms to relevant nodes. Run IP addresses to locations through the WHOIS look-up feature. Check for "exchangeable image file format" (EXIF) data on images for location tagging. Link related phone numbers to locations by country and area codes.

For this case, the online presence of the Never Better Bakery (http://www.neverbetterbakery.com/) was run using the Company Stalker machine. In Figure 34, a close-in view shows some of the technological understructure used to build this site. Based on locational leads, it was thought that this bakery was in Manhattan, Kansas. To test, the Location icon in Maltego Tungsten™ was placed into the work

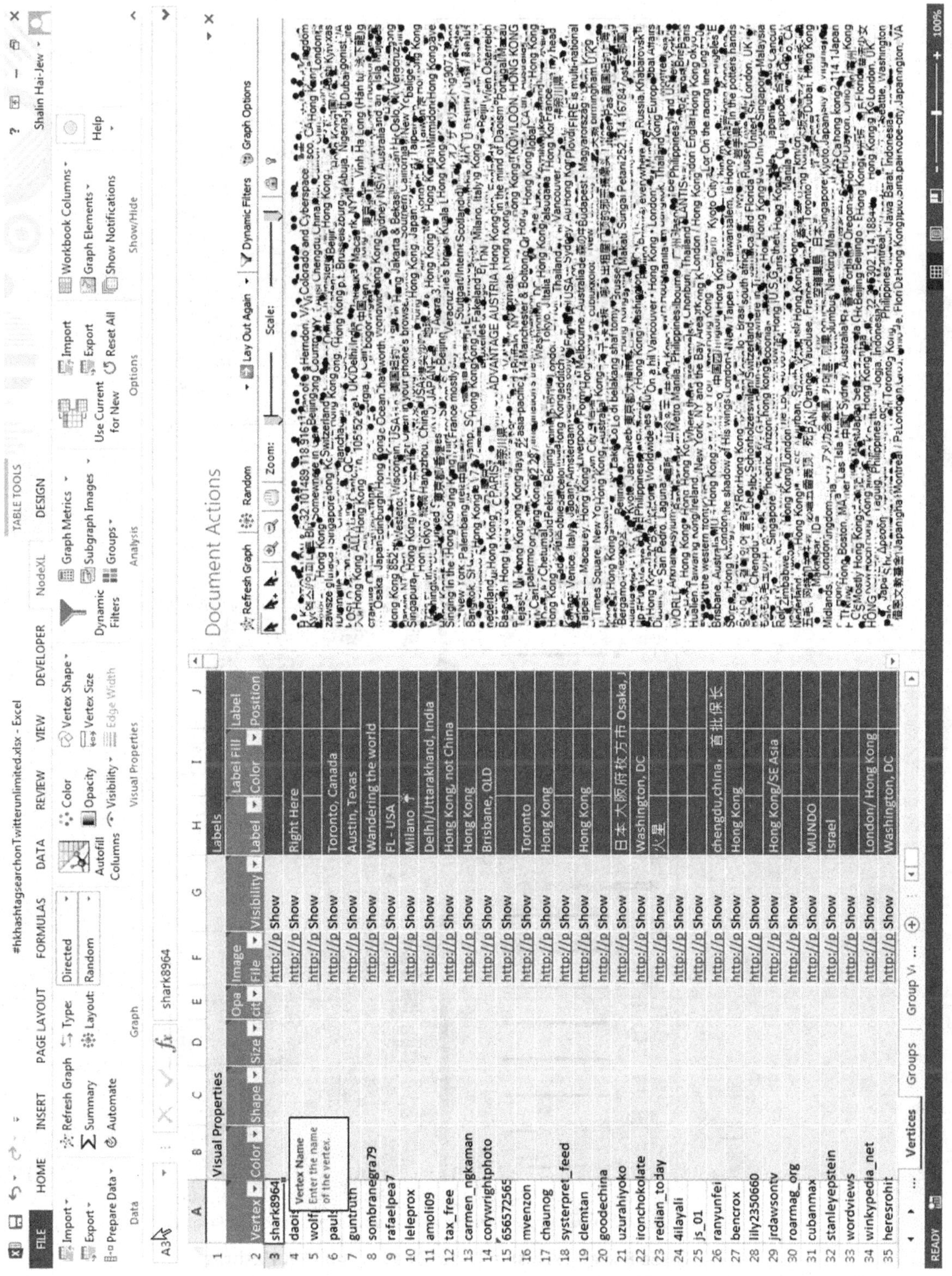

Figure 32. #HK hashtag search on Twitter with Vertices Relayed as Locations and a Highlighed Column of "Folk" Described Locations

Figure 33. Three rough exclusive time slices of the #HK hashtag conversation on Twitter (via UTC or coordinated universal time slices)

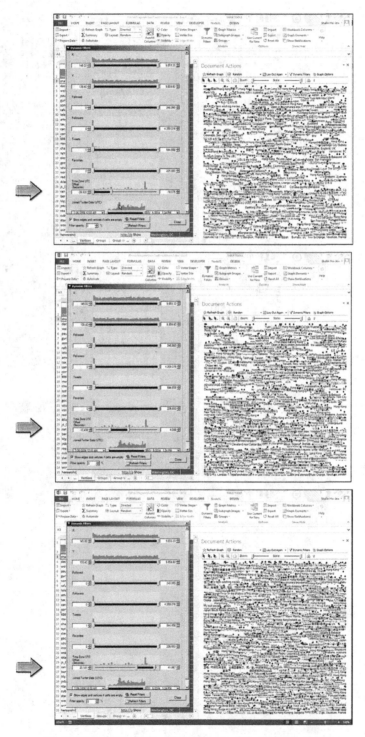

**Three Rough Exclusive Time Slices of the #HK Hashtag
Conversation on Twitter
(via UTC or Coordinated Universal Time)**

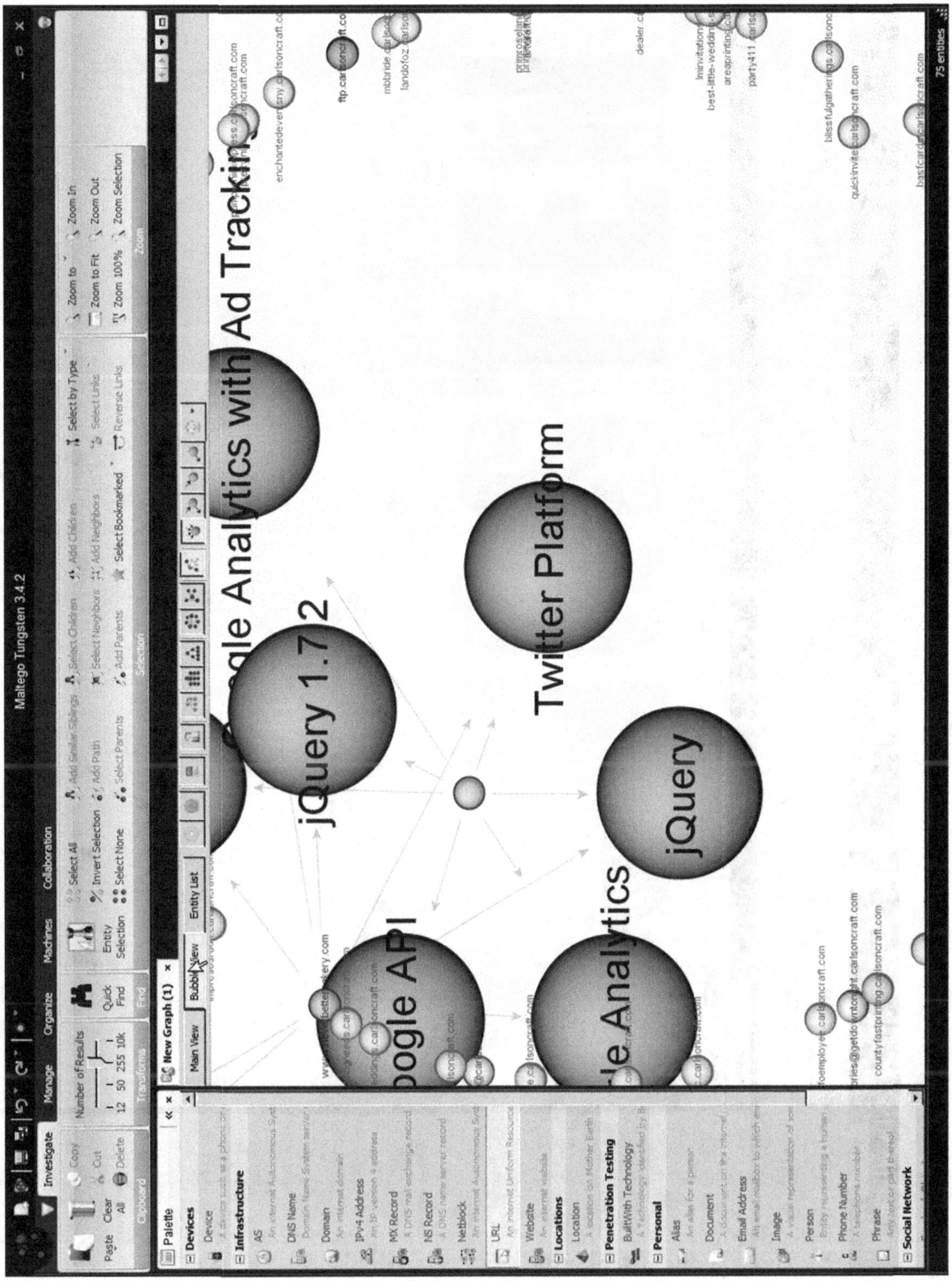

Figure 34. Linking http://www.neverbetterbakery to its physical location

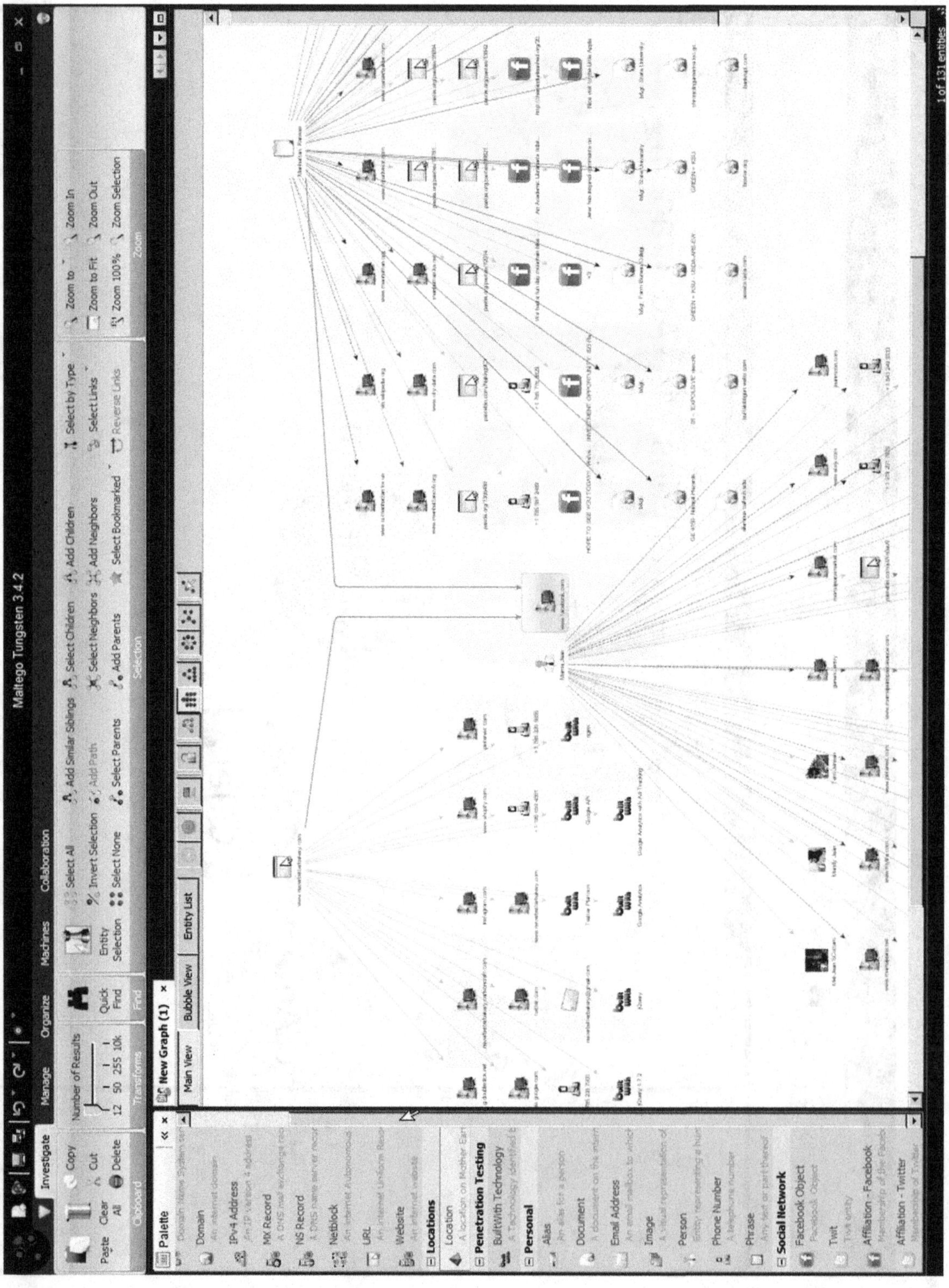

Figure 35. Never Better Bakery's website and Manhattan, Kansas, linked by Facebook entity

pane, and it was run to see if there were any overlapping nodes between that locational indicator and the links for the bakery.

In Figure 35, that guessed location panned out with a few connectors. (The location could be run as a phrase or as some other textual element, too, to see if there are connections there as well.)

CASE F: Mapping a One-Degree Ego Neighborhood (Belonging to a Focal Node) to Physical Locations

Another approach involves the mapping of an ego neighborhood (based on a focal node) to a particular location. An ego neighborhood of one-degree, in social network analysis, involves mapping the direct ties to one focal node. These direct relationships are with so-called "alters" (nodes in this ego neighborhood). A 1.5 degree mapping of an ego neighborhood is a reflection of transitivity, or the likelihood of the alters themselves being connected to each other. A two-degree extraction includes the direct ego neighborhoods of the alters. The world itself is supposedly connected through six degrees of separation based on the small world phenomena. An ego neighborhood is informative based on the concept of homophily (people preferentially forming relationships with others who are similar to themselves) and the sense that "the company you keep" reflects on the connected individual.

In this case, a public figure, Jack Ma of Alibaba renown, was selected because he was in the news at the time of the data extraction. First, a run was done to resolve the person to emails. Then, from there, a number of other connections were made. From the various linked information, interestingly, the locations resolved to Boston, Cambridge, and their environs in the state of Massachusetts. Figures 36, 37, and 38 relate to this data extraction.

The data extractions on the Web and Internet may collect data on defunct accounts that are no longer used because of residual information left on servers and in other spaces that are queried. In such cases, the long memory (some would say "the inability to forget") of the Web and Internet may lead to misleading conclusions.

CASE G: Tracking a Phrase to Physical Locations

Theoretically, a highly disambiguated phrase could also be linked to physical locations. In this case, "Chinese whispers" was selected, but it turns out that this phrase has evocations to businesses, games, phrases, pastebins, and a variety of documents. This data extraction was not particularly informative about spatiality. Another type of phrase then may be run in any number of languages enabled by Unicode. In this case, a data extraction was run on "香港"[Xiānggǎng (in pinyin) or "fragrant harbor" in Chinese). This extraction quickly resolved to the .hk domain and Hong Kong as a location. The extraction itself resulted in a multi-lingual haul of information.

Figure 40 shows a closer-in view of the 香港 phrase search.

CASE H: Mapping a Hashtagged Eventgraph to Physical Locations

An "eventgraph" is the mapping of a network that has coalesced around a planned (or unplanned) event. Such event-based conversations are hashtagged to indicate the happening. In this case, #dataweek was identified as a hashtag for an event which had wrapped several weeks prior. By the time a data extrac-

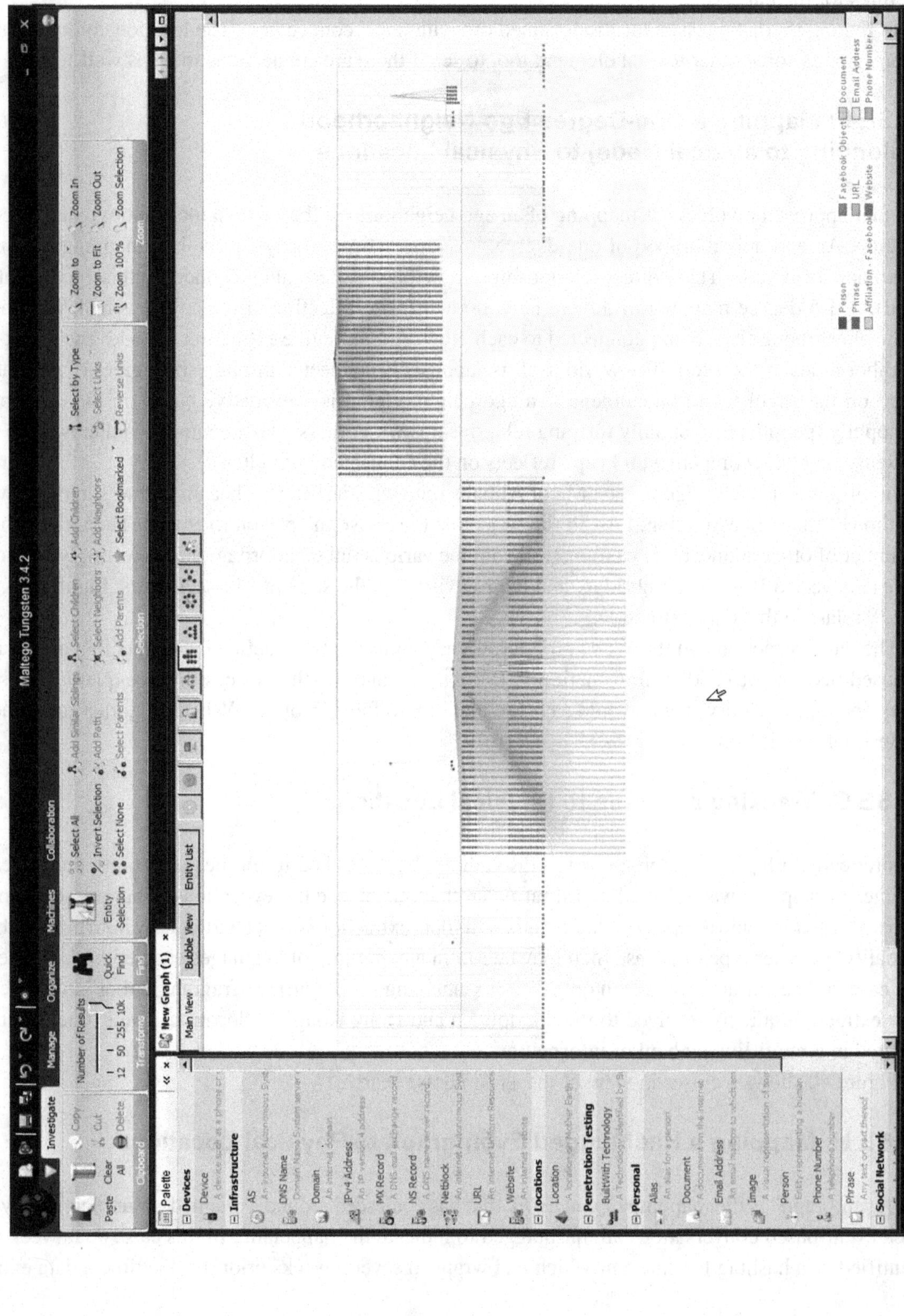

Figure 36. Jack Ma of Alibaba fame mapped to locations

Figure 37. Jack Ma of Alibaba fame mapped to cyber and physical locations

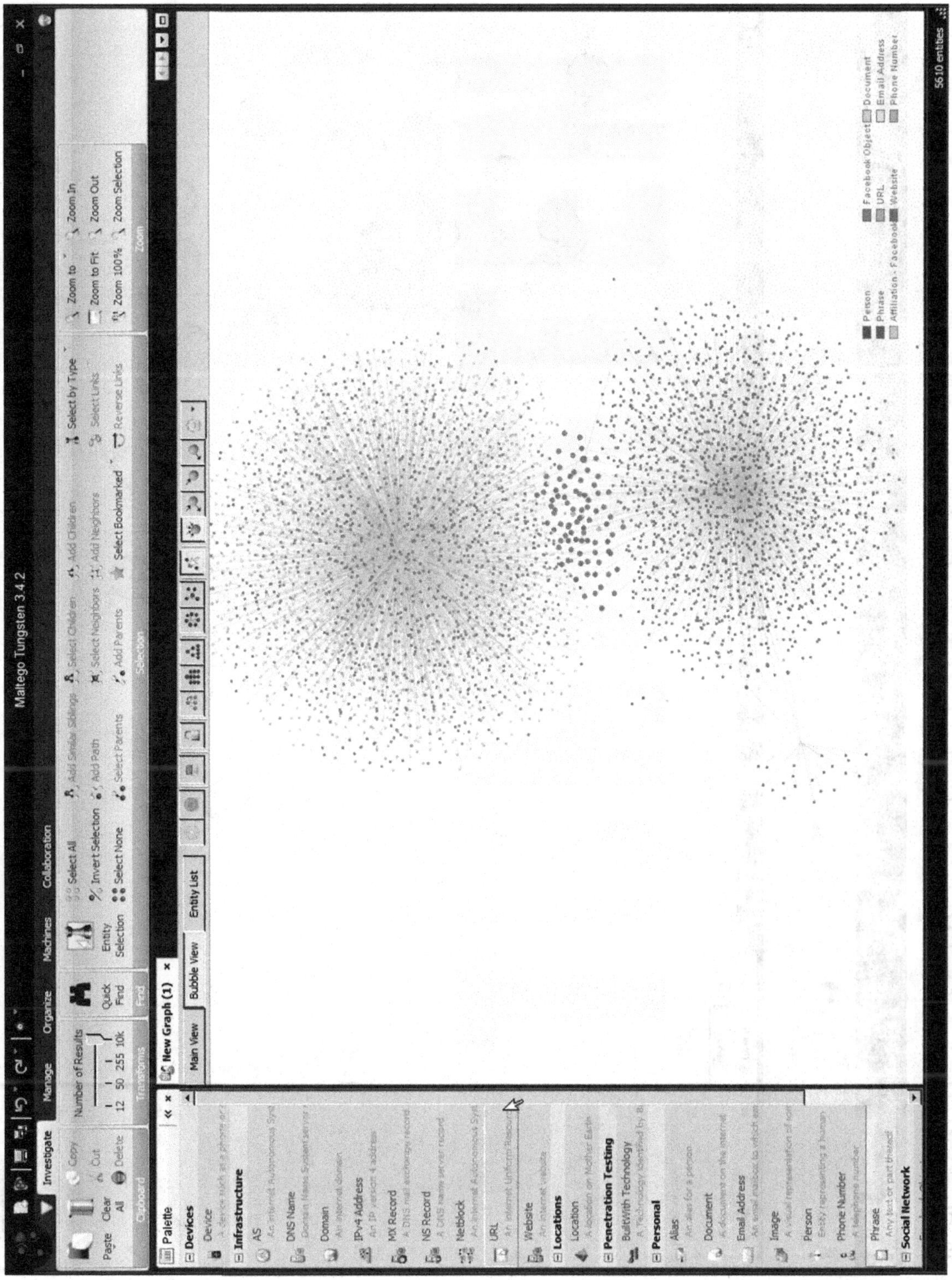

Figure 38. Close-in bubble view of Jack Ma Ego neighborhood and physical locations

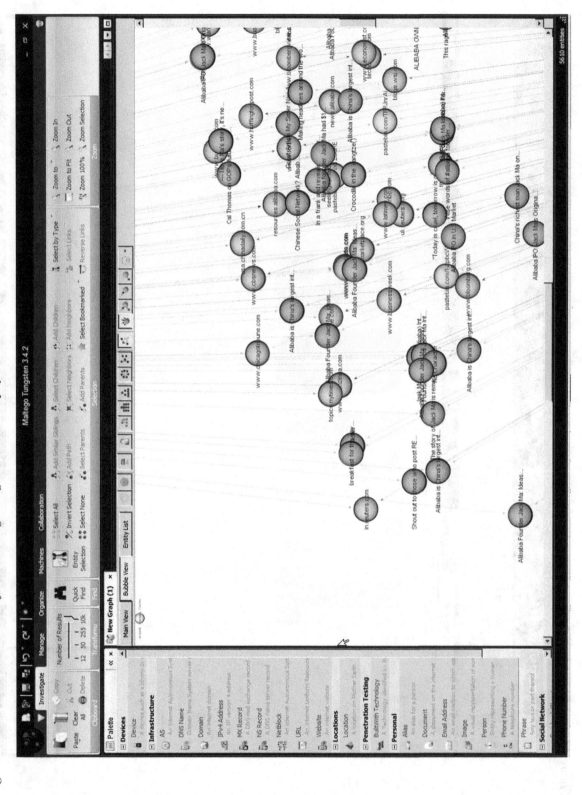

Figure 39. 香港 phrase search to location (Maltego Tungsten™)

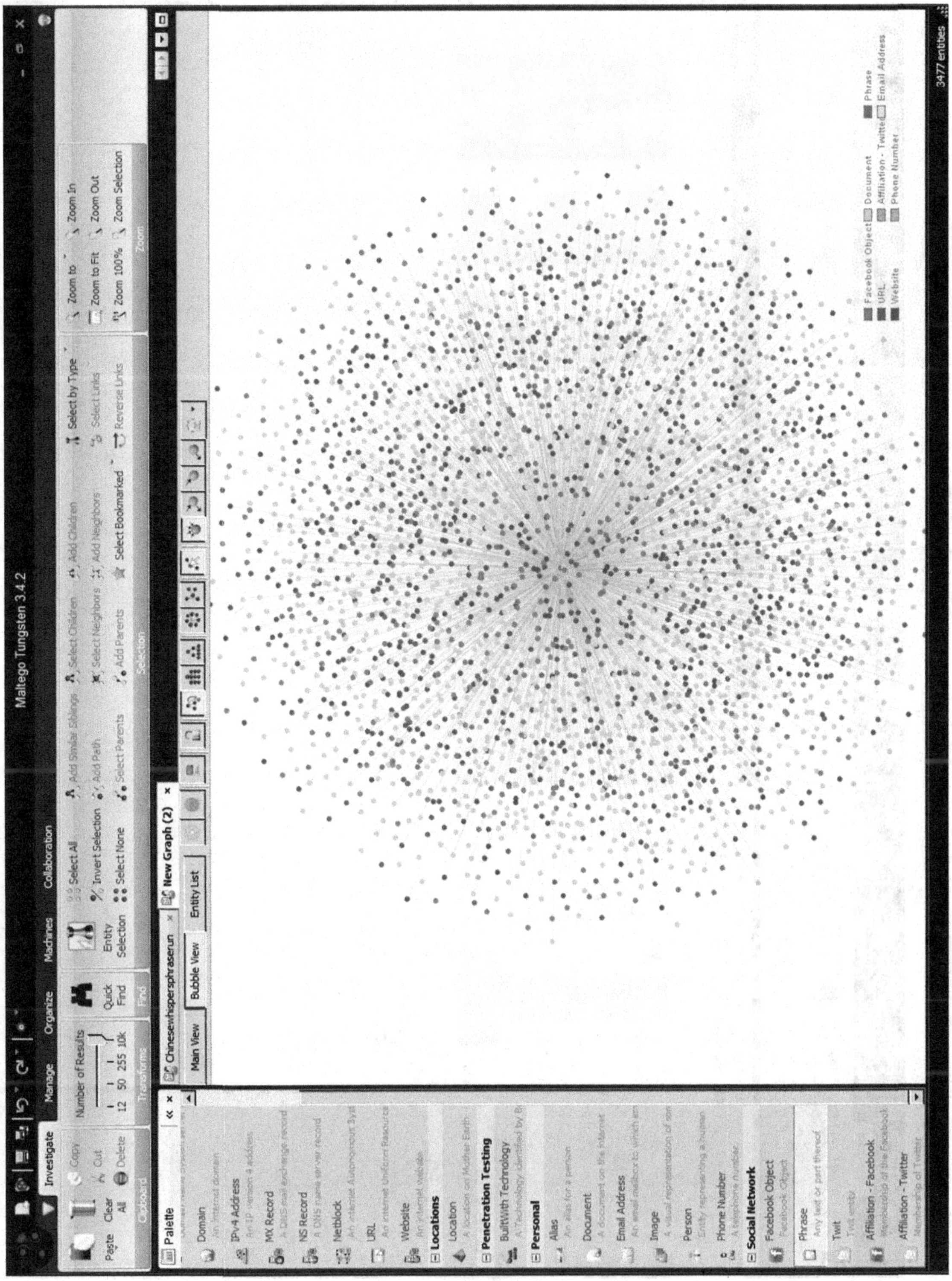

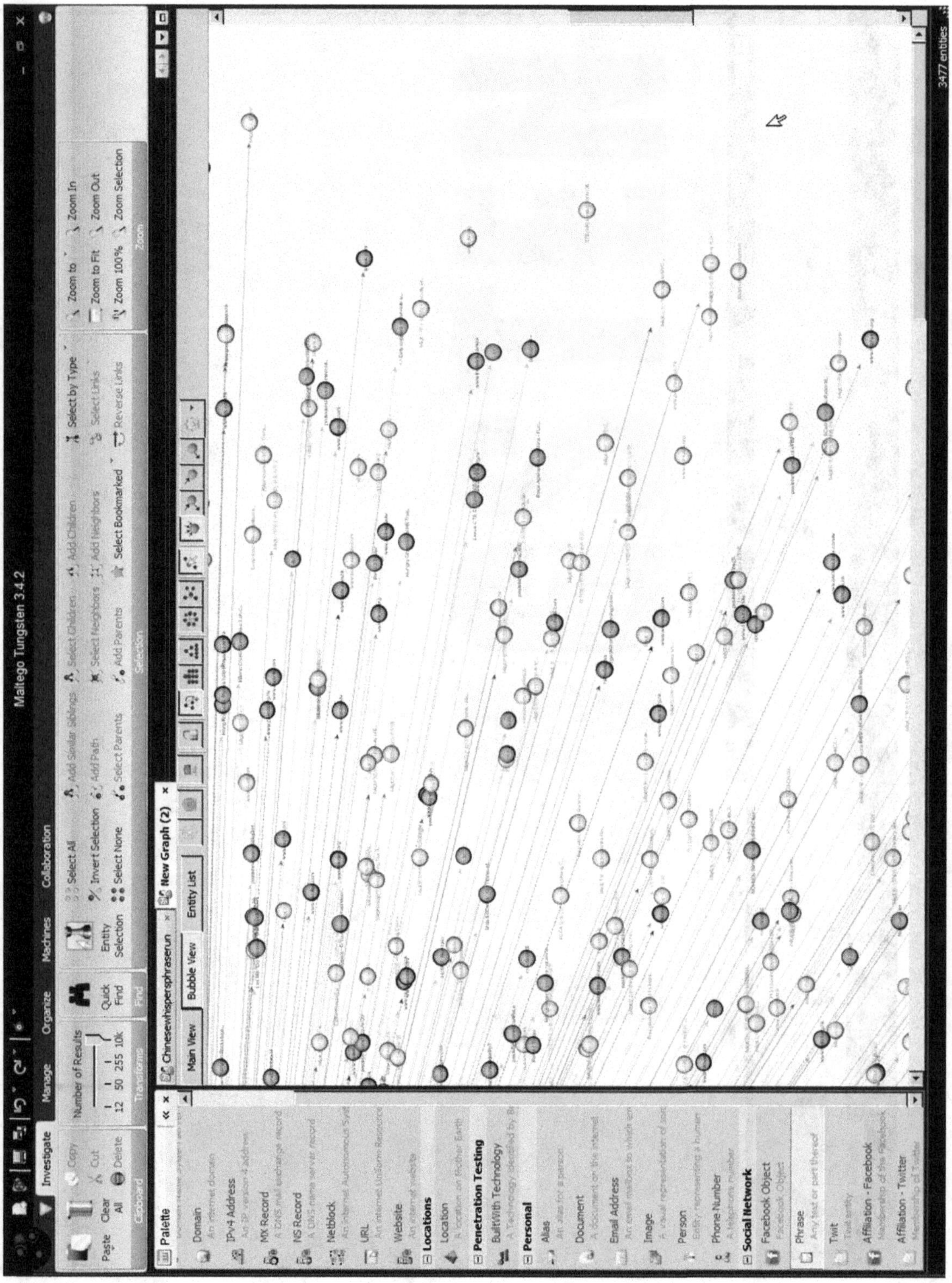

Figure 40. Xianggang close-in bubble view of phrase search to location in Maltego Tungsten

tion was conducted, the messaging had dwindled to some follow-on comments with little interactivity between individuals. A NodeXL extraction of the #dataweek hashtag resulted in Figure 41.

There was more information collected with a broadscale search of the #dataweek hashtag in Maltego Tungsten™. There were multiple sites that indicated locations, telephone numbers, and other potential leads. The event clearly brought together individuals from a variety of locations.

CASE I: Mapping a Twitter (Hashtag or Keyword) Conversation to Locations

To better understand the physical locations of the participants of a Twitter hashtag (#) conversation, a collection was made of recent short messaging labeled with #seattle (already a location name and referent to a space). The "location" column in the dataset was used in lieu of node (vertex) names, as may be seen in Figure 43.

CASE J: Mapping a Twitter Account to Physical Locations

To tie the messaging of a Twitter account holder (individual or group) to physical locations Another approach is to map a Twitter account to physical locations. Again, a Twitter account may represent an individual or a group; it may refer to people or 'bots or cyborgs. In Case J, the @TheJusticeDept user account on Twitter was explored for locations. At the time of the data extraction, the account had 1,449 Tweets, 33 photos / videos, 207 following, and 718 followers. The U.S. Justice Department had joined Twitter through this account back in September 2009. The Twitter landing page of this account indicated that this department does not collect comments through its account. A straight Twitter Geo Location machine was attempted, but the continuing OAuth challenges made that query unfruitful. The account was run as a phrase…which resulted in a wide range of connections—to U.S. government sites, media organizations, and indicators of location. (In such cases of formal government offices, their public-facing websites will often include some location information.)

CASE K: Turning an Online Alias to Personally Identifiable Information (PII) to Physical Space

An online alias may be resolved to an identified individual and then to physical space. To test this, a search was conducted for "Verax," one of the known aliases for Edward J. Snowden, the individual who leaked numerous secret documents from his work at the U.S. National Security Agency. Multiple runs were conducted on "Verax" without being able to disambiguate known aliases. There are many other instantiations of "Verax" in a variety of other contexts, some personal, some commercial.

In this case, some ties between the alias and the individual were found, but the locational ties were vague and peripheral and not to any real-time location. It would seem that the more disambiguated an alias is from the beginning, the more easily that may be linked to an identified individual. (It also helps if there is a clear statement of connection on a public website.) What finally worked in this context was dropping the known identifier in the work pane in order to see if there were any findable linkages. Given the media coverage and the prior revelations, this connection did come to light. However, if a researcher were only starting out with one part of the puzzle, the connection may well have been missed (even though a Google search would have found the link but only because journalists had surfaced it).

Figure 41. #dataweek eventgraph discussants post-event (NodeXL)

CASE L: Mapping an Email Account to a Physical Location

There is a way to link micro-level information (such as an email account) to a physical location. This endeavor is assisted by the fact that many email providers today enforce verified identities and that many have a public-facing side (which suggests that they would be mentioned on the Surface Web). The author did a data extraction using her work email which linked directly to location. Of the identified links, though, at least 1/6 (17%) of them did not have an actual tie to the known email. There is a sense that how the machine makes connections may be somewhat unknowable. Also, extant ties were not fully captured by Maltego Tungsten™ through the Paterva servers either.

Figure 42. #dataweek search on Maltego Tungsten™ to link to locations

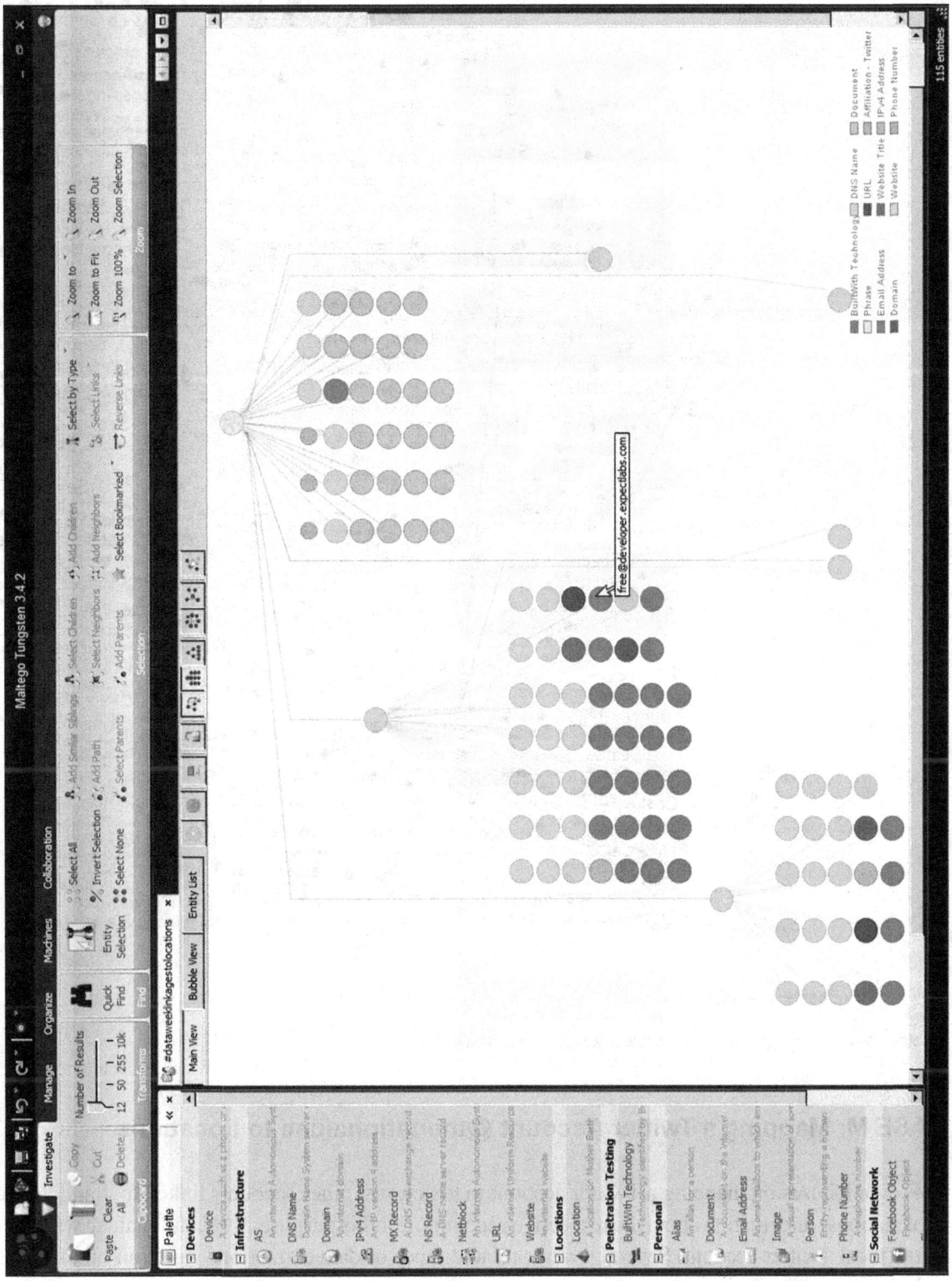

Figure 43. #seattle hashtag search on Twitter, with vertexes as locations (NodeXL)

CASE M: Mapping a Twitter Account @thenationaluae to Locations

This case focuses on mapping a Twitter account to the closest other accounts linked to it and capturing geolocational information about the respective accounts. For this purpose, @thenationaluae was selected as the focal Twitter account. Several Twitter-related types of data extractions were run on this account to little effect. The Twitter Geolocation tool was still not fully functioning and returned 0 entities even after multiple tries.

Grounding Cyber

Figure 44. *@TheJusticeDept on Twitter and into cyberspace and the world*

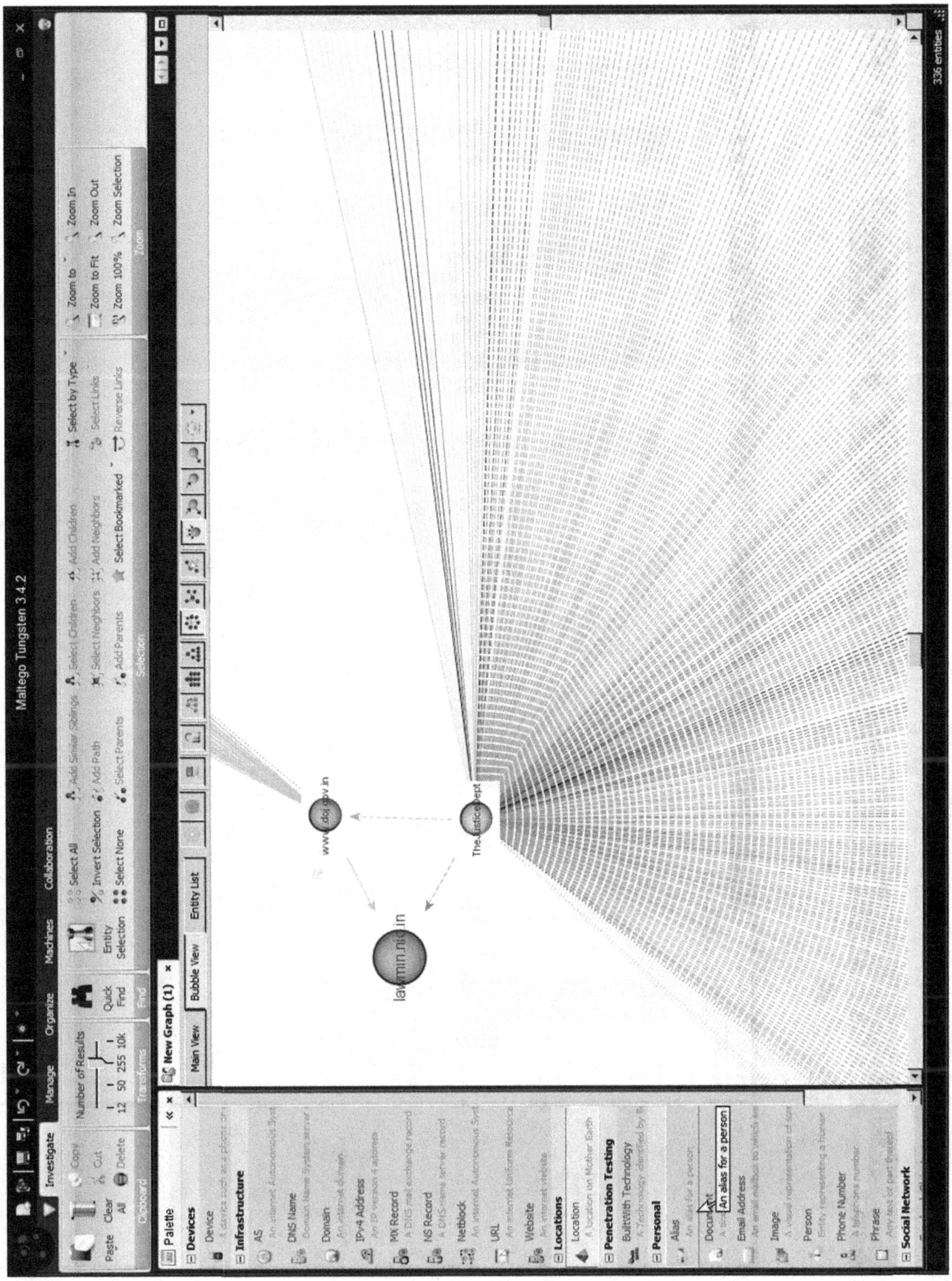

487

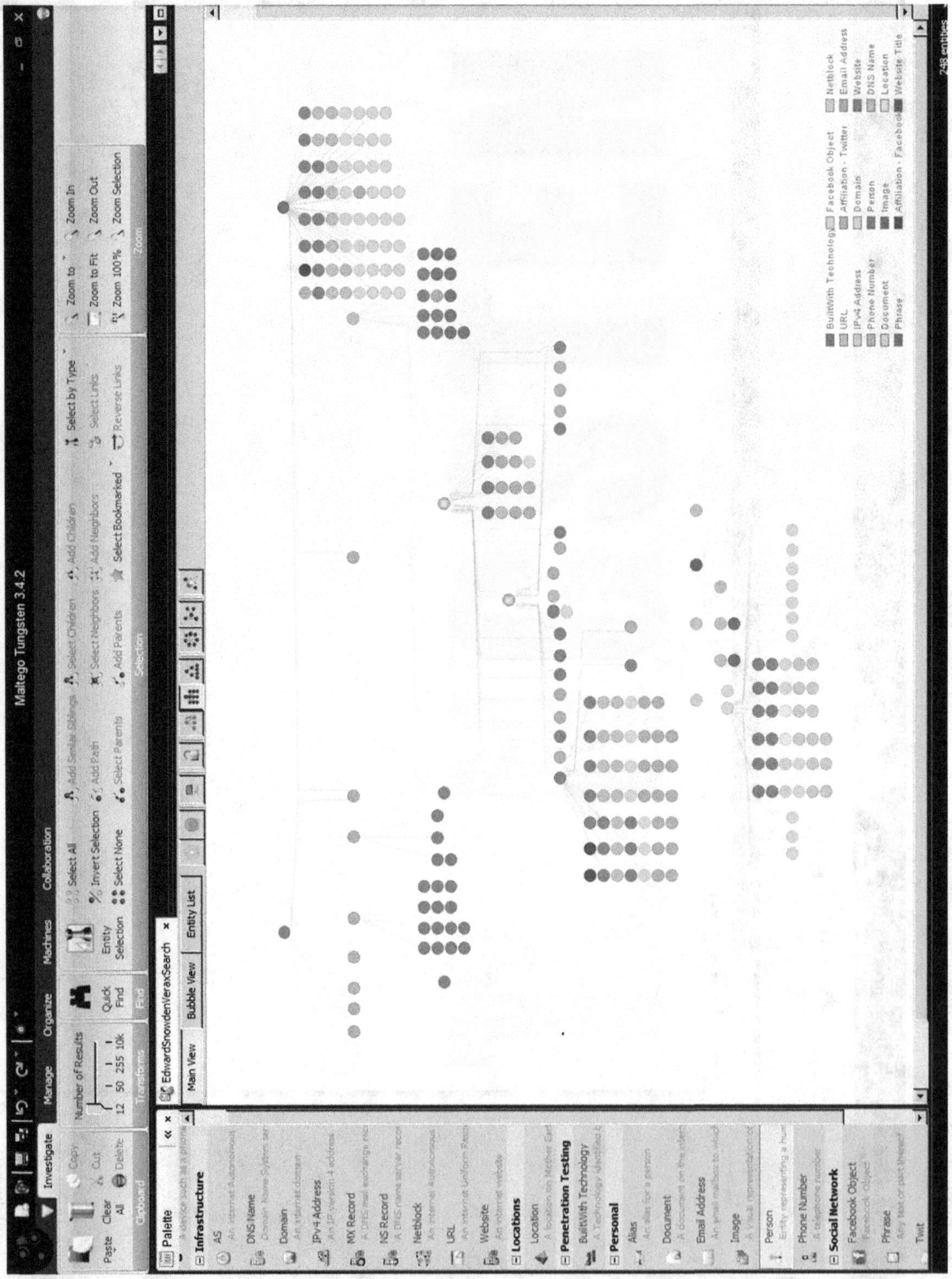

Figure 45. Verax, Edward J. Snowden, and some ambiguous online ties (Maltego Tungsten™)

Figure 46. Locating a workplace email to physical locations (Maltego Tungsten™)

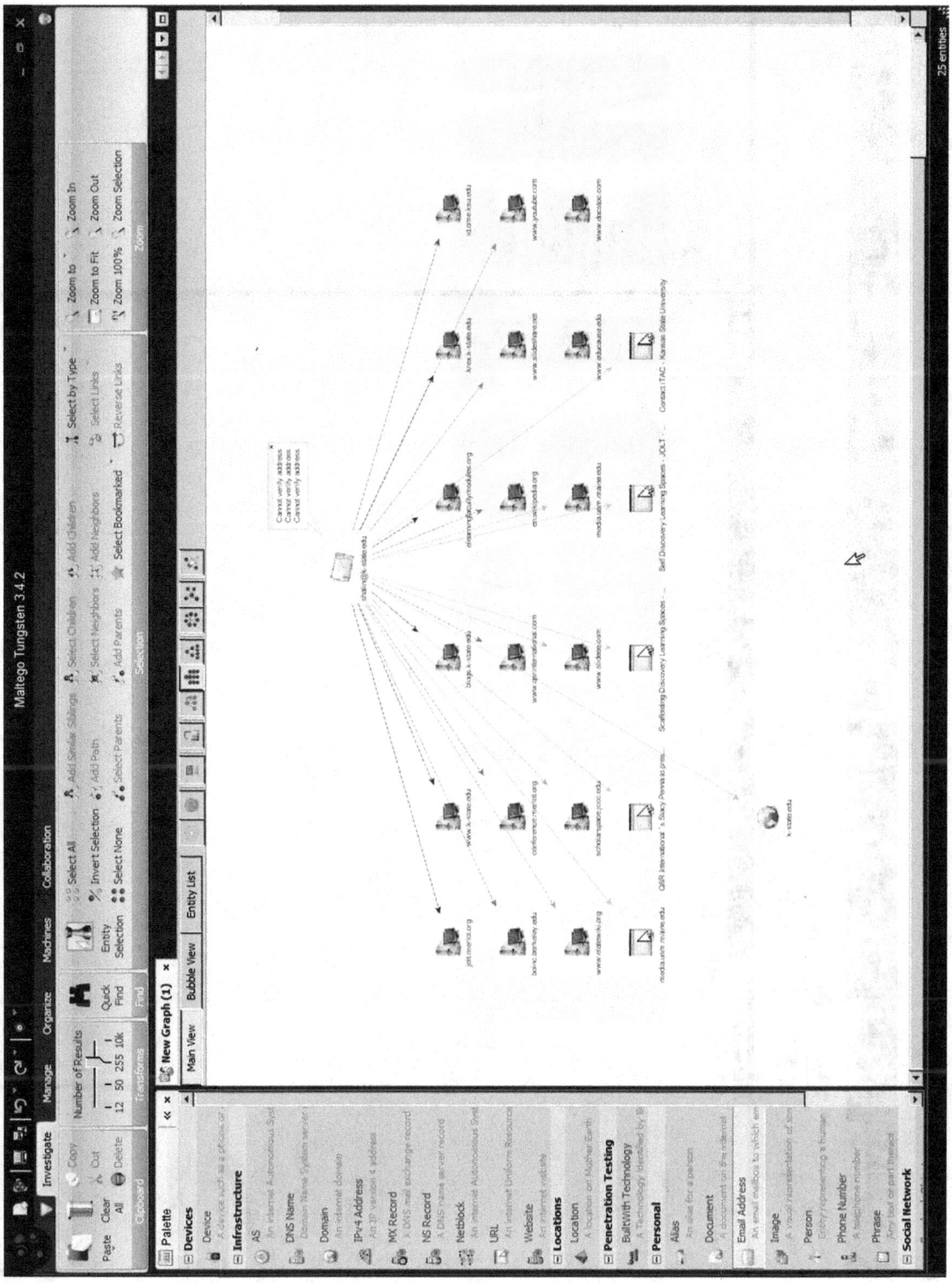

Figure 47. @thenationalUAE Twitter account networks mapped

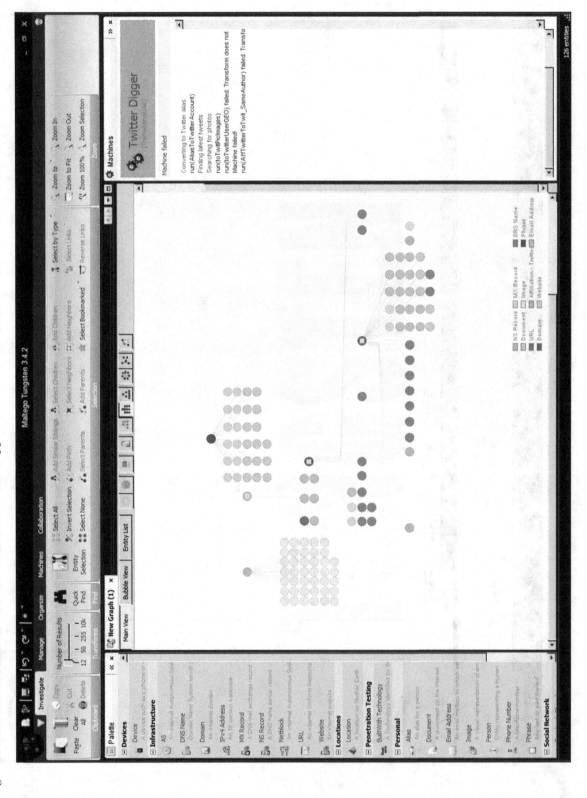

Finally, the strategy was to change the @thenationalUAE account from a Twitter account or Twit element to an alias, then a phrase, and so on, …and then running all possible "transforms" against these nodes…in order to capture as much across-the-board information as possible using Maltego Tungsten™. In Figure 48, the @thenationalUAE account was tied by its web and Internet connections to some unspecified documents on Twitter and some contact information (via email and telephone).

Finally, NodeXL was brought into play to map the one-degree ego neighborhood of @thenationalUAE account on Twitter. Three other accounts were seen to be in close proximity to the @thenationalUAE account: Lifenationaluae, Sprtnationaluae, and Ind_insights. This proximity may be seen in Figure 49.

The information of the three close nodes were run again on Maltego Tungsten in order to capture their interrelationships on the Surface Web. The placing of multiple nodes into the work space enables multiple simultaneous data extractions to look for potential inter-relationships. In Figure 50, some of the interrelationships are shown.

In Figure 51, a two-degree data crawl was conducted on the @thenationaluae account on Twitter. This shows a network with quite a few groups or clusters of interrelated entities, depicted using the Harel-Koren Fast Multiscale layout algorithm.

This two-degree network includes 2,790 vertices, with 2,172 edges. The geodesic distance or graph diameter is 4, with an average geodesic distance of 3.8, which suggests that the network itself may not be that deeply interconnected or dense.

CASE N: Related Keyword and #Hashtag Searches across a Range of Physical Spaces

Keyword searches may be used to help identify recent conversations among groups of individuals (or even just individuals with their narrowcast audiences), and then the various accounts may be mapped to physical locations. At the time of this chapter's research and writing, the news coverage was addressing an outbreak of "ebola" in parts of West Africa, with individuals carrying the virus on to other parts of the world during their travels. There were many concerns because this was a disease outbreak with pandemic potential. This case highlights the capabilities of additively bringing together multiple data extraction methods for sense-making.

Figure 52 shows a keyword search for "ebola" on Twitter using NodeXL and also using the tool's features to focus on location. Many of the accounts seem as if they are located in one region, and there are only a few nodes highlighted in a different color (light orange in the color version) to highlight a different location. By the visualization alone, it looks like there is a dominance of messaging by those in one part of the world.

A hashtag search of #ebola on Twitter ended up without any relational links, but the following Table 4 does show much more in the way of vertices or nodes (16,793).

There was also a search for an "ebola" video network on YouTube, and three main clusters were identified. The relationships between the video contents were identified based on the following three methods, with edges or links for all the following: "pair of videos that have the same category," "pair of videos commented on by the same user," and "pair of videos responded to with another video by the same user." A perusal of the authors in that video network show a range of interests: academic, scientific, and popular in Figure 53.

Figure 48. @thenationalUAE and its linked documents to its Twitter account

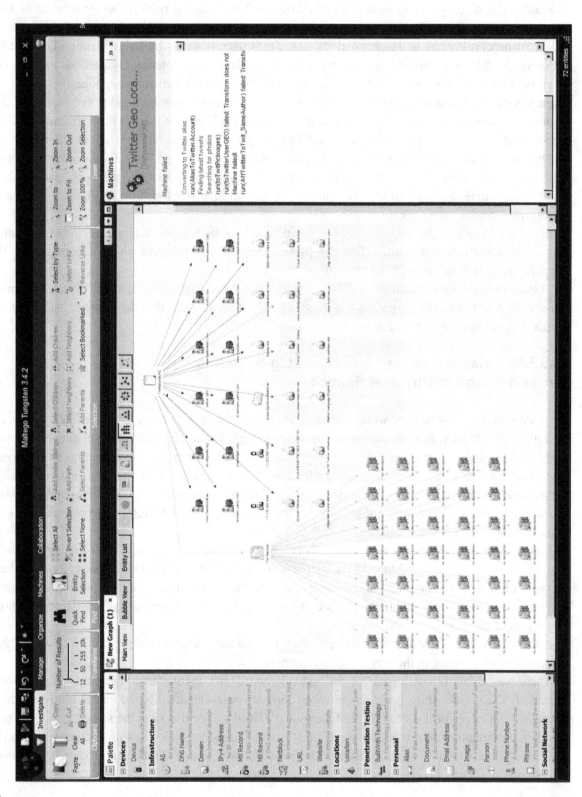

Figure 49. @TheNationalUAE ego neighborhood on Twitter (1 deg) (NodeXL)

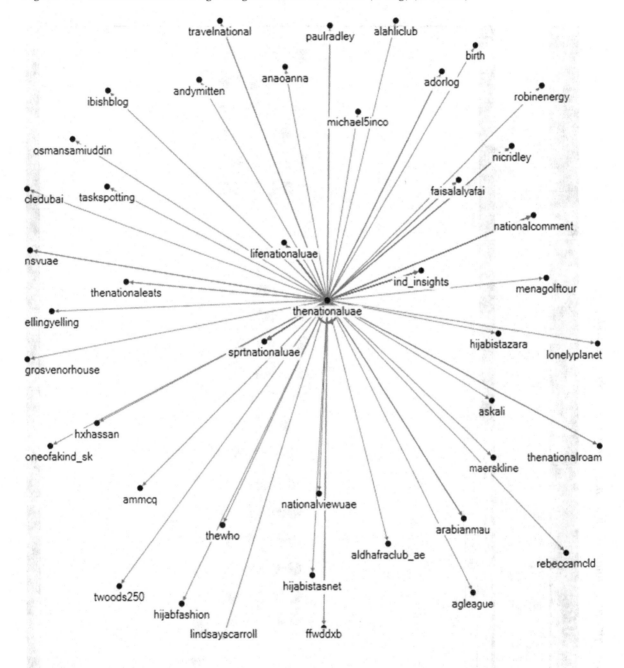

A perusal of the titles of the videos show varying degrees of hysteria in Figure 54. The titles of the videos are somewhat hyperbolic in some contexts, and fear seems to be a predominant theme given the transmissibility of the virus.

In Figure 55, some of the thumbnail images related to the respective videos have been extracted and are presented in the network.

A broad extraction of information related to "ebola" across the Web and Internet show a wide range of connections, in a Maltego Tungsten crawl. The structured visualization shows a variety of interested

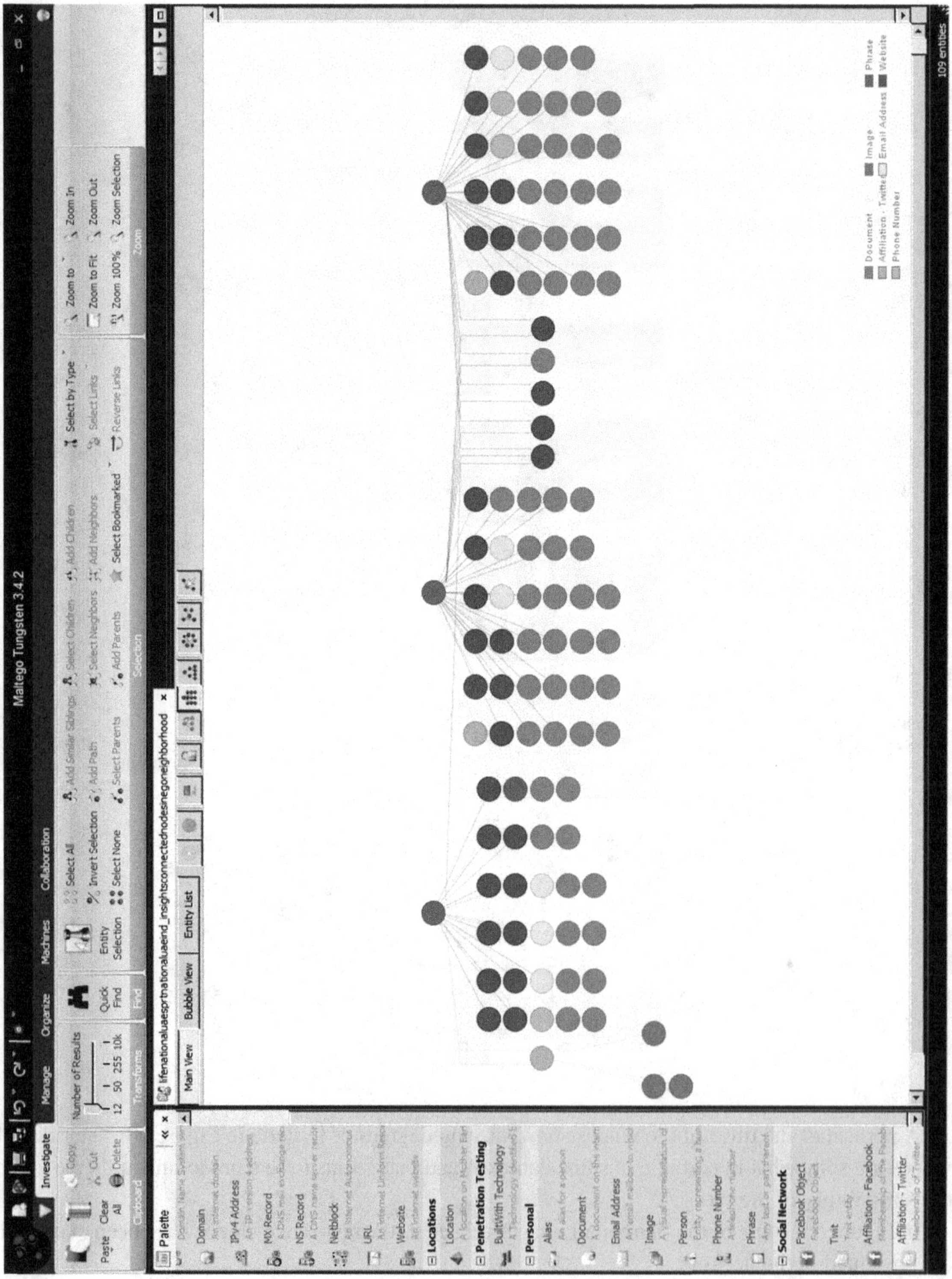

Figure 50. thenationaluae, sprtnationaluae and ind_insight run on the Surface Web

Figure 51. @TheNationalUAE ego neighborhood on Twitter (2 deg) (NodeXL)

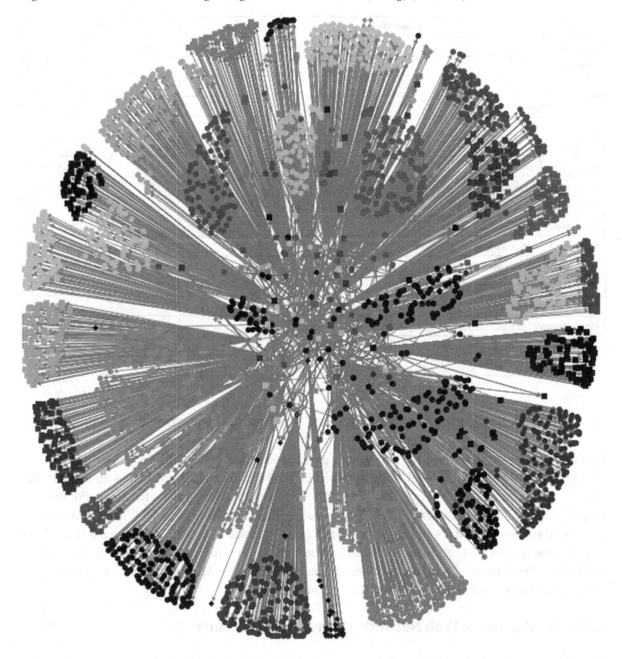

entities: media, government, medical professionals, commercial entities, and individuals; there is a range of messaging and documents. There is a lot of content, apparently, in pastebins.

There is a close-in bubble view of the same data extraction for "ebola" in Figure 57.

An effort was made to identify any keyworded or hashtagged contents about ebola on Flickr, but neither of those queries resulted in any network.

Table 2. Graph Metrics Table for the @TheNationalUAE ego neighborhood on Twitter (2 deg) (NodeXL)

Graph Metric	Value
Graph Type	Directed
Vertices	2790
Unique Edges	2172
Edges With Duplicates	8052
Total Edges	10224
Self-Loops	3586
Reciprocated Vertex Pair Ratio	0.013954964
Reciprocated Edge Ratio	0.027525805
Connected Components	1
Single-Vertex Connected Components	0
Maximum Vertices in a Connected Component	2790
Maximum Edges in a Connected Component	10224
Maximum Geodesic Distance (Diameter)	4
Average Geodesic Distance	3.792818
Graph Density	0.000410856
Modularity	Not Applicable
NodeXL Version	1.0.1.333

CASE O: Phone Number to "Transforms" to Physical Locations

It is also possible to link telephone numbers to physical locations because of the way area codes are codified in many parts of the world. People's tendencies to keep phone numbers across time, even after they've moved, means that cell or other such numbers may not link to physical locations. For this example, 1-800-RED CROSS (1-800-733 2767) was run, with no outcomes initially. When it was run as a "phrase" type, though, and not as a phone number, a range of results emerged. The general Surface Web crawl showed plenty of reverse number identification sites, but it also included successful connections to the Red Cross and its various regional centers, including some in Michigan, Iowa, and New Jersey; however, this was still a gap-filled sort of data extraction.

CASE P: Mapping a Web Network to Physical Locations

To map a web network (of interlinked websites) to physical locations to understand proximity and culture, a data extraction was created around http://themercury.com/, a local newspaper site. The http network of this site was created, which showed proximity with local newspapers. Quite a few branches were created before a location became clear. In terms of physical locations, the web network was mapped to a geographical area within the state of Kansas.

Figure 52. "ebola" keyword search on Twitter (using NodeXL)

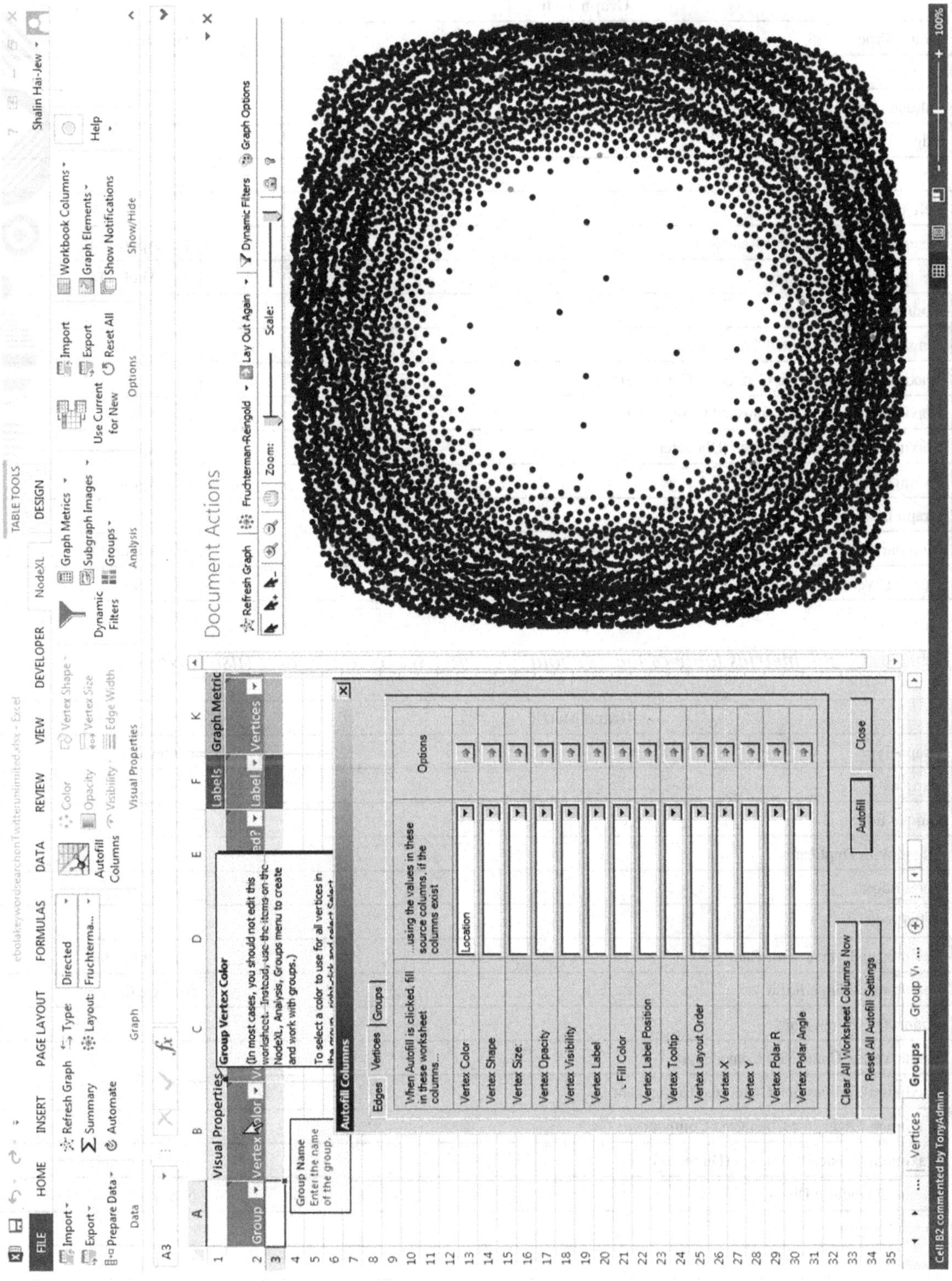

Table 3. Graph Metrics Table of the "ebola" Keyword Search on Twitter (using NodeXL)

Graph Metric	Value
Graph Type	Directed
Vertices	7311
Unique Edges	0
Edges With Duplicates	0
Total Edges	0
Self-Loops	0
Reciprocated Vertex Pair Ratio	Not Applicable
Reciprocated Edge Ratio	Not Applicable
Connected Components	7311
Single-Vertex Connected Components	7311
Maximum Vertices in a Connected Component	1
Maximum Edges in a Connected Component	0
Maximum Geodesic Distance (Diameter)	Not Applicable
Average Geodesic Distance	Not Applicable
Graph Density	0
Modularity	Not Applicable
NodeXL Version	1.0.1.333

Table 4. Graph metrics table of the "#ebola" hashtag search on Twitter (using NodeXL)

Graph Metric	Value
Graph Type	Directed
Vertices	16793
Unique Edges	0
Edges With Duplicates	0
Total Edges	0
Self-Loops	0
Reciprocated Vertex Pair Ratio	Not Applicable
Reciprocated Edge Ratio	Not Applicable
Connected Components	16793
Single-Vertex Connected Components	16793
Maximum Vertices in a Connected Component	1
Maximum Edges in a Connected Component	0
Maximum Geodesic Distance (Diameter)	Not Applicable
Average Geodesic Distance	Not Applicable
Graph Density	0
Modularity	Not Applicable
NodeXL Version	1.0.1.333

Figure 53. ebola video network authors on YouTube

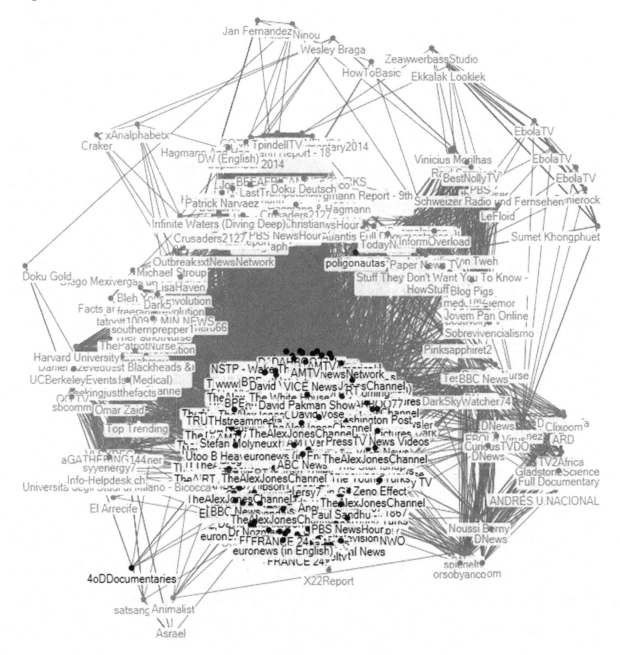

CASE Q: Mapping an Internet Protocol (IP) Address to Various Contents and Physical Locale

It is possible to map an Internet Protocol address to various contents and also ultimately physical locales. For this example, an IPv4 address was selected (175.45.179.255) that was identified to link to DPRK. In Figure 60, a data extraction based on the IPv4 address is linked to North Korea, as indicated by the pyramid glyphs in the visualization in Maltego Tungsten™.

Figure 54. "ebola" video network titles on YouTube

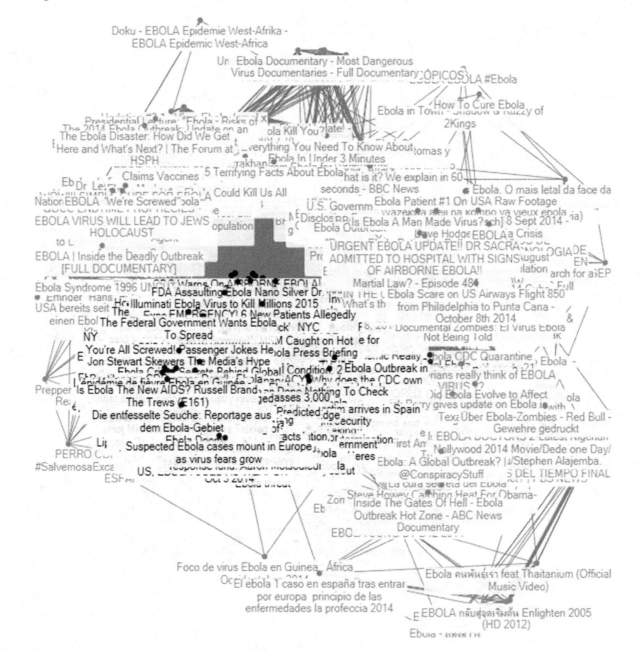

A data table of the data extraction linked to the specific IPv4 address follows in Figure 62.

OTHER VARIATIONS

The prior data extractions and visualizations are part of a limited set of geolocational types of queries based on a few software tools. These were by no means any comprehensive set. To that end, it may help to add a few more insights about ways to broaden query methodologies.

Figure 55. "ebola" video network's authors on YouTube with related thumbnail images and partitioning

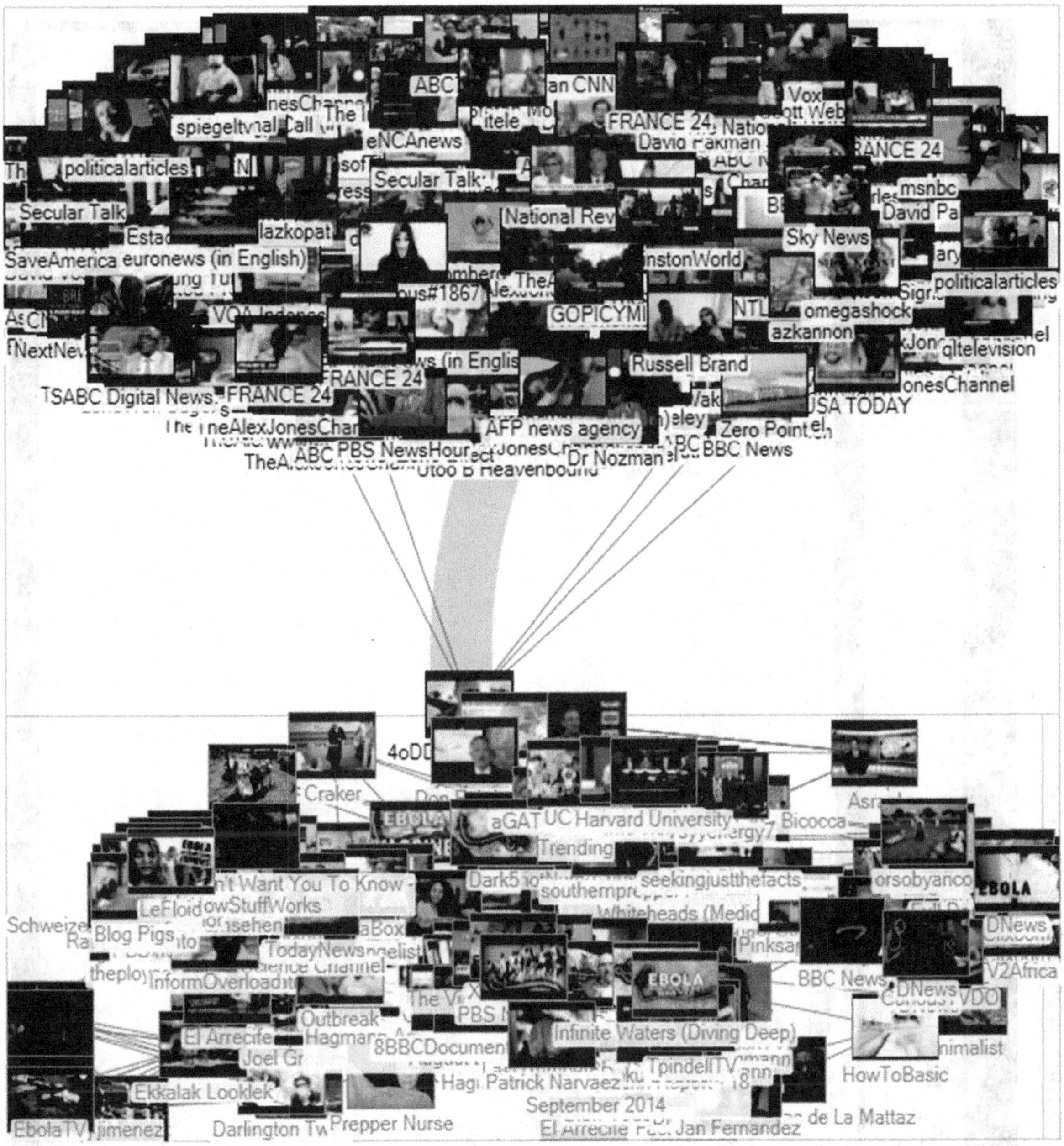

Multiple Data Extractions for One Target

One target may be queried in multiple ways for a wide range of knowing. An individual may be linked to a Twitter account, a Tweetstream dataset, hashtagged conversations, multiple websites, multiple email accounts, and all sorts of multimedia contents on social media sites, all of which may leak information about location (as well as other data). A company may be explored through multiple levels of domain footprinting, individuals (their emails, their accounts, and their phone numbers), documents, and social

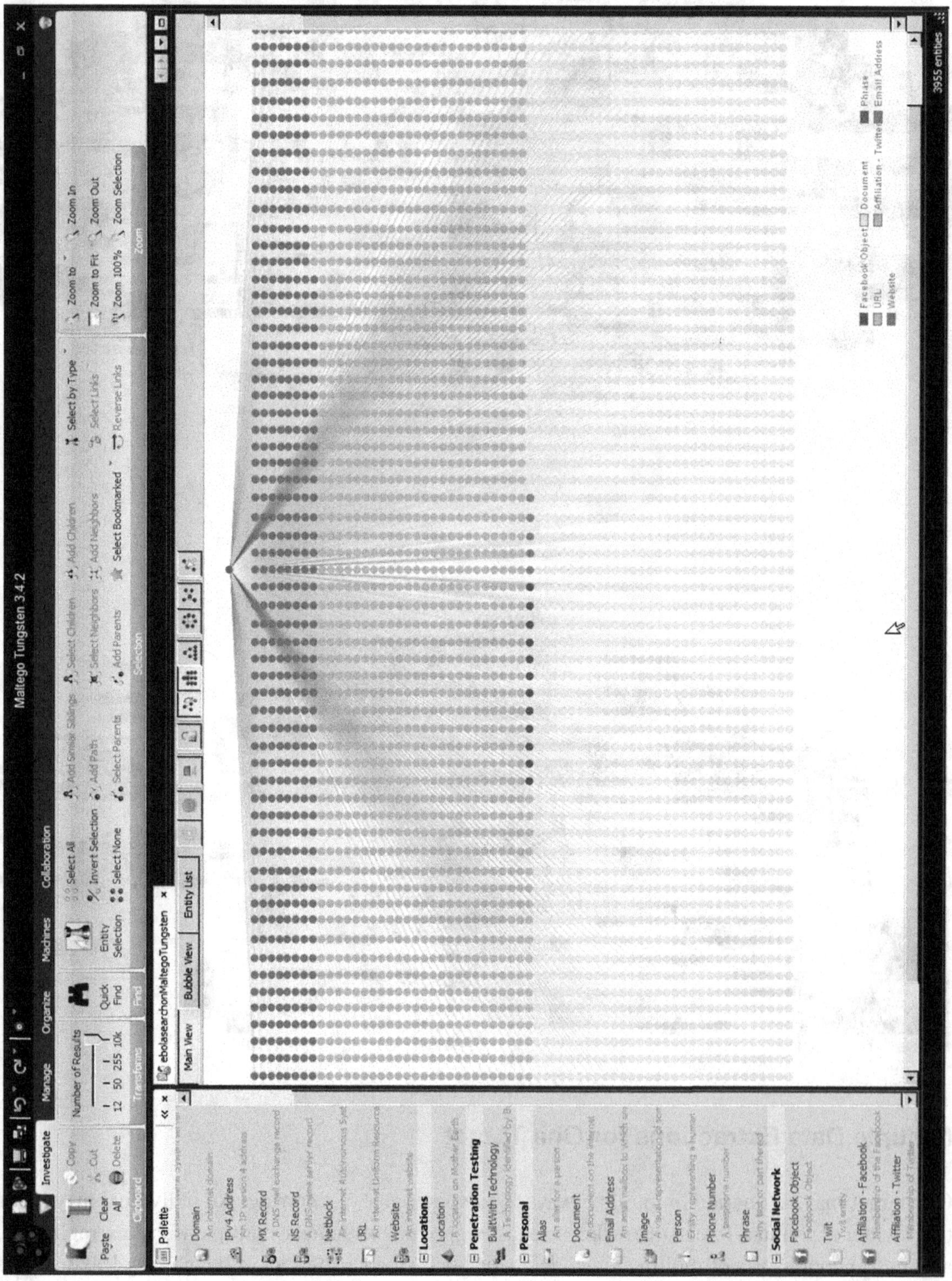

Figure 56. ebola keyword phrase search on Maltego Tungsten™

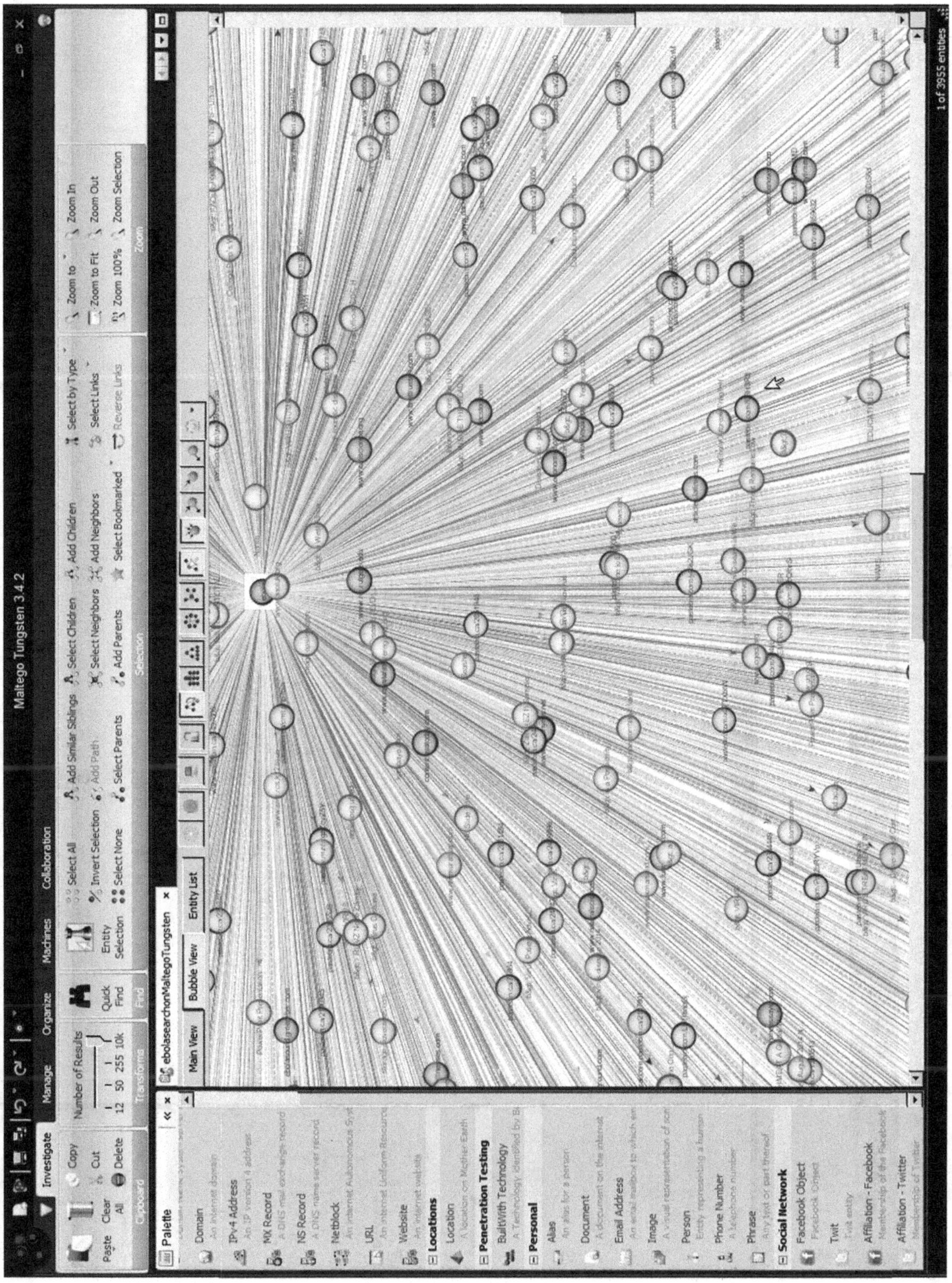

Figure 57. A close-in bubble view of the "ebola" keyword phrase search on Maltego Tungsten™

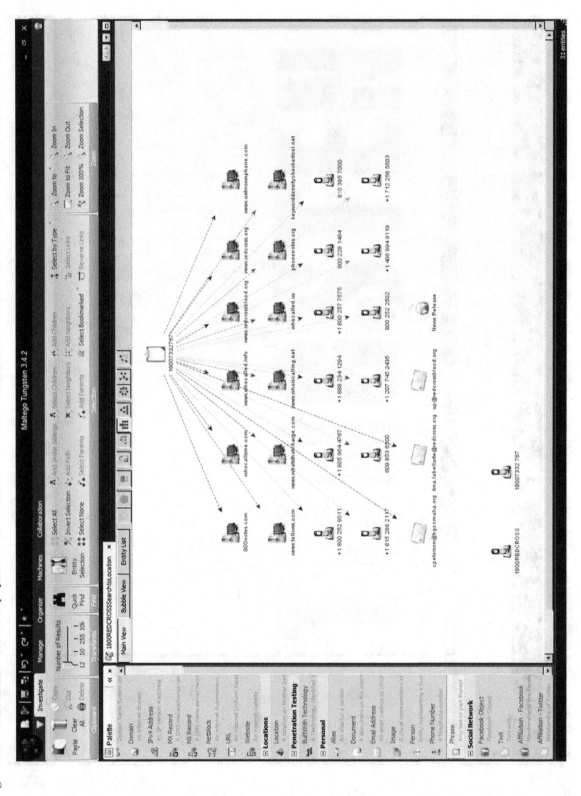

Figure 58. 1-800-RED-CROSS to physical locations

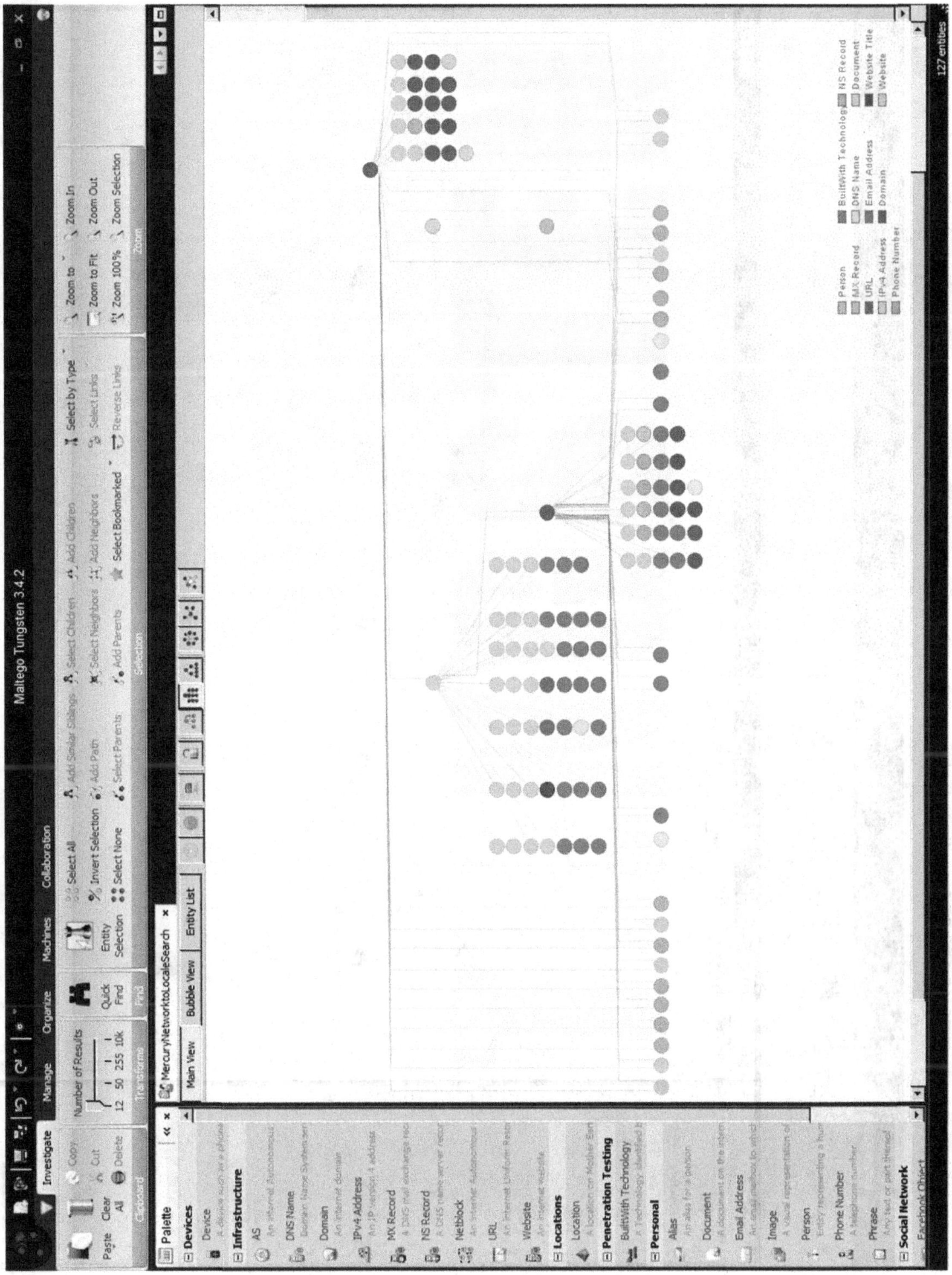

Figure 59. http://themercury.com/ to a proxemic physical location

Figure 60. An IPv4 address (175.45.179.255) linked to physical locations

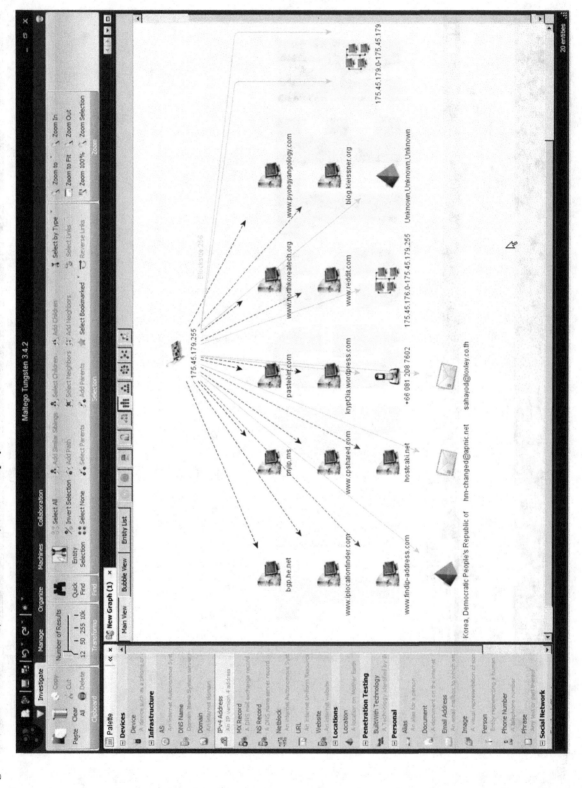

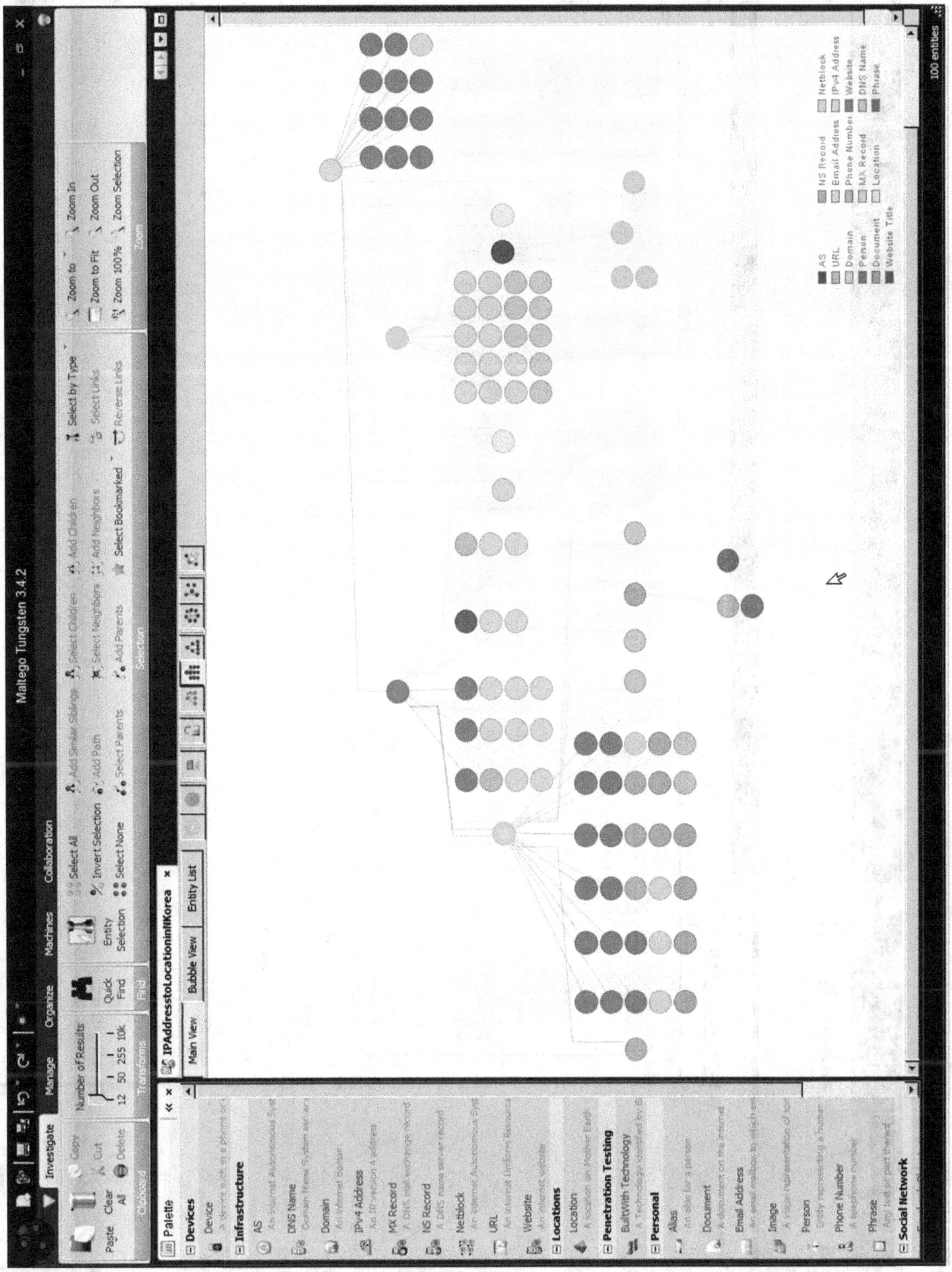

Figure 61. Further disambiguation of 175.45.179.255 linked to other cyber and real-world spaces

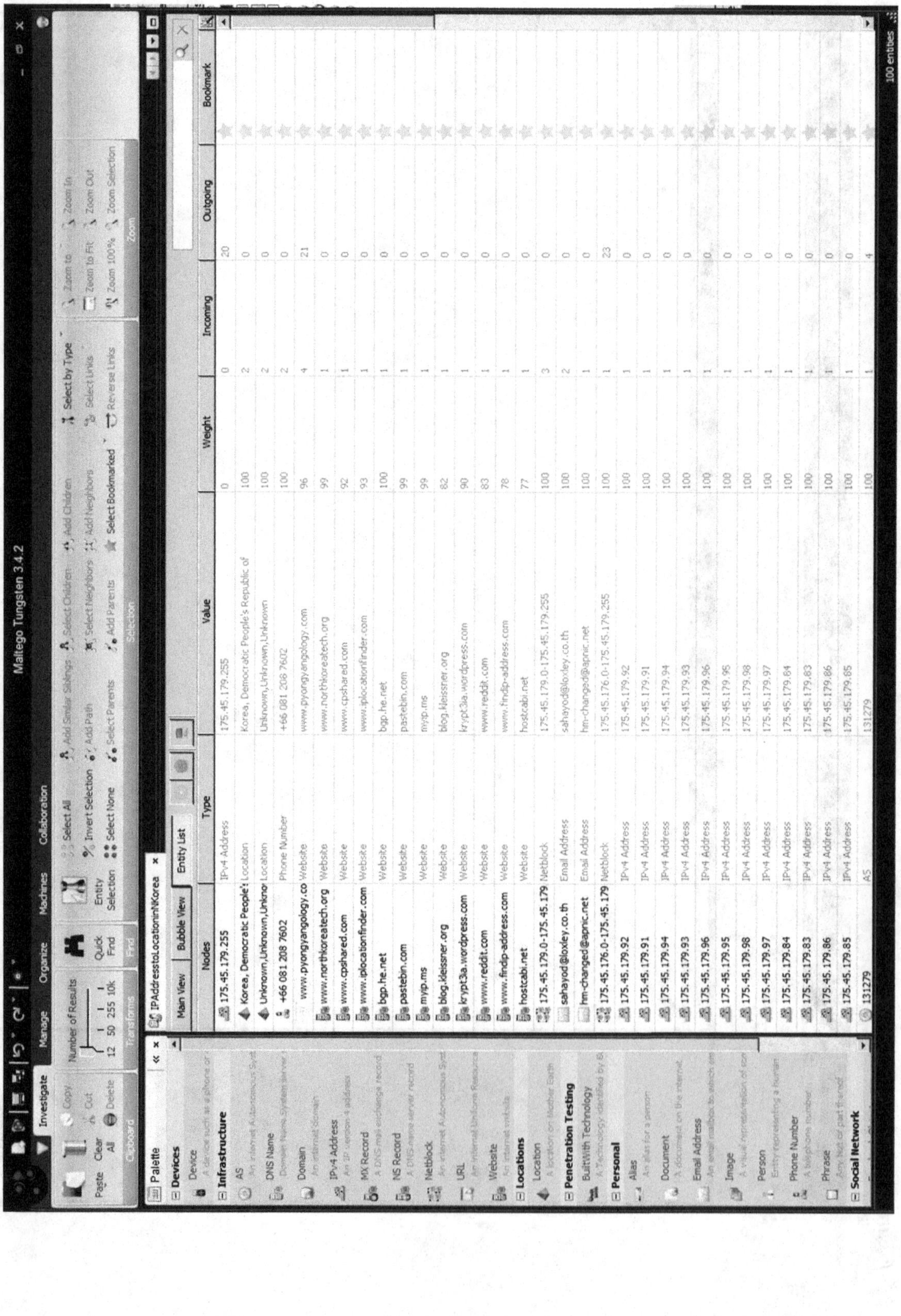

Figure 62. An IPv4 address linked to physical locations (further disambiguated) in an entity list view

media accounts. Sparse data about a target may quickly build to thick and in-depth data, and these may have to be pruned and sifted for informational value. In Figure 63, a web network was graphed for www.cdc;gov, which was found to include many ties to other sites and organizations globally. This extraction in Maltego Tungsten identified a variety of topics of interest for the site: hand hygiene, body mass index (BMI), asthma, and other health information. There were links to documents as well as images.

An NCapture (of NVivo 10) query of the CDC Twitter account @CDCgov resulted in a Tweetstream dataset of thousands of messages (2,728 recent records). The dataset contained the names of the various individuals communicating with @CDCgov, which meant that the data could be mapped as a social network of interacting accounts on Twitter around the @CDCgov account. There were time stamps on the messages. There were links to images and videos. Any of these may be content-analyzed for additional understanding and informational value.

When these were run through a word frequency count and mapped to a word cloud, various #hashtagged public health-based conversations were surfaced along with many of the issues of the day, as may be seen in Figure 65.

Formulating Leads for "Mayors" of Hashtags

One of the strengths of electronic social network analysis (E-SNA) applied to online conversations and phenomena is the ability to identify the so-called mayors of the hashtag (to borrow a term from sociologist and NodeXL-development team member Dr. Marc A. Smith). A "mayor" in the context of a hashtagged conversation is an individual or group that is a central figure in discussing a particular issue through a microblogging site (or an email network, or a wiki site, or a blogging site, etc.). The "mayor" is seen as someone who is highly connected and potentially quite knowledgeable as a proponent. E-SNA enables the identification of such important nodes with high "betweenness centrality" (structural positioning to capture a lot of the information moving through a social network because of high connectivity with others) and with high degree centrality, such as "in-degree" (incoming informational resources in terms of communications with other nodes) and "out-degree" (outgoing informational resources to other nodes). Without the work of social network analysis, the relative importance of such nodes would remain hidden or latent. In some types of research, the detailed observation of particular lead nodes may reveal rich information streams because of the potential influence of the individual given his / her / their structural placement in the network (on factors such as betweenness centrality, degree centrality, in-degree and out-degree, potential bridging functions, node-based descriptors, and other factors).

Such data captures also involve a Tweetstream set, which may be analyzed to understand what messaging is going on within the network discussing a particular issue. The discussions may be captured as either #hashtagged conversations or keyword searches (just the appearance of the keyword in the microblogging message). In Figure 66, the data visualization shows a network discussing #flight and the "mayors" with the highest connectivity in this context. (In some data extractions for both hashtagged conversations and keyword-based conversations, a researcher can run a half-dozen or more extractions before one with actual relationships may be found. In other words, on Twitter, with generic or common terms, there may be a lot of people engaging in thoughts and outgoing messages about the topic but without direct engagement with others on the issue in terms of replies-to or re-Tweeting, or other types of relating such as following or being followed. The timing also matters because if there is not a breaking or trending issue, then the levels of messaging from the present and through the prior seven days—which is what the Twitter API enables—then there may be low levels of public interest, with sometimes zero

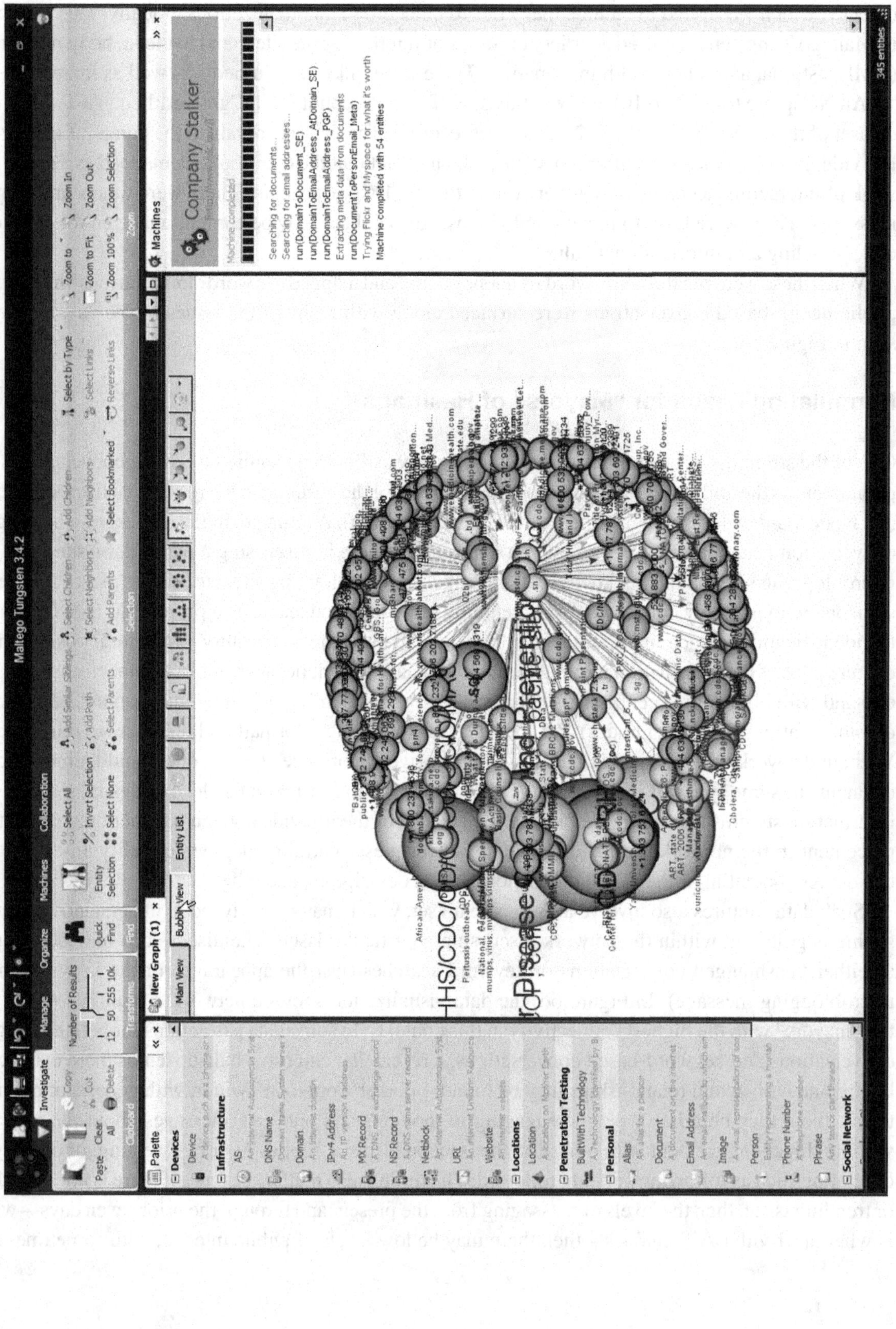

Figure 63. The web network around the www.cdc.gov Site (Maltego Tungsten™)

Figure 64. Data table view of the @CDCgov Tweetstream dataset in NVivo 10

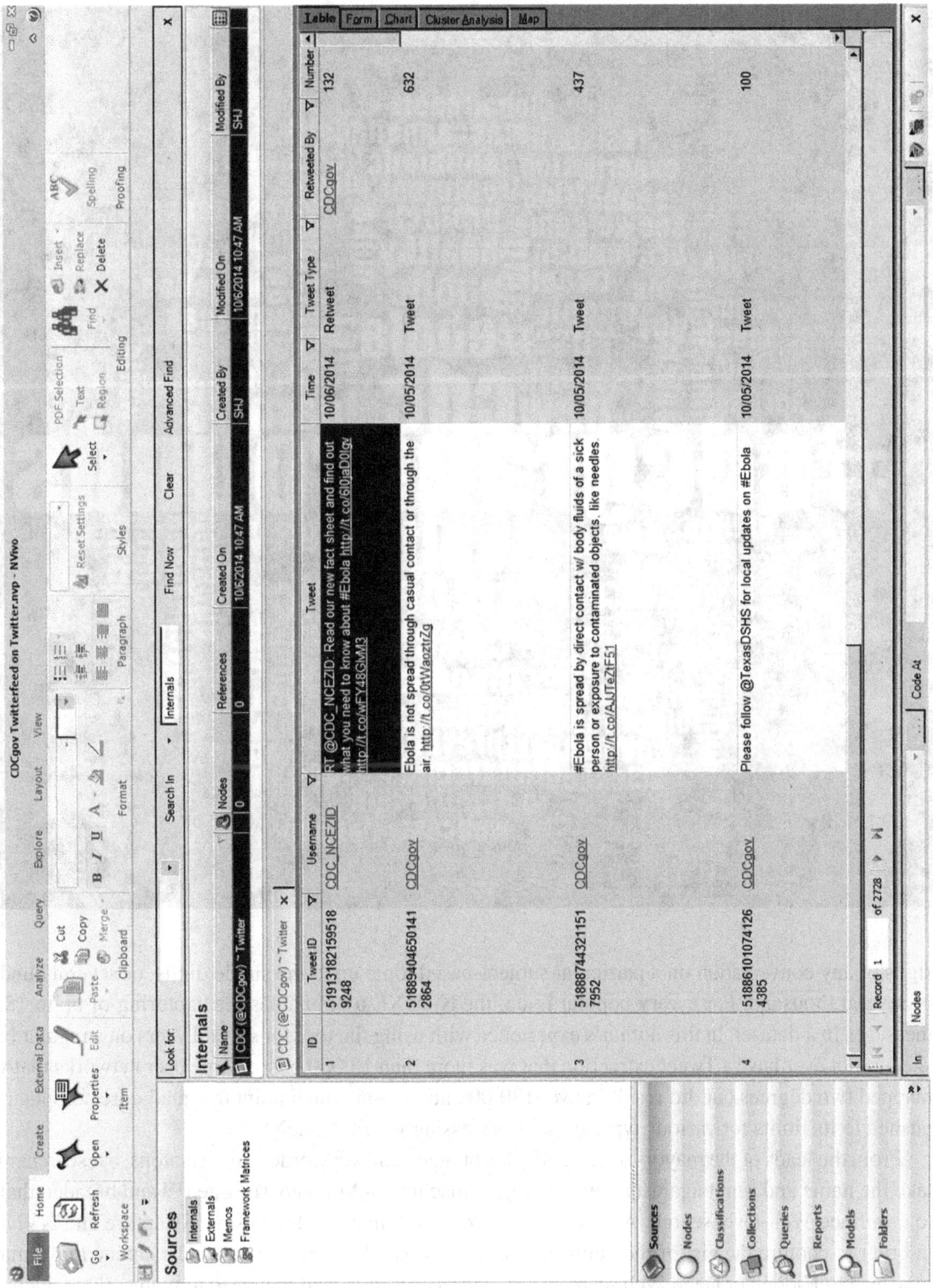

Figure 65. A word cloud from the @CDCgov user network Twitterstream

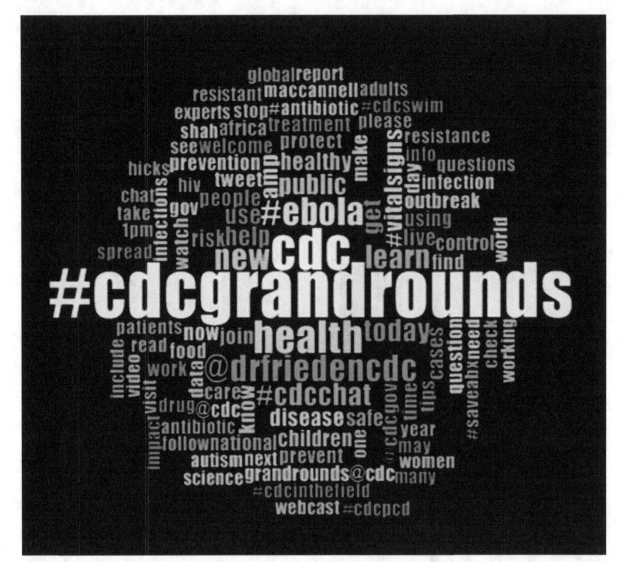

signs of any conversation on a particular subject-based topic up to the single digits, or several hundred, or several thousand. For a very popular issue, the NodeXL tool enables the capturing of up to 18,000 messages in a dataset. In this author's experience with using the tool for several years on a regular basis, she has not ever have a Tweet extraction that was more than 15,000 or so. Some user networks that were mapped two degrees out did result in over 120,000 nodes—at which point the quad-core computer was pushed to its limits for various types of data processing within NodeXL.)

From the leads of the mayors of particular hashtagged and keyworded conversatons, a researcher may take the name and run it against a Twitter Digger machine in Maltego Tungsten™ and broaden that out to a Surface Web-level search. A Tweetstream extraction may be done using NCapture and NVivo 10 in order to capture the gist of the online conversations based on that account. The chained information may lead to Hidden or Deep Web searches. In other words, one lead may lead to many others, including personally identifiable information (PII) to a verified individual and physical locations. .

Figure 66. #flight hashtag search on Twitter with some "mayors" of the hashtag conversation circled

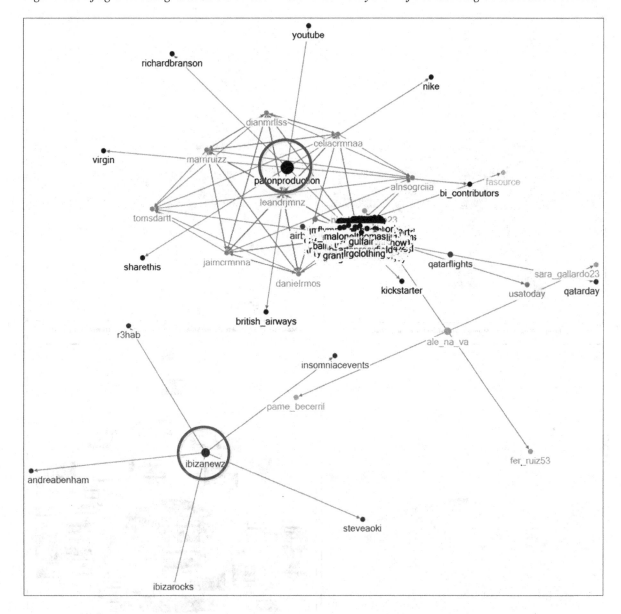

Visualizing Extracted Data in a Variety of Ways

Figure 67 shows four different versions of the graphed network based on an "ISIL" (aka "Islamic State of Iraq and the Levant") video network on YouTube. The vertexes (vertices) may be author accounts, UTC time codes, titles of the videos, or some form of text label combined with thumbnail images from those videos (or accounts). Extracted graphs may be visually depicted in a lot of different ways. In this case, only Network Overview, Discovery, and Exploration for Excel or "NodeXL" was used for the through-put. In actuality, the extracted datasets may be run through any number of other graphing tools (like Gephi, Pajek, UCINET, or others) to create different visualizations that may be more informative of certain data.

Figure 67. ISIL window network on YouTube (based on the Harel-Koren fast multiscale layout algorithm)

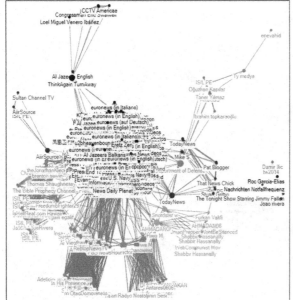

Main YouTube Accounts Sharing Videos about ISIL as Larger Nodes

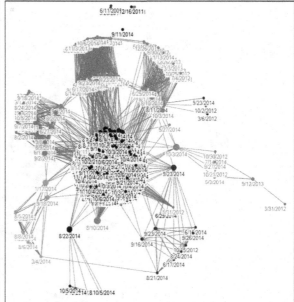

Main YouTube Accounts Sharing Videos about ISIL [vertexes as created date (in UTC)]

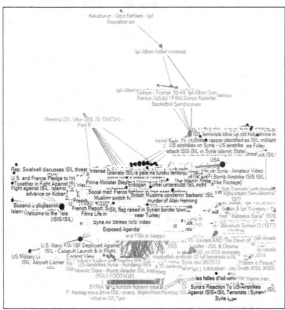

Main YouTube Accounts Sharing Videos about ISIL [vertexes as titles for gist]

Main YouTube Video Titles Sharing Videos about ISIL [vertexes as account images for gist]

Different layout algorithms will also enable researchers to view data in disparate ways and emerge with new insights.

Testing the Geolocational and Geoparsing Findings

This data extraction from social media platforms enables access to empirical in-world data that may provide insights for certain types of questions and types of knowing. As such, geolocational research has garnered recent attention from a broad range of researchers across the digital humanities and computational social sciences. Physical spaces are considered part of the situatedness and context of most of human phenomena. Geospatial technologies are used alongside qualitative and mixed methods techniques and technologies to acquire information and problem-solve for applied situations. This type of geolocation query (based on cyber information) is both structured (with *a priori* questions) and unstructured (inclusive of discovery learning). Some *a priori* questions could be:

- Where are the main servers for a multinational (or state-run, or local) company? What are the technological capabilities behind a particular website in terms of what tools are used in its building?
- What is the social network around a particular movement, and where are the various nodes located? When are the respective nodes most active?
- What are the main businesses with a cyber-presence in a particular location?
- Who are the "mayors" of a particular hashtag conversation, and what messages are they sending out, and where are they mainly located? (Are there non-locals trying to change up the dynamics of a social movement or demonstrations from remote locations?)
- Who is the "troll" behind an alias, and where is he or she or they located?
- Where are the locational hotspots where particular images or videos were shot and shared on content-sharing sites?
- What microblogging conversations are occurring based on a particular location?
- What types of digital contents are being shared about a particular location?
- What related tags are used with photos and videos shared around a particular location (from the local / micro all the way to the global / macro)?
- Who is behind a particular movement?

General data extractions and data queries may be conducted as a form of discovery. Some discovery-based questions could be:

- What are some themes that may be detected in an emergent way from this dataset?
- Are there certain patterns or trends in terms of how people communicate in certain regions?
- In generic word searches for related tags networks, are there patterns? Do such patterns align with any of the literature on the topic? Do the patterns align with any theories or models?
- Are there human research capabilities that may be enhanced by these tools—in a complementary way?

Clearly, research may entail both a mix of *a priori* designed questions and general discovery. It seems beneficial to run any possibly relevant branch, node, and data point to ground—in the multiple senses of that phrasing (to unambiguous facts as well as to physical locations).

Those who would use this process of online geolocation and geoparsing would do well to apply a high level of caution and a lot of qualifiers in making assertions. Social media platform accounts can be easily faked because of a low-level of account verification by many account providers or the reliance on "verified emails" (instead of going to multi-factor verification, such as IP addresses, name verification, and other more rigorous methods). The data in online sites may be provided by humans, robots, or cyborgs (humans and robots combined in an account). Many companies and organizations will try to manipulate their pageranks and their apparent popularity through manipulations, such as hiring individuals in the low-wage regions to create impressions of site usage or popularity through spamming or hiring programmers to create computer programs to do the same. Narrow-cast and broadcast communications are social performances, and as such, there is always a degree of egoistic subjectivity and posing—so messaging may be understood as such. There are limits to extracting data from social media platforms because there are built-in rate-limits to prevent individual users from dominating the (often-free) service. The software used for the extraction also involves limits. Then, too, there is forbidden or off-limits data which may not be seeable through a query from a public space.

Even if a full dataset could be pulled, geodata tends to be sparse. As one example, the geolocational data related to Twitter's microblogging set is about 1% to 1.5% of Tweets. The 98.5% to 99% of such messages are untagged. With growing savvy about the risks of mobility traces with tools such as Creepy and others gaining public awareness, many have chosen to silence their locational indicators on their mobile devices and to forgo the use of locational apps, which may mean a functionally impenetrable silence about location (except through more privileged means of analysis, such as through government and law enforcement powers). Geolocational information from social media platforms tends to be noisy, particularly if the data is "volunteered geographic information" (human-provided) vs. machine-reported. The "folksonomy" aspect of human-reported data means that there may be mistaken reporting; there may be intentional misreporting (such as people asserting that they're Tweeting from Mars). The noise-to-signal ratio may be quite high particularly if there are limited data extractions, limited usages of particular software tools and limited social media platforms, and limited analysis of the data.

Also, it is important to consider how people behave to better understand how to interpret the data. For example, if one uses an area code to a cell phone number as a way to tie to a location, that may not be truly indicative of place. After all, people may keep a cell phone number for many years even long after they've moved from a particular location. Using one data point alone is never advisable, and in this case, it can lead to very inaccurate conclusions.

Ways to shore up data. Even at this very moment with the tools available, there are ways to strengthen geolocation data.

1. **Asking the right questions.** The types of geolocational and other information available through such data extractions are of a type. The questions asked have to be somewhat aligned with the research methods for the answering of the questions or the testing of certain hypotheses.

2. **Understanding the strengths and weaknesses of the respective tools.** Use the software tools correctly. Most are complex, with encapsulated complexity. Test data extractions against known information to see how accurate the tool is (in a variety of settings and with a variety of parameters). Have individuals who do and don't know the real-world "answers" already run the tool to see what is knowable based on user awareness. Different data settings will result in different data outcomes. How the researcher prunes relational ties is also important to disambiguate the dataset and the findings. Indiscriminate pruning means that the researcher is losing potentially relevant information; on the other hand, non-pruning of data will mean that the dataset will contain plenty of noisy and potentially irrelevant and misleading data.

3. **Understanding the strengths and weaknesses of the respective social media platforms.** It is helpful to know "who" is delivered via the various social media platforms and what sorts of direct messaging, digital contents, and metadata may be expected from them. These datapoints are constantly changing, so the information will have to be updated regularly from reputable sources.

4. **Multiplying data extractions at different time periods…and with continuous / dynamic time instead of slice-in-time / static time.** Conduct multiple data extraction runs on the same data set

at different times of the day or week or month (or other time period) using the same tools. Another variation on this may be to run data extractions continuously for a certain time period for dynamic data extractions. This is a fairly publicly accessible capability although it may entail some cost (some social media platforms enable only commercial access for some types of their data). The extracted data may look quite different in terms of trends or messaging manifestations over time. (Both Maltego Tungsten™ and NodeXL have some limited capabilities for continuous data extractions. Those capabilities are beyond the focus of this particular chapter.)

5. **Multiplying data extractions using different software tools.** Conduct multiple data extraction runs on the same data set using different tools at the same time. Ensure that the data parameters used in the data extractions are the same across tools. Compare the results. What are the similarities? What are the differences? Why might these differences exist?

6. **Multiplying data extractions using different social media platforms.** Conduct data extractions from a range of social media platforms, and understand what demographics are represented in each social media platform.

7. **Multiplying types of data extractions.** As has been shown earlier, there are a range of types of data that may include informational value. All the following may offer insights about location: the contents of Tweetstreams; shared images; shared video; websites; online documents; server details; telephone numbers; email addresses, and other information. All of these may "transform" to other data and resolve to physical addresses. The close contacts of a target individual or entity may reveal important locational information. In other words, location may be approached in a variety of ways through online information.

8. **Testing extracted data.** Test geolocational data extractions against known information to see how accurate the tool is. What information has been left off from the data extraction? What inaccurate data has been left in from the data extraction? (It is important to see both false positives / mentions and false negatives / non-mentions.)

9. **Multiplying data points tested for consensus or dissensus.** Ensure that there are a range of datasets and datapoints, to test if there is consensus or dissensus to location(s) based on the majority of the information. How well does the online data test against the real-world and physical space? Datasets should be visualized and queried in a variety of ways. While social media platform information is often considered "big data," what is generally extracted is not an n = all, and it is not comprehensive. It is actually a kind of electronic "convenience sample."

10. **Applying rigorous analysis.** Analyze the research findings in breadth (the network, the main themes in microblogging Tweetsets) and depth (close-in views of clusters, branches, and nodes; entity analysis). Work to actively disconfirm the initial (and later) findings. What evidence is there that the findings are untrue? Has all relevant information been brought to bear?

11. **Extracting complementary data from the Deep / Hidden Web.** Draw information from the Deep Web as well. Try to locate identified individuals to real names and real locations.

12. **Acknowledging the level of certitude (or lack thereof) related to the extracted data.** Make sure not to over-claim or over-assert. Be transparent in describing the processes used in the data extractions—particularly where the data visualizations are used for analytical purposes and not just general examples or visual interest. Qualifying the data may be helpful.

In some ways, it may be difficult to resolve all ambiguity online to something that is absolutely validated. The methods and tools mentioned here provide some observational windows, but outside the windows are plenty of unseen information. However, as the data extraction tools and human methods for data extraction both improve, these geolocational and geoparsing results may become more accurate and more applicable to direct in-world problem-solving. That said, having a focus on geolocational information helps focus and parse some online data searches.

Amplifying the Value of Geolocational Data

Once some fairly solid geolocational data has been extracted from online sources, it may help to add value to that locational data (whether it is structured or unstructured, deeply precise or somewhat imprecise). One way to add value is to extract additional relevant information based on that location. What is considered relevant will depend on the particular analytical context (which would be unique to the context). Earlier on in this chapter, relevant locational data was cited such as demographic, government, business, and other types of social data. Weather and climate information may also be captured to a location—and often well into the past for long-term trends analysis. There are plenty of other types of available datasets, made available by corporations as well as government entities.

Also, additional physical location-based social media extractions may be based on topic, time period, user accounts, or hashtags. In other words, a point may be selected on a map and related social media and other information tagged to that locale may be extracted from a number of social media sites. In other words, just identifying geolocational data does not mean that the social media platforms have served their purpose. The geolocations themselves may be applied to the platforms to extract further data. Geographical information may be indexed by geographic information retrieval (GIR) systems for further analysis—such as ranking geographic information by relevance and enabling queries based on locational metadata.

Finally, place or physical location is not particularly deterministic. Place is a partial fact only. How researchers use this information will determine the value of that data. It is important to properly qualify the relevance / irrelevance of the locational information for its proper place in research.

FUTURE RESEARCH DIRECTIONS

The ability to tie probable physical locations to digital artifacts involves some guesswork at this point, even with tools like Maltego Tungsten™, NodeXL, and NVivo 10 (with its NCapture plug-in for two browsers). This work involves geolocation of Web-originated information, the refinement of that information to improve proximity, geocoding / geoparsing unstructured data to structured location references, and creating maps on the geospatial Web and elsewhere. This work involves the need for basic technological savvy, digital literacy, and analytical thinking—to link digital data to physical spaces. This process involves the ability to extract microblogging messages and images and videos through location-based searches (often through the affordances of the application programming interfaces (APIs) linked to social media platforms (through either command line data extraction requests to the Web servers or the use of middleware tools).

In terms of direct future research, some researchers may explore these and related tools for additional value-added capabilities in data extraction, data de-noising, data mining, data visualization and graphing, geographical mapping, and the application of data overlays. In more advanced work, computer scientists may be able to extract more information from both the Surface Web and the Deep or Hidden Web. It is hoped that geographical data will become more accurate on the social media platforms and that there will be improved ways to extracted related social media messaging and digital contents.

CONCLUSION

That online phenomena is grounded in the real and the physical is not the insight per se. Rather, it is just how much geolocational information is lightly embedded in online contents and how broadly this information may be accessed. This chapter highlights some of the present-day capabilities of researchers to capture data from the Surface Web and social media platforms to geolocate online data to physical spaces. These techniques may be applied to physical locations -> cyber data, and vice versa, and in any number of transformative directions. Also, this capability may be applied to the entire continuum from macro to meso to micro-scale issues. "Cyber" may be linked to actual physical spaces (and physical spaces to cyber "spaces") for enriched and grounded understandings.

ACKNOWLEDGMENT

The author first presented on this topic at the Summer Institute on Distance Learning and Instructional Technology (SIDLIT) in Overland Park, Kansas, in August 2014. The title of that presentation was "Using Maltego Tungsten™ to Explore the Cyber-Physical Confluence in Geolocation." A slideshow on this presentation is available on SlideShare at http://www.slideshare.net/ShalinHaiJew/using-maltego-tungsten-to-explore-cyberphysical-confluence-in-geolocation. The author would like to express gratitude to the few audience members who attended for both their enthusiasm and skepticism. Also, thanks to Kansas State University for funding the use of the research tool, Maltego Tungsten™.

REFERENCES

Andrejevic, M. (2007). iSpy: Surveillance and Power in the Interactive Era. Lawrence: University Press of Kansas.

Anger over hidden commercialized tracking devices. (2014, Oct. 11). *CBS News*. Retrieved from http://www.cbsnews.com/videos/anger-over-hidden-commercialized-tracking-devices/

Backstrom, L., Sun, E., & Marlow, C. (2010). Find me if you can: Improving geographical preduction with social and spatial proximity. In the proceedings of *WWW 2010*. Raleigh, North Carolina.

Blum, A. (2012). *Tubesd: A Journey to the Center of the Internet*. New York: Harper Collins.

Brunty, J., & Helenek, K. (2012) Social Media Investigation for Law Enforcement. In L.S. Miller, Series Ed. Amsterdam: Elsevier. 41–70. Retrieved from http://www.sciencedirect.com/science/book/9781455731350

Cheung, A. S. Y. (2014). Location privacy: The challenges of mobile service devices. *Computer Law & Security Report, 30*(1), 41–54. doi:10.1016/j.clsr.2013.11.005

Clare, K. (2013). The essential role of place within the creative industries: Boundaries, networks and play. *Cities (London, England), 34*, 52–57. doi:10.1016/j.cities.2012.05.009

Claval, P. (2004). At the heart of the cultural approach in geography: Thinking space. *GeoJournal, 60*(4), 321–328. doi:10.1023/B:GEJO.0000042967.76392.93

Elwood, S., & Leszczynski, A. (2011). Privacy, reconsidered: New representations, data practices, and the geoweb. *Geoforum, 42*(1), 6–15. doi:10.1016/j.geoforum.2010.08.003

Gambs, S., Killijian, M.-O., & Nuñez del Prado Cortez, M. (2014). De-anaonymization attack on geolocated data. *Journal of Computer and System Sciences, 80*(8), 1597–1614. doi:10.1016/j.jcss.2014.04.024

Garcia-Gavilanes, R., Mejova, Y., & Quercia, D. (2014). Twitter ain't without frontiers: Economic, social, and cultural boundaries in international communication. In the proceedings of CSCW 2014 Geographic Distance. Feb. 15 – 19, 2014. Baltimore, Maryland.

Hai-Jew, S. (2013, May). Maltego Radium™: Mapping Network Ties and Identities across the Internet. In the *Conference on Higher Education Computing in Kansas*. Pittsburg State University, Pittsburg, Kansas. Retrieved from http://www.slideshare.net/ShalinHaiJew/maltego-radium-mapping-network-ties-and-identities-across-the-internet

Hai-Jew, S. (2014, Aug.) Using Maltego Tungsten™ to Explore the Cyber-Physical Confluence in Geolocation. In the proceedings of the Summer Institute on Distance Learning and Instructional Technology Retrieved from http://www.slideshare.net/ShalinHaiJew/using-maltego-tungsten-to-explore-cyberphysical-confluence-in-geolocation

Holeton, R. (1998). *Composing Cyberspace: Identity, Community, and Knowledge in the Electronic Age*. Boston: McGraw Hill.

Internet in North Korea." (2014, Sept. 12) Wikipedia. Retrieved from http://en.wikipedia.org/wiki/Internet_in_North_Korea#IPv4_ranges

Jakobsson, M. (2012). *The Death of the Internet*. Hoboken: John Wiley & Sons. doi:10.1002/9781118312551

Johnson, R., Kovács, B., & Vicsek, A. (2012). A comparison of email networks and off-line social networks: A study of a medium-sized bank. *Social Networks, 34*(4), 462–469. doi:10.1016/j.socnet.2012.02.004

Lampoltshammer, T. J., Kounadi, O., Sitko, I., & Hawelka, B. (2014). Sensing the public's reaction to crime news using the 'Links Correspondence Method.'. *Applied Geography, 52*, 57–55. doi:10.1016/j.apgeog.2014.04.016 PMID:25843991

Liu, B., Yuan, Q., Cong, G., & Xu, D. (2014). *Where your photo is taken: Geolocation prediction for social images. In the proceedings of the ASIS&T 2014*. Wiley Online Library; doi:10.1002/asi.23050

My Korea Info Directory. http://my-korea.info/directory.html

Naaman, M. (2011). Geographic information from georeferenced social media data. *SIGSPATIAL Special, 3*(2), 54–61. doi:10.1145/2047296.2047308

Ponds, R., van Oort, F., & Frenken, K. (2007). The geographical and institutional proximity of research collaboration. *Papers in Regional Science, 86*(3), 423–443. doi:10.1111/j.1435-5957.2007.00126.x

Saxenian, A. (1994). Regional Advantage: Culture and Competition. Boston: Harvard University Press.

Senese, P. D., & Vasquez, J. A. (2008). *The Steps to War: An Empirical Study*. Princeton: Princeton University Press.

Shipley, T., & Bowker, A. (2014). Investigating Social Networking Sites. In *Shipley and Bowker's Investigating Internet Crimes: An Introduction to Solving Crimes in Cyberspace*. Amsterdam: Elsevier. doi:10.1016/B978-0-12-407817-8.00014-X

Torrens, P. M. (2010). Geography and computational social science. *GeoJournal, 75*(2), 133–148. doi:10.1007/s10708-010-9361-y

Tucker, P. (2014). *The Naked Future: What Happens in a World that Anticipates your Every Move?* New York: Current.

ADDITIONAL READING

Andrejevic, M. (2007). iSpy: Surveillance and Power in the Interactive Era. Lawrence: University Press of Kansas.

Blum, A. (2012). *Tubes: A Journey to the Center of the Internet*. New York: Harper Collins.

Tucker, P. (2014). *The Naked Future: What Happens in a World that Anticipates your Every Move?* New York: Current, A Penguin Random House Company.

KEY TERMS AND DEFINITIONS

Alias: An assumed identity.

Anonymity: Temporal, ephemeral or partial hiding of a real identity (linked to a personally identifiable individual).

App (Application): A program or piece of software.

Attack: An aggressive action.

Authornym: The use of a name under which a person publishes.

Betweenness Centrality: A node's connectivity in a network based on the number of shortest paths from all its nodes (vertices) to all others that link through the focal node.

Chokepoint: A geographical feature in which traffic is blocked or congested, which creates a vulnerability (and the possible of interception or compromise).

Convenience Sampling: The collection of data from an easy-to-access group of individuals in order to acquire an impression or quick information (often with limited generalizability), not often considered a rigorous research approach.

Cyber-Physical Confluence: The overlap between online and offline worlds.

Degree Centrality: The number of nodes connecting to a focal node in an undirected graph, and both in-degree (number of nodes following a focal node) and out-degree (number of nodes followed by the focal node) in a directed graph; an indicator of node connectedness and potential influence.

Disambiguation: Achieving a degree of clarity (or a clear "signal") through the removal of "noise" and other potentially ambiguating factors.

Domain Footprinting: The identification of the technological understructure ("digital footprint") to a particular Web domain (such as .com).

Doxing: Documenting information about a person as part of opposition research or another form of "attack".

Ego Neighborhood: The one-degree network of a focal node which includes the "alters" or nodes in direct-tie relationship to the focal node.

Emergent: Coming into being.

Entity List: A table or listing of captured data from the Surface Web underlying the data visualizations in Maltego Tungsten™.

Exchangeable Image File Format (Exif) Data: Metadata about digital information (imagery, audio, or video) that may include the conditions of the information capture and the physical location.

Extraction Sequence: The steps taken in order to achieve the acquiring and download of particular data

Focal Node: A main entity of interest in a network graph.

Geocode (Or "Forward Geocoding"): The application of structured location references—such as postal addresses, land parcels, or numerical coordinates—to unstructured data like place names (or more noisy spatial references).

Geolocation: Identifying the geographical location of an account, person, device, or other entity based on Internet- and Web-originated information.

Geographical Information System (GIS): A computer system managing geographical data.

Geoparsing: Extracting and resolving the meaning of physical locations in unstructured data (such as textual data) by assigning geographic identifiers.

Geosocial Network: A social network based on geographic services (geocoding, geotagging, locational awareness, and locational ambient signaling).

Geospatial Web (Geoweb): A computer network combining locational data displayed on a spatial 2D or 3D map.

GIS (Geographical Information System) Coordinate: The measures used to identify physical space in the world in three dimensions (on the x, y, and z axes).

Hashtag: An alphanumeric label for online text messages and digital contents prefaced by a hash (#) symbol.

Hashtag Conversation: The chain of related messages on microblogging sites indicated by a #hashtag (a pound sign followed by alphanumeric sequences to label conversations).

Holdership: The ability to maintain the consistent use of something.

Inference Attack: The extrapolation of meaning based on logic-based analysis of data and observations.

Internet Protocol (Ip) Address: A number representing a device on a computer network.

Keyword: A focal term.

Keyword Conversation: The extraction of microblogging messages which include a particular keyword or selected keywords to find topic-based conversations.

Latency (Hiddenness): Concealed, not yet developed.

Latitude (In The Geographical Sense): An indicator of physical location north or south of the earth's equator, expressed as degrees and minutes.

Locational Information: Any sort of structured or unstructured data that references a physical location on Earth.

Longitude: An indicator of physical location east or west of the meridian at Greenwich, England, expressed as degrees and minutes.

"Machine": A sequence of steps taken to extract information from the Surface Web (in Maltego Tungsten™).

Machine Analysis: The use of computational power to extract meaning from data.

Macro: Large-scale, web-scale.

Macros: A computerized command that activates a sequence of other actions (that were encapsulated in the initial command).

Meso: Intermediate-scale.

Micro: Granular, small, close-in level.

Network Graphs: A 2D visualization consisting of nodes and links that indicate the entities and their inter-relationships and functions in a system.

Nonymous: Publicly known, accurately named.

Open-Source Intelligence (Or "Osint"): The use of publicly available information to learn about a target.

Oppo (Opposition) Research: Surveillance and other investigations by an opposing force or adversary in order to compromise an individual or group or other entity.

Pastebin: A website to which people upload texts for sharing and archival.

Penetration (Pen) Testing: A method (using a variety of means) for detecting network vulnerabilities.

Personally Identifiable Information (PII): Information that links back (verifiably) to an actual individual.

Predictivity: The ability to forecast or project into the future.

Proximity: In close physical relationship to something, nearness.

Pseudonym: The exclusive use of an alias.

Pseudonymity: Untraceable long-term anonymity, exclusive use of a pseudonym over an extended time period.

Re-Identification: The enforcement of an inescapable identity and non-discretionary revelation.

Scrape: To extract information from a website or online data repository through automated, brute-force means with or without the permission of the site owner or publisher.

Social Awareness Streams (SASes): The ongoing status updates through microblogging, social networking messaging, and locational data that may provide streams of "social awareness" data.

Social Media Platform: A Web-based service that enables people to socialize, inter-communicate, organize, and share through digital file sharing, text-messaging, and other means.

Social Networking Site: A designed online space that enables people to exchange various types of digital information about themselves and others and to interact around shared interests.

Spatiality: Pertaining to physical space.

Spillover: A repercussion from one sphere to another.

Structure Mining: The analysis of relationships or relational topographies to understand social or other dynamics.

Surface Web: The publicly accessible web built on the http: protocol and accessible through search engines and Web browsers.

Time Stamp: An indicator of when something occurred.

Traceability: The situation in which at least one intermediary knows the actual identity of an individual behind a pseudonym or an anonymity context.

"Transform": The reversioning of input information of one type being output as multiple other types of information in Maltego Tungsten™ (such as the resolving of an alias to possible personally identifiable information).

Weak (Thin) Ties: Brief, superficial, transient, or low-degree relationships, such as the relational difference between long-time friends (with strong ties) and brief acquaintances (with weak ties); node relationships with few connectors (including low-frequency interactivity).

ZIPcode: The "Zone Improvement Plan" numbers that are added to a city and state to aid in mail routing (usually consisting of 5 – 9 numbers).

Section 6
Real-World Cases in Innovative Multimedia Applications

Chapter 13

Rolling NVivo 10 out to a University's Research Community:
Live Trainings and a Semantic Web–Friendly E–Book

Shalin Hai-Jew
Kansas State University, USA

ABSTRACT

At Kansas State University, there has been a concentrated effort to evolve the institution into one of the nation's top 50 research public universities. One small part of that involves the rollout of NVivo to the university's faculty, staff, and graduate students. By the second year of the site license, the campus was on its own to provide training. This effort involved multiple live face-to-face (F2F) trainings and the use of a multimedia e-book. "Using NVivo: An Unofficial and Unauthorized Primer" (http://scalar.usc.edu/works/using-nvivo-an-unofficial-and-unauthorized-primer/index) was written over a several week period (hyper-fast agile development) and released on the Scalar platform in Fall Semester 2014. This chapter addresses how a designed e-book, built on a Semantic Web-friendly platform, harnesses the power of multimedia, digital repositories, the Surface Web, and crowd-sourced feedback.

INTRODUCTION

"By 2025, Kansas State University will be recognized as one of the nation's Top 50 Public Research Universities." -- The visionary goal of the "K-State 2025" plan

At Kansas State University, the thematic goals of the 2025 plan include the following: research, scholarly and creative activities, and discovery; undergraduate education experience; graduate scholarly experience; engagement, extension, outreach, and service; faculty and staff; facilities and infrastructure; and athletics. The descriptor for the first goal reads: "Create a culture of excellence that results in flourishing, sustainable, and widely recognized research, scholarly and creative activities, and discovery in

DOI: 10.4018/978-1-4666-8696-0.ch013

a variety of disciplines and endeavors that benefit society as a whole." Across the goals are common elements, including technology. Universities that advocate faculty research need to provide the necessary technologies to support that work (Goodwin, Kozleski, Muth, Rhodes, & White, 2006).

On a campus with a main focus on quantitative research in the traditional "hard sciences," it can be difficult to garner sufficient resources, the political will, and the knowledge and skill sets to support the work of researchers who use qualitative and mixed methods research approaches. Often, the larger-sized grants come from funding agencies that focus on core hard sciences. Qualitative and mixed methods research on the campus may bolster research in the hard sciences, or it may be stand-alone, with costs covered as part of the faculty pay or small on-campus grants. In such a context, there is often much less credibility given to non-experimental non-bench-method types of research.

The "K-State 2025" plan helped coalesce administrator support around purchasing a multi-year site license for NVivo, a state-of-the-art data analysis tool for use by university faculty, staff, and graduate students. The initial contract with QSR International, the company that makes NVivo, involved six webinar trainings for the use of the tool in the first academic year (2013-2014). Attendance to the initial sessions in Fall 2013 were robust, with 20 – 30 attendees in the physical room and maybe a half-dozen online; however, the enthusiasm for the trainings dwindled, and by the end of the academic year, there were only a handful of attendees, and the last scheduled session was cancelled because no one showed up at the training even though the researchers who used Macintosh computers had expressed enthusiasm for having a research tool to use native to their machines. What were actual campus needs then in terms of support for NVivo? Was there a gap between felt needs and actual needs? Whatever the case, how could these needs be met?

A needs assessment. There was one course for graduate students on how to use this software tool, but the training was often specific to the discipline. Another department had lost a faculty member who had moved on to another institution of higher education. There were limited pockets of expertise. There were two small graduate student computer labs on which this software was installed. Suffice it to say that the numbers of those who had installed the software were small particularly relative to the capacity in the site license, which was to be expected, given the software tool's high learning curve. However, for the site license to be worth the cost, it was important to ensure that it had as wide use as possible. There had to be support for the tool's use without any trainer over-stepping into the realm of faculty serving as doctoral advisors or contravening the teachings of various disciplines (each with their evolved research methodologies, ideologies, theories, and ranges of attitudes about technologies). The complexity of addressing such histories and understandings would be well beyond the purview of a technology training.

From the beginning, the university had to take responsibility for integrating usage of the software tool into the research community on campus. Initially, this depended on the paid webinar trainings and the thin local resources at the various departments (there were pockets of expertise in a number of tools, with only limited transferability between software tools). There was not a natural bureaucratic position for this endeavor. The individual who ended up negotiating the contract and collecting funding came out of the Information Technology part of campus, namely, an instructional designer (the author)—and it ended up that this individual took the lead on the training. She also wrote the e-book in order to broaden the breadth and depth of expertise on campus. This was strategic, in order not to hold the "NVivo portfolio" too tightly—because of a range of other continuing professional commitments. [To elaborate, there were challenges with the instructional designer role. One faculty member handed off multiple graduate students for customized trainings, without any prior consultation with the instructional designer or formal request. Likewise, department administrators did the same for some of their faculty members and graduate students. Instructional design hours are generally paid for on grant-funded projects and are arrived at by discussions between research principal investigators and the supervisor for the instructional design team.]

Early on, there were some clear goals for the training, given the political context:

- The IT-based NVivo training had to be focused only on the research tool and its capabilities, not research theories, not methods, or anything else related to the research so as not to overstep bounds or to create any sense of exclusivity regarding the use of the tool ("the tool can only be used for this --- type of study")
- The trainings would have to focus on rigorous research practices which apply across a range of research fields (clear definitions, accurate and thorough citations, saturation-depth reviews of the literature, Institutional Review Board oversight for any human subjects research, transparent research methodology, strong logics and reasoning, fair crediting, and so on)

The two main goals are superficially paradoxical: focus on the data analysis technology alone but also encourage rigorous research practices (which are heterogeneous)—without limiting the use of the tool to particular types of research. For the training to have any credibility, the trainer would have to have a sense of the use of the tool in the larger context and the professional standards of research, presenting, and publishing, but this information would have to be soft-pedaled and only brought in as necessary. The trainer would also have to know of the tool's functionalities in comparison to the functionalities of competitor tools—as much as reasonably possible. Also, how NVivo could be used with other software programs would be important: for example, NVivo's data visualizations would be enhanced using Adobe Photoshop or Visio; NVivo's datasets would be enhanced with the use of Excel and Access; and so on.

By Y2 (Fall 2014), the campus had taken on providing campus-wide face-to-face (F2F) trainings and had launched a multimedia e-book to support the campus effort at developing a strong base of continuing expertise in both NVivo and diverse qualitative, mixed methods, and multi-methodology research practices in the various disciplines. The strategy involved event-based trainings to publicize the software tool's availability using the official *K-State Today* newsletter. The actual events were scheduled in a technology room in Hale Library that was reserved for the two-hour presentation and for the half-hour prior and after to encourage participants to make professional connections and possibly support each other's endeavors. There were customized trainings for faculty (often one-on-one) and graduate students (in small groups). All face-to-face trainings were done with the live software tool and a real-world project (with some additional add-ons to demonstrate particular additional functionalities of the tool). If client data was part of the training, the data stayed on the client machine and was handled there—to protect the client's data. Oftentimes, the hurdles were simple and small ones. One faculty member said she spent 12 hours trying to upload a dataset into her project. A graduate student could not create coherence in her coding, in part because she was coding in short word snippets without semantic meaning; when she returned to the data, she could not recall what she met with certain of her own codes.

At the time of the first F2F training in September 2014, a multimedia e-book was also rolled out. "Using NVivo: An Unofficial and Unauthorized Primer" (Hai-Jew, 2014). As a primer, this book was designed to be an elementary reference for those using different functionalities of the software tool. The online book addressed the basic elements of the software tool in the early pages but offered advancement through the more complex data queries and such functionalities later on. As such, it served as a self-training system, designed for users to acquire additional knowledge and capabilities in using the tool. The multimedia aspects of the tool include the uses of text, imagery, videos, an interactive digital photo album, an interactive glossary of terms, and dynamic data visualizations. The building of "Using NVivo…" on a platform (Scalar) that is designed for the Semantic Web enables a much broader potential use of the contents of the e-book primer (because of the added machine findability of the contents and the "atomizing" of the various content elements into disaggregated parts that may be used in other contexts).

At the training, there were slips of paper handed out with the uniform resource locator (URL) on it to encourage use of the resource. The thinking was that having a widely accessible reference would assist the work of busy university professors, graduate students, faculty librarians, and others. The electronic book itself was designed as a "primer," which meant that its users could use it to start their projects and to slowly acquire the more complex aspects of the tool. It was designed to minimize frustration, with step-by-step directions, in basic English—but also using the technology terms defined by the tool. The e-book also involved a few references to outside events affecting qualitative, mixed methods, and multi-methodology research—such as the interest in the archival of qualitative datasets (Cliggett, 2013). A main focus was to ensure that users would not at any time lose coherence or lose "their place" in the use of the tool, given its many capabilities (and requisite complexity).

In Figure 1, the image shows a 1.5 degree article network (linked articles) of the Multimedia article on Wikipedia. A one-degree network shows the direct links between the article to other articles on Wikipedia. A 1.5 degree network shows not only the "alters" of the focal node or its direct neighbor-hood but also the likelihood of connectivity between the "alters" to each other (a form of transitivity). A two-degree crawl includes the focal node, its direct ties or "alters" (in an ego neighborhood), and the respective ego neighborhood of those alters. It is helpful to think of the graph in a core-periphery way, with those at the center closer to the target or focal article and those on the outer periphery as farther away because of fewer ties or links or edges. The graph indicates some of the elements that comprise multimedia. It also suggests some relationships to innovations and even a "postliterate" society." It is important when considering such graphs to realize that the links in Wikipedia are human-created, and there are varying levels of professionalism and expertise, with many of the ties potentially "folk" ones or based on popular thinking vs. professional thinking. The graph, as one form of multimedia, serves to inform and engage readers; elicit reader insights, and provide visual interest and topical emphasis.

This chapter then provides an overview of this endeavor to roll out NVivo to Kansas State University through the strategic use of multimedia in both a live face-to-face training setting and in an electronic book built on the Scalar platform. This work provides transferable insights from a unique use case.

REVIEW OF THE LITERATURE

The academic literature itself is fairly sparse on QSR International, the company that first created NUD-IST (non-numerical unstructured data indexing, searching, and theorizing) the precursor software tool) and then NVivo. A search of its presence on the Surface Web, using Maltego Tungsten, shows a broad range of connections across a range of geographical domains. This finding of its HTTP network does reflect its front-runner status as one of the leading CAQDAS (computer-assisted qualitative data analysis software) tools on the market today (if not the leading tool).

Figure 2 was created from a "company stalker" machine crawl of the site at http://www.qsrinterna-tional.com/. This view shows the domains from a number of regions on a number of continents, and it also shows the company's role in both academia and in professional realms (.edu and .com). Figure 3 shows a close-in bubble view of the same data extraction from the Surface Web.

Figure 1. "Multimedia" article network on Wikipedia (1 deg)

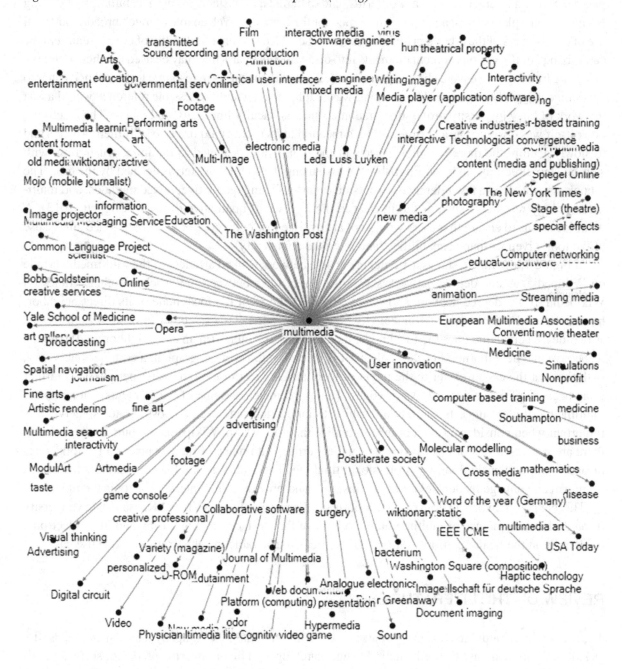

Figure 4 shows the central role of the @qsrint account on Twitter, given its centrality and its high degree. It is clearly in the interests of the company to build a strong virtual community of users online and to support their efforts through social media, including a microblogging site as popular as Twitter. In that spirit, it is important to map the user account's direct "ego neighborhood" on Twitter.

The @qsrint social network depicted in Figure 4 shows another of its accounts (@qsrsup likely for QSR Support). It shows connections to social media sites. There are connections with universities, businesses, groups, and individuals.

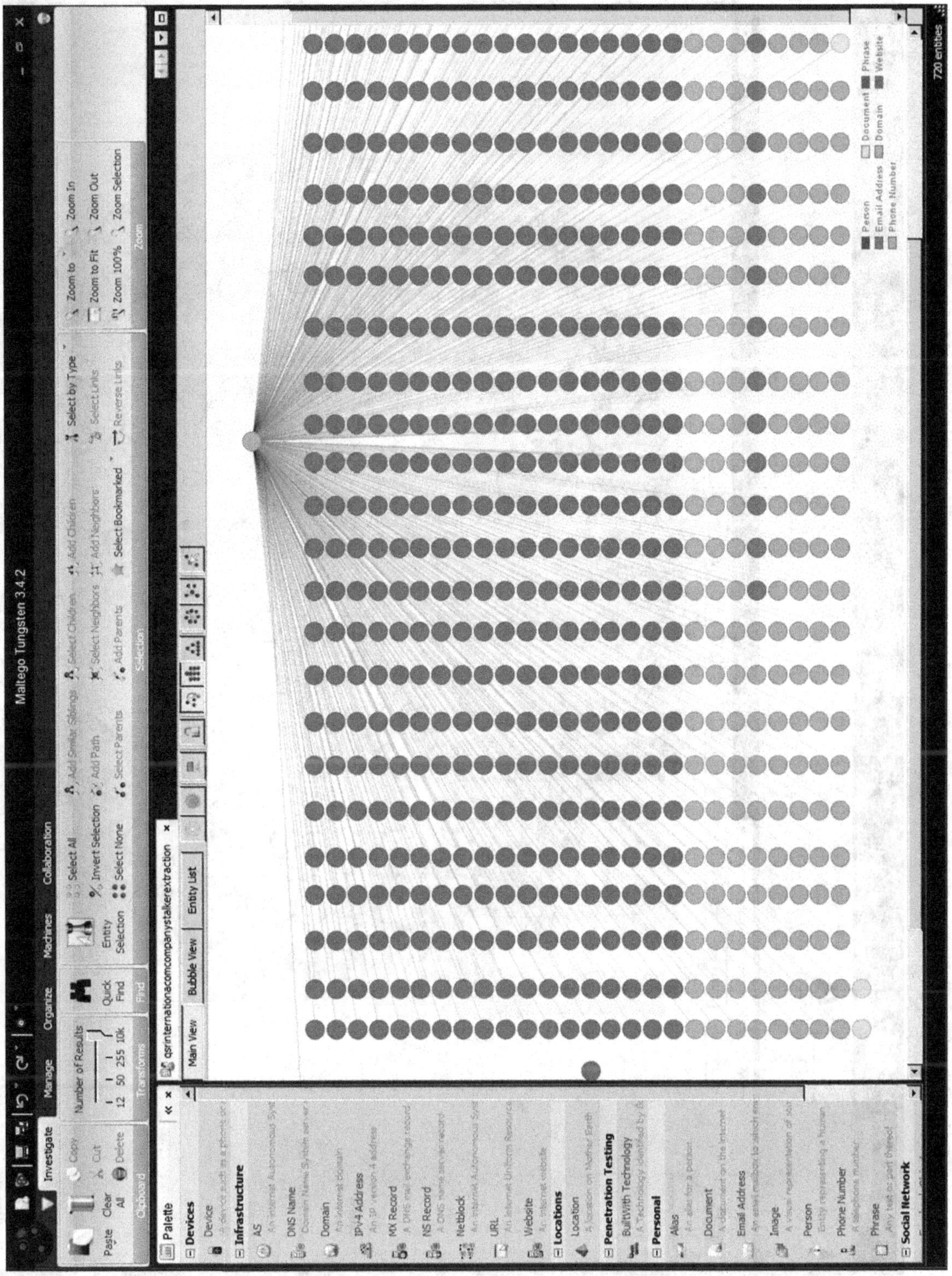

Figure 2. The HTTP Network of QSR International

Figure 3. A close-in bubble view of the http://www.qsrinternational.com company stalker view (in Maltego Tungsten)

Figure 4. @qsrint user network on Twitter (2 deg)

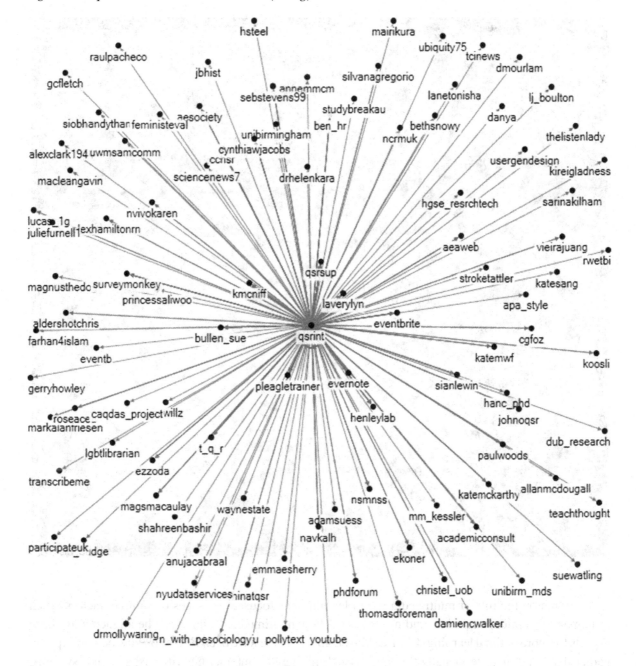

The "NVivo" article network on Wikipedia showed a wide range of ties to a variety of topics. A two-degree article-network data extraction resulted in so many links that a quad-core video-rendering machine could not fully map the network, so a version with only motif relationships extracted was visualized in a grid format. A full 197,204 unique vertices were identified. Figure 5 shows the visualized graph, with a high density of connections.

Figure 5. NVivo Article Network on Wikipedia (2 deg.)

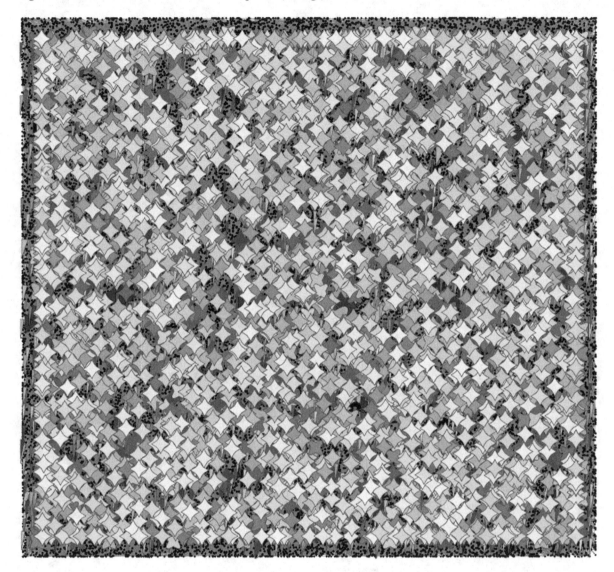

Research on the role of multimedia use in learning has focused on issues of "human factors" such as human perception, cognition, and memory, and how multimedia designs may be aligned with those aspects for more optimal learning (Clark & Mayer, 2011). There have been studies on how people explore, gather data, and analyze visually through "visual mining" by interacting with visualization systems; more specifically, people use visual mining strategies to "assess, estimate, develop options" and to find particular information and create hypotheses and identify patterns and make judgments (Mozaffari & Mudur, 2011, p. 52). There is a broad literature on a range of designs and unique applications of multimedia to particular learning contexts and defined trainee audiences. Researchers suggest the importance of "multimedia self-efficacy" for trainee perception of training effectiveness for trainings built using multimedia (Christoph, Schoenfeld, & Tansky, 2006); further, prior exposures to multimedia are helpful in creating this sense of multimedia self-efficacy.

Web 1.0 (the Read / Write Web) and Web 2.0 (the Social Web, made much more interactive and possible with the popularization of Javascript) are currently known as the non-semantic Web; currently, a large amount of the online data is unstructured or semi-structured. The meaning-making within both phases of the Web are essentially achieved by people. The Semantic Web has been an inspiring and activating concept for decades, since it was posited by Tim Berners-Lee, in 1994, in the first World Wide Web Conference. He was much-quoted from that event as saying:

"I have a dream for the Web (in which computers) become capable of analyzing all the data on the Web—the content, links, and transactions between people and computers. A 'Semantic Web', which should make this possible, has yet to emerge, but when it does, the day-to-day mechanisms of trade, bureaucracy and our daily lives will be handled by machines talking to machines. The 'intelligent agents' people have touted for ages will finally materialize" (Berners-Lee & Fischetti, 1999).

The basic concept behind the Semantic Web is that it is structured in such a way as to enable machines to autonomously extract data, make meaning based on context, and extrapolate relationships, among other functions. In the literature, there are a wide number of postulated benefits from this capability. A basic concept is that computers may access the Web and Internet as a large database and extract and exchange (machine-to-machine) desired information without direct human intervention. With the proper metadata and structuring and related technologies, machines will be able to "find, exchange, and interpret information" (Suman, 2014, p. 14). The first generations of Semantic Web browsers are available and using the formal metadata linked to the labeling of knowledge objects by libraries (De Keyser, 2012, p. 221). In terms of the stages of the Web, De Keyser points to the following: Web 1.0 consisting of HTML pages, Web 2.0 or the Social Web consisting of the write web (with "blogs, wikis, photo and video sites, folksonomies, etc."), Web 3.0 as the "web of data" or Semantic Web, and Web 4.0 of "the intelligent web" which is capable of reasoning (2012, p. 222). This author describes some possible uses of the Semantic Web:

Suppose the web is indeed this large structured database. You could formulate complex queries and get an answer in one web page instead of going through 20,000 or more links to pages that might contain only a part of the answer. A typical question that could be answered by a Semantic Web engine would be: 'Which articles on telemarketing were written in 2007 by authors working in companies with less than 100 employees? (De Keyser, 2012, pp. 225 - 226)

There has been early work on creating browser add-ins that showcase some semantic Web capabilities. For example, Magpie is one such tool that enables the highlighting of terms on a website that are linked to particular categories of information. This tool enables right-clicking on an image on the webpage in order to access its definitions. There are also connections to related images and related multimedia. This tool connects pages that are not explicitly linked. In other words, this approach enables the linking of knowledge (across sites and forms and sources) instead of mere documents to documents (Dzbor, Motta, & Domingue, 2007). Other researchers suggest that the Semantic Web may benefit follow-on learning in online assessment environments (del Mar Sanchez-Vera, Fernandez-Breis, Castellano-Nieves, Frutos-Morales, & Prendes-Espinoza, 2012). There is experimentation on different ways to rank results from semantic searches on the Web (Jindal, Bawa, & Batra, 2014). Building to the Semantic Web then would benefit from designer awareness of the ambitions for the Semantic Web and the importance of tagging and annotating data that will go online.

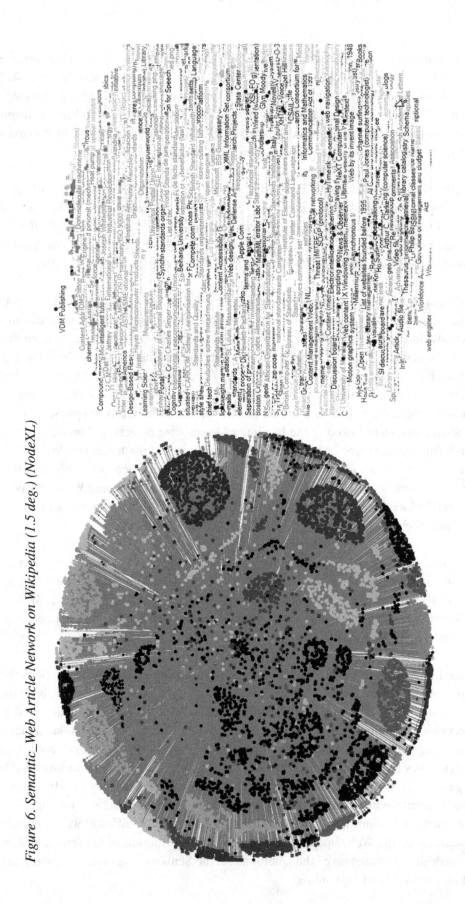

Figure 6. Semantic_Web Article Network on Wikipedia (1.5 deg.) (NodeXL)

In Figure 6, to the left is a Harel-Koren Fast Multiscale layout of the network, with various clusters of articles linked to the Semantic_Web article. To the right is the same dataset reflected as groupings with related article titles. A read-through of the right graph gives a sense of the broad interests related to the evolution of a Semantic Web.

AN EMERGENT STRATEGY (body)

In terms of how the software tool was introduced to campus in Y1, the university relied on the formal trainings provided by professional QSR International trainers, who offered five webinars to the campus. The webinars could not be recorded without the payment of thousands of extra dollars, so the campus merely had a room reserved in the library for the trainings and some online participants who joined in through the online webinar.

The live trainings hosted by K-State, starting in Fall 2014, followed the same general scheduling and room location (one Friday afternoon a month for two hours each session and a total of three sessions per semester). The trainings transitioned from basic to more advanced. Participants were not asked to RSVP; they were asked to sign up only if they wanted credit through the Human Resources Information System (HRIS). The presentations were delivered using a live NVivo 10 version (in a Windows laptop) and using a local project with some added synthetic data in order to be able to present the tool's various functionalities. All participants were encouraged to bring their laptops with the software installed. All faculty, staff, and graduate students could access the software and the annual license key off of a hosted site on the campus; the site required sign-in by electronic identification and password. Those who didn't know about the protected site could download a trial version of the software from QSR International's website. (Those using NVivo on the Mac OS did their best to follow along even though their version did not have the full functionality of the Windows version.) While there were set goals for what to cover in each session, the sessions were held in a conversational way, with participants asking questions and describing their research plans and goals.

As is typical in the Fall Semester, there was a groundswell of interest. The main point-of-entry for most into the software was a project, whether it was self-generated or assigned to them from someone else. The varying projects meant that potential users had varying degrees of need for the tool's different functionalities. Some came at the tool with no background in qualitative data analysis (QDA) or CAQ-DAS (computer-assisted qualitative data analysis software), while there were others who were quite well versed in the tool and even wanted just casual coding sessions so they would have a time and place to meet to shoot the breeze and see what others were doing.

The goal for the initial presentation was to keep it simple—and to provide sufficient information so that people in the room could get started. The presentation started with self-introductions of everyone in the room (about 20 people) along with their particular interests in the tool and what they were hoping to do with the tool. During the session, audience members brought up that they were doing a group coding project and wondered how the tool might help them. This discussion led to a brief introduction to various types of "codebooks," the setup of "event logging," the importance of proper researcher identifiers on their respective versions of NVivo, research journaling, and a short discussion of interrater reliability and Cohen's Kappa. There was discussion also of how to integrate group coding using a non-server version of NVivo (by maintaining a master project file and integrating external project files). For some of the prior, the presenter did a walk-through on the tool to show where certain settings could be achieved, and for others, she offered a raincheck to show how to achieve different ends (in order to keep the presentation sufficiently simple). Another audience question addressed whether the tool could be used to integrate multiple languages, and that led to a discussion of Unicode. In other words, while there was a clear and publicized agenda for what to cover in detail, there was plenty of room left in the two-hour sessions to go off script in order to meet the needs of the audience. A fair amount of time was spent learning about the software tool's behaviors: the 15-minute save reminders, the need to have backup copies of projects elsewhere, the terminology, the project size limits, and so on.

The presenter had listed some bullet points of concepts and practices to infuse in the presentations, with the goal of ultimately integrating these into the complete three-sets of presentations.

- Know your data well.
- Start with a small set and learn the tool. See what it can do. Understand its limits.
- (Find complementary tools that may enhance and extend your analysis.)
- Document each step that you're taking.
- Define your terms well. Be transparent about your research, your data cleaning, your thinking processes, and the implications of your research.
- Define good research habits in your field and follow them.
- Assume that the system re-sets with each new run…so pay attention to your parameters.
- Make sure that the data is ingested appropriately for the most optimal ways to query.
- Avoid data duplication.
- The coding and structuring capability is very flexible in NVivo…so it's good to use these as flexibly as possible. Be open to new ways of seeing the data.

Generally, the three face-to-face presentations were as follows.

One participant's suggestion in Session 1 was to make assignments for the participants. The presenter decided that it might be better to have an assignment in Session 3 after the users were more familiar with the platform and with some unique approaches and questions that could be asked.

To summarize, the face-to-face trainings were built on an actual NVivo project with integrated multimedia. The presentations involved a range of functionality walk-throughs to demonstrate the capabilities of the tool in an applied setting.

A Semantic Web-Friendly E-Book on Scalar

To complement the learning in the F2F trainings, an e-book was built (initially on whim) on the Scalar platform in a two-week period in September 2014 (just prior to the first presentation). The fast and agile development cycle was used of necessity because the idea was to have a slip of paper with the URL to the e-book for the first in-person presentation. Administration agreed to the primer build because of the need to ensure that the knowledge of the software tool could be preserved in the case of professional staff moving on. The book was conceptualized as a primer in order to make the software seem less threatening to new users. The purpose of the e-book was to provide an exploratory space where researchers from faculty, graduate student, administration, and staff ranks) could learn more about the tool at their own convenience. Administrators could refer to this resource in order to understand what they funded and were supporting. "Using NVivo…" was also written to affirm and backstop the presenter's expertise. It would serve as an online "calling card" for collaborative projects, whether for publishing or teaching.

Table 1. Session Descriptors for the F2F Sessions Introducing NVivo 10 in Y2 of the Campus Site License

	Session Overviews
Session 1: NVivo 10 Basic	This presentation will address the following: • how to download and install NVivo 10 and input the license key • how to download NCapture (browser add-in) • the basic parts of the NVivo 10 interface and how to navigate it • how to start and structure a research project • how to ingest various multimedia file types • how to start coding the multimedia types, and • how to back up the .nvp project file.
Session 2: NVivo 10 Advanced	This presentation will address the following: • questions from the basic introduction of NVivo • the basics of NVivo 10 (its interface, ingesting multimedia files, and coding data) (a review from NVivo Basic) • how to create relationships between nodes • how to query the collected data in an NVivo project (word frequency counts, text searches, matrix coding queries, and others) • how to create data visualizations (word trees, word clouds, dendrograms, ring lattice graphs, and others (for analysis and presentations) • how to conduct both types of auto-coding (by structured data and by machine learning), and • how to output a basic report.
Session 3: Usng NVivo 10 to Tap Social Media Streams"	This will address the following topics: • questions from the prior basic and advanced trainings in NVivo 10 • how to extract data from social media platforms (like Twitter Tweetstreams, Facebook data, YouTube video links, and the general Web and Internet) using NCapture • how to code on and query social media data using the analytical tools in NVivo 10 • how to create data visualizations from social media platforms in NVivo 10, and • what may be asserted by social media data.

The Scalar platform was chosen for a number of reasons. One reason was ideological. The Alliance for Networking Visual Culture, which develops and supports Scalar (located at http://scalar.usc.edu/) has a stated ambition of bringing scholars together with the contents of various online repositories to enhance the creation of scholarship and learning. The tool itself is open-source, but there is also a hosted solution (out of the University of Southern California). The Scalar Web interface is highly usable, with a slight learning curve and plenty of resilience against user error; the interface is so friendly that it was amenable to "cold" or on-the-fly storyboarding to the site. The platform offered rich capabilities for building a Semantic Web-friendly book—with the ability to create a wide range of overlapping book paths or navigational sequences (and a range of points-of-entry in the Table of Contents), tagging and annotation for multimedia, tagging and annotation of pages, and a number of data visualizations of the book's contents and its various elements. The platform offered some powerful "skins" for various publications. It showcased imagery and multimedia (video links) well. Those who wanted could build virtual communities within Scalar to interact around the various e-publications and artifacts. The developers themselves engaged with their users closely, and they actively sought feedback on additional functionalities to add.

There were e-book primer project standards defined for the quick design. The ideas were as follows: Each page would be comprehensive, and they would link to complementary resources broadly available on the Web and Internet; these included YouTube videos by users and by QSR International trainers, SlideShare slideshows, and websites. The e-book would have a clear trajectory. There would be step-by-step directions on how to achieve the work and screenshot illustrations. All processes would be actually tested through the software and documented. The e-book would not overlap with QSR International's tech-writing documentation, and if anything was used, it would be in quotes. The terminology used would align with QSR International's on their site but also that of the larger research community (optimally without falling into jargon). A real research project would be used for a sense of reality but with anything possibly sensitive glassed out. Visuals would include screenshots but also diagrams and digital drawings to illustrate concepts.

An actual NVivo project was used to summarize many of the software tool's functionalities, but screenshots were often "glassed" to obscure potentially sensitive data. Synthetic data was also created to communicate other functionalities that were not required in the actual real-world project.

The Table of Contents (TOC) was constructed based on a concept of how the work might unfold for a new user. NVivo was conceptualized as a tool that researchers could integrate into their familiar research processes, as described in text, visual timelines, and workflows. Within that approach, any related pages were also clustered. Some other conventions of books were followed such as having a cover, an intro, a glossary of terms, and a references list. Figure 7 shows the internal view of a Scalar page.

Digital elements—videos, screenshots, diagrams, a digital photo album, and a glossary of terms digital flashcard object were also integrated. The user interactivity included the ability to visualize the contexts of the various pages in five different ways: radial, paths, index, tags, and media. Figure 8 shows some of these direct built-in visualizations in Scalar for the primer. Users could experience digital flashcards with definitions included. They could play some embedded videos, with the typical interactivity of YouTube and Vimeo. They could also flip through a digital photo album of screenshots from the tool. They could enlarge or download any of the uploaded images (by clicking on the Details button at the bottom right of each image).

Figure 9 shows a "Details" view of one of the process sequences inside the primer. The ability to enlarge an image makes it much more readable even though the base sizes of images is limited in Scalar.

An original set of flashcards were created to enable users to acquire some of the common terms used in qualitative and mixed methods data analysis using a state-of-the-art software tool. There was a conscious effort to avoid jargon; however, there was a need to balance the use of terminology. Figure 10 shows a screenshot of the "codebook" definition in the digital flashcard.

A first iteration of the e-book had been released to the research community at K-State when a page on Drawing Relational Models was added. The emergent Table of Contents follows:

1. Cover
2. Intro
3. What is NVivo?
4. A Research Workflow with NVivo Integrations
5. Downloading, Installing, and Registering the Software
6. The NVivo User Interface
7. Starting a New NVivo Project
8. Starting a Multilingual Project
9. Research Journaling in NVivo
10. Ingesting "Internal" Source Citations
11. Ingesting "External" Source Contents
12. NCapture and the Web, YouTube, and Social Media
13. Analyzing Social Media Data in NVivo

Figure 7. Ingesting "Internal" Source Contents Page on Scalar

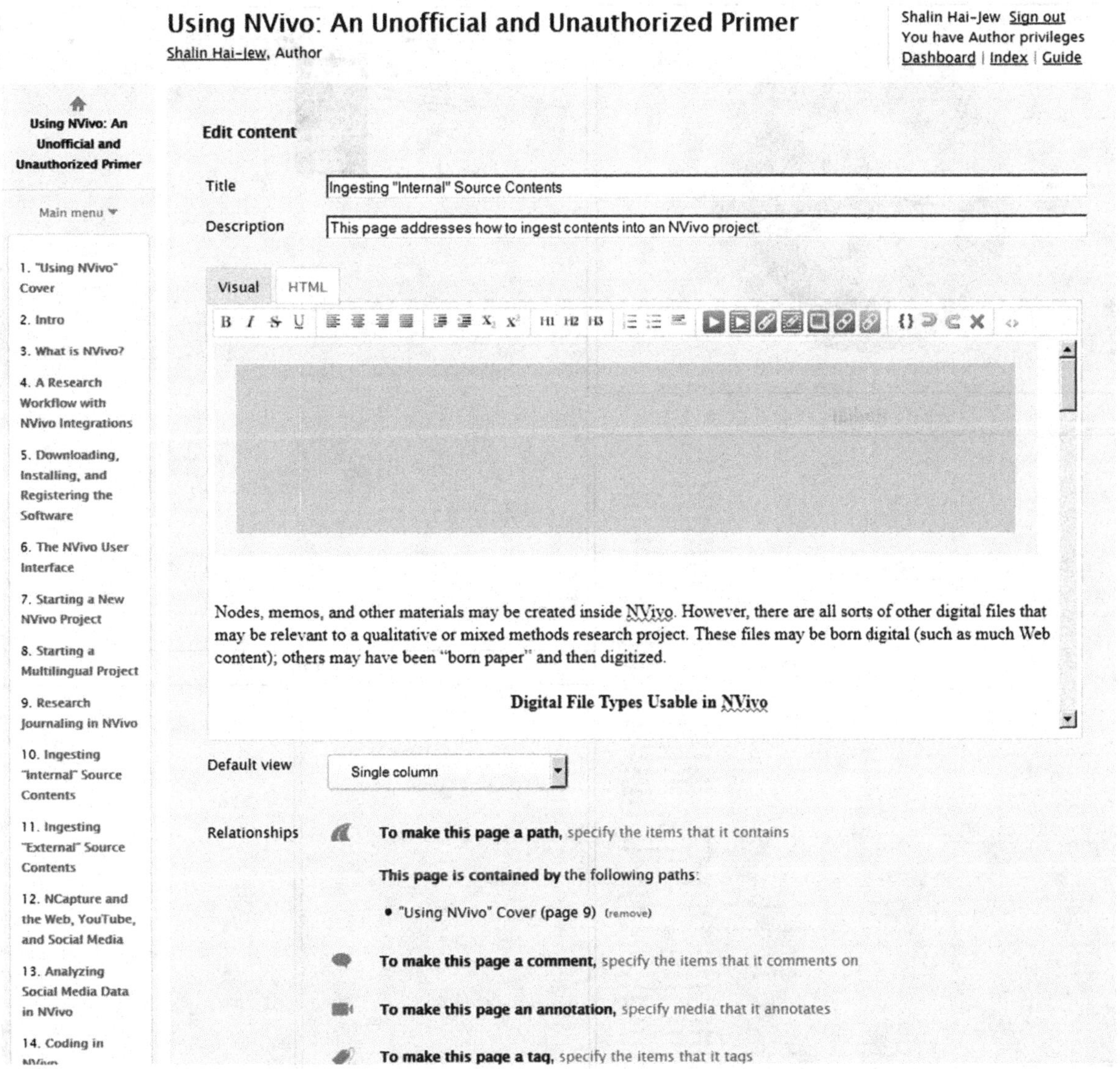

Using NVivo: An Unofficial and Unauthorized Primer
Shalin Hai-Jew, Author

Shalin Hai-Jew Sign out
You have Author privileges
Dashboard | Index | Guide

Using NVivo: An Unofficial and Unauthorized Primer

Main menu ▼

1. "Using NVivo" Cover

2. Intro

3. What is NVivo?

4. A Research Workflow with NVivo Integrations

5. Downloading, Installing, and Registering the Software

6. The NVivo User Interface

7. Starting a New NVivo Project

8. Starting a Multilingual Project

9. Research Journaling in NVivo

10. Ingesting "Internal" Source Contents

11. Ingesting "External" Source Contents

12. NCapture and the Web, YouTube, and Social Media

13. Analyzing Social Media Data in NVivo

14. Coding in NVivo

Edit content

Title   Ingesting "Internal" Source Contents

Description   This page addresses how to ingest contents into an NVivo project.

Visual   HTML

B *I* S U   ...   H1 H2 H3   ...   {} ⊃ ∈ X ‹›

Nodes, memos, and other materials may be created inside NVivo. However, there are all sorts of other digital files that may be relevant to a qualitative or mixed methods research project. These files may be born digital (such as much Web content); others may have been "born paper" and then digitized.

Digital File Types Usable in NVivo

Default view   Single column

Relationships   **To make this page a path,** specify the items that it contains

This page is contained by the following paths:

• "Using NVivo" Cover (page 9) (remove)

To make this page a comment, specify the items that it comments on

To make this page an annotation, specify media that it annotates

To make this page a tag, specify the items that it tags

14. Coding in NVivo
15. Identifying Relationships between Nodes
16. Creating Codebooks in NVivo
17. Conducting Data Queries in NVivo (Part 1 of 2)
18. Conducting Data Queries in NVivo (Part 2 of 2)
19. Data Query: Text Search Query
20. Data Query: Word Frequency Count Query
21. Data Query: Coding Query
22. Data Query: Matrix Coding Query
23. Data Query: Coding Comparison (Advanced) and Cohen's Kappa Coefficient
24. Data Query: Compound Query (Advanced)

Figure 8. Built-in data visualizations of "Using NVivo..." on Scalar

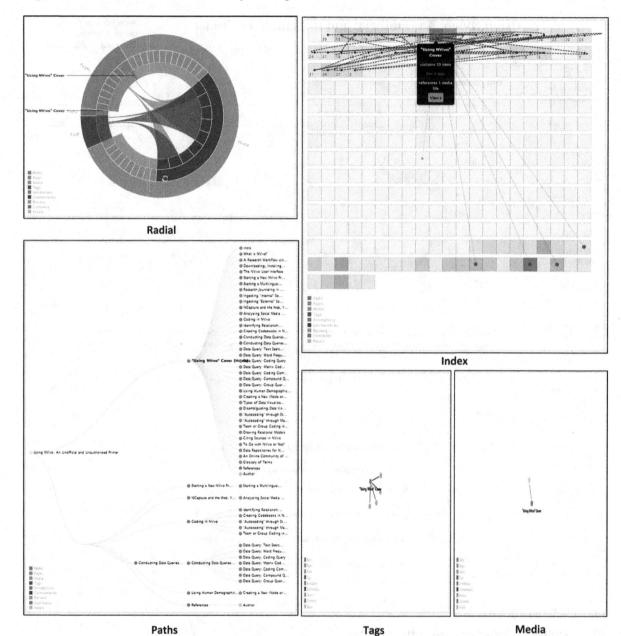

Built-In Data Visualizations of "Using Nvivo..." on Scalar

25. Data Query: Group Query (Advanced)
26. Using Human Demographics to Further Explore Interview, Survey, or Focus Group Data
27. Creating a New (Node or Source) Classification Sheet with Ingested Data
28. Types of Data Visualizations in NVivo
29. Disambiguating Data Visualizations
30. "Autocoding" through Sylted or Structured Textual Data

Figure 9. A "Details" View of a Process Sequence for Including Demographic Information into an Analysis

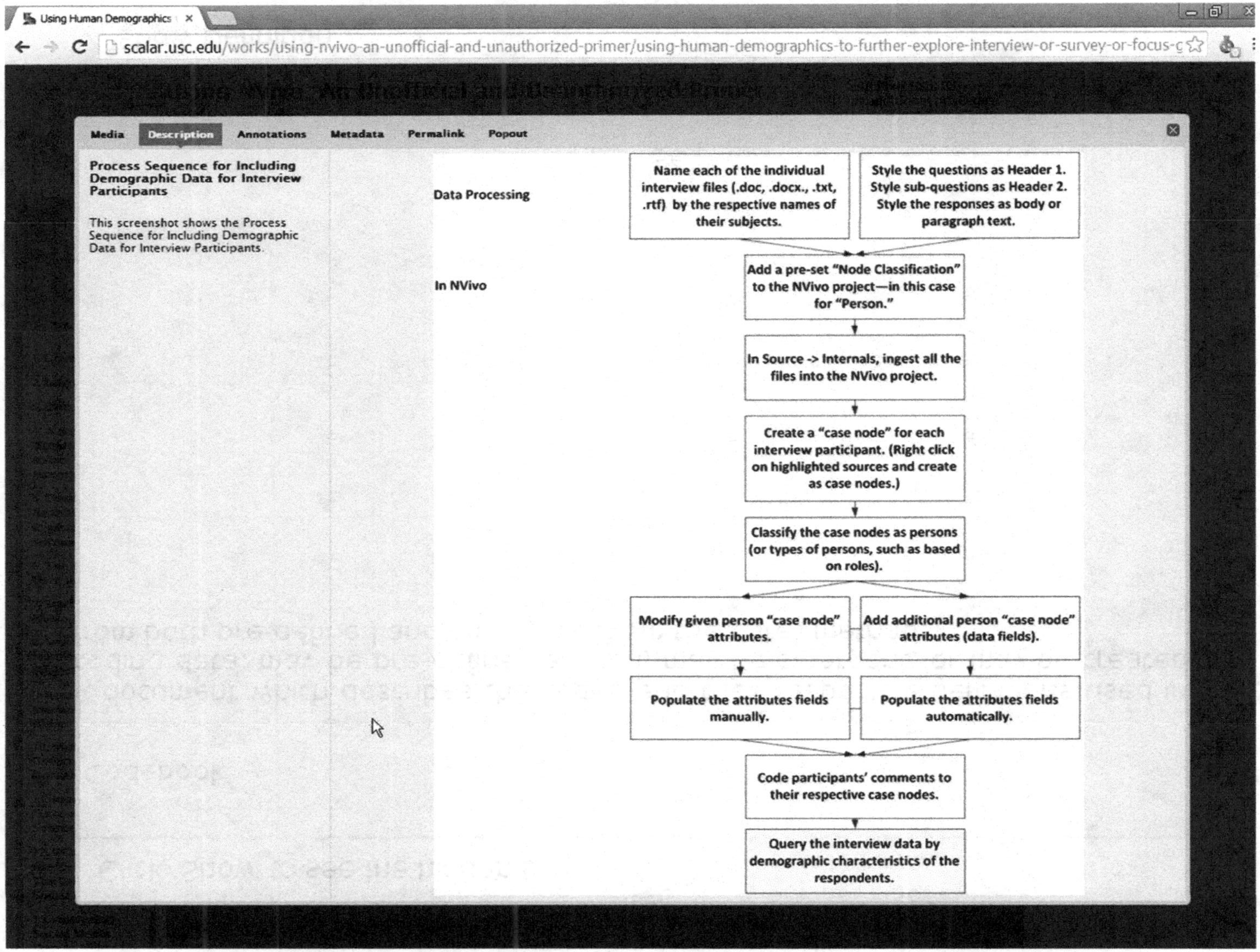

Figure 10. Glossary of Terms: Digital Flashcards for "Using NVivo…"

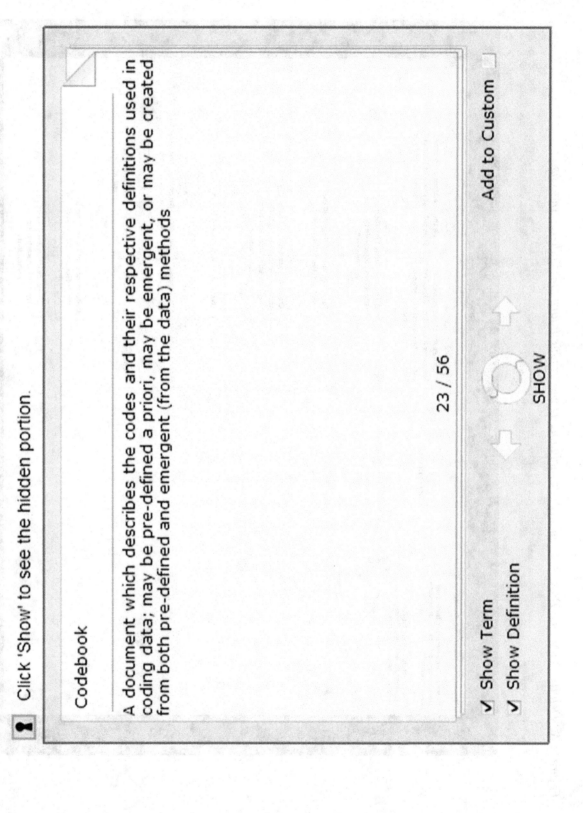

Click 'Show' to see the hidden portion.

Codebook

A document which describes the codes and their respective definitions used in coding data; may be pre-defined a priori, may be emergent, or may be created from both pre-defined and emergent (from the data) methods

23 / 56

Add to Custom

SHOW

✓ Show Term
✓ Show Definition

31. "Autocoding" through Machine Learning of Existing (Human) Coding Patterns
32. Team or Group Coding in NVivo
33. Drawing Relational Models
34. Citing Sources in NVivo
35. To Go with NVivo or Not?
36. Data Repositories for NVivo-based Data Sets?
37. An Online Community of Users and Additional Resources
38. Glossary of Terms
39. References
40. Author

The basic work went as follows. The author started a Word file and brainstormed a TOC to structure the work. She fleshed out the main contents needed in each page. She went online to find resources that could be cited. Then, she opened up NVivo 10 and started describing the sequences of work by doing a walk-through and collecting screenshots as she went. She named the images in a way that made sense and contextualized them but that were also brief; she stored the respective images in the necessary folders for easy upload. Digital learning objects (based on Flash) were created and hosted on a local server for reference, and a screenshot was taken of each to use as a signal of the resource. A book site was started in Scalar, and she sketched out the various pages and put them in some sort of initial order. (The order changed multiple times before the e-book actually went live.) Next, she started to place the book contents onto Scalar. At this stage, page names were revised as were the names of images and multimedia files. As new ideas arose for additional relevant content, that was written, and screenshots were taken, and the content was uploaded onto Scalar.

Altogether, the text had over 250 media objects. A majority were screenshots of the tool; some were hand-drawn diagrams; some were videos from YouTube and Vimeo; some were data visualizations built into Scalar (but based off the data of the book). Once the initial book was sketched out on Scalar, it was released to the public in a "soft launch." A soft launch occurs without much publicity, so it just appears quietly in a public space—and whomever may happen upon it is welcome to use it. It was estimated that Google's crawlers would take about a week-and-a-half to find it. The "going public" enabled the author to experience the pressure of an audience in order to speed up the work. ["Using NVivo: An Unofficial and Unauthorized Primer" is available at http://scalar.usc.edu/works/using-nvivo-an-unofficial-and-unauthorized-primer/index].

To create the sense of the newness of the Scalar platform and its capabilities, the "Using NVivo..." cover featured a radial diagram of the book's contents. This also helped set reader expectations for the level of visual interest on each of the pages, virtually all of which included some data visualizations. The presentation of the data was partially done to create a sense of glamor—as potentially a motivation for people to invest the hard work to learn the software tool and to apply it correctly. All imagery was informational and highlighted important points. There were no purely gratuitous images.

Figure 12 describes a matrix coding query. In this image, it shows what the basic data structure of a matrix is.

Those possibly considering use of NVivo for their work are encouraged to conduct a simple cost-benefit calculation. Those who wanted a more in-depth way of considering this were asked to consider a customized decision tree. Figure 13 shows a functions-based decision tree to help readers decide whether or not they wanted to pursue use of the technology. The software tool enables some functionalities that

Figure 11. "Using NVivo…" Book Cover

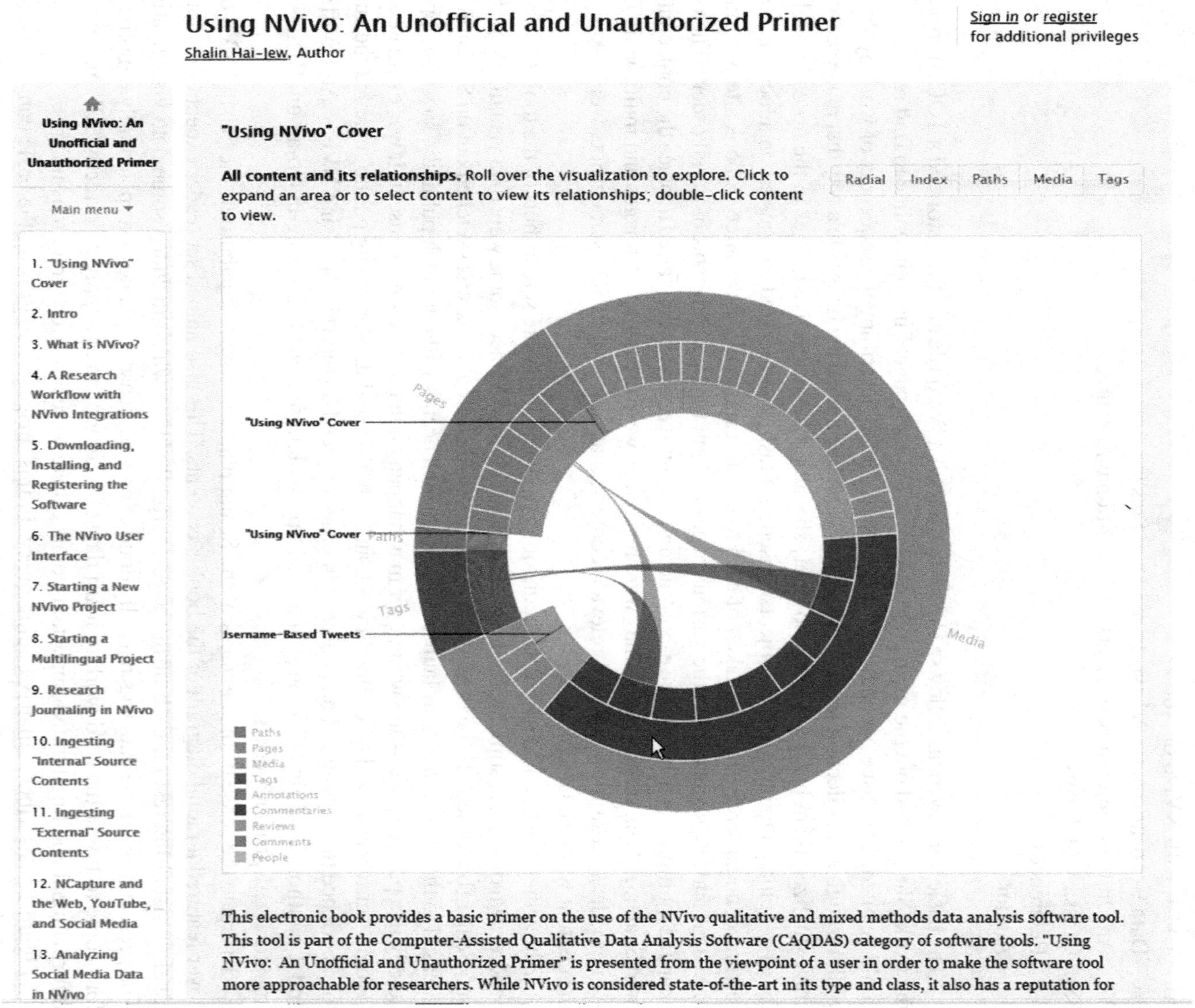

Figure 12. Data Query: Matrix Coding Query (A Page from the E-Book)

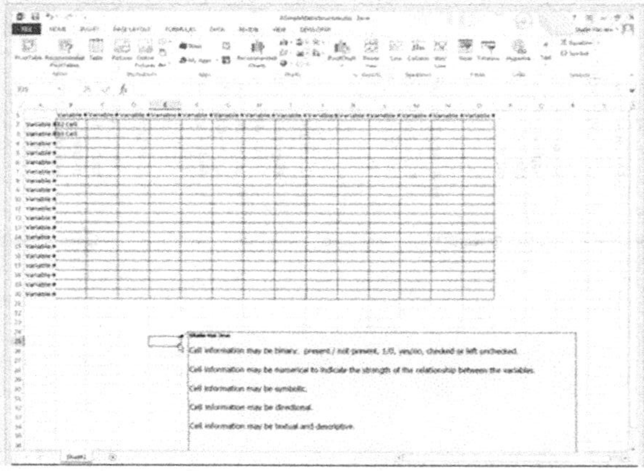

Using NVivo: An Unofficial and Unauthorized Primer

Shalin Hai-Jew, Author

Sign in or register for additional privileges

Previous page on path   Next page on path

Conducting Data Queries... (Part 2 of 2), page 4 of 7

Other paths that intersect here:

Data Query: Matrix Coding Query

Matrix Coding Query

It is important to understand what a basic matrix structure looks like. Basically, there are rows and columns of variables, and the cells contain data at the intersections of the rows and columns. Matrices are usually of a certain type in terms of how the information is represented. As noted in the visual below, cell information may be in the following forms (one type per matrix—not mixed types):

binary: such as present / not present, 1/o, yes/no, checked or unchecked

numerical: (such as to indicate strength of relationship)

symbolic: (such as any symbolic indicator representing information)

directional: ->, <-, <>, or other (such as one variable in relation to another)

textual and descriptive: described with words

or some other method...

The cells where the data would go were highlighted for clarity.

A Simple Matrix Structure

Using NVivo: An Unofficial and Unauthorized Primer

Main menu ▼

1. Cover

2. Intro

3. What is NVivo?

4. A Research Workflow with NVivo Integrations

5. Downloading, Installing, and Registering the Software

6. The NVivo User Interface

7. Starting a New NVivo Project

8. Starting a Multilingual Project

9. Research Journaling in NVivo

10. Ingesting "Internal" Source Contents

11. Ingesting "External" Source Contents

12. NCapture and the Web, YouTube, and Social Media

13. Analyzing Social Media

Figure 13. A Functions-Based Decision Tree for Considering NVivo

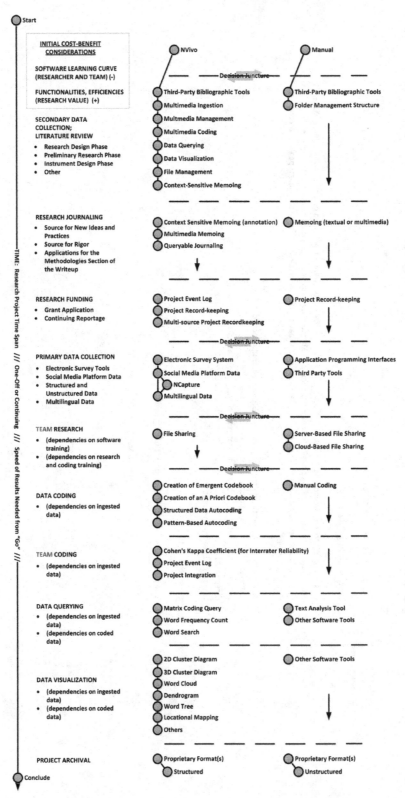

Figure 14. A virtual community of researchers discussing "NVivo" (through a keyword search on twitter using NodeXL)

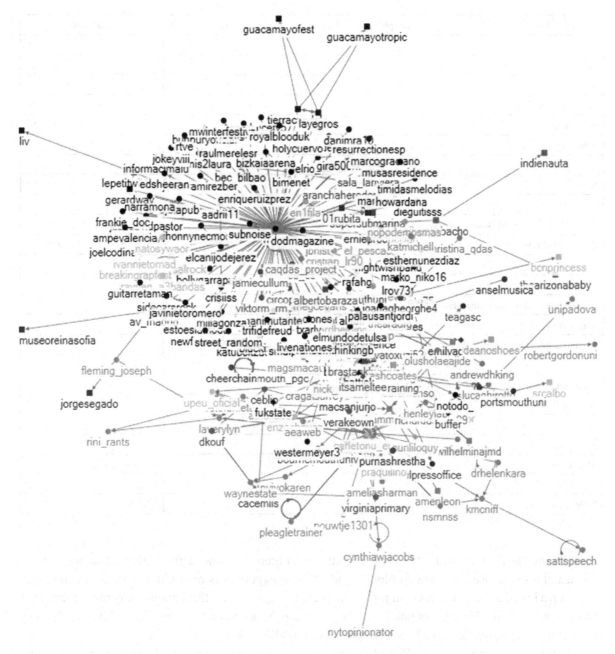

are not possible through manual means. However, the learning curve of the technology is high even if the costs of its adoption are negligible for individuals on campus. The decision tree also highlights certain decision junctures which are especially critical for projects.

Finally, users of the e-book were encouraged to use online resources related to the tool and to participate in the online community surrounding the use of NVivo. To emphasize (and illustrate) this point, a real-world data extraction of the communities surrounding the "nvivo" keyword and a hashtag

Table 2. Graph Metrics Table for A Virtual Community of Researchers Discussing "NVivo" (through a Keyword Search on Twitter using NodeXL)

Graph Type	Directed
Vertices	238
Unique Edges	288
Edges With Duplicates	80
Total Edges	368
Self-Loops	99
Reciprocated Vertex Pair Ratio	0.071428571
Reciprocated Edge Ratio	0.133333333
Connected Components	60
Single-Vertex Connected Components	35
Maximum Vertices in a Connected Component	103
Maximum Edges in a Connected Component	183
Maximum Geodesic Distance (Diameter)	4
Average Geodesic Distance	2.136022
Graph Density	0.004520796
Modularity	Not Applicable
NodeXL Version	1.0.1.333

conversation "#nvivo" community were both extracted. Figure 14 shows a graph of a virtual community of researchers who use NVivo microblogging about their experiences on Twitter. This keyword search brings up a broader span of users than just researchers though because this captures any non-hashtagged mention of "NVivo." The dataset linked to this graph may be accessed from the NodeXL Graph Gallery at http://nodexlgraphgallery.org/Pages/Graph.aspx?graphID=30866.

A "keyword" search shows a different side of a term than a hashtagged one. In a keyword search, this captures the mentions of a term anywhere in a Tweet (but not in a hashtag). Figure 14 shows a resulting graph and the various clusters or groups using "nvivo" as a keyword term. This figure was depicted using the Harel-Koren Fast Multiscale layout algorithm, in NodeXL. This graph showed 70 groups or clusters, with one main one and a lot of smaller ones.

The graph metrics for Figure 14 are reflected in Table 2. An analysis of the exchanged microblogging messages or Tweets shows a number of different languages, which reflects NVivo's global stature and broad marketshare.

Figure 15 shows a fairly active hashtag (#) conversation (#nvivo) in the week prior to the data extraction on Twitter, with users of the tool going to social media to share expertise and to ask questions. This electronic social network analysis (e-SNA) graph was depicted using the Fruchterman-Reingold force-based layout algorithm as deployed in NodeXL.

The graph metrics table related to Figure 15 follows in Table 3. This network around #nvivo included 16 different groups.

Tapping social media with NVivo. The tapping of social media for learning adds a deeper layer of complexity to NVivo. This capability is enhanced through the NCapture plug-in to Internet Explorer and Google Chrome. The extraction of data from social media platforms relies on layers of technologies, with particular functions and encapsulated complexities that may not be apparent through a cursory use of the tool.

A simple illustration that alludes to some of this complexity comes from an article network for "Social_media" on Wikipedia in Figure 16. A one-degree article network extraction shows how this concept (and practice) of social media is interrelated with so many other phenomena.

Continual updates to the e-book. It was perhaps helpful that the first version of "Using NVivo..." was created so quickly that some typographical errors got through. While corrections were made, the invitation to notify the author of any incorrect information and typos has been left on the cover (main landing page) of the e-book. It makes sense that such a primer should be continually evolved and improved upon.

Discussion

In this chapter, a use case involving the deployment of multimedia in both a live and online archival setting to promote the rollout and usage of NVivo at a university was shared. In both contexts, multimedia was part of an adaptive endeavor to meet the needs of a university's research community in learning to effectively use a complex software tool with a wide range of capabilities.

FUTURE RESEARCH DIRECTIONS

For this particular project, it will be important to create an assessment and feedback loop to understand the strengths and weaknesses of this particular approach of using an online primer to support software adoption and usage. One variable may be the numbers of downloads and installs of the software by the K-State community, of which there is already data from Y1. Help Desk tickets related to the software may be assessed. There may be elicitations of feedback at the F2F trainings. There may be surveys sent out to users to assess this as well. Another metric could involve the numbers of university publications using the tool in KREx (K-State Research Exchange), the campus repository, or in the broader academic publishing context.

Figure 15. #nvivo hashtag search on Twitter (basic network using NodeXL)

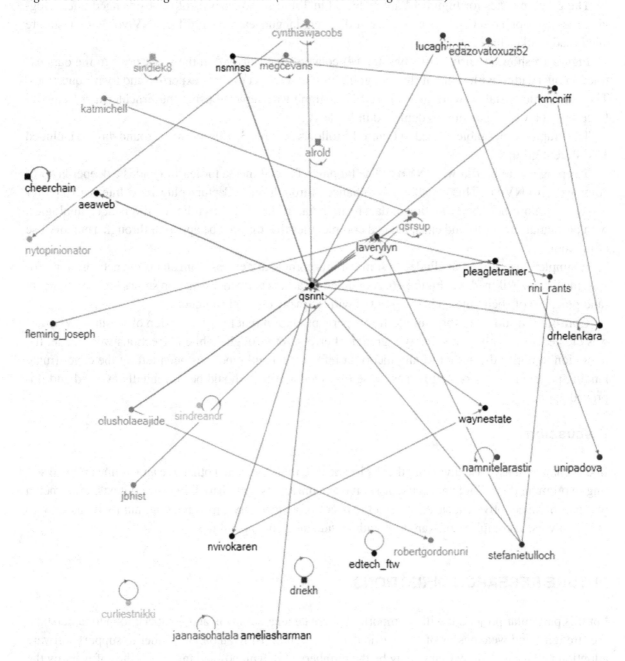

Another way to benefit the research literature would be to analyze the uses of e-publications for self-discovery learning, self-training, and trainer-led trainings (in a variety of contexts). There may be research on how to harness the Semantic Web in terms of content creation for such learning. It may help to explore ways to enhance platforms like Scalar, such as through the additional integration of Web-based repositories (such as those containing digital learning objects).

In terms of the continuing efforts to support the adoption and usage of NVivo at K-State, there will likely be a number of other efforts. It is possible that digital simulations may be created through the uses

Table 3. Graph Metrics Table for #nvivo hashtag search on Twitter (basic network using NodeXL)

Graph Metric	Value
Graph Type	Directed
Vertices	33
Unique Edges	44
Edges With Duplicates	5
Total Edges	49
Self-Loops	18
Reciprocated Vertex Pair Ratio	0.111111111
Reciprocated Edge Ratio	0.2
Connected Components	12
Single-Vertex Connected Components	11
Maximum Vertices in a Connected Component	22
Maximum Edges in a Connected Component	36
Maximum Geodesic Distance (Diameter)	4
Average Geodesic Distance	2.250505
Graph Density	0.028409091
Modularity	Not Applicable
NodeXL Version	1.0.1.333

of screen capture tools to show work-based sequences. Digital simulations that model a system or process that offer high levels of user control often result in higher senses of learner self-efficacy and learning transfer (Gegenfurtner, Queada-Pallarès, & Knogler, 2014); one sense of control in videos involves the ability to start, stop, pause, play, and replay the videos, and make other adjustments, for example. Another strategy may be to encourage learner self-experimentation with the software itself, using that as a simulation platform prior to commitment to that software for research projects. Many learn in an applied way by starting projects and learning as they go, and it may help to collect data about these types of learning experiences as well. Research on other strategies used to roll out complex software to a university community on a budget would be helpful.

Present-day multimedia has come a long way since the studies of the 1990s and 2000s. The multimedia itself has changed with the wide uses of animations, screen capture software, simulations, rich mapping, and formative learner evaluations in interactive videos. There has been integration of eye-tracking tools,

Figure 16. Social_media article network on Wikipedia 1 deg (NodeXL)

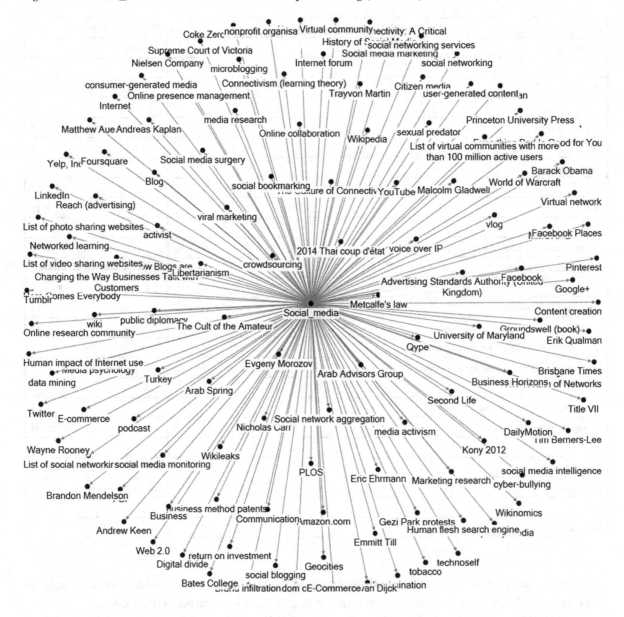

for example, to capture just what people focus on in their interactions with multimedia. The application of multimedia in trainings has broadened to a wide scale, and these experiences may be captured in case studies and cross-case studies. The uses of multimedia for self-discovery learning also holds immense promise. It is time for an in-depth look at present-day multimedia and the effects on human learning and training. This is an exciting time to study the applications of multimedia simply because there is so much potential and so many directions that this is moving in.

CONCLUSION

The "future world" projected by the ambitions of "K-State 2025" would require a much deeper bench of expertise, particularly by individuals willing to share their knowledge with others, in order to promote others' research work.

ACKNOWLEDGMENT

So much of this work would not be possible if it were not for the many who contribute to the open-source movement: funders, organizations, developers, technical writers, trainers, users (particularly those who share their work broadly through galleries and repositories), and others. This work relied on those at the Social Media Research Foundation (supporting Network Overview, Discovery, and Exploration for Excel or "NodeXL") and The Alliance for Networking Visual Culture (ANVC) (supporting Scalar). Sometimes, cost is a sufficient barrier against investing the time and effort to learn to use and deploy software that could enhance research; sometimes, "free" is a sufficient motivation to learn software tools and to share the knowledge and learning broadly. Also, the pursuit of learning may sometimes be very fragile, and the kindness of others along the way makes a big difference in the pursuit of the learning.

REFERENCES

Alliance for Networking Visual Culture. (2014). Scalar. http://scalar.usc.edu/

Berners-Lee, T., & Fischetti, M. (1999). *Weaving the Web*. San Francisco: Harper.

Christoph, R. T., Schoenfeld, G. A., & Tansky, J. W. (2006). Overcoming barriers to training utilizing technology: The influence of self-efficacy factors on multimedia-based training receptiveness. *Human Resource Development Quarterly*, 9(1), 25–38. doi:10.1002/hrdq.3920090104

Clark, R. C., & Mayer, R. E. (2011). *2008). E-Learning and the Science of Instruction: Proven Guidelines for Consumers and Designers of Multimedia Learning*. San Francisco: John Wiley & Sons. doi:10.1002/9781118255971

Cliggett, L. (2013). Qualitative data archiving in the digital age: Strategies for data preservation and sharing. *Qualitative Report*, 18(1), 1–11. Retrieved from http://www.nova.edu/ssss/QR/QR18/cliggett1.pdf

De Keyser, P. (2012). *The Semantic Web. Indexing: From Thesauri to the Semantic Web*. Oxford: Chandos.

Del Mar Sánchez-Vera, Fernández-Breis, Castellano-Nieves, Frutos-Morales, & Predes-Espinoza. (2012). Semantic Web technologies for generating feedback in online assessment environments. *Knowledge-Based Systems*, 152–165.

Dzbor, M., Motta, E., & Domingue, J. (2007). *Magpie: Experiences in supporting Semantic Web browsing. Journal of Web Semantics*. Science Direct.

Gegenfurtner, A., Quesada-Pallarès, & Knogler, M. (2014). Digital simulation-based training: A meta-analysis. *British Journal of Educational Technology*, 1–18.

Goodwin, L., Kozleski, E., Muth, R., Rhodes, L. K., & White, K. K. (2006). Establishing a center to support faculty research. *Innovative Higher Education, 30*(4). doi:10.1007/s10755-005-8347-z

Hai-Jew, S. (2014). *Using NVivo: An Unofficial and Unauthorized Primer.* Retrieved from http://scalar. usc.edu/works/using-nvivo-an-unofficial-and-unauthorized-primer/index

Jindal, V., Bawa, S., & Batra, S. (2014). A review of ranking approaches for semantic search on Web. *Information Processing and Management:* 50, 418–425.ScienceDirect. K-State 2025 Plan. Kansas State University. Retrieved from http://www.k-state.edu/2025/plan/goals.html

Mozaffari, E., & Mudur, S. (2011). A classification scheme for characterizing visual mining. In G. Salvendy & M. J. Smith (Eds.), *Human Interface, Part 2* (pp. 46–54). Springer-Verlag Berlin Heidelberg. doi:10.1007/978-3-642-21669-5_6

NodeXL: Network Overview, Discovery and Exploration for Excel. (2014). Social Media Research Foundation. http://nodexl.codeplex.com/

Suman, A. (2014). *From Knowledge Abstraction to Management: Using Ranganathanas Faceted Schema to Develop Conceptual Frameworks for Digital Libraries. Chandros Publishing (imprint).* Amsterdam: Elsevier.

ADDITIONAL READING

Alliance for Networking Visual Culture. (2014). Scalar. http://scalar.usc.edu/

InternationalQ. S. R. http://www.qsrinternational.com/

K-State 2025 Plan. Kansas State University. Retrieved from. http://www.k-state.edu/2025/plan/goals.html

KEY TERMS AND DEFINITIONS

Agnostic (As In Theory- Or Method- Agnostic): A software tool that is not designed with an underlying theory or method in mind but is sufficiently flexible to accommodate a range of theoretical or methodological approaches.

Autocoding (Automatic Coding): The computerized labeling of data to particular nodes in NVivo either based on text style or on machine learning (from extant human coding).

Bibliographic Tool: A third-party software tool that enables the ingestion of bibliographic (citation) data from formally-published contents hosted on repositories (and often contents from the Web and Internet).

Caqdas: Computer-Assisted Qualitative Data Analysis Software.

Codebook: A document which describes the codes and their respective definitions used in coding data; may be pre-defined a priori, may be emergent, or may be created from both pre-defined and emergent (from the data) methods.

Classification Sheet: A table which enables the description of types of sources or case nodes in a project and the attributes linked to the particular classification (such as a "person" type of "case node" and the respective attributes for that person such as "age," "education," and "gender".

Coding Comparison: A type of matrix query that enables comparisons-and-contrasts across coded nodes.

Coding Pattern: A machine-analysis of human coding for machine-emulated autocoding.

Cohen's Kappa Coefficient: A similarity calculation of interrater reliability that looks at the disjoint set of two coders' coded data (as compared to their agreement on what to code and what not to code).

Compound Query: A multiple-layered query of types of information in NVivo (from both sources and coded nodes).

Data Query: The mining of both structured and unstructured data in NVivo using a range of possible tools.

Data Repository: A collection of datasets or data.

Dataset: A collection of data (of a certain type or of varying types).

De-Identification: Removing the identifying features of respondents from a dataset (optimally in a way in which individuals may not be re-identified).

Disambiguation: Removing ambiguity or confusion or "noise" from data.

Dynamic: Moving, changing over time.

Event Log: A recording of the human actions taken in an NVivo project (reported out as a text file).

External Source: A category of source which contains "proxies" for data which cannot be directly transcoded and ingested into the NVivo project.

Geolocation: The relating of online data to a physical location on earth (often from noisy data to specific "structured location references".

Graph: A 2D or 3D node-link representation of entities and relationships.

Group Query: An advanced query that enables the querying of particular groupings of data for in-depth analysis.

Hashtag (#): The labeling of microblogging text messages or shared social media contents based on a shared theme or topic or conversation.

Ingest: The importation of data into an NVivo project.

Interface: The space where a human being interacts with a software tool, including the Navigation View, Ribbon, Find Bar, List View, and Detail View in the integrated workspace.

Internal Source: Any digital data related to the research project.

Inter-Rater Reliability: A similarity measure to compare how closely two coders code data (as points of agreement and points of disagreement; also known as inter-annotator reliability.

Machine Reading: The capability for computers to automatically extract relevant data based on algorithms, without human intervention.

Matrix: A table used to compare entities or variables labeled in the rows and columns (with the data in the intersecting cells).

Memo: A note related to a particular object (in terms of context-sensitive memoing).

Metadata: Information about content data.

Microblogging: The act of sharing short messages, URL links, images, and videos through a microblogging site or related app.

Mixed Methodology: A form of research which integrates or mixes qualitative and quantitative theories and methods.

Multi-Methodology: A form of research that uses more than one method of research.

Multimedia: Media that consists of a variety of content forms.

NCapture: A plug-in or add-on to Google Chrome and Internet Explorer to enable the capturing of website information for use In NVivo as well as dataset extractions from Twitter, Facebook, Linked-In and other social media platforms.

NVivo: A qualitative and mixed methods data analysis software tool.

.nvp: The extension for an NVivo project.

Node: The basic unit of "code" in NVivo, which may represent concepts, themes, individuals, demographic attributes, or a range of other informational features.

Operating System: Software that runs the basic functions of a computer, such as Windows, Mac, or Linux.

Path: A sequence of navigation through pages and multimedia (on Scalar, the platform on which the "Using NVivo" text is hosted).

Proxy: Something used to represent or stand in for something else.

Radial Diagram: A data visualization in Scalar based on a radiating pattern from a central point (in Scalar).

Relationship: An undirected or directed linkage between two nodes.

Research Journal: A chronological record of the research.

Screenshot: A screen capture of the visual contents on a computer screen.

Semantic Web: A concept of the World Wide Web in which its contents are sufficiently metadata-ed so as to be machine searchable (a concept of Tim Berners-Lee) for a wide range of information mining capabilities.

Social Media Platforms: Online spaces that enable human sharing of digital information and interactions through self-created online identities.

Static: Non-dynamic, not moving, passive.

Structured Data: Data that is pre-labeled in spreadsheets with column and / or row headers labeling the data.

Synthetic Data: Artificial data (created for exemplification or other purposes).

Tag: The folk labeling of social media contents like images, audio files, video files, slideshows, or other contents.

Text Frequency Count: A machine count of all (generally semantic) words in a document or text corpus (minus those listed in a "stopwords list" or a "delete words list").

Text Search: The extraction of all instances of a particular term or phrase (or related synonyms) in order to capture the "gist" of its usage based on proxemics terms (both prior to the term's use and following the term's use).

Unicode: A code set of characters and specifications that enables the inclusion of any written language to be used on computers and the Internet (based on the work of The Unicode Consortium available at http://www.unicode.org/).

Unstructured Data: Data that is not structured in tables with labeled rows and columns, such as textual documents, text corpuses, extracted Tweetstream datasets, images, audio files, video, and so on.

Visual Mining: The human extraction of information from often-interactive visual objects.

Compilation of References

(Ed.). Shank, P. (2011). *The online learning idea book: proven ways to enhance technology-based and blended learning, 2.* Retrieved from http://common.books24x7. com/toc.aspx?bookid=44452

"Frontiers in Massive Data Analysis." (2013). National Research Council of The National Academies. Washington, D.C.: The National Academies Press.

Abdelhaq, H., Gertz, M., & Sengstock, C. (2013). Spatio-temporal characteristics of bursty words in Twitter streams. *Proceedings ofSigspatial '13.* Orlando, Florida. doi:10.1145/2525314.2525354

About Twitter. (n.d.). Retrieved from: https://about.twitter.com/company

Adar, E., Teevan, J., Dumais, S. T., & Elsas, J. L. (2009). The Web Changes Everything: Understanding the Dynamics of Web Content. In *Proceedings of the 2nd ACM International Conference on Web Search and Data Mining, WSDM '09,* Barcelona, Spain. (pp. 282-291). doi:10.1145/1498759.1498837

Adler, B. T., & de Alfaro, L. (2007). A content-driven reputation system for the Wikipedia. In *WWW 2007* (pp. 261–270). Track E-Applications. doi:10.1145/1242572.1242608

Agostinho, S., Tindall-Ford, S., & Roodenrys, K. (2013). Adaptive diagrams: Handing control over to the learner to manage split-attention online. *Computers & Education, 64,* 52–62. doi:10.1016/j.compedu.2013.01.007

Alderman, M. K. (1990). Motivation for at-risk students. *Educational Leadership, 48,* 27–30.

Alkan, S. (2013). *Factors effecting eye tracking measures and achievement in multimedia learning* (PhD Thesis). Middle East Technical University, Ankara, Turkey.

Allen, B. L. (1998). Visualization and Cognitive Abilities. In Pauline Atherton Cochrane; Eric H. Johnson (Eds.) (1998) *Visualizing Subject Access for 21st Century Information Resources*

Allen, I. E., & Seaman, J. (2014). *Grade change: Tracking online education in the United States, 2014.* Babson Survey Research Group and Quahog Research Group, LLC.

Alliance for Networking Visual Culture. (2014). Scalar. http://scalar.usc.edu/

Ames, C. A. (1990). Motivation: What teachers need to know. *Teachers College Record, 91*(3), 409–421.

Anderson, D. R., Fite, K. V., Petrovich, N., & Hirsch, J. (2006). Cortical activation while watching video montage: An fMRI study. *Media Psychology, 8*(1), 7–24. doi:10.1207/S1532785XMEP0801_2

Anderson, N. (2013). *The Internet Police: How Crime Went Online, and the Cops Followed.* New York: W.W. Norton & Company.

Andrejevic, M. (2007). iSpy: Surveillance and Power in the Interactive Era. Lawrence: University Press of Kansas.

Andrejevic, M. (2014). The big data divide. *International Journal of Communication, 8,* 1673–1689.

Andress, J., & Winterfeld, S. (2014). Psychological Weapons. Cyber Warfare: Techniques, Tactics, and Tools for Security Practitioners. Amsterdam: Elsevier. doi:10.1016/B978-0-12-416672-1.00008-8

Anger over hidden commercialized tracking devices. (2014, Oct. 11). *CBS News.* Retrieved from http://www.cbsnews.com/videos/anger-over-hidden-commercialized-tracking-devices/

Arab, M., Dastfal, S. M., & Zareian, E. (2014). The effect of pairwise video feedback on the learning of elegant eye-hand coordination skill. *Annals of Applied Sport Science, 2*(3), 7–12.

Ares, K. (2014, Nov. 29). Social media data does not reveal true human behaviour. *Tech Analyst*. Retrieved from http://www.techanalyst.co/social-media-data-does-not-reveal-true-human-behaviour/14462/

Atkinson, R. K., Mayer, R. E., & Merrill, M. M. (2005). Fostering social agency in multimedia learning: Examining the impact of an animated agent's voice. *Contemporary Educational Psychology, 30*(1), 117–139. doi:10.1016/j.cedpsych.2004.07.001

Ayres, P. ve Sweller, J. (2005). The Split-Attention Principle in Multimedia. In R. E. Mayer (Ed.)., The Cambridge Handbook of Multimedia Learning.

Back, M. D., Stopfer, J. M., Vazire, S., Gaddis, S., Schmukle, S. C., Egloff, B., & Gosling, S. D. (2010). Facebook profiles reflect actual personality, not self-idealization. *Psychological Science*. Retrieve from: http://pss.sagepub.com/content/early/2010/01/28/0956797609360756.short?rss=1&ssource=mfc

Backstrom, L., Sun, E., & Marlow, C. (2010). Find me if you can: Improving geographical preduction with social and spatial proximity. In the proceedings of *WWW 2010*. Raleigh, North Carolina.

Baddeley, A. D. (1986). *Working memory*. New York: Oxford University Press.

Baeza-Yates, R., & Castillo, C. (2000). Caracterizando la Web Chilena. In Encuentro Chileno de Ciencias de la Computación. Sociedad Chilena de Ciencias de la Computación.

Baeza-Yates, R., & Poblete, B. (2006). Dynamics of the Chilean Web Structure. *The International Journal of Computer and Telecommunications Networking*. 50(10), 1464-1473.

Baeza-Yates, R., Castillo, C. & Lopez, V. (2005). Characteristics of the Web of Spain. *Cybermetrics*. 9(1).

Baeza-Yates, R., Castillo, C., & Efthimiadis, E. N. (2007). Characterization of National Web Domains. *Journal ACM Transactions on Internet Technology*. 7(2).

Baeza-Yates, R., Saint-Jean, F.,, & Castillo, C. (2002). Web Structure, Dynamics and Page Quality. *String Processing and Information Retrieval: Lecture Notes in Computer Science Series, 2476*, 453–461.

Bair, D., & Dickinson, M. (2011, April 21). *How Much Narration in eLearning? Our Lessons Learned*. Retrieved from: https://www.learningsolutionsmag.com/articles/666/how-much-narration-in-elearning-our-lessons-learned

Bastos, M. T., Puschmann, C., & Travitzki, R. (2013). Tweeting across hashtags: Overlapping users and the importance of language, topics, and politics. *24th ACM Conference on Hypertext and Social Media,* Paris, France.

Baucom, E., Sanjari, A., Liu, X., & Chen, M. (2013). Mirroring the real world in social media: Twitter, geolocation, and sentiment analysis. Association of Computing Machinery.

Bayram, S., & Mutlu-Bayraktar, D. (2012). Using Eye Tracking to Study on Attention and Recall in Multimedia Learning Environments: The Effects of Design in Learning. *World Journal on Educational Technology, 4*(2), 81–98.

Bazar, N. S. (2009). *Web usability or accessibility: Comparisons between people with and without intellectual disabilities in viewing complex naturalistic scenes using eye-tracking technology*. (Master Thesis). Mount St. Mary's University, Fairfax, VA.

Beilock, S. (2010). *Choke: What the Secrets of the Brain Reveal about Getting it Right When You Have To*. New York: Free Press.

Bergman, M. K. (2001). The Deep Web: Surfacing Hidden Value. *Journal of Electronic Publishing*. 7.

Bergmann, J., & Park, A. (2012). Just how small is an atom? Retrieved from http://ed.ted.com/lessons/just-how-small-is-an-atom

Bermingham, A., Conway, M., McInerney, L., O'Hare, N., & Smeaton, A. F. (2009). Combining social network analysis and sentiment analysis to explore the potential for online radicalisation (sic). *Advances in Social Networks Analysis and Mining*. Greece. Retrieve from: http://doras.dcu.ie/4554/3/DCU_asonam09.pdf

Berners-Lee, T., & Fischetti, M. (1999). *Weaving the Web*. San Francisco: Harper.

Betrancourt, M. (2005). The animation and interactivity principles in multimedia learning. In R. E. Mayer (Ed.), *The Cambridge handbook of multimedia learning* (pp. 287–296). New York: Cambridge University Press. doi:10.1017/CBO9780511816819.019

Betters, E. (2015, April 22). Virtual Reality: The VR headsets to buy in 2015, whatever your budget. Retrieved from http://www.pocket-lint.com/news/132945-virtual-reality-the-vr-headsets-to-buy-in-2015-whatever-your-budget

Bharat, K., Chang, B., Henzinger, M. R.,, & Ruhl, M. (2001). Who Links to Whom: Mining Linkage Between Web Sites.*Proceedings of the 2001 IEEE International Conference on Data Mining, ICDM '01,*IEEE Computer Society, San José, California, USA (pp. 51-58). doi:10.1109/ICDM.2001.989500

Biedert, R., Buscher, G., & Dengel, A. (2009). *Hauptbeitrag / The Eyebook.*

Bielawski, L., & Metcalf, D. (2003). *Blended elearning: integrating knowledge, performance support, and online learning.* Retrieved from: http://common.books24x7.com/toc.aspx?bookid=4920

Björneborn, L., & Ingwersen, P. (2004). Toward a Basic Framework for Webometrics. *Journal of the American Society for Information Science and Technology, 55*(14), 1216–1227. doi:10.1002/asi.20077

Black, A., Mascaro, C., Gallagher, M., & Goggins, S. P. (2012). Twitter Zombie: Architecture for capturing, socially transforming and analyzing the Twittersphere. Proceedings of *GROUP '12*, Sanibel Island, Florida.

Bliss, C. A., Kloumann, I. M., Harris, K. D., Danford, C. M., & Dodds, P. S. (2012). Twitter reciprocal reply networks exhibit assortativity with respect to happiness. *Journal of Computational Science, 3*(5), 388–397. doi:10.1016/j.jocs.2012.05.001

Blum, A. (2012). *Tubesd: A Journey to the Center of the Internet.* New York: Harper Collins.

Blumberg, P. (2009). *Developing learner-centered teaching: A practical guide for faculty.* San Francisco, CA: John Wiley & Sons.

Blumenstock, J. E. (2008). Size matters: Word count as a measure of quality on Wikipedia (Poster Paper). In the proceedings of *WWW 2008*. Beijing, China.

Bodenhausen, G., Kang, S., & Peery, D. (2012). Social categorization and the perception of social groups. In S. Fiske & C. Macrae (Eds.), *The SAGE handbook of social cognition* (pp. 311–330). London: SAGE Publications Ltd.; doi:10.4135/9781446247631.n16

Boldi, P., Codenotti, B., Santini, M.,, & Vigna, S. (2002). Structural Properties of the African Web.*Proceedings of the 11st International Conference on World Wide Web, WWW'02*, Honolulu, Hawaii, USA.

Boucheix, J., & Schneider, E. (2009). Static and animated presentations in learning dynamic mechanical systems. *Learning and Instruction, 19*(2), 112–127. doi:10.1016/j.learninstruc.2008.03.004

Bowman, N. D., Westerman, D. K., & Claus, C. J. (2012). How demanding is social media: Understanding social media diets as a function of perceived costs and benefits—A rational actor perspective. *Computers in Human Behavior, 28*(6), 2298–2305. doi:10.1016/j.chb.2012.06.037

Brenner, M., & Izquierdo, E. (2012). Social event detection and retrieval in collaborative photo collections. *Proceedings of ICMR.* Hong Kong, China. doi:10.1145/2324796.2324823

Brewington, B.,, & Cybenko, G. (2000). How Dynamic is the Web?*Proceedings of the 9th Conference on the World Wide Web.* (pp. 257-276).

Broder, A., Kumar, R., Maghoul, F., Raghavan, P., Rajagopalan, S., & Stata, R. et al. (2000). Graph Structure in the Web. Computer Networks. *The International Journal of Computer and Telecommunications Networking, 33*(1-6), 309–320.

Bruno, N. (2011). Tweet first, verify later? How real-time information is changing the coverage of worldwide crisis events. *Reuters Institute for the Study of Journalism.* University of Oxford.

Brunty, J., & Helenek, K. (2012) Social Media Investigation for Law Enforcement. In L.S. Miller, Series Ed. Amsterdam: Elsevier. 41 – 70. Retrieved from http://www.sciencedirect.com/science/book/9781455731350

Bull, P. H. (2013). Cognitive constructivist theory of multimedia: Designing teacher-made interactive digital. *Creative Education, 4*(9), 614-619. Retrieved from http://0-search.proquest.com.liucat.lib.liu.edu/docview/1448245192?accountid=12142

Bull, P. (2009). Cognitive constructivist theory of multimedia design: A theoretical analysis of instructional design for multimedia learning. In G. Siemens & C. Fulford (Eds.), *Proceedings of World Conference on educational multimedia, hypermedia and telecommunications 2009* (pp. 735–740). http://www.editlib.org/p/31581

Burnap, P., Rana, O. F., Avis, N., Williams, M., Housley, W., & Edwards, A. et al. (2013). Detecting tension in online communities with computational Twitter analysis. *Technological Forecasting and Social Change*, 1–13.

Buss, A. H., & Sánchez, P. J. (2002). Building complex models with Legos. *Proceedings of 2002 Winter Simulation Conference*. Charnes.

Buswell, G. (1922). *Fundamental reading habits: A study of their development*. Chicago: University of Chicago Press.

Buswell, G. T. (1935). *How people look at pictures*. Chicago: University of Chicago Press.

Byers, S. (2004). Information leakage caused by hidden data in published documents. *IEEE Security and Privacy, 2*(2), 23–27. doi:10.1109/MSECP.2004.1281241

Byrne, M. D., Anderson, J. R., Douglass, S., & Matessa, M. (1999). Eye tracking the visual search of click-down menus. *Human Factors in Computing Systems: Proceedings of CHI '99*.

Calandra, B., Barron, A. E., & Thompson-Sellers, I. (2008). Audio use in E-Learning: What, why, when and how? *International Journal on E-Learning, 7*(4).

Candan, K. S., Di Caro, L., & Sapino, M. L. (2008). Creating tag hierarchies for effective navigation in social media. In the proceedings of SSM '08, Napa Valley, California. (pp. 75–82). doi:10.1145/1458583.1458597

Canvas Instructor Guide. (2014). *Canvas instructor guide*, by Instructure. Retrieved from https://guides.instructure.com/m/4212/pdf

Carson, E. (2015, March 4). *The pros and cons of low-cost virtual reality headsets*. Retrieved from http://www.techrepublic.com/article/the-pros-and-cons-of-low-cost-virtual-reality-headsets

Chalk talk. (n.d.). In Merriam-Webster online dictionary. Retrieved from http://www.merriam-webster.com/dictionary/chalk%20talk

Chang, R. C., Chung, L. Y., & Huang, Y. M. (2014). Developing an interactive augmented reality system as a complement to plant education and comparing its effectiveness with video learning. *Interactive Learning Environments*, (ahead-of-print), 1-20.

Charlwood, J., Dennis, A., Gissing, A., Quick, L., & Varma, S. (2012). Use of social media during flood events. *Batemans Bay 2012*. Retrieve from: http://floods.org.au/use-of-social-media-during-flood-events/

Cheng, Z., Caverlee, J., & Lee, K. (2013). A content-driven framework for geolocating microblog users. *ACM Transactions on Intelligent Systems and Technology*: 4(1), Article 2, 2:1 – 2:27.

Chen, M.-P., Wang, L.-C., Chen, H.-J., & Chen, Y.-C. (2014). Effects of type of multimedia strategy on learning of Chinese characters for non-native novices. *Computers & Education, 70*, 41–52. doi:10.1016/j.compedu.2013.07.042

Cheung, A. S. Y. (2014). Location privacy: The challenges of mobile service devices. *Computer Law & Security Report, 30*(1), 41–54. doi:10.1016/j.clsr.2013.11.005

Cho, J., & Garcia-Molina, H. (2003a). Estimating Frequency of Change. *Journal ACM Transactions on Internet Technology, 3*(3), 256–290. doi:10.1145/857166.857170

Cho, J., & Garcia-Molina, H. (2003b). Effective Page Refresh Policies for Web Crawlers. *Journal ACM Transactions on Database Systems, 28*(4), 390–426. doi:10.1145/958942.958945

Cho, J., Shivakumar, N., & Garcia-Molina, H. (2000). Finding Replicated Web Collections. In *Proceedings of the ACM SIGMOD International Conference on Management of Data*, Dallas, Texas. (pp. 355-366).

Christoph, R. T., Schoenfeld, G. A., & Tansky, J. W. (2006). Overcoming barriers to training utilizing technology: The influence of self-efficacy factors on multimedia-based training receptiveness. *Human Resource Development Quarterly*, 9(1), 25–38. doi:10.1002/hrdq.3920090104

Cicero, S. (2012, May 30). *Cisco's VNI forecast projects the Internet will be four times as large in four years*. Retrieved from http://newsroom.cisco.com/press-release-content?amp;type=webcontent&articleId=888280

Cierniak, G., Scheiter, K., & Gerjets, P. (2009). Explaining the split-attention effect: Is the reduction of extraneous cognitive load accompanied by an increase in germane cognitive load? *Computers in Human Behavior*, 25(2), 315–324. doi:10.1016/j.chb.2008.12.020

Cisco. (2014). *Cisco visual networking index: Forecast and methodology, 2013 – 2018*, Cisco whitepaper. Retrieved from http://www.cisco.com/c/en/us/solutions/collateral/service-provider/ip-ngn-ip-next-generation-network/white_paper_c11-481360.pdf

Clare, K. (2013). The essential role of place within the creative industries: Boundaries, networks and play. *Cities (London, England)*, 34, 52–57. doi:10.1016/j.cities.2012.05.009

Clark, R. C. (2010). *Evidence-based training methods: a guide for training professionals*. Retrieved from: http://common.books24x7.com/toc.aspx?bookid=35123

Clark, R. C., & Mayer, R. E. (3rd Ed.). (2011). *e-learning and the science of instruction: proven guidelines for consumers and designers of multimedia learning*. Retrieved from: http://common.books24x7.com/toc.aspx?bookid=44340

Clark, R. C., & Mayer, R. E. (2011). *E-learning and the science of instruction: Proven guidelines for consumers and designers of multimedia learning*. San Francisco, CA: Pfeiffer. doi:10.1002/9781118255971

Clark, R. E. (1983). Reconsidering research on learning from media. *Review of Educational Research*, 53(4), 445–459. doi:10.3102/00346543053004445

Claval, P. (2004). At the heart of the cultural approach in geography: Thinking space. *GeoJournal*, 60(4), 321–328. doi:10.1023/B:GEJO.0000042967.76392.93

Cliggett, L. (2013). Qualitative data archiving in the digital age: Strategies for data preservation and sharing. *Qualitative Report*, 18(1), 1–11. Retrieved from http://www.nova.edu/ssss/QR/QR18/cliggett1.pdf

Cobb, J. (2013). *Leading the learning revolution: the expert's guide to capitalizing on the exploding lifelong education market*. Retrieved from: http://common.books24x7.com/toc.aspx?bookid=47761

Collins, C., & Carpendale, S. (2007). VisLink: Revealing relationships amongst visualizations. *IEEE Transactions on Visualization and Computer Graphics*, 13(6), 1192–1199. doi:10.1109/TVCG.2007.70521 PMID:17968064

Crone, I., & MacKay, K. (2007). Motivating today's college students. *Peer Review*, 9(1), 18–21.

Crooks, S., Inan, F., Cheon, J., Ari, F., & Flores, R. (2012). Modality and cueing in multimedia learning: Examining cognitive and perceptual explanations for the modality effect. *Computers in Human Behavior*, 28(3), 1063–1071. doi:10.1016/j.chb.2012.01.010

Cuevas, R., Gonzalez, R., Cuevas, A., & Guerrero, C. (2014). Understanding the locality effect in Twitter: Measurement and analysis. *Personal and Ubiquitous Computing*, 18(2), 397–411. doi:10.1007/s00779-013-0658-y

Cui, W., Wu, Y., Liu, S., Wei, F., Zhou, M. X., & Qu, H. (2010). Context preserving dynamic word cloud visualization. In the proceedings of the *IEEE Pacific Visualization Symposium*, Taipei, Taiwan. doi:10.1109/PACIFICVIS.2010.5429600

Dayter, D. (2014). Self-praise in microblogging. *Journal of Pragmatics*, 61, 91–102. doi:10.1016/j.pragma.2013.11.021

De Keyser, P. (2012). *The Semantic Web. Indexing: From Thesauri to the Semantic Web*. Oxford: Chandos.

de Koning, B. B., Tabbers, H., Rikers, R. M. J. P., & Paas, F. (2009). Towards a framework for attention cueing in instructional animations: Guidelines for research and design. *Educational Psychology Review*, 21(2). 113–140. doi:10.1007/s10648-009-9098-7

Deci, E. L., & Ryan, R. M. (1991). A motivational approach to self: Integration in personality. In R. Dienstbier (Ed.), Nebraska symposium on motivation: Vol. 38, Perspectives on motivation (pp. 237–288). Lincoln: University of Nebraska Press.

Del Mar Sánchez-Vera, Fernández-Breis, Castellano-Nieves, Frutos-Morales, & Predes-Espinoza. (2012). Semantic Web technologies for generating feedback in online assessment environments. *Knowledge-Based Systems*, 152–165.

Desai, P., & Vijayalakshmi, M. (2015). Flipped classroom: An efficient pedagogical tool to teach a course for final year computer science and engineering graduate students. *Journal of Engineering Education Transformations*, 306-310.

Deubel, H., & Schneider, W. (1996). Saccade target selection and object recognition: Evidence for a common attentional mechanism. *Vision Research*, *36*(12), 1827–1837. doi:10.1016/0042-6989(95)00294-4 PMID:8759451

Devine, T., & Maassarani, T. F. (2011). *The Corporate Whistleblower's Survival Guide: A Handbook for Committing the Truth*. San Francisco: Berrett-Koehler Publishers, Inc.

Diakopoulos, N., De Choudhury, M., & Naaman, M. (2012). Finding and assessing social media information sources in the context of journalism. *Proceedings of CHI 2012, Social Computing: Business & Beyond*. Austin, Texas. doi:10.1145/2207676.2208409

Dick, W., Carey, L., & Carey, J. O. (6th Ed.) (2005). *The systematic design of instruction*. Boston: Allyn & Bacon.

Dörk, M., Williamson, C., & Carpendale, S. (2012). Navigating tomorrow's web: From searching and browsing to visual exploration. ACM Transactions on the Web: 6(3). *Article*, *12*, 13–26.

Downey, A. B. (2001). The Structural Cause of File size Distributions. *Proceedings 9th International Symposium on Modeling, Analysis and Simulation of Computer and Telecommunication Systems*, Cincinnati, Ohio. (pp. 361-370).

Doyle, T. (2011). *Learner-centered teaching: Putting the research on learning into practice*. Sterling, VA: Stylus Publishing, LLC.

Driscoll, M. (2nd Ed.). (2002). Web-based training: creating e-learning experiences Retrieved from: http://common.books24x7.com/toc.aspx?bookid=3748

Drout, M., & Smith, L. (2012). How to Read a Dendrogram. Retrieved from http://wheatoncollege.edu/lexomics/files/2012/08/How-to-Read-a-Dendrogram-Web-Ready.pdf

Dunn, C., & Scheiderman, B. (2013). Motif simplification: Improving network visualization readability with fan, connector, and clique glyphs. *Proceedings of CHI 2013: Changing Perspectives*. Paris, France.

Dzbor, M., Motta, E., & Domingue, J. (2007). *Magpie: Experiences in supporting Semantic Web browsing. Journal of Web Semantics*. Science Direct.

Efthimiadis, E.,, & Castillo, C. (2004). Charting the Greek Web. *Proceedings of the Conference of the American Society for Information Science and Technology (ASIST)*, Rhode Island, USA.

Eijkman, H. (2007). Web 2.0 as a non-foundational network-centric learning space. *Campus-Wide Information Systems*, *25*(2), 93–104. doi:10.1108/10650740810866567

Elam, C., Stratton, T., & Gibson, D. (2007). Welcoming a new generation to college: The millennial students. *Journal of College Admission*, *195*, 20–25.

Elwood, S., & Leszczynski, A. (2011). Privacy, reconsidered: New representations, data practices, and the geoweb. *Geoforum*, *42*(1), 6–15. doi:10.1016/j.geoforum.2010.08.003

Evans, C., & Gibbons, N. J. (2007). The interactivity effect in multimedia learning. *Computers & Education*, *49*(4), 1147–1160. doi:10.1016/j.compedu.2006.01.008

Eyal, N., & Hoover, R. (2014). *Hooked: How to Build Habit-Forming Products*. New York: Portfolio, Penguin.

Fetterly, D., Manasse, M., & Najork, M. (2004). Spam, Damn Spam, and Statistics: Using Statistical Analysis to Locate Spam Web Pages. *Proceedings of the 7th International Workshop on the Web and Databases* WebDB '04, Paris, France. (pp. 1-6).

Fetterly, D., Manasse, M., Najork, M., & Wiener, J. (2003). A Large-Scale Study of the Evolution of Web Pages. *Proceedings of the 12th International Conference on World Wide Web, WWW '03*, Budapest, Hungary. (pp. 669-678). doi:10.1145/775152.775246

Flickr. (2014, Nov. 25). Retrieved from http://en.wikipedia.org/wiki/Flickr

Flora, C. (2013). *Friendfluence: The Surprising Ways Friends Make Us Who We Are*. New York: Doubleday.

Florax, M., & Ploetzner, R. (2010). What contributes to the split-attention effect? The role of text segmentation, picture labelling, and spatial proximity. *Learning and Instruction*, 20(3), 216–224. doi:10.1016/j.learninstruc.2009.02.021

Freberg, K., Saling, K., Vidoloff, K. G., & Eosco, G. (2013). Using value modeling to evaluate social media messages: The case of Hurricane Irene. *Public Relations Review*, 39(3), 185–192. doi:10.1016/j.pubrev.2013.02.010

Frontiers in massive data analysis. (2013). *National Research Council of the National Academies*. Washington, D.C.: The National Academies Press.

Fung, H., & Ma, W. W. (2015). Investigating the relationship between students' attitude towards video production project and their generic skills enhancement. In *New Media, Knowledge Practices and Multiliteracies* (pp. 235–248). Heidelberg, NY: Springer Singapore.

Gambs, S., Killijian, M.-O., & Nuñez del Prado Cortez, M. (2014). De-anonymization attack on geolocated data. *Journal of Computer and System Sciences*, 80(8), 1597–1614. doi:10.1016/j.jcss.2014.04.024

Garcia-Gavilanes, R., Mejova, Y., & Quercia, D. (2014). Twitter ain't without frontiers: Economic, social, and cultural boundaries in international communication. In the proceedings of CSCW 2014 Geographic Distance. Feb. 15 – 19, 2014. Baltimore, Maryland.

Gawhry, L. N. (2012). *Assessing the impact of social media on the 25 January 2011 Egyptian Revolution*. Naval Postgraduate Thesis.

Gegenfurtner, A., Quesada-Pallarès, & Knogler, M. (2014). Digital simulation-based training: A meta-analysis. *British Journal of Educational Technology*, 1–18.

Gilbert, J. K. (2005). Visualization: A metacognitive skill in science and science education. Visualization in Science Education. (pp. 9–27). Springer.

Gillen, J., & Merchant, G. (2013). Contact calls: Twitter as a dialogic social and linguistic practice. *Language Sciences*, 35, 47–58. doi:10.1016/j.langsci.2012.04.015

Gilley, A., Dixon, P., & Gilley, J. W. (2008). Characteristics of leadership effectiveness: Implementing change and driving innovation in organizations. *Human Resource Development Quarterly*, 19(2), 153–169. doi:10.1002/hrdq.1232

Glenny, M. (2011). *DarkMarket: Cyberthieves, Cybercops, and You*. New York: Alfred A. Knopf.

Gobert, J. D. (2005). Leveraging technology and cognitive theory on visualization to promote students' science. Ch. 5. In John K. Gilbert's, Visualization in Science Education: (pp. 73–90).

Goldberg, J. H., Stimson, M. J., Lewenstein, M., Scott, N., & Wichansky, A. (2002). Eye tracking in web search tasks: Design implications. *In Proceedings of the Eye Tracking and Related Applications Symposium*, 51-59. doi:10.1145/507072.507082

Goldman, R., Pea, R., Barron, B., & Derry, S. J. (Eds.). (2014). *Video research in the learning sciences*. New York, NY: Routledge.

Gomes, D., & Silva, M. J. (2005). Characterizing a National Community Web. *Journal ACM Transactions on Internet Technology*, 5(3), 508–531. doi:10.1145/1084772.1084775

Gonzálex-Bailón, S., Wang, N., Rivero, A., Borge-Holthoefer, J., & Moreno, Y. (2014). Assessing the bias in samples of large online networks. *Social Networks*, 28, 16–27. doi:10.1016/j.socnet.2014.01.004

Gonzalez-Sanchez, J., Chavez-Echeagaray, M. E., Gibson, D., & Atkinson, R. K. (2013). Multimodal affect recognition in virtual worlds: avatars mirroring user's affect, *Humaine Association Conference on Affective Computing and Intelligent Interaction*, (pp. 724–725). doi:10.1109/ACII.2013.133

Goodwin, L., Kozleski, E., Muth, R., Rhodes, L. K., & White, K. K. (2006). Establishing a center to support faculty research. *Innovative Higher Education, 30*(4). doi:10.1007/s10755-005-8347-z

Greenwald, G. (2014). *No Place to Hide: Edward Snowden, the NSA, and the U.S. Surveillance State*. New York: Metropolitan Books.

Grefenstette, G., & Nioche, J. (2000). Estimation of English and Non-English Language use on the WWW. *Proceedings of Content-Based Multimedia Information Access*, Paris, France. (pp. 237–246).

Griggs, S. A., & Dunn, R. S. (2000). Practical approaches to using learning styles in higher education: The how-to steps. In R. Dunn & S. A. Griggs (Eds.), *Practical Approaches to Using Learning Styles in Higher Education* (pp. 19–33). Westport, CT: Greenwood Press.

Groh, G., Straub, F., Eicher, J., & Grob, D. (2013). Geographic aspects of tie strength and value of information in social networking. Proceedings of ACM SIGSPATIAL LBSN'13. Orlando, Florida. 1 – 10. doi:10.1145/2536689.2536803

Guild, P. B. (2001). Diversity, learning style and culture. *New Horizons for Learning*. Retrieved at http://education.jhu.edu/PD/newhorizons/strategies/topics/Learning%20Styles/diversity.html

Gulli, A., & Signorini, A. (2005). The Indexable Web is more than 11.5 Billion Pages. *14th International Conference on World Wide Web, WWW '05* Chiba, Japan. (pp. 902-903).

Gyongyi, Z., & Garcia-Molina, H. (2005). Web Spam Taxonomy. *Proceedings of the First International Workshop on Adversarial Information Retrieval on the Web, AIRWeb 2005.* (pp. 39-47).

Haddow, G. D., & Haddow, K. S. (2014). *Disaster Communications in a Changing Media World* (2nd ed.). Amsterdam: Elsevier.

Hai-Jew, S. (2012, July 1). *Building and Analyzing Node-Link Diagrams to Understand Social Networks*. Retrieve from https://softchalkcloud.com/lesson/c4d8tSWMCwm39n

Hai-Jew, S. (2012, June 24). *Building Effective Study Guides for Online Learning and Assessment*. Retrieved from https://softchalkcloud.com/lesson/rFnD0AQX3xRVTa

Hai-Jew, S. (2012, Mar. 3). *Using Tableau Public for (Spatial and Trendline) Data Visualization (An Early Exploration and 'TMI' Musing on Data)*. Retrieved from https://softchalkcloud.com/lesson/rtNYCf1K80el9w

Hai-Jew, S. (2013, Aug. 2). Data visualization: Drawing with data, with concepts, and with rules. *Summer Institute on Distance Learning and Instructional Technology (SIDLIT) 2013*. Retrieved from http://www.k-state.edu/ID/DataVisualization/mobile_pages/DataVisualization.html

Hai-Jew, S. (2013, May). Maltego Radium™: Mapping Network Ties and Identities across the Internet. In the *Conference on Higher Education Computing in Kansas*. Pittsburg State University, Pittsburg, Kansas. Retrieved from http://www.slideshare.net/ShalinHaiJew/maltego-radium-mapping-network-ties-and-identities-across-the-internet

Hai-Jew, S. (2014). "ICT4D and its Potential Role in the Detection, Surveillance, and Prevention of Novel Zoonotic Disease Outbreaks for Global, National, and Local Pandemic Prevention." Ch. 7. In C.M. Akrivopoulou and N. Garipidis's Human Rights and the Impact of ICT in the Public Sphere: Participation, Democracy, and Political Autonomy. Hershey: IGI-Global. doi:10.4018/978-1-4666-6248-3.ch007

Hai-Jew, S. (2014). Conducting Surface Web-Based Research with Maltego Carbon. Retrieve from: http://scalar.usc.edu/works/conducting-surface-web-based-research-with-maltego-carbon/index

Hai-Jew, S. (2014). Using NVivo: An Unofficial and Unauthorized Primer. Retrieve from: http://scalar.usc.edu/works/using-nvivo-an-unofficial-and-unauthorized-primer/index

Hai-Jew, S. (2014). *Using NVivo: An Unofficial and Unauthorized Primer*. Retrieved from http://scalar.usc.edu/works/using-nvivo-an-unofficial-and-unauthorized-primer/index

Hai-Jew, S. (2014, Aug.) Using Maltego Tungsten™ to Explore the Cyber-Physical Confluence in Geolocation. In the proceedings of the Summer Institute on Distance Learning and Instructional Technology Retrieved from http://www.slideshare.net/ShalinHaiJew/using-maltego-tungsten-to-explore-cyberphysical-confluence-in-geolocation

Hai-Jew, S. (2015). Querying Social Media with NodeXL. Retrieve from: http://scalar.usc.edu/works/querying-social-media-with-nodexl/index

Hale, S. A. (2014). Global connectivity and multilinguals in the Twitter network. *Proceedings of CHI 2014, One of a CHInd*. Toronto, Ontario, Canada. 833 – 842. doi:10.1145/2556288.2557203

Handley, A., & Chapman, C. C. (2011). *Content rules: how to create killer blogs, podcasts, videos, ebooks, webinars (and more) that engage customers and ignite your business*. Retrieved from: http://common.books24x7.com/toc.aspx?bookid=40621

Hannafin, M. J., & Land, S. M. (1997). The foundations and assumptions of technology-enhanced student-centered learning environments. *Instructional Science*, *25*(3), 167–202. doi:10.1023/A:1002997414652

Hansen, D., Smith, M. A., & Schneiderman, B. (2011). EventGraphs: Charting collections of conference connections. *Proceedings of the 44th Hawaii International Conference on System Sciences*. IEEE. 1 – 10.

Hansen, D. L., Schneiderman, B., & Smith, M. A. (2011). *Analyzing Social Media Networks with NodeXL: Insights from a Connected World*. Amsterdam: Elsevier.

Harding, L. (2014). *The Snowden Files: The Inside Story of the World's Most Wanted Man*. New York: Vintage Books.

Harris, S. (2014). *War: The Rise of the Military-Internet Complex*. New York: Houghton Mifflin Harcourt Publishing.

Hasler, B. S., Kersten, B., & Sweller, J. (2007). Learner control, cognitive load and instructional animation. *Applied Cognitive Psychology*, *21*(6), 713–729. doi:10.1002/acp.1345

Hassan, Q. (2011). Demystifying Cloud Computing. *The Journal of Defense Software Engineering*, *2011*(Jan/Feb), 16–21. Retrieved from: http://www.crosstalkonline.org/storage/issue-archives/2011/201101/201101-Hassan.pdf

Heaney, M. T. (2014). Multiplex networks and interest group influence reputation: An exponential random graph model. *Social Networks*, *36*, 66–81. doi:10.1016/j.socnet.2012.11.003

Hegarty, M. (2004). Dynamic visualizations and learning: Getting to the difficult questions. *Learning and Instruction*, *14*(3), 343–351. doi:10.1016/j.learninstruc.2004.06.007

Hegarty, M., Kriz, S., & Cate, C. (2003). The roles of mental animations and external animations in understanding mechanical systems. *Cognition and Instruction*, *21*(4), 325–360. doi:10.1207/s1532690xci2104_1

Heider, F. (1958). *The psychology of interpersonal relations*. New York, NY: John Wiley & Sons. doi:10.1037/10628-000

Henry, P. (2009). Online Presentation Strategies for Visual Learners. *Proceedings of The European Conference On E-Learning*, 743-749.

Herman, J. H. (2012). Faculty development programs: The frequency and variety of professional development programs. *Journal of Asynchronous Learning Networks*, *16*(5).

Herrington, J., Reeves, T. C., Oliver, R., & Woo, Y. (2004). Designing authentic activities in web-based courses. *Journal of Computing in Higher Education*, *16*(1), 3–29. doi:10.1007/BF02960280

Hillstrom, A. P., & Chai, Y. C. (2006). Factors that guide or disrupt attentive visual processing. *Computers in Human Behavior*, *22*(4), 648–656. doi:10.1016/j.chb.2005.12.003

Hoare, C. (Ed.). (2011). *The Oxford handbook of reciprocal adult development and learning*. New York, NY: Oxford University Press. doi:10.1093/oxfordhb/9780199736300.001.0001

Hodell, C. (3rd Ed.). (2011). *Isd from the ground up: a nononsense approach to instructional design* Retrieved from http://common.books24x7.com/toc.aspx?bookid=41948

Höffler, T. N., & Leutner, D. (2007). Instructional animation versus static pictures: A meta-analysis. *Learning and Instruction*, *17*(6), 722–738. doi:10.1016/j.learninstruc.2007.09.013

Hoffman, J. E. (1998). *Visual attention and eye movements*. Hove, UK: Psychology Press.

Hofschroer, M. (2012, December 3). *Friends* helps global television audience learn English. Marketwire. Retrieved from http://www.marketwire.com/press-release/friends-helps-global-television-audience-learn-english-1732657.htm

Holeton, R. (1998). *Composing Cyberspace: Identity, Community, and Knowledge in the Electronic Age.* Boston: McGraw Hill.

Holloway, T., Bozicevic, M., & Börner, K. (2007). Analyzing and visualizing the semantic coverage of Wikipedia and its authors. *Complexity. Interscience, 12*(3), 30–40.

Honigsfeld, A., & Schiering, M. (2004). Diverse approaches to the diversity of learning styles in teacher education. *Educational Psychology, 24*(4), 487–507. doi:10.1080/0144341042000228861

Hoogterp, B. (2014). *Your perfect presentation: speak in front of any audience anytime anywhere and never be nervous again.* Retrieved from: http://common.books24x7.com/toc.aspx?bookid=65444

Huberman, B. A., & Adamic, L. A. (1999). Internet: Growth Dynamics of the World-Wide Web. *Nature, 401*(6749), 131–131. PMID:10490019

Huff, M., Bauhoff, V., & Schwan, S. (2012). Effects of split attention revisited: A new display technology for troubleshooting tasks. *Computers in Human Behavior, 28*(4), 1254–1261. doi:10.1016/j.chb.2012.02.008

Hughes, D. J., Rowe, M., Batey, M., & Lee, A. (2012). A tale of two sites: Twitter vs. Facebook and the personality predictors of social media usage. *Computers in Human Behavior, 28*(2), 561–569. doi:10.1016/j.chb.2011.11.001

Hunziker, H. W. (1970). Visuelle Informationsaufnahme und Intelligenz: Eine Untersuchung über die Augenfixationen beim Problemlösen. Schweizerische Zeitschrift für Psychologie und ihre Anwendungen. Retrieved from http://www.learning-systems.ch/multimedia/forsch1e.htm

Ikawa, Y., Enoki, M., & Tatsubori, M. (2012). Location inference using microblog messages. Proceedings of WWW 2012 – SWDM '12 Workshop. Lyon, France. 687 – 690. doi:10.1145/2187980.2188181

Internet in North Korea." (2014, Sept. 12) Wikipedia. Retrieved from http://en.wikipedia.org/wiki/Internet_in_North_Korea#IPv4_ranges

Ip, D., Keung, K. L. K., Cui, W., Qu, H., & Shen, H. (2010). A visual approach to text corpora comparison. In the proceedings of the *first international workshop on Intelligent Visual Interfaces for Text Analysis (IVITA) '10,* Hong Kong. doi:10.1145/2002353.2002361

Jacob, R. J. K., & Karn, K. S. (2003). Eye tracking in human-computer interaction and usability research: Ready to deliver the promises. In J. Hyona, R. Radach, & H. Deubel (Eds.), *The mind's eye: cognitive and applied aspects of eye movement research* (pp. 573–603). Oxford, UK: Elsevier Science. doi:10.1016/B978-044451020-4/50031-1

Jain, R. (2013). EventWeb: Towards social life networks. *Philosophical Transactions of the Royal Society, 371*(1987), 1–11. doi:10.1098/rsta.2012.0384 PMID:23419853

Jakobsson, M. (2012). *The Death of the Internet.* Hoboken: John Wiley & Sons. doi:10.1002/9781118312551

James, W. (1983). *The Principles of Psychology.* Cambridge, MA: Harvard University Press.

Jansen, B. J., Sobel, K., & Cook, G. (2010). Gen X and Y's attitudes on u sing social media platforms for opinion sharing (Work-in-Progress). Proceedings of *CHI 2010,* Atlanta, Georgia.

Jarodzka, H., Van Gog, T., Dorr, M., Scheiter, K., & Gerjets, P. (2013). Learning to see: Guiding students' attention via a Model's eye movements fosters learning. *Learning and Instruction, 25,* 62–70. doi:10.1016/j.learninstruc.2012.11.004

Jehn, K. A., & Bezrukova, K. (2010). The faultline activation process and the effects of activated faultlines on coalition formation, conflict, and group outcomes. *Organizational Behavior and Human Decision Processes, 112*(1), 24–42. doi:10.1016/j.obhdp.2009.11.008

Jennex, M. E. (2012). Social media—Truly viable for crisis response? *Proceedings of 9th International ISCRAM. Conference.* Vancouver, Canada. 1 – 5.

Jindal, V., Bawa, S., & Batra, S. (2014). A review of ranking approaches for semantic search on Web. *Information Processing and Management: 50*, 418 – 425. ScienceDirect. K-State 2025 Plan. Kansas State University. Retrieved from http://www.k-state.edu/2025/plan/goals.html

Johnson, L., Becker, S., Estrada, V., & Freeman, A. (2014). *The NMC horizon report: 2014 higher education edition.* Austin: New Media Consortium.

Johnson, R., Kovács, B., & Vicsek, A. (2012). A comparison of email networks and off-line social networks: A study of a medium-sized bank. *Social Networks, 34*(4), 462–469. doi:10.1016/j.socnet.2012.02.004

Jonassen, D. H. (1994). Thinking technology: Towards a constructivist design model. *Educational Technology,* 34–37.

Jonassen, D. H. (2nd Ed.). (1999). Designing constructivist learning environments. In C. M. Reigeluth (Ed.), *Instructional theories and models: A new paradigm of instructional theory* (pp. 215–239). Mahwah: Lawrence Erlbaum.

Junco, R., & Mastrodicasa, J. (2007). Connecting to the net generation: What higher education professionals need to know about today's college students. *National Association of Student Personnel Administrators.* Retrieved from http://blog.reyjunco.com/pdf/NetGenerationProof.pdf

Jurgenson, N. (2011). Digital dualism and the fallacy of web objectivity. *Cyborgology. The Society Pages.* Retrieve from: http://thesocietypages.org/cyborgology/2011/09/13/digital-dualism-and-the-fallacy-of-web-objectivity/

Kalyuga, S. (2007). Expertise reversal effect and its Implications for learner-tailored instruction. *Educational Psychology Review, 19*(4), 509–539. doi:10.1007/s10648-007-9054-3

Kalyuga, S., Ayres, P., Chandler, P., & Sweller, J. (2003). The expertise reversal effect. *Educational Psychologist, 38*(1), 23–31. doi:10.1207/S15326985EP3801_4

Kalyuga, S., Rikers, R., & Paas, F. (2012). Educational implications for expertise reversal effects in learning and performance of complex cognitive and sensorimotor skills. *Educational Psychology Review, 24*(2), 313–337. doi:10.1007/s10648-012-9195-x

Kamath, K. Y., Caverlee, J., Cheng, Z., & Sui, D.Z. (2012). *Spatial influence vs. community influence: Modeling the global spread of social media.*

Kaplanis, D. (2014). *8 Top Benefits of Using a Cloud Based LMS - eLearning Industry.* Retrieved from http://elearningindustry.com/8-top-benefits-of-using-a-cloud-based-lms

Karasar, N. (2007). *Bilimsel Araştırma Yöntemi. 17. Baskı.* Ankara: Nobel Yayın Dağıtım.

Kaufman, P. B., & Mohan, J. (2009). *Video use and higher education: Options for the future.* Study funded by Copyright Clearance Center and conducted by Intelligent Television in cooperation with New York University. Retrieved from https://library.nyu.edu/about/Video_Use_in_Higher_Education.pdf

Kearney, M., & Treagust, D. (2001). Constructivism as a referent in the design and development of a computer program using interactive digital video to enhance learning in physics. *Australasian Journal of Educational Technology, 17*(1), 64–79.

Keengwe, J., & Kidd, T. (2010). Towards Best Practices in Online Learning and Teaching in Higher Education. *MERLOT Journal of Online Learning and Teaching, 6*(2). Retrieved from: http://jolt.merlot.org/vol6no2/keengwe_0610.htm

Keim, D. A. (2002). Information visualization and visual data mining. *IEEE Transactions on Visualization and Computer Graphics, 8*(1), 1–8. doi:10.1109/2945.981847

Keller, J. M. (1987). Development and use of the ARCS model of instructional design. *Journal of Instructional Development, 10*(3), 2–10. doi:10.1007/BF02905780

Keller, T., Gerjets, P., Scheiter, K., & Garsoffky, B. (2006). Information visualizations for knowledge acquisition: The impact of dimensionality and color coding. *Computers in Human Behavior, 22*(1), 43–65. doi:10.1016/j.chb.2005.01.006

Kelly, R. (2009). A learner-centered emotionally engaging approach to online learning. In *Faculty Focus Special Report: Faculty Development in Distance Education: Issues, Trends and Tips.* Madison, Wisconsin: Magna Publications.

Khacharem, A., Zoudji, B., Spanjers, I. A. E., & Kalyuga, S. (2014). Improving learning from animated soccer scenes: Evidence for the expertise reversal effect. *Computers in Human Behavior*, *35*, 339–349. doi:10.1016/j.chb.2014.03.021

Kim, H. & Park, J.W. (2013). Topics on Bible visualization: Content, structure, citation. In the proceedings of *SIGGRAPH Asia 2013,* Hong Kong.

Kim, J. H. (2012). *Dropping out of high school: The role of 3D Alice programming workshop. Paper presented at Association for Educational Communication and Technology Annual International Convention.* Louisville, KY.

Kirilenko, A. P., & Stepchenkova, S. O. (2014). Public microblogging on climate change: One year of Twitter worldwide. *Global Environmental Change*, *26*, 171–182. doi:10.1016/j.gloenvcha.2014.02.008

Kirkpatrick, D. L. (1994). *Evaluating training programs*. San Francisco: Berrett-Koehler Publishers, Inc.

Kirkpatrick, D. L., & Kirkpatrick, J. D. (2006). *Evaluating training programs: The four levels*. San Francisco: Berrett-Koehler Publishers.

Knowlton, D. S. (2000). A theoretical framework for the online classroom: A defense and delineation of a student-centered pedagogy. *New Directions for Teaching and Learning*, *2000*(84), 5–14. doi:10.1002/tl.841

Koban, D. D. (2014). Accounting for uncertainty in social network analysis through replication. Thesis. North Carolina State University.

Kolb, D. (1984). *Experiential learning: Experience as the source of learning and development*. Englewood Cliffs, NJ: Prentice Hall.

Korfiatis, N. T., Poulos, M., & Bokos, G. (2006). Evaluating authoritative sources using social networks: An insight from Wikipedia. *Online Information Review*, *30*(3), 252–262. doi:10.1108/14684520610675780

Kozma, R. B. (1991). Learning with media. *Review of Educational Research*, *61*(2), 179–211. doi:10.3102/00346543061002179

Krathwohl, D. R. (2002). A revision of Bloom's taxonomy: An overview. *Theory into Practice*, *41*(4), 212–218. doi:10.1207/s15430421tip4104_2

Kühl, T., Scheiter, K., Gerjets, P., & Edelmann, J. (2011). The influence of text modality on learning with static and dynamic visualizations. *Computers in Human Behavior*, *27*(1), 29–35. doi:10.1016/j.chb.2010.05.008

Kumar, S., Morstatter, F., Zalarani, R., & Liu, H. (2013). Whom should I follow? Identifying relevant users during crises. *Proceedings of 24th ACM Conference on Hypertext and Social Media*. Paris, France. 139 – 147.

Kumar, J. P., & Govindarajulu, P. (2009). Duplicate and Near Duplicate Documents Detection: A Review. *European Journal of Scientific Research*, *32*, 514–527.

Kunneman, F., Liebrecht, C., van Mulken, M., & van den Bosch, A. (2014). Signaling sarcasm: From hyperbole to hashtag. *Information Processing and Management*. Retrieve from: http://www.businessinsider.com/library-of-congress-is-archiving-all-of-americas-tweets-2013-1

Lampoltshammer, T. J., Kounadi, O., Sitko, I., & Hawelka, B. (2014). Sensing the public's reaction to crime news using the 'Links Correspondence Method.'. *Applied Geography*, *52*, 57–55. doi:10.1016/j.apgeog.2014.04.016 PMID:25843991

Lampos, V. & Cristiannini, N. (2012). Nowcasting events from the Social Web with statistical learning. *ACM Transactions on Intelligent Systems and Technology*. 3 (4), Article 72, pp. 72:1 -72:22.

Lane, P., Hunt, J., & Farris, J. (2011). Innovate teaching to engage and challenge twenty-first century entrepreneurship students: An interdisciplinary approach. *Journal of Entrepreneurship Education*, *14*, 105–123. Retrieved from http://0-search.proquest.com.liucat.lib.liu.edu/docview/885241325?accountid=12142

Lanir, J., Booth, K. S., & Findlater, L. (2008). Observer presenters' use of visual aids to inform the design of classroom presentation software. In CHI 2008 Proceedings: Tools for Education, Florence, Italy. (pp. 695–704).

Lee, Mark J.W. & (eds), Catherine McLoughlin. (2011). *Web 2.0-based e-learning: applying social informatics for tertiary teaching*. Retrieved from: http://common.books24x7.com/toc.aspx?bookid=36761

Leuf, B., & Cunningham, W. (2001). *The wiki way: Quick collaboration on the Web*. Boston, Massachusetts: Addison-Wesley.

Lewandowski, D. (2008). A Three-year Study on the Freshness of Web Search Engine Databases. *Journal of Information Science, 34*(6), 817–831. doi:10.1177/0165551508089396

Lim, L. (2013, January 23). *Friends* will be there for you at Beijing's Central Perk. *National Public Radio*. Retrieved from http://www.npr.org/2013/01/23/170074762/friends-will-be-there-for-you-at-beijings-central-perk

Lin, C. F., Hung, Y. H., & Chang, R. I. (2013). Analyzing the Effects of Different Multimedia Materials on Learning System. *Journal of Computer Trends and Technology, 4*(5), 2145–2150.

Lin, L., & Atkinson, R. K. (2011). Using animations and visual cueing to support learning of scientific concepts and processes. *Computers & Education, 56*(3), 650–658. doi:10.1016/j.compedu.2010.10.007

Lin, L., Atkinson, R. K., Christopherson, R. M., Joseph, S. S., & Harrison, C. J. (2013). Animated agents and learning: Does the type of verbal feedback they provide matter? *Computers & Education, 67*, 239–249. doi:10.1016/j.compedu.2013.04.017

Lin, L., Atkinson, R. K., Savenye, W. C., & Nelson, B. C. (2014). The effects of visual cues and self-explanation prompts: Empirical evidence in a multimedia environment. *Interactive Learning Environments*. doi:10.1080/10494820.2014.924531

Liu, B., Yuan, Q., Cong, G., & Xu, D. (2014). *Where your photo is taken: Geolocation prediction for social images. In the proceedings of the ASIS&T 2014*. Wiley Online Library; doi:10.1002/asi.23050

Liu, H. C., Lai, M. L., & Chuang, H. H. (2011). Using eye-tracking technology to investigate the redundant effect of multimedia web pages on viewers' cognitive processes. *Computers in Human Behavior, Vol, 27*(6), 2410–2417. doi:10.1016/j.chb.2011.06.012

Lyon, D. (2003). *Surveillance as social sorting: Privacy, risk, and digital discrimination*. New York: Routledge.

Magee, C. M. (2011). A multi-case study of two studio learning environments: Technology enabled active learning at Massachusetts Institute of Technology and a Reggio Emilia studio at school within school. *INTED2011 Proceedings*, (pp. 4067-4076).

Malinick, T. E., Tindall, D. B., & Diani, M. (2013). Network centrality and social movement media coverage: A two-mode network analytic approach. *Social Networks, 35*(2), 148–158. doi:10.1016/j.socnet.2011.10.005

Mansfield-Devine, S. (2014). Masking sensitive data. *Network Security, 2014*(10), 17–21. doi:10.1016/S1353-4858(14)70104-7

Marcus, A., Bernstein, M. S., Badar, O., Karger, D. R., Madden, S., & Miller, R. C. (2011a). Tweets as data: Demonstration of TweeQL and TwitInfo. *Proceedings of SIGMOD '11*. Athens, Greece.

Marcus, A., Bernstein, M. S., Badar, O., Karger, D. R., Madden, S., & Miller, R. C. (2011b). TwitInfo: Aggregating and visualizing microblogs for event exploration. In the proceedings of CHI 2011. Twitter Systems, Vancouver, B.C., Canada. May 7 – 12, 2011.

Mason, L., Tornatora, M. C., & Pluchino, P. (2013). Do fourth graders integrate text and picture in processing and learning from an illustrated science text? Evidence from eye-movement patterns. *Computers & Education, 60*(1), 95–109. doi:10.1016/j.compedu.2012.07.011

Mayer, B. L. (2011). *Modern social media and social revolutions*. Master's thesis. U.S. Army Command and General Staff College. 1 – 127.

Mayer, R. E., & Moreno, R. (2010). Techniques that reduce extraneous cognitive load and manage intrinsic cognitive load during multimedia learning. In J. L. Plass, R. Moreno, R. Brünken, (Ed.), Cognitive load theory (s.131-153). New York: Cambridge University Press.

Mayer, R. E. (2005a). Introduction to multimedia learning. In R. E. Mayer (Ed.), *The Cambridge handbook of multimedia learning* (pp. 1–16). New York: Cambridge University Press. doi:10.1017/CBO9780511816819.002

Mayer, R. E. (2005b). Cognitive theory of multimedia learning. In R. E. Mayer (Ed.), *The Cambridge handbook of multimedia learning* (pp. 31–48). New York: Cambridge University Press. doi:10.1017/CBO9780511816819.004

Mayer, R. E. (2005c). *The Cambridge handbook of multimedia learning*. New York: Cambridge University Press. doi:10.1017/CBO9780511816819

Mayer, R. E. (2009). *Multimedia learning*. New York, USA: Cambridge University Press. doi:10.1017/CBO9780511811678

Mayer, R. E., & Chandler, P. (2001). When learning is just a click away: Does simple user interaction foster deeper understanding of multimedia messages? *Journal of Educational Psychology, 93*(2), 390–397. doi:10.1037/0022-0663.93.2.390

Mayer, R. E., Dow, G. T., & Mayer, S. (2003). Multimedia learning in an interactive self-explaining environment: What works in the design of agent-based microworlds? *Journal of Educational Psychology, 95*(4), 806–812. doi:10.1037/0022-0663.95.4.806

Mayer, R. E., Hegarty, M., Mayer, S., & Campbell, J. (2005). When static media promote active learning: Annotated illustrations versus narrated animations in multimedia instruction. *Journal of Experimental Psychology. Applied, 11*(4), 256–265. doi:10.1037/1076-898X.11.4.256 PMID:16393035

Mayer, R. E., & Moreno, R. (2002). Aids to computer-based multimedia learning. *Learning and Instruction, 12*(1), 107–119. doi:10.1016/S0959-4752(01)00018-4

Mayer, R. E., & Moreno, R. (2003). Nine ways to reduce cognitive load in multimedia learning. *Educational Psychologist, 38*(1), 43–52. doi:10.1207/S15326985EP3801_6

McCann, D. (2015). A flipped classroom using screen-capture video. *The FASEB Journal, 29*, 687–688.

McCormick, M. (2008). Data theft: A prototypical insider threat.. In S.J. Stolfo, S.M. Bellovin, S. Hershkop, A., Keromytis, S. Sinclair, & S.W. Smith, (Eds.), Advances in Information Security. SpringerLink. 53 – 67. doi:10.1007/978-0-387-77322-3_4

McCulloh, I.A. & Carley, K.M. (2008). *Social network change detection.* Carnegie Mellon University.

Mediasite Analytics. (2013). *Mediasite analytics*, Mediasite document. Retrieved from http://www.sonicfoundry.com/data-sheet/mediasite-analytics

Mendoza, M., Poblete, B., & Castillo, C. (2010). Twitter under crisis: Can we trust what we RT? *Proceedings of 1ˢᵗ Workshop on Social Media Anaalytics.*

Merchant, Z., Goetz, E. T., Cifuentes, L., Keeney-Kennicutt, W., & Davis, T. J. (2014). Effectiveness of virtual reality-based instruction on students' learning outcomes in K-12 and higher education: A meta-analysis. *Computers & Education, 70*, 29–40. doi:10.1016/j.compedu.2013.07.033

Meusburger, P. (2008). The nexus of knowledge and space. *Clashes of Knowledge.* 34 – 90.

Michalko, M. (2006). *Thinkertoys: A Handbook of Creative-Thinking Techniques* Berkeley: The Speed Press.

Miller, G. A. (1956). The magic number seven, plus or minus two: Some limits on our capacity for processing information. *Psychological Review, 63*(2), 81–97. doi:10.1037/h0043158 PMID:13310704

Miller, M. V. (2011). A system for integrating online multimedia into college curriculum. *Journal of Online Learning and Teaching, 7*(2), 294.

Miranda, J., & Gomes, D. (2009). How Are Web Characteristics Evolving? *Proceedings of the 20th ACM Conference on Hypertext and Hypermedia, HT '09,* Torino, Italy. (pp. 369-370). doi:10.1145/1557914.1557993

Modesto, M., Pereira, A., Ziviani, N., Castillo, C., & Baeza-Yates, R. (2005). Um Novo Retrato da Web Brasileira. *Proceedings of XXXII SEMISH,* São Leopoldo, Brazil. (pp. 2005-2017).

Molina, A. I., Redondo, M. A., Lacave, C., & Ortega, M. (2013). Assessing the effectiveness of new devices for accessing learning materials: An empirical analysis based on eye tracking and learner subjective perception. *Computers in Human Behavior.*

Moreno, R. (2006). Learning in high-tech and multimedia environments. *Current Directions in Psychological Science, 15*(2), 63–67. http://www.jstor.org/stable/20183078 doi:10.1111/j.0963-7214.2006.00408.x

Moreno, R., & Park, B. (2010). Cognitive load theory: Historical development and relation to other theories. In J. L. Plass, R. Moreno, & R. Brünken (Eds.), *Cognitive Load Theory.* Cambridge: Cambridge University Press. doi:10.1017/CBO9780511844744.003

Moreno, R., & Valdez, A. (2005). Cognitive load and learning effects of having students organize pictures and words in multimedia environments: The role of student interactivity and feedback. *Educational Technology Research and Development*, 53(3), 35–45. doi:10.1007/BF02504796

Morin, E., & Unesco. (2001). *Seven complex lessons in education for the future*. Paris: UNESCO.

Morin, R. (2014, July 2). Facebook's experiment causes a lot of fuss for little result. *Pew Research Center*. Retrieve from: http://www.pewresearch.org/fact-tank/2014/07/02/facebooks-experiment-is-just-the-latest-to-manipulate-you-in-the-name-of-research/

Morphological analysis. (2014, Aug. 7). Wikipedia. Retrieve from: http://en.wikipedia.org/wiki/Morphological_analysis_%28problem-solving%29

Morrison, G. R., Ross, S. M., Kalman, H. W., & Kemp, J. E. (7th ed.). (2013). *Designing effective instruction* Hoboken, NJ: John Wiley & Sons, Inc.

Mossberger, K., Wu, Y., & Crawford, J. (2013). Connecting citizens and local governments? Social media and interactivity in major U.S. cities. *Government Information Quarterly*, 30(4), 351–358. doi:10.1016/j.giq.2013.05.016

Moursund, D. (1999). *Project-based learning using information technology.International Society for Technology in Education*. Eugene, OR:

Mozaffari, E., & Mudur, S. (2011). A classification scheme for characterizing visual mining. In G. Salvendy & M. J. Smith (Eds.), *Human Interface, Part 2* (pp. 46–54). Springer-Verlag Berlin Heidelberg. doi:10.1007/978-3-642-21669-5_6

Müller-Birn, C., Dobusch, L., & Herbsleb, J. D. (2013). Work-to-rule: The emergence of algorithmic governance in Wikipedia. In the proceedings of *C&T '13*. Munich, Germany. (pp. 80–89).

Muralidharan, A., & Hearst, M. A. (2012). A sensemaking environment for literature study. In the proceedings of *CHI 2012*. Austin, Texas. doi:10.1145/2212776.2223735

Mutlu-Bayraktar, D., & Bayram, S. (2013). Using Eye Tracking to Investigate the Relationship Between Attention and Change Blindness. *World Journal on Educational Technology*, 5(2), 257–265.

My Korea Info Directory. http://my-korea.info/directory.html

Naaman, M. (2011). Geographic information from geo-referenced social media data. *SIGSPATIAL Special*, 3(2), 54–61. doi:10.1145/2047296.2047308

Nelson, B. C., Kim, Y., Foshee, C., & Slack, K. (2014). Visual signaling in virtual world-based assessments: The SAVE Science project. *Information Science*, 264, 32–40. doi:10.1016/j.ins.2013.09.011

Neo, M., & Neo, T.-K. (2009). Engaging students in multimedia-mediated constructivist learning: Students' perceptions. *Journal of Educational Technology & Society*, 12(2), 254–266.

New Media Consortium. (2014). *Horizon report: 2014 higher education*. Retrieved from http://cdn.nmc.org/media/2014-nmc-horizon-report-he-EN-SC.pdf

NodeXL: Network Overview, Discovery and Exploration for Excel. (2014). Social Media Research Foundation. http://nodexl.codeplex.com/

North, M. (2012). *Data Mining for the Masses*. A Global Text Project Book.

Ntoulas, A., Cho, J., & Olston, C. (2004). What's New on the Web?: The Evolution of the Web from a Search Engine Perspective.*Proceedings of the 13th International Conference on World Wide Web, WWW '04*,New York, NY. (pp. 1-12). doi:10.1145/988672.988674

Ntoulas, A., & Manasse, M. (2006). Detecting Spam Web Pages Through Content Analysis. In *Proceedings of the World Wide Web conference, WWW'06*,Edinburgh, UK. (pp. 83-92). doi:10.1145/1135777.1135794

Olorunnisola, A. A., & Martin, B. L. (2013). Influences of Media on social movements: Problematizing hyperbolic inferences about impacts. *Telematics and Informatics*, 30(3), 275–288. doi:10.1016/j.tele.2012.02.005

Olston, C., & Pandey, S. (2008). Recrawl Scheduling Based on Information Longevity.*Proceedings of the 17th International Conference on World Wide Web, WWW '08*,Beijing, China. (pp. 437-446). doi:10.1145/1367497.1367557

Oosterman, J., & Cockburn, A. (2010). An empirical comparison of tag clouds and tables. In the proceedings of *OZCHI 2010*. Brisbane, Australia. doi:10.1145/1952222.1952284

Oxley, A. (2013). *Security Risks in Social Media Technologies: Safe Practices in Public Service Applications*. Oxford: Chandos Publishing. doi:10.1533/9781780633800

Ozcelik, E., Arslan-Ari, I., & Cagiltay, K. (2010). Why does Signaling Enhance Multimedia Learning? Evidence from Eye Movements. *Computers in Human Behavior*, *26*(1), 110–117. doi:10.1016/j.chb.2009.09.001

Page, L., Brin, S., Motwani, R., & Winograd, T. (1998). *The Pagerank Citation Ranking: Bringing Order to the Web*. Stanford Digital Library.

Paivio, A. (1986). *Mental representations: A dual coding approach*. Oxford: Oxford University Press.

Palen, L. (2008). Online social media in crisis events. *EDUCAUSE Quarterly*, *3*, 76–78.

Pan, D., Qiu, S., & Yin, D. (2008). Web Page Content Extraction Method Based on Link Density and Statistic. *Proceedings of the 4th International Conference on Wireless Communications, Networking and Mobile Computing, WiCOM '08*, Dalian, China. (pp. 1-4). doi:10.1109/WiCom.2008.2664

Pastizzo, M. J., Erbacher, R. F., & Feldman, L. B. (2002). Multidimensional data visualization. *Behavior Research Methods, Instruments, & Computers*, *34*(2), 158–162. doi:10.3758/BF03195437 PMID:12109006

Pentzold, C. (2009). Fixing the floating gap: The online encyclopedia Wikipedia as a global memory place. *Memory Studies*, *2*(255), 255–272. doi:10.1177/1750698008102055

Plass, J. L., Moreno, R., & Brünken, R. (2010). Cognitive Load Theory. New York: Cambridge. doi:10.1017/CBO9780511844744

Plass, J. L., Heidig, S., Hayward, E. O., Homer, B. D., & Um, E. J. (2013). Emotional Design in Multimedia Learning: Effects of Shape and Color on Affect and Learning. *Learning and Instruction*; Advanced Online Publication. doi:10.1016/j.learninstruc

Plate, B. (2013). Big data opportunities and challenges for IR, text mining and NLP. In the proceedings of Unstructured NLP. San Francisco, California.

Ploetzner, R., & Lowe, R. (2012). A systematic characterization of expository animations. *Computers in Human Behavior*, *28*(3), 781–794. doi:10.1016/j.chb.2011.12.001

Ponds, R., van Oort, F., & Frenken, K. (2007). The geographical and institutional proximity of research collaboration. *Papers in Regional Science*, *86*(3), 423–443. doi:10.1111/j.1435-5957.2007.00126.x

Posner, M. I. (1980). Orienting of attention. *The Quarterly Journal of Experimental Psychology*, *32*(1), 3–25. doi:10.1080/00335558008248231 PMID:7367577

Pousman, Z. & Stasko, J.T. (2007). Casual information visualization: Depictions of data in everyday life. *IEEE Transactspi ions on Visualization and Computer Graphics:* 13(6), 1145–1152.

Prensky, M. (2001). Digital natives, digital immigrants. *On the Horizon*, *9*(5), 1–6. Retrieved from http://www.marcprensky.com/writing/Prensky%20-%20Digital%20Natives,%20Digital%20Immigrants%20-%20Part1.pdf doi:10.1108/10748120110424816

Prieto, V., Álvarez, M., & Cacheda, F. (2012). Analysis and Detection of Web Spam by Means of Web Content. *Proceedings of the 5th Information Retrieval Facility Conference, IRFC '12*, Vienna, Austria. doi:10.1007/978-3-642-31274-8_4

Prieto, V., Álvarez, M., & Cacheda, F. (2013). The Evolution of the Web. *Proceedings of the 2013 International Conference on Systems, Control and Informatics, SCI 2013* Venice, Italy. (pp. 95-104).

Prunckun, H. (2010). *Handbook of Scientific Methods of Inquiry for Intelligence Analysis*. Lanham: The Scarecrow Press, Inc.

Public Response to Alerts and Warnings using Social Media: Report of a Workshop on Current Knowledge and Research Gaps. (2013). *National Research Council of the National Academies*. Washington, D.C.: The National Academies Press.

Purves, D., Augustine, G. J., Fitzpatrick, D., et al. (Eds.). (2nd Ed.). (2001). Neuroscience. Sunderland: Sinauer Associates. Retrieved from: http://www.ncbi.nlm.nih.gov/books/NBK11126/

Qian, X., Liu, X., Zheng, C., Du, Y., & Hou, X. (2013). Tagging photos using users' vocabularies. *Neurocomputing*, *111*, 144–153. doi:10.1016/j.neucom.2012.12.021

Qiu, L., Lin, H., Ramsay, J., & Yang, F. (2012). You are what you tweet: Personality expression and perception on Twitter. *Journal of Research in Personality*, *46*(6), 710–718. doi:10.1016/j.jrp.2012.08.008

Radio, E. (2014, Sept. 12). Web Data 101. *Proceedings of Digital Humanities Forum 2014. KU Institute for Digital Research in the Humanities*. University of Kansas. Lawrence, Kansas. https://idrh.ku.edu/dhforum2014

Raghavan, S., & Garcia-Molina, H. (2001). Crawling the Hidden Web.*Proceedings of the 27th International Conference on Very Large Data Bases, VLDB '01*San Francisco, CA. (pp. 129-138).

Rayner, K. (1998). Eye movements in reading and information processing: 20 years of research. *Psychological Bulletin*, *124*(3), 372–422. doi:10.1037/0033-2909.124.3.372 PMID:9849112

REFERENCES

Richter-Levin, G., Kehat, O., & Anunu, R. (2015). Emotional tagging and long-term memory formation. In *Synaptic Tagging and Capture* (pp. 215–229). Heidelberg, NY: Springer Singapore.

Rigby, K. T. (2015). Real-time computer-based simulation as an intervention in aerodynamics education. *Journal of Aviation/Aerospace Education & Research*, *24*(2), 1–20.

Risen, J. (2006). *State of War: The Secret History of the CIA and the Bush Administration*. New York: Free Press.

Risen, J. (2014). *Pay Any Price: Greed, Power, and Endless War*. New York: Houghton Mifflin.

Ritchey, T. (2011). Modelling complex socio-technical systems using morphological analysis. *Swedish Morphological Society*. Retrieve from: http://www.swemorph.com/pdf/it-webart.pdf

Roberts, J. C., & Panëels, S. (2007). Where are we with haptic visualization? In the proceedings of the *Second Joint EuroHaptics Conference and Symposium on Haptic Interfaces for Virtual Environment and Teleoperator Systems (WHC'07)*. doi:10.1109/WHC.2007.126

Robertson, A., & Olson, S. (2013). *Sensing and shaping emerging conflicts: Report of a joint workshop of the National Academy of Engineering and the United States Institute of Peace: Roundtable on technology, science, and peacebuilding*. Washington, D.C.: The National Academies Press.

Rodrigues, E. M., & Milic-Frayling, N. (2011). Flickr: Linking people, photos, and tags. In L. Derek (Ed.), *Hansen, Ben Schneiderman, & Marc A. Smith's Analyzing Social Media Networks with NodeXL: Insights from a Connected World*. Amsterdam: Elsevier. doi:10.1016/B978-0-12-382229-1.00013-8

Rogers, M., Runyon, D., Starrett, D., & Von Holzen, R. (2006). Teaching the 21st century learner. *22nd Annual Conference on Distance Teaching and Learning*. Retrieved from http://umstrategicplan.wikispaces.com/file/view/teaching_21sC_Learner.pdf

Rogers, R. (2013). Debanalizing Twitter: The transformation of an object of study. *Proceedings of WebSci'13*, Paris, France. (pp. 356–365).

Rohan, R. J. (2011). *Social networking, counterintelligence, and cyber counterintelligence. Utica College. Treadstone 71*. Whitepaper.

Rout, D., Preotiuc-Pietro, D., Bontcheva, K., & Cohn, T. (2013). Where's @wally? A classification approach to geolocating users based on their social ties. *Proceedings of 24th ACM Conference on Hypertext and Social Media*. Paris, France. (pp. 11–20).

Rubin, A. D., & Geer, D. E. Jr. (1998). A Survey of Web Security. *The Computer Journal*, *31*(9), 34–41. doi:10.1109/2.708448

Russell, T. (2006). Cloudalicious: Folksonomy over time. In the proceedings of *JCDL '06*, Chapel Hill, North Carolina.

Russell, M. (2005). Using eye-tracking data to understand first impressions of a website. *Usability News*, *7*(1), 1–14.

Ryoo, K., & Moon, S. (2014). Inferring Twitter user locations with 10 km. accuracy. *Proceedings of the WWW '14 Companion,* Seoul, Korea. (pp. 643–648).

Sabo, K. E., Atkinson, R. K., Barrus, A. L., Joseph, S. S., & Perez, R. S. (2013). Searching for the two sigma advantage: Evaluating algebra intelligent tutors. *Computers in Human Behavior, 29*(4), 1833–1840. doi:10.1016/j.chb.2013.03.001

Salimian, M. H., Brooks, S., & Reilly, D. (2013). Examining the impact of regional familiarity and design characteristics on use of a map-based news visualization. MAPINTERACT., Orlando, Florida. doi:10.1145/2534931.2534943

Sanguanpong, S., Piamsa-nga, P., Keretho, S., Poovarawan, Y., & Warangrit, S. (2000). Measuring and Analysis of the Thai World Wide Web. *Proceeding of the Asia Pacific Advance Network.* (pp. 225-230).

Saxenian, A. (1994). Regional Advantage: Culture and Competition. Boston: Harvard University Press.

Schell, G. P., & Burns, M. (2002). Merlot: A repository of e-learning objects for higher education. *E-Service Journal, 1*(2), 53–64.

Schifferes, S., & Newman, N. (2013). Verifying news on the Social Web: Challenges and prospects. *Proceedings of WWW 2013 Companion,* Rio de Janeiro, Brazil. (pp. 875–878).

Schmidt-Weigand, F., Kohnert, A., & Glowalla, U. (2009). A closer look at split visual attention in system- and self-paced instruction in multimedia learning. *Learning and Instruction, 1,* 11.

Schmidt-Weigand, F., & Scheiter, K. (2011). The role of spatial descriptions in learning from multimedia. *Computers in Human Behavior, 27*(1), 22–28. doi:10.1016/j.chb.2010.05.007

Schoenebeck, S. Y. (2014). Giving up Twitter for Lent: How and Why We Take Breaks from Social Media. *SIGCHI Conference on Human Factors in Computing Systems.* Toronto, Ontario, Canada.

Schruben, L. (1983). Simulation modeling with event graphs. *Communications of the ACM, 26*(11), 957–963. doi:10.1145/182.358460

Schupak, A. (2015, Jan. 13). Computers know you better than your friends do. *CBS News.* Retrieve from: http://www.cbsnews.com/news/computers-know-you-better-than-your-friends-do/

Schwan, S., & Riempp, R. (2004). The cognitive benefits of interactive videos: Learning to tie nautical knots. *Learning and Instruction, 14*(3), 293–305. doi:10.1016/j.learninstruc.2004.06.005

Scott, J. (2011, June 1). The rise of online video will break the Internet. *Reel SEO.* Retrieved from http://www.reelseo.com/rise-online-video-break-internet

Screencasting Best Practices. (n.d.). Retrieved from http://www.screencast.com/help/tutorial.aspx?id=403&

Senese, P. D., & Vasquez, J. A. (2008). *The Steps to War: An Empirical Study.* Princeton: Princeton University Press.

Seo, K. K., Templeton, R., & Pellegrino, D. (2008). Creating a ripple effect: Incorporating multimedia-assisted project-based learning in teacher education. *Theory into Practice, 47*(3), 259–265. doi:10.1080/00405840802154062

Serrano, M. A., Maguitman, A., Boguñá, M., Fortunato, S. & Vespignani, A. (2007). Decoding the Structure of the WWW: A Comparative Analysis of Web Crawls. *Journal ACM Transactions on the Web, 1*(2).

Seufert, T., Schütze, M., & Brünken, R. (2009). Memory characteristics and modality in multimedia learning: An aptitude treatment interaction study. *Learning and Instruction, 19*(1), 28–42. doi:10.1016/j.learninstruc.2008.01.002

Seyranian, V. (2014). Social identity framing communication strategies for mobilizing social change. *The Leadership Quarterly, 25*(3), 468–486. doi:10.1016/j.leaqua.2013.10.013

Shahani, A. (2014, Aug. 27). Pew study: Facebook, Twitter users held back views on Snowden. *National Public Radio.* Retrieve from: http://www.npr.org/2014/08/27/343623178/pew-study-facebook-twitter-users-held-back-views-on-snowden

Shelton, T., Poorthuis, A., Graham, M., & Zook, M. (2014). Mapping the data shadows of Hurricane Sandy: Uncovering the sociospatial dimensions of big data. *Geoforum, 52,* 167–179. doi:10.1016/j.geoforum.2014.01.006

Shen, Z., Ogawa, M., Teoh, S. T., & Ma, K.-L. (2006). BiblioViz: A system for visualizing bibliography information. Australian Computer Society. Asia-Pacific Symposium on Information Visualization (APVIS2006), Tokyo, Japan. *Conferences in Research and Practice in in Information Technology: 60.*

Shestakov, D. (2011a). Sampling the National Deep Web. *Proceedings of the 22nd International Conference on Database and Expert Systems Applications, DEXA'11.* (pp. 331-340). Toulouse, France. doi:10.1007/978-3-642-23088-2_24

Shestakov, D. (2011b). Databases on the Web: National Web Domain Survey.*Proceedings of the 15th Symposium on International Database Engineering & Applications, IDEAS '11*, Lisbon, Portugal. (pp. 179-184). doi:10.1145/2076623.2076646

Shipley, T., & Bowker, A. (2014). Investigating Social Networking Sites. In *Shipley and Bowker's Investigating Internet Crimes: An Introduction to Solving Crimes in Cyberspace.* Amsterdam: Elsevier. doi:10.1016/B978-0-12-407817-8.00014-X

Shuyo, N. (2010). Language Detection Library for Java. Retrieved from http://code.google.com/p/language-detection/

Singer, P. W., & Friedman, A. (2014). *Cybersecurity and Cyberwar: What Everyone Needs to Know.* Oxford: Oxford University Press.

Singh, L. & Getoor, L. (2007). Increasing the predictive power of affiliation networks. *Bulletin of the IEEE Computer Society Technical Committee on Data Engineering.* (pp. 1–10).

Širanović, Z. (2007). *Guidelines for designing multimedia learning materials.* Varaždin: University of Zagreb.

Size of Wikipedia. (2014, Oct.21). http://en.wikipedia.org/wiki/Wikipedia:Size_of_Wikipedia

Smith, A., Halstead, B., Esposito, L., & Schlegelmilch, J. (2013). Social media and virtual platforms. New Haven Health System Center Retrieve from: http://yalenewhavenhealth.org/emergency/PDFs/SocialMediaandVirtualPlatforms.pdf

Smith, M. A. (2012, Mar. 9). NodeXL describes the networks you create: Graph Summary in v. 2013. Retrieved from http://www.connectedaction.net/2012/03/09/nodexl-describes-the-networks-you-create-graph-summary-in-v-203/

Smith, M. E., & Gevins, A. (2004). Attention and brain activity while watching television: Components of viewer engagement. *Media Psychology, 6*(3), 285–305. doi:10.1207/s1532785xmep0603_3

Solso, R. L., Maclin, M. K., & Maclin, O. H. (2008). Cognitive Psychology, Bacon, USA: Pearson.

Song, Y., Zhang, Y., Cao, J., tang, J., Gao, X., & Li, J. (2014). A unified geolocation framework for web videos. *ACM Transactions on Intelligent Systems and Technology.* 5(3), Article 49, 49: 1–49: 22.

Sorapure, M. (2010). Information visualization, Web 2.0, and the teaching of writing. *Computers and Composition, 27*(1), 59–70. doi:10.1016/j.compcom.2009.12.003

Sorden, S. D. (2005). A Cognitive Approach to Instructional Design for Multimedia Learning. *Informing Science Journal, V*, 8.

sound. (2015). In *Encyclopædia Britannica.* Retrieved from: http://www.britannica.com/EBchecked/topic/555255/sound

Sousa, D. A. (2011). *How the brain learns.* Thousand Oaks, CA: Corwin Press.

Sparks, R. L. (2006). Learning styles-Making too many 'wrong mistakes': A response to Castro and Peck. *Foreign Language Annals, 39*(3), 520–528. doi:10.1111/j.1944-9720.2006.tb02903.x

Spinellis, D., & Louridas, P. (2008). The collaborative organization of knowledge. *Communications of the ACM, 51*(8), 68–71. doi:10.1145/1378704.1378720

Stafanidis, A., Crooks, A., & Radzikowski, J. (2013). Harvesting ambient geospatial information from social media feeds. *GeoJournal, 78*(2), 319–338. doi:10.1007/s10708-011-9438-2

Starbird, K., & Palen, L. (2013). Working & sustaining the virtual 'disaster desk.' *Proceedings of CSCW '13.* San Antonio, Texas. 491 – 502.

State of Video. (2014). *The state of video in education 2014*, Kultura report. Retrieved from http://site.kaltura.com/Education_Survey_Thank_You.html?aliId=93189612

Stavredes, T. (2011). *Effective online teaching: Foundations and strategies for student success*. San Fransisco, CA: Jossey-Bass.

Steelman, J. (2005). Multimedia makes it mark: Benefits and drawbacks of including these projects in your curriculum. *Learning and Leading with Technology, 33*, 16–19.

Stein, R. L. (2012). StateTube: Anthropological reflections on social media and the Israel state. *Anthropological Quarterly, 85*(3), 893–916. doi:10.1353/anq.2012.0045

Stephens, M., & Poorthuis, A. (2014). Follow thy neighbor: Connecting the social and the spatial networks on Twitter. *Computers, Environment and Urban Systems*, 1–9.

Suel, T., & Yuan, J. (2001). Compressing the Graph Structure of the Web. *Proceedings of the Data Compression Conference, DCC '01*, Snowbird, Utah. (pp. 213-213). doi:10.1109/DCC.2001.917152

Suman, A. (2014). *From Knowledge Abstraction to Management: Using Ranganathanas Faceted Schema to Develop Conceptual Frameworks for Digital Libraries. Chandros Publishing (imprint)*. Amsterdam: Elsevier.

Sweller, J. (2004). Instructional design consequences of an analogy between evolution by natural selection and human cognitive architecture. *Instructional Science, 32*(1/2), 9–31. doi:10.1023/B:TRUC.0000021808.72598.4d

Sweller, J., van Merrienboer, J. J. G., & Paas, F. (1998). Cognitive architecture and instructional design. *Educational Psychology Review, 10*(3), 251–296. doi:10.1023/A:1022193728205

Taleb, N. N. (2010). *The Black Swan: The Impact of the Highly Improbable* New York: Random House Books

Tan, A.-H. (1999). Text mining: The state of the art and the challenges. In proceedings of the PAKDD 1999 Workshop on Knowledge Discovery from Advanced Databases. Retrieved from http://www3.ntu.edu.sg/sce/labs/erlab/publications/papers/asahtan/tm_pakdd99.pdf

Tapscott, D., & Williams, A. D. (2010). Innovating the 21st century university. *EDUCAUSE Review*. Retrieved from http://www.educause.edu/er

Tarmizi, R., & Sweller, J. (1988). Guidance during mathematical problem solving. *Journal of Educational Psychology, 80*(4), 424–436. doi:10.1037/0022-0663.80.4.424

Teeter, C., Fenton, N., Nicholson, K., Flynn, T., Kim, J., & McKay, M. et al. (2011). *Using communities of practice to foster faculty development in higher education. Collected Essays on Learning and Teaching*. CELT.

The NIST Definition of Cloud Computing". (n.d.). National Institute of Standards and Technology. Retrieved from: http://csrc.nist.gov/publications/nistpubs/800-145/SP800-145.pdf

Thelwall, M., & Wilkinson, D. (2003). Graph Structure in Three National Academic Webs: Power Laws with Anomalies. *Journal of the American Society for Information Science and Technology, 54*(8), 706–712. doi:10.1002/asi.10267

Thomas, J., Pennock, K., Fiegel, T., Wise, J., Pottier, M., Schur, A., et al. (1995, May). The visual analysis of textual information: Browsing large document sets. In the proceedings of the *DL '95 Conference*, Washington, DC. Retrieved from http://www.osti.gov/scitech/servlets/purl/71681

Tool 13: Morphological box." (2013). In *EDIC Ecodesign Manual. Innovation and EcoDesign in the Ceramic Industry*. Retrieve from: http://www.adam-europe.eu/prj/5887/prd/1/4/Tool%2013_Morphological%20box.pdf

Torrens, P. M. (2010). Geography and computational social science. *GeoJournal, 75*(2), 133–148. doi:10.1007/s10708-010-9361-y

Treasure, J. (2009, July). The 4 ways sound affects us [Video file]. Retrieved from http://www.ted.com/talks/julian_treasure_the_4_ways_sound_affects_us/transcript?language=en#t-132000

Tucker, P. (2014). *The Naked Future: What Happens in a World that Anticipates your Every Move?* New York: Current.

Tüzün, H., Akıncı, A., Kurtoğlu, M., Atal, D., & Pala, F. K. (2013). A Study on the Usability of a University Registrar's Office. *The Turkish Online Journal of Educational Technology, 12*(2).

Tversky, B., Morrison, J. B., & Betrancourt, M. (2002). Animation: Can it facilitate? *International Journal of Human-Computer Studies, 57*(4), 247–262. doi:10.1006/ijhc.2002.1017

Tyshchuk, Y., & Wallace, W. (2013). The use of social media by local government in response to an extreme event. *Proceedings of 10ᵗʰ International ISCRAM Conference*, Baden-Baden, Germany. (pp. 802–811).

Underwood, G., & Radach, R. (1998). Eye guidance and visual information processing: Reading, visual search, picture perception and driving. In G. Underwood (Ed.), *Eye guidance in reading and scene perception* (pp. 1–28). Oxford, England: Elsevier Science Ltd. doi:10.1016/B978-008043361-5/50002-X

United States Army. (2011). *The U.S. Army learning concept for 2015: Training and Doctrine Command Pamphlet 525-8-2*. Retrieved from http://wwwtradoc.army.mil/tpubs/pams/tp525-8-2.pdf

University Business. (2013). *Academic video at a tipping point: Preparing your campus for the future*, (white paper). Retrieved from http://www.sonicfoundry.com/white-paper/academic-video-tipping-point-preparing-your-campus-future

Unleash the Power of Video. (2014). *Unleash the power of video in the enterprise: A guide to building a solid video strategy*. Retrieved from http://www.sonicfoundry.com/white-paper/unleash-power-video-enterprise-guide-building-solid-video-strategy

Using eye tracking for usability testing. (2000). Brussels, Namahn.

Van Eck, N. J., & Waltman, L. (2011). Text mining and visualization using VOSviewer. ISSI Newsletter, 7(3):50-54. Retrieved from http://arxiv.org/ftp/arxiv/papers/1109/1109.2058.pdf

Van Garderen, D. (2006). Spatial visualization, visual imagery, and mathematical problem solving of students with varying abilities. *Journal of Learning Disabilities*, 39(6), 496–506. doi:10.1177/00222194060390060201 PMID:17165617

van Genuchten, E., Scheiter, K., & Schüler, A. (2012). Examining learning from text and pictures for different task types: Does the multimedia effect differ for conceptual, causal, and procedural tasks? *Computers in Human Behavior, 28*(6), 2209–2218. doi:10.1016/j.chb.2012.06.028

Vandenberg, S. G., & Kuse, A. R. (1978). Mental rotations, a group test of three-dimensional spatial visualization. *Perceptual and Motor Skills, 47*(2), 599–604. doi:10.2466/pms.1978.47.2.599 PMID:724398

Viégas, F.B. & Wattenberg, M. (2008). Tag clouds and the case for vernacular visualization. *Forum Timelines*. 49 – 52.

Viégas, F.B., Wattenberg, M., & Feinberg, J. (2009). Participatory visualization with Wordle. In the proceedings of IEEE Transactions on Visualization and Computer Graphics, 15(6), (pp. 1137 – 1144).

Vik, G. N. (2004). Breaking bad habits: Teaching effective PowerPoint use to working graduate students. *Business Communication Quarterly, 67*(2), 225–228. doi:10.1177/1080569904672012

Vogel-Walcutt, J. J., Guidice, K. D., Fiorella, L., & Nicholson, D. (2013). Using a video game as an advance organizer: Effects on development of procedural and conceptual knowledge, cognitive load, and casual adoption. *Journal of Online Learning and Teaching, 9*, 376–392.

W3C DOM IG. (2005). The Document Object Model. Retrieved from http://www.w3.org/DOM

W3C. (2014, October 28). Retrieved from http://www.w3.org/standards/techs/html#w3c_all

W3C. (2015, January 1). Retrieved from http://www.w3.org/standards/webdesign/audiovideo.html

Waggoner, Ben. (2010). *Compression for great video and audio*. Retrieved from http://common.books24x7.com/toc.aspx?bookid=36547

Wagner, C., Mitter, S., Körner, C., & Strohmaier, M. (2012). When social bots attack: Modeling susceptibility of users in online social networks. #MSM2012 workshop. Lyon, France.

Wagner, W., Valencia, J., & Elejabarrieta, F. (1996). Relevance, discourse and the 'hot' stable core of social representations—A structural analysis of word associations. *The British Journal of Social Psychology, 35*(3), 331–351. doi:10.1111/j.2044-8309.1996.tb01101.x

Ware, C. (2012). Visual thinking processes. Ch. 11. In Ware's Information Visualization: Perception for Design. Elsevier. 375 – 423.

Watson, H., & Finn, R. L. (2013). Social media and the 2013 UK heat wave. *Proceedings of 11ᵗʰ International ISCRAM Conference,* University Park, Pennsylvania. (pp. 755–759).

Wei, F., Liu, S., Song, Y., Pan, S., Zhou, M. X., Qian, W., et al. (2010). TIARA: A visual exploratory text analytic system. In the proceedings of *Knowledge Discovery and Datamining (KDD) '10.* Washington, D.C. doi:10.1145/1835804.1835827

Weimann, G. (2014). *New terrorism and new media.* Washington, D.C.: Woodrow Wilson Center for Scholars.

Weng, L. (2013, June). Virality prediction and community structure in social networks. YouTube. Retrieve from: https://www.youtube.com/watch?v=VVnN5Wm8fcE&feature=youtu.be

Weng, L., Menczer, F., & Ahn, Y.-Y. (2014). *Predicting successful memes using network and community structure* (Pre-publication version). Association for the Advancement of Artificial Intelligence. 1-11.

Weng, L., Ratkiewicz, J., Perra, N., Goncalves, B., Castillo, C., Bonchi, F., et al. (2013). The role of information diffusion in the evolution of social networks. *KDD '13,* Chicago, Illinois.

Wetzel, C. D., Radtke, P. H., Stern, H. W., Dickieson, J., & McLachlan, J. C. (1993). *Review of the effectiveness of video media in instruction, No. NPRDC-TR-93-4.* San Diego, CA: Navy Personnel Research And Development Center.

Wikipedia. Statistics. (2014, Nov. 25). Retrieved from http://en.wikipedia.org/wiki/Wikipedia:Statistics

Wilkinson, D. M., & Huberman, B. A. (2008). Assessing the value of cooperation in Wikipedia. *First Monday.* http://firstmonday.org/article/view/1763/1643

Wilkinson, D., & Thelwall, M. (2012). Trending Twitter topics in English. *Journal of the Association for Information Science and Technology, 63*(8), 1631–1646http://onlinelibrary.wiley.com/doi/10.1002/asi.22713/pdf. doi:10.1002/asi.22713

Wille, D. G. (2012). *Every soldier a messenger: Using social media in the contemporary operating environment. Monograph.* School of Advanced Military Studies.

Willerman, M., & Mac Harg, R. A. (1991). The concept map as an advance organizer. *Journal of Research in Science Teaching, 28*(8), 705–711. doi:10.1002/tea.3660280807

Wilson, C., Sala, A., Puttaswamy, K.P.N., & Zhao, B.Y. (2012). Beyond social graphs: User interactions in online social networks and their implications. *ACM Transactions on the Web:* 6(4), Article 17, 17:1–17:31.

Wilson, M. L. (2012). Learning styles, instructional strategies, and the question of matching: A literature review. *International Journal of Education, 4*(3), 67–87. Retrieved from http://0-search.proquest.com.liucat.lib.liu.edu/docview/1323309431?accountid=12142 doi:10.5296/ije.v4i3.1785

Wilson, M. W. (2012). Location-based services, conspicuous mobility, and the location-aware future. *Geoforum, 43*(6), 1266–1275. doi:10.1016/j.geoforum.2012.03.014

Wing, B. P., & Baldridge, J. (2011). Simple supervised document geolocation with geodesic grids. *Proceedings of 49ᵗʰ Annual Meeting of the Association for Computational Linguistics,* Portland, Oregon. (pp. 955– 964).

Woldkowski, R. J. (2008). *Enhancing adult motivation to learn: A comprehensive guide for teaching all adults.* San Francisco, CA: Jossey-Bass.

Wouters, P., Tabbers, H. K., & Paas, F. (2007). Interactivity in video-based models. *Educational Psychology Review, 19*(3), 327–342. doi:10.1007/s10648-007-9045-4

Wu, B., & Davison, B. D. (2005). Identifying Link Farm Spam Pages. *In 14th International Conference on World Wide Web, WWW '05*, Chiba, Japan. (pp. 820-829). doi:10.1145/1062745.1062762

Xie, K., Xia, C., Grinberg, N., Schwartz, R., & Naaman, M. (2013). Robust detection of hyper-local events from geotagged social media data. In the proceedings of MDMKDD '13, Chicago, Illinois. (pp. 1–9). doi:10.1145/2501217.2501219

Yang, J., & Leskovec, J. (2011). Patterns of temporal variation in Online Media. *WSDM '11,* Hong Kong, China. doi:10.1145/1935826.1935863

Yang, F. Y., Chang, C. Y., Chien, W. R., Chien, Y. T., & Tseng, Y. H. (2013). Tracking learners' visual attention during a multimedia presentation in a real classroom. *Computers & Education, Vol, 62*, 208–220. doi:10.1016/j.compedu.2012.10.009

Yarbus, A. L. (1967). *Eye Movements and Vision.* New York: Plenum. doi:10.1007/978-1-4899-5379-7

Yau, H. K., Cheng, A. L. F., & Ho, M. W. M. (2015). Identify the motivational factors to affect the higher education students to learn using technology. *TOJET, 14*(2).

Yi, J. S., Kang, Y. A., Stasko, J. T., & Jacko, J. A. (2007). Toward a deeper understanding of the role of interaction in information visualization. *IEEE Transactions on Visualization and Computer Graphics, 13*(6), 1224–1231. doi:10.1109/TVCG.2007.70515 PMID:17968068

YouTube Statistics. (2014). Retrieved from https://www.youtube.com/yt/press/statistics.html

Youyou, W., Kosinski, M., & Stillwell, D. (2014). *Computer-based personality judgments are more accurate than those made by humans (PNAS Early Edition). 1–5.*

Yuan, X., Zhang, X., & Trifmovsky, A. (2010). Testing visualization on the use of information systems. In the proceedings of *Information Interaction in Context Symposium (IIiX) 2010*, New Brunswick, New Jersey, USA. doi:10.1145/1840784.1840840

Zaid, M. (2013, June 24). A Legal Perspective on the Snowden Case. Spycast. International Spy Museum. Retrieved from http://www.spymuseum.org/multimedia/spycast/episode/a-legal-perspective-on-the-snowden-case/

Zesch, T., & Gurevych, I. (2007). *Analysis of the Wikipedia Category Graph for NLP Applications. TextGraphs-2: Graph-Based Algorithms for Natural Language Processing. 1 – 8.* Association for Computational Linguistics.

Zhang, D., Zhou, L., Briggs, R. O., & Nunamaker, J. F. Jr. (2006). Instructional video in e-learning: Assessing the impact of interactive video on learning effectiveness. *Information & Management, 43*(1), 15–27. doi:10.1016/j.im.2005.01.004

Zhou, X., & Chen, L. (2014). Event detection over twitter social media streams. *The VLDB Journal, 23*(3), 381–400. doi:10.1007/s00778-013-0320-3

Zipf's law. (2014, June 18). *Wikipedia*. Retrieved from http://en.wikipedia.org/wiki/Zipf%27s_law

About the Contributors

Shalin Hai-Jew works as an instructional designer at Kansas State University (K-State). She has taught at the university and college levels for many years (including four years in the People's Republic of China) and was tenured at Shoreline Community College but left tenure to pursue instructional design work. She has Bachelor's degrees in English and psychology, a Master's degree in Creative Writing from the University of Washington (Hugh Paradise Scholar), and an Ed.D in Educational Leadership with a focus on public administration from Seattle University (where she was a Morford Scholar). Hai-Jew was born in Huntsville, Alabama, in the U.S.

* * *

Víctor M. Prieto Álvarez is currently the CEO of his own business in web information services. He received his Bachelor's Degree in Computer Engineering from the Universidade da Coruña in 2007 and a Ph.D. Degree in Computer Science in Department of Information and Comunications Technologies at the same university in 2013. His main research fields are web crawling, Hidden Web and Web Spam. He has also published several papers in international journals and has participated in multiple international conferences.

Manuel Álvarez Díaz is an Associate Professor in the Department of Information and Communication Technologies, at the Universidade da Coruña (Spain). He received his Bachelor's Degree in Computer Engineering from the Universidade da Coruña in 1999 and a Ph.D. Degree in Computer Science from the same University in 2007. His research interests are related to information retrieval and data integration. Manuel has managed several projects at national and regional level in the field of data integration and Hidden Web accessing. He has also published several papers in international journals and has participated in multiple international conferences.

Brent Anders, M.Ed., is a Senior Electronic Media Coordinator for the Office of Mediated Education at Kansas State University. His work includes: educational media consulting (working directly with instructors and departments), as well as videography/filmmaking (directing, capturing, editing and final production). Additionally Anders works directly with live-webcasting and web accessibility/usability. Anders has a Bachelor's degree in Psychology (human computer interaction focus), and a Master's degree in Education with an instructional technology focus. Currently, Anders is pursuing a PhD in Adult Education. Anders also serves in the Army National Guard as a Master Sergeant. His primary military duty is that of Public Affairs First Sergeant, managing soldier journalist insuring the both video and print news stories are created promptly and accurately as well as ensuring that all necessary military training is occurring successfully. Additionally Anders works as a Senior Military Instructor, primarily teaching the 80-hour Army Basic Instructors Course (ABIC). This course teaches sergeants and officers how to properly instruct soldiers within a class setting using proven effective means of education. Anders has contributed to multiple published works dealing specifically with higher education. The focus of these publications has ranged from video and graphics, to motivation and the use of emotion to enhance educational success. Anders has been in the education field for over 15 years dealing with military training, online/distance education, educational media, and higher education in general.

Danilo M. Baylen is a tenured Professor of Media and Instructional Technology at the University of West Georgia in Carrollton, GA. His research interests include technology integration across the curriculum, visual and media literacy education, and online learning and teaching. Recent research projects focused on faculty readiness for online teaching, best practices of technology integration, and design and development of digital resources. Currently, he is exploring the convergence of emerging technologies and children's literature through interactive picture books and digital storytelling.

Servet Bayram graduated with a Bachelor degree from Department of Psychology at the Istanbul University in 1985. After receiving the Certificate of Teaching and the title of Psychologist, he worked as a Consultant/Educational Psychologist at Bogazici University in Istanbul between 1988-1992. When he completed his Masters degree in Guidance & Counseling at the Bogazici University, he went to the United States for doctoral studies. He completed his doctoral studies in "Learning and Teaching Technologies" and received a Doctorate degree from the University of Pittsburgh, Pennsylvania, in 1995. Then, as a Post Doctoral Fellow, he went to Bloomington Indiana. At the Indiana University he studied on the Electronic Performance Support and Information Systems in 1996. Between 1997-1998, he served as a Second Lieutenant & Psychologist at the Air Force Academy in İstanbul. Then as an Assistant Professor, he started to work at the Department of Computer Education & Instructional Technologies in the Marmara University. He was promoted to Associate Professorship on Computer Education & Instructional Technologies in 2000. Then, he became a full professor in the same area in 2006. He has been working as a chairman of the department since 2000. Human-Computer Interaction, Educational Software Design, Usability Engineering, Human Resource Management, Project Management, School Achievement and Motivation, Psychology of Learning, Attention, Perception and Understanding are among his research/teaching interests.

Amy Gaimaro is the Director of Online Learning and Services at St. John's University. Prior to joining St. John's, she worked as the lead instructional designer at Long Island University within the Office of Academic Affairs. Dr. Gaimaro currently oversees a team of instructional designers and online student recruitment coordinators. She is leading the university's efforts in overall quality assurance for online courses and programs. She coordinates the online faculty development program, which certifies faculty to teach hybrid and online courses. She is a recent graduate of Sloan-C's Institute for Emerging Leadership in Online Learning (IELOL). Dr. Gaimaro has served and continues to serve as a faculty member at Long Island University, teaching instructional technology and computer courses. She possesses over fifteen years of experience teaching traditional, blended and fully online courses in higher education. Dr. Gaimaro has worked in higher education administration in the areas of online learning, faculty development, assessment management systems and electronic portfolios. Dr. Gaimaro holds a B.B.A. in Finance, M.S. in Accounting, and D.B.A. in Information Systems.

Jackie Hee Young Kim, Ed.D, is an assistant professor at Armstrong State University in Savannah, GA, where she has taught online classes and childhood education courses for the past six years. She taught technology integration courses for pre-service teachers at State University of New York Cortland for two years before joining AASU in 2007. Her publications related to technology integration in the classroom and distance education have appeared in numerous professional journals and books and she has given many presentations at professional meetings. She enjoys Southern living, writing, and teaching in coastal Georgia.

Amy S. C. Leh, Ph.D., is a Professor in Instructional Technology at the College of Education at California State University San Bernardino, where she has taught instructional technology courses to credential students and graduate students during the past 16 years. In addition to teaching, she has served as interim director of the university's Office of Distributed & Online Learning and has directed several major grant projects at the institution. She has written more than 30 articles and made more than 100 presentations at international/national conventions. Her research interests include distance education, web-based instruction, interaction in web-based learning environments, computer-mediated communication (CMC) and social presence, technology integration, and telecommunication technologies in foreign (second) language acquisition.

Lijia Lin is an Assistant Professor in the School of Psychology and Cognitive Science at East China Normal University in Shanghai, China. He obtained his Ph.D. from Arizona State University's Educational Technology Program. His research focuses on learning and instruction in technology supported environments. He has published several articles in peer-reviewed journals such as Computers & Education, Interactive Learning Environments, and Journal of Educational Computing Research. He has also made dozens of presentations at the national and international conventions.

Duygu Mutlu-Bayraktar graduated with a Bachelor degree in 2007 from Computer Education and Instructional Technology Department of Cukurova University, Turkey. She received M.S. degree in 2010 from Computer Education and Instructional Technology Department Hacettepe University, Turkey. She completed her doctoral studies in Computer Education and Instructional Technology Department and received a Doctorate degree in the field of Eye Tracking Method about Multimedia Learning from the Marmara University, Turkey in 2014. Dr. Mutlu-Bayraktar has worked as a Research Assistant in Istanbul University since 2008. Her research interests include multimedia learning, instructional design, eye tracking, human computer interaction and artificial intelligence. She is currently working toward on the eye tracking about multimedia learning environment.

Fidel Cacheda Seijo is an Associate Professor in the Department of Information and Communications Technologies at the Universidade da Coruña (Spain). He received his Ph.D. and B.S. degrees in Computer Science from the University of A Coruña, in 2002 and 1996, respectively. He has been involved in several research projects related to Web information retrieval and multimedia real-time systems. His research interests include Web information retrieval and distributed architectures in information retrieval. He has published several papers in international journals and has participated in multiple international conferences.

Hattie Wiley is a Distance Learning Developer for the National Weather Service Training Center. Hattie has over 15 years of combined academic, corporate, and government experience in the eLearning, training, and leadership development industry. At the National Weather Service, she acts in a design, development, consultation, and staff development capacity. Additionally, she is actively involved in the eLearning development community and has acted as newsletter editor for the Kansas City chapter of Association for Talent Development (ATD), formerly ASTD; a workshop facilitator at the eLearning Guild's Learning Solutions conference; and at multiple local (Kansas City area) development conferences. Hattie is a doctoral candidate in Transformative Studies at the California Institute for Integral Studies and holds an MS in Instructional Design and Technology from Emporia State University. Hattie completed her BAs in Psychology, Sociology, and Philosophy from the University Missouri Kansas City. Hattie is also certified in information mapping and Lean Sigma.

Index

A

Add-On (Plug-In) 428
Ad Hoc Event 103
Affinity Diagram 301
Agnostic (As In Theory- Or Method- Agnostic) 557
Alerting 65, 69, 301
Animated Pedagogical Agent 152, 163
App (Application) 522
Application Programming Interface (API) 127, 301
Army Learning Concept 194
Audio Equipment 187
audio production 183
Auditory Learning Style 336
Autocoding (Automatic Coding) 557

B

Betweenness Centrality 382, 406, 510, 522
Bibliographic Tool 557
Blending Learning Model 336
Brainstorming Diagram (Mind Map 226, 232, 301
bubble graph 254, 261, 263

C

Center-Periphery (Core-Periphery) Dynamic 428
Chalk Talk 326, 336
Chokepoint 435, 522
Civil Liberties 428
Classification Sheet 558
Client Side Hidden Web 30
Cluster diagram 238, 242-245, 301
Coding Comparison 225, 558
Coding Pattern 558
Cognitive Constructivist Theory of Multimedia (CCTM) 327, 336
Cognitive Load 112, 169-170, 187, 211-212, 295, 339-340

Cohen's Kappa Coefficient 225, 558
Compound Query 558
Content Analysis 103, 147, 209, 216, 314, 316, 430
Content Networks 103
Content-Sharing Sites 39, 93-94, 103, 277, 281, 372, 440-441, 459
Convenience Sampling 522
Correlation Coefficient 60, 103
Crawling Systems 1, 26, 30
critical thinking 194, 297, 430, 435
Cross-Sectional 147
Crowd-Sourcing 103, 106, 109
Cyber-Physical Confluence 33, 435-436, 520, 522
Cybersecurity 374, 376-377, 385, 389-390, 392-393, 428

D

Data Analytics 204, 210, 321
Data Cube 301
Data Leakage 58, 97, 114, 125, 144, 370-372, 374-375, 377, 379, 382, 409, 422, 428, 438, 442
data leakage movement 370, 372, 379, 382
Data Matrix 285-287, 301
Data Query 548, 558
Data Repository 524, 558
Data Spinning 210, 301
Data Visualization 36, 44, 61, 93, 104, 116, 120, 204, 211-214, 216, 226, 230-231, 244, 253, 263, 269, 282, 291, 301-302, 304, 311-312, 382, 422, 510, 519, 559
Deep Web (Hidden Web) 103
Defense In Depth 377, 428
Degree Centrality 440, 510, 523
De-Identification 558
design strategies 173, 187
Discriminant Analysis 103, 296
Domain Footprinting 443, 450, 502, 523
dynamic player 196

E

Ego Neighborhood 44, 247-251, 267-269, 404, 478, 481, 492, 494, 496, 523, 530-531
Electronic Self-Talk 145, 147
Entity List 85, 261-262, 459, 509, 523
Euclidean Distance 428
Eventgraph 31, 39, 48-49, 85, 95, 103, 147, 382, 478, 485
Event Log 558
event mapping 56
Exchangeable Image File Format (Exif) Data 523
Expertise Reversal Effect 151, 163
Extraction Sequence 445, 470, 523
Eye Tracking 338, 340-341, 345, 347-349, 352, 357, 363
Eye-Tracking Method 338, 340, 368

F

F2F presentation 306, 310
face-to-face 189-190, 194, 197, 306, 309, 319, 324, 329, 527, 529-530, 539
faculty development 324, 327-328, 330, 334
Flipped Learning 324, 336
Focal Node 44, 248, 261, 263, 268-269, 291, 414, 478, 522-523, 530
Focused Attention 345-346, 349, 352-354, 357-359, 363, 368
Formative Evaluation 157, 163

G

Geocode (Or "Forward Geocoding") 523
Geographical Information System (GIS) 523
Geolocation 36, 40-41, 43, 48, 50, 62, 103, 437-438, 440-444, 468, 487, 516-517, 519-520, 523, 558
Geoparsing 438, 515-516, 519, 523
Geosocial Network 523
Geospatial Web (Geoweb) 437, 523
GIS (Geographical Information System) Coordinate 523
Group Query 558

H

Hashtag (#) 277, 382, 484, 552, 558
Hashtag Conversation 119, 127, 269, 272, 282, 288, 380-381, 416, 430, 459, 468, 475, 514, 523, 550
hashtag network graph 118, 132
Heatmap 301

Hidden Data 1, 30
Hidden Hands 103
Hidden Web 2-4, 19-20, 23, 26, 30, 95, 103, 443, 520
human sensor network 36, 54

I

Iframes 305, 310, 313-314, 316, 321
Inference Attack 523
Innovations in Web Technology 187
Insider Threat 428
Instructional Design 151-152, 157, 160, 163-165, 167-168, 173, 187-188, 269, 275, 330, 345, 529
Instructional Design Considerations 167, 187
instructional strategies 323-324, 327
Instructional Video Capturing System 189-190, 195-196, 201
Internet Protocol (Ip) Address 445, 500, 523
Inter-Rater Reliability 558

K

Kinesthetic Learning Style 337

L

Latency (Hiddenness) 523
Latitude (In The Geographical Sense) 524
Learner Control 149, 153-154, 163, 170
Learning-Centered 189-190, 194-197, 201
Learning Management System 194, 201, 329, 332
Learning Management System (LMS) 194, 201
Learning Styles 171, 195, 201, 323-324, 326-327, 330, 332, 334, 337
Listening Post 103
Locational Information 288-289, 443, 519, 524

M

Machine Analysis 35, 207-208, 282, 303, 430, 524
Maltego Tungsten™ 429, 438, 443, 445-447, 450, 459, 473, 482, 484-486, 489-490, 492, 500, 503-504, 511, 513, 519-520, 523-525
Mediawiki 393, 412, 428
Meronymy 371, 428
Microchat 106, 125, 127, 147
Mixed Methodology 558
Motif census 44, 103, 370
Motif Structure 103
multimedia e-book 527, 529
Multimedia Learning Environment 340, 345-346

N

Natural Language Processing (NLP) 302
Network Analysis 43, 45, 48, 52, 58, 111, 114, 127,
    147, 277-278, 313-316, 370-372, 379-380, 413,
    418, 420, 435, 442, 478, 510, 552
Network Graphs 41, 44, 106, 127, 137, 139, 269,
    278, 281-282, 371-372, 524
Node-Link Diagram 254, 263, 268-269, 273, 314,
    321, 428

O

Online Learning 150, 189, 197, 304, 316-317, 323-
    324, 326, 329-330, 332, 337, 357
Online Presentations 323, 328-332, 334, 337
Open Domain 147
Open-Source Intelligence (Or "Osint") 524
Operating System 13, 149, 174, 301, 559
operational environment 194
Oppo (Opposition) Research 524

P

Participatory Sensing 47, 104, 437
Part-of-Speech 302
Penetration (Pen) Testing 443, 524
Personally Identifiable Information (PII) 36, 435,
    484, 513, 524
Point-of-View (POV) 104
Pseudo-Social Event 104

R

Radial Diagram 291, 546, 559
Re-Identification 524
related tags network 78-79, 82, 89, 92, 281-284,
    389, 392, 395-398, 415, 424, 430-431, 459, 461
Research Journal 559
responsive 187
ring lattice graph 226, 243-244, 246-247, 249-250,
    269, 273, 468-469

S

Scatterplot (Scatter Diagram, Scattergraph) 302
semantic-based network analysis 370-372, 379, 413,
    418, 420
Semantic Web 530, 536, 538, 553, 559
sentiment analysis 48, 57, 89, 108, 143, 302
Server Side Hidden Web 19, 30
SME (Subject Matter Expert) 188

Social Awareness Streams (SASes) 524
Social Media Platform 35-36, 39, 44, 55, 57, 69, 85,
    93-94, 103-104, 112, 122, 125, 147, 301, 371,
    379, 386, 389, 402, 428, 430, 435, 516, 524
    402, 413, 418, 420, 422, 429, 438, 440, 442-443,
    515, 517, 519-520, 552, 559
social network analysis 43, 45, 48, 52, 58, 111, 127,
    277-278, 313-316, 370, 442, 478, 510, 552
Social Networking Site 524
Social Revolution 52-53, 104
Spanish Web 2, 30
Spatial Imagery 211, 302
Split Attention 338-340, 345-347, 352, 355-357,
    360-362, 368
Stemming (of Words) 302
Stopwords (Delete) List 302
Streamgraph 61, 104, 215, 289-294
Stream Graph 291, 302
Structured Data 559
Structured Text Data 302
Structure Mining 111, 141, 302, 435, 524
Student-Centered 189-190, 194-195, 201, 326, 331
student engagement 192, 323
Study Guide 317, 319, 321
Summative Evaluation 157-158, 163
Surface Web 87-88, 95, 103, 125, 443, 485, 492,
    495, 497, 520, 523-525, 527, 530
Synthetic Data 60, 270, 538, 541, 559

T

Tag Cloud 213, 302
Term Map 208, 302
Text Corpus 48, 205-206, 214, 216, 253, 302-303,
    371, 559
Text Frequency Count 559
Text Mining 208, 217, 302
Text Search 253-254, 559
Time Stamp 525
Tokenization 303
Twenty-First Century Learner 324-325, 337

U

Uniform Resource Locator (URL) 39, 147, 530
Unit of Analysis 37, 301, 303
Unstructured Data 48, 58, 147, 302, 437-438, 519,
    523-524, 530, 558-559
Unstructured Text Data 303
Unsupervised Machine Learning 104, 205

V

Valence (in a Psychological Sense) 104
Video Analytics 196, 201
Video Screen Capture Tools 327, 330, 337
Virtual Reality 197, 201
Visual Cueing 149, 153, 163
Visual imagery 211, 303
277, 280, 282, 284, 287, 289-291, 295-297, 301-
    304, 311-312, 314, 382, 385, 422, 430, 435,
    445, 450, 492, 494, 500, 510, 519, 524, 535,
    559
Visual Learning Style 337
Visual Mining 535, 559

W

Weak (Thin) Ties 525
Web characterization 3
Whistleblower 372, 376, 389, 395, 428
Word Art 214, 303
Word Cloud 223, 225-226, 269, 275-276, 303, 468,
    470, 510, 513
Word Frequency Count 223, 232, 258-259, 263,
    303, 510
Word Tree 226, 248, 253-254, 303

Become an IRMA Member

Members of the **Information Resources Management Association (IRMA)** understand the importance of community within their field of study. The Information Resources Management Association is an ideal venue through which professionals, students, and academicians can convene and share the latest industry innovations and scholarly research that is changing the field of information science and technology. Become a member today and enjoy the benefits of membership as well as the opportunity to collaborate and network with fellow experts in the field.

IRMA Membership Benefits:

- **One FREE Journal Subscription**

- **30% Off Additional Journal Subscriptions**

- **20% Off Book Purchases**

- Updates on the latest events and research on Information Resources Management through the IRMA-L listserv.

- Updates on new open access and downloadable content added to Research IRM.

- A copy of the Information Technology Management Newsletter twice a year.

- A certificate of membership.

IRMA Membership $195

Scan code to visit irma-international.org and begin by selecting your free journal subscription.

Membership is good for one full year.

Printed in the United States
By Bookmasters